D1519849

WESTERN REPUBLICANISM AND THE ORIENTAL PRINCE

For
Leszek Kołakowski,
John Pocock and
Quentin Skinner

Contents

WESTERN REPUBLICANISM ——AND THE—— ORIENTAL PRINCE

Patricia Springborg

UNIVERSITY OF TEXAS PRESS
AUSTIN

JA
82
.S67
1992b

Copyright © 1992 by Patricia Springborg
First published 1992 by Polity Press in association with
Blackwell Publishers

First University of Texas Press edition, 1992

All rights reserved

Requests for permission to reproduce material from this work should
be sent to Permissions, University of Texas Press, Box 7819,
Austin, TX 78713-7819.

ISBN 0-292-77664-0

Library of Congress Catalog Card Number 92-60170

Printed in Great Britain by T. J. Press Ltd., Padstow, Cornwall

JUN 23 1994

Acknowledgements

This is a story of how the West was won, which tells at the same time of the deep origins of orientalism and anti-Semitism – as it affects all Semites, Arab and Jew. Finally concluded in the throes of a war reflecting the outcome of the deep divide between East and West, as old as history itself, or at least as old as Ionian *historia*, this work has put me in debt to scholars far and wide, who work in areas as remote from one another as Bronze Age archaeology and Renaissance texts. I would like to thank Bernard Knapp and Sturt Manning for their assistance with the Bronze Age; Harold Tarrant, Godfrey Tanner, Richard Mulgan and Paul Vander Waerdt for the classics; Cary Nederman, Janet Coleman, Conal Condren, Louis Green, John Koenig and John O. Ward for the European medieval and Renaissance periods; Michael Rogin and Alastair Davidson for the modern imperial state. Looking Eastwards, I would like to thank Enid Hill and Ira Lapidus for discussions on Islam; my husband Robert Springborg for insights on modern Egypt; and Lucette Valensi for her splendid work (1987) on the observations of Venetian ambassadors on the Sublime Porte – for which, as in the case of Veyne (1976), I have provided my own translation. I owe special thanks to Martin Bernal, who has assisted me with related work; and although this particular text was largely written before *Black Athena* appeared, I have incorporated references to it where appropriate. To Sandra Donnelly, Maria Robertson, Sonja Waikawa, Lynne Thomson, John Robinson and to my excellent copy-editor Sue Ashton, and desk-editor Halina Boniszewksa, I am very thankful for overseeing the processing of the text; while to Lyn Fisher, who prepared the index, and the University of Sydney for the resources that it put at my disposal, I am especially grateful. I wish to acknowledge to both my husband and to my editor, David Held, deep indebtedness for encouragement and substantive assistance; to my children patient understanding. To John Pocock and Quentin Skinner, who read more than one version of the typescript, and who have shown unstinting generosity in reading and commenting on manuscripts and writing letters of recommendation, I owe immense gratitude; to them, and to Leszek Kołakowski, also a teacher and friend, this book is dedicated.

Introduction

Western republicanism and the myth of the oriental prince pose for us boundaries, some of which are self-erected walls, others ancient lines of demarcation between conceptual systems, and yet others are like the mirrors through which Alice in Wonderland can step – they reflect distortions which disappear under examination, and sometimes reverse images. What this study will try to accomplish is an appraisal of these boundaries, their historical basis and the purposes they serve. The critical tradition of historiography, evident at least as early as Herodotus and the logographers, tells us that the purposes for which history is written are constantly being revised. The logographers were as aware as any twentieth-century deconstructionist of the polemical purposes to which the writing of history can be put. Indeed, myth-making may prove to be one of the greatest incentives to the writing of history, just as myth-unmasking is one of the most important stimuli for its critical reassessment. I treat with suspicion the fact that Plato and Aristotle, along with certain other 'great books' of the Western civilization curriculum, have been privileged for so long. It is a sign, not of the death of our civilization (Bloom, 1987), but rather of its remarkable capacity for renewal, that these works should now be reassessed for cultural bias.

One of the more surprising features of my story is the late date at which the boundaries between East and West were fully sedimented. For most of the period under discussion here – from Antiquity to the Renaissance – the lines are still fluid. It is not until the post-Reformation period and the rise of the early modern European state that the East, as constant reference point for the West, becomes definitively different and characteristically 'despotic', due to certain historical fundamentals: the advance of the Ottoman Empire into the heartland of Europe; the late reception of certain of Aristotle's ideas to account for Ottoman rule as a patrimonial regime; and a general change in perceptions of the Turks, which we will view through the eyes of the Venetian ambassadors at the Sublime Porte (part II, chapter 20).

This is not to underestimate, however, the degree to which the East/West dichotomy drew on important distinctions made by Greek thinkers in the ancient period, particularly Aristotle, between Greeks and barbarians, freemen and slaves, types of entitlement to property and other rights. I make no apology for the fact that this is a thoroughly revisionist account. Seemingly innocent, archaically quaint or apparently arbitrary elements in the writings of some ancient philosophers, when examined in historical context, are shown to shore up racial and elite hegemony quite deliberately. Thus Aristotle's defence of slavery, treated more benignly than it deserves by conventional commentators, is shown to contain thinly veiled racial imperatives to treat 'Greeks like brothers, barbarians like plants and animals' (part I, chapter 2). The slave by nature, it emerges, was quite simply an Asiatic. In the same way Aristotle's treatment of the notable, *megalopsuchos*, the great-souled one, is an endorsement of the system of beneficence, by means of which a timocratic elite received state honours and the right to rule, in exchange for a willingness to put private resources at the disposal of the public purse.

It is curious that when Cicero comes to describe beneficence he, as one of only five new men whose families joined the senatorial oligarchy from the time of Marius, misapplies Aristotle's criteria. The notable, instead of being the big shot of Aristotle's description, given to the lavish gesture and conspicuous consumption on a grand scale, well beyond the resources of a new man, is with Cicero a moderate liberal – precisely the type Aristotle ruled out. Cicero invokes the Aristotelian mean and confines the benefactor to a middle path between niggardliness and spendthriftness, in this case mainly benefiting his friends (part I, chapter 5). The constant inveighing by Polybius against the softness and self-indulgence to which the mob inclines; his account of the formation of a sense of justice in the individual out of the experience of beneficence, and of injustice as outrage at ingratitude for benefactions received; his definition of freedom as restricted to freedom of speech, ruling out economic freedoms, all bespeak an unwillingness to see the walls of timocratic rule breached (part I, chapter 4).

Property ownership was precisely the criterion by which the slavishness of the Asiatic was so often defined: the Great King ruled his people like a household, their servility due to the lack of private property. As we see, so far is this from being true, resting as it does on confusions about the nature of entitlement in the East, that in fact the defence of property against the poor and powerless is precisely where so many of the Ancients, Aristotle, Polybius, Cicero and some Stoics included, rest their case, providing, as Quentin Skinner has so nicely put it, an *ironie de sort* (Skinner, 1990). Plato, Diogenes, some Cynics and Stoics, were willing to make radical departures – which ran to depriving the ruling class of property ownership altogether, a precept which early Islam emulated – but this served only to make these philosophers dangerous in the eyes of the orthodox. Often it was the same maverick thinkers who saw the large-scale *systemata* of the East more benevolently (part I, chapter 6). Among the realities which ancient polemicists were anxious to disguise, was a legacy of traditions concerning the Afro-Asiatic origins of the founders of Greece: Cadmus the Phoenician and Danaus the Egyptian (part I, chapter 7). While fragments of the founding myths of Greek colonization from the East are to be seen in the *Theogony* of Hesiod, the works of Homer and lost histories, this was a chapter which promoters of the proud *polis*, in which Greeks ruled and barbarians were enslaved, were keen to forget (part I, chapters 7–10). Its excavation has not been easy ever since.

It is not difficult to show that the self-assumed identities of modern Western European states were theorized in a specific historiographic tradition, that of classical republicanism. The socially constructed nature of these identities is easier to see in the early modern than in the ancient period, which has become sacrosanct in its canonized classical republican form. This is not to say that ancient writers were not already making the defence of rule of the rich over the poor, the superiority of some races over others, that later European writers were to emulate. But in the later period the ideological function of classical republican theory becomes transparent in an uneasy fit between the realities of the landed monarchies of Europe and their republican self-descriptions, in a way that in the earlier period it is not. Newly emergent European nation states were given by their theoreticians an exalted past: that of classical Greece and Rome. The struggle for an independent identity prosecuted by the small states against hegemonic claimants, the Pope and Emperor, involved a peculiar competition between East and West for the legacy of the classical Greek *polis*. It was an old contest, in which an earlier outcome saved the day for the West. Rome, the first great imitator of the Greeks, had easily assumed the authoritative mantle of Athens, even over its Hellenistic competitors, marking a divide between East and West that the Greeks had already staked out. (I state the case in the language of proprietary right, for reasons that become clear.) There was a structural fit between the city-republic of Rome and the Greek *polis* that was ignored, however, when, under the exigencies of the disintegration of the Roman Empire, early European nation states struggled in turn for legitimation.

Western early modern theory of the state is specifically ideological, then. It was generated out of the struggle between weak, concession-dispensing Crowns and the economically dominant classes, as they contested the economic power that state expansionism from the sixteenth century on created; a struggle in which the *Burgertum* marshalled an old resource: the legacy of the *polis* and Eastern city-state forms. Transmitted by the Church along with theological and philosophical texts of the classical Greek period, this legacy was mobilized by the bourgeoisie to induce the Crowns of the great landed monarchies of Europe to transform aristocratic clan councils and advisory bodies into institutions more closely resembling the genuinely participatory forms of the classical *polis*, its Mesopotamian antecedents and Hellenistic/Eastern descendants. It was a contest that the *Burgertum* ultimately won. In a series of revolutions from 1789 to 1914 the monarchies of Europe lost their Crowns and came to resemble in most formal respects the classical republican model.

The exigencies of the struggle required that any contenders for the mantle of the *polis* be displaced. There is abundant evidence now produced in the fields of archaeology and epigraphy to suggest that the ancient Middle East may well have pioneered city-republican forms, of which the Greek *polis* was only an example. These comprise the bicameral legislature, eligibility to which was decided on property qualifications and birth to free citizens; rule of law, an independent judiciary, procedures for holding magistrates to account and trial by jury; the rotation of magistracies among an isonomous elite; voting by ballot and by lot; private laws of contract and commercial law. Yet ironically, the ancient Orient was precisely the first contender to be displaced in the struggle for the mantle of the *polis*. Theories of oriental despotism grew up as a foil for classical republican theory, the permitting conditions being a profound ignorance about oriental states; certain racist attitudes inherited from Aristotle; and others that gained ground with the development in the eighteenth century of theories of racial difference based on climatological factors. Protestant fervour had its own contribution to make, deeming the Church Roman and Catholic, heir to the institutions of the corrupt Roman Empire, the 'City of Man', compared with the 'City of God', and later even the 'Whore of Babylon'. This smear rested on a distinction between East and West first made by Augustine, but extended in a very non-Augustinian way.

It is one of the most interesting aspects of these developments that the classical republican forms cloned in Europe represented the original model as very imperfectly as any colonial structure resembles the original. The hybrid republics, among which I include the Roman as essentially fake Greek, differed from city-republican forms of the *poleis* of Greece and Mesopotamia in the following way. They were agrarian, patriarchal, decentralized, non-participatory and they admitted very few to the circle of power, which was still essentially monarchical. Here they differed essentially from the urban, entrepreneurial, densely settled city-states, where classical republican forms aggregated innumerable networks of little societies. Incorporated for cultic, recreational, ethnic, occupational and other serious purposes, these groups provided recruitment agencies to man the magistracies (usually on a tribal roster), and foot the expenses of public works privately, necessary if a state possessed of few resources was to work.

To put it differently: the state in the East, which includes Greece, was essentially pluralistic, aggregating the institutions of civil society in a classically Hegelian manner. In fact, the first time the Middle East knew the authoritarian state in its pure form, as Hannah Batatu (1978) argues, was as a result of Western colonial conquest: nineteenth-century European colonizers were the first with the technological capacity and the long experience of authoritarian rule to have both the ability and the will to smash the institutions of civil society, destroy the old social order, and create the vacuum into which first the colonial power, then its stooges (transplanted and faked-up kings, shahs, etc.) and finally the revolutionary one-party state, could step. The state in the West, by contrast, was classically authoritarian: it rested on the absence of participatory structures, where even the tribal comings-together, as Marx suggested (*Grundrisse*, 1973 edn, 484), did not constitute real entities of any comparable sort with the clan organizations of classical (or modern) Greece, the ancient (or modern) Middle East.

This work, concerned as yet with only part of the story whose narration requires some care to preserve its particular contours and subtleties, approaches the historiographical problem, as John Pocock (1990) has pointed out, by the method of reverse discourse. The reader is asked to assume for the moment the hypotheses I propose: first, that the continuity of the Western European 'political' tradition is a work of imagination, or at least a social construction; secondly, that the considerable irony by which the landed monarchies of Western Europe fell heir to the classical republican traditions of Greece requires some explanation; and, thirdly, that this explanation may take the form of a critical examination of their particular histories. Paul Veyne (1988), in his excellent work on how the Greeks interpreted their myths, tells us that *mythos* was anciently a 'vulgate', respectfully repeated time out of mind, but that a critical attitude to myth arose at the time at which history as we recognize it came to be written. But myths are under constant construction and revision, while history is still being written, and, ironically, the *historia*, as opposed to the *mythoi*, of the *polis* constitute foundation myths for us, which have only recently come to be assessed critically.

I proceed in this manner because to lay out the story in the conventional hypothetico–deductive mode would require the alternative, and to my mind less desirable, methodology of asserting my case in one volume and demonstrating it in another. It would also involve reversing the chronology and telling the early modern story first – an approach adopted in the brilliantly controversial work of Martin Bernal (1987a), which has brought cries of 'where's the proof?' (Donelan, 1989). By adopting the method of reverse discourse I am, I hope, able to show that one has only to read the accounts of the Ancients from a different perspective to find an alternative, and in some cases more literal, meaning. This method has the advantage of holding to account certain authors historically privileged as founders of 'the Great Tradition', who have been exempted, as 'men who could not tell a lie', from the critical canons which have been applied to others. It has the corresponding advantage of enabling writers whose works have been eclipsed by such selectively applied criteria, conventionally approached as 'men who could not tell the truth', to be reinstated. Plato and Aristotle, more or less historically privileged for the duration of their careers, happen to be practitioners of that particular form of historiography which chronicles the past in terms of a Battle of the Giants between the Greeks and the barbarians, in which the Greeks usually win. Like many classical writers, they were not averse to altering particular outcomes to teach the general moral, as I try to demonstrate (part I, chapter 6). Herodotus, Diodorus, Isocrates and Plutarch, on the contrary, are writers who tell us things about the barbarians that for a long time we preferred not to hear.

While part I of this volume, 'The Greek *Polis* versus the "Great King"', gives the alternative reading I suggest of the ancient period, necessarily selective as it has to be, part II, 'Renaissance Republicanism and the Eastern Marcher Lord', makes corresponding adjustments to the Renaissance historiographic framework and reception of the works of Antiquity. Here a case is made that the foci of attention should be less the *polis*-centred works of Plato and Aristotle, and more the works of Hellenistic Stoic, Sceptic and Epicurean thinkers writing in the age of Empire. These latter were writers preoccupied with questions close to the Renaissance heart: the Eastern marcher lord, now individuated in the form of the Muslim conqueror. Here too the evidence is necessarily selective. I have paid rather less attention to the Roman historians and rhetoricians, Livy, Sallust, Tacitus and Cicero – in so far as I treat them at all it is to emphasize their reliance on the now lost works of Panaetius, Posidonius and Chrysippus – and rather more to Polybius, precisely to emphasize the Hellenistic character of Roman ideas as transmitted to the Renaissance.

This account will stand or fall on its merits. I am not suggesting for one moment that one can arrive by arbitrary choice at the sort of reading one gives the past. The sometimes tedious detail with which I illustrate my case attests to the fact that the normal canons of evidence apply. I am suggesting, however, that no writer or tradition is in principle exempt from the critical scrutiny with which the logographers confronted the mythographers of antiquity (see part I, chapter 8). Can we be content to deconstruct a historical account without putting something substantive in its place? To this question I would answer that historical criticism and giving an alternative substantive explanation are logically separable tasks, the latter subject to recognized canons of its own. Part of the substantive work, which concerns the Greek, Roman and Hellenistic legacy of ancient Near Eastern monarchy, is already done (Griffiths, 1960, 1970, 1975, 1980; Astour, 1967a; Bernal, 1987a; Springborg, 1990d). For a substantive account of the classical republican tradition from a sympathetic standpoint I cannot do better than refer my readers to the magisterial works of J.G.A. Pocock (1975) and Quentin Skinner (1979). A substantive statement of the revisionist account suggested here, which would focus on the symbiotic relationship between the classical republican tradition of the early modern period and theories of oriental despotism as a counterpoint, awaits the future. Its detail will stress not so much the impact of the Greek *polis*, or even that of Roman and Hellenistic writers on post-Reformation protagonists of the tradition, but rather the primitive democracy of ancient Israel, as the model to which they appealed. The appropriation by the West of the Old Testament among Eastern literatures, is only part of the story of how the West holds the East to ransom for its own legacy.

Pluralistic Structures and State Power

Many shibboleths exist about power. Since the work of Michel Foucault it has become commonplace to maintain that all social relationships are relationships of power. But such a view obscures the fact that some social systems generate more power than others. For power is created by interactions, exchanges and those structures of social life that provide a multiplicity of forums for negotiation, transactions and exchange. Some societies are inherently more transactional than others. Mediterranean and Near Eastern societies where people live more communally, fraternizing in their families and kinships, brotherhoods and syndicates, religious, cultic, trade and occupational associations, in their coffee houses and clubs, are vastly more transactional in a personal sense than the societies of Northern Europe and the New World cultures they have transplanted, lived behind closed doors in the nuclear family home, apartment, or at the office, where members visit other nuclear families, go to the cinema, go jogging, occasionally coming together in larger numbers to imbibe refreshments, standing, shouting over the noise, intoxicated by the hub-bub reminiscent more of the amorphous crowds associated with mass transport, queues, traffic jams, football crowds and band audiences – the more typical large-scale aggregations encountered in a day – than of a social gathering in societies of the ancient or modern Mediterranean world.

It is true to say that modern Western society is characterized by the ability to process commercial and financial transactions in hitherto unprecedented volume, to effect instantaneous trans-border data flows, and so on. But these are depersonalized transactions conducted in the interface between the bureaucratic hierarchies of the great transnational corporations, and national governments. The difference between a face-to-face transactional society and a depersonalized and bureaucratically controlled one represents the distinction that early social scientists tried to capture with the distinction between *Gemeinschaft* and *Gesellschaft*, status to contract (Maine, 1861; Morgan, 1877; Tönnies, 1955 edn; Marx, 1974 edn; see Springborg, 1986), except that they applied the characterizations in more or less the opposite form to that endorsed here. For, it is the great landed monarchies marking the history of Western society whose social relations have been characterized as more *Gemeinschaftlich*, status-bound and hierarchical; the social relations of Eastern *polis* society more transactional and *Gesellschaftlich*. Such monarchies generate very little power and distribute even less; what there is is usually devolved to the 'friends' of the king. But city-republics, just because of the volume of transactions that they facilitate, create a multiplicity of power sites. At the same time they provide structures and institutions capable of aggregating members of different families, clans and tribes, individuals with nothing in common initially, who become 'citizens' by virtue of membership.

Across several disciplines now scholars have observed certain shortcomings in the received historical canon to which the *Gemeinschaft/Gesellschaft* (Tönnies, 1955) distinction belongs. It posits an evolutionary schema from primitivism to *polis* to modern (Western) nation state, the states of the East constituting a residual category. Studies in Assyriology, Iranology, Egyptology, among area specialties with which I am familiar, disclose highly developed ancient civilizations, however, which exhibited considerable technological competence. More disquieting still is the fact that economic and technical competencies were accompanied by the full array of social and cultural traits that we associate with 'development' as it is currently conceived. The capacity of the 'irrigation societies', so called, of ancient Sumeria, Mesopotamia more generally, Egypt and China to make the transition from city-state to Empire, a transition that the Greek *polis*, for instance, never made (Anderson, 1974a; Mann, 1986), was a function precisely of the following developmental competencies: (a) impersonal government administered by a bureacracy; (b) the conception of man as citizen; (c) forms of political representation; (d) the creation of an economic surplus; (e) a monetarized economy, accompanied by the institutions of credit, commerical law, trade treaties and international laws of contract; (f) a standing army, equipped with advanced military technologies; (g) social stratification along functional lines, comprising classes of farmers, artisans, merchants, an administrative elite and priestly caste; (h) the concept of nature as governed by rational laws; (i) institutions for the acquisition, organization and dissemination of knowledge; (j) the development of writing and basic sciences of mathematics, geometry, astronomy, navigation, architecture, engineering and highly developed skills in construction, metal-working, pottery, textiles, sculpture and painting (Drucker, 1979; Mann, 1986).

To take the case of Sumeria, one of the earliest examples, scholars (Diakonoff, 1956, 1974; Kramer, 1963; Oppenheim, 1969; Jacobsen, 1970, 1976) now suggest that city-states like those of Lagash were adminstered by parallel temple and palace bureaucracies, agents of each required to countersign shipments in and out of the state granaries, for instance (Oppenheim, 1969, 7ff). The considerable lands of the city comprised palace and temple complexes and their holdings, noble estates and the lands of commoners, organized in 'patriarchal clans and town communities', whose property could be bought and sold by chosen family representatives in transactions for which, around 2400 BC, we already have documentary evidence (Kramer, 1963, 75–7). Corresponding to these, now classic, property divisions was a surprisingly conventional division of political power. Early evidence for representative councils in Sumer is to be found in the Gilgamesh Epic, as it also exists for Egypt in the Great Corporation of Heliopolis recorded in the mythological 'Contendings of Horus and Seth' (Anthes, 1954; Griffiths, 1960). From *c*.1894–1595 BC evidence exists for a bicameral assembly in Sippar, the upper house of which was controlled by the nobility, the lower house confined to commoners, access being granted on property qualifications. Magistracies, appointed on an annual basis, were rotated among an isonomous elite constituted by the judicial, administrative and merchant classes (Oppenheim, 1969, 9–10). Lagash has the honour of recording in its annals the first known use of the word 'freedom' (Kramer, 1963, 79), celebrated in the Urukagina Reform Document of around 2350 BC in terms strikingly reminiscent of Solon's *seisachtheia* nearly 1800 years later. Freedom meant precisely protection against the predations of the palace tax collector, as well as redress of administrative abuses by the 'ubiquitous and obnoxious bureaucracy' of the temple, Urukagina, like Solon later, promising release of those imprisoned for debt bondage.

Some of the best evidence we have for government by an impersonal bureaucracy is yielded by the third millennium Mesopotamian site of Ebla, in the form of some 20,000 clay tablets. A prosperous city of some 260,000 people, Ebla was ruled by a king (*malik*, cf. Hebrew and Arabic *malik*), a council of elders (*abbu*, see Arabic *abu*, 'father' and cf. Roman *patres*, senators) and some 11,700 bureaucrats whose ledgers, daybooks and inventories account for some 13,000 clay tablets (Bermant and Weitzman, 1979; Matthiae, 1980). Further evidence for bureaucratically administered rule of law is to be found in the provisions of a series of codifications of the common law of the area, from the Ur-Nammu Code of 2050 BC up to and including the famous Hammurabi Code. The code of Ur-Nammu upheld the rights of orphans, widows and small landholders against powerful 'grabbers of property'. It undertook regulation of the marketplace by the introduction of standard weights and measures, instituting a schedule of fines for infringement against the laws of fair trade, in line with other codes for the area, including the Hittite. Court proceedings for the period record litigation regarding 'marriage contracts, divorces, inheritance, slaves, hiring of boats, claims of all sorts, pledges and such miscellaneous items as pre-trial investigations, subpoenas, theft, damage to property, and malfeasance in office' (Kramer, 1963, 84–5). In ancient Egypt too, although perhaps a less litigious society, property transactions were a document-ridden affair, asset dossiers comprising every piece of paper associated with a given piece of property (Lloyd, 1983, 314; Pestman, 1983). Contrary to modern assumptions, ancient Egypt was a society also characterized by independent city-development in its early history

(Bietak, 1979b; Trigger, 1983, 40, 48), private and noble patronage systems (Kemp, 1983, 83–5), and a high level of individualism as attested by the personal signatures of artists to works as early as the Pyramids of Giza (Drucker, 1979, 44).

It is not necessary to list in detail the technological accomplishments of ancient Mesopotamia and Egypt. It is worth pointing out, however, that each of the instances Max Weber gives in his Preface to *The Protestant Ethic and the Spirit of Capitalism* (Weber, 1958, 15ff) for the administrative, scientific and technical superiority of the West over the East is erroneous. So ubiquitous are assumptions of Western development and Eastern underdevelopment that a thinker who spent a good deal of his life writing about Eastern systems felt no need to check his facts. He claims that Babylonian astronomy lacked a mathematical basis, neglecting to mention also the invention of geometry as Egyptian (cf. King, 1978, 1980); that Eastern legal traditions lacked the systematic quality of Roman and canonical law – whereas, in fact Roman law is derived from the law-codes of the Eastern provinces, codified by those Easterners, Papinian and Ulpian from the Beirut school of law (cf. Rostovtzeff, 1932; Driver and Miles, 1952–5; Cumont, 1956 edn). Weber (1958, 15) further claims that 'though the technical basis of our architecture came from the Orient ... the Orient lacked the solution to the problems of the dome' – quite the contrary, the Orient provided the solution not only to the problem of the dome, but also of the arch. On the subject of the compilation and dissemination of knowledge, Weber claims that Western universities are superior to those of China and Islam, 'superficially similar', but lacking 'the rational, systematic and specialized pursuit of sciences with trained and specialized personnel' (Weber, 1958, 15–16) – he neglects to point out that Islamic universities like al-Azhar were older than those of the West, which did not begin life as scientific institutes either. Evidence for the early existence of medical and law schools, to which women were also admitted, dates in fact to the third millennium Ebla site, which also furnishes lists of precious metals, minerals and other scientific information (Bermant and Weitzman, 1979, 153–5). Weber goes on to claim, rather surprisingly since this is his special subject, that it is an accomplishment of the West to staff its bureaucracies with a specially trained *organization* of officials. More startling still is his claim that the organization of labour based on freedom to contract is a triumph of the West. But stipulations regarding freedom to contract are to be found in the earliest known Mesopotamian law codes, the Hammurabi Code, for instance, including extensive treatment of both agricultural and commercial labour contracts regarding rates of hire, offences and liabilities involving oxen, husbandmen, agricultural implements, graziers, shepherds, wagons and seasonal workers; wages and rates of hire for craftsmen (Driver and Miles, 1952–5).

It is fair to say that a certain uneasiness has afflicted theorists in the face of persistent claims of Western superiority. Karl Marx was one of the first to suggest not only that Eastern development might not lie along the same spectrum as that of Western Europe, but also that there seemed to be irreconcilable differences between urban *polis* society and its putative heirs, the Western European states. To put it briefly, Marx understood that categorical differences separated forms of the state that no mere evolutionary schema could account

for, and that he tried to capture in his classification of modes of production –
not always successfully. Primary among these was the distinction between
homo politicus and *homo oeconomicus*, the former, inhabitant of the densely
settled, urban, entrepreneurial, riverine and littoral civilizations of the Eastern
Mediterranean, the Mesopotamian and Indus river valleys; the latter, member of
the decentralized patriarchal society of the Germanic and Celtic tribes scattered
in the Northern European woods. 'The history of classical antiquity is the history
of cities', he observed, 'but of cities founded on landed property and agriculture',
whereas European history, dating from the medieval German period, 'begins
with land as the seat of history, whose further development then moves forward
in the contradiction between town and country-side'. The 'modern age', he
declares categorically, 'is the urbanization of the country-side, not ruralization of
the city as in antiquity' (Marx, *Grundrisse*, 1973 edn, 479). 'Asiatic history'
requires a further category, as 'a kind of indifferent unity of town and countryside (the really large cities must be regarded here merely as royal camps, as works
of artifice erected over the economic construction proper)'. And here, of course,
Marx is referring not only to the realms of the Assyrian 'marcher lords', treated
so convincingly by Michael Mann (1986), but also to those of the great
Alexander, more oriental than Hellenic in style – a connection that Mann (1986,
138–40) also makes.

The significance of the distinction between *homo oeconomicus*, for whom the
oikos, or economy of the household, is the critical social unit, and *homo politicus*,
for whom it is the *polis*, or city, is that, in the case of the former, whatever
communal structures may be produced by the periodic comings-together of the
tribes, do not add up to a '*state*, or *political body*, as in classical antiquity, because
this community does not exist as a *city*' (Marx, *Grundrisse*, 1973 edn, 483). As
Aristotle had long ago observed, it is a mistake to assume that government of a
large household (*oikos*) and a small city (*polis*) are the same thing (Aristotle,
Politics, 1252a5–16, 1981 edn, 54). The differences between forms of rule are
more than a question of scale, they are differences in the sources of power.
Political (*politikon*), royal (*basilikon*), patriarchal (*oikonomikon*) and patrimonial
(*despotikon*) systems of power are categorically different, Aristotle (*Politics*,
1285b20–34) maintained; a distinction he himself served to obscure by charac-
terizing absolute monarchy as patrimonial rule, or the intrusion of the household into the public domain. Differences between the patriarchal rule of the
oikos and the political rule of the *polis* lie chiefly in the fact of the one being based
on a chain of command governed by the structure of the family in the self-
sufficient household; the other based on the exchange relations of the urban,
entrepreneurial *polis*. For Aristotle was the first to argue that all communities or
partnerships rest on exchange: 'if there were no exchange there would be no
association (*koinonia*), without equality there would be no exchange and without
commensurability there would be no equality' (Aristotle, *Nicomachean Ethics*,
1133b17–18, 1976 edn, 185). It was the interaction of equals, coming together to
exchange commodities for the mutual satisfaction of their needs, that established
the basis of wider participation in power and communal autonomy, which
constituted politics as the form of interaction peculiar to the *polis*. Those for
whom the characteristic form of rule was *oikonomikon*, or the patriarchal rule of

the extended household, could never make the transition to free and democratic relations of economic and social equals that characterized the ancient city, for structural reasons. They passed rather easily from the condition of serfs to that of wage slaves.

These are the reasons, Marx seems to intimate, why modern 'economic man' has never sloughed off patriarchy, and why the realm of the 'political' is an empty fiction that provides legitimacy to the untrammeled struggle of naked economic forces (Marx, 'On the Jewish Question'). The state is a residual category in *economic* society, not because Marx misunderstands the nature of power, but because he understands very well that in *economic*, as opposed to *political*, society its sources are different. In the society of the marcher lords they are different again – and if Marx seems to assume this to be the type of all oriental societies, it is a small but significant correction to slip the 'sedentary' civilizations (to use Ibn Khaldun's useful term) of Mesopotamia and the Levant back under the *polis* category, and the great household and royal economies of the Egyptians and Persians back where they belong.

Islamic society, like the Mesopotamian societies which governed its sedentary forms, was supremely contractual (Springborg, 1987a), a characteristic which underlay much of its success. By the standards of economic development, the Islamic cities achieved a size, based on the division and specialization of labour, unparalleled in Europe until the nineteenth and twentieth centuries. Charles Issawi, the economic historian, reports the population of tenth-century Baghdad at around a million, while Cairo in the fourteenth century is reported by a French traveller to have been twice the size of Paris, with four times the population. By 1800, Istanbul had a population of a million, while Baghdad and Cairo's populations had declined, compared with the population at that time of London of 400,000 (Issawi, 1969, 102–5). The Jewish historian of Islam, Sholomo Goitein (1967, 99), observes that in the Geniza documents of medieval Cairo, 'The terms for about 265 manual occupations have been identified thus far, as against 90 types of person engaged in commerce and banking and approximately the same number of professionals, officials, religious functionaries and educators.' Goitein compares this total of some 450 recognized occupations 'with the 150 or so professional corporations traced in ancient Rome by J.T. Walzing in his monumental *Corporations professionelles* on the one hand, and the 278 *corporations de métiers* listed by André Raymond [1957] for Cairo in 1801', on the other, as well as the 435 recognized occupations compiled by the Qasimis, father and son, for Damascus at the turn of this century (Goitein, 1967, 99).

But the question remains, why, with such a finely graduated division of labour, capitalism did not emerge in the East. Essentially it was because business generated a specific professional form, the partnership, neither based on a division between owners and non-owners, nor giving rise to the employer–employee relation (Goitein, 1967, 154–5, 203, 263). There were important social reasons for this, not least of which is the fact that the employer–employee distinction approximated too uncomfortably the relation between master and slave, in what were originally slave-owning societies (Goitein, 1967, 77) – the slaves, incidentally, being either black, or that other inferior class of persons, Europeans, captured on the corsair route! Centuries of small business organized in partnerships, in which some partners contributed capital, others labour, but all were happily 'owners', shut out the large-scale industrialist as a dominant type. Based on the family, the neighbourhood or the confession, these business partnerships cemented primary social ties – even women were frequently partners, whose economic independence has often been misrepresented. What can one think of the subjugation of women in a society in which mothers gave their daughters names like 'Female Ruler', 'Mistress of the Turbans', 'Mistress of the Clerks', 'Mistress of Byzantium', 'Mistress of Baghdad', 'Mistress of the Muslim West', 'She who Rules over Everyone', 'Fame', 'Victory', General', even 'King' (Goitein, 1978, 314–19)?

The conception of the city-republic as constituted out of a series of voluntarily contracted partnerships has a great ancestry, for all that the 'right to contract' is conceived as a peculiarly modern form (Maine, 1861; Morgan, 1877; Marx, 1973 edn, 1974 edn;). Not only did the ancient *poleis* of Mesopotamia and Greece draw together a mixed collection of small associations contractually construed, based on kinship, friendship, cultic, economic and commercial functions, but they were understood by their members to be so constituted. This is quite clear from the account of the foundations of the *polis* given by Aristotle (*Politics*, 1.1.), who for centuries was read as lending support to an organic theory of society in response to Plato's theoretical attempts at social engineering.

In the case of the city-republics of Sumeria, Assyria and Babylonia, the evidence is quite explicit, but articulated in a documentary rather than a theoretical mode. It lies in the innumerable records of contract preserved on clay tablets and unearthed over the last century. It can also be inferred from the rare interventions of the city as a corporate governing body to adjust the alignment of economic and social forces, where the balance of interests had broken down. The citizens of Nippur in 1900 BC won exemption from corvée duty from the king of Isin, for instance, while the citizens of Babylon in a letter to King Ashurbannipal proclaimed that 'even a dog becomes free and privileged when he enters [our] city' (Oppenheim, 1969, 7). The Babylonian conception of the city as a corporate entity, expressed in the term *alum u sibutum*, 'city-and-aldermen', in the case of Sippar, for instance, in the period *c.*1894–1595 BC, referred to all free males within the city who met and acted as a body for certain purposes (Oppenheim, 1969, 9–10).

Urbanism and Affinity

Aristotle was one of the first to theorize pluralism as the outcome of aggregated networks of participatory activity feeding into the administrative structures of the city. He was also one of the first to insist that the essence of democracy is participation and that the secret of participation is doing it (Aristotle, *Politics*, bk 3). Participation is not an activity undertaken for its own sake, however. People participate by virtue of doing things, trying to get things, and pursuing projects, not merely to keep themselves busy, or for the pleasure of talking. It is for this reason that the classical *polis* of the ancient world was participatory: because it was a small-scale society full of people in their brotherhoods, kinship organizations, phratries and clubs, trying to get things, sell people things and ideas, trade services and allegiances, just as in Mediterranean societies they still do (Ferguson, 1910, 1936, 1938; Wade-Gery, 1931; Péristiany, 1965, 1968, 1976; Goitein, 1967–83, 1969; Khuri, 1975, 1976, 1980; Bourriot, 1976; Peters, 1976; Roussel, 1976).

That such activities and transactions eventually were deemed, or became, *political* had to do with the overarching framework within which they were cast: that of the city. Innumerable small-scale familial, cultic and fraternal organizations constituted the elements which, when aggregated, gave us the city. When the sheer volume of business became sufficient to warrant government, so to speak – and the classical account of the origins of the city in Plato and Aristotle is precisely in these terms – it was these private organizational structures that carried out much of its function. So the tribes lent to the *polis* those characteristic offices that we associate with it: the *archon*, originally the tribal chief; the *gerontes*, originally a tribal council of elders; the *agora*, originally that space for the gathering of young warriors of the tribe to ratify decisions of war and peace, which eventually became the assembly or the *ecclesia* of the *polis* as a whole.

Once set up, the governmental forms of the *polis* still relied on family, clan and tribe to man the roster of magistracies in this state on a shoe-string. So, for instance, the Athenian *boule*, that agenda-setting steering committee of the *ecclesia* responsible for the day-to-day business of the city, as constituted first under Solon and then under Cleisthenes, was made up of tribal representatives on a monthly roster. One of Cleisthenes' extraordinary reforms was to reconstitute the tribes as ten, out of the four traditional tribes of Attica subdivided into *trytteis* (threes), to suit a lunar rather than a solar calendar. The *boule* was accordingly reconstituted as a council of 500, rather than the Solonian 400, made up of 50 delegates chosen by lot from the ten new tribes. These ten *prytaneis* constituted tribal committees, each serving for a month, that supplied the chairman, or chief executive officer, of the *boule*, which met daily; the agenda-setting steering committee for the *ecclesia*, which met four times a month; and coordination of the various subcommitees of the *boule*, which handled finance, the putting out of contracts for tax-farming, the collection of receipts, the accountability of magistrates and, if necessary, their prosecution, the sending and receiving of diplomatic envoys, and so on. A willingness to serve as a tribal delegate, and to act as chairman for a day, was presumed of every citizen. Such a system of high turnover among office-bearers did indeed ensure, as Aristotle stipulated, that citizenship meant ruling as well as being ruled. This is what participation meant and this is why life was *political*.

Voluntary associations, in and out of which one contracted, were so intimately related to concepts of freedom and democracy that, where traditional institutions have been unable to transform themselves in these terms, they have simply withered away. So the family, kinship and collegial networks in modern democracies, where they do not exist as multipurpose, social, economic and political forms of association, simply do not exist at all. The public space has quite literally devoured the private sphere. Institutions like the family, neighbourhood, church, collegial associations and other private networks, as primarily need-based agencies, cannot survive without resources. In societies where they flourished, and they flourished in the ancient world as they have done under monarchies and do in the Third World today, their vitality derives from the performance of essential functions.

The family, as the primary need-satisfying agency in ancient Greece, in Renaissance Italy, as recent scholarship emphasizes, and as, for instance, in modern Egypt, is no merely spiritual entity based on emotional ties of devotion and nostalgia. It is rather a robust and voracious institution, within whose confines members live out their lives, to whose resources they turn for the needs of everyday life, power within which is determined by success at meeting the demands and challenges of fellow members (Ferguson, 1910; Costello, 1938; Péristiany, 1968, 1976; Heers, 1974; Khuri, 1975, 1976, 1980; Bourriot, 1976; Peters, 1976; Roussel, 1976; Davies, 1977–8, 1981; R. Springborg, 1982; Bill and Springborg, 1990). The family is a disputatious, highly competitive, emotionally demanding, intensely interactive environment within which most of the drama of daily life is played out – referred to by Francis Kent (1977a, 297), in the case of Renaissance Florence, as 'the hothouse atmosphere of a lineage's corporate life'. It is into the family that individuals are born, within it that they are nurtured, the family marries them and buries them. More than that, immediate or extended family members provide contacts to secure an education, a career, a circle of friends, a spouse, religious affiliation and 'influence' or 'mediation' (Egyptian colloquial, *wusaata*) to steer one's way by bureaucratic and governmental road-blocks in the form of the tax man, the army recruitment agency and the inspector. Only when family resources fail one in the daily contest to satisfy one's personal requirements, to meet the demands of the state and its far-reaching bureaucracy, and to advance one's prospects a little in all this, does one turn to outside networks. One turned then to neighbourhood or collegial forms of association, or religious groups – this was as true in ancient Greece (Pusey, 1940) as it was in Renaissance Italy (F. Kent, 1977a; D. Kent 1978; D. Kent and F. Kent, 1988) and is still true of the modern East Mediterranean and Near East.

Wider non-familial social groups have a comparable durability and vitality, due to their ability to provide resources, solve problems and meet needs in daily demand. Moreover, they reinforce, rather than take away from, the resources of the family as the primary network. Networking is no zero-sum game. Larger aggregates actually enhance the status of the smaller units they contain. Such is the logic of federalism to this day, which is why it is welcomed by smaller and weaker units, minorities and small parties, who have less to fear from a confederacy than they have from a centralized state. It is the logic to which the emerging European confederate community appeals, as it was of the United States, Canada and the Commonwealth of Australia. The notion that larger social aggregates may actually reinforce, rather than subsume, subordinate entities applied also in Cairo medieval and modern (Goitein, 1969), and in Renaissance Florence (Kent, 1977a, 295). The tendency of families to cluster in neighbourhoods or quarters, to endow public buildings there, whether churches, synagogues or mosques, and to construct tombs for their veneration by descendants, resulted in overlapping affinities between family and neighbourhood that reinforced, rather than diminished, the power of the family.

In what were universally patrilineal societies, kinship relations favoured, if they were not exclusively confined to, the male side. So Florentine laws of the *quattrocento* officially recognized 'closest paternal kinsmen [*proximi consorti*]' as constituting the domestic unit (Kent, 1977a, 293), 'the Florentine constitution itself [giving] lineages a sort of political patrimony to preserve or squander as they would' (Kent, 1977a, 295). In ancient Greece consanguinity was recognized only on the male side (Davies, 1977–8; Fustel de Coulanges, 1873 edn); and in modern Egypt endogamous marriages, especially of the father's-brother's-daughter variety, tie the lineage ever closer (R. Springborg, 1975, 1982). In Renaissance Florence, just as in ancient Athens, the language of patrilineal kinship was mobilized to encompass the larger universe of social relations. So, while in ancient Greece 'the Homeric *agathos* (warrior-chieftain in charge of his own *oikos*) uses *philos* ['dear', 'beloved'] of his various faculties, possessions and fellowmen, beginning as near as possible to the man himself and working steadily outwards' (Adkins, 1963, 30); in a later period concepts of kinship (*oikeiotes*) were expanded from the family (*oikos*) to include ever larger aggregates, so that thinkers as cosmopolitan as Eratosthenes and Thucydides could think of likeness (*oikeiosis*) obtaining between different *ethnai* and even between different races, to yield eventually the Stoic *oikoumene* (Baldry, 1965, 42, 142–3, 178).

By the same logic, the network of patrilineal kinship in Renaissance Florence was extended by metaphor to include those who were not family, friends and neighbours, referred to as 'most dear like a father', or 'honoured as an elder brother' (cited in Kent and Kent, 1982, 2). The neighbourhood (*vicinanza*) was seen as 'a fundamental unit of human association', as Dante expostulating on Aristotle's *Politics*, 1.1–2, in his *Convivio*, 4.4 (1963 edn, 298) declared: 'just as a man to be fulfilled, needs the society of family life [*comagnia domestica di famiglia*], so too a house is insufficient to itself without a neighbourhood [*vicinanza*]' (Kent and Kent, 1982, 2). Family histories, or '*Ricordi*', speak in one breath of *parenti*, *vicini* and *amici*, patriarchs such as Giovanni Rucellai counselling their sons to 'be benevolent towards neighbours', to 'please neighbours, love kinsmen'.

These are aphorisms reminiscent of those endorsed by Aristotle in dealing with affinal sets: 'amity is friendship [*philotes he isotes*]' (*Nicomachean. Ethics* (*NE*), 8.5.5, 1157b 37); 'like attracts like [*isotes kai homoites philotes*]' (*NE*, 8.8.5, 1159b 1–5); and 'all things in common among friends [*koina ta philon*]' (*NE*, 8.9.1, 1159b 30–5). Aristotle's rather extensive treatment of friendship in that work suggests circles of intimacy with preferred rights that take account of affinal sets even before citizenship. So we are rather surprised to hear him announce that 'it is more shocking to defraud a comrade [*hetairos*] of money than a fellow-citizen; or to refuse aid to a brother than to do so to a stranger' (*NE*, 8.9.2–3, 1159b 30–1160a 10, 1956 edn, 487). For, as Aristotle explains:

> The claims of justice also differ in different relationships. The mutual rights of parents and children are not the same as those between brothers; the obligations of members of a comradeship are not the same as those of fellow-citizens; and similarly with other forms of friendship ... Similarly it is natural that the claims of justice should increase with the nearness of the friendship, since friendship and justice exist between the same persons and are co-extensive in range.

Aristotle's analysis of friendship discloses the nature of affinal sets in the Eastern Mediterranean, ancient and modern, institutionalized for the exchange of benefits, the protection of the in-group against the out-group, and dating from a period in which the capacity of the state to provide for the peace, welfare, security and justice of its inhabitants was relatively limited. The relationship between members of subordinate associations is explicitly contractual, according to Aristotle, but this does not mean that they are all the same: 'all friendship involves community or partnership [*koinonia*]', but relationships between members of a family and of comradeships [*hetaireiai*] and brotherhoods [*phratriai*] are 'less in the nature of partnerships than are the relationships between fellow-citizens [*politikai*], fellow-tribesmen [*phyletikai*], shipmates, and the like; since these seem to be founded as it were on a definite compact' (*NE*, 8.12.2, 1161b 10–15, 1956 edn, 497–9). Nevertheless:

> in every partnership we find mutual rights of some sort, and also friendly feeling: one notes that shipmates and fellow-soldiers speak of each other as 'my friend', and so in fact do the partners in any joint undertaking. But their friendship is limited to the extent of their association in their common business, for so also are their mutual rights as associates. (*NE*, 8.9.1, 1159b 25–35, 1956 edn, 485)

Aristotle, as is his wont, uses the metaphor of the marketplace to establish the reciprocity of friendship. In 'friendships of equality', he stresses, 'both parties render the same benefit and wish the same good to each other, or else exchange [equivalent amounts of] two different benefits' (*NE*, 8.6.7, 1158b 1–5, 1956 edn, 475–7). These friendships, like equity cases in the courts, involve transactions based on arithmetical equality. But in unequal friendships, 'which involve superiority of one party over the other', 'it is proportion ... that establishes equality and preserves the friendship; just as in the relations between fellow-citizens, the shoemaker receives payment for his shoes, and the weaver and the other craftsmen for their products, according to value rendered' (*NE*, 9.1.1, 1163b 30–1164a 5, 1956 edn, 517).

Lest one believe the barter/exchange metaphor to be overdone, it is worth recalling that affinal sets served just this primary need-satisfying activity. So great is the contribution of family, kinship and neighbourhood networks to the everyday needs of the individual that, in the case of modern Egypt, for instance, it is not unknown for lower to lower-middle class Egyptian families to be able to save virtually their entire monetary income for a year (Singerman, 1986). This means that, in fact, the daily needs of their members are more or less entirely met on the barter system that operates between affinal sets. So durable are the *duf'a*[s] – those modern Egyptian corporate entities constituted by members of the same graduating class in school, military academy or university – and *shilla*[s] – or formalized circle of friends – that they continue to bind members together even when life has taken them on very different paths (R. Springborg, 1975, 1982). A television producer, a sufi member, a novelist, a chicken farmer and lowly members of the bureaucracy are still bound to their *confrères*, just as one supposes the members of an Athenian hetairy, remarkably similar in function and said to owe its origins to 'sharers of the same tent' (Ehrenberg, 1960), were so bound. Such an association or partnership, for which Aristotle reserved the Greek term *koinonia* (Springborg, 1984a), binds its members, not by virtue of emotional ties, which follow from, rather than precede, continuous human contact, and which are far too fragile and fickle to support a lasting network; but because the form of association continues to be a resource that members of the *duf'a* or *shilla*, like those of the *hetaireia*, who honour their sworn or unsworn pledges to help one another out for the duration, can command.

The very nature of a society constituted this way out of subordinate groups which take precedence in everyday life because of their need-satisfying functions, tends to make it self-perpetuating. The complexity of society formed of a plethora of little societies, each with its own group dynamics and power networks firmly entrenched in day-to-day functions, inward-looking, intensely concerned with the solution of immediate problems, and relatively intractable to centralized control and penetration from the outside – if for no other reason than because there are so many of them and they are so relatively unimportant – gives rise to further groups with information resources on how to steer through all the forms of association whose demands one must meet in order to make one's way.

At the same time the pluralistic constitution of such a society, geared to strategic need-satisfying functions and agencies, predisposes its members to view the state too as a resource to be tapped for their private purposes. The dismay of Western governments and their commentators at the utilitarianism of immigrants from Mediterranean societies, who begin to set in place their 'key men' and establish their networks to 'work' the system immediately upon arrival, has its parallel in the dismay of commentators on the ancient *polis*, who saw that love of one's friends or love of one's faction almost always took precedence over love of the city (Calhoun, 1913; Pusey, 1940; Connor, 1971). But one can think of it differently. Perhaps this is what love of one's city meant: an admiration for the resources the city put at the disposal of one's family, one's clan, one's tribe and one's friends. Plato's frequent admonitions that justice ought to mean more than 'benefiting one's friends and harming one's enemies' (*Crito*, 45c5ff, *Meno*, 41e2ff, *Republic*, 332d) remind us that this is what it usually did mean. His was a signal attempt to make a case for justice as something over and above utilitarian interests, but whether it had any practical effect in persuading Athenians to widen the groups to which they felt affinity to include the whole city, is doubtful.

Aristotle tackles the same problem, but not in the same way, trying to show that the same result may be achieved, not by abolishing local loyalties, but by aggregating them, so that 'love of the city', although immediately willed by no one would be indirectly promoted by all, in their kinships, their phratries, their brotherhoods and partnerships of all kinds (Aristotle, *Politics*, 3.5.13–14, 1280b30–1281a15, 1932 edn, 217–19). Aristotle, more aware than Plato of the imperviousness of a fundamentally pluralist society to centralized control, could conceive of no 'general will' that might produce unanimity. The good of the city was a higher good than the good of its individual members or their traditional forms of association, not because it was a good in itself, the city being an empty collectivity apart from the good of its individual members. Rather its superiority lay in the *telos* of human beings, as individuals whose potential powers could only be realized on a wider stage than the traditional affinal networks permitted. In a sense, Aristotle's claims for the *polis* represent an attempt to justify an entity that was traditional too, historically rooted, but lacking the claim on affections and loyalties enjoyed by the interest groups it contained. The apparently *ad hoc* nature of the city, as the taken-for-granted framework of life lived out in its interstices, was a matter for reflection. In the last instance it remained true, however, that the city existed to complement the satisfactions which the more immediately need-orientated structures of daily life afforded, and not to supplant them. Its good was higher by virtue of being more universal; as a teleological good being less immediate, more remote, and for that reason less often appreciated.

Aristotle was making for the ancient city the case that modern theorists have tried to make for urbanism as a phenomenon (Williams, 1984). The customary equation between the *polis* and the nation state obscures this fact; an equation that Marx, with characteristic perspicuity, called into question, pointing out at least four times that what Aristotle meant by *zoon politikon*, was that man was a city-dweller, and no more. The observation is first to be found in Marx's piece on 'The Civic Militia Bill' of 1848 (Marx–Engels, *Collected Works*, 1977 edn, vol. 7, 264); secondly in the *Grundrisse* (1973 edn, 496); thirdly in *Capital* (vol. 1, n.d., 309), perhaps the most famous example, where he notes, 'Strictly, Aristotle's definition is that man is by nature a town-citizen. This is quite as characteristic of ancient classical society as Franklin's definition of man as a tool-making animal is characteristic of Yankeedom', Marx clearly having in mind Aristotle's remarks on slaves as human tools, which we later discuss (part I, chapter 1); and, fourthly, in *The Ethnological Notebooks* of 1880–3 (1974 edn, 196).

In ancient Greece, as in the modern state, the city as an entity tends to be underestimated because the interest groups it contains often have the power to command greater loyalty – Nathan Pusey (1940) has argued persuasively that it was with great difficulty that the ancient city competed with families, friends and fraternities for the loyalties of its citizens. And just as the city in ancient times was never coextensive with the *ethne*, or nation, so the modern city has been subsumed into a greater collectivity, that of the state. Modern cities fight not only intense localism, but also intense nationalism in the competition for loyalties. And both more local and more national institutions have a greater chance of success, due in no small measure to the greater resources, public and private, at their disposal, than the city, which is seen merely as the field in which they have their play. One recent theorist (Williams, 1984) has tried to emphasize that space, too, is a resource and that urbanism provides tangible and intangible benefits, in the form of contiguity, information flow, physical access and critical mass, as a facilitator in the innumerable transactions and exchanges on which social life is founded. However, because these benefits do not figure in the official accounting systems of individuals or governments, the privileged book-keepers of public life, they are not accounted for at all. In this respect most citizens are free riders from the point of view of the city itself.

Orientalism and Despotism

The description given here of the pluralistic *polis* points to urbanism as an essential feature of the ancient state, on which most authorities for ancient Egypt and Mesopotamia are also agreed (Oppenheim, 1969, 1977; Bietak, 1979b).

Urbanism marks an essential contrast between the societies of *homo politicus* and *homo oeconomicus*. The early modern nation states of Western Europe, enjoying the life of dispersed pastoral communities, generated very little power – since they were virtually contained within their self-sufficient households – and distributed even less. It is a supreme irony in the history of state legitimation theories, then, that the pluralist, transactional, entrepreneurial, but traditional and relatively ungovernable East, should have been deemed 'despotic' by the pastoral, quiescent, relatively underdeveloped West, whose main concession to democracy involved parliaments, to which universal access was granted as late as the twentieth century of our era. Never demonstrating the same dense networks of subordinate forms of association, and still lacking the participatory forms associated with them, Western states have nevertheless dared to characterize the East as lacking a 'civil society' – precisely what is bespoken by the pluralist forms they demonstrate.

Bryan Turner (1984), in his excellent essay 'Orientalism and the Problem of Civil Society in Islam', has shown how the absence of civil society in oriental society constitutes the basic theoretical postulate of the case for oriental despotism. Inherited from Aristotle, and transmitted through a long line of thinkers from Montesquieu's *Spirit of the Laws* of 1748, through Marx and James Mill to Durkheim, 'whose Latin dissertation on Montesquieu and Rousseau was published in 1892', and Gramsci, who applies it to Russia, the thesis constitutes an inherited estate rather than a scientific theory, but has had undiminished success in the social sciences for all that. Citing Montesquieu's characterization of republics, monarchies and despotisms as being founded on virtue, honour and fear, respectively, Turner (1984, 29) demonstrates the utility of the absence of civil society to Montesquieu's argument:

(1) while monarchy is based on the inequality of social strata, in despotism there is an equality of slavery where the mass of the population is subject to the ruler's arbitrary will; (2) in monarchy, the ruler follows customs and laws, whereas a despot dominates according to his own inclination; (3) in despotism there are no intermediary social institutions linking the individual to the state.

James Mill, writing on *The History of British India* (1972 edn, 212–13, cited in Turner, 1984, 31) observed that 'according to the Asiatic model, the government was monarchical, and, with the usual exception of religion and its ministers, absolute. No idea of any system of rule, different from the will of a single person, appears to have entered the minds of them or their legislators'. John Stuart Mill shared his father's view of the Asiatic tradition, which, combined with de Tocqueville's analysis of democracy in America, produced in him fears of oriental slavishness infecting even Britain under majority rule: the threat 'not of great liberty, but too ready submission; not of anarchy but of servility; not of too rapid change, but of Chinese stationariness' (J.S. Mill, *Dissertations and Discussions*, 1859 edn, 56, cited in Turner, 1984, 31).

Durkheim, under the influence of Montesquieu, came to see the presence or absence of civil society as crucial a determinant in state formation processes as the division of labour itself – if indeed it was not the larger outcome. Gramsci maintained the tradition to which Hegel, the Scottish political economists, influenced by the long line of theoreticians from Aristotle, and Marx had contributed, of seeing the development of civil society as 'a major indication of social progress from the state of nature to civilization' (Turner, 1984, 27). Marx had maintained: 'Civil society embraces the whole material intercourse of individuals within a definite stage of the development of productive forces. It embraces the whole commercial and industrial life of a given stage and, in so far, transcends the State and nation ...' (Marx and Engels, *The Russian Menace in Europe*, 1953 edn, 76, cited in Turner, 1984, 27). And Gramsci concluded quite simply: 'Between the economic structure and the state with its legislation and its coercion stands civil society' (*Selections from the Prison Notebooks*, 1971 edn, cited in Turner, 1984, 28).

To give an indication of how this thesis was applied, in this case to Russia, Gramsci maintained: 'the state was everything, civil society was primordial and gelatinous; in the West, there was a proper relation between state and civil society, and when the state trembled a sturdy structure of civil society was at once revealed' (Gramsci, *Selections from the Prison Notebooks*, 1971 edn, 238, cited in Turner, 1984, 28). Max Weber, surprisingly lax in checking out his facts, as we have suggested, in *The Sociology of Religion* (cited in Turner, 1984, 34) characterizes Islam as quite simply the 'national Arabic warrior religion', which is 'inherently contemptuous of bourgeois-commercial utilitarianism and considers it as sordid greediness and as the life force specifically hostile to it'. An assertion hard to reconcile with the well-known fact of Islam's commercial bias, evident both in its law, as reflecting the realities of Mohammed, its founding merchant class, and the life of its citizens based on trade and commerce (Goitein, 1967, 1969; Cook, 1974).

Perhaps the most gratuitous and transparently untrue addition to the civil society thesis applied to these Easten societies, founded so many millennia ago on the long distance trade, is the assertion, first made by Marx, and repeated by Max Weber, that in the East 'the first basic condition of bourgeois acquisition is lacking, the security of the person and the property of the trader' (Marx and Engels, *The Russian Menace*, 1953 edn, 40, cited in Turner, 1984, 34). Not only does ancient Near Eastern society have the longest recorded history of civil and private law regarding the rights and property of the trader, but it likely pioneered the contractual forms in which they are expressed (Rostovtzeff, 1932, 8–9). Such historical inversions are due less to malice or a predilection for untruth, than they are to the ideological status of the claims involved – as provisional truths staking out territory and hoping, thereby, to create facts. They are due also to the nature of stereotyping: the characterization of the East as the 'other', or merely as the negation of all that was being claimed for the West, by polemicists knowing, in fact, very little about it.

PART I

The Greek *Polis* versus the 'Great King'

1

Greeks and Barbarians, Freedom and Slavery

Among the lines of conceptual demarcation between East and West having a long prehistory, one of the most central concerns the power/property nexus. As we shall see, the most enduring characterization of Eastern regimes is that of the patrimonial state: in the words of Aristotle, Eastern kings rule their people as slaves (*Politics*, 3.14, 1285a16, 1981 edn, 217–18). This perception, grossly distorted as it is, rests, however, on differences of entitlement, and a conceptualization of power and its relation to property, that are fundamental. Aristotle's addendum that 'it is because non-Greeks are by natural character more slavish than Greeks (and the Asiatics than the Europeans) that they tolerate master-like rule without resentment' (*Politics*, 3.14, 1285a16, 1981 edn, 217–18) is where he rests his case. It is an irony worth noting that Aristotle, for whom natural slavery was a right and proper thing, should have found political slavery so abhorrent – does he not protest too much?

Light is shed on the generally vexed question of Aristotle on slavery when the Greek/non-Greek axis is examined seriously. Indeed, much of the current analytical debate on Aristotle's views of slavery, which addresses only abstract philosophical axioms and a theory of human nature in general, is rendered absurd when the contextual elements are taken into account. Fortenbaugh (1977, 137), for instance, mounts the weak defence 'that Aristotle's view of slavery is neither psychologically foolish nor morally repulsive', because 'of course there are no natural slaves in the world, so that the view remains theoretical'! This is to misconstrue entirely Aristotle's view of the matter. For it is not too much to argue that Aristotle's whole case for or against slavery is mutually entailed by his attitudes to Greeks versus non-Greeks. One can say this and still maintain the general axiom, as others have argued it, that 'slavery was not born of racism, rather racism was born of slavery' (Winks, 1972, 7).

Aristotle lived in a society in which slavery was a customary institution and where slaves were generally Asiatics captured in war, and at a time when the tide seemed about to turn and the orientalization of Hellas beginning. As Sinclair (1962, 17) has pointed out, the Greek cities had already 'lost their absolute autonomy and notably their military power, so that they could not henceforth oppose the wishes of the Syrian, Macedonian, or other monarchs within whose territory they lay'. And Alexander had begun his conquests which would produce an empire in imitation of the Persians and earlier Eastern marcher lords, on the subject of which Aristotle's silence voices what we otherwise know to have been his disapproval (Ehrenberg, 1938). It is very possible that xenophobia on the part of this outsider, who was never himself a citizen of Athens, accounts for Aristotle's protestations that barbarians deserved to be no better than slaves. Political and population pressures were growing. With the exception of Sparta, where the helots were Greek, slaves from Asia Minor in some Greek states represented double the number of native citizens (Barker, 1947, 350), so that wholesale emancipation, or even manumission, about which he promises to talk but does not, is out of the question.

Aristotle's whole treatment of slavery is fraught with anomalies. While he defends slave-raiding as a necessary, and even praiseworthy, feature of warfare, he is vehemently opposed to the rule of barbarian kings who fail to differentiate between women and slaves, or for that matter men and slaves either. This is the point that Aristotle is concerned to make, in fact, on the very first occasion on which the subject of slavery is raised, early in the *Politics* (1.2 1252a34, 1981 edn, 57): 'But non-Greeks assign to female and slave exactly the same status. This is because they have nothing by nature which is fitted to rule; their association consists of a male slave and a female slave.' It might be pointed out that on almost every occasion on which the nature and status of slaves is discussed by Aristotle, he refers to women in the same breath; and that the distinction between them does not lie too far apart as far as he is concerned. It is significant that he should go on to conclude, however, from the fact – undoubtedly false – that the barbarians do not distinguish between women and slaves at all: 'So, as the poets say, "It is proper that Greeks should rule non-Greeks" [Euripides, *Iphigeneia in Aulis*, 1400], the implication being that non-Greek and slave are by nature identical.' Greek society, said to be such a great improvement on oriental, does not pretend to put men and women on an equal footing either, as Aristotle makes clear, for he goes right on to say of it (*Politics*, 1.2 1252b9, 1981 edn, 57–8): 'Thus it was out of the association formed by men with these two, women and slaves, that a household was first formed; and the poet Hesiod was right when he wrote, "Get first a house and a wife and an ox to draw the plough [*Works and Days*, 415]." (The ox is the poor man's slave)' – and the wife is a poorer man's ox.

Aristotle's discussion of slavery, which falls within the bounds of his discussion of property and the appropriate use of natural objects for the purposes of household management, might be treated with general scepticism. Aristotle's moralistic restrictions on trade, designed, it would seem, to foster a nation of pastoralists and beekeepers, do not extend to the slave trade. The same Aristotle who puts severe constraints on mercantile shipping, the entrepôt trade and commerce in general, as involving conceptual mistakes about the relation of money-making to the good life, nevertheless has no compunction about endorsing slave-owning as a species of property management and slave-raiding as an essential function of warfare. Slave-owning is not merely a dictate of necessity, it provides an ontological proof of mastery, more compelling even than that of a man over a woman. For while a man's powers do not require the presence of women to confirm them, the powers of a master cannot be confirmed in the absence of a slave – a point which Hegel, much later, was concerned to make.

The ontological significance of property is precisely the context in which the discussion of slavery is cast – and here we have the connection which John Locke, himself involved in the slave trade, was later to make much. 'The great and *chief end* therefore, of Mens uniting into Commonwealths, and putting themselves under Government, *is the Preservation of their Property*', Locke declared (*Second Treatise on Government*, ch. 9, 1964 edn, 395), meaning their 'Lives, Liberties and Estates, which I call by the general name, *Property*'. Locke, that anti-Aristotelian in epistemology and psychology, turns a very nicely Aristotelian argument on the slave as property. A slave is one who has forfeited his right to life, surrendering himself to a master as a species of property (Locke, *Second Treatise*, ch. 4, 1964 edn, 325). Locke, like Aristotle before him, makes logic out of the reality of slave-raiding. Slavery is a consequence of a '*State of War continued, between a lawful Conqueror, and a Captive*'. For it violates the precept of life in conditions of peace that 'a Man, not having the Power of his own Life, *cannot*, by Compact, or his own Consent, *enslave himself* to any one, or put himself under the Absolute, Arbitrary Power of another, to take away his life when he pleases' (Locke, *Second Treatise*, ch. 4, 1964 edn, 325). Locke would seem to have set up the prohibition against suicide precisely to deny the right of voluntary enslavement, as if to emphasize that slavery involves a coercive relation with outsiders and is not a right to suborn one's fellow citizens, insiders. From a general prohibition on suicide it follows that 'No body can give more Power than he has himself; and he that cannot take away his own Life, cannot give another power over it.' Enslavement takes place incidentally, as it were, as a consequence of forfeiting one's right to life to another in conquest, when 'he, to whom he has forfeited it, may (when he has him in his Power) delay to take it, and make use of him to his own Service', thereby strictly '[doing] him no injury by it'. It is interesting that in the cases of nations apparently selling themselves into slavery voluntarily – technically voluntary submission 'to *Drudgery, not to Slavery*', in fact (Locke, *Second Treatise*, ch. 4, 1964 edn, 326) – only the Jews are singled out for mention by name.

Aristotle, who proceeded to excavate the roots of the state in family and household, argued similarly, including slavery under the rubric of property. He began (*Politics*, 1.4 1253b23, 1981 edn, 64): 'Now property is part of a household, and the acquisition of property part of household-management, for neither life itself nor the good life is possible without a certain minimum supply of the necessities.' Establishing that, 'like any craft', living requires tools, Aristotle asserted that 'tools may be animate or inanimate': 'So any piece of property can be regarded as a tool enabling a man to live, and his property is an assemblage of such tools; a slave is a sort of living piece of property; and like any other servant is a tool in charge of other tools' (*Politics*, 1.4 1253b23, 1981 edn, 64–5). 'Tools in the ordinary sense', he went on to argue, 'are productive tools, whereas a piece of property is meant for action.' Slaves are more in the nature of property than tools, therefore (*Politics*, 1.4 1254a1, 1981 edn, 65): 'Now life is action and not production, therefore the slave, a servant, is one of the tools that minister to action.' A slave, to reverse Kant's axiom, is precisely a person treated not as an end but as a means, and this is more or less definitional of 'the slave by nature', i.e. not by his or her nature, but by the nature of what it is to be a slave; Asiatics and only Asiatics, as far as I can determine, being slaves by their own natures:

> A piece of property is spoken of in the same way as a part is; for a part is not only part of something but belongs to it *tout court*; and so too does a piece of property. So a slave is not only his master's slave but belongs to him *tout court*, while the master is his slave's master and does not belong to him. These considerations will have shown what the nature and functions of the slave are: any human being that by nature belongs not to himself but to another is by nature a slave; and a human being belongs to another whenever, in spite of being a *man*, he is a piece of property, i.e. a tool having a separate existence and meant for action. (*Politics*, 1.4 1254a9, 1981 edn, 65)

Aristotle's justification of the method of slave acquisition is, like Locke's, in terms of slave-raiding as a species of war. After endorsing the highly questionable anthropomorphic view that plants exist for animals, animals for man (*Politics*, 1.8 1256b19, 1981 edn, 79), Aristotle goes on to make the specious generalization:

> If then nature makes nothing without some end in view, nothing to no purpose, it must be that nature has made all of them for the sake of man. This means that it is according to nature that even the art of war, since hunting is a part of it, should in a sense be a way of acquiring property; and that it must be used both against wild beasts and against such men as are by nature intended to be ruled over but refuse; for that is the kind of warfare which is by nature just. (*Politics*, 1.8 1256b20, 1981 edn, 79)

The justification, as the editor of the earlier Penguin edition (Sinclair, 1962, 38) points out, is that 'for Aristotle property, not work, is the basis of livelihood', and 'getting slaves must be considered along with getting other property'. Just how much attention is paid to slave-raiding is surprising when one reads between the lines. Returning to his argument that slaves are a species of tools, Aristotle ties the property/power nexus tight: 'wealth is a collection of tools for use in the administration of a household or a state. It is clear therefore that there is a certain natural kind of property-getting that is the natural duty of those in charge of a house or a city; and why this is so is also clear' (*Politics*, 1.8 1256b26, 1981 edn, 79).

It is not that procuring slaves, by slave-raiding or other means, is technically part of the master's know-how, which rather consists in knowing the use-value of slaves. But even this is not knowledge of great consequence:

> All such fields of knowledge [cookery and domestic service] are the business of slaves, whereas a master's knowledge consists in knowing how to put his slaves to *use*; for it is not in his acquiring of slaves but in his use of them that he is master. But the use of slaves is not a form of knowledge that has any great importance or dignity, since it consists in knowing how to direct slaves to do the tasks which they ought to know how to do. Hence those masters whose means are sufficient to exempt them from the bother employ an overseer to take on this duty, while they devote themselves to statecraft or philosophy. The knowledge of how to *acquire* slaves is different from both these, the just method of acquisition, for instance, being a kind of military or hunting skill. (*Politics*, 1.7 1255b30, 1981 edn, 75)

What is significant about mastery and slavery is, in fact, neither acquisition nor use but *being*: 'A man is not called master in virtue of what he knows but simply in virtue of the kind of person he is; similarly with slave and free' (*Politics*, 1.7

1255b20, 1981 edn, 74). Not by virtue of what sort of *moral* person a man is, we might note, but in what relation he stands to property: as the owner or the owned.

The question of the right of property-getters to enslave others is a morally vexed question, as Aristotle indeed agrees in 1.6 (1255a3, 1981 edn, 71) – and so he should since his first axiom is that 'the difference between ruling over free men and ruling over slaves is as great as the difference between the naturally free and the natural slave' (*Politics*, 7.3 1325a16, 1981 edn, 400). The Greeks stake their superiority to the barbarians on freedom versus slavery. And yet Aristotle supports the enslavement of non-Greeks by Greeks as of right. In *Politics* 7.2 1324b22 (1981 edn, 397) his racism is barely disguised:

Of course we may be sure that nature has made some things fit to be ruled by a master and others not, and if this is so, we must try to exercise master-like rule not over all people but only over those fit for such treatment – just as we should not pursue human beings for food or sacrifice, but only such wild animals as are edible and so suitable to be hunted for this purpose.

The association between barbarians, slaves and wild animals is ominous, and this is not the first time that we encounter it, as we shall see.

Our fears are not allayed when Aristotle in his discusssion at 7.3 references his definitions at 1.6. At 1.5 (1254a28, 1981 edn, 68) he has already invoked physiological criteria, when he defines 'slaves by nature' as those 'whose condition is such that their function is the use of their bodies and nothing better can be expected of them'. Note the reference to their 'condition' – not necessarily their 'nature' at all – more probably the consequence of forced enslavement than its cause. Aristotle goes on to explain that 'the "slave by nature" is he that can and therefore does belong to another, and he that participates in reason so far as to recognize it but not so as to possess it (whereas the other animals obey not reason but emotions).' Scarcely differentiated from animals in their nature 'the use made of slaves hardly differs at all from that of tame animals: they both help with their bodies to supply our essential needs' (*Politics*, 1.5 1254a28, 1981 edn, 69). Aristotle turns to more overtly physical criteria: 'It is then part of nature's intention to make the bodies of free men to differ from those of slaves, the latter strong enough to be used for necessary tasks, the former erect and useless for that kind of work, but well suited for the life of a citizen of a state.' Note the qualification that follows, reminding us that the *polis* is a quintessential warrior state: 'a life which is in turn divided between the requirements of war and peace' (*Politics*, 1.5 1254a28, 1981 edn, 69). We are reminded of the invocation by the Boers of South Africa of Biblical notions to the effect that 'the sons of Ham are hewers of wood and drawers of water'; the same Hamitic peoples earlier enslaved in some instances by the Greeks.

Of course, as Aristotle freely admits, one runs into problems when physiological and moral qualities do not seem to match and we end up with 'people who have the right kind of bodily physique for free men, but not the soul, others who have the right soul but not the body.' He concludes rather lamely that 'suppose that there were men whose bodily physique showed the same superiority as is shown by the statues of gods, then all would agree that the rest of mankind would deserve to be their slaves' (*Politics*, 1.5 1254b32, 1981 edn, 69). I suspect that Aristotle was speaking less about general physical characteristics and more about specifically racial characteristics, and that he would have been so read. He does briefly consider, however, the moral dilemmas encountered by the general endorsement of a right to enslave prisoners of war.

Aristotle broaches the subject as a corollary of the distinction he has already made between natural slavery and slavery by convention, a distinction not only suspect with respect to his motives, but highly unstable in the way that he makes it: 'The expressions "state of slavery" and "slave" have a double connotation: there exists also a *legal* slave and state of slavery. The law in question is a kind of convention which provides that all that is conquered in war is termed the property of the conquerors' (*Politics*, 1.6, 1255a3, 1981 edn, 71). Aristotle concedes that to some the right of capture is illegitimate as merely an assertion of 'might is right': 'they hold it to be indefensible that a man who has been overpowered by the violence and superior might of another should become his property' (*Politics*, 1.6 1255a3, 1981 edn, 71). The question turns, Aristotle insists, on the word 'superior':

> in a way it is virtue, when it acquires resources, that is best able actually to use force; and in the fact that anything which conquers does so because it excels in some good. It seems therefore that force is not without virtue and that the only dispute is about what is just. Consequently some think that 'just' in this connection is a nonsense, others that it means precisely this, that 'the stronger shall rule'. (*Politics*, 1.6 1255a12, 1981 edn, 71–2)

Admitting no possibility of reconciliation between the views, which casts in jeopardy 'our principle that the superior in goodness shall rule and be master', Aristotle goes on to discuss what enslavement in war means in the barbarian context – surely the only one that he has in mind:

> Some take a firm stand (as they conceive it) on 'justice' in the sense of 'law', and claim that enslavement in war is just, simply as being legal; but they simultaneously deny it, since it is quite possible that undertaking the war may have been unjust in the first place. Also one cannot use the term 'slave' properly of one who is undeserving of being a slave; otherwise we should find among slaves and descendants of slaves even men of the noblest birth, should any of them be captured and sold. For this reason they will not apply the term slave to such people but use it only for non-Greeks. But in so doing they are really seeking to define the slave by nature, which was our starting point; for one has to admit that there are some who are slaves everywhere, others who are slaves nowhere. And the same is true of noble birth: nobles regard themselves as of noble birth not only among their own people but everywhere, and they allow nobility of birth of non-Greeks to be valid only in non-Greek lands. This involves making two grades of free status and noble birth, one absolute, the other conditional. (In a play by Theodectes, Helen is made to say, 'Who would think it proper to call me a slave, who am sprung of divine lineage on both sides?') But in introducing this point they are really basing the distinction between slave and free, noble-born and base-born, upon virtue and vice. For they maintain that as man is born of man, and beast of beast, so good is born of good. But frequently, though this may be nature's intention, she is unable to realize it. (*Politics*, 1.6 1255a21, 1981 edn, 72–3)

Aristotle's are not moral qualms about just and unjust men, the principle of rule of the best versus might is right. Rather it is a question of whom the war is being fought against and who is being enslaved. If the war is against barbarians, and it is they who are being enslaved, it is always right; if it is against Greeks, never. If those of noble birth are enslaved, it depends in whose eyes they are noble. As far as the Greeks are concerned the nobility of non-Greeks is simply something locally perceived, whereas noble Greeks are universally noble and can therefore never rightfully be enslaved. Everything turns once again on the distinction between those who are slaves by nature and those who are by nature free: 'the distinction between slave and free, noble-born and base-born ... virtue and vice'; what it is, in a word, to be Greek as opposed to barbarian.

It is worth noting that the normally benign Socrates is recorded in the strange Platonic dialogue *Menexenus* 244–5, (1961 edn, 195) (strange because it is not a dialogue at all, but rather a diatribe containing some rather bad history) professing similar views on the barbarians and the right to enslave them *vis à vis* the right to enslave Hellenes. The context is the account of an encounter between the Greeks and the Persians, in which the Greeks were coming off best, and the 'Great King' offered to make an end to hostilities on condition that the Athenians allow him the Hellenes he had enslaved in Asia:

> And if a person desired to bring a deserved accusation against our city, he would find only one charge which he could justly urge – that she was too compassionate and too favorable to the weaker side. And in this instance she was not able to hold out or keep her resolution of refusing aid to her injurers when they were being enslaved [in this case other Greek cities], but she was softened, and did in fact send out aid, and delivered the Hellenes from slavery, and they were free until they afterward enslaved themselves, whereas to the Great King she refused to give the assistance of the state, for she could not forget the trophies of Marathon and Salamis and Plataea, but she allowed exiles and volunteers to assist him, and they were his salvation. And she herself, when she was compelled, entered into the war, and built walls and ships, and fought with the Lacedaemonians [Spartans] on behalf of the Parians. Now the king fearing this city and wanting to stand aloof, when he saw the Lacedaemonians growing weary of the war at sea, asked of us, as the price of his alliance with us and the other allies, to give up the Hellenes in Asia, whom the Lacedaemonians had previously handed over to him – he thinking that we should refuse, and that then he might have a pretense for withdrawing from us. About the other allies he was mistaken, for the Corinthians and Argives and Boeotians, and the other states, were quite willing to let them go, and swore and covenanted that, if he would pay them money, they would make over to him the Hellenes of the continent, and we alone refused to give them up and swear. Such was the natural nobility of this city, so sound and healthy was the spirit of freedom among us, and the instinctive dislike of the barbarian, because we are pure Hellenes, having no admixture of barbarism in us. *For we are not like many others, descendants of Pelops or Cadmus or Aegyptus or Danaus, who are by nature barbarians, and yet pass for Hellenes, and dwell in the midst of us, but we are pure Hellenes, uncontaminated by any foreign element, and therefore the hatred of the foreigner has passed unadulterated into the lifeblood of the city.* (Menexenus, 244–5, Plato, 1961 edn, 195, emphases added)

As we shall see, the reference to the descendants of Pelops, Cadmus, Aegyptus and Danaus, as 'by nature barbarians' is an extraordinary give-away. It suggests that Socrates at least believed the genealogies celebrated in the great Epic cycle and refined by the later mythographers, and that 'pure Greeks' distanced themselves from the partners to the synoecism that constituted Greece as a melting-pot of Afro-Asiatic races.

In Aristotle too, as we have suggested, the inherent racism, cued by the focus on physiological characteristics, is barely disguised by the moralistic language in which it is dressed: 'base-born' versus 'noble-born', which we know to have referred to class and status characteristics, the *agathoi* versus the *kakoi*. A comparison between slaves and beasts belongs to the very definition of what it means to be a 'slave by nature', by virtue of being 'owned' by another as a mere chattel, and by virtue of his/her 'use-value', according to Aristotle (*Politics*, 1.5, 1254b16, 1981 edn, 68–9). Sinclair (1962, 17), in his Introduction, points to the durability of these arguments among nineteenth-century defenders of slavery, adding 'the difference between black and white races gave them just that outward manifestation of nature's supposed intervention that Aristotle had looked for in vain (book 1, chapter 5)'. But had he not also found it in the determination of race? Aristotle's highly moralistic language can be misleading. He moves on from the argument of physical superiority to that of mind:

> And if this is true in relation to physical superiority, the distinction would be even more legitimately made in respect of superiority of mind. But it is much more diffi-cult to see quality of mind than it is to see quality of body. It is clear then that by nature some are free, others slaves, and that for these it is both right and expedient that they should serve as slaves. (*Politics*, 1.5 1254b32, 1981 edn, 69)

It is only clear on the assumption that there is in fact something that one can *see* to demarcate slaves from free – racial or other physical characteristics – the missing premise that would convert a very bad argument into a plausible one from Aristotle's point of view. We are justified in suspecting that Aristotle's ontological arguments for 'slaves by nature' represent nothing more than a justifi-cation of *de facto* slavery. The statement referred to above (*Politics*, 1.7 1255b20, 1981 edn, 74, translation amended), 'A man is not called master in virtue of what he knows but simply in virtue of what he is – a master; similarly with slave and free', can be given a quite literal reading then. Our suspicions are not greatly allayed by Aristotle's attempt in 1.13 (1259b18, 1981 edn, 94) to give greater ontological depth to the notion of slavery by nature: 'About slaves the first question to be asked is whether in addition to their virtue as tools and servants they have another and more valuable one. Can they possess restraint, courage, justice, and every other condition of that kind, or have they in fact nothing but the serviceable quality of their persons?' Very revealingly Aristotle responds:

> The question may be answered in either of two ways, but both present a difficulty. If we say that slaves have these virtues, how then will they differ from free men? If we say that they have not, the position is anomalous, since they are human beings and share in reason. Roughly the same question can be put in relation to wife and child. Have not these also virtues? Ought a woman to be 'restrained', 'brave', and 'just', and is a child sometimes 'intemperate', sometimes 'restrained' or not? (*Politics*, 1.13 1259b26, 1981 edn, 94)

This instability in the behaviour of inferior persons does not alter the fact that in the nature of being: 'the deliberative faculty in the soul is not present at all in a slave; in a female it is present but ineffective, in a child present but undeveloped' (*Politics*, 1.13 1259b32, 1981 edn 95).

The lines of nature and convention, slavery *de facto* and slavery *de jure*, may seem to be blurred by other distinctions that Aristotle makes: the worker as a species of slave, for instance (*Politicss*, 1.13 1260a36, 1981 edn, 96). In fact, of course, many artisans in the fourth-century Greek states were foreigners, or metics, also frequently Asiatics. It is altogether consistent for Aristotle to justify the exclusion from citizenship of workers and freed slaves in his ideal state, in the way that he does then, arguing that, although in Athens of his day workers qualified as citizens, his own position did not really 'result in any absurdity':

> After all, slaves do not belong to any of the above-mentioned categories, nor do freed slaves: true it is that we must not give the name citizen to all persons whose presence is necessary for the existence of the state ... In ancient times in certain countries the mechanics *were* slaves or foreigners, and therefore mostly still are. But the best state will not make the mechanic a citizen ... what we have called the virtue of a citizen cannot be ascribed to everyone, nor yet to free men alone, but simply to those who are in fact relieved of necessary tasks. Some tasks of this kind are discharged by services to an individual, by slaves, others by mechanics and hired labourers, who serve the public at large. (*Politics*, 3.5 1277b33, 1981 edn, 183–4)

One question Aristotle does not even attempt to answer is on what grounds, if slaves are slaves by nature, manumission, which he recommends, might be justified.

The association of slavery with racial types is once again confirmed by Aristotle's disquisition on barbarian kingships. Having described the marcher lords, where 'kingship is like a perpetual generalship held on terms of personal authority' that might be thought more typical of Asiatic rulers, Aristotle in fact gives the example of Agamemnon who, 'put up with being abused in meetings of assemblies, but once an expedition had begun ... had sovereign power of life and death' (*Politics*, 3.14 1285a3, 1981 edn, 217). Aristotle goes on to say:

> Alongside this there is another type of monarchy, such as kingships found among certain non-Greeks. All these have power approximating to that of tyrannies, but they are legally established and ancestral. For it is because non-Greeks are by natural character more slavish than Greeks (and the Asiatics than the Europeans) that they tolerate master-like rule without resentment. (*Politics*, 3.14 1285a3, 1981 edn, 217)

As we shall try to show, appeal from racial characteristics and property entitlements to make the case for the slavishness of the barbarian involved conceptual failures that were either deliberate or inadvertent. The subjects of Asiatic kings were vested with different property entitlements, never properly understood in the West, resting on a contractual agreement whereby right of usufruct was gained for the willingness to pay taxes to the central government. Now, that the property/power nexus was crucial in Aristotle's conception of the state is evident, for instance, in his discussion of kingship. Although officially grounding legitimate kingship on 'the same basis as aristocracy: merit – either individual virtue, or birth, or distinguished service, or all these together with a capacity for doing things' (*Politics*, 5.10 1310b31, 1981 edn, 335), Aristotle speaks of those who 'have been honoured with the position of king'. They include 'some, like Codrus [who] saved their people by war from slavery; others, like Cyrus [who] set them free or acquired territory or settled it, like the kings of the Lacedaemonians, of the Molossians, and of the Macedonians'. In summary: '*A king aims to be a protector – of the owners of possessions against unjust losses*, of the people against any ill-treatment. But a tyrant, as has often been said, does not look to the public interest at all, unless it happens to contribute to his personal benefit' (*Politics*, 5.10 1310b40, 1981 edn, 335, emphases added). We have here the notion of the state as a pact of property-owners that is to resurface constantly in the history of political thought, most notably in the writings of the Venetian ambassadors on the Sublime Porte, accusing the Great Turk of emasculating his people, by denying nobles a fief or peasants a vassalage!

Much twentieth-century debate has been occasioned by the question of the general relation between property and power, fuelled by Marxist reflections on the aphorism of Rousseau in the Second Discourse, that 'the man who, having enclosed a piece of ground, bethought himself of saying "This is mine", and found people simple enough to believe him, was the real founder of civil society' (Rousseau, 1913 edn, 192). Long before this, however, from the time of the pre-Socratic Democritus at least, and certainly among the Epicureans, it was conventional to see the state as a pact of property-holders. Even the etymology of the word *nomos*, in the absence of more explicit historical evidence, would suggest the property/power nexus. As the *Oxford English Dictionary* (OED) tells us, the word, from *nemo*, a feeding place for cattle, pasture, in Homer could be qualified to yield also 'woodland' and was used by Hesiod to mean more generally 'food'. Its second meaning was 'an abode alotted or assigned to one, a district, province', as in Pindar and Sophocles; and 'one of the districts into which Egypt was divided', as in Herodotus 2.91 (Lloyd, 1969). Its third meaning was 'anything assigned, a usage, custom, law, ordinance', as in Hesiod, *nomos panton basileus*, 'custom is king' (*OED*, 1971 edn, 535) – or does he mean 'property is king'?.

It is tempting to argue the case for the historical development of *nomos* along the lines of its linguistic extension (Springborg, 1990d, 167). But it is at this point that we enter the hall of mirrors. For, whatever phenomenal/linguistic connection we may posit, the experience of power, like other intangibles, is expressed through metaphor (Condren, 1989); and whatever fundamental structural continuities may exist with respect to state forms, perceptions of them and the language in which they are expressed are constantly shifting and reacting back on the phenomenon (Condren, 1989). Scholarly attention has recently focused on the terminology of Machiavelli at the historical watershed of the Florentine Renaissance state, the suggestion being mooted that the entrance of the term *lo stato* onto the historical stage may even have assisted in catalyzing the phenomenon (Hexter, 1973; Mansfield, 1979; Skinner, 1979, vol. 1; Condren, 1989). Although this is a suggestion methodologically suspect as a piece of philosophical idealism, and historically anachronistic with respect to the long prehistory of state forms, it may be true with regard to a different set of specifics: and that is the link between power and property, or territoriality.

Lo stato in Machiavelli, as several scholars have stressed (Hexter, 1973; Skinner, 1979; Condren, 1989), is as much backward-looking as forward-looking. It still moves across the boundaries of two fields, one juridical, the other more literally territorial: that is to say between the *regnum stato* of Medieval political theory, which conceded to princes extraordinary power for the maintenance and protection of their patrimony; and the notion of the state as an estate or territory to which the prince held title (Anglo, 1969, 173–4, citing Post, 1964; Condren, 1989). These two conceptions to some extent converge. Anglo (1969, 173) points out: 'That Machiavelli has come to be particularly identified with the divorce of political from private morality, with the doctrine of expediency in political action, and with the mode of justifying all political means on grounds of reason of state, is due less to his uniqueness than to the dynamic way in which he expressed these ideas.' He goes on to say: 'Medieval legal theorists and canonists did not merely employ "reason of state", or some synonymous term, literally, they also had a very clear conception as to its meaning: and used the idea that "necessity has no law" to justify the extraordinary acts to which a ruler might oftentimes resort through force of circumstances' (Anglo, 1969, 173). Anglo (1969, 174) cites Gaines Post (1964, 308 n.141):

> I must point out once more that this kind of *ragione*, the *ratio publicae utilitatis*, etc., as we have abundantly seen, was as medieval as modern; *necessitas legem non habet* was a commonplace in the twelfth century; the legists and canonists often said that the prince could make new laws because situations, circumstances and the times are constantly changing; and Terence was frequently quoted (*Phormio*, II.iv.454): '*quot homines tot sentientiae*'. And why were the Florentines more '*rational*' about politics than medieval men in subjecting *ragione* to the moral law and God? Who was more sincere, who more cynical, in calling upon God? Finally, why say that the idea of *necessità* is opposed to or limits the use of *ragione*? After all, *necessitas* is part of and enhances the force of 'reason of State'. Even the maxim, '*Dove necessita caccia non bisogna consiglio*' represents the medieval doctrine, that by reason of the safety of the State, when the necessity or danger was so urgent and imminent that delay in taking action could not be risked, there was no need of waiting for lengthy debate or the consent of all interested parties. Not only was this understood when Edward I and Philip IV taxed the clergy without waiting for the consent of Boniface VIII, but Thomas Aquinas stated it for a more ordinary immediate danger.

We may say that 'reason of state', so understood, contains a moral element of care, and is more then than rank opportunism. The prince takes the necessary measures for the protection of his state (estate), as the shepherd protects the flock, or a patriarch his people. The language of Machiavelli is not primarily the language of care, of course, but that of an aggressive and assertive masculinity characteristic of the male warrior republic. As we learn from Hexter's content analysis of *The Prince*, *lo stato* is something conquered, held, acquired, lost, redeemed, but never itself a political actor. It is a territory, not necessarily coextensive with the state as we know it, possessed, pillaged, raped or ravaged and finally governed, but itself incapable of possessing, pillaging, raping or ravishing, or even governing. Hanna Pitkin, who reflects on the feminine metaphor of power in Machiavelli (Pitkin, 1984), which is one of almost unrelieved aggression, would probably agree that the horizons of the concepts

Machiavelli invokes, paradoxically, do include care. This is in part for technical reasons: *lo stato* shares the features of 'estate', as an object of power, with the legal juridical features of *status*, as an index of rights and duties.

One has to ask from what viewpoint the state was seen in this way, and what was new about it; for the phenomenon of the state long predated *lo stato*, the word. Clearly the standpoint is that of one interested in the parameters of state power seen from above, from the point of view of the prince rather than his subjects. Just as clearly, princely title to rule was being assimilated to the prince's territorial patrimony, where formerly it had been separated from it. Were all species of state, that is to say republics as well as principalities, so viewed? Perhaps, but not certainly. The opening lines of *The Prince* are indicative: 'all the states, all the dominions under whose authority men have lived in the past and live now have been and are either republics or principalities' (Machiavelli, 1961 edn, 33) – suggesting that the referents for *lo stato* are coextensive with *dominium*, under whose aegis republics certainly fell. Just as certainly, however, *lo stato* predominates in *The Prince*, and is rarely encountered in *The Discourses*.

Reppublica, as the Italian translation of 'the public thing', would seem to be categorically different from the patrimony of a prince. In a significant passage (*Discourses*, 2.30), in which the term *lo stato* does occur, it is clearly associated with patrimonial rule. 'Among other indications of the power of a strong state one looks to the terms on which it lives with its neighbours', Machiavelli (*Discourses*, 2.30, 1970 edn, 373) says, going on to list a number, mostly kingdoms, who paid tribute to Rome: 'the Massilians, the Aedui, the Rhodians, Hiero of Syracuse, king Eumenes and king Masinissa'. He lists modern examples of dependency as well, for instance the king of France, who pays tribute to the Swiss and to the king of England, observing that dependency 'comes from depriving the people of arms, and from the fact that this king and the other states mentioned have chosen rather to enjoy the present advantage of being able to despoil their people and of being able to avoid an imaginary rather than a real danger, instead of so acting as to secure their people's goodwill and to make their state [estate/*stato*] happy forever'. A thinly veiled contrast between principalities/patrimonies and republics.

Curiously, patrimonial rule, as the primary referent of *lo stato*, suggesting that no distinction was made by the prince between rule of his household and rule of his realm, was that precisely of which the Persians and other Orientals were accused. The story told by Koenig (1982, cited in Condren, 1989, 8) about Bernabo Visconti and his hunting dogs, that he billeted them upon the citizens of Milan, who were punished with fines and confiscations if they did not care for them properly – suggesting that Bernabo made no clear distinction between the duties of his subjects and those of his household – might well have been told of the Great Turk or a Persian king. Sigificantly, however, we shall see, this perception of oriental rule did not yet predominate in the minds of the Italians, awaiting the reception of Aristotle's ideas about Asiatics that came later than we tend to think.

The property/power nexus has a long history of mutual entailment. As Janet Coleman (1985, 77) has shown, the usual meaning of *dominium*, as debated by John of Paris and Marsilius of Padua, was precisely 'lordship over property'. Title to property meant precisely that the use and disposition of it were within one's power. Power did not necessarily mean title to property, but it often did. Possession was not the only framework within which power as title could be discussed and there is a tradition in Antiquity, at least as strong, of viewing title to use or usufruct separately from title to own. Without subscribing to the notion of 'irrigation societies' discussed by Marx, Weber and Wittfogel (1957) – now largely discredited on the grounds that basin irrigation did not, in fact, require centralized systems (Butzer, 1976) – one can show that in the Near East title to land was typically maintained by the Crown, as representative of the gods, to whom it really belonged. Title to use, however, was vested with tenant farmers by a contractual arrangement whereby they agreed to furnish taxes to the central government, as well as paying a lease (Keyder, 1987). In the Islamic civil code considerable attention was paid to rights of usufruct and the protection thereof (Lambton, 1953), as also in earlier Eastern legal codes. It is possible that usufruct, as it entered Roman law codified by Easterners Paulus, Papinian and Ulpian, represented Eastern practices.

In Plato's *Republic*, again perhaps a reflection of the realities of Eastern regimes, ownership of land was also vested with the state, its use being communal. But Aristotle, whose influence is so debatable in the formation of early modern theory of the state, has a secure niche with Cicero in establishing the property/power nexus; just as surely as he is responsible for formulating the divide between Eastern and Western systems in terms, paradoxically, of the patrimonial state. The anomaly that Aristotle, theorist *par excellence* of cities and the city-state, should have been ruralized to produce an advocate of feudal kingdoms (Springborg, 1989a), can now be seen to have a basis in Aristotle's theory of property, which those who constructed the medieval Aristotle may well have intuited. For, Aristotle, in book 2, chapters 3–5 of the *Politics*, rests his critique of Plato's *Republic* on the centrality of property to the state and Plato's failure to understand the material basis of all affection and affinity in the right of possession. Scoffing at the notion of the community of women and children, where Plato by a semantic trick 'substituted for the usual meaning of "mine" ownership by any number from 2 to 10,000', Aristotle drily remarks that anyone would rather have a cousin truly a cousin than a son shared in such a manner, adding: 'there are two impulses which more than all others cause human beings to love and care for each other: "this is my own" and "this I love"' (*Politics*, 2.4, 1262b3–23, 1981 edn, 111). In chapter 5, Aristotle insists, against Plato, that property should remain in private hands, although its use can be communally shared. He precisely denies what Plato was at pains to assert, that depriving the guardians of the state of property rights was appropriate in preserving the neutrality of their interests, and would not be a source of unhappiness, once this was understood. Against this argument, later reasserted by the *falasifa* of early Islam, Aristotle argues that ownership, like love of self, is not bad, but only when it leads to selfishness and excessive greed.

Cicero, in *De officiis* and in the fragmentary allusion to Plato's communism in *De re publica* (4.5, 1928 edn, 235), endorses the enjoyment of property, even of large estates, as a right, declaring that 'envy shall not stand in the way of the rich', just as 'the poorer classes shall not be oppressed because of their helplessness' (*De officiis*, 2.24, 85, 1913 edn, 263). While declaring at the outset

that 'there is no such thing as private ownership established by nature, but
property becomes private either through long occupancy [that is to say use] ... or
through conquest ... or by due process of law, bargain, or purchase, or by
allotment', he cannot really provide a satisfactory answer to the question he
himself raises, why in the republic, the common affair, there should be large-scale
private property at all (*De officiis*, 3.12, 53, 1913 edn, 323).

There are fundamental underlying reasons why Cicero was committed to
maintaining property rights, which like Aristotle he seems to view as a necessary
entitlement, as providing the field in which the powers and capacities (of some)
have their play. This despite the fact that entry into civil society was said to
involve the renunciation of private rights and interests (Nederman, 1988, 9).
Nederman (1988, 6) is not the first to point out (see Baron, 1938a) that 'Cicero
was the only political thinker of pagan antiquity whose works continued to be
accessible to the Christian West following the collapse of Roman domination.' If
De re publica and *De legibus*, although not always directly circulated, found their
way into patristic sources such as Saint Augustine and Lactantius, *De officiis*
and *De inventione* were among the most widely circulated of all treatises in the
medieval West (Nederman, 1988, 6–7 and notes). The reception of Aristotle's
Politics was within precisely Ciceronian parameters then.

Nederman (1988, 8–9) is insistent that Cicero does not derive the *res publica*
from self-interest and the desire to protect property outright. He secures its
origins in the instinct for self-preservation, the propensity to speech, and the
gregariousness these presume. However, once in place, Cicero extends the
naturalistic argument for society as such, to specific property arrangements and
political orders that any given society exhibits, so that 'the various political and
economic byproducts of human association come to possess the stamp of nature
by virtue of their compatibility with the gregarious impulse, and whatever tends
to the disturbance of political and economic order stands opposed to man's
naturally social inclination'. Moreover, given that 'the highest calling to which
the state can aspire is the reinforcement of the full range of civil and private
rights which men have acquired through social intercourse' (Nederman, 1988,
8–9), the more territory the state can command and the greater the property-
holders that it represents, the better. Cicero was the man who proclaimed that
'cities "mighty and imperial" ["*urbes magnas atque imperiosas*"], to quote Ennius,
ought in my opinion to be considered superior to hamlets and outposts' (*De re
publica*, 1.2.3, 1928 edn, 16), and that 'those who rule such cities by wise counsel
and authority are to be deemed far superior, even in wisdom, to those who take
no part at all in the business of government.' Not surprisingly, we find an almost
direct echo of Cicero's phraseology in the salute by John of Salisbury, in the
Metalogicon (827b, cited Nederman, 1988, 13), to enlightened eloquence, which
'has borne so many outstanding cities, has made friends and allies of so many
kingdoms and has unified and bonded through love so many people'.

We have here a Ciceronian set of associations: greatness is the mark of cities,
speech is the mark of rationality, free speech the mark of freedom and eloquent
speech the mark of greatness. These are notions that we see constantly being re-
echoed – somewhat to our suprise – in the Christian writers, for whom rhetoric
and eloquence have no valorization in strictly religious sources. They are Roman

rather than classical Greek emphases, the values of the orators being incorporated into the Roman philosophical tradition, in a way that in the Greek, those of the Sophists were generally not. It is true to say that freedom of speech, *parrhesia*, captured the content of freedom for the Greek dramatists and orators, too, Nicostratus proclaiming, 'freedom of speech (*parrhesia*) is the shield of poverty' and that 'anyone who loses his freedom has thrown away the shield of life' (Nicostratus, fr.29, cited in Rahe, 1984, 272). This is a truth that represented the reality of Athenian political life, where freedom was exercised in the right to debate and deliberate in popular assemblies, and only secondarily, if at all, in the right to economic and other freedoms. Plato and Aristotle did treat property as a condition of freedom, the former negatively, the latter positively, reflecting the reality of the Athenian *polis*, where property-ownership and free birth to Athenian-born parents constituted qualifications for citizenship. We should not be surprised to find that in Polybius, and later Machiavelli, writers whose works reflect much more Ciceronian than Aristotelian preoccupations, freedom is also more Roman in its definition – freedom, of speech, the right 'to shine' in representative assemblies, 'freedom of the Greeks' as the Romans construed it, in a word.

This conception of 'greatness', so central to Roman and, as we will later see, Renaissance Italian national aspirations, presupposed a class of 'great ones', public not private figures, the great-souled *megalopsuchos* of Aristotle's *Nicomachean Ethics* book 4, and the *magnus animus* of Cicero's *De officiis*, book 1. Great-souledness, it turns out, presupposes large quantities of quite material property – resources for the 'big gesture', for 'it is the mark of the magnificent man, in expenditure of whatever kind, to produce a magnificent result (for that is a standard not easily exceeded)' (*NE*, 4.2.19, 1934 edn, 211):

> It is also characteristic of the magnificent man to furnish his house in a manner suitable to his wealth, since a fine house is a sort of distinction; and to prefer spending on permanent objects, because these are the most noble; and to spend an amount that is appropriate to the particular occasion. (*NE*, 4.2.16–17, 1934 edn, 211)

Cicero, in *De officiis* 1.26.92 (1913 edn, 95), using language suspiciously similar, stipulates that men of 'great spirit' (*magni animi*), although it is desirable that they 'direct the affairs of nations', yet it is not necessary for them to participate in public life, the *res publica*, to warrant their station as entitled to 'live in magnificence, dignity and independence'; a view with which Aristotle, we know from his dissertation on the virtues of *schole*, leisure, would concur. The conditions which Cicero sets on the *magni animi* in the enjoyment of their property – and property seems to be the primary index of great-souledness – are hardly onorous:

> But even in the life of retirement there are and there have been many high-souled men who have been engaged in important inquiries or embarked on most important enterprises and yet kept themselves within the limits of their own affairs; or, taking a middle course between philosophers on the one hand and statesmen on the other, they were content with managing their own property – not increasing it by any and every means nor debarring their kindred from the enjoyment of it, but rather, if ever there were need, sharing it with their friends and with the state. Only let it, in

the first place, be honestly acquired, by the use of no dishonest or fraudulent means; let it, in the second place, increase by wisdom, industry, and thrift; and, finally, let it be made available for the use of as many as possible (if only they are worthy) and be at the service of generosity and beneficence rather than of sensuality and excess. (*De officiis*, 1.26.92, 1913 edn, 95)

The *polis* was very much a territorial entity, unlike the *ethne*, while the Roman *urbs*, as we know from Livy's first Pentad, was the site for synoecism – the coming together of tribes that constituted the Roman city as a heterogeneous entity much greater than a sum of the tribes and clans which constituted it. The territoriality of the ancient city-state was, therefore, no incidental feature. Aristotle endorsed 'the jealous city' (Dossa, 1987), as an enclave for the 'civilized' insider, requiring strict boundary maintenance against the 'uncivilized' barbarian – that is to say those who did not live in cities, inhabiting rather sprawling empires, and who were therefore less than gods and worse than men (Aristotle, *Politics*, 1.1.8–9, 1252b30–1253a10). Citizenship of the *polis* indeed depended on ownership of the *kleros*, or small holding, as well as free birth. It is nevertheless true, as Marx has insisted, that what rendered it, like its Roman successor, the *res publica* or 'public thing', was the existence of communal property, in the case of the latter, the *ager publicus* – so 'were [one] a natural Roman citizen, he would have an ideal claim (at least) to the *ager publicus* and a real one to a certain number of *iugera* of land' (Marx, *Grundrisse*, 1973 edn, 490).

In classical Antiquity communal ownership mediated relations between citizens and the state, which far from being an estate or patrimony whose ownership was secured by heredity and by right, was rather a territory or locus of power constantly under contest by various social groupings, tribal, ethnic, aristocratic; a contest for which the republican constitution provided certain ground rules. Thus, although republics allowed for the rule of executive magistrates every bit as powerful as princes, they ruled by a different title, which the rotation of elective office ensured would be maintained. More specifically, the contractual nature of rights and duties, *beneficia* and *officia* in Roman law, circumscribed powers as emanating from a reciprocal exchange of services – in theory at least; in fact, these were entitlements almost as entrenched as rights to real property. Such reciprocity was bound to apply more readily to subjects more or less equal at the point of exchange than to a prince and his subjects, whose powers were radically asymmetrical. So we tend to have rights/duties language applying to republics and property/patrimony arguments applying to principalities.

Such a rough divide is of course overschematized in terms of given systems. In the case of the Asiatic commune, as Marx was percipient enough to observe, the real basis is not necessarily territorial at all: 'the individual has no property but only possession' (Marx, *Grundrisse*, 1973 edn, 484). Title to rule is different too, being in the case of Islam, for instance, the title of a warrior leader over the faithful (Lambton, 1981, ch. 2), not so different from the Biblical model of the militant people of God, reintroduced by the radical Protestant sects of the seventeenth century. *Dar al Islam*, the house of Islam, despite the metaphor suggesting a power site, and despite the success of its marcher lords in acquiring territory, is still much less an essentially territorial unit than either the seventeenth-century people of God on the march (Walzer, 1965) or the modern Israeli state.

For reasons that we do not fully comprehend, part theological, part economic, the lands in which Islam established itself had had an immemorial tradition of state ownership and individual use. Large-scale state systems like those of Egypt and Persia conceived of all property as state property, to which usufruct was granted as a concession. Thus the avaricious and powerful Egyptian Ptolemaic Queens Berenice, Arsinoë II and Cleopatra II were careful not to alienate Crown lands, content merely to exploit their generous concessions – in the case of Arsinoë II, the fishing rights to Lake Moeris near Alexandria, and Cleopatra II the right to transport royal grain in her own ships (cited Pomeroy, 1984, 14–15).

Roman law made the distinction between ownership and use in two specific contexts: to establish what rightly belonged to the office of the emperor, as opposed to his person; and to establish the rights of subjects to communal or indivisible goods. Thus the emperor could spend his own money as he wished, but the imperial fisc he was obligated to pass on in the condition in which it came into his care, or better. And a subject had rights to clean water, air and sunlight, so that someone who obstructed a public right of way, or a neighbour who erected a canopy on his balcony blocking one's sunlight, committed an infringement for which one had redress (Veyne, 1976, 593–6). Moreover, the Roman emperor, like most of his successors, with the exception perhaps of the Carolingians, whose territory was small enough for it to be feasible, were not understood as 'owning' their realms: they were rather seen as the protectors of the private property of others, who 'owned' it in bits and pieces, ownership in this case providing the private wealth out of which the needs of the empire could be furnished, and warranting, indeed, imperial protection. The notion of the principality as the patrimony of the prince, Weber's disquisitions (1968, vol. 2, chs 12, 13) on patrimonialism to the contrary, is an innovation that medieval thinkers achieved in principle, the Renaissance state in practice. Janet Coleman (1985, 77) has argued convincingly that John of Paris in the Prologue of his tract *De Postestate regia et papali*, 'immediately made clear that power, *potestas*, in temporal affairs, is to be taken specifically in the narrow sense, meaning that lordship over *material property* is to be discussed, i.e. *dominium in rebus*.' She comments: 'this narrowed understanding of *potestas* is one of the most significant contributions to our conception of the theme of *dominium* in fourteenth-century texts.'

The distinction between ownership and usufruct was forced on the consciousness of Western Christendom in the struggle between the spiritual Franciscans and the conventuals over whether the propertylessness of Christ was enjoined on the order as a whole or only on its individual members (Coleman, 1983, 1985; Condren, 1984, 1989). The debate turned on the distinction between the use of moveables and the use or title to real property; a contest that became generalized to the Church as a whole and its *potestas*, as opposed to *possessio*, *auctoritas*, and 'the *ius* of priests to rule' (Condren, 1989, 6). A certain fluidity, as Condren points out, allowed premodern political theorists to move between the notion of the state as an estate and the state as a trust, *potestas* rather than *possessio.* In Innocent Gentillet's *Anti-Machiavel* of 1576 (Condren, 1989, 8–9) and in the *Essayes* of Francis Bacon (1595–1625), the state is still clearly a status or estate. But in John Ponet's *Short Treatise* of 1556 power is like a legal trust (Condren, 1989, 9). Condren has advanced the compelling argument that edifice metaphors and the state as an elaborate structure, rest not only on the conception of a fundamentally law-governed system, but also on the notion of a locus of power and power as a physical property. We shall have cause to note the degree to which edifice language was employed by Venetian commentators on the Ottoman Empire, discussed none the less almost exclusively in terms of *imperium* and *dominium* rather than the smaller-scale and more patrimonial *stato*. The distinction between movable property, the personal property of the emperor, for instance, and real property, real estate, was recast by the German public law theorist Christopher Besold in his *De magistate in genere* of 1626, to yield a distinction between personal majesty, 'the moveable power of the ruler', and real majesty, 'immovable and vested in a community' (Condren, 1989, 10).

It is another curious twist in the hall of mirrors that John Locke, in his effort to promote the notion of the social contract establishing society in the trust of a ruler, should at the same time have been responsible for the definitive association between power and property as an extension of the personality, its *sine qua non*: 'in Locke property right is symbolic of all political rights as well as being a term referring to material possessions or rights of use' (Condren, 1989, citing Laslett, 1964). As Condren (1989, 11) has shown, there was a longstanding English tradition of referring to power 'in the immediate ambit of physical property', or as in fact physical property: 'like an estate to be given, entrusted, passed on like an escheat [John Humphrey, in *A Plain, Honest Easy and Brief Determination of the Late Controversy*, 1689, 4, alluding to Hooker's *Laws of the Ecclesiastical Polity* (1600)]'; something 'lost, held and maintained [George Lawson, *Politica Sacra et Civilis* (1660)]'. It is without doubt appropriate to the monarchical systems within which social contract theories of the seventeenth century were formulated that, despite attempts to domesticate Roman law concepts of power as rights to use, and duties to refrain from use, power as property should have won the day. Janet Coleman (1983, 1985), pointing to correspondences between John of Salisbury's concept of 'lordship' and Locke's theory of property, suggests how deeply rooted in European historical realities the association between *dominium* and property really was. The homology between power as a patrimony and the patrimonial state was too powerful to bear resistance, and whatever later exclusive association might be pressed between patrimonialism and the oriental prince was in the face of this unassailable fact. When Louis XIV declared, 'L'État, c'est moi', what he uttered was merely a tautology.

2

Ionian *Historia* and *Kulturgeschichte*

Concepts of republicanism and despotism, sedimented in early modern thought as boundary markers between Western and Eastern political systems, have a long history of ethnic and cultural embedding that we can now begin to reconstruct, thanks to the work of a number of scholars (Frost, 1913, Aalders, 1950; T. Brown, 1962; Cole, 1964, 1967; Astour, 1967a; Bernal, 1987a). Popular stereotypes of the cyclical conception of time in ancient society must give way to the observation that notions of linear time and progressive technological and social development are as old as history itself – or at least as old as Ionian *historia*. Due, it is speculated, to their long contact with the sophisticated cultures of the Assyrian, Babylonian, Hittite, Medean, Persian and Egyptian East, and in the tradition of the great Ionian epic, Asiatic Greeks from Hecataeus of Abdera and Herodotus of Halicarnassus, Hellanicus of Lesbos and Aristogoras of Miletus, to Diodorus of Sicily and Manetho the Egyptian, conceived of a universal history that was not confined to their own *ethne*, long before the great Hellenistic exponent of the art, Polybius, and in a manner that anticipates him (T. Brown, 1962, 269–70). Among the *topoi* of these histories, in the original meaning of *historia*, were (a) the development of larger and larger social aggregates, facilitated by (b) the expansion of needs and corresponding technological and social developments; (c) the sequence of institutional forms that accompanied these developments; (d) the accurate chronological dating of linear time; and (e) the contribution of Eastern civilizations, particularly that of Egypt, to Greece.

These preoccupations, it has been noted (T. Brown, 1962, 259), were more or less exclusive to Asiatic exponents of *historia*. Greeks from the mainland, bordered by more primitive northern neighbours, lacking the stimulus to wider enquiry that Asiatic Greeks were provided with, were smug in their sense of superiority that the latter were not. The more static view of the mainlanders, of a world bounded by the confines of the *polis* and its possible permutations, formulated cyclically, came to dominate Greek thinking, with the consequence that large-scale 'barbarian' systems like those of the Egyptians and the Persians were looked upon as 'monstrosities'. (One recalls Aristotle's barbed remark, *Politics* 1265a14, that Plato's ideal state would require a land as large as Babylon to maintain its numerous citizenry (T. Brown, 1962, 270, n.98).) Interest in these large-scale *systemata* as human experiments, and for the insights they afforded into technological development and progress, gave way to narrowly ethnic stereotypes of them as oriental despotisms or barbarous tyrannies. In this way the popular view of Greek cyclical history and its parochialism became true, although not uniformly or simply true, as we will see.

For Asiatic *archaiologia*, in the tradition of Ionian *historia*, persists in a fragmentary way right through the classical period, up to and including the Hellenistic historians, preserved early by the Greeks in Sicily, who could not insulate themselves from Carthaginian and Etruscan influence; historians like Timaeus of Tauromenium and Diodorus of Sicily (T. Brown, 1962, 270, n.100); and writers of general history like the Asiatics Ephorus and Theopompus (T. Brown, 1962, 259, n.17); as well as the historians of Assyria, Babylonia, Media, Persia, Lydia and India. It is even present, sometimes in antithesis, at other times in uneasy synthesis, in works that focus on the *polis* and the finite forms to which it gave rise, their cyclical recurrence and the most efficacious 'mix' or 'balance' of elements to prevent corruption and excess, ensuring relative longevity against the assaults of Fortune. It has been the fruit of the innovative, if controversial, work of Thomas Cole (1964, 1967) to show, by *archaiological* excavation, that in the work of the most elaborate and complex formulas for a balanced constitution both traditions are present simultaneously, notably in those of Plato and Polybius, where the specific items are remarkably similar.

In his efforts to characterize the 'static' (cyclical), as opposed to the 'progressive' (linear) view, Cole has identified certain elements. The static view contains (1) a tripartite schema of political constitutions – the one, the few and the many – in their good and bad forms: monarchy, aristocracy and democracy; and correspondingly, tyranny, oligarchy and ochlocracy. It maintains (2) an 'organic connection' between the healthy forms and the corruptions that are endemic to them. (3) Organic principles of the natural life cycle of institutions: growth, maturation and decay, cannot be permanently interrupted. But (4) they can be temporarily arrested by the institution of complex or 'mixed', rather than simple, forms, to produce a constitutional balance that holds characteristic excesses in check (Cole, 1964, 443–4).

These four elements are constitutive, we may note, of 'classical republicanism', from its earliest anticipations in Herodotus 3.82.2, and Pindar, *Pythagoras* 2.86; down through Polybius, the only survivor among Hellenistic political theorists (Cole, 1964, 440); and Machiavelli, his Renaissance successor. The tradition is primarily Peripatetic, receiving its most explicit formulation in Aristotle (*Nicomachean Ethics* 8.10 1160a31–b22; *Eudemian Ethics* 7.9 1241b27–32; *Politics*, 3.5 1279a28–b6). With variations that are insignificant for our purposes this essentially Peripatetic schema is restated by Arius Didymus (*ap.* Stobaeus, 2.7.26, cited in Cole, 1964, 444); the first book of Cicero's *De re publica* (1.44, 1.65, 1.69, cited in Cole, 1964, 445); the biological *metabole* of individuals, families and cities in Philo's *De aeternitate mundi*; and the Pythagorean forgeries ascribed to Ocellus Lucanus and Hippodamus of Miletus (cited in Cole, 1964, 445–6). The essentially Peripatetic ingredients of Polybius' *anacyclosis*, or cycle of regimes is not ruled out by the possibility of transmission through Stoic sources, such as Panaetius, or even the Pythagoreans (Cole, 1964, 447).

If Aristotle's treatment of the occupational hazards of characteristic *polis* forms, and ways to circumvent them by a balance of institutional arrangements, represents the purest statement of the type A or 'static' tradition; those of other theorists of the *polis*, including Plato, or of the *cosmopolis*, including Polybius, contain elements from the 'progressive' tradition, labelled by Cole (1964) tradition B. Ranging over a period of time as extensive as the Peripatetic tradition A, this latter 'progressive' strand is yet more heterogeneous, both for the fact that it includes a variety of Asiatic Greeks, as well as mainland Greeks, and because they come from diverse philosophical schools. Again, it should be emphasized, these antithetical traditions are analytical constructs that, in particular writers, may be present simultaneously. What tradition B represents, as Cole has shown in his later monograph (1967), is a very different focus from tradition A: that is, the attempt to account sociologically for the structural development of civilization by way of an historical reconstruction of the dynamic processes of the great nations (*ethnai*) of the past, or in terms of a *Kulturgeschichte*.

This 'progressive' account is both ancient and ageless, demonstrating ingredients that we find present in the structural analyses of cultural processes in thinkers as diverse as Democritus, Epicurus, Plato, Polybius, Diodorus, Posidonius, Seneca, Vitruvius, Tzetzes, Machiavelli, Rousseau, the Political Economists, Hegel and Marx. It begins with the concept of needs and the means of subsistence; economic and technological strategies designed to meet them; the simultaneous production of knowledge and new needs; and concomitant forms of social and political organization (Springborg, 1981). In Plato's *Laws* 3, this account receives one of its earliest and most complete statements that demonstrates the antiquity of anthropologies of the state of nature and civil society. Characteristic ingredients are already present: the notion of a cataclysm, by flood or fire; of the reconstruction of society by stranded hilltop survivors; of the loss of old technologies with the destruction of the earlier society; and the redevelopment of the new. These were notions anticipated by Plato in the more mythical reconstruction of the *Protagoras* (Cole, 1967, 8–9), and the rebuilding after catastrophe recorded in Solon's Egyptian story (*Timaeus* 22B–25D; *Critias* 109B–10D).

Among the elements that are archetypal are the transition from a hunter-gatherer mode of production to clans – developed as an extension of the patriarchal family structure – and primitive kingship. The development of moral sensibilities is said to proceed apace, Plato and Polybius giving an account of the genealogy of morals, in the observance by subjects of the benefactor king, that is almost identical (Cole, 1967, 87–91). In Hermarchus and Diodorus, similarly, the development of *logismos* arises from shared needs and reflections on the observance of shared behaviour, based on the human capacity for empathy. Elements present in earlier accounts: the significance in Democritus (B157, cited in Cole, 1967, 121) of ' "governments and polities and the friendship of kings" ' as a blessing; Herodotus's account (I.96) of Deioces, king of the Medes, the benefactor–king; are paralleled in the *reges* of Lucretius 5.1108–11 and Polybius 6.7.4 (Cole, 1967, 91, n.18); and the observations of Diodorus 1.90.3 that Egyptian deification of kings and totemization of animals represent rewards for benefactions (Cole, 1967, 93, n.20).

The utilitarian element is present in the original account in each case, the *Kulturgeschichte*, in this mode, presupposing notions of the pursuit of pleasure and avoidance of pain, on which later and more famous theories of progress were based, as the set of motivations that made the expansion of needs possible. Concomitantly, expansion of knowledge and the pursuit of science as goods in themselves, were characteristically endorsed: traits for which the accounts of the atomists Democritus and Epicurus, as well as early modern advocates of progress, were famous; both present in the less well-known sources of *Kulturgeschichte* as well.

Tradition B, as both more amorphous and heterogeneous than tradition A, deserves to be treated as an analytical construct with even greater caution. Not all the elements enumerated were present in the accounts that it characterizes. Nevertheless, Cole (1964, 1967) has made a good case for the reconstruction by Plato and Polybius of *systemata*, or social aggregates of increasing size, and their propensity to prefer corporate government of a meritorious elite to kingship or democracy, being linked to fragments of Democritus on larger aggregations, his reflections on *democratia* and *nomos* and the relative merits of superior ability as opposed to the collective will and custom. It is even probable, as Cole argues (1967, 107–9), that Plato's precise account of the progressive development of social aggregations of an increasing size, from family to clan, city to confederation (Cole, 1967, 97–8), reflects less an evolutionary primordialism – the account of society in its progress from primitive to civilized state – than it does an axiom of atomist physics: the derivation of 'the entire universe from the concourse of atoms in aggregations or "orderings" (*kosmoi*) ... believed ... by Democritus to be characterized by a tendency to become progressively larger (A40)' (Cole, 1967, 109, 107). In the same way perhaps, Plato's disquisitions on friendship, and the conventional Greek formulas, 'everything in common between friends', and 'birds of a feather flock together', may be linked to the Democritean notion that all *kosmoi* are formed of aggregations of 'like to like' (Cole, 1967, 117).

The implication of Cole's reconstruction is to drive a wedge between the Peripatetic and the Platonist traditions. And if this should be treated with considerable caution, it is nevertheless the case that this incipient breach becomes a divide of great significance in Renaissance receptions of ancient political thought. A reconstruction as novel as this serves to re-focus thought that has become fixed in pathways cemented in early modern thought. The amorphousness and relative fluidity of all systems of thought permit such reinterpretations. And they permit them to be true in ways that do not necessarily invalidate earlier interpretations, providing only a necessary correction to their exclusivity. This can be shown quite specifically. For what is startling about the thesis of these two antithetical traditions, is not that Plato and Polybius should evince a complex, and perhaps uneasy, synthesis of elements that pull in two different directions: one leading to the theorization of society based on the corporate city, the other to the great landed empires based on kingship and aristocracy. The greater departure is a call for the reconsideration of the works of those Asiatic and Hellenistic thinkers – among whom Polybius belongs – who have for so long suffered from the Attic bias in the classics that reflects the received orthodoxy of the ancient world. The net yield of this redirection is to focus on the analysis of non-Greek systems, as observed through the eyes of the Greeks and those Hellenized Asiatics who dominated the Hellenistic world.

The extensive writings still extant of Herodotus, Xenophon, Polybius, Diodorus Siculus, Stobaeus, and fragments of Hellenistic philosophers and historians preserved in anthologies, provide accounts of large-scale political systems, often much older than, and later coexistive with, the *polis*. They are accounts surprising for their informativeness, given access to sources, as we now know from the research of Egyptologists, Assyriologists, students of ancient Persia and Asia Minor. And what they provide are perceptions of the Greeks on the large-scale barbarian political systems, which vary, in fact, from reverence to ridicule. More importantly, they show beyond doubt our schematic evolutionary notions of social and political development to be misplaced. Glorification of the *polis*, as the quintessential social form of the ancient world that we claim as our ancestor, has now to be set alongside systems, some similar – like those of Mesopotamia – some quite different: the great territorial realms of Persia and Egypt, with their elaborate divisions of labour, finely tuned economic systems, large-scale bureaucracies, tax-collecting and distributional systems, military capabilities and capacities for agricultural and industrial production.

Not only did these large-scale systems precede, by several thousand years, the development of the *polis*, but they were the dominant forms into which the Greek and Roman worlds relapsed in the Hellenistic period, after its brief experiment was over. It is testimony to its marvellous literature, preserved fortuitously by a long philhellenic but Eastern intellectual tradition, that the *polis* has continued to dominate our conceptions of the ancient world to the degree that it does. Along with its literature, of course, we have tended to perpetuate Attic stereotypes of Eastern systems; and it is for this reason that notions of republicanism and despotism are paradigmatic. Concepts that, we will see, hardly do justice to the experience of ancient kingship, now revealed by archaeological and epigraphic research. Or even to the analysis of Eastern systems that less favoured ancient writers can reveal. Indeed, once the reconstruction is complete, the insights of Plato, like those of Polybius, on Egypt and the great civilized world beyond Greece's boundaries, belie these categories. The construction of the myth of oriental despotism has been the foil for classical republicanism, and its deconstruction must follow the same path.

Roman political thought, already less fluid than Greek, because imitative, has a significant contribution to make in the sedimentation of stereotypes, even though the strategies of policy-makers suggest that their perceptions took account of the complexity and levels of cultural development of the East (Badian, 1968; Gruen, 1984). Rome is peculiarly paradoxical for the fact that, as it expanded from *polis* to Empire, it personally took on attributes of the great Eastern systems, and specifically those of Egypt. The role of the Roman pharaoh has been insufficiently explored, but aspirations, first of Mark Antony, Caesar, and briefly of Augustus, to shift the Empire's capital east to Alexandria, where they would enjoy more immediately the honour of deified kingship – a shift eventually accomplished, but to Constantinople – bespoke the impact of Eastern imperialism.

As we attempt to reconstruct the alternative to the Peripatetic tradition, tradition B, it will become clear that the observation of Egypt in particular, original playground of the gods, locus of creation itself and the primeval flood, on some accounts (Plato, *Phaedrus*, 274C; Diodorus 1.9, 1933 edn, 33–7), and laboratory for social and economic development, played a role extraordinary in ancient political thought. Constant references are made in the search for indices of technological innovation to Egypt as the early experimenter with agriculture and the sedentary existence that accompanies it. Diodorus Siculus 1.14.2–3 (1933 edn, 49) suggests that the offering to Isis of the first grains of the season honours her as the discoverer of agriculture – the first Demeter, the dispenser of *cornucopia*, roles with which she is again associated in the Renaissance. The use of grass sacrifices in Egypt suggests cultivation for food (Diodorus Siculus, 1.43.2, 1933 edn, 155). The mention of reed houses as forms of early construction (Diodorus 1.34.4, 1933 edn, 155), of Hermes as the inventor of weaving, and of Osiris as the patron of mining and metallurgy, by means of which he adorned the golden chapels of Amun (Diodorus 1.15.3–5, 1933 edn, 51), suggests the methods by which a sedentary civilization was furnished with its needs. Observations of a long line of thinkers in tradition B on the significance for social and cultural development of the innovation of writing – for instance, Plato, *Timaeus*, 23AB, Lucretius 5.1444–47 (Cole, 1967, 44, 191) – often took the specific form of attribution to the Egyptian Hermes or the great god Thoth; a powerful tradition that continued into the Renaissance and beyond (Iversen, 1961, 1971). Diodorus Siculus went further in his assertion that what Hermes created for Egyptians was a *lingua franca* (*koine dialektos*) out of pre-existing materials, a synthesis of pre-existing dialects (Diodorus 1.16.1, 1933 edn, 53), a passage linked by Cole (1967, 108–9) with Plato's notion, *Laws*, 3.681A–C, of the coalescence of clans and the necessity to synthesize their *nomoi*, yet another example of Democritean atomistic conceptions of the creation of social aggregates.

It is indeed possible to put together an Egyptian version of the whole account of creation, development of technology and the arts, destruction by cataclysm and redevelopment, to be found as early as Plato and as late as Diodorus, of which universal, rather than specifically oriental, versions are to be found in the Hellenistic period in the accounts of the Cynics, Stoics and Epicureans, and even in Byzantine sources (Lovejoy and Boas, 1935; Cole, 1967). The Egyptian story, the prevalence of flood mythologies in the great epic cycles of Mesopotamia, the Asiatic origins of most Hellenistic writers who contribute to the Stoic and Cynic versions, suggest a heavily oriental bias to tradition B, which may or may not cast light on Cole's attribution to Democritus as a single source.

For Cole characterizes tradition B as essentially 'Sophist', tracing a line that runs from Protagoras to Democritus, to Hermarchus and on down to the Stoics, Epicureans and Sceptics (Cole, 1967, 123–4). The Sophists, an occupational category rather than a philosophic school, as itinerant teachers of rhetoric, represented a tradition both more individualistic and more pragmatic than the institutionalized schools. The Sophist or Democritean anthropology and genealogy of morals made only intermittent appearances after the fifth century, due primarily to the hegemony of Aristotelian teleology and Platonic idealism (Cole, 1967, 131). That it was later accepted by the Cynics, Sceptics, Stoics and Epicureans is testimony to the disfavour into which the Academic and Peripatetic universal systems fell in the Hellenistic period – a subject of great interest to Karl

Marx, and the topic of his doctoral dissertation and early notes (Marx-Engels, *Collected Works*, 1975, vol. 1).

As early as Hesiod and Xenophon there are traces of Democritean and Sophist themes: the natural origin of morality in the family; the division of labour and parallels between political and domestic economies (Cole, 1967, 132). Aristotle himself provides a phenomenology of *philia*, or affective ties, as the bond creating primary forms of community out of which the *polis* is constructed, but he is ultimately disparaging of all but ethical bases of *koinonia* (Cole, 1967, 134–5; Springborg, 1984a). Plato, who follows the *Kulturgeschichte* so far, rejects its final thrust for different reasons: his preference for the patriarchal family and kingship (Cole, 1967, 116). In *Laws* 3, the account which Polybius 6 so closely parallels, we have, Cole speculates (1967, 98–100) a composite of Plato's earlier justifications for the king as good shepherd (*Politicus*), the archaic Egyptian origins of kingship (*Timaeus* and *Critias*), along with justifications from a different, and perhaps Asiatic, tradition of kingship and rule of law.

Polybius, for whom the experience of kingship is an important stage in the development of the genealogy of morals and the social structures out of which Empire, as an aggregation of corporate structures compatible with kingly rule, is created, is ultimately more faithful to the Democritean spirit than Plato, Cole argues (1967, 116). In Polybius, like Democritus, parents, unlike animals, expect gratitude in their children; and subjects experience the beneficence of the good king, dismayed by failure to reciprocate. Here the origins of *nomos* are born, language creating the vehicle. The further expansion of the arts and music require an economic surplus. And we have the social compact of Epicureanism and the role of the family in the image of *koinonia* (Cole, 1967, 112–15). Parallels between Archytas of Tarentum and Polybius on reason (*logismos*) and harmony (*homonoia*), as principles underlying the expansion of kinship, ethnic and political boundaries, suggest a further link to Democritus in a thinker influential on Aristotle for his mathematical conceptions of proportional justice (Soudek, 1952, 54–8; Harvey, 1965, 101–40; Springborg, 1984a).

From Protagoras to Democritus and Hermarchus to Plato and Polybius, we have an account of justice (*dike*) and political science (*politike techne*) as responses to the struggle for survival in the state of nature; the experience of warfare, kingship and community as coping strategies; and a preoccupation with the kingly art of rule (*basilike techne*), that find their parallel in Epicurus and Lucretius (Cole, 1967, 123–7). Apparent similarities between Polybius' analysis of the expansion of community and the Stoic universe (*oikoumene*) differ on significant points, however. The Stoic notion of kinship, *oikeiosis*, is more abstract, positing laws of *physis*, tending toward a uniform human nature with inbuilt propensities for social harmony. Polybius' understanding is more sociological, involving the inductive development of *logismos* through experience, imitation and habit; the recognition that human nature, a product of culture as much as of nature, is as variable as history permits (Cole, 1967, 136–40).

Polybius and Diodorus differ from the Epicureans on the same score, rejecting a mechanistic atomism, just as they reject the Peripatetic *oikeiotes* and the Stoic *oikeiosis*, as favouring nature, *physis*, over convention, *nomos* – that dichotomy first articulated in the fifth century that set the parameters for social theory ever since. Polybius preserves a balance between those elements in human nature which are 'fixed' and those which are 'acquired' or cultural, that harks back to the fifth-century Sophist Antiphon and his distinction between 'natural' wrong-doing, which invites divine retribution, and that which is so by virtue of *nomos*, for which the penalties are civil (*VS* 87B44, Fr. A. col. 1.1–2.20, cited in Cole, 1967, 142); a distinction between the consequences of *physis* and *nomos* that is paralleled in Herodotus 4.110.2–117 (cited in Cole, 1967, 143). Polybius' perspective on the processes of history as open and contingent is succinctly expressed in the fragment of another late fifth-century thinker Archelaus (*VS* 60A4.6, cited in Cole, 1967, 143, n.38), that 'men were separated from the other animals and then developed leaders and lawful usages and techniques and cities'. An essentially fifth-century view that was lost to the Peripatetic and Platonist traditions in which the polarity of a universal human nature and the status of the moral individual became dominant preoccupations: 'In finally gaining his own soul Hellenic man had lost the world – or at least the possibility of understanding it' (Cole, 1967, 143).

It is a further irony that Plato's predilection for the patriarchal family as a moral entity, and for kingship as its macro-form, may have derived from his experience of Egypt, the very source of *exempla* for theories of contingent and progessive social development in the Hellenistic works of Hecataeus, Diodorus and Polybius. This turning point is not without its ramifications either. Hellenistic large-scale state systems, theorized by Polybius and Diodorus, were heavily indebted for imperial ideology to Platonist notions of the Beneficent King, the King as Shepherd; notions that have an important role in Pythagorean and Stoic thought (Goodenough, 1928; Delatte, 1942). The admirable fit between the realities of Hellenistic monarchy, more oriental than Greek, and the content of Platonic–Pythagorean theories of kingship, suggests more than the adaptation of Greek theory to Asiatic circumstances, and this consideration reflects back on Cole's schema.

For there is an unconvincingly philhellenic element to his insistence on the exclusive derivation of the 'alternative' tradition – tradition B in the earlier work (Cole, 1964), but referred to as the 'Sophist' tradition in the later work (Cole, 1967) – from Democritus. This becomes clear in his arguments for the accounts of Diodorus, Euhemerus and the priest Leo in the apocryphal letter of Alexander the Great to his mother (*FGrH* 659F5, F9, cited in Cole, 1967, 20, 153–4) as Egyptianized versions of a Hellenic anthropology (Cole, 1967, 16–20, 150–61). This even while admitting that the Egyptian accounts move the dynamics dramatically from a Democritean democratic, to a royal or court, setting (Cole, 1967, 162). The role of deified kings, in the Egyptian version, and their benefi-cence in creating technologies that gave rise to civilization, are unsatisfactorily accounted for by the proposition that 'once the divine craftsman and the deified mortal *euergetes* of Greek tradition had been fused into a single personality, and the type so created identified with the pre-dynastic god-kings, Egyptian tradition was most easily rationalized in a context suggested by Democritus' (Cole, 1967, 161).

Hardly more worthy are Cole's further contentions that Democritean distinctions between history and prehistory lent themselves to adaptation to separate the Egyptian dynastic and predynastic period; that the Democritean emphases on individual event-sequences in the *Kulturgeschichte* were easily transposed by their attribution to the work of individual Egyptian gods; that the Democritean notion of the benefactor-king could then be taken over unchanged; and that the 'pervading atmosphere of *mythos* – which would have made it sound old-fashioned if propounded in direct competition with the more "modern" anthropology of Academics and Peripatetics – was eminently suitable in an account presented, as those found in Diodorus' source and subsequent euhemerist texts regularly are, in the guise of native tradition preserved from time immemorial in priestly archives' (Cole, 1967, 161).

Cole, while postulating a possibly original oriental tradition in Democritus' own writings, on the basis of two works on kingship of doubtful authenticity attributed to him (Cole, 1967, 161, n.40), argues on balance that the adaptation of the Democritean anthropology to oriental kingship was achieved by Diodorus for propagandistic purposes. The *Kulturgeschichte* of Democritus may already have been applied this way by his follower Anaxarchus, admirer and friend of Alexander the Great, in his *Peri basileias* (*VS* 72B1–2, cited in Cole, 1961, n.41), he notes. But it is by a piece of purely circular reasoning, in the inference of a *terminus post quem* for Diodorus' source as coterminous with the establishment of a Greek dynasty in Egypt, by reading 'part of what is said in Diodorus 1.11–29 about the early god-kings ... as Lagid propaganda' (Cole, 1967, 159, n.34), that he then concludes a propagandistic success for Diodorus' source, whose adaptation of the Democritean model 'of the progressive expansion of an original social and economic unit was doubtless, once transformed into an account of the triumphal civilizing expedition of an Osiris or Dionysus, most welcome at the court of a prince who laid claim to be the heir to the universalism of Alexander and would have regarded these gods as his prototypes' (Cole, 1967, 161).

Not only is the tradition of *Kulturgeschichte* for which Cole seeks a source (*Quellenforschung*) in Democritus too heterogeneous to lend itself to such an aetiology, but the Egyptian version and the centrality to it of kingship, which shifts the locale of progress away from the city to the royal court, that Cole so badly argues as an oriental version of the Greek original, deserves consideration in its own right. Students of Egyptology have noted an uncanny acquaintance with the specifics of dynastic succession, local events and social practices in Diodorus' account, like those of Herodotus and Polybius – for instance, Diodorus 1.80, on the protection in Egyptian law of the children of slaves (Baillet, 1913, 354); Diodorus' lengthy observation (1.24.1–8, 1933 edn, 77–9) that the original Heracles was an Egyptian, after whom the son of Alcmene was named millennia later, now suggested by other epigraphic sources (Brundage, 1958); and more generally in the accounts of Herodotus, Polybius and Diodorus (Baillet, 1912, 1913; Fowden, 1986). Attribution of their sources to some priestly account, such as that of Manetho – Cole (1967, 159, n.35) rules out Manetho as a source for Diodorus, as incompatible with the former's presentation of 'the earliest Egyptian kings in so thoroughly Hellenic a guise' – only serves to push the problem back one step. What has to be recognized, because it is now quite well established by scholarly research, is the degree to which the concept of the beneficent king – '*soter*' ('saviour') and '*euergetes*' ('benefactor') according to Greek and specifically Ptolemaic appellations (Baillet, 1912, 1913; Ferguson, 1912; Nock, 1951) – accorded with both the theory and the practice of pharaonic monarchy. And what a long shadow Egyptian monarchy cast over the Hellenistic and perhaps also the Hellenic worlds. Hecataeus, like Protagoras and Democritus himself, were from the same city of Abdera in Thrace, with perhaps more contact with the Asiatic East, where Egypt's influence was felt far into Asia Minor and the kingships of Mesopotamia. The important role of the beneficent king in Plato's *Politicus* and in the genealogy of morals of Polybius cannot adequately be accounted for as the transportation to a courtly site of processes that in more 'Greek' versions took place in the city. Cole (1967, 161, n.39) notes that the benefactor king creeps into Aristotle (*Politics*, 3.1285B6–9), and 'even more strikingly, Lycurgus, *Locr.* 88, [in] the *isotheoi timai* [god-like honours] paid to early kings of Athens because of their services to the city'.

Cole (1967, 51) has observed the textural differences between the secular, utilitarian, rationalistic 'challenge-response' accounts of the origins of civilization given by Democritus, Protagoras and later the Stoics, Epicureans and Sceptics, usually accompanying an account of atomist physics, on the one hand; and the mythological accounts, on the other. The latter comprise works by Plato like the *Protagoras*, where the *demiourgike politike*, the development of technology, and *politike techne*, are gifts of the gods Prometheus and Zeus, respectively; the third-century novel of the *Sacred Scripture* by Euhemerus, written at the Macedonian court of Cassander, relaying a voyage to remote islands of the Indian Ocean where Uranus, Cronos and Zeus, great kings in their day, were worshipped as gods for their benefactions; and of Diodorus in the *Aegyptiacha*. The fit between these latter accounts and the need to justify Hellenistic ruler-cults – which certainly contributed to their historical significance – does not rule out the material belonging to traditions that antedate their use. The content of Plato's *Protagoras*, taken in conjunction with the *Timaeus* and *Critias*, would seem to provide the best evidence for the case for multiple sources for *Kulturgeschichte*, producing at least two definable types of tradition. One tends towards a secular, rationalistic, evolutionary account positing linear time; technological and social development extending into the indefinite future in unknown ways according to natural laws of *physis*, and producing ever-larger aggregations according to general principles of expansion and progress. The other is a quite specific account of the development of empire based on sacred kingship that is much more precisely historical and may have reflected both the theory and practice of Egyptian kingship.

To the first tradition belong not only fifth-century and later Hellenistic, secular, Stoic, Epicurean and Sceptic accounts, but even elements of the Peripatetic tradition and the work of Polybius to a certain extent. It is not inconceivable that this tradition, to which Democritus surely belongs, and which tends to focus on the city, its atomistic construction out of affinal sets, and the tension between individual and the collectivity, has its roots in the experience of urban development not only in Greece, but also in Mesopotamia – characterized also by a secularism, rule of law and astrological materialism not so dissimilar to

Greek atomism. The kingly tradition is quite different, its mythical and sacred dimensions no mere fancy dress for Greek concepts. The theory and practice of Egyptian kingship is perhaps more faithfully represented in the work of Plato than that of any other Greek writer, as we will presently show.

What of Cole's contention (1964) that Polybius straddles traditions A and B – and what are we now to make of traditions A and B? Cole, in both his works (1964, 1967), has pointed to a wide range of Greek accounts of the origins of society in which kingship plays a highly significant role, from Plato, Aristotle, Theophrastus and Panaetius, to Polybius, Tacitus, Lucretius and Posidonius (Cole, 1964, 450–4). Among a number of these thinkers kingship represents a form of rule natural to man and beast that is no more than a way station in the higher evolution of the species. For when customary kingship turns to tyranny it is forced to give way to rule of law. And yet the centrality of kingship to the account, the role of the benefactor in the genealogy of morals, an abiding fear of tyranny and preoccupation with the *polis–tyrannis* polarity, suggest something more than an open-ended, secular, evolutionary process. For *democratia* is valorized over against *monarchia* in a very pointed way. Cole (1964, 455–65) notes the rather difficult accomplishment of Polybius in fitting the tripartite cycle of regimes of the Peripatetic schema, tradition A, into the bipartite tradition B, in which democracy and monarchy are mother constitutions and no significant space is made for aristocracy or oligarchy. Under what pressure was Polybius placed that he did this? – for on the face of it the marriage between static, non-evolutionary, but cyclical tradition A and sociological, evolutionary, tradition B makes no sense.

Cole is probably right, that as far as Greek macro-historical schemas of the rise and fall of nations go, there are two traditions roughly coinciding with traditions A and B. Tradition A is a non-evolutionary schema; it does not presuppose primordial states or evolutionary sequences, but is concerned with urban *polis* society as a universal political form, its structures and dynamics essentially timeless within cycles of oscillation around a mean. Moreover, tradition A matches the reality of Greek and East Mediterranean experience in a peculiar way. For urban, entrepreneurial society of the riverine and littoral civilizations of Greece, Mesopotamia and the Levant produced city-republican forms that have endured from the third millennium BC, through the classical period in Greece, their greatest flowering in the Hellenistic period of city foundations (Jones, 1937, 1940; Tarn, 1952), through the Renaissance, the Islamic Middle Ages, and still perhaps are not dead (Springborg, 1987a). So much of what falls under tradition A still seems applicable to the dynamics of city and republican government, and if its timelessness is not matched by a spatial universality, this arises from very specific cultural processes of extrapolation by which the classical republican tradition was transposed to Europe, then the New World, and ultimately the Third World.

What tradition B represents, originally Sophist in its Greek formulation, is indeed an evolutionary account of expansionism. Sociological speculation on the origins of regimes classically takes the form of postulates concerning the extension of the patriarchal family in its macro-form of kingship, to meet needs for security common to man and beast. The development of new needs, once the primary needs on which civilization is founded can be met, leads to new expectations of gratification, concentrations of economic and social power, and propensities to excess and systemic imbalance which produce tyranny. Subjects, for whom the experience of social development and institutions of patriarchy and beneficent kingship have produced an awakening of cognitive processes and moral sensibilities, are able to band together to overthrow the tyrant and institutionalize customary law.

This preoccupation with human needs, utilitarian aspirations among men and the progression of social forms; as well as the hazards of excess, corruption and domination endemic to expansionism; most clearly articulated in Polybius 6; is what drives the author to subsume epicycles among forms of regime within this grand cycle of decline and fall. The apparent synthesis between traditions A and B is no mere academic exercise, but arises out of a different focus; and that focus is eastward-looking. For looking East, less parochial exponents of *archaiologia* observed large-scale social aggregates that enjoyed the palpable exercise of state power.

3

Polybius on Democracy, Freedom and Tyranny

As Greeks, these universal historians were also somewhat uneasy about oriental phenomena. The three thousand year Reich of the pharaoh was almost complete when most of them wrote and its reputation for relative invariability, and even immobility, suggested an aggregation of power in time and space quite formidable, and almost inconceivable in the small-scale world of the *polis*. The careful chronicling of the Egyptian story of creation; intelligent reflections on the institution of pharaonic kingship; and an aetiology of morals to which beneficence is central; play a role in Greek universal histories suggestive of the dominating Egyptian presence in the ancient world and of the role of the pharaoh in the evolution of morality and justice that are justly borne out by modern research (Baillet, 1912, 1913; Frankfort, 1948; Hornung, 1983; Trigger and Kemp, 1983).

How to accommodate kingship on this scale in the Greek world? The Greek experience had indeed been one in which kingship was seen as a step in the stages of evolution to more corporate forms. For city-republican government was seen as essentially different from beneficent kingship, drawing instead on a fund of localism, a plethora of participatory forms of association for cultic, familial, recreational and occupational purposes which the *polis* aggregated as an over-arching unit. The way the universal historians read it – but not, as we have seen, Aristotle or the Peripatetics – the Greek *polis* had already achieved the transition from primordial to political social forms that marked an evolutionary advance over its competitors. Nor was she alone. The city-republics of the Assyrian and Babylonian empires, even if strung together along the Tigris and Euphrates under the hegemony of the Great King, had also achieved the autarchy, autonomy and self-sufficiency as corporate entities that characterized the Greek. The rational development from patriarchal kingship to rule of law was written in the stars, Greek theorists sanguinely concluded – a theme of evolutionary historians that still rules – and even the pharaoh ultimately has his day.

But this conclusion to the evolutionary story did not sit easily with everyone. A predilection for patriarchal kingship that Cole detects in Plato may be something else: a recognition that the beneficent pharaoh did represent a form of rule both categorically different and legitimate in its own right. Plato's constant references to the model of Egypt and its laws, its education system, division and speciali-zation of labour as the economic basis for a superstructure in which a non-propertied scribal cast rules under the Just King of the *Republic*, suggest even an attempt to meld the Greek experience to this model. The mythic and religious content of the *Phaedrus*, the *Timaeus* and *Critias*, suggests at the same time an acquaintance with, and fascination for, Egyptian theology.

In less explicit ways this fascination with oriental forms of kingship is to be found in the *Sacred Scripture* of Euhemerus, the Alexander romance, the accounts of Hecataeus and Diodorus and the Osirid theogony as related by Plutarch, all significantly works of the Hellenistic period in which the Great King had become the ruling reality for most of the Greek world. Not only were the Ptolemies pharaohs in all but name, as the Roman emperors were to be after them, but the heirs of Alexander had established kingships in the Antigonid, Macedonian as well as Seleucid lands. Polybius, still nostalgic for the *polis* forms of Achaea perhaps, nevertheless faced the prospect of imperial expansion optimistically. *Democratia* no longer meant to him what it meant to Aeschylus, Herodotus or Sophocles. *Democratia*, by the second century BC represented no more than the rule of a free commonwealth, whether oligarchic or more participatory, so long as the Great King was absent, or did not stand in the way of representative government – even the kingdom of Macedonia was said to comprise four autarchic republics, despite the presence of a king, and myths abounded about his 'isonomous' companions (Larsen, 1945). The strength of the bipartite, as opposed to the tripartite model, derived from the fact that oligarchy had long come to be compatible with *democratia*, and that democracy had come to represent the only feasible challenge to kingship.

Even then the antithesis was not mutually exclusive. For if democracy and monarchy were mother constitutions – and they truly represented different regional archetypes – in their pure forms they too, despite the antiquity of the regimes in which they had been historically instantiated, were susceptible to decline and death, the fate of all mortal institutions. But the synthesis of monarchical and democratic principles might still serve to prolong the longevity of the greater social aggregates that progress produced, as Hellenistic experience suggested. Somewhat differently from Cole, then, we are suggesting a specific historical context for Polybius' conflation of the sociological, evolutionary schema of tradition B and the Peripatetic, cyclical, 'static', tradition A. And that context is constituted by Hellenistic empire in which kingship at the national level coexisted with the democratic *polis* form at the local levels of government. It also takes account of Cole's ingenious hidden model: the experience of the Achaean League.

Support for this thesis lies in both what the Polybian synthesis contains and what it lacks. Let us begin with what it contains. As Cole has noted (1964, 455–6), one of the central themes of Polybius 6 is that of the transition from monarchy, as a primary and chronologically early form of regime, to democratic constitutionalism, comprising chronologically later and more complex forms which achieve the social harmony and stability of monarchy by different means. This theme is associated with tradition B and those sociological and evolutionary accounts which proceed from primitive kingship to larger social aggregates, whether the constitutionalism of Plato's *Laws*, or in the Stoic form of the *cosmopolis* transcending national boundaries. This broad schema may be seen as a sort of motorized version of a polarity present in the Peripatetic tradition A, although essentially tripartite, between polity (*polis*) and tyranny (*tyrannis*). Or at least Polybius made it seem so.

In fact, the polarity represents something different in the Peripatetic tradition: and that is the xenophobia of the Hellenes *vis à vis* the barbarians; and their belief, reflected most acutely in Aristotle, in categorial differences between 'political' and 'hegemonic' rule, peculiar to the Greeks and barbarians respectively. Preoccupation with 'liberty–tyranny antitheses' (Cole, 1964, 456, n.39) took different forms but central to all of them was a belief that 'political' rule – rule in the *polis* – was *isonomos*, involving freedom and equality, 'the fairest names of all', no matter how broadly or narrowly defined in class terms. Thus the praises of Harmodius and Aristogeiton were sung, for 'slaying the tyrant and making the Athenians *isonomous*' (*Scolia Anonyma*, 10,13, cited in Vlastos, 1953, 341–44; Cole, 1964, 456, n.39), even though the regime they inaugurated was oligarchic and no broad-based democracy.

The fact that oligarchy as a political category disappears in the *polis/tyrannis* dichotomy may well be due to the increasing tendency to associate *isonomia* with Greek rule, *tyrannis* with that of the foreigner, particularly of oriental regimes.

> Seen from this perspective, it makes little difference whether tyrants are one, or thirty, or four hundred in number; and an oligarchy which is *isonomos* must be sharply distinguished from the *dynasteia* of a small group of men – something which verges on tyranny (cf. Thucydides 3.62.3). The terminology which appears in such contexts varies considerably. The condition of men who are *autonomoi* may be contrasted with that of those who are slaves to a tyrant or to a foreign power (cf. Herodotus 1.96.1), or Greek freedom with the rule of oriental despots (*ibid.*, 7.104.4). Health is said to be a state of *isonomia*, by contrast with the *monarchia* of one of the bodily humors which is disease (Alcmaeon of Croton, 2434). *Demokratia* is set against the rule of 'dynasts' (Democritus *FVS* 7 68B251), *tyrannides* against *poleis* (Demosthenes 2.21), *monarchia* against *politeia* (Aristotle, *Politics* 5.10 1310b1–3). Democracy and kingship are presented as the archetypes of all polities (Plato, *Laws* 3.693d) or identified with the two basic forms of government, rule by *logos* and rule by *nomos* (*Rhetorica ad Alexandrum* I 1420a19–25). (Cole, 1964, 456–7)

It is a small step, then, for Polybius to posit *democratia* as an evolutionary advance over *monarchia*, the primitive kingship of the barbarians, and to reduce the six political forms of the *anacyclosis* to an essential two, in which oligarchy or aristocracy represent merely the bridge between them of no lasting significance (Cole, 1964, 458). The aristocratic revolution merely anticipated the dynamics of the democratic one, as a widening of the circle in which *isonomous* relations reign. Since that circle was never coextensive with the whole polity under *democratia*, and decreasingly so in the Hellenistic age where its stipulations do not require an *ecclesia* as such, there was no fast line to be drawn between oligarchy and democracy at all. What the tyrannicides concluded in favour of oligarchy: that power cannot be entrusted to the lawless 'one' (Polybius 6.7.9–6.9.1); the democrats concluded for themselves: power cannot be entrusted to the lawless 'few' (Polybius 6.9.2–3).

Not only is the fact of oligarchy insignificant in the antithesis between freedom and tyranny, but in the psychological and cognitive account, an important element in Polybius 6, it is secondary too. For the democratic solution to the problem of government arises as a conclusion from experience: habituation, *synethia*, producing ideas of right and wrong first developed under monarchy, and subsequently expanded as aristocracy turns to oligarchy (Polybius 6.8.4–6.9.2–3). Democracy, too, can retain its purity only so long as the experience of its alternative is fresh (Polybius 6.9.4, 1979 edn, 309); but when in succeeding generations the rule of the dynasts is forgotten, democracy does not fail to succumb to the excessive concentration of power which is the occupational hazard of all forms of regime.

Cole is right, I think, to stress the preoccupation with the liberty–tyranny polarity, and for more reasons than he gives. It expresses at once the basic direction of the evolutionary account in tradition B, and of cognitive and moral progress in Polybius' utilitarian, empiricist psychology. At the same time it represents the abiding antithesis of the Peripatetic tradition A: the contrast between essentially Greek and barbarian regimes, seen from the standpoint of xenophobic Hellenes. What Polybius' synthesis includes from tradition B is the natural genesis of kingship in the primordial family and a division between prepolitical and political states, marked by *monarchia*, as primitive kingship, and *democratia*, as constitutional government, respectively. Something that the timeless world of men and nature does not permit in Aristotle or the Peripatetic tradition, where society neither originates in, nor relapses back to, a primordial state prior to, or outside, the political cycle of regimes – how could it since these conditions describe the state of barbarian society from which 'political' regimes are mutually excluded?

In marked contrast, Polybius posits both an original state of nature, and the ever-present possibility of its return, under the pressures of *pleonexia* and *philotimia*, greed and love of power, corrosive forces for all forms of regime, even, or perhaps especially, democratic ones. The Polybian cycle ends with the demagogue-induced rule of the mob when: 'the people having become accustomed to feed at the expense of others, and their prospects of winning a livelihood depend upon the property of their neighbours'. This is the seedbed of demaguogy, such that 'as soon as they find a leader who is sufficiently ambitious and daring, but is excluded from the honours of office because of his poverty, they will introduce a regime based on violence.' A condition of *stasis* that involves massacre and despoilation and 'finally degeneration into a state of bestiality, after which they once more find a master and a despot' (Polybius 6.9, 1979 edn, 309). Polybius' 'rule of violence' (*cheirokratia*) represents, as Cole points out (1964, 463), a theory of generalized corruption, reminiscent of Hesiod's 'rule of fists' (*Works and Days*, 1959 edn, 192), which, however, is not specifically democratic. '*Ochlokratia*, mob rule (Polybius 6.4.10), by contrast is the innate corruption of democracy' (Cole, 1964, 463).

In the transition from his account of the *anacyclosis* (6.6–9) to his account of the mixed constitution (6.9), we see the rather bad join between traditions A and B that Polybius has stitched together. Clear echoes of the cyclical, but static, tradition A are present in the organic language of 'the cycle of revolution, the law of nature according to which constitutions change, are transformed, and finally revert to their original form', 'grasp of [whose] process', although admitting of errors in the forecasting of a timespan for the process to play itself out, allows near infallible judgements 'as to the state of growth or decline which a given community has reached, or as to the form into which it will change' (Polybius 6.9, 1979 edn, 309–10). In the same breath Polybius mentions the case of Rome, whose development was incremental, by trial and error, its increasing complexity a product of pragmatic solutions to specific historical problems. Rome, Polybius declares, nevertheless 'was formed, grew and reached the zenith of its achievement as well as the changes for the worse which will follow', due to the same organic processes of growth, maturation and decline that govern all human institutions: 'this state, if any ever did ... takes its foundations and its growth from natural causes, and will pass through a natural evolution to its decay' (Polybius 6.9, 1979 edn, 310).

What Polybius' account includes from the Peripatetic tradition A is more than it comprises, for in Polybius' version states can fall right through the bottom into a state of nature that in tradition A does not exist, transported from tradition B. And it is possible by virtue of the cyclical escalator which his *anacyclosis* comprises, fabricated out of elements in tradition A. In addition, democracy as the rule of law, before its relapse into *stasis*, is the rule of a free commonwealth in a specific sense that cannot be found in either tradition B or Peripatetic tradition A texts, although perhaps in the spirit of tradition B, which postulates a collective social order in regimes that succumb to democracy even greater than that which kingship permits.

What Polybius' synthesis lacks from the Peripatetic tradition is as symptomatic as what it includes and becomes clear when we see the nature of the 'mixed constitution', capable of holding at bay for some considerable time the entropic forces to which simple regimes readily succumb. Polybius' examples are Rome, presaged by Sparta (6.10), 'mixed' due not so much to a balance of forces, like the mixed regimes of Plato and Aristotle, as to constitutional checks and a separation of powers to prevent the excessive concentration of power (Cole, 1964, 465–6). Polybius' focus on constitutional devices is to the detriment of analytical depth, by the standards of Plato and Aristotle. It seems clear that the impetus for Polybius' account does not arise from the study of Spartan or Roman institutions either (Cole, 1964, 466–7). If the perspective of Plato, Aristotle and Cicero's constitutional analyses is the creation of community (*politiea* or *res publica*) out of disparate elements and classes, irrefrangible entities which retain their identity in the greater collectivity, Polybius' imperative is rather the negative one of safeguarding the community from excessive concentrations of power. The simple solution in its starkest form is to be found in the Spartan contract between kings and people, sealed by oath, which represents to Polybius the bipartite balance of elements, monarchic/democratic, consistent with the liberty/tyranny antithesis as he understands it.

In Plato, Aristotle and subsequently Cicero, the processes of state-building were far too complex to be so reduced. Aristotle's blending of elements democratic, aristocratic and oligarchic in 'polity' as a mixed form – from which monarchy is significantly absent – has its counterpart in the complexity of Plato's conception of community as the synthesis of principles of *phronesis* (wisdom), *philia* (love, affinity) and *eleutheria* (freedom): if *phronesis* is embodied in kingship, *eleutheria* is the principle of aristocratic rule and *philia* represents the social harmony of the totality. One should not fail to note that it is Persia, the pre-eminent example of an efficacious blending of the mother constitutions of monarchy and democracy, that Plato takes as his model and whose decline he traced to the breakdown of its original constitution embodying *to despotikon, to eleutheron* and *to philon* (*Laws*, 693b–d; 697c; 701d, cited in Cole, 1964, 468). A clear counterpart to Plato's triadic principles is provided in Cicero's *consilium, libertas, potestas/caritas* formulation, where *caritas* is linked to kingship, *consilium* to aristocracy, and *libertas* to the balance of the whole (*De re publica*, 1.55; 2.15; 2.57, cited in Cole, 1964, 467); once more 'a blending of principles and qualities' rather than a set of institutional checks and balances.

Plato's principles or 'qualifications' (*axiomata*) of rule in the *Laws* are indicative of the heterogeneity of irrefrangible elements present in the community as a harmonious totality. Plato's 'seven titles to rule' – of old over young, of masters over slaves, parents over children, the wise over the foolish, the virtuous over the non-virtuous, the noble over the base (both of these latter antitheses would be construed in class terms as virtually identical), and those chosen by lot over those not so chosen (*Laws*, 690a–c, cited in Cole, 1964, 469) – have their parallel in the somewhat reduced catalogue of irreducible titles to rule in Aristotle, *Politics*, 1.3, 1253b1–14, of master over slave (*despotike*), of husband over wife (*gamike*), of father over children (*teknopoietike*); and the here unstated and categorically different title of the political ruler (*politike*) over the ruled (*Politics*, 1.1 1252a7–16). As both von Fritz (1954, 81–2) and Cole (1964, 470) observe, Polybius' account lacks both the economic and sociological depth of the Platonic and Peripatetic accounts of community as an aggregate of irrefrangible economic and class entities, the irreducible identities of subordinate forms of familial, cultic and occupational associations and principles of justice, equality, rights and duties proportionate to them: a totality into which Plato and Aristotle threw all sorts of ingredients, including Pythagorean principles of proportional and arithmetical equality, Parmenidean conceptions of 'the one' and 'the many', Democritean notions of subordinate affinal sets as atomic complexes, Orphic odes to love (*philia* and *eros*) and harmony as the music of creation.

If Polybius' selection of Sparta as the early form of the mixed constitution does not seem to reflect either Platonic or Peripatetic concepts of constitutional balance as a synthesis of disparate elements, or the realities of Spartan constitutional forms, what does it represent? Cole (1964, 473ff) sees in Polybius' election of Sparta as the proto-typical mixed regime, indebtedness to predecessors for whom Sparta was an important example of social contract between rulers and ruled. In the accounts of these predecessors certain themes – the benefactions of kings, and magistrates as *euergetes* who exercise kingly power by contract, constituting a monarchical element despite their aristocratic or oligarchic origins – may have made an important contribution to Polybius' conception. In Xenophon (*Resp. Lac.* 15.7), Isocrates (*Archidamus* 20) and Plato (*Laws* 3.684a), references are made to kings who are bound to the people by oath, and in the case of Xenophon the reference is to Sparta (Cole, 1964, 471). But in Plato, Aristotle and Herodotus, all of whom reflect on the subject of oaths between kings and people, their conclusion is that the product is a constitutional regime, as distinct from a 'mixed' constitution – a very important difference (Cole, 1964, 474).

That Polybius should have mistaken one for the other, or deliberately conflated the two, could be due to a number of factors. It may reflect the fact that the constitutional regimes of his day were for the most part binary systems in which the brake on rulers by the ruled, suggested by the epithet *democratia*, did not at the same time imply participatory rule in the classical fifth-century sense (Larsen, 1945). It may have reflected a hidden model of constitutional government in the form of the Achaean League, to which Polybius was patriotically committed but which, for obvious reasons, he did not wish to disclose, as Cole suggests (1964, 471, 477). And it may reflect, more generally, the realities of Hellenistic empire, in which kings and people were frequently bound together by oath, the rights of Alexander and his successors in foreign affairs being contractually limited by the autarchy of the municipality in its own domestic business (Ferguson, 1912).

In his account of Sparta, in which the oligarchic gerousia has such an important role to play, Polybius' conflation of the notions of 'constitutional' and 'mixed' regime may well have been more by design than by accident. As Cole (1964, 477) has noted: 'it is thus democratic theory and practice in some of its more conservative aspects which recalls Polybius' version of the Spartan constitution most closely.' Constitutional regimes in tradition B came uncannily close to the realities of second-century democracy, no longer a simple form of government in any sense of that term, and characterized more by the dominance of the *boule*, or *synedos*, effective counterpart to the *gerousia*, than the popular *ecclesia*. Recommendations, like those of Democritus, to make them more representative of the 'inner moral power of the individual' and as far removed as possible from despotism (frag.181, 248, 268, cited in Aalders, 1950, 306), tell us how oligarchic these governments probably were. Between the Spartan regime and the Achaean League of Polybius' own experience there were, moreover, specific parallels (Cole, 1964, 478).

Already in Democritus (460–370 BC) 'anti-democratic' trends are to be found that lean towards 'moderate oligarchy' or 'constitutionalism', of which Aristotle's *politeia* (*Politics*, 4.13 1297b 24; 4.7 1293a 39ff; 4.8 1293b 33ff), Plato's Eighth Letter and *Laws*, 7.793a–c (cited in Aalders, 1950, 310) are reminiscent. In fragment 255 Democritus openly declares that the best form of regime is that in which the well-to-do govern the unpropertied in a patriarchal manner. Afraid of the *kakoi*, and calling into question systems of accountability in public affairs, of which the Athenian is most well known to us, the Abderite in fragments 267 and 53a, points both to the dangers of unlimited freedom of speech, and yet the value of this freedom as a guarantee against arbitrary government when appropriately exercised (frag. 51, 252, cited in Aalders, 1950, 309, 310). Freedom in Democritus' individualistic and atomistic universe was more a principle of personal life than of politics; and politics was less valued than science, as always subordinated to the welfare of the individual (Aalders, 1950, 311, 313). Above all, the purpose of the state was to achieve concordance (*homonoia*), or social harmony of the aggregate, arrived at consensually rather than on the basis of written laws, that would reflect best the moral value of the individual (Aalders, 1950, 310, 313).

One can see very well how Polybius might be thought to belong to the Democritean tradition; a tradition that is primarily Sophist, as several commentators have pointed out (Morrison, 1941, 15; Cole, 1964, 485, n.115), popular rather than academic; a tradition that:

> takes as its starting point neither an abstract scheme of classification nor a universally applicable morphology of growth and decay, but, rather, certain feelings, slogans and programs which were deeply rooted in the actual life of the Greek polis; its desire for *homonoia*; its conviction that the barbarians, with their predominantly monarchical mode of government, represent an earlier or arrested state of political life. (Cole, 1964, 485, n.115)

The family resemblance between the views of Polybius, Democritus, Protagoras and Plato on the origins of culture, if so much a part of the popular Greek political milieu, did not presuppose any acquaintance of these thinkers with one another – the energies that have been expended on trying to decide whether Polybius had or had not read Plato concluding nothing unanimous on that score. Similarities to the *Republic* suggest at best an incorrectly remembered reading (Cole, 1964, 484 and n.113). The closer parallels to *Laws* 3 in the bipartite division of regimes suggest elements of the *Kulturgeschichte* whose ancestry is much older: a theory of constitutional balance, an account of primitive monarchy and its decline, the collapse of lawful 'democracy', leading to tyranny and return to a state of nature (Cole, 1964, 485, n.115). Family resemblance remains our best case; and if indeed tradition B did represent a popular tradition with Sophist sources we need do no better. Such theories were well dispersed by the itinerant teachers of rhetoric or debate, as Plato himself attests in many places. Moreover, we have specific parallels in the Democritean and Protagorean fragments that would attest to these continuities.

Polybius' account of the Achaean League suggests a case in point, both conforming to the contours of the tradition B account, and historically specific enough to constitute a model for constitutional government. Polybius chronicles two stages in the development of the Achaean League: first, the expulsion of the tyrants and the adoption of democracy (2.34.3); and, secondly, the introduction of the monarchical principle which renders its constitution 'mixed'. At the close of the first stage two things have been accomplished: the creation of an organic unity out of twelve separate cities, 'an allied and friendly community ... shar[ing] the same laws, weights, measure and currency, and besides these the same magistrates, council and law courts' (Polybius 2.37.10–11, 1979 edn, 149). What principle underpinned this unification movement? It was the dynamic of democracy. 'The cause, then, in my opinion', Polybius states (2.38, 1979 edn, 150), careful advocate of causal explanation despite his reverence for Fortune, 'is something like this. It would be impossible to find anywhere a political system or a guiding principle which allowed more equality and freedom of speech, or which was more genuinely representative of true democracy, than that of the Achaean League.' Animated by two guiding principles, 'the sense of humanity and equality', the union became a unity in reality as well as name.

It was, as Cole has noted (1964, 477), however, democracy heavily biased towards oligarchy. It was a democracy whose aspirations may have reflected fifth-century values of freedom and equality, but whose form was that of the second-century constitutional commonwealth (Larsen, 1945, 88–9). Constitutionality was guaranteed by the important role assigned by Polybius to the dicasts as guardians of the law, both as a court of review for legislative decrees, and as empowered by the Assembly to scrutinize magistrates (28.7.9; 38, 18.3). Parallels between the Achaean *dicasteria*, selected *aristinden* (*IG* VII 188.9 and *SIG* 665.34–5 noted by Cole, 1964, 477), the Lycurgan *gerousia* and Athenian Areopagus are apparent. They have further parallels in Plato's *Laws* which leant heavily on the law of Athens (Morrow, 1960; Harrison, 1968).

Moreover, although Polybius (6.10.7–11, 1979 edn, 310) assigns to kingship 'the inbred vice [of] despotism', he was well aware that tyranny arose out of democracy by way of the demagogue, rather than from kingship, in the cycle of regimes. The best palliative for the unmitigated violence and bestiality of ochlocracy was aristocratic constitutionality. And Sparta had always had a reputation as being '*atyrannetos*' (Thucydides 1.18.1): the traditional defender of freedom (Herodotus 5.92a), by virtue of a constitution (*politeia*), both democratic and mixed regime, as 'the ideal of a responsible and limited *arche*' (Cole, 1964, 77, n.101). It is notable that when Polybius describes democracy he focuses on equality and freedom of speech as definitive, characteristics of constitutional rather than strictly democratic regimes. For equality implied equality between equals, inequality between unequals, among citizens equal under the law but unequal in their class, status and functional designations, as Aristotle so succinctly pointed out; while freedom of speech is freedom to voice one's opinion in the assembly, and to hold private views – both negative forms of freedom. It is equally notable that Polybius considered the Achaean constitution by the close of the first phase of its (schematic) history to be incomplete, and that its completion should have taken the form of the addition of the monarchical element, in the form of 'a secretary and two generals ... elected by each city in turn' (Polybius 2.43, 1979 edn, 155), with the result that 'when in due course the country did find leaders of sufficient stature, its potentialities for good were immediately revealed by the fulfilment of that most glorious purpose, the union of the Peloponnese' (Polybius 2.40, 1979 edn, 152).

The apparently unqualified endorsement of Sparta by Polybius in 6.10–11 as the great example of the mixed constitution, devised to prevent each of the simple forms 'from degenerating into a debased form of itself', is now more credible. For the epicycles of constitutional revolution take place within a larger cycle of rise and fall in which democracy represents the acme: the last and most vulnerable point in the evolutionary cycle, from which decline into chaos, violence and anarchy is endemic. Constitutional checks and balances against the arrogation of power by the many is the only, and the temporary, sanction against ochlocracy, the fate of all simple regimes:

> Lycurgus foresaw this, and accordingly did not make his constitution simple or uniform, but combined in it all the virtues and distinctive features of the best governments, so that no one principle should become preponderant, and thus be perverted into its kindred vice, but that the power of each element should be counterbalanced by the others, so that no one of them inclines or sinks unduly to either side. In other words, the constitution should remain for a long while in a

state of equilibrium thanks to the principle of reciprocity or counteraction. Thus kingship was prevented from becoming arrogant through fear of the people who were also given a sufficiently important share in the government, while the people in their turn were restrained from showing contempt for the kings through their fear of the Senate. The members of this body were chosen on grounds of merit, and could be relied upon at all times to take the side of justice unanimously. By this means that part of the state which was at a disadvantage because of its attachment to traditional custom gained power and weight through the support and influence of the senators. For that very reason the result of the drawing-up of the constitution according to these principles was to preserve liberty for the Spartans over a longer period than for any other people of whom we have records. (Polybius 6.10, 1979 edn, 310–11)

The Achaean League as the hidden point of reference for the constitutional commonwealth has similarities of scale to recommend it that forge links to Rome. For the sociological, expansionist and evolutionary schema of tradition B was more credibly invoked to account for large-scale aggregations that lay outside the bounds of the *polis*, to which Sparta was still confined. Polybius' insistence on the unity of the Achaean League as that of a single city, whose situation 'only differs from the situation of a single city in the sense that its inhabitants are not encircled by a single wall' (6.37, 1979 edn, 149), adds an additional element of complexity that did not obtain in the classical *poleis*. Polybius refers to the Achaean League as a nation (*ethne*) and he does so in the context of remarks about the special significance of universal history accounting for the dynamics of historical aggregations that cannot be reduced to their simple components (6.37, 1979 edn, 148). Polybius' historiography owes its sophistication to this very preoccupation with complexity as the dynamic principle of historical progress – one wonders if it is not the easy slide from the assumption that complexity involves size, to the veneration of size for its own sake, that accounts for the historical progression to republics of ever-greater size and the relentless development of technologies to furnish them. Universal history cannot be arrived at by aggregating 'the histories which record isolated events', Polybius argues (1.4, 1979 edn, 45), just because the whole is greater than the sum of the parts; and the world empires of Alexander and Rome – which have created its universality – are not reducible to the components out of which they are constituted:

> one might as well try to obtain an impression of the shape, arrangement and order of the whole world by visiting each of its famous cities in turn or looking at separate plans of them … It has always seemed to me that those who believe they can obtain a just and well-proportioned view of history as a whole by reading separate and specialized reports of events, are behaving like a man who, when he has examined the dissected parts of a body which was once alive and beautiful, imagines that he has beheld the living animal in all its grace and movement … the fact is that we can obtain no more than an impression of a whole from a part, but certainly neither a thorough knowledge nor an accurate understanding. We must conclude then that specialized studies or monographs contribute very little to our grasp of the whole and our conviction of its truth. (Polybius 1.4, 1979 edn, 45)

The homology between universal history and universal empire is of crucial importance. And in the analysis of universal empire, the 'Achaean nation …

[which has] achieved a growth of power and an internal political harmony which are altogether remarkable' (Polybius 2.37, 1979 edn, 149) stands midway between Sparta and Rome, about the latter of whom Polybius (1.3, 1979 edn, 44) wishes to 'leave his readers in no doubt that [she] had from the outset sufficient reason to entertain the design of creating a world empire and sufficient resources to accomplish [her] purpose.' Rome added to the spatial complexity of empire, as a unity created out of disparate elements, the complexity of gradualness, as an entity evolved over time and incremental responses to disparate pragmatic problems. But the Roman empire was not invulnerable to decay either; and once again the contours of *anacyclosis* suggest ochlocracy as its nemesis. There is a parallel between Polybius 6.9 and 6.57 that is striking, as Cole notes (1964, 480), and prophetic. For although Polybius did not live to see it, the relentless tendency towards democratization of the empire, which eventually enfranchised all subjects as Roman citizens, leading to Spanish and even Arab incumbents on the imperial throne, is credited by historians from Gibbon to Badian as among the causes of Rome's decline and fall.

The parallel extends to a specification, in psychological and moral terms, of the dynamics, both in the simplified *polis* example, Sparta (Polybius 6.9), and the complex imperial example, Rome (Polybius 6.57). In both cases it is the insatiable appetite of the people for power and gratification that produces corruption and moral decline. For if power arises out of benefaction it is dispersed by gratification: a common dynamic unites the two ends of the circle. Polybius and all his imitators, particularly Machiavelli, make this explicit. In the case of the simple regime democracy is the acme:

> By this time the people have become accustomed to feed at the expense of others [*euergetism*], and their prospects of winning a livelihood depend upon the property of their neighbours; then as soon as they find a leader who is sufficiently daring, but is excluded from the honours of office because of his poverty, they will introduce a regime based on violence. (Polybius 6.57, 1979 edn, 309)

In the case of Empire the point is the same (Polybius 6.57, 1979 edn, 350).

If Polybius' account has been mistaken for a Stoic one, there are good reasons for this in the relentless dynamics of expansion to larger and larger aggregates, similar to the Stoic logic of *oikeiosis* and, perhaps more importantly, the psychological account of corruption common to both accounts. Polybius' focus on gratification as the logical extension of benefaction, and the moral turpitude that the latter induces, strongly echoed in Machiavelli's apparently Stoic stress on *mollizia*, or 'softness', accounts for macro-historical processes in micro-psychological terms that have been a feature of accounts of the rise of civilization from Plato to Seneca. They also close the circle between the beginnings and the ends of regimes in postulating a continuous motivational principle that extends from the beginning to the end of their lives. Motivated to contract into society by the largesse that the benefactor king, with the resources of the aggregate to dispense, can offer, individuals both learn the moral lesson of altruism essential to state-building, and the immoral lesson of power-seeking which is the state's unmaking. Each successive step in the nation-making process that leads to empire is built upon wider and securer sources of patronage, the magisterial *euergetes* offering multiple and diverse resources that cannot be matched by a king. The final logic of the dynamic is for benefactor and beneficiary, gratifyer and gratification, to be united in one body, both one and all: the *demos*.

The *pleonexia*–ochlocracy connection, in the case of great empires, preserves the homology with simple regimes, where rise and fall trace the trajectory from kingship to tyranny to democracy. And it does so by drawing on the same tension between rulers and ruled: 'The result is the "fairest of all names" – freedom and democracy – but the worst of all actualities – ochlocracy' (Polybius 6.57.9 cited in Cole, 1964, 481). We cannot mistake the reference to Herodotus (3.61) for whom equality (*isonomia*) and democracy are the 'fairest names of all'; and to Thucydides (3.82.8, cited in Cole, 1964, 481) for whom the *isonomia politike* and *aristocratia sophron*, respectively, were specious slogans to conceal the worst of all motives: party factiousness. While encapsulating the tripartite constitutional provisions of Peripatetic tradition A against regime dissolution, the Polybian *anacyclosis* revolves around the axis of the *polis/tyrannis* polarity, the bipartite struggle between rulers and ruled, when it comes right down to it. The evolutionary push to ever greater and more complex aggregates owes its impetus to the escalating needs and anticipation of benefits that account for both the micro-psychological and the macro-institutional processes described by a single dynamic.

In Polybius' grand account of the emergence of world empire, dominated by the hegemonic rule of the great Alexander, and the entry into history of large-scale complex *systemata* with resources not merely to thwart Fortune or Fate, but actively to assail her by an aggressive grasp of opportunities, the beneficent king, so prominent in the *Kulturgeschichte* of tradition B, is a residual character. In the second-century world BC, dominated by constitutional republicanism, as democracy had come to be, it is surprising that he continues to be as prominent as he is. Were it not for the fact that the great kingdoms of the Eastern monarchies continued to be an enduring reality, kingship perhaps would have vanished without trace in the evolutionary progress of mankind, as it has done in the modern republican *Gestalt*. This would reflect the tendencies of tradition A, the Peripatetic tradition, where kingship has already disappeared from Aristotle's 'mixed' constitution, and *hegemonia* was the rule of oriental monarchies; but not, however, of tradition B, the evolutionary tendencies of this strand notwithstanding. The imperishable legacy of kingship in the Polybian genealogy of morals reflects, it would seem, the historical significance of kingship in at least one tradition of Greek thought, which is to live on, revitalized, in Neoplatonism. The specificity of the accounts of Plato, Diodorus and the Hellenistic Neoplatonists, suggests that the kingship they have in mind may well have been particular, and that it may also have been Egyptian. Whatever the case, this experience of beneficent monarchy was sufficiently profound to leave a residue that sets the Platonist tradition definitely apart from the Peripatetic; in the latter the suggestion of kingship as a non-Greek category in the contemporaneous world, hinting at a theory of oriental despotism. It is a testament to the pervasiveness of the Platonist tradition, as I shall refer to it – for the role of kingship is much less evident in Democritus, Protagoras or Sophist strands of thought – that Polybius should have taken the role of the beneficent king as seriously as he did.

The contours of Polybius' account, as Cole has noted (1967), faithfully reflect the outlines of *Kulturgeschichte* in Plato's *Laws* 3, Diodorus' *Aegyptiacha* and the later accounts of Vitruvius and Tzetzes. The beginnings of political society are reconstructed from the observation of its emergence after periodic catastrophe, flood, crop failure or similar causes, 'discussed in the greatest detail by Plato and certain other philosophers':

> From time to time, as a result of floods, plagues, failures of crops or other similar causes, there occurs a catastrophic destruction of the human race, in which all knowledge of the arts and social institutions is lost. Such disasters, tradition [B?] tells us, have often befallen mankind, and must reasonably be expected to recur. Then in the course of time the population renews itself from the survivors as if from seeds, men increase once more in numbers and, like other animals, proceed to form herds. (Polybius 6.5, 1979 edn, 305)

The herd develops as a pragmatic solution to the problem of individual weakness, and *monarchia*, the rule of one man, follows the logic of rule of the strong over the weak (Polybius 6.5, 1979 edn, 306). Kingship, as a moral institution, Polybius distinguishes from primeval one-man rule, for the former presupposes the development of social relationships, the family and the community, absent in the case of the latter: 'and then for the first time mankind conceives the notions of goodness, of justice, and of their opposites' (Polybius 6.5, 1979 edn, 306). Moral progress and social development are simultaneous processes: adults, reflecting, thanks to the faculty of reason, on the gratitude they owe their parents for nurture, form a sense of duty generalized to the whole community, reinforced by experiences of benevolence bestowed by neighbours. Dereliction of duty and instances in which a beneficiary 'so far from showing gratitude to his benefactor actually tries to do him harm', create similar resentment when done to one's neighbour as when done to one's self (Polybius 6.6, 1979 edn, 306), due to a capacity for empathy born of the experience of mutual interdependence: 'In this way each individual begins to form an idea of the theory and meaning of duty, which is the beginning and end of justice.'

The institution of beneficent kingship belongs to this process: the gratitude of companions, defended from danger as 'the onslaught of the most powerful wild beasts', expresses itself in the bestowal of authority, based on moral conceptions of 'the noble [and] ... the base', on a leader (Polybius 6.6, 1979 edn, 306). So long as they experience his authority in a manner consistent with conceptions of justice that have developed, 'reward[ing] or punish[ing] each according to his deserts, then they will do his bidding not through fear of violence, but because their judgement approves him'; and he will receive life-long support. 'In this way, and almost imperceptibly, the monarch develops into a king when reason becomes more powerful than ferocity or force ... the first ideas of goodness and of justice and of their opposites are formed among men, and this is the origin and the genesis of true kingship' (Polybius 6.6–7, 1979 edn, 307). Heroic kingship of ancient times, when 'those who had been singled out for royal authority continued in their functions until they grew old ... built imposing strongholds, fortified them with walls, and acquired lands to provide for their subjects both security and an abundance of the necessities of life' (Polybius 6.7, 1979 edn, 307), conformed to this model. So long as kings 'were pursuing these aims they were never the objects of envy nor of abuse, because they did not indulge in distinctions of dress or of food or drink at the expense of others, but lived very much in the same fashion as the rest of their subjects, and kept in touch with the people in their daily activities'. The institution of hereditary monarchy changed all this due to the accumulated power and resources that kings inherited, which provided security, food in excess of their needs, and a general 'superabundance [that] tempted them to indulge their appetites' (Polybius 6.7, 1979 edn, 307). Corruption followed the age-old path and the people, seeing their trust betrayed and the beneficent king degenerate into the self-indulgent tyrant, soon conspired to overthrow him. Aristocracy provided only a temporary improvement: the aristocrats, born with a silver spoon in their mouths,

> had no experience of misfortunes and no tradition of civil equality and freedom of speech, since they had been reared from the cradle in an atmosphere of authority and privilege. And so they abandoned their high responsibilities, some in favour of avarice and unscrupulous money-making, others of drinking and convivial excesses that go with it, and others the violation of women and the rape of boys. In this way they transformed an aristocracy into an oligarchy, and soon provoked the people to a pitch of resentment similar to that which I have already described, with the result that their regime suffered the same disastrous end as had befallen tyrants. (Polybius 6.8, 1979 edn, 308)

Democracy followed the same path of moral degeneration, in each case due to lack of a palpable sense of gratitude for benefits conferred, owing to a lapse of time between the original beneficent acts, as recompense for which authority had been bestowed, and new generations of power-seeking democrats (Polybius 6.9, 1979 edn, 309).

Not only are all the items in Polybius' summary *Kulturgeschichte* to be found in Plato's *Laws*, but they appear in the same mix of 'static' and 'progressive' elements (Cole, 1967, 98). The evolutionary account, which if Cole (1967, 99) is right is the older of the two, dating back to Protagoras and Democritus, includes the standard items of catastrophe by flood, plague or famine; the destruction of all except scattered mountain-dwelling herdsmen; the regeneration of the population in a patriarchal agrarian setting in which earlier technologies had been lost; the absence of cities or laws and correspondingly underdeveloped conceptions of good and evil (*Laws* 677E–78A) – an account which later characterizes Hellenistic critiques of civilization from the Epicurean to the Stoic Seneca's Ninetieth Letter on Progress, pure Posidonius in fact (Springborg, 1981, ch. 2). Plato, most curiously, refers to this sort of regime as *dynasteia* (680B), a usage of the term as unusual as Polybius' *monarchia*, and with the same meaning, to designate primordial, herd-like society, which he in fact compares to that of birds living in flocks. Only with the development of larger aggregations in settled communities, agriculture and walled-towns, did *dynasteia* give way to law-governed society ruled either by kingship or aristocracy (681D) and eventually the *ethnai* founded on alliances between cities (682D–83A). This completes the list of items in the evolutionary account, tradition B, which Plato has elaborated further in the concepts of *demiourgike techne* and *politike techne* of the *Protagoras* (Cole, 1967, 50–1).

A different set of elements, which Cole refers to as 'static' or 'regressive' (Cole, 1967, 97–101), but which, to avoid confusing them with the Peripatetic account, to which they certainly do not belong, I will simply refer to as 'primitivist', coexists in *Laws* 3, but uneasily. This set of elements comprises moral constraints and a theory of corruption that would seem to look back to a golden age of beneficent kingship. So the absence of technology in the post-cataclysmic society is read by Plato as absence of vehicles of greed and competition characteristic of cities (667A–B); a veneration on his part of simple primordial society that is extended to comment on the friendship and mutual affection of mountain dwellers; whose decentralized existence made their periodic meetings happy ones; whose few needs could be met from existing resources due to their small numbers; and whom the loss of developed technology deprived of the means of warfare, leaving them only the simple arts of weaving and pottery. Living the self-sufficient existence of patriarchal families organized more broadly in clans (680A), this primordial society enjoyed the absence of great differentials in wealth or poverty that are the stimulus to envy and greed. Their acceptance of received wisdom on the subject of the human and the divine, a kind of natural justice and rustic discipline, obviated the necessity for a law-giver or codified law; the customary law of their ancestors and the principle of patriarchy sufficing to produce the justest of all kingships (680D–E). Only when they ventured out of their mountain fastnesses into the plains, did these men become subject to all the vicissitudes and misfortunes (*pathemai*) of government, to which urban (*polis*) society is susceptible.

4

Patronage, Magnificence and Title to Rule

In successive treatments of the problem of tyranny and the transition from the rule of kings to that of notables from Thucydides, Aristotle, the Anonymus Iamblichi and Theophrastus, to Polybius himself, the notion of the benefactor king is a guiding principle (Cole, 1964, 453). Aristotle's account in *Politics* 3.14 1285b4–19 (1981 edn, 218–19) of the fourth type of kingship, that of the Greek heroic age, is archetypal: there ancestral monarchy came into being by virtue of 'kings [being] benefactors of the mass of the people in the arts of peace or in warfare, or in welding the people together, or in providing them with land'. Customary kings ruling over willing subjects exercised a peculiar combination of religious, military and judicial powers familiar to us from the accounts of cultic kingship in Aeschylus and Herodotus – the dramatic power of Aeschylus' *Suppliants* and Sophocles' *Antigone*, for instance, turning on the possible conflict of allegiances that these roles may create (Ehrenberg, 1950, 515–48).

Aristotle mentions binding by oath in his account of the kings' judicial function: 'They also gave judgements at law; some did this on oath, some without oath, the oath being the raising aloft of the royal sceptre.' The residual duties of kings, once they have either 'relinquished some of their duties' or 'been deprived of them by the populace', were 'the duty of offering sacrifices' – 'in some states the only one which was left in the hands of the kings'; and even in the cases 'where one could justifiably say a kingship did still exist, they retained only the leadership of armies on expeditions beyond the borders' (Aristotle, *Politics*, 3.14 1285b3–19, 1981 edn, 219). In other words, municipal autonomy reduced the kingly functions to those of chief priest of the state cult, the military function of border maintenance, and foreign diplomacy. To whom did the functions of domestic government pass? They passed to *euergetai*: notables, whose resources for patronage were more diversified than those of a king, and whose benefactions were institutionalized in the municipal instruments of the liturgy and *antidosis*. A matter on which Aristotle is quite specific in his account of *megalopsuchos*, the notable, 'great-souled one', whose profile is constituted by his munificence, grandeur and sense of honour (Aristotle, *NE*, 4.3 1123b1–1125a15, 1976 edn, 153–8).

We may push the proposition that the final 'democratic' or 'constitutional' form of Aristotle's political theory was actually generated out of monarchical theory more or less far. Godfrey Tanner, in two seminal papers (Tanner,

1990a,b), suggests a reconstruction of the development of Aristotle's non-scientific writings that would both account for the period in which he served as an instructor to Alexander, and show how the later teachings at the Athenian Lyceum were developed out of earlier doctrines. Such an account, if it could be substantiated, would also go some distance towards exlaining the hitherto inexplicable coexistence of a 'monarchical Aristotle', to which the Peripatetic and medieval Aristotelian traditions give witness, alongside the 'republican Aristotle', resuscitated first by Aquinas and thirteenth-century commentators on the city state, and later by seventeenth- and eighteenth-century classical republicans. Tanner's account extends the circle of Aristotle's early instruction beyond Alexander to include the Royal Pages, the future rulers of the Seleucid and Ptolemaic kingdoms in particular, which would go some way towards explaining the extraordinary accomplishment of Alexander's 'companions' in holding together an empire barely conquered and certainly not yet held at the time of his death, as grounded in the common teaching of their master Aristotle on creating and maintaining colonies. On this reading, then, the mature *Nicomachean Ethics* and the *Politics* are the outcome of an evolutionary process whose phases can be charted, at least speculatively. Generated initially out of Aristotle's instructions to Alexander and the Royal Pages, they represent the necessity to adapt advice to monarchs to the exigencies of Athenian democratic politics; the *megalopsuchos* or notable, for instance, representing that class of ruler or magistrate on whom Aristotle would have been forced to depend for protection were Alexander or the companions to fail (Tanner, 1990b, remarks).

The distinctive features of Aristotle's politics may date even earlier, to his teachings in Assos 347–5 BC, under the patronage of a tyrant who produced a liberal constitution which worked quite successfully, until he was put to death by the Persians (Tanner, 1990b, 1). Werner Jaeger (1961, edn, cited in Tanner, 1990b, 1) has argued, for instance, that the Ethics in five books mentioned by Diogenes Laertius date to this period. The specific form of Aristotle's mature works of instruction, as comprising a *Poetics*, *Rhetoric*, an *Ethics* and *Politics*, was perhaps early shaped by the demands placed on Aristotle in his role of *grammaticus* to the young Alexander and contemporary Royal Pages, possibly Ptolemy and Hephaestion, in the Nympheion at the Mieza palace in Pella between 343 and 337 BC. Scholars have noted the significance of Aristotle's role as super-Sophist, or *grammaticus* (Ross, 1949, cited in Tanner, 1990b, remarks); the high level of poetic illustration in the *Ethics* (Long, 1974, cited in Tanner, 1990b, 1) as suitable for the 'musical' education of young men and consistent with Aristotle's reputation for having prepared an edition of Homer specifically for the education of Alexander; and Aristotle's propensity for group teaching, which he continued in the Athenian Lyceum (Tanner, 1990b, 1). Tanner (1990a, 1; 1990b, 1–2) endorses the view of Thomas Case (1910, *Encyclopaedia Britannica*, 11, pp. 515ff), that the evidence for dating the *Rhetorica ad Alexandrum* before 340 BC, the last date mentioned in that work, is compelling, suggesting that the work of instruction to a future king and his ministers, predating the regency of Alexander, and comprising advice on ' "Privy Council" procedures' as well as standard matters of rhetoric, may well have provided the basis of the mature *Rhetorica* (Tanner, 1990a, 6). Tanner goes on to argue that just as the 'Ethics in 5 books' mentioned by Diogenes Laertius and dating to the Assos period, became the *Eudemian Ethics* 1–3, 7–8; so the work 'On Justice in 4 books', likely dated to the Mieza period, may have constituted books 5–7 of the Lyceum *Nicomachean Ethics* (Tanner, 1990b, 1–2); and that, moreover, 'in addition to preparing *On Justice* for Alexander and the Pages, Aristotle had ordered or directly prepared a summary of the 5-book *Proto-Eudemians* incorporating a similar summary of *on Justice* in 4 books' (Tanner, 1990b, 2). The content of *Eudemian Ethics* 4 and *Nicomachean Ethics* 5, on justice, dealing with royal duty, would suggest this provenance, as would *Eudemian Ethics* 6 and *Nicomachean Ethics* 7, on self-control, as 'precepts for the great' (Tanner, 1990b, 2 and remarks). When it comes to the *Politics*, Tanner maintains of the Lyceum version:

> Our *Politics* appears to incorporate *Alexander on Colonies* reshaped as Book VII on the Ideal State, whilst *on Monarchy* also seems to be embedded there as Book III. Book VIII may abridge Diogenes' list item *On Paedeia*. Books IV-VI explain Greek *polis* structures and ideas of citizenship, constitutional change, and devices for preserving convenient constitutions, and were probably greatly developed at the Lyceum. But originally their first draft may have been advice on controlling client Greek states for a Macedonian king! (Tanner, 1990b, 2)

Tanner (1990b, 2) concludes: 'Our present *Politics* is likely to post-date the death of Callisthenes' in 327, brought about by the Conspiracy of the Pages, which had soured Aristotle's relationship with Alexander. It would thus have been 'designed to conciliate Athenian moderate conservative opinion towards a School likely to appear as a Macedonian foreign implant in Athens – hence its concern with constitutions more than kings as it stands.'

Tanner (1990a, 3–4) speculates that Alexander's *grammaticus* would un-doubtedly have left in the prince's possession copies of the textbooks of instruction that he had prepared for him and the Royal Pages. These may have found their way to the Alexandrian Library, or the Library at Pergamum, accounting for the extensive list of manuscripts eventually recorded, as a compilation of works from both the Pella-Mieza and Athenian-Lyceum periods. The Eastern seats of learning may well have been the repositories then of early Aristotle's monarchical writings that fed the Peripatetic tradition. Tanner (1990a, 2) also suggests a plausible reconstruction of the strange history of the Lyceum manuscripts, which, comprising copies of both the earlier and the mature works of Aristotle, along with those of Theophrastus, were bequeathed in 285 BC to Neleus of Scepsis in the Troad:

> Neleus' kinsfolk buried the books to protect them from the agents of Attalus who was seizing books by royal warrant to stock his Pergamene Library between 238 and 198 BC. This family then sold them to the Athenian bibliophile Apellicon about a century later, and he took them to his house in Athens. When Sulla took Athens he seized them and sent the collection to Rome where Tyrannio and Andronicus edited them about 70 BC. Some works survived only in highly conjectural copies of damaged originals made by Apellicon and the rest had suffered from moths and damp. Plutarch's *Life of Sulla* (26) echoes this account, and both insist that after Neleus took the collection, the Lyceum had copies of only a small part of the master's work, chiefly exoteric works, no doubt in part the dialogues now lost to us

rather than much of our present corpus of philosophical essays inspired by problems of teaching in the Lyceum. (Tanner, 1990a, 2)

Tanner (1990a, 2) considers this account 'too substantial for fabrication', speculating that Theophrastus' action in bequeathing the archive to a scholar in the Troad, thereby burying it far from royal procuring agents, may well have been inspired by his visit to Ptolemy Soter to advise him on the Alexandrian Library. There he probably met Philadelphus and Arsinöe and may have had cause to fear 'that they would intervene in Greece and take occasion to seize the Lyceum collection for Alexandria' (Tanner, 1990a, 2). Tanner notes in addition that Theophrastus' death at about the time that Ptolemy Soter's exiled son sought haven in Macedonia, thereby 'rendering all allies of Macedon open to Ptolemaic revenge', provided a particular occasion to fear a Ptolemaic invasion of Attica to carry off the Lyceum Library to Alexandria.

Paul Vander Waerdt in a fine paper (1990) on Aristotle's *politike* or political science, while avoiding the problem of the provenance of Aristotle's manuscripts, presents the *Nicomachean Ethics* and the *Politics* as a continuous project which sought to uncover the foundations of the best regime in an appropriate fit between constitutional forms and racial qualities or aptitudes. Books 5 and 6 of the *Politics*, concerned with the problem of the good man and the good citizen, receive a symptomatic elaboration in books 7 and 8, where Aristotle presents a taxonomy of existing regimes and ways to improve them with respect to the good. Such a project, in which, Vander Waerdt argues, the conventional distinction between *ethica* and *politike* simply is not made – being likely a Peripatetic innovation, evident already in the *Magna Moralia*, for which we may be indebted to Theophrastus or his school – tilts in favour of the *polis* as the examplar of the good life, as the cognate *politike* would suggest, barbarian regimes being strictly speaking neither cities nor political. The project may well have been related to the imperial project of Philip – if not Alexander – and the specific task of governing colonies, as his programmatic statement *Politics* (1327b23–38, cited in Vander Waerdt, 1990, 19) suggests:

> That nations in cold places, and particularly those in Europe, are filled with spiritedness (*thymos*), but are relatively lacking in intelligence (*dianoia*) and art (*techne*); hence they remain freer, but lack political institutions and are unable to rule their neighbours. Those in Asia, on the other hand, have souls endowed with intelligence and art, but lacking in *thymos*; hence they remain ruled and enslaved. But the race of Greeks shares in both qualitites, just as it occupies the middle position in space. For it is endowed with both intelligence and *thymos*; hence it remains free, possesses the best political institutions, and is capable of ruling over all, if it should obtain a single regime (*politeia*).

Due perhaps to the fate of the Aristotelian manuscripts, and coinciding with a Hellenistic rejection of grand metaphysical theory and a retreat into empiricism, materialism and localism (Kerferd, 1967; Barber, 1970), the Peripatetics, although nominally transmitters of Aristotle's legacy and heirs to his school, abandoned the doctrines of the Lyceum. Aristotle's scientific writings continued to have an impact in the great centres of learning of the Hellenistic world, Pergamum and Alexandria. The geographer Ptolemy and the physician Galen, the former of Alexandria, the latter of Pergamum, reflect the Aristotelian empirical legacy. But the fate of the non-scientific writings is mixed. There are circumstantial reasons for this, as Tanner (1990a, 2) suggests. Circulation of an edited version of the Lyceum manuscripts dates from 70 BC when Sulla, upon capturing Athens, seized them from the house of the bibliophile Apellicon and took them to Rome, where Tyrannio and Andronicus of Rhodes produced 'an edition of the treatises in the order in which they have survived to us' (Kerferd, 1967, 92). There, it is assumed, Cicero had access to the collection. Cicero's philosophical friends of the Academy and the Stoa were doubtless well acquainted with the peripatos, strongly represented in Rome at this time. But there are good reasons why Cicero, after having thrown in his support with Sulla, and given his attitude to Caesar and his apology for the tyrannicides in *De officiis*, would have skirted around the monarchical treatises (Tanner, 1990b, remarks). That the Lyceum–Apellicon writings are poorly represented in Cicero's writings, too, has to do with the fact that Cicero, after Caesar came to power, worked over his books in exile, drawing on the sources he knew well, relying therefore on Panaetius rather than Aristotle on ethical subjects (Tanner, 1990b, remarks). This is not to minimize Aristotle's general influence on Cicero, however, who, as we shall see, owes a great deal to him on questions of constitutional form, patronage and the function of magistrates.

To conclude the story of the peripatos, after Alexander of Aphrodisias, who produced commentaries on the principal treatises around AD 200, this tradition of commentary passed to Boethius of Sidon and then to the Byzantine scholars, Themistius, Ammonius and Simplicius – all of whom are more Platonists than Aristotelians – influenced to some extent by Stoic doctrines (Kerferd, 1967, 92). In the crowded capitals of the Hellenistic monarchies, with their mixed populations, it is not surprising that the Aristotle of the Lyceum–Apellicon writings, apparent spokesman of a parochial Hellenism, should have found little favour. Eratosthenes, the great librarian of Alexandria, is the most likely source of the upbraiding Aristotle receives for his advice to Alexander to treat Greeks as a leader, non-Greeks as a despot, in Plutarch's symptomatic work *On the Fortune or the Virtue of Alexander* (Bury, 1923, 27). In a typically Hellenistic presentation, recreated in Renaissance texts, Alexander is shown responding to Fortune (Tyche), who 'would try to inscribe her name on his successes' in the boldest terms: ' "Slander not my virtues, nor take away my fair fame by detraction. Darius was your handiwork: he who was a slave and courier of the king, him did you make the mighty lord of Persia ... Adorn yourself, proud Fortune, and vaunt your dominion over kings that never felt a wound nor shed a drop of blood" ' (Plutarch, 326e–f, 1936 edn, 383–5). Alexander then goes on to record his trials and victories, in Asia, among the Indians, and in opening up 'the broad land of Egypt'. Although Plutarch dares to claim for Alexander's virtue, as a philosopher, that 'the equipment that he had from Aristotle his teacher when he crossed over into Asia was more than what he had from his father Philip' (Plutarch 327e–f, 1936 edn, 391), the programme that Alexander, king of the Greeks and Lord of Asia is seen to execute, is not that of Aristotle, but of Zeno the Stoic, a Semite and probably a Phoenician, which 'may be summed up in this one main principle':

that all the inhabitants of this world of ours should not live differentiated by their respective rules of justice into separate cities and communities, but that we should consider all men to be of one community and one polity, and that we should have a common life and an order common to us all, even as a herd that feeds together and shares the pasturage of a common field. This Zeno wrote, giving shape to a dream or, as it were, shadowy picture of a well-ordered and philosophic common-wealth; but it was Alexander who gave effect to the idea. For Alexander did not follow Aristotle's advice to treat the Greeks as if he were their leader, and other peoples as if he were their master; to have regard for the Greeks as for friends and kindred, but to conduct himself toward other peoples as though they were plants or animals; for to do so would have been to cumber his leadership with numerous battles and banishments and festering seditions. But as he believed that he came as a heaven-sent governor to all, and as a mediator for the whole world, those whom he could not persuade to unite with him, he conquered by force of arms, and he brought together into one body all men everywhere, uniting and mixing in one great loving-cup, as it were, men's lives, their characters, their marriages, their very habits of life. He bade them all consider as their fatherland the whole inhabited earth, as their stronghold and protection his camp, as akin to them all good men, and as foreigners only the wicked; they should not distinguish between Grecian and foreigner by Grecian cloak and targe, or scimitar and jacket; but the distinguishing mark of the Grecian should be seen in virtue, and that of the foreigner in iniquity; clothing and food, marriage and manner of life they should regard as common to all, being blended into one by ties of blood and children. (Plutarch, *On the Fortune of Alexander*, 329b–d, 1936 edn, 397–9)

Plutarch would seem to be referring in the last lines quoted to Alexander's bigamous marriage to Roxane, the Persian. As for the heroization of Alexander, architect of the 'unity of mankind', this has been standard from the flatterers of Hellenistic times – initiated by Callisthenes, relative and protegée of Aristotle (Pearson, 1960, 5). For this particular passage of *De Fortuna Alexandri*, Plutarch is probably indebted to Eratosthenes, who owed his position to the Ptolemies of Egypt, and whose commentary on Zeno's *Republic* may have been contemporary with the reforms of Cleomenes in Sparta, designed to show the superiority of Alexander's policy to that of the Spartan reformers. It is speculated that Plutarch's chapter too was written during the Spartan reforms, with the same propagandistic purpose: veneration of the Great King, set over against egalitarian reform (Reesor, 1951, 17, citing Tarn, 1933, 151, n.25; cf. Baldry, 1965, 114–27). The image of the Great King, projected onto Alexander, and an image which he strove for himself in his imitations of the Persian monarch, derives from the Peripatetic Aristotelian tradition, as much as from Alexander's propagandists. For in the Hellenistic period, Aristotelian theories of kingship, once transposed from their strictly Greek context to the heterogeneous Eastern kingdoms, could find wider support in the 'ideal of the "socially-minded" king, helping, and providing for, his subjects – an ideal originating from oriental ideas which was, in Hellenistic times, proclaimed in many parts and exalted by Greek public opinion [in the] ideal of the sovereign *soter* and *euergetes*' (Ehrenberg, 1938, 93–4).

Disentangling the mutual, and reciprocal, influences of Aristotle and Alexander on theories of Hellenistic kingship is not easy, but whatever their precise delineations, we may concur with Ehrenberg's general comment that 'since the fourth century the Greeks, disappointed and distrustful of the *nomos poleos*, felt drawn to the belief in the *nomos empsuchos*, in the true monarch as Law incarnate'; that 'political ideas began to develop in that direction long before the times of Philip and Alexander'; and that 'the outlines they assumed later on, after Aristotle, were decisively influenced by the unique personality of the great king and lord of the world', Alexander (Ehrenberg, 1938, 83). Ehrenberg believes that whatever the status and content of Aristotle's works *peri Basileias* and *Alexandros he huper apoikon* (Diogenes Laertius 5.22, no. 17) and their relation to Alexander, the treatment of kingship contained in them concerns the best constitution, *politeia* and not the best man, and is thus consistent with the analysis of kingship in the *Politics*, book 7. This is probably true given Aristotle's penchant for systemic analysis. It does not follow from Aristotle's tutorship of Alexander that he subsequently approved of his projects. If the late Aristotle, who trimmed his sails to the winds of Athenian democracy, represents the true Aristotle, then it follows that: 'The Greek ideal was very remote indeed from the national king of the Macedonian people, who never allowed his fervent love of Hellenism to interfere with political and military necessities; more remote still from the "King of Asia", who more and more gave access to Orientalism and became the successor of the Persian kings' (Ehrenberg, 1938, 84).

Leaving aside controversial questions of the evolution, dating and provenance of Aristotle's manuscripts and the relationship between the tutor and his most famous pupil – questions that evidence may never permit us to resolve – the issue whether Aristotle's theory of constitutional rule could in principle be generated out of a handbook for kings turns on a different consideration, and that is the substantive question of the nature of rule. *Euergetism*, the patronage relation between benefactor and beneficiary – so crucial in the case of Aristotle and Alexander, Aristotle and Athens – was the mode in which leadership in the ancient world was conceived (Veyne 1976). It created a continuum connecting the king as magistrate bound by oath to his people to the notables as *euergetai*, also so bound. Magistracy, on such a reading, represented an extension of the royal principle. What oaths sealing the contract between benefactor and beneficiary in Sparta, for instance, presaged for Aristotle and Polybius was constitutional oligarchy. Plato in the Eighth Letter (355e–56b) urged a similar contractual arrangement on the contending factions at Syracuse, suggesting the sharing of a triple kingship analogous to the power-sharing of Spartan kings. This would reserve to the kings ancient religious functions and 'as many other things as are appropriate for men who were once benefactors' (356d); while dividing the remaining governmental functions among assembly, council and board of *nomophylakes* (cited in Cole, 1964, 473).

Aristotle defines the notables (*euergetai*), the 'well-to-do', as 'those who render public services (*leitourgiai*) by their possessions'; 'persons capable of holding office and rendering service (*leitourgiai*) of this kind to the state, either continuously or by turns' (Aristotle, *Politics*, 4.4 1291a33–39, 1981 edn, 248). It is by virtue of the distinction between beneficiaries and benefactors: 'on the one hand the people, on the other the notables, as we call them' (Aristotle, *Politics*, 4.4 1291b14–20, 1981 edn, 249), that the distinction between oligarchy and democracy, so crucial to the mixed constitution, *politeia*, arises. Aristotle argues against Plato's primary distinction between the virtuous (*aristoi*) and the non-virtuous. More democratically – and very much against the 'one man one job' principle of Plato – Aristotle observes that the various capacities of individuals for office, often multiple in any given individual, which qualify 'the people' (*demos*), in fact, for most of the offices, do not allow discrimination between 'the few and the many on the grounds of virtue (*arete*)'. But the numerical distinction does have crucial, and different, significance: 'the same people cannot be both rich and poor, and that is why the prime division of the state into parts seems to be into poor and the well-to-do.' It just so happens that the poor are many and the rich are few: 'so the constitutions are accordingly constructed to reflect the predominance of one or other of these, and there seem to be two constitutions – democracy and oligarchy' (Aristotle, *Politics*, 4.4 1291a40–b13, 1981 edn, 249).

Oligarchy and timarchy were constitutive forms of economic dependency in the ancient world, represented by the phenomenon of *euergetism*. Patronage justified a division between the haves and have-nots as a basis for the relation between rulers and ruled; this Aristotle makes explicit. It expressed the prevailing reality of Greek politics, where the great landed families controlled politics, as Plato freely admits in the *Protagoras* 326c–d and the Seventh Letter; a reality long justified by arguments like those of the Old Oligarch, 1.3 and 13, who noted the willingness of the inferior (*kakoi*) to let the superior (*chrestoi*) rule, as long as they continued to profit from the regime (noted in Cole, 1964, 474). In the anonymous *Rhetorica ad Alexandrum*, the author urges on democracies the time-honoured strategy of choosing minor officials by lot and major ones by election, as gratifying both the demands of the people, who will not be envious, and of the wealthier citizens, who will be happy to perform services (*leitourgiai*) in exchange for the honour and reputation that accrue (1424a12–25, cited in Cole, 1964, 475). The lot is cheap; electoral campaigns favour the wealthy.

Standards by which officials as *euergetai*, or patrons, were held to account were every bit as strict as those for the benefactor king, although the oligarchs, as a corporate body, were less vulnerable to despoliation and more inclined to clientage. Nevertheless, the proscription of magistrates and their trials for extortion in the Roman period were testimony to the fact that patronage was a justifiable duty and no mere charity on the part of the ruler (Veyne, 1976, 47–8). The vulnerability of powerful officials is plain in the smear on Pericles and his circle as Pisistratids (tyrants) (Ehrenberg, 1954, 84–91, cited in Cole, 1964, 475, n.95); in the fear engendered by the career of Alcibiades; and in the suggested reforms of Hippodamus of Miletus (cited in Aristotle, *Politics*, 2.8 1267b39–68a1). He, like Democritus (B253 and 266), recommended a court of appeal reminiscent of Polybius' *gerousia* to deal with cases involving extortion that resulted from the scrutinizing of magistrates after their term in office; as well as ways to make officials less vulnerable to the malice of the masses (Cole, 1964, 476). The Spartan *gerousia*, incidentally, was praised by Isocrates (*Panathenaicus* 153–4) as having been modelled on the Athenian Areopagus instituted by Solon, who according to Aristotle (*Politics*, 2.12 1273b35–41) was credited by some thinkers with 'mixing the constitution well' (cited in Cole, 1964, 476).

That mixture is in fact oligarchic, and Aristotle specifies the patronage of notables as necessary for the preservation of oligarchies (*Politics*, 6.7

1321a26–b3, 1981 edn, 379). Oligarchies require a demonstration effect for their success: the people need to see that the regime does indeed justify itself by its benefactions. If it does not do so and the notables seek to benefit themselves from office, rather than bestowing benefits on others as the price of the right to rule, they are not strictly speaking oligarchies at all, but 'democracies in miniature'. For 'to hold office for profit rather than honour is a characteristic of democracy' (editor's note, 379, n.5, Aristotle, 1981 edn). Of oligarchy, Aristotle says:

> the most supreme offices, which must be held by those who are members of the constitution, should have public services (*leitourgia*) associated with them. This will reconcile the people to having no share in office, and make them think the more kindly of officials who pay heavily for their position. It is appropriate, too, that newcomers to office should offer magnificent sacrificial banquets and execute some public work. The object is that the people, when they share in the banquets and see their city being adorned with votive offerings and with buildings, may be satisfied to see the constitution continue. There is the further result that these will remain as memorials to the notables' expenditure. But nowadays those who are connected with an oligarchy do not do this, but rather the reverse, for it is the gains they are after, no less than the honour. Such oligarchies are well named 'democracies in miniature'. (*Politics*, 6.7 1321a26–b3, 1981 edn, 379)

In the *Nicomachean Ethics*, Aristotle gives a more complete list of the liturgies the notables were required to perform: the *choregia*, or furnishing the training and accoutrements for a choral or dramatic performance (*NE*, 1101a15, 1122b22, 1123a23, 1177a30, 1178a24, 1179a11); the *trierarchia*, or the manning, equipping and maintenance of a warship (*NE*, 1122a24, b23); the *architheoria*, which involves sending a foreign delegation to a festival abroad (*NE*, 1122a25); *hestiasis*, or the furnishing of a banquet to one's tribe (*phyle*) (*NE*, 1122b23, 1160a18) (Aristotle, 1976 edn, editor's Appendix I, 362).

Oligarchy, by virtue of the primary distinction between the rich and the poor, is a regime in its own right then, and not necessarily lacking in virtue either, although, for the reasons given, virtue can never be the discriminating principle. Anomalies in the distribution of honours, and the power of the notables who weigh in, either with the people or against them, are major causes of revolutions (Aristotle, *Politics*, 5.4 1304a17–32, 1981 edn, 308). Oligarchy cannot function without liberality and beneficence; the latter among the first in Aristotle's taxonomy of virtues in the *Nicomachean Ethics*, and, if length is any indication, the most central; leading directly into his description of *megalopsuchos*, the moral and social profile of the notable, whose characteristic virtues are magnificence (*megaloprepeia*) and its correlative magnanimity (*megalopsuchia*). The connection to oligarchy is clearly made, Aristotle declaring that magnificence, 'unlike liberality ... does not extend to all financial transactions, but only to such as involve expenditure'; that 'in these it surpasses liberality in scale, because (as its very name implies) it is befitting expenditure on a large scale'; and that the types of expenditure it involves are those typical of an *euergetes*: 'maintain[ing] a warship' or 'lead[ing] a delegation to a festival' (*NE*, 4.2 1122a189–20, 1976 edn, 149).

Euergetism is thus constitutive of an aristocratic – if not in fact a timocratic – as opposed to a democratic, social order, its original connection to kingship, which lived on under the Roman Emperor, lingering in Aristotle only in the *majestas* of the grandee. Aristotle prevails on the desire for fame and fortune of the timocratic elite for public purposes, reminding it constantly that these are honours to which the poor cannot aspire:

> Now there are some kinds of expenditure that we describe as honourable, e.g. services paid to the gods – votive offerings, buildings and sacrifices – and similarly with anything of a religious nature; and all objects of public-spirited ambition e.g. in any case where it is thought to be a duty to make a fine show by the provision of a chorus, or the maintenance of a warship, or even by entertaining the whole city at a banquet. But in every case the expenditure is related to the position and resources of the agent; because it must be worthy of these, and appropriate not only to the result produced but also to the man who produces it. Hence a poor man cannot be magnificent, because he has not the means to meet heavy expenses suitably ... But such expenditure befits those who have appropriate resources, acquired either by themselves or from ancestors or connections, and persons of noble birth or great reputation or other such qualities, because these all involve grandeur and distinction. These are the primary requirements for the magnificent man, and it is chiefly in outlays of this sort that magnificence is exercised (as we have said), because they are the grandest and most highly esteemed ... for the magnificent man spends not upon himself but upon public objects, and his gifts have some resemblance to votive offerings. (Aristotle, *NE*, 4.2 1122b21–1123a10, 1976 edn, 150–1).

The public nature of private display, constitutive of magnificence, does not rule out private occasions as worthy of lavish patronage, particularly 'any event that excites the interest of the whole community, or of people in high positions'. The notable's private indulgence in conspicuous consumption is not deprecated, so long as the purposes are public image and reputation:

> It is also characteristic of him to furnish his house in a way suitable to his wealth (because even this is a kind of ornament), and to spend his money for preference upon results that are long-lasting (because they are the finest), and in every set of circumstances to spend what is appropriate (because the same expenditure is not equally due to gods and men, nor is the same outlay proper in the case of a temple as in that of a tomb). (Aristotle, *NE*, 4.2 1123a1–11, 1976 edn, 151)

In these magnificent displays by the *megalopsuchos* it is not characteristic of him to count the cost, the mark of the 'petty'; rather 'he will consider how he can achieve the finest and most appropriate result'. In fact, in the determination of magnificence monetary value is irrelevant: the excellence of a possession relates to its cost, but the excellence of an achievement relates only to the admiration it excites in others. *Arete*, or excellence, is precisely the virtue of the *aristoi*, a virtue of action, not of possession, although possession is related, as the necessary but not sufficient condition. It follows that 'magnificence as an achievement is excellence on a grand scale' (Aristotle, *NE*, 4.2 1122a18–1122b20, 1976 edn, 149–50).

Aristotle has no difficulty with the concentration of wealth that patronage requires. Not only is the poor man incapable of magnificence but even the liberal man may be disqualified, 'because the man who spends duly in small or moderate transactions ... is not called magnificent – only the one who does so on a grand scale'; so, 'although the magnificent man is liberal, the liberal man is not necessarily magnificent.' It is true that magnificence may run to excess in the opposite direction, as 'vulgarity, lack of taste', 'ostentatious outlay in wrong circumstances and in a wrong manner'. For magnificence, like *megalopsuchia*, depends on fine judgements of taste and the sort of breeding and demeanour that characterize the aristocracy: 'the magnificent man is a sort of connoisseur; he has an eye for fitness, and can spend large sums with good taste'; indeed, he is required to do so. Appropriateness is always and everywhere the measure, which does not suggest in this case moderation or a mean, but rather tastefully lavish display. Aristotle makes a fine point of contrast to the vulgar man, who 'uses trivial occasions to spend large sums of money and make a jarring display: e.g. by entertaining the members of his club as if they were wedding-guests, and (if he is financing a comedy) by bringing on the chorus in purple robes at their first entrance, as they do at Megara' (Aristotle, *NE*, 4.2 1123a11–30, 1976 edn, 152).

There is perfect symmetry between the magnificent and the magnanimous man on Aristotle's account: in each case the virtue requires fitness in the candidate due to factors of birth and social position that define it as a class attribute. At the same time these virtues appeal to values of honour and glory that excite interest in the whole community. Moreover, since the candidate pays for his superiority by the patronage expected of him in his public capacity, his private indulgences are justified as appropriate forms of self-love and honour owed his social standing:

> Greatness of soul, as the very name suggests, is concerned with things that are great, and we must first grasp of what sort these are ... Well, a person is considered to be magnanimous if he thinks that he is worthy of great things, provided that he *is* worthy of them ... because magnanimity implies greatness, just as beauty implies a well-developed body: i.e. small people can be neat and well-proportioned, but not beautiful ... (Aristotle, *NE*, 4.3 1123b1–25, 1976 edn, 153–4)

It is quite clear that the honours to which 'greatness' pertains are public honours, and that they belong to a system of honours that, far from being incidental to, actually constitutes the basis of economic and political power. *Euergetism* or patronage, as the economic system of the ancient world, generalized *timarchy* well beyond the confines of what Plato and Aristotle were prepared theoretically to concede. Thus even innocently high-minded claims to paying one's class dues to the gods reflect the status due to the notable: 'If then, the magnanimous man makes, and deservedly makes, great claims, and especially the greatest claims, he must have one special object in view' – and that is honour. Aristotle points out that the virtue of the magnanimous man cannot be honour in the absence of virtue: 'Since the magnanimous man has the greatest deserts, he must be the best man of all; because the better a man is the greater his deserts are, and the best man's deserts are the greatest. So the truly magnanimous man must be good'. A most specious form of reasoning, we should note, which would suggest that everywhere wealth is a mark of goodness. But Aristotle persists: indeed, he says, 'if one considers all the various departments of conduct it will be obvious that the idea of a magnanimous man's not being good is utterly ridiculous'. Moreover, his goodness will be an 'all-round excellence':

It would seem that the magnanimous man is characterized by greatness in every virtue. It would not be at all fitting for him to run away at top speed, or to do a wrong; for what motive could induce one so imperturbable ['one to whom nothing is great'] to behave disgracefully? ... So magnanimity seems to be a sort of crown of the virtues, because it enhances them and is never found apart from them. (Aristotle, *NE*, 4.3 1123b26–1124a5, 1976 edn, 154–5)

Aristotle appeals to the self-esteem of the notable, his sense of his own worthiness, and the preservation of his reputation and image to safeguard virtue. The profile of *megalopsuchos* is a quaint portrait of the ancient grandee, who talks with a low voice, walks with a slow gait, preserving his dignity and reserving his honour for worthy projects, part aristocrat, part Stoic sage of a later age. A man greatly removed from the democratic character of his day – as portrayed by Plato, for instance, in *Republic*, 559–61 – rather representing the 'timarchic' character of Plato's more negative depiction (*Republic*, 549–505). By any canons that we would recognize for the public deportment of the privately wealthy today, Aristotle's notable is a faintly ridiculous, if not a vain and despicable character:

It is chiefly with honours and dishonours, then, that the magnanimous man is concerned. At great honours bestowed by responsible persons he will feel pleasure, but only a moderate one, because he will feel that he is getting no more than his due, or rather less, since no honour can be enough for perfect excellence. Nevertheless he will accept such honours, on the ground that there is nothing greater that they can give him. But honour conferred by ordinary people for trivial reasons he will utterly despise, because that sort of thing is beneath his dignity ... but he will also be moderately disposed towards wealth, power, and every kind of good and bad fortune, however it befalls him: that is, he will neither be overjoyed at good nor over-distressed at bad fortune, since he does not regard even honour as a very great thing ... This is why magnanimous people are thought to be supercilious ... The magnanimous man's disdain is justifiable, because his estimate is true; but most people's disdain is capricious. The magnanimous man does not take petty risks, nor does he court danger, because there are few things that he values highly; but he takes great risks, and when he faces danger he is unsparing of his life, because to him there are some circumstances in which it is not worth living. (Aristotle, *NE*, 4.3, 1124a6–1124b10, 1976 edn, 155–6)

Aristotle makes the link between the magnanimous one as *euergetes* explicitly, and precisely in the context of the exchange of benefits for honours and power:

He is disposed to confer benefits, but is ashamed to accept them, because the one is the act of a superior and the other that of an inferior. When he repays a service he does so with interest, because in this way the original benefactor will become his debtor and beneficiary. People of this kind are thought to remember the benefits they have conferred, but not those that they have received (because the beneficiary is inferior to the benefactor, and the magnanimous man wants to be superior), and to enjoy being reminded of the former, but not of the latter ... (Aristotle, *NE*, 4.3, 1124b11–1125a20, 1976 edn, 157–8)

Once again, the personal demeanour of the notable is less an expression of private emotion, than it is a public registration of the receipt of appropriate (class) honours:

He is haughty towards those who are influential and successful, but moderate towards those who have an intermediate position in society, because in the former case to be superior is difficult and impressive, but in the latter it is easy; and to create an impression at the expense of the former is not ill-bred, but to do so among the humble is vulgar – like using one's strength against the weak. He does not enter for popular contests, or ones in which others distinguish themselves; he hangs back or does nothing at all, except where the honour or the feat is a great one. The tasks he undertakes are few, but grand and celebrated. He is bound to be open in his likes and dislikes ... his superior attitude makes him outspoken and candid – ... and he cannot bear to live in dependence upon somebody else, except a friend, because such conduct is servile; which is why all flatterers are of the lowest class, and humble people are flatterers. He is not prone to express admiration, because nothing is great in his eyes. He does not nurse resentment, because it is beneath a magnanimous man to remember things against people, especially wrongs ... For this reason he is not abusive either, not even of his enemies, unless he intends to be insulting. In troubles that are unavoidable or of minor importance he is the last person to complain or ask for help, because such an attitude would imply that he took them seriously ... The accepted view of the magnanimous person is that his gait is measured, his voice deep, and his speech unhurried. For since he takes few things seriously, he is not excitable, and since he regards nothing as great, he is not highly strung; and those are the qualities that make for shrillness of voice and hastiness of movement. Such, then, is the magnanimous man. (Aristotle, *NE*, 4.3, 1124b11–1125a20, 1976 edn, 157–8)

The magnanimous one is easily recognized as the Stoic sage, virtuous, wise, self-sufficient and at peace with himself. Aristotle's account of *megalopsuchos* has more worthy, and certainly more palatable, counterparts in Epictetus' advice to the wise man, and Marcus Aurelius' Roman Emperor and Stoic philosopher's reflections on virtue and one's attitudes to Fortune and one's fellows. We should not be surprised to find an almost direct parallel in the descriptions of the virtues of the ideal courtier recorded on the stele of Intef, son of Set, in the reign of Sesostris I, Twelfth Dynasty king of Egypt (*c*.1975 BC):

> I am cool, free of haste,
> Knowing the outcome, expecting what comes
> I am a speaker in situations of strife,
> One who knows which phrase causes anger.
> I am friendly when I hear my name
> To him who would tell me (his) concern.
> I am controlled, kind, friendly,
> One who calms the weeper with good words.
> I am one bright-faced [generous] to his client,
> Beneficent to his equal.
> (Lichtheim, 1973, 122)

5

Polybius, Stoicism and the Benefactor King

Polybius was by no means the first, then, to make the connection between the beneficent king and the notable, *euergetes*, which would render oligarchy a phenomenon continuous with kingship, magistrates enjoying the exercise of kingly functions. Patronage, the mechanism underpinning the ancient economy, accounted for the dynamics of civil society as an all-embracing principle. For in a world in which 'democracy' prescribed political freedoms, but economic unfreedom, 'beneficence' – bread and circuses – was the principle by which the people lived. In Polybius, as in Cicero, benefits (*beneficia*) and their complement, *officia*, or duties, summarized not only this fundamental economic interchange, but the moral obligations, concepts of virtue and duty, to which it gives rise. The experience of beneficence in the life of the individual was said at the same time to account for the development of moral sensibilities, of good and evil, welfare and injury. In Polybius 6.6 (1979 edn, 306), the ungrateful youth who, 'so far from showing gratitude [by] helping to protect those who have brought him up, deliberately injures them by word or deed', becomes the paradigm for an ungrateful people who, nurtured by beneficent rulers, show their ingratitude by claiming economic independence and right, in excess of the 'privileges of equality and freedom of speech', which constitute democracy in its only legitimate form (Polybius 6.9, 1979 edn, 309). It is precisely on the principle of ingratitude that Polybius rests his case against freedom in any sense except the negative 'freedom of speech', and against equality in any form except equally free speech.

The case for justice is correspondingly narrowly construed. Premised on a capacity for empathy, a sense of justice emerges at the experience of ingratitude for beneficence that one witnesses in others: 'when a man who has been helped, or rescued from some difficulty, so far from showing gratitude to his benefactor actually tries to do him harm, it is clear that those who hear of the affair will naturally be displeased and offended at his behaviour, will share the resentment of their neighbour, and will imagine themselves to be placed in his position' (Polybius 6.6, 1979 edn, 306). The capacity for empathy, in Polybius, as in Adam Smith's theory of moral sentiments, accounts for the way in which 'each individual begins to form an idea of the theory and meaning of duty, which is the beginning and end of justice' (Polybius 6.6, 1979 edn, 306). It is no more than giving to each his due in a timarchic system.

Polybius' theory of moral sentiments is essentially Stoic, but his concept of justice would seem to be quite restrictive by the standards of the Stoa. Much has been written about the natural sociability of men based on the self-preservation instinct and capacity for empathy to be found in Cicero. As transmitter of the organic theory of society to the Middle Ages (Nederman, 1988), Cicero is certainly historically more important than Polybius. But the degree to which these notions belong to a constellation of ideas that includes the theory of the mixed constitution, natural justice based on desert and the rule of the wise, derived from works of the Stoics that have since been lost to us, has been insufficiently stressed. This even in cases where the debt is specifically acknowledged, as Cicero acknowledges his first two books of *On Duties* to be indebted to the work by Panaetius of that title, and the theory of the mixed constitution, to have been the subject of discussion by the Scipionic Circle to which Polybius also belonged.

Relevant works of Stoic political philosophy include those of the Old Stoa more generally: Zeno of Citium, (*fl.* 277/6–243 BC), Sphaerus, active at the court of Cleomenes of Sparta (236–222 BC), Cleanthes of Assos (331/0–232/1 BC), Chrysippus from Cilicia (d. 204/8 BC), Diogenes of Babylon (visited Rome 155 BC), Antipater of Rhodes (resident in Rome around 33 BC); and those of the Middle Stoa specifically: the works of Panaetius of Rhodes (who accompanied Scipio on his embassy to Alexandria 140 BC), Hecaton of Rhodes (a pupil of Panaetius and friend of the Roman Stoic Q. Aelius Tubero), Blossius of Cumae (associate of Tiberius Gracchus in 134 BC), and Posidonius of Rhodes (visitor to Rome in 87 and 51 BC) (Reesor, 1951, 1–3). This school of philosophers was confusingly heterogeneous, both in political orientation and degree of personal involvement in politics. It comprised not only representatives of the Eastern provinces, often Semitic, and in some cases specifically associated with Hellenistic kings and their official propaganda machines, but also participants in the land reform programmes in Sparta – there being in some cases a direct connection between Sparta and the Hellenistic regimes, especially Egypt.

Chrysippus, in his book *Concerning Lives* (*Peri Bion*), had openly argued that of the three possible ways of life for a wise man, advising kings, living with friends or teaching students, the first was the best: 'The wise man will voluntarily receive a kingdom, drawing money from it. If he himself cannot be king, he will live with a king and will serve in the army with a king' (*Stoicorum Veterum Fragmenta*, 1964 edn, 3.691, 3.693, cited in Reesor, 1951, 23). So Eratosthenes, who is said to have influenced Plutarch's views on Zeno and the *cosmopolis* as a family of races (Plutarch, *De Fortuna Alexandri*, cited in Tarn, 1933, 151, n.25; Reesor, 1951, 17), was a client of the Ptolemies of Egypt, while Cleomenes of Sparta, patron of Sphaerus, had deified Ptolemy Philopator before his death (Reesor, 1951, 17, n.14). Sphaerus himself participated in the land reform movement of Agis and Cleomenes at Sparta, which allowed Stoicism to be associated with the cause for economic equality (Polybius, 2.62; Plutarch, *Agis* 13.3; cited in Reesor, 1951, 16–17). If there was a core of beliefs common to the Stoa, what they represented is primarily a response to the exigencies of empire, and the ethical problems of choice and economic distribution that it posed, premised on a physics and logic that accommodated the notion of nature well regulated.

Polybius' notion of justice based on natural sympathy and the moral power of emulation, to be found also in Cicero, had a specifically Stoic source in the belief that kinship (*oikeiosis*) is the source of justice. A fragment of Zeno's (*St. V. Fr.*, 1.197, cited in Reesor, 1951, 13) runs: 'Perception is the source of all kinship and estrangement; Zeno and his school assume that kinship is the source of justice.' From further fragments (*St. V. Fr.*, 3.178, 3.179) we know that Chrysippus used the term for kinship, *oikeiosis*, as Homer had originally used the word *philos* (Adkins, 1963, 30), to refer equally to the relation between a man and the parts of his body, or to a man and his relation to his offspring. A consideration that goes some way to explaining both the notion of 'natural' justice and the distinction, carefully made by Chrysippus, between charity *charis*, and service (*opheleia*), or beneficence: beneficence for the equal, charity for the unequal, both dispensed through a chain of fellowship. The English word 'freedom', as Hanna Pitkin (1988, 259, citing Benveniste, 1973, 266–7) points out, has a curiously similar etymology, deriving from the Indo-European adjective **priyos*, meaning 'one's own, the personal, but with a connotation of affection or closeness rather than of legal property'; 'used of personal possessions, of parts of one's body, but also of people with whom one had an emotional connection ... "according to context, it can be translated sometimes by 'his own' and sometimes by 'dear, beloved' " '; 'its various European derivatives also include words for wife, friend, to delight or endear, and – in religious discourse – "a sort of mutual belonging between gods and humans" '; 'in Gothic, however, the derivatives of **priyos* split into two distinct families, one of which includes words for *love* and *friendship*, the other words meaning *free* and *freedom* (or liberty)'.

Beneficence, according to two fragments of Chrysippus (*St. V. Fr.*, 3.246, 3.627, cited in Reesor, 1951, 21), accounts both for the transactions between gods and men and between wise men. In the first we find the king involved in reciprocal exchange with the gods, in Persian and Egyptian fashion: 'In virtue Zeus does not surpass Dion, but Zeus and Dion are helped by one another in the same way, since they are both wise, whenever the one finds the other disturbed' (*St. V. Fr.*, 3.246, cited in Reesor, 1951, 21). In the second, we have a chain of beneficence activated by the wise man: 'If one wise man anywhere stretches out his finger prudently, all wise men throughout the world are bene-fited' (*St. V. Fr.*, 3.627). Services (*opheleia*), or beneficence (*euergetism*) concern only the wise; the mass receive only charity (*charis*): 'But those who are not wise (*phauloi*) are not benefited when they obtain these things, nor are they well-treated, nor do they have benefactors, nor neglect their benefactors' (*St. V. Fr.*, 3.672, cited in Reesor, 1951, 21). Chrysippus had written a book on charity, *Concerning Acts of Kindness* (*Peri Chariton*), largely concerned with mythology and genealogy, we are told, but which also discussed receiving and returning kindness (*St. V. Fr.*, 2.1082, cited in Reesor, 1951, 21).

The concept of the wise man also governed the Stoic sovereignty of the good, a notion which we find in a mild form in Polybius' emphasis on the natural superiority of the leader. It goes back to Zeno, who distinguished between the wise (*sophoi*) and the unwise (*phauloi*), and an intermediate class, those on the way to becoming wise, about whom less is said. Only the wise were 'capable of being citizens, friends, kindred and free' (*St. V. Fr.*, 1.222, cited in Reesor, 1951,

10), a proviso which qualifies the precept on which Zeno's *Republic* is based, 'that we may not live by cities or demes, severally divided according to our own ideas of what is just, but may consider all men our demesmen and fellow citizens, and that there may be one life and one world just as a herd feeding together, nurtured by common law' (*St. V. Fr.*, 1.262, cited in Reesor, 1951, 10). One is tempted to wonder if the notion of the sovereignty of the good did not find fertile ground precisely due to the experience of colonial elites in the Hellenistic empires; as a justification of the Emperor and his companions; and of affinity as the ruling principle. Certainly there is much to suggest a close fit between Stoicism and exigencies of the empires over which its influence swept, as commentators have noted (Tarn, 1933, 1948; Reesor, 1951).

This is true of the Roman Empire and its senatorial caste, as it was of the Hellenistic. Stoicism, as one commentator has stressed (Earl, 1967, ch. 2) was the philosophy of new men, those who defined nobility as an individual rather than a class attribute, an achievement based on *virtus* rather than *genus*. Of such *novi homini*, Marius' speech in Sallust's *Bellum Jugurthine* (*BJ*, 85.4; 85.29; 85.37; 85.38; cited in Earl, 1967, 48) is said to be representative. But it is worth noting that Marius was a client of the Caecilii Metelli until their paths crossed (Earl, 1967, 51), and a combination of luck and intrigue gave him the consulship, so that the individualism of the Roman Stoics did not run essentially counter to notions of affinity based on class and clientage, or even noble birth and kinship. Thus it is that Cicero ends up affirming the strange principle endorsed by Hecaton of Rhodes, Panaetius' pupil, that even though a man's duty to his country is greater than that to his family, a son should defend his father caught robbing shrines or the state treasury, on the grounds that 'it is to our country's interest to have citizens who are loyal to their parents' (*De officiis*, 3.90, 1913 edn, 367 = Hecaton fr. 10, cited in Reesor, 1951, 35).

We are again reminded of the Ancients' preoccupation with property, money and resources for patronage as an institution. The same Hecaton, personally endorsed by Cicero (*De officiis*, 3.63–4), defended private property and the duty of each individual to look after his property: 'For we are rich not only for ourselves, but for our children, our relatives, friends and especially for the state. The resources and property of individuals constitute the welfare of the state' (Hecaton fr. 9 = Cicero, *De officiis*, 3.63, cited in Reesor, 1951, 35). Cicero, having discusssed the naturalness of human sociability and the growth of community based on reason and speech in book 1 of *De officiis*, very much after the manner of Panaetius as commentators agree (Reesor, 1951; Brunt, 1973, Appendix: 'Panaetius and Cicero, "De officiis" I.150f.': 16–34), in book 2 goes on to discuss duties as they relate to service, *beneficientia*, in the technical sense. From the standpoint of the new man his discussion is rather pointed. Having posited society as based on an exchange of goods and services in a thoroughly Aristotelian vein, he goes on to ask how a statesman is to win honour and confidence from the people. A question to which *beneficientia* is the answer. 'Who is there,' he asks, 'to whom that point which is argued at great length by Panaetius is not clear, that no leader in war or statesman at home could conduct important affairs of state in safety without the help of other men?' (Cicero, *De officiis*, 2.16, cited in Reesor, 1951, 27).

Beneficientia may be manifested in two ways: by giving money to the community, or offering personal service by interpreting the laws and serving in the courts. Discussing the benefactor who would put his private means at the public disposal, Cicero invokes Aristotle's concept of the liberal man, steering a middle path between niggardliness and spendthriftness. He defines liberality as typical of generous men 'who employ their own means to ransom captives from brigands, or who assume their friends' debts or help in providing dowries for their daughters, or assist them in acquiring property or increasing what they have' (Cicero, *De officiis*, 2.56, 1913 edn, 227). It is worth noting two things: first that these liberal men are notably benefiting friends rather than the state, on the sort of scale that new men could afford; and, secondly, that Aristotle's *megalopsuchos*, exhibiting magnificence on an awesome scale, is not a moderate liberal at all, but a wealthy aristocrat given to the big gesture. Cicero has turned Aristotle's categories around to define spendthrifts as 'those who squander their money on public banquets, doles of meat among the people, gladiatorial shows, magnificent games, and wild-beast fights – vanities of which but a brief recollection will remain, or none at all' (*De officiis*, 2.55, 1913 edn, 227).

But this is precisely the *euergetes* Aristotle had in mind; bread and circuses at work. Cicero is not altogether comfortable with his revisionist view: 'Out of respect for Pompey's memory', he says, 'I am rather diffident about expressing any criticism of theatres, colonnades, and new temples; and yet the greatest philosophers do not approve of them – our Panaetius himself, for example, whom I am following, not slavishly translating in these books' (Cicero, *De officiis*, 2.60, 1913 edn, 233). Cicero is clear, as Panaetius before him we can guess, that it is not the institution of patronage as such, but rather its excessive scale – well beyond the means of new men – that he is criticizing: 'To conclude, the whole system of public bounties (*talium largitionum*) in such extravagant amount is intrinsically wrong; but it may under certain circumstances be necessary to make them; even then they must be proportioned by our ability regulated by the golden mean' (*De officiis*, 2.60, 1913 edn, 233).

There may well have been a connection between Aristotle's doctrine of the mean, invoked by Cicero to put a brake on the excesses of the senatorial class, and the Stoic doctrine of 'mixed government' as the preferred constitutional form. Not only did Aristotle endorse a politics of 'balance' (*Politics*, 1297a) after the manner of Plato's *Laws* (693D), but the notion of the 'mixed constitution', combining the best features of kingship, aristocracy and democracy, so famously stated in Polybius 6, was considered by Diogenes Laertius characteristic of the Stoics (*St. V. Fr.*, 3.700 = Diogenes Laertius 7.131, cited in Reesor, 1951, 20). Thus Polybius 6.10–11 was certainly not the only source of the doctrine available to later Renaissance thinkers, which may cast light on the puzzle of the missing manuscripts (see below part II, chapter 16), for the doctrine is clearly stated in book 1 of Cicero's *De re publica*. Moreover, both Polybius 6 and Cicero on the mixed constitution are believed to be heavily indebted to Panaetius.

In the debate on the sources of Polybius 6.12–18, Svoboda and Kornemann point out that these chapters may in fact have been written later, and interpolated around 146 BC, the time of publication and a time at which both Panaetius and Polybius were members of the Scipionic circle (Svoboda 1913, 465–83;

Kornemann, 1931, 169–84, cited in Reesor, 1951, 29). These commentators note inconsistencies between 6.11, where Polybius claims that Rome was a mixed constitution and 6.51, where it is regarded as an aristocracy; between 6.8 where the permanence of the Roman constitution is remarked on, and 6.9, 12–14; 6.51, 4–8; and 6.57, 1–9, where it is regarded as susceptible to change. Passages of striking similarity, on the other hand – for instance, Polybius 6.6 and Cicero *De officiis*, book 1, ch. 11 – as well as shared common tenets concerning natural sympathy, sociability, justice and 'service' as the foundations of society, on which we have remarked, suggest a common source for wider aspects of their theories (Reesor, 1951, 29–30). The 'mixed' nature of government that as crypto-Stoics they endorsed was heavily tilted in the direction of the propertied classes, just as it had been with Aristotle – and here Stoicism is seen to be more innately conservative than its post-Enlightenment reputation would suggest.

Like Aristotle, anciently, Cicero and apologists for the oligarchs, contemporaneously, then, Polybius believed honour to be inseparable from the ruling caste of aristocrats who were its historical bearers. Thus he saw intimations everywhere that demagogy and the incursions of the *novi homini* would bring the glories of the Republic to an end. Commenting on the policy of land redistribution among Roman citizens in Gaul, Polybius remarked: 'this policy of colonization was a demagogic measure introduced by Gaius Flaminius, which may be said to have marked the first step in the demoralization of the Roman people' (Polybius 2.21, 1979 edn, 132). It would be a mistake to believe, however, that Polybius' economic conservatism was merely self-serving, or designed to please his senatorial friends. It represents, rather, a conceptual inability to break out of the framework in terms of which the causality of political decline was traditionally discussed: a framework in which ethical prescriptions and aetiological argument were conflated. Polybius registered the adjustments to the definition of democracy that represented his age: freedom equalled *parresia*, freedom of speech, and neither the ancient hoplite right to rule as well as being ruled; nor equality in its most minimal form as 'equality before the law' (Ehrenberg, 1950; Vlastos, 1953). Paul Veyne puts it nicely: 'If one were required to write a book on the Romano-Hellenistic notion of liberty, one could adopt as an epigram Polybius' words: "Men are intractable when it comes to their right to speak as equals, the right of free speech, which is what everybody takes liberty to be" ' (Polybius 4.31.4, cited in Veyne, 1976, 710).

Polybius' fear of defining freedom so as to include economic goods arises from a primitivism that attributes to wealth, luxury, the escalation of human needs and the enlargement of the appetites, the causes of tyranny and civic decline. Dread of luxury as the corrupter of republics is a theme that played itself out for a millennium or more in political theory, exiting in the eighteenth century, just when it had achieved supremacy in the works of Swift, Rousseau and Montesquieu, under the pressure of a more precise definition of economic causality, attributable to the pioneering work of the political economists (Veyne, 1976, 472; Springborg, 1981). (Gibbon, for instance, refused to invoke luxury in the conventional sense to account for the decline and fall of Rome, relying on more intrinsic factors of civic culture such as religion.) To the degree that the conventional moralistic analysis of corruption admitted of differences in interpretation, Polybius represented the more conservative tendency. Thus, if Juvenal, the 'democrat', bemoaned the decline of civic virtue that the popular distribution of public benefits ushered in, so that 'the same people who once distributed power, the fasces, the legions, finally all have learned in our day to stay in their place and desire for nothing more earnestly than two things: bread and circuses' (cited in Veyne, 1976, 474); Polybius concluded from the fact of patronage on such a scale something different: it killed docility. To him civic virtue was predicated on keeping the people poor, an essentially conservative view according to which uniformity and immobility were the only guarantees against the potential conflict that competition, engendered by social differentiation and the psychological expansion of needs, would produce. Keeping the people poor meant killing off aspirations to power and participation that might unsettle that caste of superiors who guaranteed a nation greatness:

> When a state, after warding off many great perils, achieves supremacy and uncontested sovereignty, it is evident that under the influence of long-established prosperity life will become more luxurious, and among the citizens themselves rivalry for office and in other spheres of activity will become fiercer than it should. As these symptoms become more marked, the craving for office and the sense of humiliation which obscurity imposes, together with the spread of ostentation and extravagance, will usher in a period of general deterioration. The principal authors of this change will be the masses, who at some moments will believe that they have a grievance against the greed of other members of society, and at others are made conceited by the flattery of those who aspire to office. By this stage they will have been roused to fury and their deliberations will constantly be swayed by passion, so that they will no longer consent to obey or even to be the equals of their leaders, but will demand everything or by far the greatest share for themselves. When this happens, the constitution will change its name to the one which sounds the most imposing of all, that of freedom and democracy, but its nature to that which is the worst of all, that is the rule of the mob. (Polybius 6.57, 1979 edn, 350)

Polybius' slighting reference to Herodotus 3.82, that democracy and equality (*isonomia*) 'are the fairest names of all', is symptomatic. If his analysis of the nature of democracy superficially resembles the famous account in Plato, *Republic* 7, of the psychological profile of the democrat among character types, even Plato did not rule out aspiration to office on the part of the citizen as a sign of corruption; it was only the abuse of office for personal enrichment that discredited democracy as a form of government in which wide citizen participation was constitutive of the type. But Polybius, while referencing both Plato and Herodotus, brings to his analysis the observation of Hellenistic kingdoms, where the patronage of a more moderate oligarchy had created a level of public wealth and the sort of animated competition for power to which he attributed all the economic and political crises of the age (Veyne, 1976, 472, citing Polybius 6.9):

> But as soon as a new generation has succeeded and the democracy falls into the hands of the grandchildren of its founders, they have become by this time so accustomed to equality and freedom of speech that they cease to value them and seek to raise themselves above their fellow-citizens, and it is noticeable that the people most liable to this temptation are the rich. So when they begin to hanker

after office, and find that they cannot achieve it through their own efforts or on their merits, they begin to seduce and corrupt the people in every possible way, and thus ruin their estates. The result is that through their senseless craving for prominence they stimulate among the masses both an appetite for bribes and the habit of receiving them, and then the rule of democracy is transformed into government by violence and strong-arm methods. By this time the people have become accustomed to feed at the expense of others and their prospects of winning a livelihood depend upon the property of their neighbours; then as soon as they find a leader who is sufficiently ambitious and daring, but is excluded from the honours of office because of his poverty, they will introduce a regime based on violence. After this they unite their forces, and proceed to massacre, banish and despoil their opponents, and finally degenerate into a state of bestiality, after which they once more find a master and a despot. (Polybius 6.9, 1979 edn, 309).

If Plato in *Republic* 8, 5629–565c, hinted at the corruption of the appetites that democracy interpreted as economic freedom might induce, Polybius, in the Stoic tradition of the Roman oligarchy, found in this possibility the single greatest argument against the devolution of political or economic power. So insistent is he that civic discipline depends on subjugation that, like all subsequent thinkers who have found the corruption of civilization to be predicated on an expansion of needs, he believes civil order to depend on levelling all tall poppies. Potential demagogues, like rambunctious subjects, threaten the prevailing civic virtue, and its aristocratic bearers, the *nobilissimi*, *clarissimi* or *optimates*, because they too rise up on the strength of inflated appetites.

Thus *monarchia*, or one man rule, which Polybius, using the term *dynasteia*, like Plato, distinguishes from hereditary sacral kingship elsewhere in the *Histories*, also describes original primitive kingship, uncorrupted by the habits of absolutism that institutionalization can bring. Polybius, in this usage which has puzzled commentators (Walbank, 1957, vol. 1, 656; 1972, 140 ff; Cole, 1964, 461; 1967, 102 ff), preserves all the ambiguities of *tyrannos*, for which *monarchos* stands as an interchangeable term. Tyranny, as the primitive kingship of tribal chiefs or marcher lords, served to establish or consolidate territorial nations. These founder kings opened up the possibility of a constitutional monarchy moderated by the participation of the aristocratic class in some form, on the one hand, like his own Acheans – and this is what a 'mixed' regime essentially looked like; or rule by demagogues over the mob, on the other. Perhaps Polybius already saw Rome going the latter way, classifying the Republic as a 'democracy', as Dio Cassius, in a less malignant sense, was later to do (Larsen, 1945, 89–90; Cole, 1964, 457, 483, n.109). Whatever the case, those who embraced freedom as unlimited economic acquisition, whether by the appetitive many or the gluttonous one, succumbed to the same evil, excessive desire. Essentially the relation between the partners in corruption was a symbiotic one. Whether benefi-cent notables, who maintained their right to rule by distributions to the many, or kings who maintained themselves in power as living embodiments of the personal gratification that peace and economic progress could procure, those of the ruling class who risked the destabilization of social order that an expansion of needs and rising aspirations to participation in economic and political power promised, ended up not only corrupting the public, but also corrupting themselves. So, primitive kings, while they pursued their state-building tasks and constructed:

> imposing strongholds, fortified them with walls, and acquired lands to provide for their subjects both security and an abundance of the necessities of life ... were never the objects of envy nor of abuse, because they did not indulge in distinctions of dress or of food or drink at the expense of others, but lived very much in the same fashion as the rest of their subjects, and kept in close touch with the people in their daily activities. But when rulers received their power by inheritance, and found that their safety was well provided for and their food was more than sufficient, this superabundance tempted them to indulge their appetites. They assumed that rulers should be distinguished from their subjects by a special dress, that they should enjoy additional luxury and variety in the preparation and serving of their food, and that they should be denied nothing in the pursuit of their love affairs, however lawless these might be. These vices provoked envy and indignation in the first case, and an outburst of passionate hatred and anger in the second, with the result that kingship became a tyranny. (Polybius 6.7, 1979 edn, 307)

Polybius was probably mindful of the ostentatious Eastern ceremonial and dress, adopted by Roman governors returning from their tours of duty in the Hellenistic kingdoms, where they were treated like monarchs. He was undoubtedly acquainted with the fact that the great Alexander, elsewhere praised by him as having founded the most powerful monarchy in the world, affected the elaborate dress of a Persian king, and was reputed even to have instituted the *proskynesis*, ruler worship in the Persian form of prostration, among his companions at Bactria (Tarn, 1927; Ehrenberg, 1938; Taylor, 1975, Appendices 1 and 2, 247–66).

One would think, indeed, that Philip and Alexander might represent the very epitome of the *monarchos* in its tyrannical sense. Alexander, who ruled not as *strategos* or *hegemon*, but as king, had ordered that the oligarchies go and the conquered cities enjoy democratic rule, the restoration of freedom and independence (*eleutheria kai autonomia*) for all (Ehrenberg, 1938, 11–13). Thus Alexander created the precedent for the 'freedom of the Greeks' that the Roman *princeps* so wisely followed. And while it is not true to maintain that Macedonian enlightenment went so far as to establish *symmachia*, or rule as between equals, in the conquered realms; members of the Corinthian League did enjoy real independence, other Greek cities immunities that they treated for individually and the non-Greeks a relative autonomy that compared favourably with their position under more ancient imperiums. Thus could Alexander justly claim the epithets by which he was praised: King of Macedon, Lord of Asia, Owner of the Asiatic *chora*, Liberator and Benefactor of *poleis* (Ehrenberg, 1938, 33–5). Rather than follow Aristotle's advice to be *hegemon* to the Greeks, but to the Asiatics *despotes*, Alexander went the other way, banishing to Elephantine, in Upper Egypt, the oligarchs who at the time he assumed power ruled most Greek cities, and inaugurating democratic regimes that put no intermediaries between himself and the people. A policy motivated not by pan-Hellenic idealism, but by considerations of *Realpolitik*, in a period less *polis*-minded and more prone to disaffection.

Thus Alexander stood as king, supreme above the faction fights of the cities, the one who could promise liberty against subjection, security against sedition. It is not surprising then that the Macedonian conqueror should have inspired spontaneous movements to divinize him, with a little encouragement from their idol (Ehrenberg, 1938, 39ff), even among the Greek cities. If Antigonus and his Seleucid successors maintained this tradition of 'freedom and autonomy' for conquered cities, it is not surprising either, since the formula for success worked so well. Only the Ptolemies refused to grant their peoples independence and municipal self-government; but everywhere Hellenistic kings were hailed as *soter*, saviour, and *euergetes*, benefactor, terms which defined the relations between king and subjects as those of *philia*, appropriate to a ruler cult (Ferguson, 1912; Ehrenberg, 1938, 47–9; Nock, 1942, 1951).

Polybius was not blind to the reports of lasciviousness and excess which everywhere followed the Macedonian rulers in their peregrinations. The corruption that is legendary among absolute monarchs certainly was reported to surround them, as he relates in salacious detail (Polybius 8.9–10, 1979 edn, 370–72), chiding Theopompus for portraying Philip:

> first of all as having been so promiscuous in his relations with women that he did everything in his power to ruin his own household by his passionate and ostentatious cravings ... secondly, as having behaved with the utmost injustice and lack of scruple in his schemes for forming friendships and alliances; thirdly, as having treacherously seized and enslaved a great number of cities by deceit and by force; and finally, as having been so addicted to strong drink that he was often seen by his friends openly drunk even during the hours of daylight. (Polybius 8.9, 1979 edn., 370)

To quote Theopompus' own words: ' "Anyone in Greece or among the barbarians whose character was thoroughly lascivious or shameless could be expected to gravitate to Philip's court in Macedonia, where he would earn the title of one of 'the King's companions'. For Philip made it his custom to turn away men of good reputation who took care of their property, but to honour and promote those who were spendthrifts and passed their time drinking and gambling" ' (Polybius 8.9, 1979 edn, 370). Theopompus repeats other scurrilous details of homosexual practices, of those who shaved and depilated their bodies to make love to bearded men, rightly condemned as 'courtesans rather than courtiers and male prostitutes rather than men at arms' who, 'being by their nature man-eaters ... became through their practices man-whores' (Polybius, citing Theopompus 8.9, 1979 edn, 370–1).

Polybius had his reasons, at which we can only guess, for wishing to preserve Philip's reputation from this, not unattested, taint. Was it from pan-Hellenic aspirations in turn? – which never, in fact, prompted him to praise the Athenians or other contenders for the title, Leader of the Greeks. Or was it because the Achaeans in general fared rather well out of an imperial policy that left them with their ancient freedoms in return for considerable security? (Polybius 2.41–2, 1979 edn, 152–5) – a policy inaugurated by Alexander but happily continued by the Romans. Or was it for reasons of *Realpolitik* and an admiration of those who could seize the moment for national goals? Polybius has the same praise for the

Macedonians as the 'rulers of Asia', as he had for the Persians as among 'the most celebrated empires of the past which have provided historians with their principal themes', and which provide the context for an analysis of the success of the Romans, who 'have brought not just mere portions but almost the whole of the world under their rule, and have left an empire which far surpasses any that exists today or is likely to succeed it' (Polybius 1.2, 1979 edn, 42). Philip and Alexander created the reality which made a Universal History possible. For, 'in earlier times the world's history had consisted, so to speak, of a series of unrelated episodes, the origins and results of each being as widely separated as their localities, but from this point onwards history becomes an organic whole: the affairs of Italy and of Africa are connected with those of Asia and of Greece, and all events bear a relationship and contribute to a single end' (Polybius 1.3, 1979 edn, 43).

Important as it is to rescue the reputation of Philip, if this momentous development is to be a tribute to something other than tyranny, it is more important still to rescue his 'companions'. For they represent the consultative elite which can render the Macedonian regime – on a rather generous reading – constitutional. This Polybius unabashedly does, declaring:

> when we come to speak of Philip and his friends, the problem is not merely that we should hesitate to accuse them of cowardice, effeminacy and shameless immorality. It is rather that when we set ourselves the task of honouring their achievements we might well fail to find words adequate to describe their courage, their perseverance, and, in a word, the manly virtue of their character. For there can be no doubt that by their indefatigable energy and daring they raised Macedonia from the status of a petty kingdom to that of the greatest and most glorious monarchy in the world. And apart from what was accomplished during Philip's lifetime, the successes that were achieved by Alexander after his father's death won for them a reputation for valour which has been universally recognized by posterity. (Polybius 8.10, 1979 edn, 371)

Having given due credit to the young Alexander as commander-in-chief, Polybius very pointedly exonerates the royal 'companions':

> who overcame the enemy in many battles against all expectation, and endured many extraordinary toils, dangers and hardships. Later, even though they came into possession of vast wealth and enjoyed unlimited opportunities to satisfy every desire, none of them suffered any deterioration of their physical strength for that reason, nor did they commit any unjust or licentious actions to gratify the demands of passion. On the contrary, all those who were associated with Philip and later with Alexander showed themselves by their magnanimity, their daring and their self-discipline to be truly royal. We need not mention any of these men by name. But after Alexander's death, when they became rivals for the possession of an empire which covered the greater part of the earth, the glory of their achievements was such as to fill chronicle after chronicle with the record of their exploits. (Polybius 8.10, 1979 edn, 371–2)

One may compare the indulgence with which Polybius treats Philip, Alexander, who died of drink, and the 'royal companions', with the harshness with which he treated the Boeotians, as lacking any sense of national mission or desire for glory, content rather with drink and good cheer, so that by the individual pursuit of private goods, they lost, little by little, the public goods that accrue from honour and power (Polybius 20.4–6, cited in Veyne, 1976, 464). In fact, the Boeotians were not less enamoured 'than Polybius of Roman glory, or less oligarchical by inclination, their laws having no other end but to secure from Rome the popular support' necessary to a programme of imperialistic grandeur. At the same time these very Boeotians, were 'one of the bastions of Greek resistance to Roman hegemony, while Polybius himself actively collaborated with the conqueror' (Veyne, 1976, 464). By an irony of history, perhaps due to Polybius' calumny, the very name Boeotia has come to be synonymous with bovine stupidity. As Veyne points out, in order to understand Polybius' judgement, it is necessary to 'deploy an ideological map of the area'. The secret lies in Polybius' resistance to the idea that an oligarchic elite born with the right to rule, might be legitimately supplanted, or surreptitiously corrupted (Veyne, 1976, 464–5). Either possibility arises from the wider dispersal of wealth that the mechanisms of patronage and beneficence permitted in the Hellenistic world. Boeotian popular independence stood for an erosion of hegemony and a threat to the *status quo* that could not be tolerated. The fraternal rule of Philip and Alexander's 'manly' companions, by contrast, represented the old social order of 'balanced' government: rule by a hegemonic oligarchy.

For Polybius, the possibility of Philip's own depravity could only be exceeded in enormity by the depravity of his companions, that bulwark of oligarchy that legitimized the marcher lord, and marked the small step between *monarchia* as nation-building by the founder prince, primal king, and the absolutism of the tyrant (*monarchos*). It is perhaps due to Polybius that the legend of Macedonian primitive democracy, balanced on the tribal assembly of clan chiefs and 'companion' elders, has persisted so long, Larsen (1945, 66–7) pointing out that Polybius not only registered the changed connotations of 'democracy', as referring to the representative government of contemporary feudal states, but held up the example of the Macedonian republics as fine specimens (Polybius 31.2, discussed by Larsen, 1945, 66–70, 90–1).

This reasoning would explain why it was that Polybius saw, neither in the Macedonians, nor in the Seleucids, the corruption and depravity that marks the fine line between absolute monarchy and tyranny, but rather in the Ptolemies. And if, one suspects, Philip and Alexander represent *monarchia* as the nation-building institution of the marcher lords, primitive kingship in all its pristine splendour, the Ptolemies, who lacked 'companions' and ruled as a one-man band, were seen by him to represent the model of the depraved tyrant – *monarchia* in its more usual sense. Polybius emphasizes, significantly, both the gratifications with which the Ptolemies bought the quiescence of the public, as well as the personal indulgences which are said to have characterized their reign. Ptolemy IV, Philopator, feeling secure in his possessions, 'began to conduct his reign as if it were a perpetual festival' (Polybius 5.34, 1979 edn, 291). At the same time, 'he neglected the business of state, made himself difficult to approach, hardly deigned to receive the members of his court or the officials responsible for internal affairs, and treated with contempt or indifference whose who handled his country's interests abroad, to which his predecessors had given more attention than to the administration even of Egypt itself' (Polybius 5.34, 1979 edn, 291). Polybius, noting the success with which former Egyptian kings had extended their hegemony into Asia Minor, Anatolia and the Fertile Cresent, observed that 'since they had extended their power to such remote regions and had long ago established such a far-flung system of client states to protect them, the Kings of Egypt had never felt anxiety concerning their rule at home, but had naturally attached great importance to the handling of foreign affairs' (Polybius 5.34, 1979 edn, 292). All of this Ptolemy IV was said to have sacrificed: 'Philopator, however, neglected all these areas of his authority, and gave his whole attention to ignoble love affairs, and to senseless and continuous drinking. And so, as might have been expected, it was not long before conspiracies began to be formed, against both the King's life and his throne' (Polybius 5.34, 1979 edn, 292) – the classic story of the tyrant and his downfall.

6

Plato and the Egyptian Story

The spectre of Egypt looms over the writings of certain Hellenistic thinkers, as it does over Plato. The series of developments producing 'the justest of all kingships', which Greek society departed for an uncertain future of city-development, according to *Laws* 3, may have reference to other historical models of his acquaintance. Here the example of Egypt seems peculiarly appropriate, Plato having been long fabled to have sojourned there, along with Solon and other seekers of wisdom in different periods. Diogenes Laertius (*Life of Plato*, 3.6, cited in Forsyth, 1980, 32) reports the point of Plato's Egyptian visit being 'to see those who interpret the will of the gods', but as he puts him in the company of Euripides, who was long dead at the time, this could hardly be considered proof; which leaves us only with the remark of Plutarch (*Life of Solon*, 2, cited in Forsyth, 1980, 32) that 'Plato paid for the expenses of his stay in Egypt by selling oil'. For Solon's visit we have stronger evidence, Plutarch twice maintains it, in *De Iside et Osiride*, 10.354e and his *Life of Solon*, 26 and 31, where he speaks of him as having studied with the priests Psenophis of Heliopolis and Sonchis of Sais, corroborating Plato's account. Herodotus (1.30) put Solon's visit during the reign of Amasis (569–25 BC, cited in Forsyth, 1980, 39), a view supported by Diogenes Laertius (1.50), but contradicted by Aristotle (*Constitution of Athens* 11, cited in Forsyth, 1980, 39). In the *Timaeus–Critias* Plato actually relates the story Solon was said to have told on his return. It is suggested that the projected, but unfinished, *Timaeus/Critias/Hermocrates* trilogy was a work intended to provide a bridge, perhaps as much historical as allegorical, between the *Republic* – to which the *Timaeus–Critias* is clearly connected – and the *Laws*, which may be a completed or revised version of the unfinished trilogy (Lee, 1971, 47; Cornford, 1975).

The *Timaeus* (17, 1971 edn, 29) opens with the remarks that it is to be a continuation of the discussion of the previous day on the ideal society and its laws, namely the *Republic*. It outlines the basic features of that society as being the separation of agriculture, industry and defence functions; the division into classes based on occupational categories; and the education of a guardian class so as to combine justice and gentleness toward the community with sufficient toughness to maintain power. This is to be achieved by combining philosophical training with the communal way of life of a corporate caste that could own property collectively but not individually (*Tim.*, 18, 1971 edn, 30). Socrates recapitulates the provisions made in the *Republic* to ensure both the integrity of the caste and its rule of meritocracy, stipulating 'that marriages and children should be shared in common' (*Tim.*, 18, 1971 edn, 30) and that the educational system should be devised to 'promote the worthy and demote the unworthy' (*Tim.*, 19, 1971 edn, 31). However, Socrates expresses some reservations about this depiction of the ideal society, as a lifeless portrait lacking the cut and thrust of interaction between states, or any demonstration of 'the qualities we would expect from its system of education and training, both in action and negotiation with its rivals' (*Tim.*, 19, 1971 edn, 31). The sort of realistic picture of which the poets and Sophists are equally incapable, he adds (*Tim.*, 19, 1971 edn, 32). Socrates turns to the foreigner Timaeus from the Italian city Locris to help him out, but before he can do so, Critias volunteers a story that will flesh out the account historically: an odd tale of Solon's experience of Egypt and the mythical Atlantis.

The setting of Solon's tale is significant: 'It was Children's Day in the festival of Apatouria', the old Ionian festival celebrated by the phratries. On the third day, Children's Day, the young adult males with newly married wives were enrolled in the phratry or clan, and thus registered as citizens under the aegis of a patrimonial organization (Ferguson, 1910; Nilsson, 1970, 79); 'and there were the customary ceremonies for the boys, including prizes given by the fathers for reciting' (*Tim.*, 21, 1971 edn, 33). It was also the day dedicated to the goddess Aethra, daughter of Pittheus, king of Troezen, in the old mythology, mother of Theseus by Aegeus, by a strange union. Aethra, sent by Athena to the island of Hiera or Sphairia, was 'visited' on the same night by Poseidon the god, and her husband Aegeus – hence known as Apatouria, 'the Deceitful' (Pausanias 2.33.1; Apollodorus 3.208, cited in Rose and Robertson, 1970a, 20). The 'Goddess [celebrated] on her festival day [by] a just and truthful hymn of praise', like the poem that Solon offers her, telling of ancient Egyptian and Athenian days (*Tim.*, 21, 1971 edn, 33), is thus the mother of Theseus who slew the Minotaur, as well as the patron of the phratries through Athena. Her festival was the occasion for the recitation of foundation epics, hymns of national integration (Gordon, 1953) of the type of Homer and Solon. Of the latter Critias remarks: 'if he had finished the story he brought back from Egypt, and hadn't been compelled to neglect it because of the class struggles and other evils he found here on his return, I don't think any poet, even Homer or Hesiod, would have been more famous' (*Tim.*, 21, 1971 edn, 34).

Solon heard his tale in the Egyptian delta city of Sais, where he spent time after leaving Athens in 594 BC for his ten-year peregrination in the Mediterranean, reportedly meeting the Pharaoh Amasis, a philhellene responsible for founding the Greek city Naucratis on Egyptian soil. Solon had also spent time with Egyptian priests, learning from them about their history and his own, of which 'he and all his countrymen were almost entirely ignorant' (*Tim.*, 22, 1971 edn, 34). In order to encourage the priests to divulge more, Solon relates to them the Greek mythical account of Phoroneus and Niobe, the first man and woman to have survived the flood, and their descendants, trying 'by reckoning up the generations to calculate how long ago the events in question had taken place' (*Tim.*, 22, 1971 edn, 34). This exercise provokes an interesting response in one old Egyptian priest who exclaims, ' "O Solon, Solon, you Greeks are all children, and there's no such thing as an old Greek" ' (*Tim.*, 22, 1971 edn, 34). When pressed, he continues: ' "You are young in mind ... you have no belief rooted in old tradition and old knowledge hoary with age. And the reason is this. There have been and will be many different calamities to destroy mankind, the greatest of them by fire and water, lesser ones by countless other means" ' (*Tim.*, 22, 1971 edn, 35). Greek mythology provides an allegorical version of these catastrophes, but a historical reconstruction is impossible in the absence of records that in Greece have not survived (*Tim.*, 22–23, 1971 edn, 35).

The old Egyptian priest proceeds with an account, the outlines of which are now familiar: destruction by fire (due to planetary variations and perhaps meteorites?), or by flood, and the regeneration of civilization from the survivors. The difference in the case of Egypt is that, due to geophysical advantages, her civilization and records remain intact, the art of writing is not lost and even Greek history is better preserved there than in its homeland (*Tim.*, 22–3, 1971 edn, 35): 'You remember only one deluge, though there have been many, and you do not know that the finest and best race of men that ever existed lived in your country; you and your fellow citizens are descended from the few survivors that remained, but you know nothing about it because so many succeeding generations left no record in writing.' As we shall see, Plato may here be referring to floods caused by volcanic activity for which we have independent evidence (Doumas, 1974, 1978, 1980, 1983; Manning, 1988, 21–2), and from which Lower Egypt at least was not altogether spared (Stanley and Sheng, 1986), the seventeenth century BC barely represented in the Egyptian archive, perhaps for this very reason (Bernal, 1987a, 42).

Egypt's reputation for preserving written records, and for having developed the art of writing is legendary, and attested to elsewhere in Plato. In the *Philebus*, 18b–d, (Plato, 1961 edn, 1094–5), Socrates discusses in some detail the recognition by the great god Thoth of Egyptian phonemes and the attempt to categorize them by means of 'letters'. In the *Phaedrus* (274c–275d, 1961 edn, 520–1), once again on the subject of memory, Socrates tells a tale relayed from the Greek city of Naucratis in Egypt, about 'the god to whom the bird called Ibis is sacred, his own name being Theuth', who 'invented number and calculation, geometry and astronomy, not to speak of draughts and dice, and above all writing'. Thoth was reputed to have told the king of Egyptian Thebes, Thamus, whose local name was Amun: ' "Here, O king, is a branch of learning that will make the people of Egypt wiser and improve their memories; my discovery provides a recipe for memory and wisdom." ' It is interesting that the king should be referred to as Amun, whom he would, according to the Egyptian theology, have embodied in his divine aspect (Hornung, 1983; Bell, 1985a). The king responds to Thoth: ' "O man full of arts, to one it is given to create the things of arts, and to another to judge what measure of harm and profit they have for those that shall employ them" ' (*Phaedrus*, 274e, Plato, 1961 edn, 520) – it is interesting, too, that the king should refer to Thoth as a judge, an independently attested aspect of this god (Bleeker, 1973). Thamus then proceeds to argue that the arts are a double-edged sword. What Thoth has discovered is ' "a recipe not for memory, but for reminder, calling things to remembrance no longer from within themselves, but by means of external marks" '. By the same token, the recipe for wisdom, ' "is no true wisdom ... but only its semblance, for, by telling [your disciples] of many things without teaching them you will make them seem to know much, while for the most part they know nothing" '.

Phaedrus expresses scepticism about 'tales from Egypt' incorporated in the Greek oral tradition, and is challenged by Socrates' most extraordinary rebuke that he pays too much attention to 'who the speaker is, and what country he comes from' and not enough to whether 'what he says is true or false' (*Phaedrus*, 275c, 1961 edn, 520). Plato implies that the nationality and status of the speaker should not be a warrant for the truth of what he/she says – although it usually was – one of the very rare ancient criticisms of the customary citation of authorities. Socrates goes on to contrast 'the simplicity of belief of the authorities of the temple of Zeus at Dodona, who said that the first prophetic utterances came from an oak tree'. This is the famous oracle, mentioned also by Homer (*Iliad*, 16.233), 'the most ancient and, at that period, the only oracle in Greece', whom Herodotus (2.55, 1972 edn, 150) cites as evidence that 'the names of the gods were brought into Greece from Egypt and the Pelasgians learnt them'. Dodona, for which archaeology confirms remarkable parallels to the site of the oracle of Amun at Siwa Oasis (Bernal, 1987a, 65, 78, 82, 99, 452), was in fact a Pelasgian site in north-west Greece, where, if we accept Bernal's thesis, aboriginal Greeks spoke their native language. Herodotus (2.49–52, 1972 edn, 149–51) tells us that the Dodonans did not differentiate the gods by name, referring to them only as *theoi*, certainly a Greek word, but that once Egyptian names were introduced they adopted them, having first consulted the oracle, who confirmed the appropriateness of their action. 'At Dodona', he says, 'the priestesses who deliver the oracles' tell of:

> two black doves, [who] they say flew away from Thebes to Egypt, and one of them alighted at Dodona, the other in Libya. The former, perched on an oak, and speaking with a human voice, told them that that there, on that very spot, there should be an oracle of Zeus. Those who heard her understood the words to be a command from heaven, and at once obeyed. Similarly the dove which flew to Libya told the Libyans to found the oracle of Ammon – which is also an oracle of Zeus. (Herodotus, 2.55, 1972 edn, 151)

This was the oracle at Siwa which Alexander was to consult.

The point that Socrates has to make in the *Phaedrus* (275c, 1961 edn, 520) is that 'the people of those days, lacking the wisdom of you young people, were content in their simplicity to listen to trees or rocks, provided these told the truth', whereas Phaedrus himself is concerned only with who the speaker is. Phaedrus, faced with this challenge, is prompted to concede the case, acknowledging that 'the man of Thebes is right in what he said about writing' and to concur with Socrates that 'anyone who leaves behind him a written manual, and likewise anyone who takes it over from him, on the supposition that such writing will provide something reliable and permanent, must be exceedingly simple-minded; he must really be ignorant of Ammon's utterance, if he imagines that written words can do anything more than remind one who knows that which the writing is concerned with' (*Phaedrus*, 275d–e, 1961 edn, 521).

Socrates leads the discussion into the subject of representation and semiotics, which, like a number of later Neoplatonists, he uses the examples of Egyptian art and hieroglyphics to illustrate (Iversen, 1961, 1971). Observing that 'the painter's products stand before us as though they were alive, but if you question them, they maintain a most majestic silence', he maintains that 'it is the same with written words; but if you ask them anything about what they say, from a desire to be instructed, they go on telling you the same thing forever' (*Phaedrus*, 275d, 1961 edn, 521). Socrates seems to be referring to mysteries or esoteric wisdom, which, he goes on to argue – in written form so much more easily disseminated to the wrong people than in oral form – must be confined to the circle of initiates: 'once a thing is put in writing, the composition, whatever it may be, drifts all over the place, getting into the hands not only of those who understand it, but equally of those who have no business with it; it doesn't know how to address the right people and not address the wrong' (*Phaedrus*, 275d–e, 1961 edn, 521). This was a view shared not only by the initiates of the Pythagorean, Orphic and later Gnostic mysteries, but also by the Egyptian priestly caste. The Egyptians, like a number of Asiatic cultures, some of which still preserve the tradition today, considered some forms of knowledge so privileged that access to them was closed by virtue of class-restricted written or spoken languages: hieroglyphics, for instance, a 'holy' language as the particle 'hiero' suggests; other examples being courtly languages in China and South East Asia, some still extant.

Socrates' remarks on imitation and the representation of reality in art, *mimesis*, are very far from being governed by aesthetic considerations primarily, for art in the ancient world, like writing, constituted a system of signs, whose interpretation presupposed a special relation between the sign and the signifier. The Hellenistic Neoplatonists, commenting significantly on the semiotic power of hieroglyphics, self-consciously addressed the question of the relation between the sign, the signifier and the signified. Iamblichus, in *De Mysteriis Egyptorum*, and Plotinus, *Enneads*, 5.8.6., argued explicitly that hieroglyphics were endowed with performative power as *aenigmata* which revealed their essential meaning only to initiates (Iversen, 1971, 175); just as Celsus maintained animals to be sacred signs of deities, *aenigmata* that revealed the manifold aspects of divinity permeating the earthly realm (Origen, *Contra Celsum*, 3.19); both features of Egyptian theology which saw revelations of the gods in words, kings, queens, shadows, bulls, birds and sphinxes (Hornung, 1983; Bell, 1985a,b; Springborg, 1990d).

Thus when Plato, in *The Laws*, 656–7 (1970 edn, 91–2), praised Egypt as during the course of 10,000 years of civilization having achieved a stylization and stability in the canons of representation unmatched in Athens, his point is not merely the moralistic one that Egypt thereby obviated the harmful effects on the young that anarchy in representation of the dramatic and poetic arts can produce – against which he was known to enveigh. It concerned also the fundamental questions of ontology and epistemology in the sacred realm. Moreover, these achievements in the fields of music and the plastic arts, laid 10,000 years ago '(and I'm not speaking loosely: I mean literally ten thousand)', are not said to be anything other than 'a supreme achievement of legislation and statesmen'

(*Laws*, 656–7, 1970 edn, 91). And if Plato's treatment of the arts focuses on the conservativeness of Egyptian practices, his account of the Egyptian educational system stresses its innovativeness. In *Laws*, 7.819 (1970 edn, 313), he paints an engaging picture of the devices by which the Egyptians teach mathematics to 'tiny tots', that has a biting edge in his condemnation of the lack of sophistication of Athenian mathematical education: 'So we should insist that gentlemen should study each of these subjects [algebra, geometry and astronomy] to at least the same level as very many children in Egypt, who acquire such knowledge at the same time as they learn to read and write' (*Laws*, 819, 1970 edn, 313).

In the Egyptian tale of the *Timaeus* and *Critias*, Plato's references to Egypt are no longer haphazard and allusive, but take the form of a full-blown comparison between the social structures, specialization and division of labour, the institution of kingship and ancient history of Egypt, compared with those of Athens and the mysterious Atlantis. And in these fragmentary works, part of the late projected trilogy never completed, bridges are built back to *The Republic*, of which Marx is on record as saying that its class structure was but an 'idealization' of the Egyptian caste system (Marx, *Capital*, n.d. ch. 14, 346): 'Egypt ... served as the model of an industrial country to many of [Plato's] contemporaries also, amongst others to Isocrates, and it continued to have this importance to the Greeks of the Roman Empire.' Herodotus (2.166–7, 1972 edn, 195–6) gives an account of the seven Egyptian classes – 'priests, warriors, cowherds, swineherds, tradesmen, interpreters, pilots' – remarkably similar to the class structure of the *Republic* (370–1, 1974 edn, 118–19), comprised of agricultural and industrial producers, merchants, sailors and ship-owners, retail traders, wage-earners, auxiliaries and guardians. We know that for Plato the latter two classes were not permitted the personal ownership of property or to engage in manual labour of any sort. Correspondingly, Herodotus (2.166–7, 1972 edn, 195–6) notes of members of the Egyptian warrior class that 'none of them touch trade of any kind, but all have a purely military education ... son following father'; and that although private property may have been ruled out, members of 'the Egyptian warrior-class had certain privileges, shared by no other class except the priests', that included a small grant of tax-free land, 'a daily allowance of 5 lb of bread, 2 lb of beef and 4 cupfuls of wine'.

As the tale of Solon's visit to the Egyptian priests of Sais unfolds in the *Timaeus*, Plato is concerned at the outset to stress the antiquity of Athenian institutions according to Egyptian priestly records, and the similarity in the class structures of the two societies. The old priest tells Solon that while Egyptian records date back 8,000 years for Egyptian institutions, they show the earliest Athenian society being a thousand years older. These dates, important in placing Atlantis, are roughly congruent with the calculation in the *Laws* of 10,000 years of Egyptian culture, assuming the events Solon describes to be set back in time. That Plato, on Solon's authority, dated the ancient Athenians even earlier than the earliest Egyptian dynasties would fit with further evidence we have in the epic tradition of a tendency to favour Hellenic culture over that of the barbarians. There is, of course, a problem with the dates Plato gives, which would seem to have inflated by a factor of ten the age of archaic Athens and Egypt as a systematic record-keeping society, which dates only to the middle second millennium New Kingdom (Forsyth, 1980, 160). The reason may be a transcription error, either from the original Minoan–Mycenaean to the Egyptian or from the Egyptian to the Greek, facilitated by the fact that 'the Linear A and B symbol for 100 is ○ and that for 1,000 is ✧' (Forsyth, 1980, 160). Or, it could be due to a deliberately archaizing tendency in Plato, as we will see; while the wealth and luxury of Atlantis as Plato describes it fit better the Aegean Bronze Age, there is just a chance that Plato did want to place Archaic Athens in the Neolithic, around 9,600 BC.

The old Egyptian priest begins his account of these ancient Greeks by admonishing Solon:

> Consider their laws compared with ours; for you will find today among us many parallels to your institutions in those days. First, our priestly class is kept distinct from the others, as is also our artisan class; next, each class of craftsmen – shepherds, hunters, farmers – performs its function in isolation from others. And of course you will have noticed that our soldier-class is kept separate from all others, being forbidden by the law to undertake any duties other than military: moreover their armament consists of shield and spear, which we were the first people in Asia to adopt, under the instruction of the Goddess, as you were in your part of the world. And again you see what great attention our law devotes from the beginning to learning, deriving from the divine principles of cosmology everything needed for human life down to divination and medicine for our health, and acquiring all other related branches of knowledge. The Goddess founded this whole order and system when she framed your society. (*Tim.*, 24, 1971 edn, 36–7)

Reference to the founder-goddess, Bendix, amidst whose celebrations the *Republic* too is set, is of considerable significance. As 'the Destroyer' (Walker, 1983, 95), the same martial Afro-Asiatic goddess worshipped by the Babylonians and Hyksos as Anath and by the Egyptians as Neith, she appears in Greece under the related name of Athena (Bernal, 1987a, 21). The Ras Shamra texts from the ancient Canaanite capital of Ugarit, tell us that Anath was fertilized by men's blood, and worshipped in primitive sacrificial rites which date back to Neolithic times (Walker, 1983, 30): 'Anath hung the shorn penises of her victims on her goatskin apron or *aegis*.' Once 'transplanted to Greece and permanently virginized as *Athene*, her *aegis* was transformed from the ceremonial apron of Libyan priestesses into a breastplate'; but Athena continued to wear ' "serpents" (phalli) on her aegis, along with the Gorgon head of her Destroyer aspect'. Anath 'annually cast her death-curse, *anathema*, on the Canaanite god who became Lord of Death: Mot, the castrated "Sterility" aspect of the fertile Baal', whom she slew, scattering his pieces over the fields to regenerate them with his blood (Walker, 1983, 30–1). Elements from the history of 'the Destroyer', known in her 'diabolized' form to Abyssinian Christians as Aynat, 'the evil eye of the earth', are common both to the Egyptian myths of Hathor and the dying god Osiris, resurrected by Isis (Griffiths, 1960, 1980), as well as to the death of Christ, another Near Eastern 'dying god' (Gaster, 1969, 416; Walker, 1983, 31; Springborg, 1990d, chs 9 and 11).

The substance of the Egyptian priest's tale in the *Timaeus* is the myth of the legendary Atlantis, which Critias then repeats in the second part of the projected trilogy, that which is named after him. There he supplements the priest's account with family gossip passed down from Dropides, Solon's contemporary, a relative and close friend, father of the dramatic Critias, grandfather of the younger Critias who narrates the tale to Socrates. It is the story of a great sea-based power, located in the 'Atlantic', 'an island larger than Libya and Asia combined', 'opposite the strait which ... [the Greeks] call the Pillars of Hercules', 'ruled by a powerful and remarkable dynasty of kings', 'which arrogantly advanced from its base in the Atlantic Ocean to attack the cities of Europe and Asia' (*Tim.*, 24–5, 1971 edn, 37). This great dynasty, already controlling the [Greek] islands and most of the continent of Asia, 'in addition ... controlled, within the strait, Libya up to the borders of Egypt and Europe as far as Tyrrhenia' and, 'gathering its whole power together', was on the point of enslaving 'at a single stroke' both Egypt and mainland Greece, when 'the power and courage and strength' of the Athenians came to bear. Advancing at the head of a league of Greek states, Athens, even when deserted in the event by her allies, nevertheless succeeded in overcoming the invaders, 'rescued those not yet enslaved from the slavery threatening them, and ... generously freed all others living within the Pillars of Hercules'. Later, however, the Athenians succumbed to catastrophe along with the Atlantans (*Tim.*, 25, 1971 edn, 37–8): 'there were earthquakes and floods of extraordinary violence, and in a single dreadful day and night all your fighting men were swallowed up by the earth, and the island of Atlantis was similarly swallowed up by the sea and vanished; this is why the sea in that area is to this day impassable to navigation, which is hindered by mud just below the surface, the remains of the sunken island' – Aristotle in the *Meteorologica* 354a.22, mentioning 'shallows due to mud' outside the Pillars of Hercules (editor's note, *Timaeus*, 1971 edn, 38, n.1).

Judgements of the Ancients on the status of Plato's Atlantis story is mixed. Strabo (*Geography*, 2.102, and 13.598) records that Posidonius believed it was better to accept Plato's view that 'Atlantis did once exist, but disappeared', than to accept the judgement attributed to Aristotle that ' "Its inventor caused it to disappear, just as did the Poet the wall of the Archaeans" ' – meaning that 'Solon avoided the historical consequences of his fiction by sinking Atlantis, just as Homer did by making Poseidon and Apollo sweep away with a flood the wall built by the Achaeans in front of their ships (see *Iliad* 7.433,44 and 12.1–33)' (Strabo, *Geography*, 2.102, 1989 edn, 391–3). Furthermore, Crantor, editor of the *Timaeus*, according to Proclus (*In Platonis Timaeum Commentaria*, 24a–b, cited in Forsyth, 1980, 1), believed every word about Atlantis to be true.

Among the many recent analyses of Plato's Atlantis story, some regard it as a creation of pure fiction, dismissing all attempts at historical reconstruction (Ross, 1977); others treat it as a historical account (Luce, 1969; Raubitschek, 1978); and yet others treat it as a species of *mythos*, incorporating both historical and fictional elements (Vidal-Naquet, 1964; Gill, 1976, 1977, 1980; Forsyth, 1980; Tarrant, 1985). Of the latter type, Gill (1976, 1977) argues convincingly that the archaizing Plato is intent on presenting a primordial Athens, land-based, with an impressive citizen army of sturdy farmer–soldiers, having 'no harbor, no market-place, no mines and no elaborate temple architecture' – the direct antithesis of Pericles' Athens as presented by Plato in the *Gorgias* 518E3–519A4 (cited in Gill, 1977, 297), filled, 'by successive democratic politicians', with 'harbors, dockyards, walls, tribute and rubbish like that'. For such enticements to grandiose desire and overweaning pride were to symptomize her eventual downfall. What we have then in archaic Athens set back almost a millennium in time, is 'a graphic picture of Athens, the victor at Marathon, of Athens *before* Pericles, that conservative upholders of the *patrios politeia*, like the historical Critias, held as a model' (Gill, 1977, 295, emphasis added).

Consistent with the thrust of *mythos* as pictorializing a moral struggle, Atlantis, too, is more than 'simply a dream island in the mythical west, but the dream of Athens in the later fifth century, above all, the dream or ideal ... Periclean Athens had about itself' (Gill, 1977, 295–6). Gill adduces evidence: 'For one thing, Atlantis is an island (what Pericles wanted the Athenians, in war, to consider Athens [Thucydides, 1.143.5]). For another, it has a fantastic concentration of wealth, accumulated chiefly by water-borne trade and by sea-borne military power over a neighboring empire in the Mediterranean' (Gill, 1977, 296).

Solon's tale is then *mythos* in the truest sense: it is a cautionary tale, 'an indictment of a *politeia* which permits the "burden" of great wealth to be placed on human nature'. Gill (1977, 297) interprets Plato's intention thus: 'The Athenians were wholly human from the time of the foundation of the city, but their *politeia*, with its denial of gold and silver to the rulers, at least (*Criti.*, 112C), pre-empted such temptations.' Moreover, it is a *mythos* with a sufficiently high level of realism to be able to bridge the gap between myth and reality that the *Republic* could not. In this respect the *Timaeus–Critias* comes closest in genre to the *Menexenus*, 'a eulogistic account of a glorious event in recent Athenian history, transposed into prehistoric time and presented as the act of the ideal state' (Gill, 1977, 294). Gill stresses the historical details which lend to the Atlantis story the necessary degree of realism. These include reminiscences of Herodotus' description of Ecbatana (1.98) and Babylon (1.180 ff, cf. 189–90, cited in Gill, 1977, 292); 'Plato's seemingly authentic interest in prehistory (his account of soil erosion in Attica, *Criti.* 110E ff., does not seem to be motivated only by his political theme)' (Gill, 1977, 299). There are telling parallels to Sparta, as if it were 'a picture of Sparta lodged in an Attic locale', characterized by a Spartan ruling caste supported by hardy farmers (Gill, 1977, 295); the moral decline of the Atlantans would seem to foreshadow the later account of Persian decline in *Laws*, 695–98 (Gill, 1977, 294, n.32). And the very Hermocrates who complained that once Persia was vanquished Athens became the new Persia, the new tyrant state from whom the Greeks required liberation (Thucydides, 6.76.4, cited in Gill, 1977, 298, n.53), and who was influential in Syracuse, his daughter marrying Dionysius the tyrant, Plato's protégé (Forsyth, 1980, 175), is actually standing by to complete the third part of the *Timaeus–Critias–Hermocrates* trilogy, suggesting a link to the cautionary tale of Plato's fateful involvement in Sicily.

Such an account of the *Timaeus–Critias* would accord with the function of *mythos* to endow cities with great and glorious deeds and to tell their citizens the sort of cautionary tales that nurses and mothers tell their children before going to sleep (Veyne, 1988, 28, 42–3). The function of myth to mimic reality without actually replicating it, so as to produce a cleaned-up, larger than life account of the triumph of good over evil, would fit with the historical detail, as Gill (1977, 302) suggests. In some sense Plato's myths involve the same sort of magic performed by the wall paintings of the ancient Egyptians and decorations on their funerary vases. Pictorial recreations actually re-enacted the purified versions of events in the life of the king; just as the little boat on a funerary jar could transport the deceased one's body back to her place of birth, that beloved spot where everyone wished to be buried, but frequently lacked the material means to effect (Springborg, 1990d, 117). Platonic myth through the function of *mimesis* had the same almost magically edifying effect: it could induce in its subjects the piety it required them to have for the good city and its ruling values. Thus the *Menexenus* 'another eulogistic history of Athens ... idealizes Athens by misdescribing her history and omitting discreditable actions, while the Atlantis story does so by projecting the undesirable features of Athens onto "Atlantis"; but both can be taken as warning Athens from certain courses and advocating others' (Gill, 1977, 298, n.54).

Such an account of the magical–mimetic function of myth does not, however, do full justice the specificity of the items in the historical account, upon which we will now focus. Why Egypt? Is there a connection between Egypt and Sparta, as Bernal (1987a, 53, 109–10) has promised to explain, in some way analagous to the connection Plato posits between archaic Greece and Egypt? Did Plato have privileged access to records through the family of Critias (Rosenmeyer, 1949)? And was the flood story, interwoven in the *Timaeus–Critias*, as in the *Laws*, derived from an Asiatic mythic source? Anthony Raubitschek has asked a further set of questions:

> Did Plato unconsciously imitate the organization of Minoan Crete in his Ideal State in the Republic? Did Aristotle and Plato believe that the Dorians in Crete took over the social order from the Minoans, and that the Spartans under Lycurgus imitated this organization in their own country? Was the social political and economic life in Minoan Crete really somewhat similar to that of the Doran Cretans and of the Spartans, and of the ruling class of Plato's Ideal State? (Raubitschek, 1976, 233)

To all of these questions he gives the answer 'yes'. The specificity of these items and their more general significance in the cautionary tale is our subject.

The immediate point of the priest's tale is to stress the 'miraculous chance' by which ancient Athenian society as preserved in Egyptian records corresponds to the society described by Socrates the day before in the *Republic*. It was the *Republic* which had jogged his memory, and he wonders at the powers of recall that allow a tale told to a child by an old man to be recovered in such detail. Critias sets up the structure of the rest of the *Timaeus*, and that of the *Critias*, within the frame of reference of the *Republic*, observing to Socrates:

> We will transfer the imaginary citizens and city which you described yesterday to the real world, and say that your city is the city of my story and your citizens those historical ancestors of ours whom the priest described. They will fit exactly, and there will be no disharmony if we speak as if they really were the men who lived at that time. We will divide the work between us and try to fulfil your instructions to the best of our ability. So tell us, Socrates, do you think this story will suit our purpose, or must we look for another instead? (*Tim.*, 26, 1971 edn, 39)

Critias notes that Timaeus, 'who knows more about astronomy than the rest of us', an expert in the study of the universe, will begin with 'the origin of the cosmic system bring[ing] the story down to man'; and that he, Critias, will then take over, 'assuming that human beings have come into existence as he has described and that some of them have had [Socrates'] excellent education'; and these he 'will bring to judgement before us here by making them citizens of Athens governed as she was in the days of Solon's story – an Athens whose disappearance is accounted for in the priestly writings, and about whose citizens [he] shall in the rest of what [he has] to say assume [to be] speaking' (*Tim.*, 27, 1971 edn, 39). Here Critias does speak as if the priestly account is fictional, or at least amenable to alteration to fit the form of Plato's *Republic*. Socrates refers in the same vein to Critias' proposed account as 'splendid entertainment in return for mine' (*Tim.*, 27, 1971 edn, 39). This has led some critics to maintain that the Atlantis legend provides an excellent opening gambit with which to capture an audience for the rather dry and technical cosmology which follows in the *Timaeus*. However, we have Socrates' word that Critias' tale is no more fiction (or entertainment) than the *Republic* which has been taken rather seriously; and within the *Critias* itself rather serious historical claims are advanced, even if Plato shows a typical unwillingness to commit himself on whether or not this is to be taken at an ideal, or mythical, level, or as fact.

In the *Critias*, the tale is taken up where it was left off in the *Timaeus*, and is once again presented as a (more elaborate) account of the 'story which the priests told Solon and he brought home with him' (*Crit.*, 108, 1971 edn, 129), never in fact transformed into the epic poem that would make Solon a poet greater even than Hesiod or Homer, as Socrates earlier observed (*Tim.*, 21, 1971 edn, 34), but recorded privately in the annals of Critias' family. Several points are worth noting in advance of this expanded account in the *Critias*. First, it does indeed follow rather closely the structure of other examples of the great epic cycle, for instance Homer's *Iliad*, while the *Timaeus* may be seen as a counterpart to Hesiod's *Theogony*. Secondly, it presents essentially two classic forms of regime whose strength is pitted one against the other: the Asiatic dynastic monarchy of Atlantis and the aristocratic warrior society of the ancient Athenians, *with which the Egyptian is said to be so closely parallel*. Thirdly, this account is very much, as appropriate to the Greek epic tradition, yet another tale of the battle of the giants between the Greeks and barbarians (Frost, 1913, 204). And, fourthly, the dialogue discloses something apparently not perceived by Solon, the Egyptian priest or by Critias (about Plato we cannot be sure), and that is that both Greek and Egyptian legends independently record the same events, corroborated in the Greek Homeric epic (Frost, 1913, 206) – for instance in the tale of Theseus and the Minotaur.

So Critias begins by noting that 'the course of our narrative as it unfolds will give particulars about the various barbarian and Greek nations of the day' (*Crit.*, 109, 1971 edn, 129) and then proceeds systematically to describe the respective 'resources and constitutions' of the protagonists, Athenian and Asiatic in that order. The account of the Athenians begins in mythic prehistory with the partition of the earth among the gods. Hephaestos and Athene, as brother and sister united in 'love of knowledge and skill, were allotted this land of ours as their joint sphere and as a suitable and natural one for excellence and wisdom' (*Crit.*, 109, 1971 edn, 130). The race of men that they produced by this brother–sister marriage, of the type of Egyptian consanguineous royal marriages (Cerny, 1954), is remembered by their names and by very little else. 'For as we said before [*Timaeus*, 23, 1971 edn, 35], the survivors of this destruction were an unlettered mountain race who had just heard the names of the rulers of the land but knew little of their achievements. They were glad enough to give their names to their own children, but they knew nothing of the virtues and institutions of their predecessors, except for a few hazy reports' (*Crit.*, 109, 1971 edn, 130).

Critias attributes the ignorance of the Athenians about their origins to the conditions of basic subsistence, where 'for many generations [the ancient Athenians] and their children were short of bare necessities and their minds and thoughts were occupied with providing for them, to the neglect of earlier history and tradition.' Ancient Egyptian society by contrast, was never seen by Plato, Isocrates or Herodotus as a subsistence economy, but rather one characterized by a highly sophisticated specialization and division of labour. Evidence for the preservation of names is also rather specific, Critias observing that 'most of the [ancient] names recorded before Theseus, occurred, according to Solon, in the narrative of the [Egyptian] priests' and he gives as examples the names Cecrops, Erectheus, Erichthonios, Erusichthon (*Crit.*, 110, 1971 edn, 130–1).

Cecrops, mythical early Athenian king, is thought to have been Egyptian or Cretan by late classical writers (Apollodorus, 3.177ff; Pausanias 1.5.3; cited in Fontenrose, 1970, 218) and is represented with a serpent shape. Significantly, he is credited as being a great benefactor king, who instituted monogamy, writing and the burial of the dead. The names Erectheus, Erichthonios, Erusichthon are different, and some authorities believe more ethnically Greek, than those of the heroes of the genealogical–ethnographic tales like Danaus, Aegyptus, Cadmus, and so on (Meyer, 1906, cited in Astour, 1967a, 149, n.2). Erechtheus, another fabled early Athenian king, sacrificed his daughter Chthonia to the underworld; while Erichthonius, usually credited as being the son of Hephaestus, once born, was put into the charge of Athena who put him in a chest and passed him on to the care of the daughters of Cecrops. They, disobeying orders, opened the chest to find, Pandora-like, a serpent creature, were driven mad and leapt off the Acropolis. Erichthonius went on to become a great king of early Athens, who promoted the cult of Athena (Rose, 1970b, 406). Elements of this story are not too far removed from the fabulous tales of 'arks' and 'boxes' of Babylonian, Egyptian and syncretistic Greek myths, as well as the later Arabian Nights (Attar, 1989).

What is known from Athenian prehistory is both selective and highly signifi-cant on Plato's account. It is known, for instance, that men and women jointly participated in military exercises, that the emblem of the goddess was accordingly that of a figure in full military dress, and that this fact signified the appropriate excellence that each sex contributed to the community (*Crit.*, 110, 1971 edn, 131). This is one point at which the ancient Athenians are seen to prefigure the society of the *Republic*, infamous for its adoption of Spartan and Amazonian female equality.

A second link between prehistoric Athenian society on this account and the society of the *Republic* is the functional division of classes along lines typical of Asiatic and Egyptian society, into manufacturing, agricultural and military occupations, the military being segregated:

> The military class lived apart, having been from the beginning separated from the others by godlike men. They were provided with what was necessary for their maintenance and training, they had no private property but regarded their possessions as common to all, they did not look to the rest of the citizens for anything beyond their basic maintenance; in fact they followed in all things the regime we laid down yesterday when we were talking about our hypothetical Guardians. (*Crit.*, 110, 1971 edn, 131)

Sequestered on the Acropolis near the temples of Athena and Hephaestos, surrounded in their precinct 'by a single wall like the garden of a single house':

> On the northern side they built their common dwelling-houses and winter mess-rooms, and everything else required by their communal life in the way of buildings and temples. They had no gold or silver, and never used them for any purpose, but aimed at a balance between extravagance and meanness in the houses they built, in which they and their descendants grew old and which they handed on unchanged to succeeding generations who resembled themselves ... This is how they lived; and they acted as Guardians of their own citizens, and were voluntarily recognized as leaders of the rest of Greece. They kept the numbers of those of military age, men and women, so far as possible always constant at about twenty thousand. This then was the sort of people they were and this the way in which they administered their own affairs and those of Greece; their reputation and name stood higher than any other in Europe or Asia for qualities both of body and character. (*Crit.*, 112, 1971 edn, 133)

Critias provides geophysical information as a prelude to his account of the Athenian system, of considerable significance for the theory of periodic cataclysm (*Crit.*, 111, 1971 edn, 131–2). He compares contemporary Greece with the prehistoric period:

> So the result of the many floods that have taken place in the last nine thousand years (the time that has elapsed since then) is that the soil washed away from the high land in these periodical catastrophes forms no alluvial deposit of consequence as in other places, but is carried out and lost in the deeps. You are left (as with little islands) with something rather like the skeleton of a body wasted by disease; the rich, soft soil has all run away leaving the land nothing but skin and bone.

In the prehistoric period, before this damage had taken place, the Greek landscape had afforded agriculture at an appropriate level of subsistence 'and it was cultivated with the skill you would expect from a class of genuine full-time agriculturalists with good natural talents and high standards, who had an excellent soil, an abundant water supply and a well-balanced climate' (*Crit.*, 111, 1971 edn, 132).

    In fact, archaeologists suggest very little variation in the geophysical and climatological conditions of Greece in the prehistoric period of human habitation. But they do attest, on the basis of the excavation of the Bronze Age settlement of Akrotiri on the island of Thera, to a long history of volcanic eruptions, destruction and rebuilding from the late Cycladic I period through to the major eruption of the seventeenth entury BC (Manning, 1988, 21–2), which would certainly vindicate Plato's claim that the area had experienced catastrophic flooding in prehistoric times, sufficient to wipe out entire settlements. Archaeological evidence for the eruptions of Thera, which has provided a veritable outpouring of recent publications (Marinatos, 1968–76; Bond and Sparks, 1976; Doumas, 1978, 1980, 1983; Watkins et al., 1978; Renfrew, 1979; Sparks, 1985; Stanley and Sheng, 1986; Cadogan, 1987; Hammer, et al., 1987; Baille and Munro, 1988; Manning, 1988), includes tree rings from Irish bog oaks and Californian bristle cone pines, ice-sheet evidence in Greenland, Minoan tephra from deep-sea sediment cores and the water-worn pumice rubble used as floor packing in late Minoan IA houses. The overwhelming scientific evidence for these eruptions and the subsequent dislocation of civilizations widely dispersed in the area is matched in the literary field only by relics of flood myths, of which Plato's Atlantis story may be one of the most significant.

Critias' account of Atlantis also begins with a methodological note on the translation of names that impresses on the reader his sensitivity to historical accuracy. The reason why the names of foreigners appear in their Greek equivalents is that 'Solon [had] intended to use the story in his own poem. And when, on inquiring about the significance of the names, he learned that the Egyptians had translated the originals into their own language, he went through the reverse process, and as he learned the meaning of a name wrote it down in Greek' (*Crit.*, 113, 1971 edn, 134). We may note two things: first, that foreign names are being rendered in Greek by Solon to facilitate poetic euphony, which is relevant when it comes to identifying Atlantis; and, secondly, that Plato's assertion that as a matter of historical fact these names were Greek originally, translated by Egyptians for their records, is a moot point. A matter to which we will return in part I, chapter 9 on the philological evidence: gods, goddesses, river and place names. In other words, there was an etymological connection between Egyptian and Greek names that was problematic and could be derived either way – the Greeks tending to give priority to Greek origins.

According to the structure of Solon's account the story of Atlantis began in prehistory, with the lands of the earth being distributed among the gods, 'Poseidon's share was the island of Atlantis and he settled the children borne to him by a mortal woman in a particular district of it.' The woman was Cleito, who 'was just of marriageable age when her father and mother ["original earth-born inhabitants"] died, and Poseidon was attracted to her and had intercourse with her, and fortified the hill where she lived by enclosing it with concentric rings of sea and land' (*Crit.*, 113, 1971 edn, 134). Of the union 'five pairs of male twins' were born, among whom Poseidon distributed the land of Atlantis in ten parts. 'He allotted the elder of the eldest pair of twins his mother's home district and the land surrounding it, the biggest and best allocation, and he made him king over the others'; and 'the eldest, the King, he gave a name from which the whole island and surrounding ocean took their designation of "Atlantic", deriving it from Atlas the first King' (*Crit.*, 114, 1971 edn, 135). Atlas went on to establish a hereditary monarchy that produced 'a long and distinguished line of descendants, eldest son succeeding eldest son and maintaining the succession unbroken for many generations; their wealth was greater than that possessed by any previous dynasty of kings or likely to be accumulated by any later, and both in the city and countryside they were provided with everything they could require.' Their hegemony extended to 'controll[ing] the populations this side of the straits as far as Egypt and Tyrrhenia', and their powers of requisition allowed them 'many imports, but for most of their needs the island itself provided' (*Crit.*, 114, 1971 edn, 135). Critias' account of the Atlantan economy parallels, without replicating, the self-sufficiency of the Athenian (*Crit.*, 115, 1971 edn, 136). It was an economy based on metallurgy as well as agriculture, its mineral resources including the usual ones as well as one known only to us by the name 'orichalc', more precious to the Atlantans than gold (*Crit.*, 1143, 1971 edn, 135). It had all the timber necessary for construction and 'every kind of animal domesticated and wild, among them numerous elephants' (*Crit.*, 114, 1971 edn, 136). This reference to elephants, noted by the editor as the second only in Greek recorded literature, after Herodotus' and before Aristotle's in his *Historia Animalum* (Lee, 1971 edn, 136, n.1), is oddly out of place were Atlantis truly an Atlantic island. So too is the admission that there 'the earth bore freely all the aromatic substances it bears today, roots, herbs, bushes and gums exuded by flowers or fruit' (*Crit.*, 115, 1971 edn, 136), suggestive rather of a Mediterranean climate.

It is time to try to identify Atlantis, which a number of classical scholars (Frost, 1913; Carpenter, 1965; Luce, 1969; Page, 1970; Lee, 1971; Ross, 1977; Forsyth, 1980) have associated with Crete and the civilization of Minoa. Assuming the Pillars of Hercules to be the Straits of Gibraltar, and given that Atlantis is said to be outside the pillars, it would seem that it should indeed be located in the Atlantic. But the association with Atlas suggests a different connection: and that is to the battle of the giants, as representing the Asiatic and Greek powers respectively. If the location of Atlantis appears to be too far west to be Asiatic, this in Egyptian terminology, for which Atlantis is the Greek equivalent, would not be inappropriate. For Egyptians Crete, the land of Minos, was most probably that designated by the term *Kefti*, which means 'behind', 'away back'. Inhabitants of the Minoan world on this assumption are *Keftiu*, 'the men from afar', or from the 'Far West'.

The identification Caphtor/Keftiu/Crete is provisionally accepted by Bronze Age archaeologists (Knapp, 1985a, 1988b), which does not put it beyond dispute. (A recent work [Strange, 1980; cf. Knapp, 1985a] argues rather for the identification Alashiya/Caphtor/Keftiu, that is to say the identity of Atlantis as Cyprus, but inconclusively.) It is possible that 'an Egyptian phrase which placed the Keftiu beyond the Four Pillars of the world' – an important concept in ancient Egyptian geography and mythology – became translated by Solon into a kingdom 'beyond the Pillars of Hercules' (Frost, 1913, 189–9). The transposition of names would, according to Critias' methodological note already referred to, not be inappropriate; and, as Frost (1913, 199) notes, Atlantis, besides the connection to Atlas, provides a trisyllabic name 'that can be used with ease and dignity in hexameter lines, and [that] conveys a hint of the magic and mystery of that boundless ocean which stretched beyond the limits of human travel. It is thus a Greek equivalent to the name Keft' (Frost, 1913, 199). More convincingly still, Gill (1977, 295, n.41) argues: 'The name "Atlantis" (= Atlas' island) may have been suitable for this island because of its ambivalent mythic associations: those of a favorable ideal, a garden or orchard of the Hesperides, or Atlas' daughter (Hom. *Od.* 1.50–54, 5.63–74; Hes. *Th.* 518); and those of a Titanic struggle (cf. *Leg.* 701C), settled by Zeus' intervention (Hes. *Th.* 687 ff.; cf. *Criti.* 121C), after which Atlas (or his island, *Criti.* 25D) was sunk beneath the sea (Hes. *Th.* 746).'

Mythological references, in particular those to Poseidon and Theseus, the latter of whom received mysterious mention by Critias, as noted, strongly connect Atlantis to Minoan Crete. For Theseus, who slew the Minotaur, was known in legend as the son of Poseidon. His exploits are remarkably reminiscent of Heracles, that imported Asiatic hero, as commentators point out (Frost, 1913, 196–7; Brundage, 1958); and he could well have belonged to one of the Cretan colonies on the mainland that produced later Mycenaean civilization (Frost, 1913, 195). The fabled Labyrinth, which may refer only to the network of corridors in the great palace of Knossos, might also have been influenced by the Egyptian Labyrinth described in detail by Herodotus (2.150, 1972 edn, 188–9; see Bernal, 1987a, 61). The point of the story of Theseus and the Minotaur is very interesting: it establishes mainland supremacy over Crete. If Atlantis is indeed Crete, Plato's account in the *Critias* is congruent with the Theseus myth, although not with the historical record, which credits the Egyptians with vanquishing Crete in the encounter to which he refers.

This was an age of great mutual contact between Egypt and Crete, attested archaeologically (Pomerance, 1973; Kemp, 1977; Bietak, 1979a, 1984; Kemp and Merrillees, 1980; Stanley and Sheng, 1986; Wachsmann, 1987). Indeed, the three chief periods of Minoan history established by modern periodization – as a matter of convenience because of the heavy reliance on material from Egyptian tombs to establish Minoan dating (Manning, 1988, 24; see also Bietak, 1984; Helck, 1987; Hornung, 1987; Kemp and Merrillees, 1980; Palmer, 1981; Pomerance, 1973, 1984b; Wachsmann, 1987; Warren, 1985) – are roughly contemporaneous with the Egyptian Old, Middle and New Kingdoms. Manning (1988, 33, table 3) gives a list of Late Minoan IB and Late Helladic IIA pottery from datable Egyptian/Near Eastern sites, which includes a pithoid jar from the reign of Tuthmosis III or Hatshepsut (*c.*1503/1498–1483 BC) at Thebes (Hankey, 1987, 46) and an alabastron and cup from Sakkara, dated to the reign of Tuthmosis III. From Crete itself Egyptian artifacts important in establishing Minoan dating include a scarab of Queen Tye, wife of Amenophis III (*c.*1417–1379 BC), from Haghia Triadha, and two red-lustrous spindle bottles from LMIB contexts at Gournia and Kommos (Manning, 1988, 32).

As Plato describes the city of Atlantis, it does indeed exhibit Asiatic elements: it is an extraordinarily contrived city, ringed with man-made canals, its buildings constructed out of bands of different coloured stone, white, black and yellow, the outermost city wall sheathed in bronze, the inner side sheathed in tin, the acropolis in orichalc, 'gleaming like fire' (*Crit.*, 116, 1971 edn, 137). Plato then goes on to describe its distribution of political power, cultic elements, including the bull chase and sacrifice, royal oath-taking; the degeneration of the royal line and Zeus' decision to punish the Atlantans, the dialogue breaking off, however, before the story of Athenian conquest contained in the *Timaeus* can be related.

Elements in this account are of considerable significance. Critias' account of 'the ten kings [each with] absolute power, in his own region and city, over persons and in general over laws, [able] to punish or execute at will ... the distribution of power between them and their mutual relations [being] governed by the injunctions of Poseidon, enshrined in the law and engraved by the first kings on an orichalc pillar in the temple of Poseidon in the middle of the island' (*Crit.*, 119, 1971 edn, 141), brings to mind the distributions of power in the Mesopotamian, as well as Mycenaean, city-states, regional kings subordinate to the law of the great king, engraved on a stele of black basalt in the sacred city. Critias' aside that 'on the pillar there was engraved, in addition to the laws, an oath invoking aweful curses on those who disobeyed it', is strikingly evocative of the string of ritual curses, to ensure compliance where reason would not prevail, on the Hammurabi stele and others (Driver and Miles, 1952–5). The federal nature of authority which Critias' account describes, and which apparently also obtained in the Assyrian and Babylonian systems (Oppenheim, 1969, 1977; Sabloff and Lamberg-Karlovsky, 1976; Adams, 1981; Mann, 1986), looks forward in important ways to the larger social aggregate that Polybius was recommending in the Achaean League, setting indeed, if it was historically accurate, the pattern for Hellenistic kingships that aggregated regionally autonomous areas (Rostovtzeff, 1941; Tarn, 1952). Forsyth (1980, 165) cites evidence to suggest that Bronze Age Crete also knew feudal kingdoms, and that Knossos was supreme over the other palaces, the rules of Phaestos, Mallia and Zakros owing allegiance to King Minos.

Cultic elements of the primordial kingly assemblies, held 'alternately every fifth and sixth year (thereby showing equal respect to both odd and even numbers)' (*Crit.*, 119, 1971 edn, 141), suggest an interest in omens and numerology that could as easily be Mesopotamian or Egyptian as Pythagorean. The significance of these meetings, whose purpose was 'consultation on matters of mutual interest', but more importantly, the affirmation of a common law, is underscored by the cultic aspect expressed in the bull ceremony and oath-taking located at the site of the sacred stele on which the laws were engraved. They are ceremonies similar to the purification rites of oriental kingship to which oath-taking was also critical, the details of the bull cult (*Crit.*, 119–20, 1971 edn, 141–2) being suggestive of Egypt and Crete specifically (Bernal, 1987a, 64–5).

Frost's judgement that 'the city of Atlantis becomes a medley of marvels from all the non-Hellenic world' seems fair:

> The great temple with its 'strange Asiatic look' seems to be inspired by the Babylon that Nebuchadnezzar was building to the wonder of the world, and the facing of the city walls may be a glorification of the glazed tiles which covered the walls of some of the Babylonian fortified palaces. The vast canals are derived from those of Egypt and Babylonia. Horses and chariots were used in Crete as well as in most of the ancient world. The elephants may have come from Egyptian records of the wars of Thothmes, or may have been contributed by the Carthaginians. None of these non-Minoan wonders appear in the *Timaeus*, but they are exactly what would have struck a Greek traveller most and are exactly suited to embellish an epic of the struggle of Hellenism against Barbarism. (Frost, 1913, 204–5)

And yet there are a sufficient number of Minoan parallels to justify the identification: 'the large harbour ... crowded with vast numbers of merchant ships from all quarters, from which rose a constant din of shouting and noise day and night'

(*Crit.*, 117, 1971 edn, 139); the stadium and bath houses (*Crit.*, 117, 1971 edn, 138); the great temple of Poseidon, adorned with ivory, gold, silver and orichalc (*Crit.*, 116, 1971 edn, 137).

The secretness of this latter shrine, 'surrounded by a golden wall through which entry was forbidden, as it was the place where the family of the ten kings was conceived and begotten', as well as its function, suggest the Egyptian royal cult and its sacred and forbidden 'birth houses', or *mammisi*. Other Egyptian royal parallels are striking: the five sets of twin founder kings, for instance, twins being representative in pharaonic iconography of the eternity of kingship, the living king and his *ka* – *doppelgänger*, or alter-ego (Bell, 1985a; Springborg, 1990d). The royal incarnation, birth, coronation and apotheosis of the immortal king, the pharaoh and his *ka*, were celebrated at Luxor Temple in the most secret and sacred of rites at the annual Opet festival. They were also the object, in the same temple, of the periodic Sed or New Year Festivals, to which provincial delegations brought offerings, and the gods in their sacred barques were ferried for an elaborate concluding procession (Murnane, 1975, 1981; Bell, 1985a).

The account of the decline of the great kingdom, part Cretan, part Asiatic, which Critias outlines (*Crit.* 120–21, 1971 edn, 142–3) would appear to be pure Plato, corresponding as it does to the pattern of cultural nemesis in the *Republic*: 'when the divine element in [the ruling class] became weakened by frequent admixture with mortal stock, and their human traits became predominant, they ceased to carry their prosperity with moderation.' These themes, victory of the mortal over the immortal element by defective breeding, the consequent release of the appetite instincts and corruption by wealth, become standard in subsequent accounts of royal corruption; but here they add nothing to the general account contained in the *Republic* on the degeneration of regimes, except specific context. Zeus decided to punish these degenerate Atlantan kings, and summoning the gods to his sacred court, was about to address them when the dialogue breaks off, as Frost remarks, (1913, 204), 'exactly where an epic poet would naturally pause in composition': for, 'the *Critias* starts from the beginning as an unbroken narrative cast in the regular form of an epic poem, with Invocation of the Muse, detailed description of the combatants, careful mention of dates and numbers and a Council of the Gods.'

In other words, Plato's prose transcript of Solon's epic, like his unfinished, was perhaps intended for reworking as a dialogue, or to be incorporated in the *Laws* itself; but for various reasons was left unfinished by Plato, unchanged except perhaps for a few modifications 'to make it further symbolical of the Persian Wars' (Frost, 1913, 204). In the origins of civilization out of cataclysm, processes of cultural development and decline, there are certainly important parallels to the *Laws*; while, in this Plato's last work, there are striking similarities between his rule of law and Mesopotamian regimes that shared a continuous common law over several millennia, modified for local variations in successive codifications (Driver and Miles, 1935, 1952, 1955). Nor is this inconsistent with the fact, now argued by scholars, that Plato's *Laws* reflect on many points the law of Athens (Morrow, 1941, 1960; Harrison, 1968; Stalley, 1983), since curious parallels have been observed between Mesopotamian common law and the law of Athens on a range of subjects (Lacey, 1966). The connection between the *Laws* and Crete is explicit, occasioned as that work is by the fact that Cleinias, one of the principal interlocutors, is a Cretan appointed to a legislative commission to draw up laws for a new Cretan colony (Stalley, 1983, 89–91). One may speculate, therefore that the *Laws* stand to the projected *Timaeus/Critias/Hermocrates* trilogy as an account of Mycenaean rule of law established in the wake of mainland supremacy over the Minoan kingdoms, of whose prehistory the *Timaeus* and *Critias* give an account.

The mythic element so strongly present in the *Timaeus* and *Critias* is, of course, absent in the *Laws*, a treatment analytic to the point of dryness. One could speculate on how his version of the Egyptian tale finally sat with Plato, for clearly the historical record was doctored for national purposes by someone. Like Homer, whose account of Minoan civilization dissociates it from Crete, and who has Odysseus pretend to be the son of Deucalion, son of Minos in turn, and therefore brother of Idomeneus (Frost, 1913, 201), Solon's story of Minoan civilization has already assimilated it to Greek national myth. Except that in Homer, unlike the Theseus and the Minotaur myth and Solon's story, the great Mycenaean civilization had not yet fallen. When it did fall, it succumbed not, as Plato and the Theseus myth so conveniently have it, to Greek supremacy, but rather, almost by accident, to Egyptian. The great battle, whose unnamed Athenian heroes, like Theseus of whose marvels it is so reminiscent, single-handedly turned back the might of this great Asian power (*Tim.*, 25, 1971 edn, 37–8), is likely to be, in fact, conquest by Ramses III, although 'great battle' is certainly overdoing it. Around 1194 BC Ramses III undertook a defensive military operation to Palestine, which, although mostly by land, also involved some action at sea, conducted against 'a motley crew that included many Mediterranean/Anatolian folk, mostly turned pirate or refugee in the face of the widening economic collapse that befell the East Mediterranean from *c*.1250–1150 BC' (Knapp, 1988b). On no account was it a great victory. If, as Frost (1913, 196–7) suggests, Ramses III hoped to defeat the Mycenaean raiders once and for all, reviving the glory of the Ramesside heyday under Ramses II, he certainly did not achieve this, but simply 'delayed the inevitable crumbling of the Egyptian state under Ramses IV, his successor' (Knapp, 1988b).

It would not have been at all uncharacteristic of the Greek epic tradition to turn the Egyptian story round completely and record a victory for Egypt's enemies. But, in fact, if we examine the Egyptian priest's account in the *Timaeus* closely, we see that the contours of the real story are rather faithfully preserved, even if it emphasizes Greek supremacy over the Asiatic barbarians. For in each of the accounts, that of the Egyptian historical record, independently verified, that of the Egyptian priest according to Solon, and even the Theseus myth, a two-stage process, the collapse of the Minoan civilization to the Mycenaean, and the collapse of the Mycenaean to the Egyptian, is telescoped (Frost, 1913, 196–7, 206). This does not mean, as Frost in fact suggests, that the Egyptians did not distinguish between them. The Egyptians, in tomb paintings, clearly discriminate between Minoan and Mycenaean peoples (Wachsmann, 1987; Knapp, 1988b). An instructive current debate between Egyptologists and Bronze Age Mediterranean archaeologists turns on the question whether or not parts of the figures in the Sakkaran tomb of the famous Tuthmoside notable Rekhmire were repainted to represent a change in the composition of the delegations to Egypt, from Minoan to Mycenaean, after the Mycenaean conquest of Knossos (Betancourt and Weinstein, 1976, 338; cited in Manning, 1988, 35; Ström, 1984, 192, n.9). Although this debate is not conclusively resolved, at the very least we can say that the Egyptians distinguished the Keftiu, (Minoans), a twin superpower and trading partner, from the raiding 'Sea Peoples', who made their attack on Egypt around the time of the Trojan Wars. It was very possibly this invasion which features in Solon's story of the Egyptian priest as the great test of Greek supremacy, an ultimately short-lived victory, Mycenaean civilization doomed to succumb to flood and fire, like the Minoan that it conquered – and like the Egyptian that conquered it in turn. In Greek legend too, significantly, residual elements remain of an earlier and later Minos, an earlier and later Theseus (Frost, 1913, 106), whose history has been condensed for the purposes of epic.

Inscriptional evidence abounds for the Keftiu in the Egyptian Ramesside period. In an inscription of Ramses III, the strategic designs and composition of forces of the refugees, pirates and raiders is given as follows: 'Their main support was Peleset [Philistine], Thekel, Shekelesh [Sicilian], Denyen [Danunan], and Weshesh. These lands were united, and they laid their hands upon the land as far as the Circle of the Earth. Their hearts were confident, full of plans' (Breasted, 1906, 4.34, cited in Frost, 1913, 196). This valuable reference to the Peleset and Denyens – whose real identity will also concern us – is interpreted by Frost as referring to the Peleset as Cretans who invaded and then settled Palestine, a remnant remaining even after Ramses III's conquest.

The name, Peleset, from which 'Palestine' and the biblical 'Philistine', by which Palestinians today still refer to themselves, are derived, are those people of whom it is said in Jeremiah 47.4 that they were the '*Remnant* of the country (or island) of Caphtor' (emphasis added; see also Genesis 10.6, 13, 14; Deuteronomy, 2.23; Amos, 9.7; cited in Frost, 1913, 197, n.22; and Bernal, 1987a, 75–83). Various accounts are given of the origins of the Peleset by modern archaeologists and ancient historians, ancient authors speaking of them as the earliest inhabitants of Greece, converted under pressure to become Danunans by colonizing Hyksos overlords. Bernal's thesis that they were Indo-Europeans would suggest that the Biblical reference to them as remnants of Caphtor regards them as Mycenaeans who took over from the Minoans; as part of the motley crew known as the Sea Peoples they settled Philistia between the twelfth and tenth centuries BC (Bernal, 1987a, Appendix, 447–8). Direct reference to the Keftiu drops out of Egyptian inscriptions after Ramses III's defeat of the sea-borne raiders and the destruction of Knossos recorded eliptically by Solon's priest, being replaced by various tribal names of the Sea People, and possibly losing completely its original sense of Minoan Crete by the Hellenistic period (Frost, 1913, 202). But Proclus describes references he sees on Egyptian monuments as designating 'Atlantans' – which suggests that the connection was still made somehow – thereby stretching the credulity of the great classical scholar and philhellene, Dr Jowett, to the point where he attributes to the Neoplatonists the forging of stone monuments, as well as of books! (Frost, 1913, 202).

The catastrophic end to both the 'ancient Athenians' and Atlantis – 'there were earthquakes and floods of extraordinary violence, and in a single dreadful day and night all your fighting men were swallowed up by the earth, and the island of Atlantis was similarly swallowed up by the sea and vanished' (*Tim.*, 25, 1971 edn, 38) – has an explanation independent of Egyptian or any other conquest. It could quite simply have been the result of a volcanic eruption. Some time between the seventeenth and sixteenth centuries BC – recent frost ring data suggesting 1628–26 BC (LaMarche and Hirschboek, 1984; Warren, 1984; Bernal, 1987a, 42 and n.18; Betancourt, 1987; Cadogan, 1987; Hammer, et al., 1987; Baille and Munro, 1988; Manning, 1988, 65–7) – on the island of Thera, now known as Santorini, which had been the site of a long history of volcanic eruptions from the late Cycladic period on, a catastrophic eruption took place such that an average ash fall of 20 cm covered the sea bed, and widespread flooding (*tsumanis*), which would not necessarily have been uniform in effect in the Aegean (Forsyth, 1980, 130–1), took place. An ash fall of this magnitude, attested by deep sea sediment cores (Watkins et al. 1978) would have destroyed vegetation over a wide area, making it uninhabitable for as much as a generation (Lee, 1971, 159). This discovery first made in the late nineteenth century, and investigated by successive archaeologists (Marinatos, 1968–76; Luce, 1969; Doumas, 1974, 1978, 1980, 1983; Bond and Sparks, 1976; Renfrew, 1979; LaMarche and Hirshchboeck, 1984; Manning, 1988), would seem to be sufficient to explain the widespread destruction in Crete in this period and the rapid decline of Minoan civilization. The latter process cannot be attributed to Egypt, whose efforts were confined to the repulsion of the sea raiders, and who could take no credit for the overthrow of Knossos and the sack of the Cretan palaces (Frost, 1913, 203). Bernal (1987a, 41–2) points out, in fact, that one piece of evidence for the dating of the eruption of Thera around 1626 BC is the virtual absence of records for Egypt of the seventeenth century BC, suggesting considerable devastation in the Delta from flooding. Around 1450 BC, the conventional dating of the eruption, Crete is still sending tributory missions to Egypt, in whose extensive records for this period no mention of such an event is to be found. Bernal (1987a, 41) insists that the arrival of the Mycenaeans on Crete, appropriately dated at around 1450 BC (Vercoutter, 1956; Popham, 1970b; Palmer, 1984; Wachsmann, 1987; cited in Manning, 1988, 35), and the destruction caused by the eruption of Thera, are events separated by as much as 200 years.

That Plato alone among contemporaries should have chronicled the catastrophic end to Minoan civilization is not surprising given some of the internal evidence in the dialogues as to the transmission of the priest's tale. We have it on the authority of several sources, from the anonymous *Prolegomena* (Teubner text, vol. 15), from Olympiodorus's *Life of Plato*, to Proclus's *Commentary*, 25 ff (cited in Frost, 1913, 203), that Plato belonged to the family of Solon. The close relationship between Solon's family and that of Critias is also independently attested (Suidas, *Lexicon*, s.v. 'Solon'), Plato himself in the *Charmides*, 15E, mentioning the panegyrics composed by Solon and others to honour Critias, son of Dropidas (Frost, 1913, 203; Rosenmeyer, 1949). The contours of the legend as an epic defeat by Hellas of Asiatic kingship, telescoping a series of events whose distinct phases are still just discernible, would fit with the notion of this being information about historical events whose record is preserved in family legend to which Plato had privileged access. And it is not at all clear that Plato looks unfavourably upon Asiatic kingships. Obviously it is the modern Athenians who come off worst in the tale, the generic similarities he stresses between the ancient Egyptian society of the priest, the great federal system of kingships of Atlantis and the society of Greece in the heroic age, suggesting that this, contrary to what Frost may suggest (1913, 203), is no simple tale of the triumph of 'Hellenism against Barbarism, cosmic in scope like the Battle of the Gods and Giants', which Plato might have made 'a proto-type of the Persian Wars'.

Moreover, the substance of Timaeus' cosmology, sandwiched in between the first and the second versions of the priestly tale, and presented by Plato, like the Myth of Er to which it is related, as central to the metaphysical framework of his philosophical system, contains a striking number of elements in common with Eastern cosmologies. The world as the product of a creator god, new to the Greeks, which made the *Timaeus* appear to Christian medievalists an anticipation of monotheism, was also a feature of Mesopotamian and Egyptian creation myths. The *Timaeus* is theological in a way that Greek thought, even in the Ionian cosmologies of Empedocles, Leucippus and Democritus, with which Plato's *Timaeus* shares much, are not (Lee, 1971, 7, 15; Cornford, 1975 edn). Plato's atomism; his attempt to reconcile mathematical and geometrical realities; the perennial elements of matter: earth, air, fire and water; his aetiology; although shared by Ionian, Mesopotamian and Egyptian cosmologies, do not necessarily mark out the *Timaeus* as specifically influenced by oriental traditions. But the creator god does, and the religious character of the work requires us to rethink the current, primarily rationalist, interpretation, which views Plato's metaphysics in terms of abstract ontological and epistemological entities.

7

Hesiod and Oriental Cosmogonies

Much has now been written on the general relation between Mesopotamian creation myths and the cosmogony of Hesiod. Similarities in the great Epic cycle shared by Homer and Mesopotamian transmitters; and specific parallels between the Babylonian Enuma Elish epic and Hesiod's *Theogony*, telling the story of the creation, the generation of the gods and their genealogies, the creation of mankind and the appearance of early kingship, are too close for coincidence (Walcot, 1966; West, 1966, 22–3). It is worth pointing out that in the Babylonian creation myths, too, a personal god is missing. We have to look elsewhere to find him; and in so doing we find extraordinary parallels that tie together both Greece and Mycenae, Mycenae and Egypt. Not only do the correspondences in Egyptian mythology extend to the general outline of Hesiod's *Theogony* and the cosmology of Plato's *Timaeus* on important points, but the specific intervention of the creator god in the fashioning of Pandora in both the *Theogony* and *Works and Days* has a particular parallel in the creation of humans by the ram-headed Egyptian god Khnum on his potter's wheel. The correspondences between Pandora and Egyptian mythology do not stop there, as Walcot (1966, 64–79) has pointed out, and the implications for Greek kingship are profound. Moreover, the Egyptian evidence is presented in such a way that its centrality to official royal propaganda cannot be doubted: it is epigraphic in form, to be found in the reliefs inscribed on the walls of the great temple of Hatshepsut, the Egyptian woman on the throne of Egypt, who reigned in the Tuthmoside period, that fateful sixteenth century BC.

To take the general study of creation first. Hesiod's *Theogony* tells the epic story of the birth of the gods, their struggles for succession and supremacy as dynasties in a primitive kingship: Ouranos, being overcome by Kronos, who as ruler of the Titans, that mythical race of giants, is eventually overcome by Zeus. Creation began with Chaos, Gaia the earth mother, and Eros in the Hesiodic order (*Theog.*, 116–22, 1959 edn, 130). 'From Chaos was born Erebos, the dark, and black Night'; and Gaia lay with Erebos to produce Aither and Hemera, the day. But her first born, Ouranos, 'the starry sky' (*Theog.*, 122–7, 1959 edn, 130), was her real match, and, having brought forth the tall hills and Pontos, the sea, 'without any sweet act of love', she then lay with Ouranos and conceived with him a total of 18 children (*Theog.*, 129–49, 1959 edn, 130–2). Ouranos, by sexual predations, tried to prevent Gaia's children from being born, and 'every time each one was beginning to come out, he would push them back again, deep inside Gaia, and would not let them into the light'; 'but great Gaia, groan[ing] within for pressure of pain ... thought of an evil and treacherous attack' and, fashioning a sickle from stone, spoke encouragement to each of her children in turn to kill their 'criminal father ... the first to think of shameful dealing' (*Theog.*, 156–66, 1959 edn, 132–3). Kronos, the first to undertake the ritual parricide, ambushed and castrated the lustful Ouranos, caught *in flagrante delicto*, allowing Gaia's children to be born and Kronos and his own dynasty to rule. From the severed members tossed into the sea grew a beautiful girl, Aphrodite, the 'foam-born goddess', who made her way 'to holy Kythera' and thence 'to sea-washed Cyprus' (*Theog.*, 180–96, 1959 edn, 134–5). Kronos, as determined as his father to prevent the birth of contenders for his power, lay with Rheia and conceived six children by her, but, when each of the first five – Histia and Demeter 'of the golden sandals', Hera, 'strong Hades' and Zeus – was born, 'great Kronos swallowed it down with the intention that no other of the proud children of Ouranos should ever hold the king's position among the immortals' (*Theog.*, 460–63, 1959 edn, 150). He had in fact been tipped off by the gods that Zeus, his son, would overpower him; and Rheia conspired with Gaia and 'starry Ouranos' to ensure that this was so, forcing her husband to disgorge his remaining children (*Theog.*, 465–505, 1959 edn, 150–3). A battle between Kronos and the Titans, Zeus and his supporters ensued.

Among the elements of this creation story those which are common to the Egyptian creation myths have received far less comment than the parallels between the Hesiodic and the Hittite Kumarbi and Ullikummi myths or the Babylonian Enuma Elish theogony (Walcot, 1966, chs 1 and 2). And some have received no comment at all. The untitled Hittite Kumarbi story, known as the Kingship in Heaven myth, significantly concerns gods of earth and sky already connected to the Greek gods, Kumarbi, for instance, believed by Philo of Byblos of the first century AD to be equivalent to the Greek Kronos. It too concerns the struggle for dynastic succession between the established king of heaven, in this case Alalu, and Anu the Sumerian sky god and pretender, who rules for nine years until pursued by Kumarbi, who bites off and swallows the usurper's genitals. Anu warns him that he has in fact swallowed three gods, Kumarbi spits up two, one of whom is the river god Tigris, but the third, the weather god – cult god of the Hittites and Hurrians – refuses to be disgorged. When he does come forth, he and his supporters are ready for battle, a conflict the outcome of which is not furnished in the text, but bound to favour him, given the centrality of the weather god to the Hittite cults.

The Hittite, an Indo-European cosmogony, has a Semitic parallel in the Akkadian Enuma Elish epic, concerned like it and Hesiod's *Theogony* with the creation of the gods, primitive kingship and the struggle for world domination, in this case of Marduk. In the beginning the world was constituted of watery substances, Apsu, 'the sweet male waters', and Tiamat, 'the bitter female waters of the sea' (West, 1966, 22). In this medium, the first gods came into being, among them the sky god Anu and his son Ea, 'the wise and the strong', who dethrones Apsu, determined to destroy his children for fear of a threat to his succession. Ea begets Marduk and Tiamat, the latter incited by the older gods to go to war with Marduk, who slays her, cleaves her monstrous body in two, and out of the broken remains creates heaven and earth, the constellations and the moon. Thus we have in the Babylonian epic the primeval parents: Apsu and Tiamat, equivalent to Ouranos and Gaia. The children begotten by them are in each case loved by the mother, rejected and threatened by the father as a challenge to his power. In both cases the fear of the children is relieved when Ea the wise god, Kronos, the mighty, respectively, overcome the tyrannical father: by magic sleep in the former case, by an ambush in his marital bed in the latter. Although the specific detail of castration in the Greek cosmogony is without parallel in the Babylonian, unlike the Hittite one, and the earth mother in the Babylonian story is herself a monstrous opponent of her children, unlike the benevolent Gaia in the Hesiodic theogony, commentators have seen sufficient parallels in the succession myths of both to believe mutual transmission of original material to be present (Cornford, 1950, 112–14; West, 1966, 22–3). The Babylonian succession myth is widely believed, on the basis of later epigraphic evidence, to be a canonical text recited at the Babylonian New Year festival. And Cornford was among the first brilliantly to connect both the Greek and Babylonian theogonies to the Mystery Play of the Succession of the Pharaoh at Abydos (Frankfort, 1948, 105; Cornford, 1950, 108).

Although the connection between the Babylonian creation myth, recording the struggle of Marduk against Tiamat, the dragon woman, and the chapters of Genesis recording the creation epic and the struggle between Jaweh and the dragon Leviathan, were noted as early as Frazer's *Golden Bough* (The Dying God, cited in Cornford, 1950, 105), the case for these works representing ritual hymns associated with New Year rites was not made until Cornford's intuitive work. Persuaded, he confesses, by works on Near Eastern ritual, he argues that the power of Greek epics, and specifically that of Hesiod, derives not from 'baseless "fancies" and speculation', but from the debris of ritual, once palpably extant, and still capable of generating poetic power in the dramatic events they describe, when ethnologically defunct. Cornford is emphatic that their original power was categorically different from their poetic power as epics; for originally they were not descriptive but performative: they were hymns and as such they brought into being the rite that they celebrated. Their performative power lay in the re-enactment of sacred rites which constituted the periodic renewal of creative power. And 'there is only one fundamental theme behind all these: renewal of life; rebirth; the young king superseding the old' (Cornford, 1950, 116).

Behind the general structural similarities between the Hittite, Hurrian and Babylonian creation myths and Hesiod's *Theogony*, there is something explicit, then: the legitimization of sacred monarchy. And this is as true in the case of Egyptian official ritual as for the other cases. Not only are there general similarities in the Egyptian theology of the Pyramid Texts: the creation by Atum of the original pair, Shu and Tefnut, his female counterpart; the separation of the earth god Geb from the sky god Nut, by the air god Shu (1248a–d; 1992a, cited in Walcot, 1966, 77). But the connection to kingly ritual is particularly close, as suggested by the inscriptions at Abydos and Deir el-Bahari. Moreover, the specific correspondences between the conception and birth of Queen Hatshepsut and the Greek Pandora are without parallel in the Mesopotamian cases, involving intervention of a personal creator god, which Walcot (1966, 64–79) is the first to my knowledge to have pointed out.

In the *Theogony*, 570–614 (1959 edn, 157–9), Hesiod recounts the story of Pandora, presented by name and in some detail in *Works and Days*, 80–2 (1959 edn, 27). In Pandora we have the equivalent of the earth-goddess/dragon-lady Tiamat, creative mother and source of evil and corruption, referred to variously by Hesiod as 'an evil thing for mankind', 'this beautiful evil thing', the original of woman – 'for mortal men an evil thing' (*Theog.*, 570, 585, 600, 1959 edn, 157, 158, 159). And at greater length: 'For from her originates the breed of female women, and they live with mortal men, and are a great sorrow to them, and hateful poverty they will not share, but only luxury' (*Theog.*, 590–3, 1959 edn, 158). Hesiod goes on (595–9, 1959 edn, 158) to compare her to the drones who idle while busy bees do their work, due undoubtedly to a case of mistaken identity in the sex of the 'king bee', which he shares with Aristotle. In *Works and Days*, that celebration of the golden age before luxury and the corruptions of civilization, Pandora's heart is full of 'lies, and wheedling words of falsehood, and a treacherous nature', planted by Hermes, the guide, on the instructions of Zeus:

> and he, the gods' herald,
> put a voice inside her, and gave her the name of woman,
> Pandora, because all the gods who have their homes on Olympos
> had given her each a gift, to be a sorrow to men
> who eat bread (*WD*, 79–82, 1959 edn, 27)

Pandora is fashioned out of clay (*WD*, 61, *Theog.*, 571, 1959 edn, 25, 157), like the creations of the ram-headed Egyptian god Khnum, depicted in the fabrication of Hatshepsut. But, and this is indeed significant, nothing evil is suggested in the idea of a woman on the throne of Egypt, which knew the powerful queens: Neith-Hetep, Mer Neith, Tiye, Netocris, Nefertiti and Ahmose-Nefertere, the latter Hatshepsut's mother.

The reliefs in Hatshepsut's temple at Deir el-Bahari record the divine conception and birth of the great queen in terms of which events in Greek mythology are remarkably reminiscent. A conference between the creator god Amun and Thoth, the Egyptian Hermes, leads to a meeting between Amun and Queen Ahmose, wife of Thutmose I, for which the inscription tells us that Amun, assuming the likeness of the Queen's husband, 'visited' her; that the fragrance of the god – known to us as a sign of divinity (Hornung, 1983, 133–4; Bell, 1985a, 281, 283, citing Brunner, 1977) – aroused her from her sleep and the two were united. According to the inscription: 'He caused that she should see him in his form of a god. When he came before her, she rejoiced at the sight of his beauty, his love passed into her limbs, which the fragrance of the god flooded; all his odours were from Punt' (Brunner, 1964, 42–4, cited in Walcot, 1966, 66, 135, n.24). Heracles, that god common to Greece and the Near East (Brundage, 1958), was similarly born of a union between 'fair-ankled Alcmene' (*Theog.*, 950–55) and Zeus, who assumed the likeness of her husband, Amphitryon. And Zeus, in the form of birds, animals and even a shower of golden rain – gold, like fragrance, and Egyptian symbol of divinity along with totemistic animals, fans to create the Royal Shade and sphinxes (Bell, 1985b) – was known surreptitiously to have seduced others (Walcot, 1966, 67).

Hatshepsut in the fifth in the series of wall reliefs at Deir el-Bahari is actually depicted as being shaped by Khnum on the potter's wheel at the insistence of Amun, who ordered: 'Go, to make her, together with her ka from these limbs which are in me; go, to fashion her better than all gods; shape for me, this my daughter, whom I have begotten. I have given to her all life and satisfaction, all stability, all joy of heart from me, all offerings, and all bread, like Re, forever' (Brunner, 1964, 61, cited in Walcot, 1966, 67). The mention of the *ka* raises a fascinating suggestion which neither Walcot nor other commentators on Hesiod raise, but which may well explain the 18 children of Gaia struggling to be born. For the *ka*, sign of the vital essence of all living things and the immortality of kings through the continuity of succession (Frankfort, 1948; Bell, 1985a; Springborg, 1990d, ch. 6), took the form of a child, still-born, the royal twin. And by the Eighteenth Dynasty there were typically 14 of them – remnants, perhaps, of the 14 parts of the slain god Osiris resurrected by Isis – established in royal theology (Frankfort, 1948, 66). At Hatshepsut's temple in Deir el-Bahari, reliefs show the suckling not only of the infant queen, but also of her *ka*s, 12 royal infants embraced by the *ka* arms of the hieroglyphic symbol, two privileged ones being suckled by cow goddesses, royal wet-nurses and personifications of Hathor. The inscription is quite explicit, Amun declaring: 'I have commanded (you) to nurse Her Majesty and all her Ka's, with all life and good fortune, all permanence, all health, all joy, and the passing of millions of years on the throne of Horus of all the living forever' (cited in Frankfort, 1948, 74). The following scene sees her presentation to the assembly of the gods, the Ennead, who acclaim her: 'head of all the living Ka's together with her Ka as King of Upper and Lower Egypt on the throne of Horus, like unto Re, forever and ever' (cited in Frankfort, 1948, 77). Indeed Hatshepsut's name, 'Powerful of *Ka*s' marked her out as the only Egyptian pharaoh 'to include direct reference to her *ka* in this part of her titulary' (Bell, 1985a, 290).

One wonders if in each of these theogonies: that of Hesiod, of the Hittite 'Kingship of Heaven' and the Babylonian Enuma Elish epic, the struggles of Gaia, Kumarbi and Tiamat, respectively, against the jealous power of the patriarchal father, do not represent vestiges of the same material as the pharaoh and his/her *ka*: the violence of royal succession; the *Götterdammerung*: a twilight of the gods brought on by the death of the old pharaoh and before the accession of the new, during which the world was plunged back into Chaos, that tangible reality between earth and sky, created first among finite entities, and typified by the dragon god Apopis in the Egyptian theology (Hornung, 1983, 163). In each case a triumphant king emerges from the birth struggle; and his suppressed siblings are later disgorged or revivified, members perhaps of the eternal family of living and dead members which each dynasty constituted.

The Deir el-Bahari reliefs depict first the infant queen presented with her *ka* in the form of a male child, to the divine Ennead – like their counterpart the Greek pantheon 12 in number; Hatshepsut being presented by Amun to Egypt as his gift; and finally her journey to the North to accept homage. Hatshepsut appears Pandora-like in her beauty. According to the inscription 'her form was like a god, she did everything as a god, her splendour was like a god; her majesty was a maiden, beautiful, blooming, Buto in her time' (Brunner, 1964, cited in Walcot, 1966, 68). What follows of the coronation scenes has been badly mutilated by her defilers, subsequent pharaohs, but we can guess at the glory of her presentation from the image preserved of her decked out as pharaoh, wearing the double crown of Upper and Lower Egypt. Like Pandora, of whom it is said:

> The goddess gray-eyed Athene dressed and arrayed her; the Graces, who are goddesses, and hallowed Persuasion put necklaces of gold upon her body, while the Seasons, with glorious tresses, put upon her head a coronal of spring flowers, [and Pallas Athene put all decor upon her body]. (*WD*, 72–3, 1959 edn, 27)

Walcot is the first to point to the coronation of Hatshepsut as the key to the symbolism of Pandora's presentation, in particular the symbolism of the crown, more explicit still in the *Theogony*, 573–84 (1959 edn, 157–8):

> and the goddess gray-eyed Athene dressed her and decked her in silverish clothing, and over her head she held with her hands, an intricately wrought veil in place, a wonder to look at: wild animals, such as the mainland and the sea also produce in numbers, and he put many on, the imitations of living things, that have voices, wonderful, and it flashed in its beauty.

Thus adorned Pandora too was presented to the gods as their gift, which Hesiod explains in the etymology of her name (*WD*, 80–2); in the same way that the reigning pharaoh was granted by the gods with all their gifts (Walcot, 1966, 69).

In this case Hesiod's material would seem to be the debris of rituals once living; poetic remnants taking abstract form, once dead, that is the mark of poetry as we know it; images that, having lost their original specificity, retain a power with which their living past once endowed them. Cornford's prescience in locating these origins for Hesiod's *Theogony* did not extend to the Pandora story, which would seem to be the best case. Nor did he have any specific examples to give for the Egyptian case except to point in a sentence to the Mystery Play of the Succession at Abydos where the power of Osiris, as at once earthly king and god, is dramatically challenged by a representation of the murderous Seth and his band attacking Osiris's procession to his shrine, only to be repelled by Horus and his followers (Cornford, 1950, 108); a ritual re-enactment of the original empowering events in the Egyptian theology of the Pyramid Texts. The homology between radiant Hatshepsut and the powers of Pandora, gift of the gods, depends on an understanding of the function of kingship as beneficence, for which Cornford gives us a clue in the Biblical version of the succession myths. The prophet Zechariah (xiv.16) foretells that under the reign of the Lord as King of the earth, all those former challengers to Jerusalem's power shall come yearly to worship the King, Lord of Hosts, at the feast of the Tabernacles: 'And it shall be, that whosoever will not come up ... *upon them shall be no rain*' (cited Cornford, 1950, 109). Cornford comments:

> But at the advanced stage of civilisation we are now considering in Babylon, Egypt and Palestine, the king has become much more than rain-making magician. To control the rain is to control the procession of the seasons and their powers of drought and moisture, heat and cold; and these again are linked with the orderly

revolutions of sun, moon and stars. The king is thus regarded as the living embodiment of the god who instituted this natural order and must perpetually renew and maintain its functioning for the benefit of man. The king embodies that power and also the life-force of his people, concentrated in his official person. He is the maintainer of the social order; and the prosperity of the nation depends upon his righteousness, the Hebrew *Sedek*, the Greek *dike* [and he might have added the Egyptian *ma'at*]. He protects his people from the evil powers of death and disorder, as well as leading them in war to victory over their enemies. The purpose of the New Year festival is to renovate – to recreate – the ordered life of the social group and of the world of nature, after the darkness and defeat of winter. The power which gives one more turn to the wheel of the revolving year is vested in the king, but derived from the god whom he embodies, the god who first set the wheel in motion. So the rites are regarded as an annual re-enactment of Creation. (Cornford, 1950, 109)

It is a stroke of genius on Cornford's part to add in the last lines of his essay (p. 215): 'Further research in Crete and Asia Minor may show whether there is any ground for the guess that the New Year festival in question was once performed in the palace of King Minos.'

Pandora, as a figure for queenly beneficence, possibly derived from the remnants of real ritual, is already an ambivalent figure, between good and evil, reflecting perhaps the characteristic misogyny of Greek culture and the fear of the Mother, who in the twin person of Queen concentrated fearful power for husbands (Slater, 1968; Arthur, 1973; Humphreys, 1977; Okin, 1977; Saxonhouse, 1980; Hartsock, 1983) – so much so that her sons had to be stifled, at birth if need be. Pandora is indeed a double-faced, female Janus, prefigured in the goddess Hathor, as much feared as loved (Springborg, 1990d, ch. 10). As a vision of queenly magnificence she is both an object of reverence and terror, as Hesiod makes clear:

> But when, to replace good, he had made this beautiful evil thing, he led her out where the rest of the gods and mortals were, in the pride and glory that the gray-eyed daughter of a great father had given; wonder seized both immortals and mortals as they gazed on this sheer deception, more than mortals can deal with. (*Theog.*, 585–9, 1959 edn, 158)

Are we witnessing here the moment of queenly apotheosis? The presentation of Pandora before gods and men in her crowned magnificence, decked out in silver and gold, symbols of divinity, would suggest it. In the same way the Pharaoh of shining face appeared in radiant glory after his meeting with Amun in the innermost sanctum of Luxor Temple during the Opet festival, rehearsing his apotheosis for purposes of the renewal of divine powers (Otto, 1968; Bell, 1985a, 251 ff). And the moment of apotheosis was signalled by diffusion of the fragrance of flowers (Brunner, 1977; Hornung, 1983, 133–4; Bell, 1985a, 282, 283). Charged with power and creation imagery of all sorts that included the *ka* names of 'Mighty Bull', 'Golden One', 'Horus', 'Master of the Two Lands'; even androgynous ones, like 'Two Ladies'; and names that celebrate his immortality: 'Image of Re', 'Radiant of Appearances' and 'Great of Majesty', 'Great of Miracles', 'Celebrating Hundreds-of-Thousands of Festivals', 'Reigning for Millions-of-Years' (Bell, 1985a, 285–6); replete with imagery of the suckling of the royal *ka* by mother goddesses, depictions of the Holy Family, Mother, Father and Son, the Opet festival celebrated the renewal of royal power that kept gods and men in being. For the pharaoh, as intermediary between the realms of earth and sky, kept the gods alive on earth by creating images within which they could dwell, in the statue cults, feeding and tending them in his role as high priest and caretaker of the royal temples. At the same time he dispensed divine beneficence to men, as lord of the harvest, of the waters of the Nile, and the seasons. If the rains were late, the earth did not bear or the crops were spoiled, the king was blamed (Baillet, 1912, 224, 234–5, 253; Posener, 1960, 11–12, 37–41; Veyne, 1976, 558, 735, n.43). As bread-giver and life-giver, the Pharaoh guaranteed peace and well-being (Baillet, 1912, 224, 253). Symbol of beneficence and cosmic order, the pharaoh, himself constrained by his role as a divinity (Baillet, 1913, 631–2; Posener, 1960, 37–9), offered up to the gods *Ma'at*: the figure of a suppliant woman on a basket, ideogram of justice (Hornung, 1983, 213). Throughout the lands he was known by these titles, Bread-giver, Giver of Life, Giver of Justice, that refer to a grand and perpetual gift exchange in which the people too participated by bringing the fruits of the harvest as offerings, receiving in turn state guarantee of their sustenance (Posener, 1960, 40–1; Janssen, 1982).

Knowledge of the sacred ceremonies of Luxor temple, by which the pharaoh recharged his divine powers, was well diffused throughout the Mediterranean world, we know from the fact that Alexander and the Ptolemies contributed to the restoration of the barque chapels at Luxor, in which the sacred effigies of gods and pharaohs were honoured, and that the Romans kept a permanent embassy in the same temple, which they made their headquarters in Thebes (Nims, 1965, 128; L. Bell, 1985a, 254–5, 274). Earlier diffusions for which we do not have inscriptional evidence are also likely, and it is speculated that Mesopotamian divine kingship was an Egyptian borrowing dating to the period of Naram-Sin. It is altogether possible that the Pandora story represents the vestiges of a legend of apotheosis that dates to the great Queen Hatshepsut, as Walcot (1966, 65–79) argues. There are parallels in the imagery scattered throughout the *Theogony*: the moment of apotheosis in Luxor temple was marked by the diffusion of the fragrance of flowers; Hesiod in the account in *Works and Days* of the Pandora story mentions flowers as part of her raiment (75, 1959 edn, 27); and Walcot (1966, 67) suggests that among the Greeks fragrance was an aspect under which divinity manifested itself, so when in the Hymn to Demeter, verses 277–8, the goddess changed back from her appearance as an old woman to present her true form, 'from her perfumed robes there spread a lovely fragrance'.

The possible references to the royal *ka*, which I advance on my own account, are particularly interesting, for here the Greek ambivalence towards woman and the vestiges of Egyptian iconography appear to be fused. Gaia and Rheia, as goddesses and dynastic mothers, were technically queens. In each case the fathers of their children, Ouranos and Kronos, contrived to ensure that their children would either be still-born or killed at birth. Now the Egyptian royal *ka*, for which the hieroglyph is a royal standard, or flag, supported by protective *ka* arms, symbolizing the nurturing goddess, derived from the placenta, one and the same with the still-born twin (Frankfort, 1948, 66–9; Kaplony, 1975, 275). Flags as strips of cloth on a pole replicated the original written sign for the gods which took the form of a wrapped stick, strips of cloth symbolizing 'numinous objects', perhaps the wrappings of gods, mummies and royal babies? (Hornung, 1983, 33–8). The *ka*, as the symbol of the animate essence of each living person, was also the peculiar sign of the immortality of monarchy – the former meaning perhaps deriving from the latter, as Egyptologists suggest (Frankfort, 1948, 69). Innumerable royal inscriptions depict the pharaoh and his/her *ka*, born with the king, being suckled by the royal nursemaids, and mysteriously disappearing as the child king assumes his/her patrimony – Hatshepsut is among those female monarchs who have historically referred to themselves as king. And classicists and others have speculated on the Greek legacy of the *ka* in the concept of *daimon* and the Roman notion of the Emperor and his *genius* (Goodenough, 1928; Nock, 1947; Kantorowicz, 1957; L. Bell, 1985a; Springborg, 1990d, ch. 12).

Were the 18 children of Gaia related then to the 14 *kas* of an Egyptian pharaoh as depicted during the Ramesside period? And if the Pandora story contains relics of Egyptian apotheosis, why should a deified queen strike terror in the Greeks in a way that it did not for the Egyptians? The two questions are interconnected. That the jealousy of the threatened father should take precedence in the depiction of Gaia, would be a significant Greek contribution to the Egyptian notion of the *ka* as a still-born child. The role of the Queen Mother, like Isis both mother and wife of her children, giving birth to kings and *kas*, recedes as vestiges of a half-forgotten tale – or the half-forgotten commemorative ritual of kingship – and the passions of the succession struggle take over. We can hazard a guess that this reflects the state of mind of the less stable kingships of Mycenaean Greece, compared with the relatively well-institutionalized pharaonic rule, which nevertheless suffered something of a crisis of nerves in the Ramesside New Kingdom, as it established itself after the turmoil of the Amarna experiment; hence perhaps the reason for the effulgent protestations of divinity and extravagant titulary of a period exceeded only by the hyperbole of the imitative Ptolemies.

There is indeed a parallel for the second example of the suppression of the royal children, the children of Rheia devoured by Kronos, in Egyptian royal iconography. In the roof of the sarcophagus room in the temple of Seti I at Abydos, dating to around 1300 BC, an inscription records a quarrel leading to separation between the sky god Nut and her husband Geb, the earth, brought about because Nut caused the stars to disappear during the day by devouring them. Geb accuses her as the 'Sow who eats her piglets'. But her father Shu cautioned her: 'Beware of Geb. Let him not quarrel with her because she eats their children. She shall give birth to them and they shall live again, and they shall come forth in the place at her hinder part in the East every day, even as she gave birth the first time' (Frankfort, 1933, 83, cited in Walcot, 1966, 78). Nut is both like Ouranos a sky god, and like Kronos a god who devours her children.

Walcot (1966, 69) poses the question: 'what evidence is there to suggest that the Greeks knew and were influenced by the Egyptian concept of kingship?' And he answers it by postulating an indirect connection in the diffusion of Egyptian influence through Palestine and Syria, producing the Canaanite tradition of divine kingship and birth oracles to which the Genesis story of Abraham as fruit of the union of Sarah and Yaweh, who 'visits' her (Walcot, 1966, 70, 136, n.36), is said to belong. The birth story of Heracles, with parallels to the divine conception of Hatshepsut, is another version; and Heracles, in at least two of his manifestations, is said to have come from the Near East (Brundage, 1958; Walcot, 1966, 67). From Palestine and Syria further diffusion to Greece is not difficult to conceive.

But a second set of connections, and the more interesting for our purposes, depends on a theory of direct contact between Egypt and the Greeks some time after 1500 BC. Walcot (1966, 71) postulates: 'There is a considerable body of evidence to suggest that the Mycenaean kings were sacral kings in the full Egyptian sense'; and that this may mean, if the story of Danaus' flight from Egypt is taken as more than myth, that Mycenae was actually colonized from Egypt – by a fleeing Hyksos who carved out new territory in the Argolid, or by a Greek mercenary on the Egyptian side returning home. Archaeological evidence from the grave shafts at Mycenae strongly suggest Egyptian influence, both in the funerary function and furnishing of the grave sites, their decorative style and inscriptional evidence (Palmer, 1963, 338–63, cited in Walcot, 1966, 71–2). The role of the Mycenaean god-king, although not established in its specifics, is reminiscent of the beneficence of Near Eastern kings, of whom the pharaoh is a prototype. Thus in the *Odyssey*, XIX, 108–14, in a curious example that concerns Penelope, disguised Odysseus addresses his faithful wife, both on her own account, and as the mirror of his own kingship, thus:

> Queen, no mortal upon the boundless earth could find fault with you, for indeed your fame goes up to wide heaven like that of a virtuous king who fears the gods and who rules a strong well-peopled kingdom. He upholds justice, and under him the dark soil yields wheat and barley; trees are weighed down with fruit, sheep never fail to bear young and the sea abounds in fish – all this because of his righteous rule, so that thanks to him his people prosper. (Homer, *Odyssey*, XIX, 108–14, 1980 edn, 230)

And Hesiod too, describing in *Works and Days*, 232–7 (1959 edn, 45–7) the city which flourishes 'under men who issue [just] decrees to their people', includes a litany of beneficences that nature supplies, reminiscent of Egyptian wisdom literature:

> the earth gives them great livelihood, on their mountains the oaks bear acorns for them in their crowns, and bees in their middles. Their wool-bearing sheep are weighted down with fleecy burdens. Their women bear them children who resemble their parents. They prosper in good things throughout. They need have no traffic with ships, for their own grain-giving land yields them its harvest.

In Homer there is no clue as to the parallel between Egyptian beneficent kingship and Mycenaean monarchy beyond the mention of Danaans (*Odyssey*, 1980 edn, 9, 41, 51, 53, 62, 86, 138, 139, 140, 287) and Cadmeans (*Iliad*, 4.388), referring to the peoples of the eponymous founder gods, the Egyptian Danaus and the Phoenician Cadmus (*Odyssey*, 1980 edn, 2, 63, 134). In Hesiod there is not much more to link them, although frequent reference to Phoenix as an eponym for Phoenician (found also in Homer) and a reference to Europa as daughter of 'a noble Phoenician', in a fragment of the *Catalogue of Women* (Merkelbach and West, 1967, frs 141 and 143, cited in Bernal, 1987a, 86), suggest

Asiatic origins. We have fragmentary elements of a chronicle, perhaps in the Greek mythological accounts of the founding of Greek Thebes by Cadmus the Phoenician, and of Athens by Danaus the Egyptian. And when we come to Herodotus, Hecataeus, Isocrates and Diodorus these events are taken as part of the mytho-historical record.

Of the mythological accounts, several versions survive. The genealogies involve two different basic lines of descent, one from Nilus, father of Agenor, king of Tyre, who gave birth to Cadmus and Europa; the second from Bellus, hellenized Ba'al, founder-ancestor of the Heraclidae in Lydia (Herodotus 1.7.3), father of Aegyptus, Danaus and Damno. Agenor and Damno married to produce Phoenix, Isaee and Melia; Danaus and Melia married to produce the Danaids; and Aegyptus and Isaee married to produce 50 sons (Rose, 1970a, 311–12). Classicists have never denied that the names Nilus, Belus, Aegyptus, Danaus and Phoenix are eponyms. The Egypto-Phoenician-Hellenic synoecism that the genealogies suggest is compounded by a North African element in the ancestry of Danaus, born of a line beginning with the union of Zeus and Io, which produced Epaphus, his daughter Libya, who, making union with Poseidon, gave birth to Belus and Agenor (Aeschylus, *Suppliants*, 313 ff, cited in Rose, 1970a, 312). Aeschylus further chronicles the attempt by Aegyptus to tie the genealogies tighter by the endogamous marriage of his 50 sons to the 50 daughters of Danaus, an attempt that received the stout resistance of the latter. (Rose, 1970a, 312 claims these proposed marriages to be of 'no sociological significance', which I doubt, knowing the importance of endogamous marriage in Middle Eastern cultures, attested in brother–sister marriage in the Egyptian theology for which there are important Greek counterparts, and cousin marriage, which survives to this very day – Springborg, 1982.)

As we have suggested, archaeological and epigraphic evidence encourages the interpretation of myths increasingly in terms of the debris of an historical account, or of kingly rituals that relate to a historical account, or of both. The mythological genealogies of the founder-kings of Greece are no exception. On the evidence of the shaft graves at Mycenae, F. Stubbings (1963, vol. 2, 14.11 ff) has argued for Danaus as a Hyksos refugee and founder of the Mycenaean dynasty. The famous cup yielded up from the shaft graves, and compared with Nestor's cup of the *Iliad*, is decorated with Horus symbols, symbolizing an Egyptian deified king (Walcot, 1966, 71, 136, n.39); and scenes on the Haghia Triadha sarcophagus suggest 'that the [Mycenaean] king was worshipped after his death as a god' (Nilsson, 1950, 426–43, cited in Walcot, 1966, 71, 136, n.40). Recent archaeological excavations at Tel ed Daba'a in the Eastern Delta, the site of Avaris, the Hyksos capital, have revealed 'a composite West Semitic–Egyptian material culture showing clear resemblances to that of the Shaft Graves' of Mycenae (Bernal, 1987a, 45, citing Bietak, 1979a). Bernal (1987a, 51) notes that a West Semitic etymology can be given the name Mycenae itself – from Mahaneh, 'camp' or Mahanayim, 'two camps' – more plausible than the commonly given Greek derivation from *mykes*, 'mushroom'. Avaris may well have been the Egyptian capital to which the name Thebes, from *teba* (ark, chest), was originally given, in the absence of any record of the Upper Egyptian capital, Luxor, being known locally by that name (Bernal, 1987a, 51). Correspondingly, Egyptian tomb paintings for the period, and significantly those of Hatshepsut's famous minister Senmut, portray Minoan–Mycenaeans (Schachermeyr, 1964, 112–15, cited in Walcot, 1966, 136, n.38; Wachsmann, 1987). Europa, too, after her death was worshipped as a goddess; Cretan myths closely resemble hers; and a fayence plaque from Dendra shows her seated on a bull, with which her cult is associated (Nilsson, 1950, 480 ff; cited in Rose, 1970c, 422).

Literary evidence for these connections dates back at least to the lost epic *Danais* (Rose, 1964, 69; Rose, 1970a, 312), for which we have a fragment locating the daughters of Danaus on the banks of the Nile. And Aeschylus' trilogy or tetralogy, of which only *The Suppliants* – interestingly *Hyketides* in Greek, from the singular *hikesios*, or suppliant (Bernal, 1987a, 97), plausibly a Greek case of paranomasia, or punning – survives, comprised two other parts: *The Egyptians* and *The Danaids* (Garvie, 1969, 163–83; Bernal, 1987a, 88). Although at least one commentator sees 'the Egyptian and oriental dresses in The *Supplices* and *Persae* [as] of piece with [Aeschylus'] enjoyment of the geography of strange lands' (Pickard-Cambridge and Winnington-Ingram, 1970, 18), others treat more seriously the clear parallels to Egyptian mythology and religion. The ancestry of Danaus derives from the union of Zeus with the daughter of Inachus, Io, who to conceal her from jealous Hera, gave her the form of a heifer, reminiscent of Hathor, cow-god of love in Egyptian mythology. Io indeed, plagued by gadflies, makes her way eventually to Egypt, where she is restored by a touch of the hand of Zeus, and bears a son of this name, Epaphus, among whose descendants Danaus numbers.

The parallel has added weight in the identification of Io with Isis (Rose, 1970d, 549; Apollodorus 2.5–91, 1975 edn, 29–30), and Isis' identification in turn with cow-headed Hathor. 'The statues of Isis', Herodotus tells us (2.42, 1972 edn, 145), 'show a female figure with cow's horns, like the Greek representations of Io'; and he gives the various versions of Io's connection with Egypt. 'Greek and Persian writers agree in calling Io, daughter of Inachus, the Argive king', but in not much else about her. The Phoenicians who, 'loaded with Egyptian and Assyrian goods', traded along the Greek coastal ports, including 'Argos ... now called Hellas', according to the Persian version, succeeded in capturing Io, when she came to sample their wares, and bundled her off to Egypt (Herodotus 1.1, 1972 edn, 41). In retaliation, as the Persian story goes, Greeks – 'probably Cretans – put into the Phoenician port of Tyre and carried off the king's daughter Europa, thus giving them tit for tat' (Herodotus, 1.1–2, 1972 edn, 41–2), and delivering the opening shots in the long contest beween the Greeks and the barbarians that Herodotus chronicles. (The Phoenician version is a little different: Io, pregnant by the Phoenician trader's captain, fled voluntarily to Egypt; a version that, like the Persian, Herodotus (1.7, 1972 edn, 43) wishes neither to confirm nor deny.)

The Greek mythical version has eponymous elements connecting the Mycenaeans, Phoenicians and Egyptians, particularly evident in the full account given by Apollodorus of Athens, in Books 2 and 3 of his *Library of Greek Mythology* written in the first century BC. Apollodorus chronicles the descendants of Inachus and Belus, Inachus, after whom the river in Argos was named, said to have been born of Oceanus and Tethys, and, by Melia, daughter of Oceanus, to

have fathered Phoroneus, who ruled the Peloponnese and, by a nymph named
Teledice, fathered Apis and Niobe in turn (Apollodorus 2.1–2, 1975 edn, 29).
Apollodorus is the first to identify Apis with Serapis, the god of the Ptolemaic
bull cult: Apis, who became 'a harsh tyrant' and 'died childless, was
acknowledged to be a god, and was called Serapis'. Niobe 'the first mortal
woman' to be 'united' with Zeus, bore him two sons, Argus, who ruled
the Peloponnese and named it Argos, and Pelasgus, after 'whom those who
lived in the Peloponnesus were called Pelasgians' (Apollodorus 2.2, 1975
edn, 29), and whose line of descent Apollodorus defers to Book 3.96 ff (1975 edn,
70 f).

He meanwhile tells how Io, daughter of Inachus, was seduced by Zeus, while
still a priestess of Hera; how Zeus, to accord Hera her revenge, changed Io into a
white cow, tethered 'to an olive tree in the grove of the Mycenaeans'; how
Zeus instructed Hermes to steal her; and how, afflicted by Hera with a gadfly,
she made her way to the Ionian gulf; thence swimming her way to Egypt
(Apollodorus 2.5–7, 1975 edn, 30). Having regained her original shape in Egypt,
Io gave birth to Epaphus by the Nile – Herodotus (2.38, 3.27–9) tells us that
Epaphus is the Greek name for Apis – but he in turn is kidnapped by Hera. Io
seeks her son all over Syria and, learning that the wife of the king of the Byblians
is taking care of him, brings him back to Egypt with her, where she marries
Telegonus, king of the Egyptians at the time (Apollodorus 2.8–9, 1975 edn, 30).
Parallels to the story of Moses (Griffiths, 1953) are undoubtedly significant here;
but similarities to the myth of Osiris as related by Plutarch, where the Byblians
take custody of Osiris in his coffin (*teba*) (Plutarch, *De Iside et Osiride*, 357, 1970
edn, 141–3; Springborg, 1990d, ch. 11), are even more striking.

In gratitude to the gods for her successful quest, Io 'dedicated an image to
Demeter, called Isis by the Egyptians, as also they called Io herself' (Apollodorus
2.9, 1975 edn, 30). Epaphus, ruler of Egypt in his turn, 'married Nile's daughter
Memphis, and in her honour founded the polis of Memphis, and fathered a
daughter Libya, after whom the country Libya is named'; Libya and Poseidon,
having twin sons Agenor and Belus; of whom 'Agenor left for Phoenicia where he
became king', and was 'the founder of a great line'; while 'Belus remained to
become king of Egypt, and married Nile's daughter Achinoe, who gave him twin
sons Aegyptus and Danaus' (Apollodorus 2.10–11, 1975 edn, 30). The account
would seem to contain garbled elements of the Osiride theogony, in which a
quarrel between the brothers Osiris and Seth leads to the killing of Osiris by his
jealous brother, who sets Osiris' body afloat in a coffin near the Tanitic mouth.
Weeping Isis, seeking her husband's body, journeys as far afield as Byblos, where
she finds it (Plutarch, *De Iside et Osiride*, 356–7, 1970 edn, 139–43).

Apollodorus goes on to recount the chronicle of the 50 sons of Aegyptus and
the 50 daughters of Danaus, familiar to us from Aeschylus' *Suppliants*, and which
reflects Babylonian numerology and references to the lunar year that are a
constant in Greek mythology. A dispute over the succession leads to the flight of
the 50 daughters by ship, under Athena's supervision, to Argos, after a stop in
Rhodes. The 50 sons follow in hot pursuit and, after some side play, marriages
are arranged. Apollodorus' account (2.13–16, 1975 edn, 31) of the match between
the daughters of Danaus by the royal mother Europa, and the sons of Aegyptus

by the royal mother Argyphia, includes the name of the Egyptian king Busiris, known to the Greeks as the son of Poseidon, and xenophobic to the point of murdering foreigners, only to be killed in turn by Heracles in Egypt, according to Herodotus, Euripides, Isocrates – for whom he is the subject of the work that bears his name – Diodorus, Virgil and Appian (Brady, 1970, 185). Among the daughters and sons who did not share royal mothers, more eponyms crop up: two of the daughters were born to Elephantis; 'ten of the sons had an Arabian mother', among them Agenor, who was matched with Cleopatra, Chalcidon, matched to Rhodia, Hippolytus to Rhode; the mothers of these daughters being variously the Hamadryad nymphs, Atlanteia and Phoebe. A further seven sons by a Phoenician mother were born to daughters by an Ethiopian, while 'without drawing lots the sons of Tyria received the daughters of Memphis because of their identical names: Cleite went to Cleitus, Sthenele to Sthenelus, and Chrysippe to Chrysippus (Apollodorus 2.13–20, 1975 edn, 31).

This carefully arranged selection of spouses was to no avail: 'Danaus distributed hand-knives to his daughters' and all but Hypermnestra, who spared Lynceus because he had honored her virginity', 'slew their husbands as they lay sleeping' (Apollodorus 2.21–2, 1975 edn, 32). 'After Danaus, Lynceus ruled Argos', and Hypermnestra bore him a son, Abas, literally) father (Akkadian, *Abbu*; Arabic, *Abu*; Hebrew, *Abba*) in turn of twin sons, Acrisius and Proetus, who fought, divided 'all of Argeia between them and settled down, Acrisius lord of Argos, and Proetus lord of Tiryns' (Apollodorus 2.24–5, 1975 edn, 32). From this line of descendants of Inachus and Belus, descended both Perseus, who 'ruled Tiryns as well as Mideia and Mycenae, both of which he walled' (Apollodorus, 2.48, 1975 edn, 36), and Heracles, whose history and labours comprise what remains of Book 2 of Apollodorus (61–180, 1975 edn, 38–56). Perseus was the issue of Zeus's visitation 'in a shower of gold', to Danae, the daughter of Acrisius, shut up in a bronze chamber to forestall the prophecy that her son would kill her father. Acrisius, 'not believing that Zeus had seduced her ... cast his daughter out to sea with her son on an ark which drifted ashore at Seriphos, where Dictys recovered the child and brought him up' (Apollodorus 2.34–5, 1975 edn, 34). Among Perseus' adventures were the beheading of Medusa (2.40–2, 1975 edn, 35), and the freeing of his daughter Andromeda, 'laid out as a meal for a sea monster' in Ethiopia to fulfil a prophecy of the oracle of Amun at Siwa (Apollodorus 2.43–4, 1975 edn, 35). Perseus slaughtered the monster and rescued his daughter, as a blow for freedom in defiance of Eastern power, perhaps.

The labours of Heracles are hardly less famous, but in this case evidence abounds of syncretism between the legend of the local Argive hero and Mediterranean heroes of this name as far afield as Egypt and Cadiz (Brundage, 1958; Rose and Robertson, 1970b). That he was a hero, rather than a god, is attested by his name, which means 'Hera's glory', or 'gift of Hera'. Six of his labours identify him as being from the Peloponnese, perhaps a prince or baron of Tiryns under the overlordship of the king of Argos or Mycenae:

> The seventh, the Cretan Bull, and the eighth, the Horses of Diomedes ... are in or near the Greek world, but the other four are quite outside it, and so about equally

remote wherever we suppose Heracles' home to have been; they are (9) The Girdle of the Amazon, (10) Geryon, (11) Cerberus, (12) The Apples of the Hesperides. All of these last three are variants of one theme, the conquest of Death. (Rose and Robertson, 1970b, 498)

The specifics of this confrontation with death are of great interest: 'The hero must go to an island in the extreme west, Erytheia ['the red, or blushing one', i.e. sunset-coloured] and there overcome a triple-bodied monster, Geryon, and his attendants and take his cattle; or he must descend to the House of Hades and steal the infernal watch-dog; or finally, he must pluck the golden apples from the dragon-guarded tree at the world's end'. The reference to the 'West', identified with the After-world by the Egyptians, put Heracles' labours, like those of Odysseus in the category of the Egyptian Book of the Dead, a suggestion (Rose and Robertson, 1970b, 498) reinforced by the appearance of the 'infernal watch-dog', Jackal-headed Anubis, god of the Underworld. But elements from Mesopotamian epic cycles are evident too, leading Rose and Robertson to conclude (1970b, 498):

> All these are manifestly more elaborate forms of the simple and ancient tale that on one occasion Heracles met Hades and worsted him (*Il.* 5.395 ff, cf. Pind. *Ol.* 9.33). The fact that they are variants of one another indicates that the cycle of the twelve Labours is artificial, made up to the round number, familiar anywhere in the wide region which used the Babylonian sexegesimal counting, by including duplicates.

Apollodorus, having completed the chronicle of 'the family of Inachus to the Heracleidae' – the Dorians who adopted Heracles as their eponymous ancestor – in Book 2 of his *Library of Greek Mythology*, turns, in Book 3, to the family of Agenor, brother of Belus who ruled the Egyptians, born out of Libya by Poseidon. Agenor, who migrated to Phoenicia, married Telephassa, who bore him a daughter named Europa and sons: Cadmus, Phoenix and Cilix (Apollodorus 3.1–2, 1975 edn, 57). Europa, who may have been the daughter of Phoenix rather than Agenor, Apollodorus admits (3.2, 1975 edn, 57), was one of the many subjects of Zeus's attentions, and he visited her 'in the form of a gentle bull, put her on his back and carried her through the sea to Crete, where he slept with her'. Her mother and brothers, Telephassa, Cadmus, Cilix and (perhaps husband) Phoenix, went in search of her, but failing to find her, returned home, each settling in a different place: Phoenix in Phoenicia, Celix in Celicia, Cadmus and Telephassa in Thrace (Apollodorus 3.214, 1975 edn, 57), where Cadmus founded Thebes amid more cow and bull imagery. For, after the death of his mother Telephassa, Cadmus went to Delphi to consult the oracle about Europa:

> The god, however, told him not to bother about her, but rather to let a cow be his guide, and to found a polis wherever it grew tired and fell. With such an oracle in his possession, Cadmus journeyed through the Phocians' land, and came across a cow in the herds of Pelagon, which he trailed. It went across Boeotia and lay down where now the polis of Thebes is situated. Cadmus wanted to sacrifice the cow to Athena, and sent some of his men to fetch water from the spring of Ares, but a serpent, said by some to be a child of Ares, guarded the spring and destroyed most of those who had been sent. In outrage Cadmus killed the serpent, and then,

following the instructions of Athena, planted its teeth. From this sowing there sprang from the earth armed men, called Sparti. (Apollodorus 3.21, 1975 edn, 60)

Modern scholars give as the more likely derivation 'Spanish broom' or 'spartos'. In any event the area was more typically known from Homer on as Lakedaimon, dwelling place of Menelaus; its fabled twin kings, for whom we have king lists that date to 800 BC, being the product of Dorian synoecism, rationalized in the dual kingship of the Agiads and Euryponids (Woodward and Forrest, 1970, 1006–7). Once again, however, the mythological account, even at the point at which it alters the historical record, does so to incorporate eponyms that would fix in the memory historical associations easily lost in an oral tradition.

Europa, meanwhile, had born to Zeus the children Minos, Sarpedon and Rhademanthys, although Homer has Sarpedon as son of Zeus by Bellerophon's daughter Laodameia, Apollodorus acknowledges (3.3, 1975 edn, 57); and Diodorus (4.60.2 f) links him to the famous Trojan ally of the *Iliad*. Europa married the Cretan ruler Asterius to legitimize her children and Asterius himself died without issue (Apollodorus 3.4–5, 1975 edn, 29), to whose throne Minos, 'who lived in Crete and wrote laws, and married Pasiphae' (3.7, 1975 edn, 58), aspired, claiming divine right, for which he demanded Poseidon's sanction:

So while sacrificing to Poseidon, he prayed for a bull to appear from the depths of the sea, and promised to sacrifice it upon its appearance. And Poseidon did send up to him a splendid bull. Thus Minos received the rule, but he sent the bull to his herds and sacrificed another one. Minos was the first to gain control of the sea, and ruled over nearly all the islands. Poseidon was angry that the bull was not sacrificed, and turned it wild. He also devised that Pasiphae should develop a lust for it. In her passion for the bull she took on as her accomplice an architect named Daedalus, who had fled from Athens on a murder charge. He built a wooden cow on wheels ... skinned a real cow, and sewed the contraption into the skin, and then, after placing Pasiphae inside, set it in a meadow where the bull normally grazed. The bull came up and had intercourse with it, as if with a real cow. Pasiphae gave birth to Astrius, who was called Minotaurus. He had the face of a bull, but was otherwise human. Minos, following certain oracular instructions, kept him confined and under guard in the labyrinth. This labyrinth, which Daedalus built, was a 'cage with convoluted flexions that disorders debouchment'. (Apollodorus 3.8–11, 1975 edn, 58)

Apollodorus promises to tell the story of the Minotaur later, in his account of Theseus, and moves on to tell of Minos's children, bedevilled by oracles, cow, dog and snake images (Apollodorus 3.13–20, 1975 edn, 59–60).

The exploits of the children of Cadmus are hardly less fantastic; for 'Athena provided Cadmus with the sovereignty, and Zeus gave him Harmonia, daughter of Aphrodite and Ares, as a wife. Then all the gods left the sky for a wedding feast in the Cadmeia, where they sang hymns' (Apollodorus 3.25; 1975 edn, 60). Semele his daughter, being 'visited' by Zeus, died of fright at Hera's retribution – another visitation from Zeus, this time in the form of an electrical storm (Apollodorus 3.27, 1975 edn, 61). Semele's aborted baby was sewn by Zeus into his thigh for further incubation and, 'at the proper time Zeus loosed the stitches and gave birth to Dionysus, whom he entrusted to Hermes' (Apollodorus 3.28,

1975 edn, 61). After considerably more deer, goat and dog transformations, and retributions from Hera, we learn that 'Dionysus was the discoverer of the grapevine' and, in madness inflicted by Hera, 'wandered over Egypt and Syria', where he was purified by 'mystic rites of initiation', thence becoming master of a cult that spread with him to Thrace and Grecian Thebes.

8

Foundation Myths and their Modes

Recent accounts of mythology, of which we have a plethora (Fontenrose, 1971; Kirk, 1975; Detienne, 1977; O'Flaherty, 1980; Gimbutas, 1982, 1989; Vernant, 1982, 1983; Lefkowitz, 1986), vary greatly with respect to their claims. Uncovering the truth of myth is an ancient project, as we will see, and there have been those who reduce it to history *tout court*, and those who reject the historical or ritual theory of myth in equally short order (Fontenrose, 1971). Of recent treatments, leaving aside for the moment feminist accounts (Gimbutas, 1982; Arthur, 1983; Bergren, 1983; Springborg, 1990d), the most convincing in its treatment of myth as a genre of truth is the study by the distinguished Romanist, Paul Veyne (1988), *Did the Greeks Believe in their Myths?*, first published in French in 1983. According to Veyne (1988, 28), myth is a *tertium quid*, a third way, neither exactly fact nor wholly fiction. The world of myth was that familiar world into which one was inducted by mothers and nurses, of tales told before going to sleep, and songs sung, about ghosts, goblins, centaurs and minotaurs: 'the heroes were only men, to whom credulity had lent supernatural traits' (Veyne, 1988, 42–3). The world of myth was the world of the marvellous, the astounding, of creatures both man-like and god-like, but it was not a fictitious realm. Its analogue is still the supernatural realm of the oriental religions, full of saints and martyrs, miracles and apparitions, divine birth, heroic life, death and resurrection. It was the religious realm of antiquity.

Moreover, its treatment in written texts was analogous to the treatment of religious authorities by the pre-Reformation Christian church. Myth, as Veyne (1988, 11) states, was the 'vulgate' of antiquity, it was endlessly repeated, ancient authorities being reverently cited without acknowledgement, respected as men who could not tell a lie. Even among the Sceptics, of whom there were always some, and in increasing numbers as the tradition developed, myths contained truth. But where, and in what proportion to the accretions of falsity, was the question. Pausanias, who belongs among the critics, and yet took the trouble to travel throughout Greece to collect its myths and record them (Veyne, 1988, 46), 'in the eighth of the ten books that make up his great work ... finally writes':

> When I began to write my history, I was inclined to count these legends as foolishness; but on getting as far as Arcadia I grew to hold a more thoughtful view of them, which is this: in the days of old, those Greeks who were considered wise

spoke their sayings not straight out but in riddles, and so the legends about Cronos I conjectured to be one sort of Greek wisdom. (Pausanias 8.8.3, cited in Veyne, 1988, 11)

There came a stage in the development of the tradition when aristocratic doubt emerged in the face of popular credulity, a development that corresponded to the emergence of 'professional centers of truth' (Veyne, 1988, 31). Mythographers prefaced their claims with the phrase 'men say'. Herodotus, who with Aristotle, Xenophanes and Pausanias belonged to those who express 'aristocratic lack of credulity' (Veyne, 1988, 31), went further, declaring, 'My business is to record what people say; but I am by no means bound to believe it – and that may be taken to apply to this book as a whole' (Herodotus 7.152.3, cited in Veyne, 1988, 12).

While the critical school cast doubt on the 'absolute objectivity' of classical texts, aristocratic doubt and popular credulity did not run on entirely separate tracks. Many of the doubters, while expressing general scepticism in one breath, asserted historical veracity with respect to particulars, in another. Thus Pausanias (1.3.3, cited in Veyne, 1988, 13) insists:

There are many false beliefs current among the mass of mankind, since they are ignorant of historical science and consider trustworthy whatever they have heard from childhood in choruses and tragedies; one of these is about Theseus, who in fact himself became king, and afterwards, when Menestheus was dead, the descendants of Theseus remained rulers even to the fourth generation.

Scrupulous in flagging suspect mythic items with the phrases 'people say that' or 'according to what people believe' (Veyne, 1988, 52), Aristotle nevertheless stands firm on certain mythically expressed facts. Like Pausanias (Veyne, 1988, 14, 133, n.23), 'Aristotle does not doubt the historicity of Theseus; he sees in him the founder of Athenian democracy (*Constitution of Athens* 41.2) and reduces to verisimilitude the myth of the Athenian children deported to Crete and delivered to the Minotaur ([Aristotle] *Constitution of the Bottiaeans*, cited by Plutarch, Life of Theseus 16.2).' Theseus and the Minotaur may have been historically privileged as we shall later see. Veyne goes on to point out: 'As for the Minotaur, more than four centuries before Pausanias the historian Philochorus also reduced him to verisimilitude'; he claimed to have found a tradition (he does not specify whether it is oral or transcribed) among the Cretans according to which these children were not devoured by the Minotaur but were given as prizes to the victors in a gymnastic competition; this contest being won by a cruel and very vigorous man named Taurus (cited by Plutarch 16.1). 'Since this Taurus commanded the army of Minos, he was really the Tauros of Minos: Minotaur', Veyne (1988, 133–4, n.23) ingeniously suggests, confirming perhaps the analysis of Bernal (1987a, 64) concerning the Minotaur, the labyrinth and the bull cult of Min in Crete.

Thucydides, who along with Polybius was one of those who generally recorded only 'technically safe information that will always produce data useful to politicians and military men' (Veyne, 1988, 12), and castigated the historian Timaeus as ' "full of dreams, prodigies, incredible tales, and, to put it shortly, craven superstition and womanish love of the marvellous" ' (Polybius 12.24.5, cited in Veyne, 1988, 46), believed in the historicity of Theseus too. To give another example of an euhemerizing thinker, who nevertheless retains some belief in myths, Cicero, whom Veyne (1988, 49) refers to as 'religiously cold', while in the *Republic* (2.2.4 and 10.18, cited in Veyne, 1988, 50) professing disbelief in the supposed parentage of Romulus as 'son of a god who had impregnated a Vestal Virgin', and in *De Legibus* casting doubt on the supposed epiphany of Rome's divinized founder king, in the *Republic* however maintains 'that Rome is enough of a big city for people to respect the tale with which she adorned her origins' (Veyne, 1988, 83).

For what was the truth of myth if it was not history overlaid with falsity? 'All through the ages, many events that occurred in the past, and even some that occur today, have been generally discredited because of the lies built up on a foundation of fact ... Those who like to listen to the miraculous are themselves apt to add to the marvel, and so they ruin truth by mixing it with falsehood' (Pausanias 7.2.6–7, cited in Veyne, 1988, 59). And the older the historical tradition, the more *mythodes* encumbering it. Myth, as most mythographers were aware, was a search for origins and the aetiology of cities. The reason why myth could not be fiction or lies was because it was generated in the pursuit of truth. Menander, the Alexandrian rhetorician, in *On the Discourses of the Apparatus* (*Rhetores Graeci*, vol. 3: 359, cited in Veyne, 1988, 51), noting that different cities owe their origins to the eponymous god, hero or man, respectively, who founded them, went on to say: 'of these different etiologies, those which are divine or heroic are legendary [*mythodes*], and those which are human are more worthy of belief.'

Myth was not generated, however, in the pursuit of an unsituated truth, which is why the rhetorician played such a large part in its development. Myth provided the personality of cities by endowing them with a fabulous history. This is why Plato could castigate Homer, Hesiod and the poets, privileged as mythographers, 'for it is they, undoubtedly, who gave men these false tales' (Plato, *Republic*, 377D, cited in Veyne, 1988, 61). Plato has much to say about the frightening tales told by nurses and mothers (*Republic*, 378C, *Laws*, 887D, cited in Veyne, 1988, 139, n.56), and we know that the nurse, or suckling goddess of love, influenced men in other undesirable ways. But, generally, the tales the nurses and mothers told were not regarded as false, even if they were not true in the same way that tales about ordinary mortals were true. They told symptomatic truths that had been handed down glorifying the past, creating out of eponymous gods and heroes worthy ancestors for great cities. As Plutarch says: 'truth and myth have the same relationship as the sun to the rainbow, which dissipates light into an iridescent variety' (Plutarch, *De Iside*, 20.358F, cited in Veyne, 1988, 66; see also Plotinus, *Enneads*, 3.3.9, 24; and Springborg, 1990d, 178). The aetiological truth of myths was something that Machiavelli (*Prince*, ch. 61, *Discourses*, 3.30, cited in Veyne, 1988, 66) understood when he maintained that history (*mythodes?*) was 'the politics of olden times', full of recognizable types, whether its sources be Biblical, Greek, Roman or Persian, its heroes Moses, Cyrus, Romulus or Theseus, its cities Israelite, Roman, Persian or Greek.

The context in which myth was created enables us to see why even the most critical historians could not give it all away:

In 480 B.C., the day after their triumph over the Persians at Salamis, the Greeks convened a congress. The definitive victory was in sight, and already Athens, which had saved all of Hellas from the barbarians, appeared as the hegemonical city. It had the power and possessed the language for it. When another city decided to oppose to this new primacy its own traditional privileges, the Athenians replied that their own rights were no less ancient. For Athens had been victorious in the times of the Heraclidae, the wars recounted in the *Thebaid*, and the invasion of the Amazons. Everyone understood what the speechifying meant, and Athens won its case. The mythical titles had served to designate relations of force by justifying them. Is this an ideological cover? The relationship is not one of superposition, as that between a blanket and what lies beneath. It is the relationship between the paper money of words and the gold depository of power. Was it a threat couched in praise? It was more than that. By referring to lofty reasons instead of making a show of force, one encourages the other to submit willingly and for honorable reasons, which saves face. Ideology is not a mere echo of reality; it works like a coin inserted in a machine. In international society, mythical titles to glory, as well as legendary kinship among peoples, served as ceremonial salutes. Each city would state its legendary origins to its partners, who took care not to be skeptical. It was a way of affirming oneself as a person. The society of cities thus was composed of noble persons who had their bonds of kinship. Accepting these fictions as articles of faith signaled recognition of the rules of the international life of civilized cities. (Veyne, 1988, 80)

Now we know why so often in the stories of the battle of the giants the historical outcome is reversed to favour the Greeks over the barbarians; and why Herodotus could openly admit that 'the Greeks have many stories with no basis of fact. One of the silliest is the story of how Heracles came to Egypt and was taken away by the Egyptians to be sacrificed to Zeus' (Herodotus 2.45, 1972 edn, 147, cited in Dossa, 1987, 345; and Veyne, 1988, 32). Why the content of myth should take the form of genealogies is a story in itself:

> But why was the thread of time genealogical? Because myths recount the biographies of heroes, kings, and archetypes. This old oral literature spoke only of origins, foundations, and warlike exploits, of family dramas with princely actors. We have seen that archetypes, such as Hellen or Pelasgus, were considered ancient kings the moment that myth was interpreted as historical tradition. The history of the city was the history of its royal family. The heroes, too, were princely personalities. It was concluded from this that 'everywhere in Greece of ancient times, kingship and not democracy was the established form of government' (Paus. 9.1.2). (Veyne, 1988, 32)

It would seem, in fact, that there are important differences to be found between foundation literatures of monarchies and republics. It is not so much that kingship was archetypal, even for the Greek democracies – although it was – as that the search for origins required a credible account of the settling together of the eponymous tribes or *ethnai* out of which the *polis* was constituted. And this is precisely what the *Theogony* of Hesiod, the dramas of Aeschylus and Euripides, for instance, do give – a quasi-factual account of the creation of the gods, kings, their subsequent exploits and dynastic struggles; and, the settlement of the Greek cities, in some cases by colonizers of Afro-Asiatic origins: Cadmus the Phoenician and Danaus the Egyptian. Synoicism, Max Weber pointed out, as the settling together of tribes, is a characteristic process of state formation for republics; and the Eastern Mediterranean, in which republicanism was born, was traditionally inhabited by a plurality of tribal groupings (Weber, 1968, vol. 3: 1285).

The great epic literature to which it gave rise in the epic cycles of Mesopotamia, including the epic of Gilgamesh, the Homeric poems, and Ugaritic epic – probably the bridge between them – along with their successors, the various works of the Old Testament, was, as one scholar has pointed out, literature of national unity for essentially heterogeneous societies (Gordon, 1953, 54–6). Thus the *Iliad* of Homer and the Pentateuch, as epic stories of ethnic integration, were probably designed to be read aloud in their entirety at periodic comings-together of the tribes. The heroic theme of the unity of mankind, which they celebrate, was no mere endorsement of abstract virtue. It was a polemical principle on which the life of the ethnically divided nation depended. The dream of national unity which they promise was brought to fruition in the programme of Alexander.

The great monarchies arose, by contrast, in ethnically homogeneous realms. Their literature demonstrates a certain anti-heroism (Gresseth, 1975, 12–13), being described as the earliest manifestations of humanism, involving desacralization of the hero and his confinement within distinctly human bounds. The characteristic literature of the early monarchies records the perigrinations of a hero, whose eventual return to hearth and homeland has no parallel in the tragic or heroic epics of the *Iliad* or the Pentateuch, but a curious parallel in the *Odyssey* as a synthesis of earlier literary traditions which the author of the Homeric poems co-opted (Gordon, 1953, 56–7; Gresseth, 1975, 13–15). The Egyptian epics of Wenamon, Sinuhe and the ship-wrecked sailor, share point-by-point similarities with the *Odyssey*, while the Labours of Heracles, in its various versions, shares the same parallels of detail with the Epic of Gilgamesh and its Sumerian predecessors (Brundage, 1958, 225–36). Lacking the imperative which gave urgency to the heroic literature of national integration – or perhaps having experienced it in a much earlier period – the literature of monarchy celebrated more pacific virtues: the homely values of the hearth and love of fatherland, not to speak of the desire to entertain (Gordon, 1953, 58–9).

That the Homeric poems could straddle both traditions is evidence both of their eclectic nature as a synthesis of a large body of ethnically shared folk tales; and further attests that the distance between the monarchical and republican traditions at this stage was not great. East Mediterranean society, whether essentially monarchical or republican, exhibited a large noble caste, for and by whom the epic poems were written. Not until much later – Egyptian Middle Kingdom – did its literatures embrace the causes of the common man. Geopolitical conditions, and the differences between a heterogeneous and homogeneous population base, determined whether these nobles were capable of uniting to produce a unified kingdom or not, and whether its form would be monarchical, or turn on the power sharing of notables.

The Homeric aristocracy shared much of its Minoan–Mycenaean past, which brought it close to the Mesopotamian antecedents of these cultures; and probably more than it shared with Greek democracy of a later age. These common characteristics include rule by a noble class in an essentially agrarian society;

heroic values expressed in an epic literature; charismatic kingship and dynastic instability; legitimization for status purposes by pedigree and genealogy; traditions of hospitality, gift-exchange and guest friendship; and the high status of women (Gordon, 1953, 64–81; Finley, 1954, 1955). Recurrent themes in epic literature reflecting these social realities include the 'curse of Cain' motif and banishment incurred by the killing of one's kinsman, testimony to the governing value of fratriarchy. Unlike the later democratic age, this male dominance was paralleled by evidence of sororarchy (Gordon, 1953, 94–5) and the heroization of women, either quasi-immortal like the ageless Sarah of the Old Testament, or conferring immortality, like the suckling goddess who nurses the king in the mythologies of Hathor and Isis of Egypt (Gordon, 1953, 64–5; Springborg, 1990a). Magnification of the virtues of women, braver in battle than men, was a recurrent theme of which the Amazons are only one example (Gordon, 1953, 78–9). The heroization of noble males and females compares with the romanticization of the male–female relationship that one encounters in the literature of the sedentary civilizations of Egypt and Mesopotamia, where *Frauengeschichte* tend to focus on the 'stolen belle' and her rescue by the hero (Gordon, 1953, 80–81).

Charismatic kingship of the Eastern Mediterranean aristocratic regimes was unstable compared with the great monarchies of Babylon and Egypt, but these different societies shared a belief in the divine nature of kings and their divine election, signified by the suckling goddess (Gordon, 1953, 64; Springborg, 1990d, ch. 10). Correspondingly, belief that the behaviour and deportment of kings was of cosmic significance affecting every aspect of the realm: weather, harvest yield, the material and spiritual well-being of subjects, was common to both types of society (Gordon, 1953, 65). Plato tells us, citing Pindar in the *Meno* 81b–c (1956 edn, 129), about the solar origins of divine kings, from whom all bounty flows:

> Persephone requires requital for ancient doom,
> In the ninth year she restores again
> Their souls to the sun above.
> From whom rise noble kings
> And the swift in strength and greatest in wisdom;
> And for the rest of time
> They are called heroes and sanctified by men.

Perhaps the best account of the Cadmus legend, and one of the oldest in modern scholarship, is the long essay by Gomme (1913, 53–72, 223–45), written in refutation. Referring to earlier work (1911, 1912), where he 'endeavoured to show that the geography of Boeotia lends no support to the theory that the Cadmeans were Phoenicians', Gomme feels obliged, nevertheless, to account for the development of the legend: 'Yet from the fifth century onward at least, there was a firmly established and, as far as we know, universally accepted tradition that they were – a tradition indeed lightly put aside by most modern scholars as unimportant' (1913, 53). Concluding that 'if the arguments from geography are sound, then this traditon must be learned theory, and theory only', Gomme nevertheless expresses appropriate reservations about his conclusions: 'That this is so cannot of course be proved; for the authors by whom it was established, if it was established, are lost to us. We cannot even show, for this theory itself, that it is probable; for the methods even of Herodotus, and his reasons for his theories, are often obscure.' Gomme's argument constitutes, then, an assertion of the legend's improbability on geographical grounds, but an affirmation of its universality. His exegesis is of considerable interest; showing a development in the critical attitude to myth consistent with Veyne's very recent account; and postulating the elaboration of oriental eponyms and genealogies belonging to that process. In other words, what we have in those authors who put particular emphasis on the literal truth of Cadmus being Phoenician and Danaus being Egyptian, is an 'improvement' in the truth of the myths by logographers, who had travelled widely and were critical of the insularity of Hesiod and Homer, both of whom give hints to the origins of the Cadmeans and Danaeans as being Phoenician and Egyptian, but no positive identification. Personally, Gomme (1913, 55) rejects the suggestion that the Cadmean legend in Hesiod's *Theogony* and the 'Catalogues' might be only a local Boeotian tradition: 'The *Theogony* and the fragments are cosmopolitan.'

Among the poets and mythographers a growing proportion of their material was constituted out of the oriental genealogies. Aeschylus wrote the Egyptian trilogy, the *Supplices, Aegyptii* and *Danaides*, of which only the first survives. Euripides, author of his own *Supplices, Medea*, the *Bacchae* and *Phoenissae*, states boldly the Phoenician origins of Cadmus in the introduction to the *Phrixus*, ignores it in the *Supplices*, mentions it in the *Bacchae*, where Cadmus is a central character and the whole play is designed to show the oriental origins of Dionysus; and 'no less emphatic is he in the *Phoenissae*: the title suggests the theory, and he harps on it throughout' (Gomme, 1913, 68–9). Gomme believes that insistence on the historical truth of the Cadmus legend is a point with Euripides; his statement in the *Phrixus* 'is clear and emphatic: Euripides wished to make the theory known to the audience.' Moreover, 'Euripides wrote other plays concerning the House of Cadmus', including the *Chrysippus*, 'but fragments relevant to the present question have not survived' (Gomme, 1913, 69). 'In one play, perhaps the *Andromeda*, he called Cepheus and Phineus sons of Belus, and brothers of Aegyptus and Danaus, and so brought them into the Cadmean genealogy' (Gomme, 1913, 69).

Giving the genealogies and their variations contained in Hesiod (Gomme, 1913, 54), the late epic poet Asius of Samos (Gomme, 1913, 58) and the Scholiast on Euripides *Phoenissae* (Gomme, 1913, 59, n.38), as well as the genealogy contained in the 'Homeric Hymn to Dionysus', Gomme (1913, 60) concludes that in the early poets, although we have most of the elements of the legend of Cadmus as a Phoenician, 'all of which may have been originally in the Hesiodic or Cyclic epic ... it is as yet inchoate'. But as soon as 'we come to consider the evidence of the Logographi, we arrive almost at once at the fully developed Phoenician theory' (Gomme, 1913, 61); that is to say, in the works of Hecataeus, Hellanicus, Josephus and particularly Herodotus.

Pointing out that 'the object of the logographi, according to the now generally received opinion, was only to write down the legends of the Epic in prose', Gomme (1913, 223) shows, in fact, that a critical posture accompanied this transition. He suggests that the criticism of the logographers may not be an isolated instance: 'it is still possible that the fifth century writers represent an older and better tradition than the poets before them' (Gomme, 1913, 223); a subject on which the authorities differ. Clement of Alexandria declared that the Greek authors shamelessly copied from one another without acknowledgement, Homer borrowing from Orpheus, Hesiod from Musaeus, Aristophanes from Craninus, Plato from Comicus, Comicus from Plato, and so on (Gomme, 1913, 224). Josephus argued just the opposite: 'It is foolish to suppose that the Greeks alone know anything about antiquity; for they have no old records, as the Egyptians, Chaldeans and Phoenicians have; and they learnt even their letters late, and boast of taking them from Cadmus and his Phoenicians' (cited in Gomme, 1913, 224). But Dionysus of Halicarnassus gave a taxonomy of the practitioners of *historia* down to Herodotus that is quite impressive:

> I will say a word or two about the predecessors of Thucydides, to show the pre-eminence of the latter. There were many ancient writers in different parts of Greece before the Peloponnesian War; among them Eugeon of Samos, Deiochus of Proconessus, Eudemus of Miletus, Damocles of Phygaleia, Hecataeus of Miletus, Acusilaus of Argos, Charon of Lampsacus, and Melesagoras of Chalcedon. Nearer Thucydides' own day were Hellanicus of Lesbos, Damastes of Sigeum, Xenomedes of Chios, Zanthus the Lydian ... They wrote in a simple unaffected style, with no elaboration ... Herodotus was the first to write a complete history in a suitable style. (Dionysus of Halicarnassus *de Thuc. iudic.* 5, cited in Gomme, 1913, 225)

That the logographers took a complex but independent stance toward the Epic tradition is something for which we have evidence. Dionysus of Halicarnassus claimed that the historians 'neither added to nor took away from the records which they copied' (*de Thuc. iudic.* 5, cited in Gomme, 1913, 225; cf 23 for the genuineness of writings attributed to still earlier authors). Strabo talks about 'the value of myths in early training, how even the cities and the lawgivers sanctioned them'. But 'when he says that the logographi, dropping the metre, preserved the poetic, he is referring, not to their treatment of the myths of the Epic, but to their love of the marvellous, their recounting of miracles, their tales of one-eyed men, of dog-headed [Anubis?] and headless men with eyes in their chests, wild men and women ... stories that Herodotus would not swallow' (Gomme, 1913, 226, citing Strabo, 1.2,6; Herodotus, 4.191, 4.13, 32).

Hecataeus in his *Genealogiae* is representative of the more scientific approach. He was not one who conceived his task merely to render in prose the contents of the Epic cycle:

> Rather it is clear that his interest is to correct the errors of the Greeks, and substitute for them scientific theory. We may guess that one of those errors was the attribution of the invention of writing to Palamedes; Hecataeus had been to Egypt and knew better; he had seen in Egyptian Thebes inscriptions far older than Palamedes, and lists of priests that put to shame his own claim to be descended from a god in sixteen generations. It was Danaus who introduced writing into Greece, from Egypt. (Gomme, 1913, 227)

The fifth century was a turning point and the silence of Pindar, Aeschylus and Sophocles on the Phoenician origins of Cadmus, along with the insistence on it by Herodotus and Euripides, may have meant 'that the theory had not long been formulated, nor as yet universally accepted' (Gomme, 1913, 72). Gomme gives more attention than most to the credentials of Herodotus: 'for he was a painstaking man, not easily credulous ... learning from interpreters the meaning of inscriptions'; and again: 'the results of his *historia* are the *logoi*' (Gomme, 1913, 229). This does not mean, however, that Herodotus, more than any other ancient historian, felt obliged to disclose his sources, for the very reasons we have already discussed: 'But though he tells us that where his inference differs from popular tradition, it is the result not of an arbitrary judgement but of deep enquiry, he seldom lets us know what line his enquiries took; though we may often infer it' (Gomme, 1913, 229). Thus, 'his assertion that the names of nearly all the Greek gods came from abroad [Herodotus, 2.50] ... we may reasonably infer to be based on "enquiries" of the priestesses at Dodona; for originally the Pelasgians had no names for their gods ... and only learnt their origins and forms the other day, as it were [Herodotus, 2.52, 53]' (Gomme, 1913, 229–30).

Gomme has made an excellent case for the universality of the Cadmus myth, and the even better credentials of the myth of Danaus the Egyptian and efforts of historians to 'improve' their 'veracity': 'Closely parallel [to the myth of Cadmus] is that of Aegyptus and Danaus; and it has a far more respectable history, going back to Hesiod [Frr. 24–5] and the Epic [*Danais*]; it was like others accepted by the logographi' (Gomme, 1913, 240). Is it then sufficient for Gomme to conclude that in fact these myths were merely fabrications to provide a cosmopolitan ancestry for Greek heroes?: Gomme, citing an earlier scholar Macan (Note, vol. 5, p. 58), concludes rather cautiously:

> The Egyptian origin of the Hercleids, is, perhaps, largely a product of the attempt to connect the Greeks and their civilization with the oldest and wisest folk of antiquity, of which we have other examples in the Dodona legend, and the Egyptian origin of the Hellenic nomenclature of the Deities. At the same time it should be recognized that not merely tradition but archaeology points to a real intercourse between Egypt and Greece, particularly Argos, long before the days of Psamatik I. The Phoenicians may have been the carriers or go-betweens in a later 'middle-age', but the probabilities now point more and more to a belief in early movements and intercourse between Europe and Egypt, though it is not at present credible that any Egyptian dynasty was established in Greece. (Gomme, 1913, 241)

9

Philological Evidence: Gods, Goddesses and Place Names

Extreme caution is, of course, required in the extrapolation of historical material from the oral tradition of myth preserved in the ancient epic cycle. As Michael Astour, percipient analyst of myth, has remarked (1967a, 69–70): 'In the absence of regular analistic records and of uninterrupted continuity of written tradition, it is hard to expect that late constructions of poets, mythographers and logographers should correctly render facts about the rise and political history of ancient tribes and realms which have perished long ago in historic changes and catastrophes.' And yet, the very form and content of the myths are symptomatic in their own right:

> The basic keepers of the tradition were priests and temple personnel, as the intellectually most developed class of that time – but, in conformity with their function of cult attendants, this tradition was not a political, but a religious one. What they kept and transmitted from generation to generation were myths, poems, and dramatic mysteries about gods and divine heroes with whom the cult of the given temples was connected. Such myths and legends had more chance of being preserved during the centuries. (Astour, 1967a, 70)

What myth reveals is not statements of historical fact. The form and function of myth forbid such a banal interpretation. For if the great epics of the Mesopotamian and Homeric epic cycles – and of the Bible, in the same tradition, as Gordon (1953) has so persuasively argued – constituted a literature of national liberation to be read aloud on occasions of national celebration, the mythological content represented the sacral interpretation of ethnic and cultic origins, mediated by a long oral transmission chain. We would not expect, therefore, to find factual material as such. What we do find, by what is termed '*the method of relics* ... [are] vestigial motifs which do not [necessarily] play a rôle in the preserved version of the myth and whose very occurrence there is not justified, but which do have a sense and a justification in other versions of the basic theme, known from other sources' that may be epigraphic, archaeological or historical (Astour, 1967a, 70–1):

> On the other hand, most myths – even if they are but tales about astral, elemental or chthonic deities – reflect in certain measure the historical epoch and the geographic environment where they were born. Precisely in this respect, in an indirect way, they are precious for the modern investigator. The details of the story

may be, in the main, the free creation of poets who worked on old mythical material; but the thematic pivot which often has analogies in the myths of other peoples can be separated, and its comparative analysis can reveal its origin. (Astour, 1967a, 70)

Astour demonstrates the use of such a methodology to produce startling insights into the coincidences of content in the Greek Danaus myth, the West Semitic Ugaritic hero Danel, and the Biblical epic of the tribe of Dan. The Ugaritic connection, made possible only by the discovery of the Ras Shamra tablets, excavated in 1929 in Northern Syria from the ancient capital of Ugarit, is particularly important as providing the locale of Hellenic and Semitic encounter in a great trading centre that linked Mesopotamia, Phoenicia, Syria and the Aegean. The Biblical Daniel (Ezek. 14.14; 28.3), is both referred to as a judge and compared to a serpent (Gen. 49. 16–17), which puts him in line with the 'agrarian–chthonic personage' of the Ugaritic Aqht epic, responsible at once for fertility, the harvests, threshing-floors and vineyards; and at the same time, soothsayer, healer connected to the underworld, and judge (1 Aqht 24–5; 2 Aqht 5.7–8, cited in Astour, 1967a, 71–2). Parallels to the Argive Danaus are not lacking either: the Danaids, his daughters, found springs to water the lands, and carried water in bottomless buckets as a punishment for killing their husbands; in the underworld they represented both the water-carriers of Hades and the souls of those who had not been initiated into the Orphic mysteries (Astour, 1967a, 73).

The Ugaritic Aqht epic involves the daughter of Danel in a vengeance plot with strong similarities to the daughters of Danaus: concealing a knife in her clothing, she visits her brother, Aqht's murderer, and drinks wine with him, at which point the epic breaks off (Astour, 1967a, 74). In the Biblical 'Shechem myth' (Gen. 34, cited in Astour, 1967a, 75), a further element is present: Dinah (feminine form of Dan) is raped by Shechem, who wants not only to marry her but to arrange a clan inter-marriage between the Jacobites and the Shechemites (Astour, 1967a, 75–6). In this case the vengeance is slightly more complicated than the case of the 50 sons of Aegyptus and the 50 daughters of Danaus. Jacob's sons demand the sons of Shechem be circumcised preliminary to their marriage and, while they are incapacitated, kill them all – an early version of the ubiquitous Mediterranean tale of luring lambs to the slaughter with women, good food and strong wine.

Astour notes both the durability of, and discrepancies in, the skeletal theme between the Ugaritic and the Greek versions of the Danaus/Danel epic, due in no small part to the Aqht poem having been composed some 900 years before the first composition of the Greek version in Aeschylus' *Suppliants*, of around 479–2 BC. Quite simply, some of the detail of the Aqht version had dropped out, for instance, the motif of Aqht's murder. Astour's explanation (1967, 76) of the multiplication of the Aegyptiads and Danaids, in the form of 50 sons and daughters, corresponding to the weeks of the lunar year, is especially ingenious. He points out (Astour, 1967a, 78) that in the *Odyssey* (XII, 129–30) too, where Helios is credited with 7 herds of 50 cows and 7 herds of 50 sheep, the analogue to the days and weeks of the lunar year is transparent. Actaeon, the harvest god in the Aqht epic is torn apart by 50 dogs, and Heracles, the sun hero is said to have deflowered and impregnated 50 daughters of the king Thespios in one night, signifying the year-cycle as much as his own potency. It is not surprising that the Danaids, connected to the agricultural cycle too, should have represented its numerology, but what is interesting to note is that: 'in the final count, the symbolical figure 50 is also of Oriental origin; the Greeks did not count in seven-day weeks, while the Babylonians and the Western Semites did' – hence 'the Biblical agrarian jubilee cycle of 50 years ($7 \times 7 + 1$) to which the same chronological pattern applies', and the standard military unit of 50 customary among the Western Semites and the Arabs (Astour, 1967a, 78).

How does the Danaus/Danel myth relate to Egypt then, whence the Danaans are said in Greek tradition to have come? Astour argues on philological grounds that the Io myth belongs to the West Asian, rather than the Egyptian cultural complex. Io, signifying 'moon' in Argos, from *ienai*, to wander, is a transliteration, he suggests, of the Western Semitic (Ugaritic *arh*, Akkadian *arhu*) 'wild cow or heifer', from the root (Akkadian *arahu*, Hebrew *arah*), 'to wander, hasten, move fast' (Astour, 1967a, 84). Akkadian myths of Babylonia record the coupling of the moon-god Sin with a beautiful cow Amat-Sin (maidservant of the moon-god) to produce an offspring, Amarga, 'suckling calf'. The Hurrians, nearby, have a similar tale of the sun-god infatuated with a heifer, who gives birth to a human child, reared by a childless fisherman and his wife (Astour, 1967a, 85). In an Ugaritic version, the poem of Baal's hunt, the heroine, 'maidservant of the moon', banished to the desert by her mistress, the supreme goddess Asherah, wife of El, bears 'bull-like children with faces like Baal' (*Ugaritic Manual*, I.30–33, 1953 edn, 75). Astour (1967a, 86) notes the parallel with the story of the Biblical Hagar – 'from the Arabic *hagara* "to flee, to emigrate" ... etymologically equivalent to *arh* "heifer" of the Ugaritic myths (from *arahu*) and to *Io* (from *ienai*)'. Hagar, pregnant by Sarah's husband Abraham, flees to the desert to escape the vengeance of her mistress and gives birth to Ishmael, in Gen. 16.12, an 'onager' or wild man (from the Greek 'onagros', wild ass (Astour, 1967a, 86). Hagar, curiously, is presented as an Egyptian; Io settled in Egypt; while the names Hathor and Hagar are etymologically similar, suggesting that the link to Egypt may be closer than Astour allows.

Ugarit has a myth about the mating of god and heifer preserved in three variants, all of which involve Baal; and, in two, the goddess Anath, possibly transformed as a heifer, 'bears a Bull to Baal, yea a buffalo to the Rider of the Clouds' (*Ugaritic Manual*, 76, cited in Astour, 1967a, 87). Elsewhere, in a hymn to Anath, where she is involved in the mutilation of young men, she is called a heifer, whose son, born to Baal is named 'the Royal Appointee', 'the first born appointee', 'healer of Baal', 'the healing Lord', who as chief of the spirits of the Netherworld in his subsequent role, is often referred to as 'the young one' (Astour, 1967a, 88). The Ugaritic myth is strikingly similar to the older Sumerian myth of Enlil and Ninlil, Enlil being banished to the Netherworld for having seduced Ninlil, who follows in search of him. Enlil, to save the offspring of Ninlil, his child Nanna (Sin), from imprisonment in the Underworld, first assumes the shape of the Gatekeeper, god of the Netherworld, to impregnate her with the chthonic god Ninazu – reminiscent of Uranus, who kept reimpregnating Gaia to prevent her children being born; going on to assume the shapes of the god of the river and the ferry-man to impregnate her with more chthonic gods. In the later Akkadian texts Ninlil is described as 'the lordly Wild Cow, the most heroic among the goddesses', who 'was butting my enemies with her mightly horns', 'a description which would fit Anath as well' (Astour, 1967a, 89), while Ninazu, 'the lord healer', corresponds to Anath's son in the Ugaritic version, 'Royal Appointee', 'healer of Baal'.

There are further Biblical parallels in the reference to the son of Baal and the heifer of one version of the Ugaritic myth (*Ugaritic Manual*, 67, cited in Astour, 1967a, 89) as *Mš*, for which there is no local explanation, but which corresponds to the Egyptian *mš*, 'child', and also the Sumero–Babylonian Muš or serpent god. Astour (1967a, 89, n.4) notes that '*Mš* is basically the same name as the Hebrew *Moše*, Moses – and the close connection of Moses with the serpent-motif is well known' (Griffiths, 1953). The ancestry of the Israelites includes Leah, whose name means 'wild cow', from the Akkadian *li'tu*, *littu* (feminine form of *li'u*, 'wild bull') (Astour, 1967a, 90). The same epithet appears in the name of a Canaanite goddess and the king of the Phoenician city of Arwad under Sennacherib: *Abdi-li'ti*, meaning son of the 'wild cow', 'strong one', etc. One of Leah's sons, and perhaps the pre-eminent, 'was Levi (*Lewi*), whose name strikingly resembles that of the mythical serpent Leviathan (*Lewyatan*) and was repeatedly explained as "serpent" (from the root *lwy* "to coil")' (Astour, 1967a, 90). Furthermore:

> The Israelite priests, who were also oracle-explainers and physicians, claimed descent from Levi, and the most important of Levi's descendants, the head and organizer of the Levite priestdom, was Moses, the possessor of a miraculous serpent-staff and the creator of the healing bronze serpent on a stake. The sons of Leah migrated to Egypt – among them Levi – and were brought out from there by Moses, Levi's fourth generation descendant. (Astour, 1967a, 90–1)

Of the 11 different variants of the Io myth Astour refers to, three Sumero–Akkadian, one Hurrian, four Ugaritic, two Hebrew and one Greco–Semitic, all originate from Western Asia, for which, he claims, there is no immediate parallel in Egyptian mythology as such. For, 'although the image of the cow-goddess was well known to the Egyptians since ancient times ... Only during the New Kingdom, under Syrian influence, [did] the cow-goddess Hathor [assume] some features of the W[estern] S[emitic] Astarte ... but not, as far as we know, anything of the motif of "a god's love-affair with a cow"' (Astour, 1967a, 92, 92, n.3). On the contrary, the 'sacred marriage' between Hathor and the Creator-god Amun formed an important item in the Egyptian New Kingdom royal cult, prototype for the divine impregnation of queens (Springborg, 1990d, ch. 10). It is true that the cow-goddess, Ninhursag-become-Hathor/Mehetweret, made the journey from Mesopotamia very early, probably, it is argued (Stock, 1948), during the Memphite period, when the capital of Egypt was closer to Mediterranean routes of diffusion than Upper Egyptian sites. In fact, Hathor the cow-goddess appears already on the predynastic Narmer palette from Hierakonpolis in Upper Egypt, which would suggest that the Red Sea was also a route of diffusion (Trigger, 1983, 44–6). Here she is little more than a personified womb symbol: an oval featureless face with cow's ears, patroness of the falcon folk who unified the Two Kingdoms; but by the Fourth Dynasty she is already a fully fledged goddess (Hornblower, 1929, 38–9).

Most forms of the Western Semitic cow-goddess myth, like the Greek myth of Io, connect it to Egypt. Astour, on the basis of some intuitions of earlier scholars (Movers, 1841; Schaeffer, 1938; Schachermeyr, 1949; Bérard, 1957), explains the connection in terms of the Hyksos, who for 150 years occupied Egypt, and went on to colonize Greece. The Hyksos, worshippers of Baal – 'no wonder Belos in the myth of Danaos is represented as the king of Egypt' (Astour, 1967a, 93) – numbered among their kings more than one Apopis (or Aphophis), who lent his name, after the restoration of indigenous rulers, to the serpent god of Chaos – a comment on how the Hyksos were subsequently viewed. Apopis (Aphophis) is clearly the origin of the Greek Epaphos, usually given a Greek etymology as derived from *epaptein*, 'to touch', the touch of Zeus that transformed Io into a woman again. (Astour, 1967a, 388, n.94, denies that Epaphos can be derived etymologically from Apis, the Egyptian bull of the Serapis cult.)

The exact sequence of migrations is impossible to establish on the basis of myth. Astour notes:

> Just as the Greek and Germanic epics have reflected – though in a fragmentary, condensed and confused form – the conditions of two critical turning-point epochs, full of events of extraordinary significance and impact, two epochs of great migrations of peoples, so also the Hyksos epoch, the traces of which are visible in vestiges of the Danaan myth cycle, was a turning-point epoch for the whole of the Near East. We have very little written information on that epoch, but according to the archaeological data this was a time of enormous shocks, destructions, and displacements of entire populations. (Astour, 1967a, 95)

And he cites the archaeologist Clarence Schaeffer (1938, 262 ff; Astour, 1967a, 95): 'it becomes more and more evident that the Hyksos movement was not just an episode of the Egyptian history and of its relations with Palestine. It was an event of much larger bearing, which has profoundly modified the political and ethnic structure of the whole Western Asia. It had repercussions up to the island of Cyprus and probably even in Crete.'

Astour argues that the Danaus myth of the Hyksos and the Jewish account of the Exodus are different versions of one and the same event-sequence. Hecataeus of Abdera in the Hellenistic period had already made this point, preserved in Diodorus Siculus 40.3.2 (cited in Astour, 1967a, 98) and corroborated in the letter written by the Spartan king Areus (309–265) to the High Priest Onias I (1 Macc. 12.7, cited in Astour, 1967a, 98, n.3) to the effect that 'the Spartans (whose kings, through Heracles and Perseus, claimed descent from Danaos) are brothers of the Jews and descend from Abraham's kindred.' Both the Greek and the Jewish attempts to turn the story of Hyksos migration to account for nationalistic purposes are recorded in Josephus, *Contra Apionem*, I.15, who bases his account on Manetho, *for whom the events originate and terminate in Egypt* – while in some Greek versions, tailored to bolster national pride, they are wholly confined within Greece, and Danaus never leaves the shores of Argos (Astour, 1967a, 82). According to Manetho, as recorded by Josephus:

Sethosis, also called Ramesses ... who possessed an army of cavalry and a strong fleet, made his brother Harmais viceroy of Egypt ... He then departed on a campaign against Cyprus and Phoenicia, and later against the Assyrians and Medes ... Meanwhile, some time after his departure, Harmais, whom he left in Egypt, unscrupulously defied all his brother's injunctions ... and rose in revolt against his brother ... Sethosis instantly returned to Pelusium and recovered his kingdom; and the country was called after him Aigyptos. For Manetho states that Sethos was called Aigyptos and his brother Harmais Danaos.

Later in the same work, *Contra Apionem*, I.26 (cited in Astour, 1967a, 96, n.3), Josephus mentions 'Sethos and Hermaios, the former of whom, he [Manetho] says, took the name of Aigyptos and the latter that of Danaos. Sethos, after expelling Hermaios, reigned fifty-nine years, and his eldest son Rampses, who succeeded him, sixty-six.' This is clearly the Osiris legend that tells of the contendings of Horus and Seth (Griffiths, 1960, 1980), the only extraneous item being the well-attested Greek name for Horus, Hermes. The name Aegyptus has from immemorial time been the name by which the Egyptians refer to themselves – along with the triconsonantal *Msr*, to be found already in the Minoan Linear B tablets – and it is from Aegyptus that the indigenous Christians of Egypt, the Copts, also derive their name.

Astour (1967a, 98) sensibly concludes: 'For us, in this context, it is absolutely indifferent whether some tribes of the future Israelite confederation directly participated in the Hyksos invasion [Breasted, 1912, 220], or the Israelites adopted these reminiscences from the real participants, the Canaanites [Weill, 1918, 185–91; Dussaud, 1946–8, 45 ff], or the Hyksos motifs were borrowed from the Egyptians themselves by Judaean settlers in Egypt since the VIIIth century – what interests us is the resemblance of the essential thematic skeletons.' He reconstructs the skeletal account as follows:

Abstraction made from details and developments that have grown during the centuries of separate evolution of Argive and Hebrew legends about Egypt, their common thematic pivot can be summarized thus: the ancestor of the tribe migrates to Egypt, attains power there; his descendants stay in Egypt for four generations, but then the Egyptians prevail over the strangers, begin to oppress them, and they flee from Egypt; Egyptians pursue them, but perish; the fugitives safely return to their old home-country and again become its rulers. By an interesting coincidence, the number of generations spent in Egypt is the same in both cases: according to the scheme of Pentateuch, four generations – Levi, Qehat, Amram, Moses, and Exodus under the latter, according to the genealogy of the Danaan dynasty also four generations – Epaphos, Libya, Belos, Danaos, and flight from Egypt under the latter. Moreover, this roughly coincides with the real duration of the Hyksos rule over Egypt – approximately 150, maximum 160 years, from 1730 to 1720, when the cult of Baal was established in Tanis-Avaris, to 1580 or, according to some, 1570, when Ahmose I took Avaris, and the Hyksos retreated to Palestine. This is just four conventional generations of 40 years each, as was admitted both by the Bible and Greek logographers. This may be a mere coincidence, but it may as well be a common literary feature reflecting a tradition that really existed with both peoples. (Astour, 1967a, 98–9)

Other cognate features include the upbringing of Moses in the court of an Egyptian king, his slaying of an Egyptian and flight, paralleling Danaus' flight from Egypt after the slaying of the Aegyptiads. 'The same number of generations separates Leah the "wild cow" and Danaos from the cow Io. Still more characteristic is that both Moses and Danaos find and create springs in a waterless region; the story how Poseidon, on the request of the Danaide Amymona, struck out with his trident springs from the Lerna rock, particularly resembles Moses producing a spring from a rock by the stroke of his staff' (Astour, 1967a, 99). Furthermore, common features in the Ugaritic poem of Danel suggest it to be 'the prototype of the Danaos myth'. They include the constant interweaving of names: Aqht, son of Danel, turns up as grandfather of Moses, the brother of whom in turn bears the name of the place where Aqht was killed; the daughter of Danel, and devoted sister of Aqht, lends her name to Pu'a, midwife who saved Moses' life; Moses' own name appears in the feminine form in the Ugaritic poem as the first element of Danel's wife's name, while the second 'corresponds to the name of Levi's sister Dinah' related in turn to the Danaids (Astour, 1967, 99–100). The serpent emblem of the tribe of Dan and of Moses corresponds, and 'Danaë – another Argive heroine of the Danaid stock is thrown into the sea in a chest with her newborn son – as Moses in his ark (*teba*) – and lands on the Serpent island of Seriphos (Heb. *saraph*, applied i.a. to the bronze serpent made by Moses)' (Astour, 1967a, 100).

The association between ark, raft, box (Hebrew and West Semitic *teba*, ancient Egyptian *dbt* or *db3*) stories and Egypt include not only Osiris in his coffin, but Moses in the bullrushes, raised in the court of an Egyptian king, just as Osiris, in Plutarch's version of the story, is given haven in the court of the Byblian king Melcarth (Plutarch, *De Iside et Osiride*, 357, 1970 edn, 141–3). A set of equally tightly interlocking connections, involving eponyms, motifs and event-sequences, connects Moses, 'judge: in his sacred precinct, the Kadesh oasis, which was also called … "spring of judgement" (Gen. 14:7)', to Danel, also 'a healer, a prophet, a miracle-worker', pronouncing curses with his staff; and to Danaus too, preserved in the relic of the myth as a judge (Astour, 1967a, 100).

These reconstructions from mythology would be much less significant were they unsubstantiated in the historical record. But in fact Egyptian eyewitnesses refer to the existence of the Danunians as a living people. Thus in a letter by a vassal, Abimilki, king of Tyre, to Pharaoh Amenhotep IV, found in the Amarna archives, we hear: 'The king, my lord, has written to me: "What thou hearest from Kinahna write to me." The king of Danuna is dead, and his brother has become king in his stead, and his land is quiet. And fire has consumed Ugarit, the city (*bit?*) of the king; half of it it has consumed and its (other) half is not' (Astour, 1967a, 4–5). In 1945–7, in Eastern Cilicia, near the border with ancient Syria, a bilingual inscription, in both Phoenician and Hittite-hieroglyphic, was found, recording the founding by Azitawadd, king of the Danunians, of a new city bearing his name at Karatepe, sometime near the end of the eighth century (Astour, 1967a, 1–2). Astour (1967a, 102 ff) believes that if not the Danunians specifically, then more broadly the Canaanite, Syrian, Palestinian area provided the Hyksos invaders of Egypt, who were drawn perhaps to Ugarit, a cosmopolitan gathering point for traders and immigrants. Name lists in the Amarna tablets specify among the inhabitants of Ugarit, migrants from Southern Phoenicia and Palestine, in fact.

Ugarit, one of the large feudal second millennium Western Semitic territorial kingdoms, like Alalah and the Cilician Plain of Adana, lay to the north of the city-states of classical Phoenicia, Tyre and Arwad, and, as Astour (1967a, 105) points out, was categorically different from them. Three times the size of Attica and twice the size of the whole of the Argolid, Ugarit comprised a huge palace complex and a hinterland of some 200 towns and villages. It was only exceeded in size by the lands of the king of Halab (still the Arabic name for Aleppo), who in the time of Hammurabi was already reckoned to have more vassals than his more famous Babylonian counterpart (Astour, 1967a, 106–7). Such kingdoms, permeated and to some extent supported by the Akkadian cultural dominance of the whole Western Semitic area, together with the strength of the Phoenician city-states, would have been quite capable of mounting invasions, both south, to Egypt, and west, to the Argolid.

The pre-existence of the Ugaritic, Hebrew and Greek versions of the Western Semitic Danel myth, and the late incorporation of the Egyptian material in 'the legendary reminiscences of the Hyksos rule in Egypt', are claimed by Astour (1967a, 104) as proof of a sort, then, of a thesis that has archaeological and epigraphic support. Conventional classicists, such as Stubbings (1962, 74; cited in Astour, 1967a, 331), have dated the migrations of Danaus, the Egyptian, and Cadmus, the Syrian, at the beginning of the heroic age around 1582 BC, at the time of the expulsion of the Hyksos from Egypt:

> there is a case for inferring the arrival in Greece at this time of new rulers from abroad, such as are indeed ascribed by legend to the beginnings of the first heroic age. Some of those immigrant founder heroes are of origins too improbable to be fictitious – Danaus, for example, from Egypt; Cadmus from Syria. The only probable juncture for such immigration which can be recognized in the archaeological record is at the transition from Middle Helladic to Late Helladic; while in terms of external history no time is so likely as the period of the expulsion of the Hyksos overlords from Egypt. It seems more than fortuitous coincidence that the heroic era of Athens, according to the *Marmor Parium*, begins at 1582 B.C., and that Danaus is in that document placed at least in the same century. Several, consequently, of the principal legends of the earlier heroic age may be set in relation to the archaeological history as events of the period of settlement in Greece after the first immigrations, a period of internal conflict leading ultimately to the supremacy of Mycenae. (Stubbings, 1962, 74; cited in Astour, 1967a, 331)

Martin Bernal (1987a, 20ff) has called for a revision of this dating 'to put Danaos' landing in Greece near the beginning of the Hyksos period, at around 1720 BC, not near its end – in or after 1575 – as set out in the ancient chronographies' (Bernal, 1987a, 20). Granting that 'ever since late Antiquity, writers have seen links between the Egyptian records of the explusion of the hated Hyksos by the Egyptian 18th Dynasty, the Biblical tradition of the exodus from Egypt after the Israelite sojourn there, and the Greek legends of the arrival in Argos of Danaos', Bernal nevertheless calls into question the telescoping of these events. His revision fits with the telescoping of an event-series in the case of the Theseus myth, Plato's account of the fall of Minoan civilization and the eruption of Thera, that we have already discussed (part I, chapter 6), which recent techniques of radiocarbon dating and dendrochronology would suggest were far apart. Bernal provides considerable literary and archaeological detail for his revised schema, according to which the Hyksos colonization of Greece is not the first important Afro-Asiatic influence, following, in fact, on earlier twenty-first century incursions made by the powerful Eleventh Dynasty Middle Kingdom Egyptian kings Menthotpe, who may have established the bull cults and the legend of King Minos in Crete, referred to by Herodotus as Min – the name of the first lawgiver and pharaoh of Egypt, Menes, whose reign dates to *c*.3250 BC (Bernal, 1987a, 63–4). To these same Eleventh Dynasty invaders has been attributed an earthen stepped-pyramid north of Greek Thebes, which causes one archaeologist (Spyropoulos, 1972, 1973, cited in Bernal, 1987a, 18) to postulate the existence of an Egyptian colony in Boeotia as early as the twenty-first century BC. This pyramid, interestingly, has long been known as the tomb of Amphion and Zethos, named by Homer as founders of Boeotian Thebes long before the arrival of Cadmus, Zethos being the Greek equivalent of Seth, Osiris' wicked brother. There is further evidence of incursions into Greece by the powerful Twelfth Dynasty pharaohs, Senwosret – rendered Sesostris by Herodotus – and Ammenemes – or Memnon – whose alternative name *Hpr k3 Re* yields Kekrops, name of the legendary founder of Athens, believed by the ancients to be Egyptian (Bernal, 1987a, 19).

Michael Astour's deconstruction of the myth of Cadmus and Europa and the founding of Greek Thebes, like his treatment of the Danaus myth, follows the hypothesis that ancient historical records, whose repository was the temple, and whose transmitters the temple priests, took a mythico-religious form (Astour, 1967a, 70). His analysis is therefore in terms of continuities in epic motif, religious symbolism and the meaning of names. Names have enormous significance in an oral tradition, as pegs on which the memory hangs ethnic and genealogical information, on the one hand – still in some cases transparent – or as esoteric religious signs to initiates, on the other. In the first case we are dealing with eponyms, of great assistance in our historical deconstruction, because of 'an Ancient Eastern onomastical habit: calling the leading gods of alien peoples, even if they are adopted into the native religion, not (or not only) by their direct names, but by the title "god of this or that people", as a result of which the ethnic name becomes the name of the god' (Astour, 1967, 145).

The combination of these two onomastic techniques has its own explanation, stated long ago by Eduard Meyer (1906, 251, cited in Astour, 1967a, 149, n.2):

> Genuine myths and original sagas of the gods ... were transformed into genealogic-ethnographic tales reflecting the destinies of the corresponding tribes, tales in which along with purely genealogical figures as Tros and Ilos, Aegyptos and Danaos, Hellen, Doros, Ion and their sons, stand much more ancient names of a different character, as Priamos and Aeneas, Danaë and Perseus, Deucalion and Erechtheus ... Myth and heroic saga which evolved from it are older than genealogic poetry.

It is worth noting that Ruth Edwards (1979), who has undertaken a searching and sceptical reassessment of Astour's thesis on the Cadmus legend, neither discounts legendary evidence, nor the antiquity of this particular legend, which she believes to contain genuine Mycenaean elements, referring possibly to a sixteenth-century BC Hyksos colonization of Greece or, alternatively, a fourteenth-century trading settlement (Edwards, 1979, 17–113, especially ch. 1, n 52–7, cited in Bernal, 1987a, 424–5). Edwards goes out of her way to stress that legend is not an inherently more subjective source of evidence than archaeology itself, where items of material culture require interpretation:

> It is sometimes assumed by those who urge us to disregard legend and concentrate on these other sources that they are in some way more *objective* than the traditions. But we must emphasize that archaeology, language and documents are only objective within a very restricted compass, in fact only so long as they are concerned with mere observation and description of data. Once they aspire to interpretation, a subjective element enters in. This is particularly worth illustrating in regard to archaeology: the same assemblage of artefacts, the very same destruction levels, may be interpreted in different ways by different archaeologists. There is, moreover, a tendency for archaeological interpretations to run in fashions ... The other sources, then, are not in themselves objective *for the purpose of reconstructing prehistory*; they are subject to limitations of precisely the same order as the legendary tradition. The prehistorian is always working from imperfect and ambiguous material and there is ... nothing basically illogical or unsound about using legendary evidence, provided one recognizes what one is doing. (Edwards, 1979, 201–3, cited in Bernal, 1987a, 424–5)

Edward's style of refutation is generally overcautious, expressing scepticism without offering an alternative:

> To sum up: there is no means of demonstrating that any element in the [Cadmus–Europa] legend has as its basis the memory of historical events of the Mycenaean Age, but the arguments in favour of regarding Kadmos's oriental origin as a pure invention are inconclusive, and our other sources of information suggest not that the story bears no relation to historical fact, but rather that it is consistent with several possible reconstructions of events, not all of which need be mutually exclusive. (Edwards, 1979, 191)

She concedes, nevertheless,: 'Of the main interpretations, the oriental appears to be the most plausible' (Edwards, 1979, 191).

The Cadmus and Europa myth, not surprisingly, yields information of a genealogical and onomastic sort. Astour (1967a, 113) begins his reconstruction with a passage from Herodotus 4.147, that is replete with onomastica significant for our purposes:

> There were in the island now called Thera, but then Calliste, descendants of Membliaros the son of Poikiles, a Phoenician; for Cadmos son of Agenor, in his search for Europa, had put in at the place now called Thera; and having put in, either because the land pleased him, or because for some other reason he desired so to do, he left in this island, among other Phoenicians, his own kinsman Membliaros. These dwelt in the island Calliste for eight generations before Theras came from Lacedaemon.

Now Membliaros, a toponym, not for Thera, but for an island close by, Anaphe, is a composite name which can be reduced to Western Semitic (Ugaritic or archaic Phoenician) elements: '*mem-bli-'ar*, "waters without light", or, shorter, *bli-'ar* "without light" = darkness' (Astour, 1967a, 114); being immediately evocative of Eastern cosmologies: the 'waters of darkness', and 'the spirit of God mov[ing] upon the face of the waters' of Genesis 1.2. The Phoenician version presented by Philo of Byblos runs: 'As the beginning of all things he supposes dark and windy air, or a gust of dark air, and obscure, Erebos-like chaos' (*Praep. Ev.*, I.10.1, cited in Astour, 1967a, 115); a darkness known as *Baau*, 'the same word as *bohu* in the cosmogony of Genesis', rendered *Boeth* in a Latin inscription to designate the sacred pool of the important Phoenician sanctuary of Astarte and Adonis in Aphaca. This is the same temple at which the goddess was believed to descend as a fiery star, falling into the pool, celebrated in fire festivals, and reminiscent of *fiat lux* and the bursting of divine light into the watery chaos of Genesis 1.3, or the Phoenician version, itself reminiscent of the Egyptian: 'And Mot was shaped like an egg and burst forth into light' (Philo, *Praep Ev.*, 1.10.2, cited in Astour, 1967a, 116). These cosmogonies belonged to New Year liturgies performed by the Phoenicians at Aphaca; recorded in the Babylonian Enuma Elish creation epic, recited on the fourth day of the Akitu festival. The Hebrew Near Year Festival and Feast of the Tabernacles, at which Genesis may well have been recited as 'a repetition of the Creation', along with psalms commemorating the victory of Yahwe and re-enacting his enthronement, were further examples (Astour, 1967a, 116–17).

Why did Herodotus locate Membliaros on Thera, rather than Anaphe? Apollonius of Rhodes in the *Argonautica* includes a passage dedicated to Anaphe (*Argonautica*, 4.1694–8, cited in Astour, 1967a, 118), highly suggestive of a liturgical myth. It features the Argonauts caught on the way to Crete on 'that night which they name the Pall of Darkness', when 'the stars pierced not that fatal night nor the beams of the moon, but black chaos descended from heaven, or haply some other darkness came, rising from the nethermost depths.' But, upon Jason's invocation to Phoebus Apollo (*Argonautica*, 4.1699–1705, cited in Astour, 1967a, 118): 'darting upon one of the twin peaks, thou raisedst aloft in thy right hand thy golden bow; and the bow flashed a dazzling gleam all round', in whose light they spied a small island to which they applied for shelter: 'and they made [there] for Apollo a glorious abode in a shady wood, and a shady altar, calling on Phoebus the "Gleamer" (*Aigletes*) because of the gleam far-seen; and that bare island they called Anaphe, for that Phoebus had revealed it to men sore bewildered.'

As Astour (1967a, 118) notes, this passage contains a dramatic power, 'so unlike the general, rather slack style of Apollonios', as to suggest the relics of a cosmogonic myth. The dark waters (*Membliaros?*) pierced by the 'gleamer', so reminiscent of Marduk's bow – his only weapon in his epic struggle with Tiamat, representative of watery chaos – in the *Enuma Elish* epic, recalls also Yahwe's bow, placed upon a cloud when the waters of the flood retreated, in Genesis 9. 11–14, as a symbol of hope to men with whom he had covenanted (Astour, 1967a, 119). Membliaros would seem very clearly to be linked to a Phoenician shrine at Anaphe, as further parallels between the water rite at Anaphe, recounted by Apollonius (*Argonautica*, 1719–30, cited in Astour, 1967a, 119–20), and the Semitic rites of the Day of the Willows, climax of the Feast of the Tabernacles, would confirm.

But what about Thera? If as Astour ingeniously suggests, Anaphe was associated with the first creative act: light out of darkness; the mythology connected with Thera corresponds to the second: the emergence of land out of the primeval waters. The very name Anaphe may be derived from *anaphaino*, to appear or reveal, confirming the *fiat lux* mythological element (Astour, 1967a, 123). Thera has a similar derivation, but from the Western Semitic *te'ira*, 'lit, illuminated', and in this case the product of the creative act was land 'from a clod'. The hero of Thera, corresponding to Apollo Aigletes of Anaphe, is Euphemus, 'whom, most swift-footed of men, Europa, daughter of mighty Tityus, bare to Poseidon' (Apollonius, *Argonautica*, 1.179–84, cited in Astour, 1967a, 121). Euphemus, the cosmic wind born of Europa, signifying darkness, and Poseidon, the watery deep, received from Triton in Libya a clod of earth, which he threw into the sea; and 'therefrom rose up an island, Calliste, sacred nurse of the sons of Euphemos', which was named Thera when Theras came there with the Argonauts (Apollonius, 4.1756–64 cited in Astour, 1967a, 122).

The paired meaning of their names, Anaphe and Thera, and the complementary nature of their mythologies, suggest to Astour (1967a, 122) that these proximate islands, 'or rather their ancient sanctuaries, must have formed a sort of cultic pair where cosmogonic epics had been ritually recited or dramatically performed during the New Year Festival: in Anaphe – the first part, dealing with the primaeval chaos and the victory of light over darkness, in Thera – the second part, describing the creation of dry land out of the boundless sea'. He notes that 'this arrangement corresponds to a certain degree to the distribution of liturgic services between the two sacred mountains in Shechem: Gerizim, for blessings, and Ebal, for curses' (Deut. 28.12–13, cited in Astour, 1967a, 122). Thus 'Anaphe-Membliaros symbolized the "waters without light", Thera, the miniature of the earth, formed after the creation of light, is her antonym.' Pairing, an important mythological device with possible religious significance, may also render a Semitic derivation for Anaphe. The Greek island of Cos owes its name to the Western Semitic, Hebrew, *kos*, 'owl' (Akk. *kasu*). Now Anaphe lies west of Cos and corresponds to another word for owl, Hebrew *anapha*, Akkadian *anpatu*; and Athena, whose symbol is the owl is not an impossible derivation (Astour, 1967a, 246). The owl of Minerva flies truly only at dusk, and westward!

Once these associations are made, a chain of correspondences in the Cadmus–Europa mythology falls into place. Poikiles, father of Membliaros, can be given a Western Semitic etymology, from *pi-kol*, both 'mouth of all' and 'womb of all', symbol of the abyss in Ugaritic mythological poems, evocative of the mouth of Tiamat that swallowed Marduk in *Enuma Elish* (Astour, 1967a, 123–5). 'The original cosmogonic expression can thus be restored as *mem-bli-'ar pi-kol* 'dark water of the womb of all', yielding the patronymic *Membliaros Poikileo*, a creation from the debris of most ancient myth, rather than an eponym. The etymology of Europa herself, Phoenician princess, daughter of Agenor or Phoenix, and sister of Cadmus, is particularly instructive. In Greek the name came to mean 'wide-eyed', 'broad-faced', but its derivation is most probably from the Akkadian *erebu*, evening, which yielded the Greek *erebos*, the dark land of the dead, lying for them, as for the Egyptians, to the west (Astour, 1967a, 130). Not only does this derivation fit with Europa the mother of Euphemus, demiurge and son of Darkness and Water – Europa and Poseidon – but in the Boeotian town of Lebadeia – apparently a Phoenician name – *Demeter Europa*, the dark chthonic deity sometimes known also as *Melaina*, 'black', was worshipped (Astour, 1967, 131–2). The Ras Shamra texts discovered in 1929 reveal a deity of the Sunset–Evening–Night, for which there are parallel Babylonian and Ugaritic versions, appealed to in spells for protection against witchcraft: most notably 'the veiled goddess Ishtar', and 'our Lady, the goddess of the night', of whom the Ugaritic hymn sings:

1. I sing our Lady, the god [dess]
    of the night, of the night, the vei [led] bride,
    In the evening thou enterst into the sunset [ ]
    ... I sing. *His answer is* ... [ ]
5. When thou hast shone O Night, bride [ ]
    of the night, veiled bride [... thou en–]
    terst into the sunset. May I sing thee [...]
    They invoke thee, the herds of ... [ ]
    [ ] ... and the cattle of ... [ ]
10. [ ] ... not to forget [...]
    [.. A] nu, the Lord of the g [ods]
    [.. Lord] of Wisdom ... [ ]
    (*Ugaritic Manual*, 104, cited in Astour, 1967a, 134)

The veil is the standard iconographic attribute of Europa on coins of Gortyn and Sidon 'and on figurines ... usually represented blown out by the wind over Europa's head.' Although an innovation of the Hellenistic period, the veiled goddess 'was first introduced by the Sidonians – probably on the basis of their own traditions which are already found in the Ugaritic hymn of the XIVth century' cited above (Astour, 1967a, 134–5) – and of course Cretan Gortyn was the cult centre for Europa (Astour, 1967a, 131).

It is worth pointing out that the question of the veil is one on which Ruth Edwards (1979, 145ff) chooses to focus in her general refutation of Astour, noting that 'the wind-blown veil [said to be] first introduced by the Sidonians ... in fact ... appears slightly earlier on the coins of Knossos than those of Sidon, and may well be an artistic development from older representations of Europe holding her billowing mantle ... Even if Astour were right that the motif of Europe's veil originated in Sidon, this need be only the result of late syncretism, since it was here that Europe was identified in Hellenistic times with Sidonian Astarte, the same goddess as Ishtar.' She concludes, 'A veil is in any case a common motif in representations of divine and semi-divine personages, and can surely have little claim to provide us with any clue to Europe's original role.' In fact, evidence abounds that the veil in the ancient Middle East had a rather specific signification, as a screen for hierogamy and the 'visitation' of the father-god – which Astour's examination of the 'veiled lady of the night' of the Ugaritic poem, and Astral Aphrodite (Astour, 1967a, 134–7), as well as the analysis by Doresse (1971, 1973, 1979; see Springborg, 1990d, 141, 219) of images of the veiled 'Amun', would confirm. Veiling, it is argued, in the ancient, as in the modern Middle East (Abu-Lughod, 1986) was also a protection against incest, and much is made of the veil of Isis, described most lavishly in Lucius' account of the epiphany of Isis by Apuleius of Madauros (*Metamorphoses*, book 11, 1975 edn, 101–3), as befitting her modesty (Griffiths, 1970, 284); an item transferred along with other aspects of her regalia to the Virgin Mary.

The Semitic counterpart of Europa in the Ugaritic hymn, if Astour is right (1967, 134–5), represents the goddess not of darkness but of the starry skies, and this is borne out in both the Ugaritic and Hellenistic versions: 'When thou has shone, O Night, bride of ... the night, veiled bride'. The Semitic epithets *kuttumtum* or *mukkatimtum*, 'veiled', from the Akkadian *katamu*, to veil, yield the Cretan personal name *Tektamos*, in late mythology the designation of Europa's Cretan husband (Astour, 1967a, 135). Stephanos of Byzantium gives the variant *Tektaphos*, related to the Semitic *tihtaph*, from *hataph* (Arab. *hatafa*), 'to carry off', as in Judg. 21.21, which is what happened to Europa, carried off by a bull (Astour, 1967a, 136). The reference to the Divine Bull, in Ugaritic *El*, father of the gods, is of course highly significant. As the product of an incestuous union between El and two wives, at the same time daughters, two children are born, *Shr* and *Šlm*, Dawn and Dusk, 'islanders', born on a sea shore – could it be Crete, and could they be Cadmus and Europa? (Astour, 1967a, 137).

There are striking parallels between this incest story and the birth of Adonis to Myrrha by Theias, her father, as well as the incestuous union of the Biblical Lot and her father that produced two daughters (Gen. 19.30–38) and Tamar's veiled union with her father-in-law Judah (Gen. 38.14–30, cited in Astour, 1967a, 137). Lot means 'veil' in Hebrew, and this disguise which permitted incest in the Biblical tales, may explain 'Night, the veiled bride' of the Ugaritic hymn and veiled Europa, wife of Tektamos (Astour, 1967a, 137). Other elements in these incestuous tales correspond as well: Myrrha was changed into a myrrh tree; Tamar means date-palm; Europa's union with Zeus was consumated under a plane-tree in Gortynian tradition; and on a Babylonian cylinder seal from Lagash the Theias–Myrrha story seems to be repeated in the birth of Tammuz out of a tree referred to in the inscription as 'house of the Evening (goddess)' (Astour, 1967a, 137–8). Europa was also the goddess Evening Star, worshipped at Gortyn as *Hellotis*, 'shining one', from Western Semitic *halal*, 'to shine', related to the Arabic *hilal*, crescent moon; to *Helel*, son of *Šahar*, the god of Dawn of the Ugaritic poem already mentioned; and to Babylonian astrology in which Venus appears in two aspects: 'female as evening star, male as morning star', the Akkadian name of Venus, DIL.BAD, transcribed by Hesychios as *Delephat*, perhaps yielding *Telephassa* (Attic pronunciation **Telephatta*), 'the far-shining', the name of Europa's mother (and hypostase) in the Greek myth (Astour, 1967, 139, n.4). A torch race accompanied the annual feast (*Hellotia*) of Europa *Hellotis* of Gortyn, known there alternatively as *Phoinike*; and a similar festival was celebrated at Corinth for a goddess known as *Athena Hellotis*, who also had a cult centre at Marathon, connected in mythology with the Cretan bull.

We have in the case of Europa, therefore, 'proofs of an actual existence of a Western Semitic goddess of the Evening Star and Sunset, whose name offers an etymology in keeping with all semantic and mythical features of the Greek Europa', Astour concludes (1967, 140). But what of Phoenix and Cadmus? Phoenix is clearly an ethnographic-genealogical title, perhaps the abbreviated form of *theos Phoinix*, 'the Phoenician god' – like *Zeus Karios*, the Carian Zeus of Herodotus 5.66 (cited in Astour, 1967a, 145) – probably designating the 'Phoenician god', El, lord of the West Semitic pantheon. The name Phoenix itself is widely believed to refer to the colour of purple dye, from Hebrew *puwwa*, Arabic *fuwwa*, dyer's madder, the herbaceous plant of Syria, Palestine and Egypt, which yield the Greek *phoenix* and *porphyra*, purple, the Latin *poenus* and *punicus*, both of which have the same ethnographic usage (Astour, 1967a, 146–7). The primarily ethnic reference of the eponym explains in addition the attribution to Phoenix by Stephen of Byzantium in his carefully detailed lexicon, of the paternity of Itanos, Carnos and Cytheros, eponyms for the port city of Eastern Crete, the town Karne in Phoenicia proper, and the Greek island Cythera, respectively (Astour, 1967a, 140–2). Karne, rendered *Cornu Phenices* in the Roman imperial age, represents an interesting linguistic shift, 'Semitic *qarn* and Latin *cornu* form[ing] a remarkable pair, one of the very few Semito-Indo-European lexical coincidences' (Astour, 1967a, 142), both meaning 'horn'. Not only are all three places associated with Phoenician trade and purple-dying, but the names of both Carnos and Cythera have Semitic derivations. Herodotus, 1. 105, notes the foundation at Cythera of a shrine to Aphrodite Urania on the model of the great temple at Ascalon; cuneiform records of a dedication to Naram-Sin, king of Eshnunna, were found in Cythera as long ago as 1849; a small bay is known there as *Phoinikus*; and Skandeia, the harbour of Cythera is named for its shape, designating a head-dress, crown or coronet: *keter*, *koteret*, in Hebrew (Astour, 1967a, 142–3), to complete the doublet and provide the island's (Semitic) name!

The name Cadmus presents the complement to Europa we are looking for but cannot find in Phoenix. Deriving from the Western Semitic *qadm*, literally 'in front', which applied to time meant 'earlier', to space meant 'east', it corresponds, as Victor Bérard (1927, vol. 2, 359 ff) guessed, to the two aspects of the planet Venus, known to us from the Babylonian and Ugaritic myth as the Morning and Evening Stars (Astour, 1967a, 153): 'According to the Babylonian conception the planet Venus as the Morning Star was male, as the Evening Star female. That is exactly the situation with the sexes of Cadmus and Europa. The Evening Star goes away to the west (as was sung in the Ugaritic–Akkadian hymn), disappears beyond the sea; the Morning Star, her brother, rushes to her search, but the two can never meet', which is why Cadmus' search for Europa must be fruitless. In Babylonia a god *Qa-ad-mu* is in fact attested, named as 'vizier of Sataran', the serpent god (Astour, 1967a, 153–4). We know from the Ugaritic poem that the god *Šhr*, Dawn, has a brother *Šlm* (*Shalom*), meaning Peace, but also in some Semitic languages 'Dusk'. *Šhr*, has a female form in Hebrew, *šahar*, 'the doe of the dawn' (Ps. 22.1), and a Middle Assyrian female appears on one of the lists of the gods, *Šulmitu*, or *Šulmanitu*, 'defined as *Ištar Uru-silim-ma*, Ihstar of Jerusalem' (Astour, 1967a, 154). As Astour (1967a, 154–5) observes: 'The fact that the [Western Semitic] goddess *Šulmitu* was identified with Ishtar, whose planet was Venus, speaks for considering this Sulmitu as the female counterpart of the dusk-god *Šlm* in Ugarit, and one may easily imagine the variant *Šahar-Šulmitu* instead of *Šhr-Šlm*.' Other parallels between Cadmus, as the Morning Star, counterpart of the female Evening Star, include the hierogamy of Ishtar, five times repeated to produce a total of seven gods (including *Šhr* and *Šlm*); gods of the sea, fertility figures and 'probably islanders' (*Ugaritic Manual*, 52.57, cited in Astour, 1967a, 155). They were close in nature to the mysterious Cabiri, known to the Greeks by their Semitic name – from Hebrew and Arabic, *kabbir*, 'great, mighty'. Their cult centres were Boeotian Thebes and Samothrace, where they were specifically connected with Cadmus; and their worship as seven Cabiri – with a possible eighth brother, Asclepius-Ešmun – is reported in the Phoenician city of Berytos, by Philo of Byblos (Eusebius, *Praep. Evang.* 1.10.38, cited in Astour, 1967a, 155).

Cadmus is not exclusively god of the dawn, and his Orphic side is reflected in his transformation, and that of his wife Harmonia, into snakes, settling among the Encheleians, whose name means 'eels' or 'snake-like fish' (Astour, 1967a, 156). Here Cadmus is reminiscent of the Sumerian chthonic fertility god Ningišzida, whose emblem is that of copulating snakes, recalling the role of the dragon in the Cadmeian myth of the foundation of Thebes. (Ningišzida was also the personification of the Sunrise.) This suggests ancient origins of the Cadmus myth that go well beyond the immediate identification with the Western Semitic *Šhr/Qdm*, back in fact to Sumerian legend. Thus, if the name of Phoenix belongs to the genealogical-ethnographic genre, overlaid on original ancestral myth, the name of Cadmus belongs to the latter, Astour concludes, referring to the distinction made by Edward Meyer (1906, 251, cited in Astour, 1967a, 149), 'between the late schematic figures of genealogies and the old genuine characters of the heroic saga':

> Cadmos, the hero of a very dramatic myth, saturated with adventures, events, and epic motifs, obviously belongs to the category of the latter. The relation between Cadmos, Cadmeia and the Cadmeians is the same as between Dan–Danel and the tribe and town of Dan and the people of Danaans–Danunians; as between the goddess Anath and the inhabitants of the towns 'Anat (on the Euphrates), 'Anatot and Bet-'Anat (in Palestine); as between Astarte and the town of 'Aštarot in Transjordan; or, in Greece, as between Athena and Athens, Heracles and the Heracleia. Then it cannot be proven that the worship of Europa was "secondarily" transferred to Crete from Boeotia; Europa certainly belonged to the original mythical figures of the pre-Dorian Crete, and her appearance both in Crete and in Boeotia can much more plausibly be ascribed to her simultaneous introduction from the East through a maritime route. We also have seen ... that the excuse of Phoenix having been mistaken for a Phoenician is not valid: on the contrary, wherever Phoenix appears, either as a person or as a toponym, he is clearly connected with Semitic names, myths and cults.

This thesis requires further demonstration, that is readily forthcoming. One of the more interesting Western Semitic motifs in the myth of Cadmus is the injunction to him to follow an unyoked cow to the place where she rested, and there to found Thebes. Philistine princes put the ark of Yahwe on a wagon driven by cows never yoked before, which were subsequently sacrificed at Bet Šemeš, just as Cadmus' cow was sacrificed to Athena at Thebes (Astour, 1967a, 157–8). In Euripides *Bacchae* 1333–35, Dionysus foretells that Cadmus and Harmonia will both be changed into snakes and 'in a wagon (driven) by heifers (*moschoi*), says Zeus' oracle, thou and thy wife shall lead barbarians', suggesting a sacred procession that would draw the barbarians after it, as the Philistine princes were drawn by the ark (I Sam. 6.7–12, cited in Astour, 1967a, 158). Now the Hebrew word for 'ark' or 'chest' is *teba*, Semitic prototype of the name given to the spot *'Theba* (so in Homer, later *Thebai*)' chosen by Cadmus' cow. We know from Egyptian theology the important role of portable shrines in the form of sacred barques with carrying poles to suit river-orientated processions; in Mesopotamia, it seems the equivalent was the tabernacle, or ark, the latter possibly also in the form of a small boat. The sacred barque played an important role in pharaonic processions, not merely as a mode of display, but as the shrine in which the king assumed an aspect of the supreme god Amun, to whom he stood as deified Osiris: hence the designation of the king, in temples with which he was associated, as Amun-Re of 'United-with-Eternity', referring, for instance, to Ramses III in his Medinet Habu temple; 'Seti-Merenptah-is-Glorious', referring to Seti I in his Gurnah temple; 'United-with-Thebes', referring to Ramses II's Ramesseum (Nelson, 1942, 127). The chance of such sacred shrines having made their way into the Greek mysteries opens up all sorts of possibilities. Astour notes:

> Sacred chests with mystical emblems, whose opening was strongly forbidden, played a great role in Greek mysteries celebration, and Gruppe [1906, 1.61] derived the name of Thebes from such chests in the Cabiri mysteries. According to other hypotheses, the name originated from the ark in which the local Noah, King Ogygos, survived the flood [Nork, 1845, 4.365: 'Thebes, according to its name, the Ship-city']. Both motifs possibly played a rôle, for both the floating and the portable chest have a common cultic origin, though in Hebrew they were designated by different terms. (Astour, 1967a, 158)

Cadmus is thus strongly identified both as the god of sunrise and the chthonic fertility god, builder of cities, symbolized by entwined serpents, Sumerian Ningišzida. Astour concludes:

> Only the motif of armed men grown from the dragon's teeth which were sown by Cadmos, has no parallel in Oriental myths discovered so far, and is probably a local Greek addition aiming to satisfy the inhabitants' claim of descent from the aborigines. However, the idea of the first human beings having grown from the soil like plants is found, in a primitive form, in the Sumerian myth of Enlil and the pick-axe. (Astour, 1967a, 159)

Moreover, 'Cadmos is not an isolated figure, and ... all characters linked with him by the myth have the same origin.' Thus Harmonia, Cadmus' wife, changed into a serpent, has all the marks of the counterpart of Ningišzida's wife Ba-u (Ba-ba), known also in Sumerian as Geštinanna, 'the heavenly vine', and in Akkadian as 'Belit-seri', 'the lady of the steppe'. 'This latter goddess, notwithstanding her Sumerian name, was an underground chthonic deity and, in the classical system of the Babylonian pantheon, was assigned the function of the scribe of the Nether World, the secretary of the infernal queen Ereškigal, who registered not only the already dead, but also those who were doomed by the Nether World judges to die in the current year' (Astour, 1967a, 159). Astour notes the significance then of Harmonia's fatal necklace and peplos, dooming those who wore them. Oriental parallels do not stop there:

> Like Cadmos, Harmonia was considered in Thebes, up to Roman times, as the founding heroine of shrines. To her was ascribed the erection of three archaic

statues, *xoana*, of the triple Aphrodite – Urania 'the heavenly', Pandemos 'of the entire people', and Apostrophia 'the returning' (Paus. IX.16.3), in whom V. Bérard [1927, 2.364, 367] correctly recognized three attributes of Ištar – 'queen of heaven', 'ruler of all men', and she who returned from the Land Without Return. (Astour, 1967a, 160)

Harmonia was also recognized as 'owner of the house of the goddess', Demeter Thesmophorus, at Thebes, corresponding therefore to the Sumerian and Western Semitic goddess known variously as *Nin-e-gal*, 'the lady of the palace', and *Nin-uru*, 'the lady of the city', translated into Akkadian as *Belit-ekallim* (Astour, 1967a, 160). Hathor, literally *Hat-hor*, 'house of Horus', had just such a name (Bleeker, 1973). Did it symptomize what we otherwise know to have been her role as an anthropomorphized womb symbol (Barb, 1953)? Or did it simply signify her role as patroness of a royal house? Or was it both? Clearly Harmonia, in so many ways similar to these goddesses, both astralized and progenitors of a line of kings, the archetypal 'beautiful women' of mythology (Springborg, 1990d, ch. 9), bore a name to suit.

In Ugarit the goddesses of cities and palaces were also known: 'Nin-gal under the Semitized name of Nikkal (*Nkl*), and Nin-e-gal or Belit-ekallim under the Western Semitic name of *B'lt-bt*, or *B'lt-bhtm*, where the plural *bhtm* signifies "palace"'. Astour goes on to make the startling suggestion that 'if *ekallum* were translated not by *bt* or *bhtm*, but by another Western Semitic word for 'palace', *'armon*, the derivate of it would be *'Armoni* – which is actually attested in II Sam. 21.8 as the name of one of Saul's sons, a well-fitting name for a royal child. The feminine form of it would be *'Armonit* [there actually existed a god *Ar-man-nu* in Babylonia], or, with the ending of several female names in Ugarit, *'Armoniya*. This is exactly the Greek name of *Harmonia!*' (Astour, 1967a, 160–1). The aspirated Greek form follows the pattern which yielded *Hierosolyma* out of *Yerušalem*, *Hieromykes*, out of Yarmuk: 'the Greek ear associated the first sounds of these names with *hieros* "holy", and in the same way *'Armoniya* was perceived as Greek *harmonia* "fastening, tie, clamp", then "alliance, treaty", and finally "concord, harmony".' The 'lady of the palace' in her other form, *Hekale*, 'from *hekal*, the Western Semitic form of *ekallum*', actually turns up in the form of a hospitable old woman – the 'lady of the house' – in Plutarch, *Theseus*, 5 s, 14, and Callimachos, *Hecale* (R. Pfeiffer, *Callimachos*, I. frg. 230–64, cited in Astour, 1967a, 161, n.5).

A later Near Eastern epic, not usually associated with this series of motifs, comes closest of all to a syncretism of all the elements of 'beautiful woman' and 'box' stories, including the Egyptian myth of Osiris, the 'Tale of Two Brothers', the Cadmean and Pandora myths. It is the famed One Thousand and One Nights, recorded in English by Richard Burton in the nineteenth century. Even the name of the female protagonist, Shaharazad, is evocative of Mesopotamian astral goddesses, for whom the elements *Šhr* are critical. The story goes like this: two kings, brothers, upon finding that their wives have betrayed them, seek solace on the outskirts of civilization; a demonic monster carrying a box emerges and out of the box comes a beautiful woman, Shaharazad; abducted on her wedding day, she had been sent to the bottom of the sea in a box with seven strong locks; but such is the power of desire that the woman was able to break out of the box, despite the seven locks, and escape from the depths of the sea; the beautiful woman, now in a tree, forces the kings to make love to her or she will waken the monster (Attar, 1989).

Not all the names of those associated with the Cadmus story have Semitic origins, but they usually tie in to a connection of some sort. Thus Teiresias, the blind soothsayer of Thebes, has an obvious derivation in 'the Greek *teirea* (pl. tantum) "stars, constellations", cognate to *teras* "sign, omen, miracle, atmospheric phenomena [such] as thunder, lightning or rainbow, dream etc. as signs of divine will and presage of future events"' (Astour, 1967a, 162). But the Western Semitic word for 'blind', *'iwwer* in Hebrew, supplies the name of his father, *Eueres* – originally perhaps his own epithet, Astour suggests (1967a, 162) – and other oriental connections for Teiresias abound. His bisexuality, which allowed him to change from a man to a woman for seven years and back to a man, was characteristic of Babylonian gods of healing and death, for instance the Babylonian Damu and the Hellenistic Syrian god Ešmun-Asclepius. Transvestite gods and goddesses in Syria and Babylonia make their way, for instance, into the Laws of Hammurabi no. 178–80 and the prohibitions against transvestism in Deuteronomy 22.5 (Astour, 1967a, 162–3). Dionysus, Cadmus' grandson, was notoriously sexually ambivalent; and the Egyptian–Phoenician dying god Bata revealed of himself: 'I am not a man but a woman' (Astour, 1967a, 163). Teiresias' sex changes, the last engendered by his act of killing the male of two copulating serpents, follow both Eastern symbolism of the seven-year fertility rotation and the motif of the serpent.

As we might now expect, Astour claims (1967a, 164) that 'all mythological motifs and most names in the myths of Semele, Ino, and all four (or five) of Cadmos's grandsons are borrowed, with great accuracy, from Western-Semitic mythology.' Actaeon, son of Autnonoë and Aristaeos, mighty hunter, in his deer form torn apart by 50 hounds, parallels in all important respects, even name, the Ugaritic hero *Aqht*, torn apart by eagles (Astour, 1967a, 164–6). His father Aristaeos is a god of harvest and abundance, like Aqht's father Danel. Actaeon's death, like that of Aqht's, brought on a seven-year drought. Actaeon's connection to the mythical king of that name, said to have ruled Attica before Cecrops, is confused: the name may be eponymous, the early name for Attica having been Actica, but, as Astour (1967a, 168) points out, 'is it not remarkable that his daughter was named *Phoinike* and that in her honour he gave to the letters he had invented the name *phoinikeia grammata* (an Attic variant of the Phoenician Cadmos who allegedly introduced the Phoenician alphabet in Greece)'?

The case of Dionysus, whose Bacchic rites have long been associated with the East, is a fascinating one. His mother, Semele, may derive her name from *Sml*, the she-eagle in the poem of Aqht, who fell to the ground after Baal, at Danel's request, had broken her wings. For Aqht had been killed by eagles which were systematically dissected and then resurrected by Danel, searching for the remains of his son. Only in the she-eagle's innards were they to be found; and she was not resurrected. Like Semele, daughter of Cadmus, killed by Zeus' lightning to extract the foetus of Dionysus, she was sacrificed. To tie the parallels closer, in one version of the story, told by Hyginus (*Fabulae* 167, cited in Astour, 1967a,

172), Semele ingests the heart of Dionysus, as *Sml* swallowed the remains of *Aqht*: 'And when Semele became pregnant because of it', and the child was extracted from her womb, he 'received the name of Dionysos and began to be called "born by two mothers"'. Hyginus' version, belonging to the Roman period, as Astour (1967a, 172) remarks, may be a late one, but it harks back to 'immemorial archaic times when it was believed that pregnancy could be caused by absorbing magic food', considered perhaps 'by the tragedy-writers and mythographers of the classical Greek epoch ... too naive and primitive for their refined tastes' and so not incorporated. (Had the climate changed in Hellenistic times, when mystery cults and table-fellowship [Nock, 1952] reintroduced the magical dimension of the sacred, which even the Christian sacrament of the Eucharist reflects?) Astour (1967a, 172) notes a continuity of motif in the second millennium myth of Kumarbi, who ingested the genitalia of his father, Anu, to become pregnant; and the Egypto-Phoenician tale of the two brothers, in which Bata, killed in the form of a bull, sows two persea trees from his blood, which his treacherous wife, who had married the pharaoh, ordered to be cut down. A wood chip flew into her mouth in the process, impregnating her and reincarnating Bata, who inherited the pharaoh's throne. The tale entered Egypt in the Nineteenth Dynasty, at the same time as other Phoenician myths like that of Astarte and the Sea-god Yamm; it contains obvious Phoenician elements, such as the cedar grove in which the action takes place (Astour, 1967a, 186, n.4).

In the interpretation of the Dionysus myth doublets play an important role. For instance, Cadmus' grandson Pentheus, cousin of Dionysus, is told by Euripides in the *Bacchae* to have been ceded Thebes by Cadmus, but challenged in his rule by Dionysus, who brought with him his orgiastic cult; Theban women, including his mother and aunts, carried away in Bacchic frenzy, took to the Cithaeron mountains, rending raw animals and devouring them; and Pentheus, when he chased them, disguised as a woman, was mistaken for a lion and torn to pieces (Astour, 1967a, 173). There is something characteristic about this sacrificial death. As the great nineteenth-century anthropologists, Robertson Smith and James Frazer have pointed out:

> In the Bacchic cult, the sacrifice still remained in its first, magic stage, and did not evolve to its second, religious stage: the sacrifice was not a gift to the god, not his share at the sacrificial meal of the clan, but it represented the god himself, killed to maintain the world order and eaten in a sacramental communion in order that all participants may partake and absorb his divine essence. The victim of the bloody Bacchic rites impersonated the god; god was sacrificed to himself. One of the most important personalities of the Dionysiac cult, Orpheus, perished the same death as Pentheus; and he has many features of a dying god, including his descent to and return from Hades. So Pentheus is a doublet of Dionysos, and their separation and the justification of Pentheus' death because of his enmity toward Dionysos is a common aetiological mode of mythology. Thus the boar who killed Adonis and was sacrificed to him in special cases, originally was Adonis himself, killed in the rite of communion; thus sacrificing goats to Dionysos was aetiologically motivated by Dionysos' hatred for the goats who damage the vines, although Dionysos himself was worshipped in the shape of a goat.
>
> Pentheus is a doublet of Dionysos–Zagreus not only in his death, but in his birth

as well. As Zagreus was conceived by Persephone from Zeus who took the shape of a dragon, as the Sumerian Tammuz (Dumuzi) was the son of Ningiszida, the serpent and dragon god, so Pentheus, too, was the son of the Echion 'the serpent man'. As Euripides emphatically expresses it (*Bacchae* 537–44), 'Pentheus betrays the chthonic race, brought up once by the dragon; begotten by the chthonic Echion, he is a grim-visaged monster and not a scion of mortals.' And from his mother's side he was the grandson of Cadmos, changed into (i.e. symbolized by) a serpent. (Astour, 1967a, 173–4)

Philological evidence supports the notion of the Pentheus–Dionysus doublet, which links these two to the dying god Orpheus. Pentheus derives his name from the Greek verb *pentheo*, 'to grieve, to wail', and 'weeping for the dying gods was the essential rite of their liturgy' (Astour, 1967a, 174). One among the popular names for Dionysus was Bacchus (*Bakchos, Bakcheus*), which can be derived from the common Semitic root *bky* (Akk. *baku*, Ugar. *bky*, Heb. *baka*) 'to weep, to wail' (Astour, 1967, 174–5). Astour adds (p. 175): 'There is, besides, clear and undeniable proof of the phonetic correctness of our etymology in a lexical statement by Hesychios: *bakchon: klauthmon: Phoinikes; klauthmon* or *klauthmos* means "weeping, howling, wailing, especially at a funeral".'

The central Bacchic orgiastic rituals involving initiates in the dismemberment and devouring (*sparagmos* and *omophagia*) of raw animal flesh, are attested as practices of the Sinaitic Saracens and Israelite tribes from earliest recorded times and have been the object of study by scholars of Semitic religion from Pseudo-Nilus of the fourth century AD to the nineteenth-century Wellhausen (1897) and Robertson Smith (1894) (cited in Astour, 1967a, 178). In almost identical ceremonies (Robertson Smith, 1894, 282, 338, 491), the Arab warriors, like the Israelites, celebrated victory in battle by eating the raw flesh, sometimes of humans, more frequently of animals, taken as spoils. Thus was the Israelite victory over the Philistines (Palestinians) celebrated (I Sam. 14.32–5); so 'possessed' by God, i.e. 'ecstatic', Saul cut to pieces an oxen and sent its parts all over the country (I. Sam. 11.6–7), and even sacrificed the captive king of Amalek, Agag, by having Samuel cut him to pieces (I. Sam. 15.33, cited in Astour, 1967a, 179). We have the record in a newly excavated Ras Shamra tablet (*RS* 22.225, cited in Astour, 1967a, 180) of the fearsome Ugaritic goddess Anath, who was known to have chopped up the god of the Nether World, Mot, and mutilated various mortals by chopping off heads and hands and bathing in their blood. Admiring 'her brother's timbrel and her brother's grace as most beautiful', in the same breath 'She ate his flesh without a knife, She drank his blood without a cup'!

Ecstatic feasts are attested everywhere as part of the Bacchic cult, said to bring initiates, especially female ones, to a 'hieratic state of holy madness' (Harrison, 1957, 395, cited in Astour, 1967a, 181) – hence their names *Maenads* (*Mainades*), from *mainomai* 'to be in a frenzy'. By a combination of 'shrill music, dancing, shouting, running, jumping and whirling, they were supposed to perform strange and extraordinary acts in a state of complete temporary madness, without realizing or being responsible for their deeds' (Astour, 1967a, 81) and were thus reminiscent of the orgiastic Hathor ceremonies (Springborg, 1990d, ch. 9), Sufi cults and the Ethiopian and Egyptian *zar* ceremonies of female exorcism, of a later age. Perhaps less well known is the connection between the ecstatic (temporary) madness induced by the Bacchic cults and the soothsayers of the ancient orient. For in Euripides' *Bacchae* (551) the Bacchants are clearly referred to as prophets (*prophetai*) of Dionysus; and yet more explicitly is it claimed by the blind Teiresias of Dionysus (*Bacchae*, 298–301, cited in Astour, 1967a, 183): 'A prophet (*mantis*) is this deity: the Bacchic frenzy and madness are full of prophecy (*mantike*); for, when the god in his fullness enters their bodies, he makes his maddened ones tell the future.'

Now Babylonian *mahhu*-priests 'were indubitable ecstatics and ... their very name signified "madmen"'; while in Western Semitic Mari in the eighteenth century BC soothsayers known as *muhhum* were influential (Astour, 1967a, 182). Ecstatic prophecy in ancient Israel is also well attested. For instance, at I Sam. 10.5b–6 (cited in Astour, 1967a, 183), Samuel says to Saul:

> when thou wilt enter the town, thou wilt meet a swarm of prophets descending the holy height, and in front of them are a harp, and a timbrel, and a flute, and a lyre, and they are prophesying. And thou wilt be seized by the spirit of Yahwe, and thou wilt prophesy with them, and thou wilt be changed into a different man.

The Hebrew verb 'to prophesy', *hitnabbe, from nabi*, 'prophet', also meant 'to be crazy' (Astour, 1967a, 183). 'To be among the prophets' (I Sam. 10.11–12, cited in Astour, 1967a, 183), was hardly respectable for an aristocrat like Saul. The query 'is Saul, too, among the prophets?', was an implied indictment that assumed prophecy to be a form of contagious mass hysteria: being 'seized by the spirit of God'. And in fact Saul was so 'seized'; 'and he too took off his clothes, and he too prophesied in front of Samuel, and he fell down naked, all that day and all night'. (I Sam. 19. 20–24, cited in Astour, 1967a, 183).

Much evidence connects the Old Testament prophets with ecstatic practices. In I Kings 18.12 we learn that prophecy carries prophets away one knows not wither; in II Kings 2.16 it carries them away into mountains and valleys – like the 'rushing' Bacchants (Euripides, *Bacchae*, 114–19); in II Kings 9.1, 11, prophets, as members of a 'brotherhood', are synonymous with 'madmen' (Astour, 1967a, 184). In I Kings 18.22, 450 Phoenician prophets of Baal are said to have assembled on Mount Carmel, and 400 Israelite prophets to have worshipped to Yahwe. The former, dancing around the altar, calling for apparitions, mutilated themselves with knives; while among the latter one donned iron horns like the 'horn-wearing' female Bacchants on Boeotian Mount Laphystos (Astour, 1967a, 184) – horns being once again the emblem of the celestial cow-goddesses of Mesopotamia and Egypt who produced the Milky Way, variously Ninhursag, Hathor, Io and Isis (Walker, 1983, 181).

The notion that both Hebrew prophets and Greek Bacchants might constitute brotherhoods or sororities is an interesting one, Astour (1967a, 184) noting that 'in historical times every city had its own college of women called *Thyiades* ("rushing ones") to perform the biennial orgies of Dionysos on Mount Parnassos.' Brotherhoods of flagellants in the Shia Ashura rites of Bahrain (Ashura from *Aššur* and the rites of the Assyrian goddess?) have been nicely documented for us as a modern legacy of these age-old cultic practices (Khuri, 1980). Nor were women priestesses unknown in Israel, being mentioned in II Kings 22.14 and Isa. 8.3, where Isaiah bears a son by a priestess whom he violated on Yahwe's orders, and probably not his wife (Astour, 1967a, 184–5). Deborah, the prophetess, is referred to in Judg. 4.4 as *eset Lappidot*, wife of Lappidot, which Astour (1967, 185) sees as more than a man's proper name, and perhaps a plural of *lappid*, torch, recalling the ancient torch festivals common also to the Bacchanalia. In Gen. 35.8, 'Deborah, the wet nurse of Rebecca, died and was buried below Bethel, under the terebinth; and he (Jacob) called it the "terebinth of wailing" (*'allon bakut*)' (cited in Astour, 1967a, 185). Now the Maenads of Dionysus are referred to in *Iliad* 6.130 ff as 'nurses of the maddened Bacchos', *bakut*, wailing, supplying the Hebrew element of his name. The name Deborah, on the other hand, is Hebrew for bee (*debora*), and the priestesses of Ephesian Artemis, the nurses of Hermes as of Dionysus were represented as bees (*Homeric Hymn to Hermes* 551–63, cited in Astour, 1967a, 185).

Among the attributes and accessories of Dionysus there are striking parallels to Egyptian and Semitic mythologies. Plutarch (*De Iside et Osiride*, 355, 1970 edn, 135–7) clearly states that Dionysus is Osiris, giving the Greek equivalents of other members of the Egyptian pantheon as well. Dionysus is represented by Pausanias as the giver of water from whose wand (*thyrsos*) a spring is struck (Pausanias 4.36.7, cited in Astour, 1967a, 186). The Bacchants drew water from the hills (Euripides *Bacchae* 764 ff), milk and honey from rivers (Plato, *Ion* 534a); at their ceremonies the earth ran with wine, milk and honey (Euripides, *Bacchae* 141, cited in Astour, 1967a, 186); and they carried wands, *thyrsi*, surmounted with pine cones.

> Like the Babylonian Tammuz, the Phoenician Adonis and the Byblian god identified by the Egyptians with Osiris, Dionysos was thought to be within a tree; in Boeotia, he was named *Endendros* (Hesychios). His principal tree was the pine; this related him not only to Osiris, whose corpse grew into the trunk of a pine, but also to Bata, the hero of an Egypto-Phoenician myth, who appears in the well-known 'Tale of the Two Brothers', and presents a considerable similarity to many details of the myth of Dionysos. Bata, in this tale, places his heart among the cones of a pine and dies when the pine is cut. Of the animals, the favorite symbol of Dionysos was the bull; in Crete, he was killed in the shape of a bull both in myth as Zagreus, and in ritual in the rite of omophagy; Bata, too, transformed himself into a bull and was killed in its shape, but was revived as two persea-trees which grew from drops of blood of the slain bull. (Astour, 1967a, 186)

10
Herodotus, Diodorus, Isocrates and the Historical Record

It is likely that the eponymous heroes, gods and their animistic images recorded most fully by Apollodorus, but corroborated in the accounts of Homer, Hesiod, Pausanias, Pindar, Strabo, Diodorus Siculus and the Latin poets, Apuleius, Ovid, Pliny, Propertius, Horace and Lucian, derive from an oral tradition chronicling the colonization and settlement of Greece, often distorted by the nationalistic aspirations of a people anxious to take centre stage – and perhaps doctor the historical record to ensure that this was so. Herodotus, unjustly pilloried by Plutarch as 'the father of lies', suggests as a matter of historical fact that the mythical heroes, Danaus and Cadmus, did indeed colonize Greece from the East. Herodotus, for whom the Dorian chieftains of the accepted Greek version of the origins of the Spartan royal house are genuine Egyptians, can give us some clue as to the significance of Sparta in Polybius, her twin kings descended from the mythical royal twins, reminiscent of Egyptian kings and their *ka*s, and her similar caste system.

Referring perhaps to the mythologies we have discussed, and almost certainly to other chronicles now lost to us, Herodotus gives various versions of the historiography of the Spartans, all or which, however, agree that their origins are in fact Egyptian:

> The common Greek tradition is, that the Dorian kings as far back as Perseus, the son of Danae (thus not including the god), are as they stand in the accepted Greek lists, and are rightly considered as of Greek nationality, because even at this early date they ranked as such … If, on the other hand, we trace the ancestry of Danae, the daughter of Acrisius, we find that the Dorian chieftains are genuine Egyptians. This is the accepted Greek version of the genealogy of the Spartan royal house; the Persians, however, maintain that Perseus was an Assyrian who adopted Greek nationality; his ancestry, therefore, was not Greek; and the forebears of Acrisius were not related to Perseus at all, but were Egyptian – which accords with the Greek version of the story. But there is no need to pursue the subject further. How it happened that Egyptians came to the Peloponnese, and what they did to make themselves kings in that part of Greece, has been chronicled by other writers; I will add nothing, therefore, but proceed to mention some points which no one else has yet touched upon. (Herodotus 6.55, 1972 edn, 406)

The story of the twin kings is perhaps an ingenious attempt to explain a derived institution indigenously: Argeia, great great grand-daughter of Polynices, 'gave birth to twins', of whom she forebore to disclose the elder, 'in the hope that both of them might somehow be made kings' (Herodotus 6.52, 1972 edn, 405). The oracle at Delphi, when consulted, allowed that this could pass so long as the elder received the greater honours – which did nothing to solve the problem. But a little ethnological research allowed the Spartans to conclude that because the mother always tended the needs of the twins in the same order, her order of preference reflected the order of birth. Eurysthenes was established as the elder and Procles the younger, on this basis, and although brothers, or perhaps because of it, they quarrelled, leading to a feud between the twin kings and their families that extended over generations (Herodotus 6.52, 1972 edn, 405–6).

The relationship between the twin kings of Sparta and the Egyptian pharaoh and his *ka* is not entirely fanciful, if we bear in mind institutional continuities in other areas between the Spartans and Egyptians, in particular in the important area of professional specialization (Herodotus 6.60, 1972 edn, 408): 'The Spartans resemble the Egyptians in that they make certain callings hereditary: town-criers, flute-players, and cooks are all, respectively, sons of fathers who followed the same profession.' Nor is Sparta a special case. Herodotus is insistent (2.49, 1972 edn, 149) that 'the names of nearly all the gods came to Greece from Egypt'; and the *Histories* are sprinkled with references to Danaus and Cadmus as colonizers. At 2.172 he says that as an initiate he 'proposes to hold [his] tongue about the mysterious rites of Demeter', associated we know with Isis, divulging only 'that it was the daughters of Danaus who brought this ceremony from Egypt and instructed the Pelasgian women in it, and that after the Dorian conquest of the Peloponnese it was lost; only the Arcadians, who were not driven from their homes by the invaders continued the celebration of it' (Herodotus 2.175, 1972 edn, 197). Another mention of the fleeing Danaans also comes in the context of the continuity of cultic practices. The temple of Athena at Lindos on Rhodes is said by Herodotus to have been 'founded by the daughter of Danaus, who touched at the island during their flight from the sons of Aegyptus' (2.182, 1972 edn, 201).

Interestingly, this observation, which sounds mythological out of context, is made in the course of a rather matter of fact discussion of the relations between the pharaoh Amasis and Greece. Having described the privileges that Amasis bestowed on the Greeks, the greatest of them being 'the gift of Naucratis as a commercial headquarters' (2.178, 1972 edn, 200), Herodotus goes on to record Amasis' pact of friendship sealed with Cyrene by his taking a Greek wife Ladice from that city; their early sexual incompatibility alleviated by Aphrodite on a promise to install her statue in the temple of the goddess of Cyrene. This success caused Amasis to endow further Greek temples, sometimes, as at Cyrene and Samos with effigies of himself, and at others with rich, even gold-plated, statues of the gods. Amasis, Herodotus observes, 'was also the first man to take Cyprus and compel it to pay tribute' (2.182, 1972 edn, 201), an indication of the diffusion of Egyptian influence in the Mediterranean.

Among the similarities between Greek and Egyptian cultic practices due to direct borrowing, the bull cults, the Egyptian Hercules, the Passion Play of Osiris and the rites of Dionysus are of great significance. Herodotus, dealing with bull and cow fetishes specifically, makes the link between the Egyptian god Apis and

Epaphus, the son of Zeus by Io, restored 'by a touch of his hand' from her cow shape. 'Bulls are considered the property of the god Epaphus – or Apis', Herodotus notes (2.37, 1972 edn, 144), while 'the statues of Isis show a female figure with cow's horns, like the Greek representations of Io, and of all animals cows are universally held by Egyptians in the greatest reverence' (2.143, 1972 edn, 145). 'This', he curiously adds, 'is the reason why no Egyptian, man or woman, will kiss a Greek, or use a Greek knife, spit, or cauldron, or even eat the flesh of a bull known to be clean, if it has been cut with Greek knife.' 'Beware of the Greeks ...' as the famous Virgilian epithet was later to run. In the case of the ancient Egyptians it was simply feared that Greeks did not respect sufficiently the rites, described in great detail by Herodotus (2.37–42, 1972 edn, 144–5), for sacrificial cleanliness. So, for instance, in a throw-away remark in the course of the account of the bull sacrifice, Herodotus indicates the contempt with which Egyptians regarded the Greeks in these matters: 'they [the Egyptians] take the beast (one of those marked with the seal) to the appropriate altar and light a fire; then, after pouring a libation of wine and invoking the god by name, they slaughter it, cut off its head, and flay the carcase. The head is loaded with curses and taken away – if there happen to be Greek traders in the market, it is sold to them; if not, it is thrown into the river ... Both the libation and the practice of cutting off the heads of sacrificial beasts are common to all Egyptians in all their sacrifices, and the latter explains why it is that no Egyptian will use the head of any sort of animal for food' – but will not hesitate to sell it to a Greek.

Herodotus explains similarities in the association of Io, like Isis, with the cow-goddess, as due to transmission from Egypt to Greece and not vice versa, consistent with his depiction of Egyptian culture as older and more revered. When it comes to the case of Hercules, Herodotus is explicit about the lines of transmission:

> it was not the Egyptians who took the name Heracles from the Greeks. The opposite is true: it was the Greeks who took it from the Egyptians – those Greeks, I mean, who gave the name to the son of Amphitryon. There is plenty of evidence to prove the truth of this, in particular the fact that both the parents of Heracles – Amphitryon and Alcmene – were of Egyptian origin. (Herodotus 2.44–5, 1972 edn, 146)

Taking the opportunity to deal a side-swipe at Hecataeus, often his source, Herodotus discusses among '[Greek] stories with no basis in fact ... one of the silliest', the story told about an imaginary King Busiris 'of how Heracles came to Egypt and was taken away by the Egyptians to be sacrificed to Zeus, with all due pomp and a sacrificial wreath upon his head'. Herodotus, who voyaged to Tyre to check out stories of a Phoenician Heracles, is willing to recognize more than one god of this name, but not this one. He is confident that 'the Egyptians have had a god named Heracles from time immemorial' and that he is one of the original Ennead: 'they say that seventeen thousand years before the reign of Amasis the twelve gods were produced from the eight; and of the twelve they hold Heracles to be one' (Herodotus 2.45, 1972 edn, 147).

The Egyptian Heracles is associated with the ram symbol of Amun, and represented in the names of his titulary and that of the pharaoh. Herodotus gives his version of the origins, which links the ram cults of Egypt and of Libya. Heracles, wishing to visit Amun, but being refused entry, persisted, causing Zeus to devise a strategy to frustrate his ends:

> His plan was to skin a ram and cut off its head; then, holding the head before him and covering himself in the fleece, he showed himself to Heracles. This story explains why the Egyptians represent Zeus with a ram's head – a practice which had extended to the Ammonians, who are a joint colony of Egyptians and Ethiopians and speak a language which has points of resemblance to both. So far as I can see, the Ammonians took their name from this circumstance; for *Amun* is the Egyptian name for Zeus. (Herodotus 2.42, 1972 edn, 146)

If the account of Zeus' deception bears striking resemblances to cultic deceptions in Euripides' *Bacchae*, Herodotus actually traces 'the reason why the Thebans do not sacrifice rams but consider them to be sacred animals' to this event. He then recounts a ram festival of Greek Thebes, with structural similarities to the original Ammonian performance and all the features of an oriental animal cult:

> Nevertheless on the festival of Zeus, which occurs once a year, they break this custom and do, in fact, slaughter a ram – but only one. They cut the animal in pieces, skin it, and put the fleece upon the statue of Zeus, just as Zeus once put it upon himself, and then confront the statue of Zeus with a statue of Heracles. Then all who are engaged in the ceremony beat their breasts as if in mourning for the ram's death, and afterwards bury the carcase in a sacred sepulchre. (Herodotus 2.43, 1972 edn, 146)

The self-flagellation bears resemblances to the Dionysian cults, as well as to Sufi cults and Shia Ashura rites that persist in the Middle East to this day (Khuri, 1980).

Diffusion of the Heracles legend and the puzzle of the derivation of the names of the gods, Herodotus puts down to the fact that 'the Egyptians were already at that time a sea-faring nation, and that some of the Greeks, too, used the sea.' Pursuing the notion of maritime diffusion, he tells how to satisfy his curiosity about another Heracles' story, he 'made a voyage to Tyre in Phoenicia, because [he] had heard that there was a temple there, of great sanctity, dedicated to Heracles' (Herodotus 2.45, 1972 edn, 147). There he found the temple, said to be as old as Tyre itself – and Tyre was said to have 'already stood for two thousand three hundred years'. Among its rich adornments, and 'not the least remarkable', were 'two pillars, one of pure gold, the other of emerald which gleamed in the dark with a strange radiance', for all the world like the electrum sheathed obelisks of the great Hatshepsut. Herodotus goes on to speak of another temple in Tyre dedicated this time to the Thasian Heracles, and of his visit to 'Thasos, where [he] found a temple of Heracles built by the Phoenicians who settled there after they had sailed in search of Europa'. 'Even this', he remarks, 'was five generations before Heracles the son of Amphitryon made his appearance in Greece.' 'The result of these researches is a plain proof that the worship of Heracles is very ancient', he concludes, and the possibility of multiple Heracles' figures is a real one. A view with which modern scholarship concurs (Brundage, 1958, 225–36). So 'the wisest course is taken by those Greeks who maintain a double cult of this deity, with two temples, in one of which they worship him as Olympian and divine, and in the other pay him such honour as is due to a demi-god, or hero' (Herodotus 2.45, 1972 edn, 147).

Having dealt with Egyptian origins of Greek ram and bull cults, Herodotus turns to the goat, noting the Egyptian taboo on the sacrifice of this sacred animal:

> The reason is this: they [those Egyptians who are known as the Mendesians] believe Pan to be one of the eight gods who existed before the subsequent twelve, and painters and sculptors represent him just as the Greeks do, with the face and legs of a goat. Not that they think he is, in fact, like that – on the contrary they do not believe he differs in form from the rest of the gods. But that is how they paint him – why, I should prefer not to mention. (Herodotus 2.46, 1972 edn, 148)

Once again Herodotus intimates the esoteric knowledge of an initiate. At any rate, he can state categorically that 'the Mendesians', named for Min of Chemmis, and inhabitants of the province of Mendes, 'hold all goats in veneration, especially male ones, whose keepers enjoy special honours'. Such is the 'particular reverence' with which they are held, that 'when [one] dies the whole province goes into mourning'. By a curiosity of etymology that is significant in itself, 'Mendes is the Egyptian name for both Pan and a goat'. And Herodotus gratuitously adds (2.47, 148): 'In this province not long ago a goat tupped a woman in full view of everybody – a most surprising incident.'

But Egyptian animal taboos vary from place to place; thus: 'the Egyptians who possess a temple dedicated to the Theban Zeus [Amun], or live in the province of Thebes, never sacrifice sheep but only goats; for not all Egyptians worship the same gods – the only two to be universally worshipped are Isis and Osiris, who, they say, is Dionysus' (Herodotus 2.42, 1972 edn, 145). Herodotus gives an account of the sacred practices associated with these gods in both their Egyptian and Greek versions. He tells the story, for instance, of the transmission of the rites of the Theban Zeus (Amun), to Dodona in Greece and to Siwa oasis, site of the great oracle later consulted by Alexander. According to the priests of the Theban Zeus, whom he claims to have consulted in person, 'two women connected with the service of the temple were carried off by the Phoenicians and sold, one in Libya and the other in Greece, and it was these women who founded the oracles in the two countries':

> At Dodona, however, the priestesses who deliver the oracles have a different [but related] version of the story: two black doves, they say flew away from Thebes in Egypt, and one of them alighted at Dodona, the other in Libya. The former, perched on an oak, and speaking with a human voice, told them that there, on that very spot, there should be an oracle of Zeus. Those who heard her understood the words to be a command from heaven, and at once obeyed. Similarly the dove which flew to Libya told the Libyans to found the oracle of Ammon – which is also an oracle of Zeus. (Herodotus 2.55, 1972 edn, 151)

Herodotus gives his own reconstruction of the establishment of the oracle in Greece – 'or Pelasgia as it was then called' – for Dodona as a cult centre was old, attested in Homer, *Iliad* 16.233, and *Odyssey* XIV (1980 edn, 172) and XIX (1980 edn, 235), where Odysseus confesses to Penelope that he 'had gone to Dodona to hear from the tall and leafy oak what Zeus himself counselled to him'

(*Odyssey*, XIX, 1980 edn, 235). Dodona is also known to us as a site of the oracle from the innumerable specimens of petition that have been excavated by archaeologists (Parke, 1970, 358). Assuming that 'the Phoenicians really carried off the women from the temple and sold them respectively in Libya and Greece', Herodotus speculates:

> the one who was brought to Greece (or Pelasgia as it was then called) must have been sold to the Thesprotians; and later, while she was working as a slave in that part of the country, she built, under an oak that happened to be growing there, a shrine to Zeus; for she would naturally remember in her exile the god whom she had served in her native Thebes. Subsequently, when she had learned to speak Greek, she established an oracle there, and mentioned, in addition, that the same Phoenicians who had sold her, also sold her sister in Libya. (Herodotus 2.60, 1972 edn, 152)

It is interesting to note that Herodotus has already established the connection between Egyptian and Greek Thebes, which share more than a name, as we now know (Astour, 1967a, 158; Bernal, 1987a, 51). He speculates on the form of the oracles as birds, suggesting:

> The story which the people of Dodona tell about the doves came, I should say, from the fact that the women were foreigners, whose language sounded to them like the twittering of birds; later on the dove spoke with a human voice, because by that time the woman had stopped twittering and learned to talk intelligibly. That at least, is how I should explain the obvious impossibility of a dove using the language of men. (Herodotus 2.60, 1972 edn, 152)

In a most pregnant comment, he further speculates: 'As to the bird being black, they merely signify by this that the woman was an Egyptian', concluding: 'it is certainly true that the oracles at Thebes and Dodona are similar in character' (Herodotus 2.60, 1972 edn, 152).

Greece is indebted to Egypt for the great range of cultic practices: 'ceremonial meetings, processions, and liturgies: a fact which can be inferred', Herodotus claims (2.61, 1972 edn, 152), 'from the obvious antiquity of such ceremonies in Egypt, compared with Greece, where they have only recently been introduced'. He goes on to record the festival of Artemis at Bubastis (bu = city, Bastis = Artemis), which includes a procession down the Nile on barges with music and sacrifices (Herodotus, 2.63, 1972 edn, 153); the festival of Isis at Busiris, where 'tens of thousands of men and women – when the sacrifice is over, beat their breasts: in whose honour, however, he does not feel it is proper for him to say' – of course it is Osiris, and this is his 'passion play', that Herodotus (2.63, 1972 edn, 152–3) describes; the festival of the lamps at Sais in honour of Athena (Neith) (2.63, 1972 edn, 153); of the Sun (Re) at Heliopolis; of Leto (Uat) at Buto; and of Ares (Set) at Papremis (2.62, 1972 edn, 152).

In the first of these, the festival of Artemis at Bubastis, we see all of the colour and commotion of cultic life in which women, as well as men, participate:

> The procedure at Bubastis is this: they come in barges, men and women together, a great number in each boat; on the way, some of the women keep up a continual clatter with castanets and some of the men play flutes, while the rest, both men and

women, sing and clap their hands. Whenever they pass a town on the river-bank, they bring the barge close in-shore, some of the women continuing to act as I have said, while others shout abuse at the women of the place, or start dancing, or stand up and hitch up their skirts. When they reach Bubastis they celebrate the festival with elaborate sacrifices, and more wine is consumed than during all the rest of the year. The numbers that meet there, are, according to native report, as many as seven thousand men and women – excluding children. (Herodotus 2.63, 1972 edn, 152–3)

If this account, almost exaggeratedly Nilotic in flavour, represents river-bound festivities on which Islam has subsequently imposed some decorum, Herodotus' account of the procession of the cult-figure of the god, Set, probably in a sacred barque, is reminiscent of the river processions of the pharaonic Sed and Opet festivals, for which we have corroborative evidence (Nelson, 1942; Murnane, 1975–, 574; 1981; Bell, 1985a). The festival of Set (Ares) at Papremis is singled out by Herodotus for mention as being of peculiar significance, and we see in its contours the outline of the struggle between the brothers, Seth and Horus for the attention of the mother, Isis, which led to the slaying of Osiris:

As the sun draws towards setting, only a few of the priests continue to employ themselves about the image of the god, while the majority, armed with wooden clubs, take their stand at the entrance of the temple; opposite these is another crowd of men, more than a thousand strong, also armed with clubs and consisting of men who have vows to perform. The image of the god, in a little wooden gold-plated shrine, is conveyed to another sacred building on the day before the ceremony. The few priests who are left to attend to it, put it, together with the shrine which contains it, in a four-wheeled cart which they drag along towards the temple. The others, waiting at the temple gate, try to prevent it from coming in, while the votaries take the god's side and set upon them with their clubs. The assault is resisted, and a vigorous tussle ensues in which heads are broken and not a few actually die of the wounds they receive. That, at least, is what I believe, though the Egyptians told me that nobody is ever killed. The origin of this festival is explained locally by the story that the mother Isis of Ares Seth once lived in the temple; Ares Seth himself was brought up elsewhere, but when he grew to manhood he wished to get to know his mother and for that purpose came to the temple where she was. Her attendants, however, not knowing him by sight, refused him admission, and succeeded in keeping him out until he fetched help from another town and forced his way in by violence. This, they say, is why the battle with clubs is part of the ceremony at the festival of Ares Seth. (Herodotus 2.63, 1972 edn, 153–4)

It cannot be missed that the barque shrine which Herodotus describes bears striking resemblances to the ark or 'chest' (Heb. *teba*) of Yahwe, placed by the Philistine princes on a wagon drawn by cows never yoked before, which perhaps lends its name to the spot, Thebes, to which Cadmus' cow led him; and the procession of 'a wagon (driven) by heifers (*moschoi*), [by which] says Zeus's oracle, [Cadmus and Harmonia] ... shall lead the barbarians' in Euripides' *Bacchae*, 1333–5 (Astour, 1967a, 158). The procession and mock battle have a modern parallel in the Mouled of Abu'l Hajjaj in Luxor temple, celebrated to this day on the site of the old Opet procession (Wickett, 1990).

Herodotus also records the ceremonies of the sacred crocodile god, Sobek (2.67–8, 1972 edn, 155–7), known to us from the Graeco-Roman temple at

Komombo in Upper Egypt; and he gives an account of a sacred phoenix rite, involving one of these legendary birds bringing 'its parent in a lump of myrrh all the way from Arabia and bur[ying] the body in the temple of the Sun in Heliopolis'; a rite which he does not claim to have witnessed, since it is reputed to take place only once every 500 years; and for which he relies on depictions on temple walls (Herodotus 2.75, 1972 edn, 157). One of the most central of Egyptian sacred rites, and one on whose subject Herodotus is most insistent that Greek parallels come about due to the transmission being from Egypt to Greece, and not vice versa, is the worship of Dionysus, or Osiris. Describing the ritual sacrifice, procession, the phallic puppet show and hymns to Dionysus, Herodotus observes that, 'the Egyptian method of celebrating the festival of Dionysus is much the same as the Greek, except that the Egyptians have no choric dance.' And he concludes:

> I will never admit that the similar ceremonies performed in Greece and Egypt are the result of mere coincidence – had that been so, our ties would have been more Greek in character and less recent in origin. Nor will I allow that the Egyptians ever took over from Greece either this custom or any other. Probably Melampus got his knowledge of the worship of Dionysus through Cadmus of Tyre and the people who came with him from Phoenicia to the country now called Boeotia. The names of nearly all the gods came to Greece from Egypt, I know from the inquiries I have made that they came from abroad, and it seems most likely that it was from Egypt, for the names of all the gods have been known in Egypt from the beginning of time, with the exception (as I have already said) of Poseidon and the Dioscuri – and also of Hera, Hestia, Themis, the Graces and Nereids. I have the authority of the Egyptians themselves for this. I think that the gods of whom they profess no knowledge were named by the Pelasgians – with the exception of Poseidon, of whom they learnt the name from the Libyans; for the Libyans are the only people who have always known Poseidon's name, and always worshipped him. Heroes have no place in the religion of Egypt. (Herodotus 2.49, 1972 edn, 149)

Herodotus links the transmission of the Egyptian gods specifically through the Pelasgians and their cult centre at Dodona, giving this as the route through which both Homer and Hesiod gained knowledge of the theogonies:

> In ancient times, as I know from what I was told at Dodona, the Pelasgians offered sacrifices of all kinds, and prayed to the gods, but without any distinction of name or title – for they had not yet heard of any such thing. They called the gods by the Greek word *theoi* – 'disposers' – because they had 'disposed' and arranged everything in due order, and assigned each thing to its proper division. Long afterwards the names of the gods were brought into Greece from Egypt and the Pelasgians learned them – with the exception of Dionysus, about whom they knew nothing until much later; then, as time went on, they sent to the oracle at Dodona (the most ancient and, at that period, the only oracle in Greece) to ask advice about the propriety of adopting names which had come into the country from abroad. The oracle replied that they would be right to use them. From that time onward, therefore, the Pelasgians used the names of the gods in their sacrifices, and from the Pelasgians the names passed to Greece. (Herodotus 2.50–55, 1972 edn, 150–1)

Herodotus is quite specific that the genealogies of these borrowed gods that Homer and Hesiod give us are correct, cuing us that this information has been checked and cross-checked, and that for him its veracity is a serious matter:

But it was only – if I may so put it – the day before yesterday that the Greeks came to know the origin and form of the various gods, and whether or not all of them had always existed; for Homer and Hesiod are the poets who composed our theogonies and described the gods for us, giving them all their appropriate titles, offices, and powers, and they lived, as I believe, not more than four hundred years ago. The poets who are said to have preceded them were, I think, in point of fact later. This is my personal opinion, but for the former part of the statement on these matters I have the authority of the priestesses of Dodona. (Herodotus 2.55, 1972 edn, 151)

Later Herodotus (2.141, 1972 edn, 186) refers to the attempt at historical reconstruction of Hecataeus, noting that in Egyptian Thebes he consulted the priests of Zeus (Amun) in order 'to trace his family back to a god in the sixteenth generation'. Hecataeus was given the same treatment as Herodotus himself, although the latter 'kept clear of personal genealogies'. The priests gave both the same demonstration: taking each 'into the great hall of the temple, and show[ing] [him] the wooden statues there', effigies of the high priests of the temple arrayed 'in hereditary succession. The object lesson, once the statues had been counted, was to point out that each man was a ' "piromis" (a word which means something like "gentleman") who was son of another "piromis" ... and far from being gods [or demi-gods] – they were men' (Herodotus 2.141–6, 1972 edn, 186–7). The age of the gods long predated this, for there was a time when 'Egypt was, indeed, ruled by gods, who lived on earth amongst men, sometimes one of them, sometimes another being supreme above the rest' (Herodotus 2.146, 1972 edn, 187). According to his reckoning 'the last of them was Horus the son of Osiris – Horus is the Apollo, Osiris the Dionysus, of the Greeks.' Herodotus (2.146, 1972 edn, 187) tries to establish the time frame for this mytho-history, that is to say myth construed as history:

In Greece, the youngest of the gods are thought to be Heracles, Dionysus and Pan; but in Egypt Pan is very ancient, and one of the 'eight gods' who existed before the rest; Heracles is one of the 'twelve' who appeared later, and Dionysus one of the third order who were descended from the twelve. I have already mentioned the length of time which by the Egyptian reckoning elapsed between the coming of Heracles and the reign of Amasis; Pan is said to be still more ancient, and even Dionysus, the youngest of the three, appeared, they say, 15,000 years before Amasis.

Once again Herodotus (2.146, 1972 edn, 187) is quite emphatic about the veracity of his account and the careful method by which records were kept:

They claim to be quite certain of these dates, for they have always kept a careful written record of the passage of time. But from the birth of Dionysus, the son of Semele, daughter of Cadmus, to the present day is a period of about 1600 years only; from Heracles the son of Alcmena, about 900 years; from Pan the son of Penelope – he is supposed by the Greeks to be the son of Penelope and Hermes – not more than about 800 years, a shorter time than has elapsed since the Trojan war.

There is further mention of Cadmus at 4.147 (1972 edn, 319) where Herodotus notes that Theras, the maternal uncle and regent during infancy, of the twin Spartan kings Eurysthenes and Procles 'was a Cadmeian by descent', who, on

their coming to majority, 'resented finding himself, after a taste of power, in a
subordinate position' and betook himself off to the island of Thera, 'which used
to be known as Callista', a Phoenician settlement. For, 'Cadmus the son of
Agenor touched at it during his search for Europa and, whether because he
liked the place or for some other reason, left there a number of Phoenicians
with his own kinsmen Membliarus amongst them' (Herodotus 4.147, 1972 edn,
319). Cadmus is further mentioned at 4.60, (1972 edn, 361) concerning the
tyrannicides, Harmodius and Aristogeiton who killed Hipparchus, the son of
the tyrant Pisistratus, of whom Herodotus makes the extraordinary claim: 'The
Gephyraei, to whom the two men who killed Hipparchus belonged, came, by
their own account, originally from Eretria; but I have myself looked into the
matter and find that they were really Phoenicians, descendants of those who came
with Cadmus to what is now Boeotia.' Moreover, it was these very 'Phoenicians
who came with Cadmus – amongst whom were the Gephryaei – [who]
introduced into Greece, after their settlement in the country, a number of
accomplishments, of which the most important was writing' (Herodotus 5.60,
1972 edn, 361).

A curious mixture of mytho-history, which none of his disclaimers concerning
one's right to hold what opinions one likes about them serves to inhibit, informs
Herodotus' work; to be found most notably at 2.146 (1972 edn, 187) where he
reaffirms his belief that the gods came to Greece from Egypt, before launching
into a fairly standard Greek chronology of the Egyptian age of kings:

> It is open to anyone to believe whichever of these two traditions he prefers; I have
> already stated my own opinion. If indeed these gods had been publicly known and
> had grown old in Greece, like Heracles, the son of Amphitryon, and Dionysus, the
> son of Semele, and Pan, the son of Penelope, it might have been said that the two
> last-mentioned were men who bore the names of previously existing gods; but the
> Greek tradition is that Dionysus, as soon as he was born, was sewn in Zeus' thigh
> and taken to Nysa, which is in Ethiopia above Egypt; and as to what happened after
> the birth of Pan, tradition is silent. It is clear to me, therefore, that the names of
> these gods became known in Greece later than the rest, and that the Greeks trace
> their genealogy from the time when they first acquired the knowledge of them.

What are we to make of Herodotus' theogonies and genealogies – strikingly
similar in tone as they are to those of the poets and mythographers who precede
the logographers? Is it too euhemerist to suggest that religion had sanctified the
remnants of folk-memory, recorded in saga and song, of eponymous founder
kings and their colonization of Greece from the East? Whatever the Greeks
believed about their myths, there is consistent information stored in the names
and places they record, which neither imagination nor the fabrication of exotic
histories worthy of great cities would serve to explain.

In the *Busiris* of Isocrates, indebted as it is to the work of Herodotus, we have
a construction of mytho-history that similarly moves between genealogies of the
gods and chronologies of kings, the celestial realm of the *theoi* and the world of
temporal history. The name Busiris, a corruption of Osiris – perhaps a form of
the Semitic *bet Osiris*, 'the place of Osiris' – was given to the delta city where the
rites of Osiris were celebrated, as Herodotus (2.56–63, 1972 edn, 152–3) tells us.
Indeed, the calumny against Busiris, the legendary king, which it is Isocrates'

purpose to refute, is the same referred to by Herodotus as 'the silly story' told by Hecataeus of how Heracles came to Egypt and, when taken away to be sacrificed by the Egyptians, turned on his captors, 'exerted his strength, and killed them all' (Herodotus 2.45, 1972 edn, 147). Herodotus had dismissed the story on the grounds that elaborate Egyptian purification rites would not permit human sacrifice, and that 'such a tale is proof enough that the Greeks know nothing whatever about Egyptian character and custom.' Isocrates is not content with this quick repost, however, perhaps because the *Defence of Busiris* written by Polycrates, to whom he addresses his dialogue, has raised the subject anew.

What follows, then, is a eulogy to Egyptian customs and kingship. It begins with the standard genealogy linking gods and kings: 'Of the noble lineage of Busiris who would not find it easy to speak? His father was Poseidon, his mother Libya the daugher of Epaphus the son of Zeus, and she, they say, was the first woman to rule as queen and to give her own name to her country' (*Busiris*, 10, 1945 edn, 109). Busiris, it seems, considered Libya 'too small for one of his endowment' and after 'he had conquered many peoples and had acquired supreme power, he established his royal seat in Egypt, because he judged that country to be far superior as his place of residence, not only to the lands which then were his, but even to all other countries in the world' (*Busiris*, 11, 1945 edn, 109). Isocrates proceeds to praise Egypt, the fructifying Nile, and the abundance of the land, reminscent of the praise of Egypt in Plato's *Timaeus* 22D. Egyptians live in an ecosystem capable of furnishing the conditions for a 'perfect state of happiness' (*Busiris*, 14, 1945 edn, 111). Into this situation Busiris stepped, the beneficent king. And how did he ensure the well-being of his subjects? 'He divided them into classes', after the manner of Plato's *Republic*, on the principle of one man one job, because 'those who apply themselves constantly to the same activities perform each thing they do surpassingly well':

> Hence we shall find that in the arts the Egyptians surpass those who work at the same skilled occupations elsewhere more than artisans in general excel the laymen; also with respect to the system which enables them to preserve royalty and their political institutions in general, they have been so successful that philosophers [e.g. Plato, editor's note] who undertake to discuss such topics and have won the greatest reputation prefer above all others the Egyptian form of government, and that the Lacedaemonians, on the other hand, govern their own city in admirable fashion because they imitate certain of the Egyptian customs. (*Busiris*, 16–17, 1945 edn, 113)

It is a matter of considerable interest that Isocrates should attribute the formation of the Spartan military caste system to Egyptian influence. Similarities include compulsory military service, common messes, 'the training of the body' and professional specialization (*Busiris*, 18, 1945 edn, 113); the differences being, it would seem, that Spartan professional soldiers are concerned with property acquisition, whereas Egyptian, much closer to the Platonist ideal, are not:

> But the Lacedaemonians have made so much worse use of these institutions that all of them, being professional soldiers, claim the right to seize by force the property of everybody else, whereas the Egyptians live as people who should neither neglect their own possessions, nor plot how they may acquire the property of others. (*Busiris*, 19, 1945 edn, 113)

Remarks Isocrates makes about the superiority of the Egyptian education system recall those made by Plato in the *Laws* and already cited. Noting that the Egyptians had perfected care of the body, he goes on to discuss what they did for the soul:

> for the soul they introduced philosophy's training, a pursuit which has the power, not only to establish laws, but also to investigate the nature of the universe. The older men Busiris appointed to have charge of the most important matters, but the younger he persuaded to forgo all pleasures and devote themselves to the study of the stars, to arithmetic and to geometry; the value of these sciences some praise for their utility in certain ways, while others demonstrate that they are conducive in the highest measure to the attainment of virtue. (*Busiris*, 22–3, 1945 edn, 115)

After a good deal to say about the piety and religiosity of the Egyptians, including the remark that 'oaths taken in their sanctuaries are more binding than is the case elsewhere' (*Busiris*, 26, 1945 edn, 117), Isocrates discusses the impact of Egypt on Pythagoras, transmitter of Egyptian philosophy to the Greeks:

> On a visit to Egypt he became a student of the religion of the people, and was first to bring to the Greeks all philosophy, and more conspicuously than others he seriously interested himself in sacrifices and ceremonial purity, since he believed that even if he should gain thereby no greater reward from the gods, among men, at any rate, his reputation would be greatly enhanced. (*Busiris*, 28, 1945 edn, 119)

Isocrates' rebuttal of the calumnies against Busiris, like that of Herodotus, takes the form of revising genealogies, 'improving the truth' of myth (*Busiris*, 36–7, 1945 edn, 123): 'For the same writers who accuse Busiris of slaying strangers, also assert that he died at the hands of Heracles; but all chroniclers agree that Heracles was later by four generations than Perseus, son of Zeus and Danae, and that Busiris lived more than two hundred years earlier than Perseus.' What 'improving the truth' of myth further means for Isocrates, as for Plato, is expunging from the theogonies the 'calumnies of the poets, who declare that the offspring of immortals have perpetrated as well as suffered things more atrocious than any perpetrated or suffered by the offspring of the most impious of mortals' (*Busiris*, 38, 1945 edn, 123). And here Isocrates refers to the mouth–womb symbolism of the theogonies, on which we have already commented as related to the legitimacy and dynastic struggles of tribal and totemistic kings: 'For not only have they imputed to them thefts and adulteries, and vassalage among men, but they have fabricated tales of the eating of children, the castrations of fathers, the fetterings of mothers, and many other crimes' (*Busiris*, 38, 1945 edn, 123–5). A perhaps not disingenuous fundamentalism forbids that such wrongdoings be attributed to the gods, who are in their nature perfect, Isocrates insists. Moreover, the gods wreak their revenge – and we see a hint of the pragmatism that Isocrates reports of Pythagoras, who felt that if purification ceremonies did him no good they did him no harm either:

> For these blasphemies the poets, it is true, did not pay the penalty they deserved, but assuredly they did not escape punishment altogether: some became vagabonds begging for their daily bread; others became blind; another spent all his life in exile from his fatherland and in warring with his kinsmen; and Orpheus, who made a

point of rehearsing these tales, died by being torn asunder. Therefore, if we are wise we shall not imitate their tales ...

For Isocrates too, then, improving the truth of myth involves sanitizing it of those 'atrocities' with which the poets have embroidered it, and restoring the genealogies in accordance with the scientific canons of *historia*:

since the question is open to the judgement of all and one must resort to conjecture, who, reasoning from what is probable, would be considered to have a better claim to the authorship of the institutions of Egypt rather than a son of Poseidon, a descendant of Zeus on his mother's side, the most powerful personage of his time and the most renowned among all other peoples? (*Busiris*, 35, 1945 edn, 123)

This means that the credentials of 'those who know' come before 'the counsels of older men or of the most intimate friends' (*Busiris*, 50, 1945 edn, 131). It is another case of the 'radical' restoration of a tradition against the received wisdom. Are Plato and Isocrates so naive that they did not know the functions the epic cycle and its 'atrocious tales' served? Or is this yet another attempt to clean up the past, to make it fit for the consumption of the virtuous ones: the Greek *agathoi*, noble by birth and noble by deed?

PART II

Renaissance Republicanism and the Eastern Marcher Lord

11

Republic and Empire

If the term 'despotism' gained its current referents to Asiatic regimes of a patrimonial character quite early, the term 'democracy' acquired its present connotations of 'constitutional' or 'representative' government earlier that we tend to think. When Titus Quinctius Flamininus, proconsul, declared at the Isthmian games of 196 BC the intention of the Senate and the Roman people to leave the conquered Greek cities of Philip and the Macedonians 'free, without garrisons, subject to no tribute and in full enjoyment of their ancestral laws' (Polybius, 18.46, 1979 edn, 516), he laid the seal of Roman approval on a system of democratic government in the Hellenistic world, already constituted under the Hellenistic kings. Under the royal aegis, and named for the kings who founded them, Greek cities of the first three centuries BC, one of the most prolific periods of city foundations, were typically given democratic constitutions. They had a representative assembly, whether *boule*, *koina* or *synodos*, rarely if ever the *ecclesia* or primary assembly of classical Athens; the classic roster of magistracies, more or less; a judicial system and autonomy in internal affairs (Jones, 1937, 1940; Larsen, 1945; Tarn, 1952).

This form of representative government, and not rule of the *demos*, is what the term democracy had, by the second century BC, come to mean. The need of a ruling Greek caste to maintain its control of municipal government, probably militated against the very suggestion of wider participation, or extension of the suffrage beyond the barrier of race to native inhabitants. But the presence of the distant king, centred in Antioch many days march away, in Alexandria or, later, in Rome, was no impediment to 'democracy' either. For democracy had already come to mean that form of constitutional rule associated with stability and conducive to economic growth and development, with which monarchy was not incompatible, although this would have been inconceivable to Aristotle and the theorists of the classical *polis*.

Not only did the Romans condone democratic government in the Empire, but they actively promoted it, so that 'the freedom of the Greeks' became a crusading slogan under which they established representative town councils for the first time, in Egypt for instance, on the classic model of the *boule* (Bowman, 1971). Of course, they did not extend 'freedom and autonomy' to the Western Empire because, unaccustomed to self-government, and deemed culturally inferior, the kingdoms of the Germanic and Celtic tribes were easily held by garrisons.

For these reasons, too, they tended to base the Empire in the easily secured West. But their Eastern policy, in guaranteeing ancient freedoms, was not one of capitulation. Although it was indeed impossible to monitor these widely dispersed republics too closely, and colonial independence was a policy of pragmatism, it brought with it positive benefits that were primarily economic.

For 'democracy' soon acquired its present predominantly economic sense: freedom to trade; freedom to acquire; freedom to accumulate – something officially ruled out under its classical definition. And Roman practitioners, like Hellenistic theorists, were attuned to the superiority of republican, or 'democratic', government over monarchy in economic terms. A constitution that facilitated the dispersal of wealth among the ruling 'many', as opposed to the monarchical or aristocratic 'few', provided great incentive to economic development and political expansionism. A fact that Machiavelli, steeped in the writers, Roman and perhaps Greek, of the Hellenistic period, was quick to perceive. From the point of view of the rulers, rather than the ruled, whose perspective had long dropped from sight in systems where 'freedom' was defined by representation rather than by participation, republicanism, or representative democracy, offered unparalleled economic and political advantages over its competitors. And it was in terms of these advantages that Hellenistic writers and their early modern successors, abandoning the 'moralistic' stance of the classical Greek writers, made their judgements.

In fact, of course, the classical writers had their hidden agendas too, Aristotle and Plato displaying the scarcely veiled contempt for popular politics that characterized members of the old aristocratic families, whose ideal was stoic withdrawal when power was not actually in their hands (Adkins, 1963; Lateiner, 1982). But their purposes were only incidentally economic. As representative of old money and the values of an ancient ruling caste, they valued leisure, the pursuit of wisdom and cultivation of the arts, abhoring the commercialism and aspirations to expansionism of new blood and new money. It is almost certain that Aristotle did not condone the aspirations of Alexander, if he could even understand them, and although a Stagirite, he displayed all the conservatism and complacency of the foreigner who could 'pass' in Athenian society. Plato, although by no means the small-minded Greek, had intimations of the origins of empire, rejecting the 'city of pigs' based on subsistence needs, and was greatly admiring of Egypt, her laws and just kings. He nevertheless believed that the stability of the fragile *polis* depended on the careful curtailment of expansionist forces, and maintenance of the delicate class balance on which it was founded.

But by Polybius' day – and that of Machiavelli, his rightful successor – the *polis* as such was an obsolete social form. Deprived of its brief buffers against the incursions of the great empires of the East, the classical city-republic rapidly succumbed to internal tensions and external pressures. Hellenistic writers, once the obligatory period of mourning had passed for the 'golden age', turned to a celebration of Empire that was to last well into the early modern period. The economic vitality and improvement in the conditions of daily life, that the opening to the East and its unparalleled social developments permitted, became the object of praise rather than Spartan moralizing. And if the East had for millennia been the repository of all images of luxury and decadence, as it continues to be today, this was not considered such a bad thing (Said, 1978;

Grosrichard, 1979). The excitement engendered by constantly expanding economic and social vistas captured the imagination of all those who followed the great Alexander, who led the march East. And it rekindled interest in his predecessors, Cyrus and the great marcher lords of Assyria and Babylonia, further back again.

In the long interval between the Hellenistic 'democracies' and the Renaissance revival of 'republicanism', the incursions of the Muslims from the desert, their lightning strikes on the sedentary civilizations of the Eastern cities, and their successful conversion from raiders to emperors, impressed itself on the minds of thoughtful Western observers, who nevertheless maintained the fiction of 'oriental despotism' to hide divided loyalties. Inhabitants of smaller and more parochial polities once again raised the Polybian questions: what constitution facilitated the acquisition of empire on a world scale? And was it justified? The answer, and it was a time-honoured one, was 'republicanism', by now indistinguishable, as a term, from 'democracy' (Larsen, 1945; Jones, 1965). For what 'republicanism' promised, as Aristotle had appreciated in his discussion of 'polity', was that stability which comes from the spread of power among a ruling elite, sufficient to solve the problems of succession and acquisition that monarchy itself is too fragile to solve. On the other side, this new 'republicanism', which did not rule out a remote *imperium*, or even the marcher lord and his successors as a vehicle of economic development and territorial expansion, did not suffer from the limitations of the *polis* as a small-scale stationary state. Indeed, those long vistas of progress and development, believed to have been opened up by the revolutions of the late eighteenth and early nineteenth centuries, were already opened up here. And we have been feeling their effects ever since.

If republicanism and despotism seem to lie uncomfortably close together on the Machiavellian spectrum, the context of incipient empire perhaps explains why. Even in Florentine practice, the more liberal of the Renaissance states, they did not lie far apart. The distance was approximately that between Ghibelline and Guelf; between old money and new. Republican Florence spread power to a group that was newer, but just as narrowly based, as the old party of oligarchs who brought the Medicean despots to power. And although the *popolo*, as a party, governed as an oligarchic elite in its turn, the phenomenon of the 'new prince', a catalyst for expansionism, when tamed by constitutional government was a development that excited the old Republican. It reminded him of Cyrus, praised by Plato for having combined the maximum democracy consistent with stability, and the great Alexander, whose successors instituted constitutional regimes that carved up the old Eastern Empires and contained them.

Thus Machiavelli further eroded the already narrow space between democracy and despotism by taming the prince, tying him to constitutional government, and retaining the old term *tiranno* with its old meaning 'rule without laws' (Strauss, 1948, 93, 119, n.4) for those who, due to incapacity or malevolence, failed to make the transition to constitutional government. That he makes the distinction at all is not from moral but from strategic considerations. In fact, he is more classical than we like to think, for good tyrants were by no means an ancient contradiction in terms. Xenophon's *Hiero*, among Machiavelli's most cited authorities, sets as its subject the question 'how tyranny can best be preserved or rather improved'; and even Aristotle maintained that piety is more necessary to a tyrannical government than any other form, noting that the government of Cyrus, although no tyranny, became more pious as it became more absolute (Aristotle, *Politics*, 1314b39 ff; Xenophon, *Cyropaedia* VIII 1.23, and Machiavelli, *Prince*, XVIII, cited in Strauss, 1948, 93, 119, n.4). This, too, was an observation made from strategic rather than moral considerations.

A long interval separated Machiavellian republicanism from Aristotelian polity. Into the hiatus fell medieval 'Aristotelian' hierarchy and Hellenistic crusading democracy. When classical republicanism re-emerges with the resurrection of its political forms, it includes a bit of both. On the one hand, it cannot dispense with the services of monarchy in providing leadership and a focus of national loyalties – anathema to Athenian democracy or even oligarchy. On the other, it incorporates a more broadly based constitutionalism, anchored on the solid footing of bourgeois wealth, and here it emulates Aristotelian 'polity'. What makes for the signal differentiation between Renaissance republicanism and the classical *polis* is the economic orientation of the former. Government by the bourgeoisie for the bourgeoisie is the aim to which it aspired, whereas the ancient *polis* moved between government by the old aristocrats, whose wealth was landed – and did not involve soiling one's hands – and government by demagogues on behalf of the hoplite soldier.

Machiavelli is remarkably open about the economic advantages that accrue from republicanism synthesized with monarchy. So while the new prince makes the lightning strikes, constitutional government conserves the gains. Considerations of benefit to the ruled, the nature of the 'good life', peace and well-being are believed to flow from political success in laying claim to and securing a territory, and not from moral ethos or any equally abstract notion. Machiavelli, in his assertion that in 'free countries, riches multiply and abound', because 'everybody is eager to acquire such things and to obtain property, provided he be convinced that he will enjoy it when it has been acquired', comes close to the classic economic defence of democracy:

> it thus comes about that, in competition one with the other, men look both to their own advantage and to that of the public; so that in both respects wonderful progress is made. The contrary of this happens in countries which live in servitude; and the harder the servitude the more does the well-being to which they are accustomed, dwindle. (Machiavelli, *Discourses*, 2.2, 1974 edn, 280)

More extraordinary still, if Machiavelli divines the motor of progress as that restless desire for acquisition upon acquisition, founded in the fact that 'human appetites are insatiable – for by nature we are so constituted that there is nothing we cannot long for' (*Discourses*, 2, Introd., 1974 edn, 268) – he at the same time realizes that there is a definite limit to acquisitiveness compatible with stability and the longevity of the polity. The great republic is that which can resist the temptations to indulgence which conquest brings, and, by the stout assertion of sturdy rustic manners, can resist foreign manners and exotic customs that will corrupt it. History has proven that conquests can 'do no small harm even to a well-ordered republic when the province or city it has acquired is given to luxurious habits which can be taken up by those who have intercourse with it', as happened to Rome. Machiavelli cites Juvenal, who in his *Satires* maintained that, due to familiarity with (Eastern) luxurious custom, this ancient Republic, whose safeguard had lain in the rustic citizen warrior, succumbed: ' "gluttony and self-indulgence took possession of [her] and avenged the world [she] had conquered" ' (Machiavelli, *Discourses*, 2.19, 1974 edn, 338).

The spectre of 'oriental despotism' continues to be the mirror held up to expansionist democracies to remind them of the dangers of excess. As the vehicle for a cautionary tale, the concept has substance more as a foil for the failings of republicanism, than by virtue of intrinsic properties. As a highly transportable form, 'oriental despotism' moves from Moscow to Teheran, Damascus to Baghdad, as the occasion suits. But everywhere it performs the same function: the grim reminder to those who would take the logic of economic expansionism too far, that corruption ultimately leads to tyranny. So the despot is always accompanied by the concubine; crown and *seraglio* go together. If pressure as far north as Moscow is momentarily relaxed, it is reapplied further East – in Baghdad or Teheran. If in the twentieth century oriental despotism has been melded to the phenomenon of totalitarianism, this reminds us that Western economic acquisitiveness has reached correspondingly gargantuan proportions, that it needs such a spectre to legitimize it. So much so that borrowing against the future to fulfil the promises of economic freedom made in the present threatens the very stability and longevity of 'democracy'.

As the political dimension of participation in power has receded further and further from the everyday life of the citizen, the opportunities for economic freedom become ever more highly valued. Max Weber, it was, who first pointed out that competition for honour and prestige can, under certain circumstances, substitute for power (Weber, 1958). The European bourgeoisie, heir to the burghers of the early modern city, who gained economic but not political independence from feudal lords in the countryside, found in the professionalization of work, opportunities for status and honour that access to the political arena denied them. They were, in this respect, the first economically dominant class that did not rule (Veyne, 1976, 117). And the continuous economically rationalizing activity in which they engaged laid the basis for a capitalist system where, contrary to Marxist opinion, the status and prestige that accrue from wealth to an economic elite do not have to be cashiered into political power in order to be satisfying. Economic power brings with it visible trappings of status, in the form of conspicuous consumption, that cannot be matched by political power in polities so large that all but the few who capture the media are faceless and nameless. Political power, to be a compelling motivation, requires the face-to-face society in which it can be recognized (Olson, 1971). Economic power, since it carries with it identifying accoutrements, can both be more widely spread and more immediately enjoyed. The genius of modern democracy – not so modern, as we have observed – is that it hitched its wagon to the economic stars, leaving political participation and influence far behind as obsolete vestiges of an ancient form: the *polis*. This development did not necessarily presuppose conscious choice, but it was not made in ignorance either. The classical curriculum kept ancient models before early modern eyes. But the lure of empire was too great.

12
Aristotelian Republicanism or Renaissance Platonism?

All the states, all the dominions under whose authority men have lived in the past and live now have been and are either republics or principalities.

Machiavelli, *The Prince*

Two things are clear about the ancient antithesis between monarchy and republicanism, which Machiavelli here invokes. First, the polarity is binary, harking back to Plato and Herodotus, and eschewing the tripartite typology of regimes – monarchy, aristocracy and democracy – which had found favour with Aristotle. Secondly, and just as importantly, both republics and principalities are species of *dominium* or *stato*. That is to say, they are above all subject to power as objects for those who wield it – and here *res publica*, or literally 'the public thing', loses its ancient connection to the *ager publicus*, as the open field of public participation, and is lumped together with the *stato*, or the estate of a prince as a power object.

The question of Aristotle as a model for Renaissance republicanism is a complicated one. It has been customary for recent scholars to argue that classical republicanism, as a phenomenon, is indebted to Aristotle, its spokesman; and that Renaissance republicanism, flourishing in the aftermath of the mid-thirteenth century rediscovery and translation of Aristotle's social and political works, is Aristotelian in this sense. Thus John Pocock, in his magisterial account of the classical republican tradition from Athens to Philadelphia, maintains: 'As we complete this study of the last phase of Florentine political theory, the most vivid impression remaining should be that of the continuity of a basically Aristotelian republicanism from which Machiavelli did not seem ... to have greatly departed' (Pocock, 1975, 316). And again: 'It was in the Aristotelian and civic humanist channel that the stream of republican tradition was to flow, and Machiavelli as a historical figure, to whom theorists like Harrington and Adams referred, was to swim quite successfully in that channel' (Pocock, 1975, 317).

Quentin Skinner in two seminal pieces (Skinner, 1986, 1989) has reassessed the impact of Aristotle, including the scholastic Aristotle, on humanist and prehumanist Italian thought. Citing the excellent work of Nederman (1987, 1988) on the comparative impact of Aristotle and Cicero on late medieval European political thought, he shows that indigenous Latin and Italian sources can be given for many of the ideas hitherto thought to be Aristotelian. Indeed, it can be shown that in many cases humanist and prehumanist writers did not have access to the

Aristotelian texts to which they were assumed to be indebted. Primary Italian sources for Renaissance humanism of the *quattrocento* are not Greek treatises at all, but letters and model speeches in the local rhetorical tradition of *Ars dictaminis*, published by *Dictatores*, teachers of rhetoric, for the instruction and use of city magistrates (Skinner, 1989, 5). These works belonged to the same genre as the letters and speeches which constitute the overwhelming bulk of the surviving political writings of republican Rome; and not surprisingly, since in form and content they perform much the same function – practical instruction informed with the necessary amount of theory, and no more, for effective and responsible government. Discussing a representative sample of these Italian humanist and prehumanist writings, Skinner points out:

> None of these writers had any direct acquaintance with the works of Aristotle. Orfino da Lodi, Giovanni da Viterbo, Guido Faba, and the author of the *Oculus* all completed their treatises before the earliest Latin version of the full *Nicomachean Ethics* started to circulate in the early 1250s, and considerably before William of Moerbeke issued the first Latin translation of the *Politics* a decade later. Even Brunetto Latini, writing in the 1260s, still had access only to the brief and inaccurate paraphrase of the *Ethics* translated from the Arabic by Hermannus Alemannus in 1243–4. Still more striking is the fact that, among writers of *Dictamina* and similar compilations in the ensuing generations, the doctrines of Aristotle and his modern disciples appear to have had virtually no impact. When Geremia da Montagnone, for example, assembled his *Compendium moralium notabilium* between 1295 and his death in *c.*1320, he showed a full awareness of the Aristotelian texts, but made no attempt to integrate them with, or use them to displace, the more traditional authorities he continued to cite. Finally if we turn to the moral and political assumptions embodied in such products of the *Ars dictaminis* as Matteo de' Libri's *Arringhe* of *c.*1275, or Giovanni da Vignano's *Flore de parlare* of *c.*1290, or Filippo Ceffi's *Dicerie* of *c.*1330, we encounter in every case an exclusive reliance on traditional authorities, with no mention or even awareness of the Aristotelian texts at all. The moralists on whom these writers continued to rely were the moralists not of Greece but of Rome. (Skinner, 1986, 4–5)

Renaissance theorists of the city-republic seem to cite Aristotle's *Politics* very infrequently. Passages can be found in Guiccardini saluting Aristotle's metaphysics. Unreferenced comments are to be found in writers on the government of republics like Gianotti, to the effect that Aristotle, as the author of so many doctrines and so much wisdom, would certainly condemn both Venice and Florence for failure to enlist the *popolari* as citizens (cited in Pocock, 1975, 268, 312–13). But in the writings of Machiavelli, the greatest republican of them all, references to Aristotle are significantly absent. His only mention of him in the *Discourses* (3.26, 1974 edn, 477) concerns, typically, women as the downfall of whoring, rapine and adulterous tyrants, which would seem to refer to *Politics* 1314b27 and 1303b17–1304a18, with characteristic Machiavellian embellishments (see Mansfield, 1979, 391).

A number of reasons may be given. The first, and not the least, is the fact that Aristotle's name, despite rather than because of Aquinas, was irrevocably associated with feudalism and hierarchy (Kramnick, 1982, 653; Brown, 1986, 387). As at least one modern medievalist (Nederman, 1987) has shown, the bulk of scholastic references to Aristotle are not to the *Politics* or the *Ethics*, both lost to the Aristotelian corpus probably from the time of the destruction of the Alexandrian Library – if not from the death of Theophrastus and the removal of his copies of Aristotle's works to Neleus of Scepsis in the Troad – but to Aristotle's writings on peripheral subjects. His works, the *Physics*, the *Metaphysics* and the biological treatise on *The Motion of Animals*, provided organic principles and metaphors available for political extension, more aptly suited to the conceptualization of feudal society than the principles of the *Politics*. When, after 1250, the lost *Politics* and *Nicomachean Ethics* once more became available, and accessible in Latin translations, old habits died hard. Cary Nederman points out that the writings of major medieval political theorists writing after 1250, Pierre d'Auvergne and Pierre Dubois, writing between 1290 and 1310; Marsiglio of Padua, writing in the 1320s; and John Fortescue, writing late in the fifteenth century; 'rely for their authority upon Aristotelian texts dealing with metaphysics, nature and language rather than political philosophy'. The reason being that Aristotle did not address the questions which his works were put to work to answer: questions such as '(1) the establishment of a principle of limitation upon govermental powers of taxation: (2) the introduction of a unitary order among superior and inferior forms of jurisdiction; and (3) the discovery of comparative techniques for the analysis of nation-states' (Nederman, 1987, 32).

This ingenious explanation is surpassed in boldness by the view, more plausible if it can be substantiated, of Godfrey Tanner (1990a,b), who suggests that the substance of Aristotle's political and rhetorical writings may date to the period at which he developed a course of instruction for Alexander, and presumably the Royal Pages, at the Mieza Palace in Pergamum between 343 and 337 BC. The central non-scientific writings originally would have taken the explicit form of handbooks for princes, then, which in some respects they never lost – accounting for the anomalous and apparently quaint profile of the grandee (*megalopsuchos*), so central to the account of timocratic rule; the theory of kingship as an extension of princely beneficence; and the typology of Eastern kingships as belonging to a manual on colonial rule. Tanner's theory has the advantage of explaining both the attenuated ancient lists of Aristotle's works, and the Hellenistic diffusion of his monarchical theories. For if, as he maintains (Tanner, 1990a, 1–5), royal copies of the Mieza writings had been deposited with Alexander, that may have found their way to the Alexandrian library after 332 BC, this may account for some of the 100 works alleged in 550 books by a Peripatetic Ptolemy, probably of the second century AD and referred to in a thirteenth-century Arabic text, as comprising both the works in earlier lists and our established corpus (Tanner, 1990a, 3). Tanner suggests that the banishment to the Troad of the later Lyceum-Apellicon writings, which date from the period, after 335 BC, at which Aristotle adapted his doctrines to the more democratic climate of Athens, may be explained by a desire to escape the clutches of those rapacious curators, first the Ptolemies, on the hunt for the remainder of the Aristotle collection to complete the Alexandrian archive, and later the Attalids, anxious to complete the collection at Pergamum (Tanner, 1990a, 3–4). This explanation would certainly go further than any other toward explaining the unity of Hellenistic political theory that held together the diverse kingdoms ruled by the 'companions' of Alexander, the Attalids, the Seleucids, and the Ptolemies – as Royal Pages some of them not only shared Alexander's instruction by Aristotle, but they also enjoyed the legacy of his princely writings.

For the marriage of Greek theory and Macedonian practice had been fused under the powerful heat of Platonism in Hellenistic notions of kingship. The ascription to Aristotle of pseudonymous works like the Platonist *De Mundo*, describing a world order governed by a transcendent god, impersonal and exercising undefined powers (Kerford, 1967, 92), is evidence of the assimilation of Aristotle to the Platonist tradition in the Hellenistic period. Plato, who revered the wisdom and laws of the Egyptians, who displayed a knowledge of the Egyptian education system and social structure that may well have been acquired first hand from his reputed sojourn in Heliopolis, and who praised the Persian king, gained a cult following in Alexandria and Eastern capitals. Connections between Platonism, pharaonic theology, Persian court ceremonial and magic, some of which may well have existed in the mind of the philosopher himself, were given written expression in the fabrication of the Hermetic writings and the persona of Hermes Trismegistus, which were to exercise such an important influence in the Renaissance period that Cosimo de Medici ordered Marsilio Ficino to translate the Greek manuscripts containing the Hermetic writings into Latin before embarking on the translations even of Plato which were to set the Renaissance on its path (Kristeller, 1944a; Yates, 1964, 12–13; 1979). For it is no exaggeration to maintain that the Renaissance classical legacy is primarily Platonist, established fortuitously by the reintroduction at the Ferrara–Florence conference of 1438–9 of the Plato transmitted by the Byzantines in the person of Gemisthus Pletho. It is worth noting that the occasion was an opportunity for pan-Hellenic propaganda on the part of the Byzantine and that Florentine humanists present, including Marsilio Ficino and Cosimo de Medici himself, were at least as receptive to the imperial possilities of the Byzantine Plato as they were to the theological teachings which were the pretext for their introduction. The Plato to whom they were introduced was the Plato of the great Hellenisitic centres of learning, to which, as we have seen, the early Aristotle also belonged. Thus in a curious case of anachronism, the Peripatetic monarchical Aristotle had prepared the way for the rebirth of Platonism. To the extent that Aristotle himself was revivified, and then, as I later show (part II, chapter 20), it was mainly for his view on Asiatics and patrimonial rule, it was primarily through the Paduan School.

At the philosophical level the Renaissance and Platonism were more or less coextensive phenomena, as the Italian tradition of Renaissance scholarship, exemplified by Garin (1965) and others has always stressed. Recent studies have demonstrated the extent to which the Italian Renaissance drew on the Byzantine Palaeologan 'revival of learning'. Byzantine emigrés were pressed into service in the *quattrocento* (Geanakoplos, 1988, 350–1) to retranslate those texts translated from Greek to Latin on the rather unsatisfactory 'word for word' (*verbum ad verbum*) method employed by Aristotle's translator, William of Moerbeke, for instance. Dating from the appointment of the southern Italian Byzantine, Leontius Pilatus to the Greek chair in the Florentine *studium*, due to the good offices of Boccaccio, Greek studies in that city flourished. In 1397 the Byzantine Manuel Chrysoloras took up the invitation of the Florentine *signoria* to teach in their city, beginning his enterprise by constructing a Graeco-Latin grammar. Among his many students was the famous Leonardo Bruni, who undertook his own retranslation of Aristotle's *Politics* to replace the unsatisfactory Moerbeke edition (Geanakoplos, 1988, 354–5). Chrysoloras himself began the task of translating Plato that Florentine humanists, notably Marsilio Ficino, were to complete. Interestingly, Chrysoloras recommended to his students the late Platonist Plutarch as the best Greek author with whom to begin their studies, because 'he most successfully bridged the gap between Greeks and Romans' (Geanakoplos, 1988, 355).

Early indications of the political interests of the humanists in Greek texts are evident in the case of Leonardo Bruni, who sought out the writings of the Greek orator Aelius Aristides 'to draw the analogy between the democracy of Athens, which had saved Greek culture from the Persians, and the republicanism of Florence, then locked in struggle with the despotic Visconti of Milan' (Geanakoplos, 1988, 355). Ushered in dramatically by a philosophy conference, convened in Ferrara/Florence in 1438–9 by the Church of Rome and the Eastern Patriarchate as a last ditch attempt at reconciliation, Platonism was popularized in Florence by the lectures of Gemistus Pletho, a Byzantine scholar, polytheist, educated in the Arabic commentaries on Aristotle, as well as in Chaldaic astronomy and astrology and the doctrines of the Pythagoreans (Barker, 1957; Gill, 1959; Geanakoplos, 1966, 1967, 1976, 1978, 1988). More than just a philosopher, Pletho, who had pursued his Arabic studies at the Turkish court, and who spent most of his life in the great cultural and administrative centre of the Byzantine Empire, Mistra, in the Peloponnese near Sparta, wedded his philosophical speculations to a plan for the social and economic revivification of Greece. His lectures in Ferrara and Florence, not surprisingly, fell on fertile ground. Among the Latin humanists present were Leonardo Bruni, Ambrogio Traversari – 'the first Latin since Burgundio of Pisa in the twelfth century to translate Byzantine church fathers into Latin' (Geanakoplos, 1988, 356) – Poggio Bracciolini, Lorenzo Valla, Leon Battista Alberti and Nicholas of Cusa. Interest in the Greek church fathers, as scholars have remarked, ran a close second to Plato among humanists who attended (Geanakoplos, 1976, 270; 1988, 356).

Pletho preferred the company of Florentine humanists to the proceedings of the ecclesiastical council and was said, 'at banquets hosted by Cosimo de' Medici', to have 'held forth on the pagan philosophic doctrines not only of Plato but of his Neoplatonic followers Iamblicus and Proclus, no few of whom the West now learned of for the first time' (Geanakoplos, 1988, 356). The programmatic statements he made we find echoed constantly in the writings of Marsilio Ficino and other Florentine Platonists. In his treatise 'On the Differences Between Plato and Aristotle', for example, he asserts the superiority of Platonism over Aristotelianism, which gave rise to a polarization between those thinkers that was not evident in the nascent Byzantine tradition, but which was exhibited by Marsilio Ficino (Geanakoplos, 1967, 350–51; 1988, 356–7), for instance. Ficino, who refers in the introduction to his *Questiones de luce* to 'our Plato', elsewhere in the work claims Plato as the greatest authority (f.16, cited in

Kristeller, 1944b, 47). As Kristeller has pointed out, Ficino's enthusiasm for Plato is overlaid on a solidly Aristotelian schooling and a thorough knowledge of the scholastic tradition of Aristotle that contrasts strangely with 'his admiration for Plato [which] is apparently greater than his direct knowledge of his works' (p. 47). Ficino knew the *Timaeus*, the *Phaedo*, the *Phaedrus* and perhaps the *Republic*, from Latin translations before he began, around 1456, to study Greek. We may speculate that Pletho's secularism, his political orientation, the wafting spirit of the Orient, his criticisms of Christianity as responsible for decay of Greek institutions and the collapse of the Byzantine Empire, created a context for Platonism suggesting new beginnings in a fund of wisdom that was venerably old. Aristotelianism, by contrast, was old-fashioned and taken for granted – and as such, of course it lived on – for the Aristotle of the *Politics*, prevailing wisdom to the contrary, had never succeeded in dislodging the Aristotle of the Schoolmen, and so had never captured imaginations in the way that Platonism managed to do (Kristeller, 1944a, b, 1944–5, 1946; Skinner, 1979).

One reason for this is the fact that the European Aristotle was Latin and not Greek. Long acclimated to Latin-speaking Europe, Aristotle had been so thoroughly adapted to feudal purposes that centuries were to elapse before he would again seem Hellenic. But Plato, whose influence in the Latin world was kept alive only intermittently in the writings of Augustine and Eastern Fathers, was definitely Greek; and what was Greek was exotic, for in Western Europe, divided from the East by schism, the facility for Greek and access to Greek texts had largely been lost, just as in Eastern Europe few Byzantine scholars read Latin (Geanakoplos, 1988, 369). Manuel Chrysoloras, Gemistus Pletho, Janus Lascaris, Cardinal Bessarion, George of Trebizond and Theodore Gaza, the latter rivals at the papal court, were prominent among the Byzantine scholars who introduced Renaissance Europe to the long absent Greek heritage (Holmes, 1973, 113), as well as to a hidden tradition of oriental philosophizing, to some extent authentically Platonist, and so melded to it as to constitute part of the milieu in which Platonism was now presented. They were accompanied by lesser known, but in some cases equally important, Byzantine emigré scholars: John Argyropoulos and his successor in the Florentine *studium*, Demetrius Chalcondyles, Pletho's former student at Mistra. Argyropoulos, in the opinion of Deno Geanakoplos (1974b, 28; 1988, 357) 'deserves primary credit for the shift in the focus of Florentine humanism from rhetoric – that is, eloquence – to metaphysical philosophy, particularly Platonism'. And if Platonism, which as we have asserted virtually constituted the philosophical phenomenon of the Renaissance, was ushered in by Byzantine scholars, it was ushered out by the Reformation, whose scholars deplored the Greek and the ungodly in Renaissance thought, turning instead to the Hebrew tradition as the only true repository of wisdom in the Orient. Counter-Reformation theorists did not disagree, and Europe settled back into the insularity of its Latinity, or better still, the vernacular tongues.

The Renaissance, to use that convenient label to sum up these currents of change, had a political, as well as philosophical and artistic dimensions, and this too favoured Platonism. For if Aristotle in the popular mind represented hierarchy and privilege, Plato could be plumbed to defend the rule of the new technocrats. The Republican Aristotle had a limited run, as respository of doctrines of popular sovereignty. But the exigencies of the new politics, and the structural location of the new political scientists, militated against this form of republicanism becoming a full-scale movement. To begin with, Aristotle the Stagirite, despite his connections to the Macedonian monarchy, adopted the stance of the detached observer, and not the political advisor. He made even less claim to political influence than Plato, whose withdrawal from the traditional family role of notable and supporter of oligarchs was reluctant – as we know from the Seventh Letter – and whose intervention in Syracuse, renowned for its tyrants, was disastrous. Aristotle, in the Lyceum texts, viewed politics from the perspective of the citizen, his welfare, and the characteristic benefits of various forms of regime to his all-round development and happiness; whereas for Plato, for all that he professes the happiness of the good man to be the goal of his political analysis, the focus is on problems of order and harmony – politics seen from above.

Renaissance commentators were even more closely tied to specific regimes than Aristotle and much more political than Plato. But they found in the disquisitions of the latter on knowledge and power a defence for the role of technocrats and experts that fitted their situation as the advisors of new princes. And no matter how republican they might profess to be, their stance could never be that of the 'people' who, even in the form of the *popolo*, had never been admitted to power in Europe. What interested them was not the moral welfare of the citizen as a person, but the larger questions of order, peace and stability; the virtues of an expansionist, rather than a contractionist, politics; the role of the leader, of notables; and the allocation of resources between military and administrative functions, that the newly emergent European city-state opened up. The prevalent air of *Realpolitik*, upon which generations of historians of political thought have commented, reflects the involvement of Renaissance theoreticians in the political restructurings of their day.

At the same time, one should not underestimate the continuities between the Renaissance and what had gone before. If in the writings of its most prominent Platonists, Marsilio Ficino and others, the bedrock of Aristotelian scholasticism endures (Kristeller, 1943a, 1944b, 1944–5), among its historians and political commentators, the Latin tradition also lives on. Echoing Augustine's comment, that like Sallust he believed that the Greeks, especially compared with the Assyrians, were somewhat over-rated in their achievements, due to the brilliant account of them given by their own historians (Augustine, *Civ. Dei.*, 18.2), Renaissance historians believed the Romans to have shown considerable advance over the Greeks. Thus Bernardo Rucellai, after a visit to Naples around 1494 to consult with the great humanist Pontano on the writing of a history of the French invasion of Italy, records in his description of the meeting with Pontano the view that Roman writers of the Augustan age furnished the most excellent models to historians, among them Sallust and Livy, the latter being 'equal to the Greeks whom he imitated, and superior to those who came later' (Rucellai, 1727, 2.202, cited in Gilbert, 1965, 203–5). Bernardo Rucellai, around whom had gathered Florentine habitués of the Orti Oricellari, or the Rucellai Gardens, the group to which Machiavelli, Francesco da Diacceto, Marsilio Ficino's student, and possibly Janus Lascaris briefly belonged in a later generation, was the grandfather of Cosimo Rucellai, to whom Machiavelli dedicated his *Discourses on Livy* (Kristeller, 1946, 301, 321; Gilbert, 1949, 101–3; 1953, 150–2; 1965, 203–5; Hexter, 1956, 89–92).

It was this strange brew – Aristotelian and Platonic concepts of kingship, the figure of Alexander, Platonist magic and mysticism – and not the orderly analysis of social forms to be found in Aristotle's *Politics*, or *Ethics*, which constituted the milieu of Renaissance political theory. In Machiavelli, its most famous exponent, we find none of the references to oriental despotism that we might expect, were he the student of Aristotle that he is purported to be. Rather, after paying homage to the wisdom and good laws of the Egyptians and their 'most excellent men, whose names, if they had not been lost in antiquity, would be even more celebrated than that of Alexander the Great, and than those of many others whose memory is still fresh' (*Discourses*, 1.1, 1970 edn, 103), he rushes on to give an account of the best forms of government that is dominated by Hellenistic and Roman strong men and the person of Alexander himself. It is not too much to claim that Machiavelli's political writings are Hellenistic in essence, reflecting the world into which Rome itself blended, and of whose political theory we have one lonely representative: Polybius (Barber, 1970; Gruen, 1984).

Between the republican Aristotle and Polybius of the 'mixed constitution' lay a world of difference. At the most elementary level, Aristotle valued poetry above history, maintaining that 'poetry is something more philosophic and of graver import than history, since its statements are of the nature rather of universals, whereas those of history are singulars' (Aristotle, *Poetics*, 9, 5–10, 1941 edn, 1464). Either Aristotle had not heard of didactic history or his opinion of Herodotus is higher than later ages were to appraise him, for he explains further: 'The distinction between historian and poet is not in the one writing prose and the other verse – you might put the work of Herodotus into verse, and it would still be a species of history; it consists really in this, that the one describes the thing that has been, and the other a kind of thing that might be' (*Poetics*, 9, 1–5, 1941 edn, 1463). Aristotle, in preferring poetry over history in this way, bespeaks a preference for metaphysical subjects over ephemera.

But Hellenistic thinkers were turning their back on the moral speculations of Plato and Aristotle, just as they turned their back on the small-scale *polis*. Their concerns were both more empirical at the philosophical level, and more global at the political, than those of Aristotle. Alexander by his military adventurism had opened up new worlds to conquer and to hold. Against all the moral exhortations of the small-state Hellene, success and not virtue had won the day. And if the current antithesis on the tongues of Hellenistic sages is that between Fortune and Virtue, let no one be mistaken, virtue is the mark of the successful strong man, and not of the traditional *nobiles* who withdraws into his world of contemplation (Lateiner, 1982). Politics is respectable again, this time not in the form of the control of the city-state by a ruling class of notables and limited participation by the hoplite soldier. Politics in the Hellenistic age had burst out of the confines of the *polis* and took on a meaning much closer to our own as the machinations of strong men who throw their weight against Fortune and dare to succeed. (An interpretation against which Marxists and structuralists constantly enveigh, suffering the hidden influence of an Aristotelian concept of class politics that Marx, the classicist and heir to the nineteenth-century revival of Aristotle, has transmitted to them.)

Historians of the Hellenistic world emphasize the uncertainties, the ferment and experimentation that the conquests of Alexander unleashed, the rejection of ancient forms and preoccupation with the present, the concrete, the local and the specific. A restless spirit that we find also in Machiavelli, who opens the *Discourses* by irreverently dismissing the admonitions of Plato (*Laws*, 4.704–5, 1926 edn, 255–7) to site the ideal city inland, away from the temptations of the coast, with its harbours and foreign merchants, endorsing the decision of Alexander to reject similar advice, who laughing, 'and, leaving the mountain alone, built Alexandria where inhabitants would be glad to live owing to the richness of the land and to the conveniences afforded by the sea and by the Nile' (*Discourses*, 1.1, 1974 edn, 103–4). Nevertheless, classical authorities continued to be important in the legitimization of new theories, and Platonism provided a fund for the legitimization of new men and technocrats, with which these new theories were concerned. Cosimo de' Medici, who rode from lowly merchant to new prince on the back of Platonism, produced a reaction in more republically minded men like Machiavelli, that did not involve abandoning the new terms of reference, however. And these were Polybian as well as Platonist.

The relation in which Machiavelli stands to Platonism is an ambivalent one. Evidence in both *The Prince* and the *Discourses* suggests acquaintance with Plato's writings. The reference to the ancient legislators of Egypt, who would deserve more praise than the greatly praised Alexander, were their names not buried in oblivion (*Discourses* 1.1, 1974 edn, 103), may well refer to the tale of the Egyptian priest told to Solon on his visit to the Delta city of Sais, concerning the antiquity of Egyptian laws and institutions, compared with which the traditions of Greece are those of children, which prefaces the *Timaeus* (21a–27b) and which is repeated in the *Critias* (109–121). The *Timaeus* was widely read in humanist circles, Latin translations being available early. Its appeal gained much from the Pythagorean and Orphic elements that it contained as a cosmology that attracted Neoplatonist commentary by writers such as Proclus, Plotinus, Posidonius and Plutarch, who were also favoured in the sixteenth century (Walker, 1953).

Plato's account of the Demiurge and Egyptian and Babylonian creation myths demonstrate striking correspondences, but Machiavelli's interest in this work would, we surmise, owe less to a curiosity in oriental mysticism, than it would to the account given in the Egyptian tale to the origins of ancient civilization, its destruction by flood and fire, and its regenerative capacity. That Machiavelli had an interest in this subject, which he shared with Polybius, we know from his chapter in the *Discourses* on the age of the world, periodic cataclysms and ancient historians' accounts of them; and the regeneration of civilization by the survivors, 'rude mountain-dwellers who have no knowledge of antiquity and so cannot hand it down to posterity' (*Discourses* 2.5, 1974 edn, 290).

Interestingly, Machiavelli cites Diodorus Siculus here, who in his *Library of History* book 1, the *Aegyptiaca*, gives an account remarkably similar to that of Polybius, book 6, and Plato, *Laws* book 3, on rebuilding culture from the foundations, after the flood. Just how carefully Machiavelli had in fact read

Diodorus is a good question, because he greatly inflates Diodorus' figures on the antiquity of civilization as being 'some forty or fifty thousand years', which Machiavelli then proceeds to reject as mendacious. In fact, Diodorus, in his Egyptian history, gives 'the number of years from Osiris and Isis ... to the reign of Alexander' as around 10,000 – noting that some would put it at 'a little less than 23,000' (Diodorus 1.23, 1–5, 1933 edn, 73) – which more or less agrees with the figure given by Solon, in Plato's account of the *Timaeus* of 9,000 years of civilization; and with Plato's account in the *Laws* of 10,000 years of Egyptian culture and the arts (*Laws*, 2.656).

Moreover, we have to ask the more general question, how far was Machiavelli interested in ancient history? His passing remarks on the ancient virtue that 'first found a home in Assyria, then flourished in Media and later in Persia, and at length arrived in Italy and Rome' (*Discourses*, 2. Introd., 1974 edn, 267), are no more than that. For his antecedents as a historian are not the Ionian exponents of *historia*, whose efforts to reconstruct the history of mankind matched the cosmologies of the great epic cycle (Gordon, 1953). Machiavelli is rather in the tradition of those more recent Greek and Hellenistic writers who believed that nothing of significance took place before their day, as Thucydides had so modestly claimed on the opening page of his *History* (Brown, 1962, 257). Of course, Machiavelli did not go so far, but then neither in practice did Thucydides. The fact remains that he modelled himself on those Hellenistic and Roman historians who believed that a new age had dawned, to which the frameworks of Ionian *historia* as practised by Herodotus, Hecataeus, Hellanicus, Aristarchus – counterpart to the more mythic efforts of Homer and Hesiod to recapture the infancy of Hellenic culture and the Eastern genesis – no longer were relevant. Machiavelli does use historical examples, but to illustrate contemporary cases, and his examples rarely go back further than the Roman republic, the great bulk dating in fact to the Hellenistic period. His attempt to reconstruct the history of Roman republicanism would seem to give the lie to this claim that his interest lies in contemporary history. But Machiavelli's history of Rome is as schematic and didactic as those of Polybius and Livy on which it is modelled. Its purposes lie in the present.

If Machiavelli's Platonist references on historical subjects demonstrate a passing knowledge of, and interest in, such matters, his references to Plato's political theory, although more rare, are also more negative. Paul Kristeller has speculated that Machiavelli's pregnant silence on Platonism, except for the programmatic statement in *The Prince* 15, may well be due to a realization that his views were incompatible with those of members of the Rucellai Garden group, such as Francesco da Diacceto, with whom he would not wish to clash. The statement in *The Prince* 15 is guarded enough and prompted, Kristeller suggests, by Diacceto's views (Kristeller, 1946, 323). Machiavelli prefaces it with apologetic remarks to the effect that his views may be seen as 'presumptuous, differing as I do, especially in this matter, from the opinions of others'. He goes on to absolve himself:

> But since my intention is to say something that will prove of practical use to the inquirer, I have thought it proper to represent things as they are in real truth,

rather than as they are imagined. Many have dreamed up republics and principalities which have never in truth been known to exist; the gulf between how one should live and how one does live is so wide that a man who neglects what is actually done for what should be done learns the way to self-destruction rather than self-preservation. The fact is that a man who wants to act virtuously in every way necessarily comes to grief among so many who are not virtuous. Therefore if a prince wants to maintain his rule he must learn how not to be virtuous, and to make use of this or not according to need. (*Prince*, 15, 1961 edn, 90–1)

Machiavelli's target, most commentators agree, is Plato's *Republic* and its programme of just rule (Kristeller, 1946, 323; Strauss, 1948, 2–3; cf. Gilbert, 1939, 450, n.3, who believes rather that Machiavelli is referring to contemporary thinkers). But the philosopher to whom Machiavelli most frequently addresses himself, accruing more citations than Plato and Aristotle put together (Strauss, 1948, 95, n.3), is Xenophon, and Leo Strauss is right to point out that Xenophon's *Hiero* and *Cyropaedia* stand as two poles of attraction and repulsion to *The Prince* as no other models do (Strauss, 1948, 2–3) – he need only add the Platonist Plutarch, whose *De Alexandri magni fortuna aut virtute*, although unmentioned by name among the works of an author much cited by Machiavelli, represents another great model of the fearless leader who challenges fortune to undo him, and thus takes credit himself for his accomplishments as an incomparable war lord. It is significant, as Strauss points out (1948, 95, n.3), that Machiavelli should introduce his programmatic statement on the Platonic tradition of just rule in *The Prince* 15, with remarks, at the close of chapter 14, on the *Cyropaedia* (*Prince*, 1961 edn, 89–90). Recommending the prince to 'read history, studying the actions of eminent men to see how they conducted themselves during war and to discover the reasons for their victories or their defeats, so that he can avoid the latter and imitate the former', Machiavelli counsels him above all to 'do what eminent men have done before him: taken as their model some historical figure who has been praised and honoured; and always kept his deeds and actions before them':

> In this way, it is said, Alexander the Great imitated Achilles; Caesar imitated Alexander; and Scipio, Cyrus. And anyone who reads the life of Cyrus, written by Xenophon, will then see how much glory won by Scipio can be attributed to his emulation of Cyrus, and how much, in his high moral standards, courtesy, humanity, and generosity, Scipio conformed to the picture which Xenophon drew of Cyrus. (*Prince*, 1961 edn, 89–90)

While Scipio burned Carthage and incurred charges of corruption, he was no Hiero, and we have no reason to agree with Strauss, on the basis of these remarks, that Hiero is the hidden model for *The Prince*, or that Machiavelli was deliberately indifferent to the distinction between king and tyrant (Strauss, 1948, 2–3). Machiavelli's rejection of Plato and classical criteria of good government certainly did not go this far.

13

The Roman Legacy: Justice, Peace, Harmony and *Grandezza*

In his fine essay 'Greece and Rome in Renaissance Political Thought' (1989), Skinner systematically explores prehumanist and humanist elements in the thought of Machiavelli, giving chapter and verse in the indigenous Latin and Italian sources. It would seem, indeed, that what Machiavelli contributed to Renaissance republican theory was not novel in terms of the elements, although characteristically bold as a synthesis. By characteristic I mean that it vindicates the traditional view of Machiavellian pragmatism to the point of opportunism. Machiavelli was also responsible for a small but significant innovation, in the new usage of the term *res publica*, which had hitherto retained its Roman and specifically Ciceronian meaning of any lawfully established polity (Skinner, 1989, 28). Only with Machiavelli did *repubblica* become synomous with communal government in which freedom was guaranteed by the principle of elective magistrates.

Not that this innovation in any way departed from the sentiment of his humanist predecessors, it was just that Machiavelli made it definitive. Even Machiavelli's pragmatism is to some extent foreshadowed by his forebears, and this due to aspects of their thought also characteristically Roman. It is instructive to note that in their writings values endorsed by Plato and Aristotle as final goods are merely instrumental; whereas values which do not appear in the Greek writers as ultimately duty-worthy have pride of place. The value of greatness, or *grandezza*, is a very good example. Greatness is not a value much emphasized by writers of the *polis*, and certainly did not accompany, as it does in the Latin and Italian writers, the notions of expansion, or 'increase'. In fact, Plato situated Magnesia, in the *Laws*, as far away from the coast as possible to prevent trade-based affluence and expansionism – for which Machiavelli ridiculed him; both Plato and Aristotle constantly remonstrated against commerce-based wealth; and both would seem intent on frustrating the sort of greatness and increase that the Roman and Latin writers so greatly prized.

Greatness enters the writings of Aristotle as the noble virtue of an aristocrat, the 'magnificence' of the 'great-souled one' (*megalopsuchos*), *megalopsuchia*. Its meaning here is rather technical, however, referring to the characteristic disposition of nobles toward the state as that of beneficence (*euergetism*), to which specific economic mechanisms were attached. This particular meaning of greatness is appropriately translated into Latin as *magnificentia*, with a correspondingly technical sense. *Grandezza*, or greatness, as the final good to which nation states aspire, is a typically Latin, Roman and Renaissance value, as we may briefly show. In the first place, the Roman republic differed specifically from the classical *polis* by virtue of its capacity for expansionism: both its salvation and the ultimate cause of its demise. For all the limitations that Roman historians as analysts may exhibit, this fact was not lost on them, and when they extol the 'greatness' of Rome this is what they have in mind – something literally spatial.

Prehumanist and humanist *Dictatores*, or practitioners of the *Ars dictaminis* practised by the law schools of medieval Italy (Skinner, 1989, 5), were also, it seems, in admiration of the territorial achievements of Rome. But Rome's 'greatness' was inherently ambivalent: having pioneered the large-scale state in Europe, Rome terminated its career with Caesarism and monstrous empire, enjoining in later observers the sort of pragmatism and politics of balance which with Machiavelli become an artform. It is hardly surprising, then, that humanist and prehumanist rhetoricians should have drawn on Sallust, the critic not only of Roman decline but commentator on non-Roman systems and their fragility in the *Bellum Catilinae*. When, in that work, Sallust discusses the rise of Rome to greatness he uses specifically spatial language: '*respublica crevit*' (Sallust, 1921a edn, 10.1, p. 16, cited in Skinner, 1989, 8). When in the counterpart work, the *Bellum Jugurthinum* (1921b edn, 10.6: 148, cited in Skinner, 1989, 8) the king of Numidia counsels Jugurtha on the necessity of those who have achieved honour and glory to recall the small origins of greatness, he uses the same language: '*parvae res crescunt*'.

Among the prehumanist writers the same terminology abounds. The anonymous *Oculus pastoralis*, earliest in the genre of model speeches designed for the use and guidance of magistrates, and dated to the 1220s, counsels a rule conducive '*ad incrementum et gloriam et honorem*', to guarantee 'that the city grows to greatness': '*excrescit civitas*' (Skinner, 1989, 6, 8, 34, n.39). Giovanni Viterbo (1901 edn, 231, col. 2, 232, col. 1, cited in Skinner, 1989, 34, n.40), also writing in Latin, speaks of '*civitates crescunt*' and '*incrementum*' and '*maximum incrementum*'. By the close of the thirteenth century these ideas, which have enjoyed continuity in the rhetorical writers, are now stated in the vernacular, Matteo de' Libri advising magistrates on their duty to guarantee 'bon stato, grandeça et acresemento' (Libri, 1974 edn, 70, cited in Skinner, 1989, 34, n.41). Giovanni da Vignano, in a model speech for outgoing magistrates, bids hope that the city they have administered 'will at all times grow and increase' ('*che questa terra sempre acresca*'), in prosperity especially (Vignano, 1974 edn, 286, cited in Skinner, 1989, 8, 34, n.42).

The worldliness of this hope is expressed by the term *grandezza*, a neologism 'evidently coined to supply the lack, in classical Latin, of an expression at once denoting grandeur and magnitude' (Skinner, 1989, 8–9). From Guido Faba's *Parlamenti ed Epistole*, of the early 1240s, to Giovanni da Viterbo's *Liber de regimine civitatum*, written in Latin, we have vernacular passages expressing what could not otherwise be expressed in the language of the classical republican theorists from Cicero to Seneca: a preoccupation with 'good standing, repose and *grandecca*', 'honour, *grandecca* and welfare', 'exultation, *grandecca* and honour', expressed in the various formulations of its publicists. (Skinner, 1989, 9).

Justice, peace and concord marked the path to *grandezza*. The logical order of these virtues is not in too much doubt. The *Oculus* was the first on record to state that 'only through quiet and tranquillity and peace can a city grow great' (cited in Skinner, 1989, 10). Matteo de' Libri and Filippo Ceffi see the fruit of good public administration to be a state's ability 'to live in total tranquillity', as the path to 'honour and *grandezza*' (Libri, 1974 edn, 79; Ceffi, 1942 edn, 27; cited in Skinner, 1989, 10, 35). But not all writers saw peace, defined at the outset as an instrumental virtue, even as an unqualified good. Sallust had foreshadowed an important theme in Machiavelli when, in the *Bellum Catilinae*, he emphasized the benefits of war, attributing the greatness of Rome to her necessity to wage war against 'savage neighbouring peoples', specifically the Carthaginians; and attributing her decline to the softness, self-interest and avarice fostered by peace. Machiavelli was doubtless mindful of this analysis when in the *Discourses* (1970 edn, 3.6, 420, cited in Skinner, 1989, 3) he remarked that 'everyone has read Sallust's account of the Catilinarian conspiracy.'

The essential referents of republican *grandeça* for the humanist and prehumanist publicists, were rule of elected magistrates and the regular rotation of office as guarantees of liberty. Chief magistrates, or *podestà*, named for the supreme power they wielded, were rotated in and out of office for periods of six months to a year and they ruled by executive councils (Skinner, 1989, 1). This, we see, is rule by the formula to which Titus Quinctius Flamininus applied the epithet 'the freedom of the Greeks'. It fairly represented Greek forms of representative government of the Hellenistic period and the Roman legacy of incremental republicanism, which finally conceded representation to the people in their military tribes and tribunes of the plebs. At any rate it was far from being rule by the *demos* or the poor folk. And when in the early fourteenth century the rise of the *Signori* displaced even the *popolo* of communal governments, Sallust's fears about the indulgences of peace as a cause of Roman republican decline were echoed by the Italian historical writers, reflecting on the collapse of civic liberty in a later period (Skinner, 1989, 11).

Albertino Mussato, in the case of Padua, and Poggio Bracciolini in his *History of the Florentine People*, both conceded that peace might be a threat to liberty and that external war might be an inducement to the preservation of freedom and promote *grandezza* (Skinner, 1989, 11). One distinction that they were careful to make, however, was between war waged against external enemies and internal discord. Here too they echoed a distinction of Sallust's, who in the *Bellum Jugurthinum* makes it clear that if external wars are functional, internal strife is dysfunctional for greatness, the king of the Numidians counselling Jugurtha that if 'it is by way of concord that small communities rise to greatness, it is as a result of discord that even the greatest communities fall into collapse' (Sallust, 1921b, 10.7, 148, cited in Skinner, 1989, 12).

It was precisely internal harmony that the term *concordia* designated, and much effort was expended by Giovani de Viterbo, and by Brunetto – who more or less plagiarized him (Skinner, 1989, 6) – in showing how ancient Rome, Renaissance Florence and Venice, had destroyed themselves by faction. Latini (1948 edn, 404) admonished magistrates: 'You must point out how concord brings greatness to cities and enriches their citizens, while war destroys them; and you must recall how Rome and other great cities ruined themselves by internal strife.' A sentiment strongly expressed by Machiavelli, whose counsels against faction in *The Prince* are among the most memorable.

The Guelf–Ghibelline polarity was undoubtedly reminiscent to humanists and prehumanists of the factiousness caused by the Roman war lords, Marius and Sulla, Sulla and Pompey, Pompey and Caesar. The strategy of *The Prince* may well have reflected observations as old as Herodotus concerning the greater liability of aristocracy to factionalism than monarchy. Herodotus makes the argument most famously in the debate between the Persian notables (3.79–82, 1972 edn, 238–40). It is curious that precisely in the great chapter of the *Discourses*, 3.6 on Conspiracies, where Machiavelli raises the problem of the Cataline conspiracy, he should also introduce the case dealt with by Otanes and Darius – the very characters Herodotus presented in the Persian debate.

Machiavelli's pragmatism, not entirely singular in the tradition in which he wrote, prepares us for republicanism, where possible, and princely rule, where necessary. Generally speaking, where the polarization between factions was not already too great, government by elected magistrates regularly rotated was the best guarantee against entrenched interests establishing themselves and attracting sedition. Cicero, for whom in *De officiis*, book 1, 'the ideal of *concordia ordinum* had been of such overriding importance' (Skinner, 1989, 13), states the thesis succinctly: 'to introduce sedition and discord into a city is to look after the interests of only one part of the citizenry, while neglecting the rest.' Thus, Cicero (1.25.85, 1913 edn, 86, cited in Skinner, 1989, 13) maintained, claiming that he took the precept from Plato, magistrates have two priorities: 'First they must look after the welfare of every citizen to such a degree that, in everything they do, they make this their highest priority, without any consideration for their own advantage. Secondly, they must look after the welfare of the whole body politic, never allowing themselves to care only for one part of the citizens while betraying the rest.' This is a passage quoted in its entirety by Viterbo (1901 edn, 268, col. 2, cited in Skinner, 1989, 14), and referred to by Latini (1948 edn, 267, cited in Skinner, 1989, 14), who follows it up with a chapter 'On Concord'.

Cicero, in book 1 of *De officiis*, concurred with Seneca, *De clementia*, 1.3.2 (cited in Skinner, 1986, 10), in defining the good of the community as that point at which 'the common good and the wise man's good are the same', giving to the notion of man as a social animal a very un-Aristotelian meaning. Cicero (*De officiis*, 1.7.22, cited in Skinner, 1986, 10) went further: 'We are not born simply for ourselves, for our country and friends are both able to claim a share in us. People are born for the sake of other people, in order that they can mutually benefit one another. We ought therefore to follow Nature's lead and place the *communes utilitates* at the heart of our concerns.' In seeking to establish the conditions for *communes utilitates* Cicero, in *De officiis* 2.22.78 (trans. Skinner 1986, 11) had summarized 'the two *fundamenta* of public life, the first being *concordia*, the second *aequitas*'.

Concordia, as we have already seen, was a figure as much Eastern as Greek and Roman, known to us as Harmonia and her harbingers in the figures of Hathor, Isis, Ishtar and Astarte. In the rich analysis Quentin Skinner (1986) gives of iconographic details of the Lorenzetti frescoes in the Palazzo Pubblico, Siena, lavish in their display in a manner quite untypical of Greek republicanism of the *polis*, for instance, items from the Eastern panoply of Concordia as Harmonia are clearly present. One is impressed by 'the feminine principle' in Renaissance iconography, evident in characterizations of Florence as both 'the scent of lilies' and 'the beautiful woman with golden hair' (Gombrich, 1945, 1972; Weinstein, 1968; Springborg, 1990d). But iconography could also replicate more literal forms of expression. Skinner shows very convincingly that the order of the virtues as portrayed by Lorenzetti in the Sala del Nove, of the Palazza Pubblico, follows the order in both Cicero's *De officiis* and later Italian writers like Brunetto Latini.

In his elaboration of the virtue *concordia*, Cicero makes much of rope and knot imagery, graphically depicted in the Lorenzetti frescoes, that ties back to the legendary Harmonia and the womb symbolism of her Eastern ancestors (Frankfort, 1944, 1948; Barb, 1953; Astour, 1967a; Springborg, 1990d). In *De finibus* 2.33.117 (cited in Skinner, 1986, 12) Cicero speaks of the twin 'bonds of concord' (*vincula concordiae*), as the giving and receiving of benefits which tie us together as a group. A sentiment once again expressed in *De officiis* 1.7.22 (cited in Skinner, 1986, 12), where benefits received and disposed '[link] each individual in society together with everyone else'. In *De republica* Cicero defines *concordia* as 'the best and lightest rope of safety in society', a metaphor included by Saint Augustine in the *De civitate dei* (2.21 on *concordia*, cited in Skinner, 1986, 12), of which prehumanist writers were to make much – and much more than Aquinas and his followers, as Skinner (1986, 13) emphasizes.

The references to beneficence as the cement of a community, to be found in these reflections on the common good, are, we should note, further specified in the virtue of *aequalitas*, which refers to the symmetry established between citizens by exchange, emphasized in the later disquisitions of Latini (book 2, ch. 28, 199, 205 of the *Livres du Tresor*, cited in Skinner, 1986, 16–17). Latini, very much in the spirit of Aristotle, *Nicomachean Ethics*, book 5 on justice, as Skinner (1986, 16) notes, suggests that 'citizens and people who live together in cities [i.e. even those who are not citizens, like women and foreigners] engage in mutual exchanges with each other', referring specifically to the equalization effected by *entreservices*, whereby 'metal-workers can hope to exchange their wares with cordwainers or with carpenters in accordance with the precepts of justice'. The author of the anonymous *Moralium Dogma Philosophorum* of the twelfth century follows Cicero in declaring among 'the obligations of concord, that of binding men together in society by a reciprocity of duties, giving and receiving alternately' (cited in Skinner, 1986, 13). And in Libri's *Arringhe* (p. 92, cited in Skinner, 1986, 13), as in the *Dictamina* of Giovanni da Vignano, it is pointed out that 'a rope is much stronger when it is redoubled'.

These reflections would seem to extend in metaphor Aristotelian notions of *euergetism*, the exchange of benefits underlying the economic functions of the city. Latini's specification of magnanimity, for instance, defined the magnanimous one, as he who, unconcerned with small things, lives by the precept that 'it is a nobler thing to give than receive'. Moreover, Latini here makes a specific reference to Averroes' paraphrase of the *Nicomachean Ethics* (Latini, *Tresor*, 194, cited in Skinner, 1986, 30). The iconographic expression of concord in relation to peace and *aequalitas* in the Lorenzetti frescoes, for instance, is, however, decidedly Roman and not Greek; while the rope, knot and even snake symbolism (Skinner, 1986, 23, 43, 47), buttressed by further icons of the Virgin, gemination in the form of twins, gemstones with magical properties (Skinner, 1986, 51; see, Barb, 1953), lavish robes, staffs, sceptres, are all strikingly Near Eastern, transmitted through Rome at the height of Empire.

Let me illustrate: Peace sits at the centre of Lorenzetti's canvas (Skinner, 1986, 33), 'leaning back on her right elbow, pressing against a large cushion which in turn presses down upon a full suit of armour and holds it in place; she is represented as a victorious force, her repose the outcome of a battle won against her darkest enemies.' The very enemies over whom she has triumphed are, of course, 'external *Guerra* and internal *Discordia*, the latter being a product partly of factious *Divisio* and partly of the *Furor* of the masses' (Skinner, 1986, 33). In the Lorenzetti frescoes we have personifications of these elements, as we know from Kantorowicz's study (1957), and earlier Near Eastern examples (Springborg, 1990d), likely to be feminized.

> If we turn to the left or 'sinister' side of Lorenzetti's frescoes, we encounter just these companions of tyranny and enemies of peace ... They are seated upon the left hand – again the 'sinister' side – of the demonic central figure, behind whose head a titulus in silver lettering reads TYRANNIDES. To his extreme left, dressed in dark blue robes, we see the helmeted figure of War, a gold-hilted sword upraised in his right hand and the word GUERRA inscribed on his shield. Next to him sits a figure marked [D]IVISIO, dressed in black and white, with golden hair falling loose and dishevelled in contrast with the carefully plaited hair on the figure of Peace. She is holding a carpenter's saw, using it to cut an object held in her left hand, an evident allusion to Sallust's dire warning that *Divisio* will always serve to tear a body-politic to pieces. Finally, standing closest to the enthroned central figure, we see a black hybrid beast marked FUROR. (Skinner, 1986, 33)

From the 'black hybrid beast', decidedly occult, we move to the iconography of Concordia, replete with red robes (are they those of Hathor, the Ugaritic astral Virgin, or the Roman bride?), knots and ropes. Skinner (1986, 34), noting that in the frescoes 'we see, most prominently, a representation of the Ciceronian claim that *concordia* constitutes one of the two *fundamenta* of public life', goes on to describe her, tied to a 'mysterious regal figure', who has been thought to be 'the common good':

> Beneath the mysterious regal figure, and upon his 'good' side, we see a group of twenty-four citizens holding a double rope – one strand red, the other grey – which is handed to them by a seated female figure marked CONCORDIA. The allusion is clearly to the *vinculum concordiae*, the double bond of concord mentioned in several of the pre-humanist treatises on city government. (Skinner, 1986, 34)

The iconography emphasizes equality by way of levelling – not a Greek idea at all:

> We also see a representation of *aequitas*, the quality Cicero had described as the other *fundamentum* of civic peace. The figure of Concord holds in her lap a large *runcina* or carpenter's plane. Now a plane is of course an implement specifically designed to level out roughnesses and produce a smooth surface. So the appearance of a *runcina*, especially in such close association with *concordia*, must surely be

intended to symbolize the Ciceronian view of *aequitas* – the view that we must smooth out our differences as citizens rather than accentuate any divisions between us if we are to enjoy the blessings of peace.

Skinner points out, moreover, on the subject of levelling, that 'the citizens processing together in concord are all exactly uniform in height', each 'on level terms' with everyone else in just the manner that the Ciceronian analysis of *aequitas* prescribed (Skinner, 1986, 34). The prominence of Concordia does not mean, however, that Justice is dislodged from her ruling seat:

> As we have seen, the double rope of concord held by the procession of citizens is handed to them by the figure of Concord. She in turn receives it, however, from the two angels of justice. The red cord originates as the girdle worn by the angel on the left, the grey as the girdle of the one on the right. Each cord passes through one of the pans in the scales of justice; both are then gathered by the figure of Concord, in whose hand they are woven into a single rope. Justice is thus depicted as the source from which the rope of concord ultimately derives, and hence as the ultimate bond of human society. (Skinner, 1986, 40)

The 'mysterious regal figure', has been interpreted by Nicolai Rubinstein (1957, 181), who first analysed the political-theoretical content of the Lorenzetti frescoes, to be 'the common good'. Skinner (1986, 45–6), demurs, arguing convincingly that he represents rather the *signore* or senatorial class who can guarantee it. He has 'the red strand of the rope encircl[ing] his hand, while the end of the rope hangs down to the left – two indications that we are to think of it as knotted around his wrist', and he holds a sceptre in the same hand (Skinner, 1986, 43). Describing him further as 'grey-bearded, white-haired, and thus ... *senex* or old – a possible allusion to Sena, the Latin name for the city of which he is head ... [he is] dressed in black and white, the heraldic colours of the commune of Siena.' Skinner further notes that he has:

> At his feet a she-wolf suckl[ing] a pair of twins, the ancient symbol of the Roman republic which the Sienese had adopted and emblazoned on the arms of their city in 1297. Finally, on his shield we can still faintly discern an image of the Virgin Mary, chosen by the Sienese as their special patron just before their victory over the Florentines at Montaperti in 1260. The Virgin sits enthroned with the infant Jesus upon her left hand, and with two haloed supporters kneeling on either side of her. (Skinner, 1986, 43–4)

The overwhelmingly Roman constellation of motifs, with their ancient Near Eastern overtones in these iconographic depictions of republicanism, leaves little room for the influence of the Greek *polis*; and Plato and Aristotle, in the vernacular writings of the genre live on mainly as learned footnotes. Personifications of the virtues have on their horizons the spectre of Greek goddesses transmitted from the East too, of course. But the fundamentalism of Plato and Aristotle did not permit these shadowy features to take centre stage in the iconography of Greek republics. Not so the Italians, however. Thus, magnanimity in Lorenzetti's frescoes, although one of the most Aristotelian virtues, thought by Seneca to be 'perhaps the most dominant and splendid of the virtues' (Skinner, 1986, 48), is 'depicted: dominantly positioned, her garments a more brilliant white than those of Peace herself'. And we are reminded of white-robed Isis in Apuleius' depiction (*Metamorphoses*, 11.3–4, 1975 edn, 73–5) of the epiphany of Isis.

Iconographic items from the Isis processions described by Apuleius, by Herodotus at Bubastis, by Diodorus (6.6) and by Plutarch (*De Iside et Osiride*, 35.365a), including snakes, jars, oil lamps, cornucopia-shaped vessels and the *cista mystica* (Harrison, 1903, 296–7, 307, 318–20), abound also in Lorenzetti's depictions of the virtues. Prudence, 'among Tuscan painters and sculptors of this period ... generally pictured with a book, a pair of dividers, or sometimes a snake', in Lorenzetti's depiction is shown 'cradling in her left hand a small black lamp, the three flames of which illuminate the three words inscribed on her cartouche' (Skinner, 1989, 48). And Temperance, 'usually depicted with a vessel in each hand, often in the act of pouring liquid from one to another' (Skinner, 1989, 49) is shown by Lorenzetti with an hour glass, to express the same idea. Fortitude 'almost always depicted by Tuscan artists of this period as a Herculean hero, draped with the skin of a lion and carrying a club' – an image 'which clearly owes much to Ovid and Virgil' (Skinner, 1986, 51) – is presented by Lorenzetti 'in a different and even more belligerent [Roman] pose. A black-robed female figure, wearing a cuirass underneath her robes, she is shown carrying a shield in her left hand, a staff in her right, closely accompanied by two soldiers on horseback, each of them fully armoured and helmeted.' One feels that she has the might of Rome behind her to lend muscle to whatever moral fibre she might otherwise exhibit. These personifications would seem to demonstrate nothing if not continuity between the Roman virtues of the classical republic and Renaissance *virtù*. With Greek *arete* they share only martial excellence – even the aristocratic bias is missing given the Italian emphasis on 'levelling' – and very little in the way of iconographic items. Skinner (1986, 56) concludes of the indigenous origins of Renaissance Italian republicanism: 'It was from these humble origins, far more than from the impact of Aristotelianism, that the classical republicanism of Machiavelli, Guicciardini, and their contemporaries originally stemmed. The political theory of the Renaissance, at all phases of its history, owes a far deeper debt to Rome than to Greece.'

That greatness, according to the Roman order, was the queen of all the virtues, we shall presently see. For if Peace and 'the common good' were ruling values, how to know the common good was the question. The humanists and prehumanists concurred with the Roman orators and moralists on the formula 'giving to each his due', *ius suum cuique*, a precept enshrined in Roman law that was also Platonic. But their application of the precept was not at all Platonic, the Italian writers, like Cicero and Sallust, valuing justice, peace and concord, as instrumental and not final goods – a status that only honour and greatness enjoyed. Sallust, in *Bellum Catalinae* 10.1 (1921a edn, 16, cited in Skinner, 1989, 14–15) states it baldly: it was 'by acting with justice as well as with industry that the Roman republic grew to greatness'. Cicero in *De officiis* 1.7.20 (1913 edn, 20, cited in Skinner, 1989, 15) is just as blunt: justice represents the primary instrument 'by which the community of men and, as it were, their common unity, is preserved'.

Let us see what the Italian writers make of this. Giovanni da Viterbo (1901 edn, 220, col. 1, cited in Skinner, 1989, 15) begins his treatise by repeating the precept: it is the foremost duty of the _podestà_ 'to render to each person his due, in order that the city may be governed in justice and equity'. Latini, likewise, at the outset of his chapter 'On the Government of Cities' (1948 edn, 392, 403, cited in Skinner, 1989, 15), states that 'justice ought to be so well established in the heart of every _signor_ that he assigns to everyone his right'; and he goes on to show to what purposes this precept is instrumental: 'a city which is governed according to right and truth, such that everyone has what he ought to have, will certainly grow and multiply, both in people and in wealth, and will endure for ever in a good state of peace, to its honour and that of its friends.' Matteo de' Libri (1974 edn, 34, cited in Skinner, 1989, 15–16), in perhaps the most explicit statement of the connection between justice and greatness, proclaims: 'He who loves justice loves a constant and perpetual will to give to each his right; and he who loves to give to each his right loves tranquillity and repose, by means of which countries rise to the highest _grandeça_.' And Giovanni da Vignano (1974 edn, 296, cited in Skinner, 1989, 16) just as succinctly links justice as the basis of good government, giving to each his due as insurance against discord, and _grandezza_ as the outcome, concluding: 'it is by means of all these things that countries are able to rise to _grandeça_.'

In the order of virtues so far enumerated: expansion or increase, greatness, concord and justice, perhaps only freedom stands with greatness as a value not to be compromised. It was on the twin grounds of freedom and greatness that the _Dictatores_ stood firm in their desire to navigate between strategies conducive to these ends. Their commitment to communal rule, characterized by elective magistrates and executive councils, was made against the alternative of hereditary rule, whether by princes or aristocrats. Indeed, the principle of election, as opposed to heredity, is perhaps more crucial than the distinction between republics and princes. It accounts both for the venom expressed by Machiavelli towards the old aristocracy of Italy and his preparedness to use elective princes, as long as one could be sure to be rid of them as soon as possible. Ancient monarchy was as frequently elective as hereditary, as we are reminded by Aristotle. His distinction between tyrants, as elective kings who come to power on the basis of a party, and hereditary princes, is preserved by Machiavelli in _Discourses_ 1.7 (1960 edn, 147, cited in Skinner, 1989, 26), for whom tyranny poses the special threat of rule by faction: that which has the capacity to 'ruin a free way of life'.

The _Dictatores_ were explicit in their endorsement of the principle of election against hereditary rule by princes or _Signori_, as the primary means to uphold just rule – 'giving to each his due' – and civic greatness (Skinner, 1989, 16). Mindful of Sallust's observation in the _Bellum Catilinae_ (7.3, 1921a edn, 12, cited in Skinner, 1989, 17), that 'it was only when the city of Rome managed to become liberated from its kings that it was able, in such short space of time, to rise to such greatness', prehumanist and humanist writers, and Machiavelli in particular, enclosed the conclusion that Sallust drew: 'to kings, good men are objects of even greater suspicion than the wicked'. The positional inability of kings or hereditary rulers to consider the interests of others or of the city as a whole, was constantly re-echoed, most notably by Latini, who says of France, and those countries where kings and princes rule, that they rule only in their own interests, 'selling offices and assigning them to those who pay most for them, with little consideration for the good or benefit of the townsfolk [*des borgois*]' (Latini, 1948 edn, 392, cited in Skinner, 1989, 17).

Elective systems, not yet characterized by the term *res publica*, but referred to simply as a type of *reggimen* or *reggimento* (Skinner, 1989, 18), were superior precisely because they guaranteed equality before the law and 'free governments' The *Signori* spelled servitude, the commune freedom safeguarded by the elective principle. Mussato (1727 edn, 658, cited in Skinner, 1989, 19), writing in Latin, saw the purpose of the citizens in fending off the challenge to the *res publica* posed by the Della Scala, as 'defense of the liberty of our native land'. Filippo Ceffi, in the melancholy model speech designed for capitulation to a *signore* recorded in his *Dicerie*, has the leaders of the commune declare: 'due to the harshness of war, we find ourselves obliged to hand over our liberty and our system of justice, which have been in our possession for many years' (Ceffi, 1942 edn, 61, cited in Skinner, 1989, 19–20).

Machiavelli is both blunter and bolder in stating his strategies for freedom and peace. Once again, 'freedom of the Greeks' according to the Roman conception, where the rotation of magistrates among an isonomous elite, rather than direct democracy on the model of the *ecclesia*, constituted the model. In some sense he turned the tables on the traditional writers, arguing from the benefits of external war to the benefits of internal tumults and upheavals, as instrumental in building the tough moral fibre of a republic, so long as they produced – as they produced in the case of Rome – ultimately resolvable crises. The politics of balance, and constitutional provisions for the control of incipient factionalism, were prophylactic against the inevitable tendencies of party politics. But where they failed and polarization on the Roman Marius/Sulla model (*Discourses*, 3.6) resulted, Caesarism was endemic and the sternest measures were then sanctioned. Machiavelli's unabashed pragmatism, his willingness to take one step further the instrumentalism of his predecessors, earned him a reputation for boldness to the point of ruthlessness. A just reputation as we see from this programmatic pronouncement:

> No discerning person will ever criticise anyome for taking any action, however extreme, which is undertaken with the aim of organising a kingdom or constituting a republic. For it is right that, although the fact of extreme action may accuse him, its effect should excuse him. It is those who use violence to destroy things, not to reconstitute them, who alone deserve blame. (Machiavelli, *Discourses*, 1.9, 1960 edn, 153–4, cited in Skinner, 1989, 23)

This is far cry from the high-mindedness of Plato and Aristotle, authorities who had withdrawn from public life because of the disgust which politicking engendered in them. Theirs is, of course, a high-mindedness quite unrepresentative of the spirit of Athenian politics, which like that of all participatory, interactive, transactional politics, thrives precisely on negotiations and deals, the strategies and tactics of the back-room boys. But very little of this can be read into Plato and Aristotle's analyses, lofty models of conduct. Roman historians, rhetoricians and publicists, like the Greek Sophists, orators and historians, are a much better guide to the push and pull of day-to-day politics. In Aristotle's *Politics*, it is true, we have structural analyses of the elements of various types of regime, unparalleled for their acuity. But the reception of the *Politics* was prejudiced by the prevailing image of Aristotelianism as hierarchical, even feudal.

In Machiavelli, for whom justice, even *concordia* can be violated where the common good requires it, *grandezza*, coupled with *libertà*, as Skinner (1989, 21–30) has very well shown, are values concerning which he admits no compromise. Comparing cities which were founded by citizens 'without having any particular prince to direct them' with cities founded by princes, he takes Athens and Venice as examples of the former, observing that 'both of [them] managed to rise from these small beginnings to the *grandezza* they now enjoy' (*Discourses*, 1.1, 1960 edn, 126, cited in Skinner, 1989, 24). By contrast, in princely realms, he declares, 'due to the fact such cities do not have free beginnings, it very seldom happens that they are able to rise to greatness.' Among the epithets applied to Rome, *grandezza* is one of the most respected. The subject of book 1 of the *Discourses* is to enquire what constitution would enable a new republic 'to attain Roman *grandezza*' (*Discourses*, 1.6, 1960 edn, 146, cited in Skinner, 1989, 250), 'to come to its ultimate *grandezza*' (*Discourses*, 1.20, 1960 edn, 185, cited in Skinner, 1989, 25), or 'to arrive at the *grandezza* which it acquired' (*Discourses*, 1.6, 1960 edn, 143, cited in Skinner, 1989, 143). In book 2 the stated aim is to show what martial strategies the Romans employed 'to attain *grandezza*' (*Discourses*, 2.13, 1960 edn, 312, cited in Skinner, 1989, 25), or more grandly, as Skinner (1989, 25, citing *Discourses*, 2.6, 1960 edn, 294) points out, 'to help themselves on the way towards supreme *grandezza*'. And in book 3 the design is 'to show how much the actions of individual men contributed to making Rome great, and brought about in that city so many good effects' (*Discourses*, 3.1, 1960 edn, 383–4, cited in Skinner, 1989, 25).

Virtù, as Skinner shows, is primarily efficacious for *grandezza*, not that of the individual, but of his city: it is not the pursuit of individual goods, but rather pursuit of the common good, that brings greatness to cities (*Discourses*, 2.2, 1960 edn, 280, cited in Skinner, 1989, 26). Romulus, despite his fratricide, excused as 'something that was done for the common good, and not out of ambitiousness' (*Discourses*, 1.9, 1960 edn, 154, cited in Skinner, 1989, 26), is joined by Fabius, Manlius, Camillus and others as having assisted Rome to greatness 'by acting "entirely in favour of the public", "placing the public welfare" and "the public benefit" above all other values' (*Discourses*, 3.23, 3.30, 3.47, 1960 edn, 452, 467, 502, cited in Skinner, 199, 26).

Party faction, corruption and tyranny all turn on the inabilty to put the communal good and promotion of the greatness of the city above personal ambition. Thus 'Sulla and Marius managed to find troops willing to follow them in actions contrary to the common good, and it was by these means that Caesar was then able to place his country in subjection' (*Discourses*, 3.25, 1960 edn, 456, cited in Skinner, 1989, 27). For the same reasons 'it is usually the case whenever there is a princely form of rule, that the prince's behaviour is harmful to the city, while the behaviour of the city is harmful to the prince' (*Discourses*, 2.2, 1960 edn, 280, cited in Skinner, 1989, 27). Tyrannies, even a virtuous tyrant, have the defining feature that 'no benefit to the body politic can possibly result', because 'no one exercising a tyranny can ever confer honours on any citizens under his rule who are truly good and capable, since he will never wish to have cause to fear them' (*Discourses*, 2.2, 1960 edn, 280, cited in Skinner, 1989, 27). The same logic usually applies in the case of princes, as Machiavelli's prehumanist forebears had constantly observed. Liberation and freedom meant precisely this: 'Above all it is most marvellous to consider the greatness to which Rome rose after she had liberated herself from her kings' (*Discourses*, 2.2, 1960 edn, 280, cited in Skinner, 1989, 29), Machiavelli expostulates, echoing the lines of Sallust in the *Bellum Catilinae*, who had declared: 'it was only when the city of Rome managed to become liberated from its kings that it was able, in such a short space of time, to rise to such greatness.'

Machiavelli's disquisitions on 'a free way of life' come from the heart: 'it is easy to understand', he says, 'how an affection for living a free way of life springs up in peoples. For one sees by experience that cities have never increased either in power or in wealth unless they have been established in liberty' (*Discourses*, 2.2, 1960 edn, 280, cited in Skinner, 1989, 28–9); even liberty on a strict reading might be seen as instrumental to *grandezza*. But Machiavelli's commitment goes deeper than this. Freedom is to be valued for its own sake, which is why even though 'Romulus and the other kings enacted many good laws of a kind conformable to a free way of life. Nevertheless, their aim was to establish a kingdom and not a republic, with the consequence that, when the city became free, it still lacked many things that needed to be established in favour of liberty' (*Discourses*, 1.2, 1960 edn, 134, cited in Skinner, 1989, 29). The replacement of kings by consuls signalled the missing step – when Rome first 'elected two consuls in place of their king', this marked 'the beginning of their free way of life' (*Discourses*, 1.25, 1960 edn, 192, cited in Skinner, 1989, 30). The equivalent rule by *podestà* and executive councils was seen to guarantee freedom in the communes of Renaissance Italy, whose peoples 'were all of them free' in the time 'when one never hears tell of there being any kings' (*Discourses*, 2.2, 1960 edn, 279, cited in Skinner, 1989, 30).

What was this freedom? Machiavelli's concept of freedom, as Skinner (1981, 53–73; 1983) has very well argued, is the classical *autarkia*, negative freedom, and no libertarian notion; this in part because the concept of individual rights as such post-dates Hobbes, being notoriously unknown to the ancients, for whom benefits and duties commanded the field. Freedom for Machiavelli, to the extent that it is an individual right at all, was the right – and duty – to endeavour to control one's destiny by electing a principle of behaviour and following it – as indeed it was for the Stoics before him, and that Stoical Rousseau after him. And for the community, it meant rule of law. Freedom for the individual is a moral project; for the community it is programmatic too: the institutionalization of procedures to ensure the common good against despots and tyrants, predicated on a willingness in the citizen to serve. Sallust had given a definition of liberty, which classically emphasized the priority of the group over the individual: 'the *libertas* of the *res publica*, and thus of its members, can only be maintained if the *virtus* of all the citizens is such that they are willing to devote all their *curia* and *labor* to serving the community in war and peace' (Skinner, 1983, 13, n.12, paraphrasing Sallust, 1921a, 6.5 and 10–11); a claim whose constitutional implications Livy, in

2.1–2, had explored. For Machiavelli, too, liberty lay in the interstices of *beneficia* and *officia*. In *Discourses* book 1, on the subject of Rome's greatness, he declared programmatically: 'a republic can never hope to be perfect unless she provides for everything by means of her laws and furnishes a legal method for dealing with every unexpected event' as the means 'to establish the city's liberty on a firm base' (Skinner, 1983, citing Machiavelli, 1965 edn, 268–9, 280). Outwitting Fortune, like circumventing the Stoic Fate, was a matter of institutional prudence to ensure corporate liberty, from which that of the individual flowed, as Machiavelli fully realized, hoping, in the case of Florence, to see instituted 'a special magistracy charged with the duty of acting as "guardian of our liberty" against any who seek to undermine it' (Skinner, 1983, citing Machiavelli, 1965 edn, 204).

14

Machiavelli on Hellenistic Expansionism and Economic Needs

Machiavelli's realism belongs to the Hellenistic and Roman tradition of constitutional government consonant with territorial empire, and to this extent he rejects the standards and the values of the *polis* as a social form outmoded by progress. In the theorization of the Hellenistic empire, Platonism had had a significant role to play. Not only did Plato provide an account, missing in Aristotle, of expansion from the origins of civilization to larger and larger political aggregates, in which the bases of empire could be located, but he provided at the same time the model of the beneficent king, who stood above the laws of local regimes, gathering his flock into the fold. For these models Hellenistic writers turned not to the *Republic*, but to the *Statesman*, the *Timaeus*, the *Critias* and the *Laws*, Plato's later and more sociological works, in which he demonstrates a wide knowledge of the realities of Athenian politics and its laws, and an understanding of the ancient oriental world, that could be applied to orientalized Hellas – which, after all, is what Hellenistic culture constituted.

In prevailing Hellenistic theories of good government no incompatibility was posited between monarchy and republicanism. And we dare to postulate that in Machiavelli's case none was seen to exist either; which means that the tension between *The Prince* and the *Discourses* is more subtle than this. The failure of the *polis* form to generate stable governments and a lasting peace had encouraged the rush to monarchy and federation under the larger imperial umbrella. What costs this development brought in terms of popular participation were believed to be adequately compensated by gains in order, stability and pacific progress. Thus by Polybius' time 'republicanism' had come to mean autonomy in local government and 'democracy' a constitutional regime with some form of representative assembly. This certainly did not require an equivalent of the Athenian *ecclesia*. In the account of the four Macedonian republics founded in 167 BC as the cornerstone of Hellenistic federalism, for which our chief source is Livy, whose version 'in turn, certainly is based on Polybius' (Larsen, 1945, 69), representative government rested on the *synedrion*. Although much heated debate has been expended on the question whether the *synodoi* of the Achaean League, the *koina* of the Eastern provinces of the Roman Empire, founded under the Hellenistic monarchies, or the Macedonian *synedrion*, as chief organs of government were representative assemblies, there is no question of them being 'democratic' in the fifth- and fourth-century meaning of that term (Larsen, 1945, 66–7). Livy

(14.32.2) refers to those 'whom they call *synedroi*', as 'senators', elected and responsible for the government of the state (cited in Larsen, 1945, 69), undoubtedly using the term which Polybius had used, and one foreign to Livy's Roman readers. And Polybius (31.2.12), we know, deemed the Macedonian republics 'democratic', assuming, it would seem, their form of government to be the norm for federal states (Larsen, 1945, 69, 67).

As a number of scholars have noted, *democratia*, that magnificent ideal of the fifth and fourth centuries BC, had by the second and first come 'to be watered down so that it meant little more than constitutional republican government' (Jones, 1940, 170, cited in Larsen, 1945, 88), the rule of a free commonwealth as opposed to *tyrannos*. It was in the spirit of freedom and democracy understood in this sense, that the proconsul Titus Quinctius Flamininus stunned the participants at the Isthmian games of 196 with the announcement that the Senate of Rome had determined to leave the Greek cities 'free, without garrisons, subject to no tribute and in full enjoyment of their ancestral laws' (Polybius 66.5., 1979 edn, 516; Jones, 1940, 95–102; Gruen, 1984, 132–3). The 'freedom of the Greeks' became a resonant slogan in Roman propaganda, as we know from classical sources (Livy 33.32.5, 33.33.5–7, 34.41.3, 39.37.10, cited in Gruen, 1984, 132, n.1). That it began life in a policy statement by the conqueror of Philip of Macedon addressing his conquered cities is significant. The form of government it announced was new to Rome, but old to the Greeks. Rome was slipping easily into Macedonian shoes, adopting a policy that combined imperial hegemony with local autonomy in an age-old tradition that went back to the Mesopotamian Empires.

It is noteworthy that scholars have concluded from Polybius' usage of the term democracy as the antithesis of tyranny, and specifically from the treatment of the contrast between royal and democratic government in Polybius 22.8.6., that the tripartite classifications of governments, for which he is more famous, had now been replaced by a bipartite classification in which the contrast is between one-man and representative regimes (Larsen, 1945, 88). Thus F.W. Walbank, the Polybius scholar, early concludes from his study of the Amphictionic decree of 184/3 BC that in this decree the term 'democratic' 'seems to be used without any implied contrast to "oligarchic", but almost as a synonym for "self-governing"' (Walbank, 1940, 225, n.2, cited in Larsen, 1945, 88). Other scholars have pointed out that 'in the second century many states were called "democratic" which in the late fifth century would have been called "oligarchic"' (Larsen, 1945, 89). In another Amphictionic decree Antiochus III is congratulated for protecting the democracy and peace, if not the freedom, of the people of Antioch, whose status as a free city was, however, never in doubt (*Orientis Graeci Inscriptiones Selectae*, 234, 21–22, cited in Larsen, 1945, 89). And Dio Cassius (52.5.4) puts into the mouth of Agrippa a speech before Augustus in favour of the Republic – under the name of democracy – which refers to Rome's allies and subjects, as some being democracies from ancient times, others owing their freedom to the Romans (cited in Larsen, 1945, 89). Indeed Dio Cassius (52.1.1., cited in Larsen, 1945, 90) referred to the Roman Republic throughout its duration as 'democratic'; others deeming states under Roman rule 'free' and 'democratic' by virtue of municipal self-government, so that 'the mere transfer from subjection to a king to the control of Rome' was seen to be 'an act of liberation', even if the king were local (Larsen, 1945, 90, citing Livy, *Epitome LIX*).

Machiavelli, in commencing *The Prince* with a paradigmatic statement to the effect that all polities are constituted either as principalities or republics, writes from the Polybian perspective, which raises the question of the dating of *The Prince* and the *Discourses*, to which we will presently come, and the even thornier problem of his access to Polybius. What must be noted in the meantime is that whatever Machiavelli's half-apologetic rejection of ideal republics like those of earlier theorists, and presumably Plato, amounts to – and too much should not be made of it – it certainly does not mean that Machiavelli abandoned the distinction between monarchy and tyranny. Rather, the only important distinction remaining, once Hellenistic terms of reference were accepted, was between republicanism and tyranny, monarchy having been absorbed by republicanism; and republicanism connoting the rule of 'freedom' and 'democracy', where democracy was no longer tied to the *demos*, or freedom to the absence of monarchy.

In this respect Machiavelli also remained a Platonist. His depiction of King David, 'who heaped riches upon the needy, and dismissed the wealthy empty-handed', invokes the image of the beneficent king. The more malignant picture of Philip of Macedon who 'moved men from province to province as shepherds move their sheep', drawn in the same chapter (*Discourses*, 1.26, 1974 edn, 177), nevertheless plays on Platonic images of kingship. Strauss is right to point out that Machiavelli in *The Prince* seems to avoid the term '*tirrano*', and that individuals called '*tirrani*' in the *Discourses* are called '*principi*' in *The Prince* (Strauss, 1948, 48). Even in the *Discourses*, Machiavelli gives only two examples: Nabis, the ruler of Sparta around 200 BC, who in *The Prince* 9 is called '*principe*' and in *Discourses* 1.40 is called '*tiranno*'; and Pandolfo Petruzzi, the ruler of Siena around AD 1500 with whom Machiavelli was several times sent to negotiate, called '*principe*' in *The Prince* 20 and 22, and '*tiranno*' in *Discourses* 3.6 (Strauss, 1948, 107, n.2) – his ambivalence to whom could be explained on other grounds. It is nevertheless true that tyranny is a preoccupation in the *Discourses* that it is not in *The Prince*.

This bespeaks a shift in emphasis, however, and not a wholesale reversal in values. For the problematic of *The Prince*, like that of the *Discourses*, is the Polybian problematic. How are these new political aggregations, introduced by the Roman and Hellenistic empires, to establish and maintain themselves? Is the price paid for political expansionism too high, or is expansion the rule of life, contraction the sign of death? What degrees of freedom and participation are compatible with political order and stability? And what are the moral constraints on political leaders? These are not questions that could be answered within the framework of theories of the *polis*, a framework within which Aristotle, although witness to the birth – and even unwilling midwife, as Alexander's tutor – to these new social forms, insisted on remaining. But Plato, more widely travelled, conversant with the political systems of oriental states which had known empire for millennia, could furnish some clues, if once again reluctantly. The Hellenistic world, dominated by oriental thinkers with Greek ideals, seized on Platonist notions, which they fashioned into philosophies that produced a curious amalgam

of indigenous and exotic elements – although no more curious than some of the
more mystical works of Plato that seem to have drawn on the same fund. In the
interstices between politics and religion, the divine king finds his role in most
Hellenistic philosophies, whether Platonist, Stoic or Epicurean, and whether or
not they favour active political participation or ataraxic withdrawal. No matter
how transcendent or otherworldly their concerns, most of these theorists bow
before the reality of the age, which is that of a large-scale territorial empire and
not the self-sufficient *polis*. The question of the day is no longer how to avoid
monarchy, or even oligarchy, but how to avoid tyranny, since monarchy and
aristocracy have long been incorporated into the constitutional provisions of their
regimes.

What Machiavelli rejected in Plato was his otherworldliness, his insistence on
supererogation as the ruling political value, and his lack of political realism, in the
Republic, at least. Plato represented the 'ubiquitous Hellenic ideal' among men of
substance to minimize their involvement in politics beyond the fulfilment of state
obligations, such as the liturgies – which were onerous enough (Lateiner, 1982,
1). And this ideal found no favour with Machiavelli, as we know from his attack
on the 'proud indolence' (*ozio*) of Christianity and its philosophy of withdrawal
(*Discourses*, 1, Introduction, 1974 edn, 98, and 2.2, 278). A feature of Christianity
that owes much to the Stoic reverence for *otio*, and even the Platonic and
Aristotelian *schole*, which permitted the life of ataraxia and contemplation.
Renaissance Platonists were known to echo these sentiments which Machiavelli
rejects, Marsilio Ficino being reported by Guiccardini to have declared: 'When
cities are well governed, my Plato said good men should flee as far as possible
from involvement in government' (Guiccardini, *Dialogues and Discourses on
Florentine Government*, 1932 edn, 53, cited in Brown, 1986, 383, n.1).

But the enduring legacy of Platonism, as a doctrine self-consciously harnessed
to political purposes by Cosimo de Medici, at whose instigation Marsilio Ficino
undertook his translations from 1463 to 1484, was not this. The excitement that
Gemistus Pletho generated by his lectures at the Council of Florence, which
Cosimo is reputed to have attended, gained wings from its political content, to
which Pletho was well attuned. 'The spirit of Plato living in his writings left
Byzantium for Florence ... and flew to Cosimo de Medici', Ficino remarked in
the preface to his 1464 translation of ten Platonic dialogues dedicated to that
prince (cited in Brown, 1986, 389–90). Plato, in the *Republic*, and consistently in
his writings, taught three lessons about the well-governed polity: that power is
justified by knowledge; that the good ruler transcends good laws; and that a
functional division of labour is essential to social order and harmony.

These lessons were read by Florentine republicans in the following way. The
lesson on knowledge and power was the pre-eminent lesson that the Medicis and
their advisors drew, by means of which a humble merchant, Cosimo, propelled
himself to princely status, a leap from an inferior class in Plato's typology that he
would in fact be unlikely to condone (Brown, 1986, 394). That this lesson was
quite specifically Platonist, we know from tracts which refer to Cosimo as leader
of the guardian class and, by implication, philosopher ruler (Brown, 1986, 394).
The propaganda of the Medicis, official and unofficial, from Cosimo to Giuliano,
sought to legitimize the rule of these upstart princes as wise men, growing more

extravagant with repetition, so that kingship – as practised it is implied, by Lorenzo and Giuliano – was praised in terms that are purely Platonist: 'The king and the wise man are above the stars, whence I am beyond this vain law ... I will follow, shepherd of this flock' (Lorenzo de' Medici, *Opere*, 1914 edn, vol. 2, 114, cited in Gilbert, 1939, 476, and Brown, 1986, 401). The appeal, in this case to the prince of Plato's *Statesman*, rather than the philosopher ruler of the *Republic*, represents a Renaissance trend whereby the new prince, legitimized by his knowledge and access to expertise, is melded to the Stoic 'wise man', as well as the beneficent king as shepherd, a Platonist conception much elaborated in Hellenistic thought.

In *quattrocento* mirrors of princes we find disquisitions on the personality of the prince indicating the tendencies to individualism and voluntarism that are predominant in Hellenistic sources with their emphasis on leadership. They combine catalogues of princely virtues that are characteristically Aristotelian and Stoic, with appeals to the prince's magnificence and *majestas* that are patently from the Hellenistic Neoplatonist tradition and its medieval legacy. Thus in the mirror of Egidio Colonna, with which Machiavelli's *Prince* is most frequently compared as representative of the genre, the cardinal virtues, listed as *prudentia*, *justitia*, *fortitudo*, *temperantia*, are supplemented by the minor virtues, *magnificentia*, *magnanamitas* and so on (Gilbert, 1939, 463, n.31). Egidio, who is rather suspicious of power and worldly display, does not amplify *magnificentia*, but the same is not true for other exponents of the genre. The Venetian Pontano shows his hand by entitling his work on the prince *De majestate*, and his elaboration of the concept involves prescriptions regarding the prince's deportment, elaborate court ceremonial and etiquette (Gilbert, 1939, 466) that are more reminiscent of the Persian court and the innovations of Alexander than anything from the Greek or Roman world hitherto, governed as the latter was by sumptuary laws and notions of propriety that excluded what they deemed to be oriental hocus pocus.

This connection to Persia and the oriental courts is not entirely fanciful. The ceremonial and etiquette of the Persian court had made its entrance to Europe through the influence of the Sublime Porte; the degree to which Sasanian royal practices, by which the conventions of the Byzantine court in turn were formed, ultimately affected European monarchical convention, being a factor which, as one historian of the Hellenistic age points out, has been consistently underestimated (Bury, 1970, 14–15). Just as the courts of the Ptolemies and the Seleucids were, due in no small part to the aspirations of Alexander, imitative of the Achaemenid royal court, so the oriental ceremonial adopted by Aurelian, Diocletian and Constantine, owed its origins to the Sasanians (Bury, 1970, 14–15). New princes of the *quattrocento*, heavily indebted to the Hellenistic experience, were schooled on literature designed for the oriental prince. So Xenophon's *Cyropaedia*, and *Hiero*, its foil, were among the most cited ancient examples of the *speculum regum*.

From Xenophon it was learned that hunts, tournaments and conspicuous royal display were the outward marks of *majestas* as expressions of *magnificentia*. It is no surprise, then, to find Machiavelli (*Discourses*, 3.39, 1974 edn, 511; cf. Mansfield, 1979, 422–3) expounding on the wisdom of those ancient writers who 'tell us that the heroes who ruled the world in their day were brought up in the forests and on the chase', and citing 'Xenophon [who] in his Life of Cyrus tells us [that] ... a hunting expedition is very like a war, and that, consequently, great men look on this sport as honourable and necessary.' The other great lesson to be learned from Xenophon on Cyrus, in Machiavelli's book, is the indispensability of deception (*Discourses* 2.13, 1974 edn, 310), a lesson that one reads also in the lives of 'Philip of Macedon or that of Agathocles the Sicilian, for instance, or others of that ilk, [who] ... from an extremely low, or at any rate a low position ... rose either to a kingdom or to very great power'. It is worth noting that in Persian and Arabic manuals for princes, to which, as we will see, Machiavelli's shows striking parallels, deception, in Arabic *taqiyya*, is both a recognized and legitimate princely ploy – one invoked in the twentieth century by practitioners of *Realpolitik* as different as the Ayatollah Khomeini and Saddam Hussein of Iraq.

Machiavelli, read with some justice as the consistent exponent of *Realpolitik*, has no regard for magnificence for its own sake, as smacking too much perhaps of the imperial mantle that Italy was sloughing off with difficulty. For him the prowess of the prince, sharpened by schooling in the royal arts, had purely pragmatic purposes: the necessity of the new prince to establish his hegemony and maintain it by means of good laws, good institutions and good arms. Thus the beneficent monarch of more pacific Platonist theory is transformed by Machiavelli, as by Polybius, in the image of Philip, Alexander, Cyrus and Agathocles, military adventurers, renowned as much for their cruelty as their courage, who nevertheless succeeded in pioneering the great Hellenistic experiment at empire, of which he is so much in admiration.

Before addressing the main question which Machiavelli's notions of the expansionist state and imperial hegemony raise – the question of how far in the direction of tyranny the prince is permitted to go in order to protect liberty – we must note the use to which the third lesson from Plato's *Republic*, that political order rests on a functional division of labour, was put. One of the most recurrent themes in the political works of Plato, this emphasis on the connection between justice and functional specialization was declared by Marx, a percipient observer of the ancient world, to represent 'merely the Athenian idealisation of the Egyptian system of castes, Egypt having served as the model of an industrial country to many of his contemporaries also, amongst others to Isocrates, and it continued to have this importance to the Greeks of the Roman Empire' (Marx, *Capital*, n.d., ch. 14, 5, 346). Marx cites from Isocrates *Busiris*, 8, earlier in date than the account Plato gives of the division of labour in Egypt in the *Timaeus*, and possibly its source. There Isocrates concludes from his account of the strict division of labour in Egypt, the basis for its political and economic superiority, that 'the contrivances for maintaining the monarchy and the other institutions of their State are so admirable that the most celebrated philosophers who treat of this subject praise the constitution of the Egyptian State above all others' (Isocrates, *Busiris*, 8, cited in Marx, *Capital*, n.d., ch. 14, 5, 346, n.1.). Isocrates, available to Renaissance humanists in Latin translations, was author of 'the best known ancient example of a "mirror of princes"', his *Address to Nicocles*, which Machiavelli is believed to have imitated in his dedication of *The Prince*, to Lorenzo de Medici (Gilbert, 1939, 478).

Oriental civilization, for countless centuries the source for imagery both benign and malignant of luxury and opulence, owed its riches, as authors both ancient and modern have observed, to a highly articulated division and specialization of labour, which had its counterpart in the administrative apparatuses of government. Marx quotes from Xenophon, who in the *Cyropaedia*, 1.8, had already made this analysis in the case of Persia. Xenophon remarks that 'it is not only an honour to receive food from the table of the King of Persia, but such food is much more tasty than other food', and this due to the division and specialization of labour that brings this art, like so many others, 'to special perfection in the great towns' that cannot be matched in more simple economies (Xenphon, *Cyrop.*, 1.8.2, cited in Marx, *Capital*, ch. 14, 5, 345–6, n.3).

The connection between politics and economics was not lost on the new merchant bourgeoisie of the Italian city-states, whose republicanism rested on commerce, and whose commerce depended on expansionism. Their traditional trading rivals in the Mediterranean had for centuries been the Islamic states, whose economic institutions and commercial practices they emulated. The urban, entrepreneurial, Italian merchant states broke from the fold of the Christian Emperor, by drawing on the support of an affluent and energetic new middle class, who found support in Plato's analysis of the economic foundations of republicanism and the expertise to which the division and specialization of labour gives rise. These same principles were applied to political leadership and the new princes, upstarts for the most part, tended to be legitimized in one of two ways; either as technocrats, that is to say as 'chief magistrates', or as 'democratic' princes.

For both of these paths, Platonic references could be found. In the dialogue on monarchy of Leon Battista Alberti, *De iciarchia*, for instance, the prince stands to the community in the same relation as the father to his family: as supreme magistrate, responsible for, but not apart from, the community that he guards, performing the patriotic duty of the 'good citizen' (Gilbert, 1939, 472–3). Republican Platonism reached its apogee with the political theory of Marsilio Ficino, who in his commentaries on Plato's *Statesman*, interpreted Plato's desire to describe his world-monarch as *politikos*, rather than *monarchos*, as indicating that Plato desired for his prince none of the ostentatious trappings of monarchy, and perhaps not even its external form, but rather a statesman who reigned by his 'inner deportment' ('Argumentum Marsilii Ficini in librum Platonis de regno, vel civilem', in *Marsilii Ficine opera*, 2nd ed, Basle, 1576, vol. 2, 1294 ff, cited in Gilbert, 1939, 474). Felix Gilbert makes the pointed observation that the concept of 'mixed government', so important in the republicanism of Guicciardini and Gianotti, as well as of Machiavelli, 'was regarded as Platonic ... and, although known to the earlier humanists, began to arouse greater interest only after the Platonic revival' (Gilbert, 1939, 475, n.75). He notes at the same time the significance of the new figure of the legislator, the emphasis on constitutionality and the ability to translate philosophical principles into legal forms, which can be dated precisely to the works of Gemistus Pletho, 'first Platonist of the Renaissance', and author of his own treatise on *The Laws* (Gilbert, 1939, 475, nn. 74, 75).

This tradition of republican Platonism is one to which Machiavelli both belongs, and from which he stands apart. In this ambivalence much of the complexity of his relations to monarchy and tyranny may be seen to lie. For the alternative, absolutist, interpretation of princely power which was open to him, and which took a Platonist form too, that of the Hellenistic divine king, theocratically sanctioned, was not one to which Machiavelli, as the member of an old republican family, was predisposed to incline – it smacked too much of the emperor and divine right of kings of official propaganda. As Felix Gilbert (1939, 481–3) and others have pointed out, there is a definite break in *The Prince*, and what we have after the first 11 chapters, which follow the mirror of princes model, is a critique in the following 15. Thus it would seem that Machiavelli is mimicking the genre, both Platonist and humanist, in order insolently to satirize it. This would fit with his contemporary reputation for deviousness, as well as with some of the more audacious recent interpretations of his work (Dietz, 1986). But it leaves unresolved the puzzle of Machiavelli's deeper purposes, and his real stance on the question of republicanism and despotism. If, in fact, Machiavelli parodies the traditional humanist catalogue of princely virtues, rejecting the criteria of good and evil that it invokes, what standards does he apply to the question of tyranny instead? Careful analysis of the relevant passages shows that while retaining the conventional humanist framework for government that incorporates the innovative prince in a constitutional regime, Machiavelli rings some startling changes, suggestive of an alternative, and so far hidden, tradition of the mirror of princes genre.

Machiavelli's view of human nature militates against any simple distinction between liberty and tyranny, and this is just his first departure from the classical tradition. In *Discourses* 1.3 (1974 edn, 111–12), Machiavelli, who has already alerted us to allusions to Plato's *Laws* in 1.1, indicates how widely he differs from the master in his assessment of human nature. As if pointing to Plato's practical failure in the *Republic*, he declares that: 'All writers on politics have pointed out, and throughout history there are plenty of examples which indicate, that in constituting and legislating for a commonwealth it must needs be taken for granted that all men are wicked and that they will always give vent to the malignity that is in their minds when opportunity offers.' It follows 'that men never do good unless necessity drives them to it', and that whenever men have choice, liberty becomes licence (*Discourses*, 1.3, 1974 edn, 112). It further follows, those theorizing on the foundation of states have concluded, that if 'hunger and poverty make men industrious' then 'laws make them good' (1.3, 1974 edn, 112).

Machiavelli displays a tendency toward primitivism (Waley, 1970, 90–9), that we find in Stoic and Epicurean writers, their Enlightenment successors, Rousseau and the early socialists, in his emulation of the man of few needs. There are numerous references scattered throughout his works to the virtue of *uomini rozzi*, 'rough men' and mountain people, as men whose needs are few, uncorrupted by civilization, a view that perhaps more accurately expresses his position than the bold but blanket assertion of *Discourses* 1.3, that men are evil *tout court*. Explaining the force of civic religion in ensuring popular compliance in the early days of the Roman Republic, Machiavelli remarks that because in that time the people with whom they had to deal were 'simple' (*grossi*), it was easy to impress new forms on them, from which he concludes that 'anyone seeking to establish a republic at the present time would find it easier to do so among uncultured men of the mountains than among dwellers in cities where civilization is corrupt; just as a sculptor will more easily carve a beautiful statue from rough (*rozzo*) marble than from marble already spoiled by a bungling workman' (*Discourses*, 1.11, 1974 edn, 141; Waley, 1970, 91). Demonstrating a consistent admiration for toughness, even to the point of cruelty, and contempt for 'softness' (*mollizie*), Machiavelli in *The Prince*, 19, praises the Emperor Antoninus, son of Severus – 'upstart' and 'pacifier of the East', who combined 'the qualities of a ferocious lion and a very cunning fox' – as 'a military man' like his father, 'capable of any exertion', who 'scorned softness (*mollizie*) of any kind, at the table or elsewhere' (*Prince*, 19, 1961 edn, 110). While in the following chapter Machiavelli advises the new prince to quash potential opposition by rendering his citizens *molle e effeminati* (*Prince*, 20, 1961 edn, 115, cited in Waley, 1979, 93).

Machiavelli's most memorable remarks on the virtues of simplicity and men of few needs are reserved for the Germans, the special subject of the Roman primitivists, Tacitus in the *Germania*, and Sallust. Machiavelli would seem, in the opinion of his commentators, (Walker, 1975, vol. 2, 67; Waley, 1970, 93; Crick, 1974, 534), to make direct reference to Sallust's aphorism in *Bellum Catilinae* (52.22), attributed to Cato: *publice egestatem privatim opulentiam*, in his twice repeated prescription (*Discourses*, 1.37, and 2.19, 1974 edn, 201, 335) for 'well-ordered republics': 'to keep the public [i.e. the treasury] rich but the people poor'. This is an unwavering maxim with Machiavelli, who illustrates its wisdom time and again, as exemplified by the great Roman leader Cincinnatus (*Discourses*, 3.25, 1974 edn, 475), but contravened by the great Carthaginian Hannibal (2.19, 1974 edn, 338). That it was an early preoccupation of Machiavelli's is demonstrated by his comments in his short piece on the Germans, *Rapporto delle cose della Magna* of 1508, where he argues that poverty does not necessarily cause discontent among them: 'It is enough for them to have plenty of bread and meat and a stove to give protection against the cold ... their necessities are a lot fewer than ours ... they enjoy this rough (*rozza*), free life of theirs and are not willing to engage in war unless they are very well paid for it' (trans. Waley, 1970, 93). Remarks which he repeats almost without alteration in his later work on the same subject (the *Ritratto delle cose della Magna*, 210, cited in Waley, 1970, 93, n.8, both works contained in *Arte della Guerra e scritti politici minori*, 1961 edn).

Machiavelli follows those primitivists, principally the Roman Stoics and Epicureans, who believed, however, that the life 'according to nature' is no solution to the problem of corruption in any simple sense. Just as Seneca in his Ninetieth Letter on progress, heavily reliant as it is on the theories of the Hellenistic writer Posidonius, postulated an inherent tendency to conflict and corruption in the expansion of needs, which civilization induces; so the Epicurean Lucretius, postulated competitiveness, conflict and corruption in the same source. Machiavelli, in his account of ambition, and the demand for a share in the distribution of honours and property (*la sustanze*), that grew like a 'disease', leading to 'the dispute about the Agrarian Law and in the end caused the destruction of the republic', hypothesizes in human nature a restless desire for satisfaction after satisfaction, that knows no limit: 'The reason is that nature has so constituted men that, though all things are objects of desire, not all things are attainable; so that desire always exceeds the power of attainment, with the result that men are ill content with what they possess and their present state brings them little satisfaction.' It is this inbuilt frailty that makes them vulnerable to fortune and destruction: 'For, since some desire to have more and others are afraid to lose what they have already acquired, enmities and wars are begotten, and this brings about the ruin of one province and the exultation of its rival' (*Discourses*, 1.37, 1974 edn, 200).

Machiavelli's is the classical view with a twist, as he makes clear, challenging the views of the 'ancient writers', that men although frustrated by adversity are easily sated by prosperity (*Discourses*, 1.37, 1974 edn, 200). Not so at all, he declares, 'human appetites are insatiable, for by nature we are so constituted that there is nothing we cannot long for' (*Discourses*, 2, Introd., 1974 edn, 268). The sad fact is that if men are so by nature, 'by fortune [they] are such that of these things [they] can obtain but few. The result is that the human mind is perpetually discontented, and of its possessions is apt to grow weary.' But if this is a fact of nature, Machiavelli draws the appropriate conclusion that it is in itself neither good nor bad, abandoning the categories of the Stoic moralists in favour of his own criteria for human conduct: the ordinary versus the extraordinary (Mansfield, 1979, 97). This restless spirit, induced by the growth of new needs as more primitive needs are satisfied, which causes men to 'find fault with the present, praise the past, and long for the future' (*Discourses*, 2, Introd., 1974 edn, 268), if the source of individual weakness, is at the same time civilization's strength. It sets the challenge to the new prince, providing the energy that he must harness, and representing the driving force of culture that social institutions ignore at their peril.

Social theorists dare not look back to the golden age of the small-scale impregnable city-state, Machiavelli implies. If the examples of Sparta and Venice point to a remarkable success in holding the forces of corruption at bay in a static balance that endured, the underlying realities of human nature have been borne out by Hellenistic experience and the emergence of territorial empire propelled by expansionism and progress. Sparta succeeded due to the smallness of its population, 'which made it possible for a few to rule', by shutting foreigners out and by an egalitarian regime based on the principle that 'poverty was shared by all alike' (*Discourses*, 1.6, 1974 edn, 120–1). Venice, ruled by the gentry (*Gentiluomini*), maintained a balance by ensuring that newcomers never outnumbered this established ruling class (1.6, 119–20). Even so, Sparta, 'having subjugated almost the whole of Greece, revealed, on an occasion of slight importance in itself, how weak its foundation was', and 'entirely collapsed' under the Theban revolt; while Venice, 'having occupied the greater part of Italy ... when its strength was put to the test, lost everything in a single battle' (*Discourses*, 1.6, 1974 edn, 122).

The truth is, Machiavelli asserts, 'expansion is poison to republics of this type' and must perforce be held at bay.

> Since, however, all human affairs are ever in a state of flux and cannot stand still, either there will be improvement or decline, and necessity will lead you to do many things which reason does not recommend. Hence if a commonwealth be constituted with a view to its maintaining the *status quo*, but not with a view to expansion, and

by necessity it be led to expand, its basic principles will be subverted and it will soon be faced with ruin. (*Discourses*, 1.6, 1974 edn, 122–3)

Machiavelli elsewhere leaves us with the striking image of the small republic that gains empire being like a tree whose trunk is too small for its branches (*Discourses*, 2.3, 1974 edn, 283). Ignorant of human nature and outmoded by fortune, the *polis* fell victim to the forces of history. Athens, hardly worth mentioning, failed 'because with democracy Solon had not blended either princely power or that of the aristocracy' (*Discourses*, 1.2, 1974 edn, 110). Sparta and Venice, faced with the eternal question of all republics, divided as they are between 'an upper and a lower class', 'into whose hands it is best to place the guardianship of liberty', answered it by entrusting it to the nobles (*Discourses*, 1.5, 1974 edn, 115–16). By depriving the lower class of any realistic aspirations to power, they at the same time cut themselves off from the conflicts and class struggle on which an expansionist republic thrives. Rome, by contrast, made the plebs the guardians of liberty, and brought into play all those 'endless squabbles' and tumults that were to be the cause of its greatness (*Discourses*, 1.5, 1974 edn, 116).

Liberty for Machiavelli may also be an instrumental value, which is why the old antithesis between freedom and despotism does not take its classic form in his writings. Those who desire liberty, he argues in *Discourses*, 1.16, may be divided into those who hope to use it in order to command, and the remainder, who desire it for 'the possibility of enjoying what one has, freely and without incurring suspicion'; for the assurance that one's wife and children will be secure, and for 'the absence of fear for oneself' (*Discourses*, 1.16, 1974 edn, 154; Mansfield, 1979, 193). But both ruling class and ruled desire freedom for the increase in wealth and dominion that it permits; and the real difference between self-government (*uno vivere libero*) and tyranny is that under the latter the body politic 'ceases to make progress and to grow in power and wealth: more often than not, nay always, what happens is that it declines' (*Discourses*, 2.2, 1974 edn, 276). 'And should fate decree the rise of an efficient (*virtuoso*) tyrant, so energetic and so proficient in warfare that he enlarges his dominions, no advantage will accrue to the commonwealth, but only to himself', so they are no better off. It is in the logic of tyranny that 'he alone profits by his acquisitions, not his country', and 'should anyone desire to confirm this view by a host of further arguments', Machiavelli advises, 'let him read Xenophon's treatise *On Tyrannicide*' (*Discourses*, 2.2, 1974 edn, 276).

But let us not be misled by the classical reference: Machiavelli is not making the classical case that riches are to be valued for the freedom that they bring, but rather the opposite, that freedom is to be valued for the wealth and power that accrue! And the classic case against tyrants, that they rule not in the interests of the commonwealth, but treat the commonwealth as their personal property, has been interpreted by Machiavelli in purely economic terms. This is the thinker who argues against the ancients that 'men set much greater store on property than on honours' (*Discourses*, 1.37, 1974 edn, 204), a fundamental precept of his proud 'modernism'. We should not infer from this principle a norm, however. Machiavelli, consciously or not, reflects a Hellenistic legacy of speculation on the instincts, that draws conclusions about the energy derived from individual motivations for cultural purposes, not seriously discussed again until the psychological writings of the Enlightenment period, to which Sigmund Freud was a most famous heir. The view of human nature as appetitive, proprietary, combative, but capable of cold rationality, that we find in Thomas Hobbes, for instance, shows none of this subtlety, despite the latter's Epicurean connections through Gassendi – the conclusion he draws from the negative traits of human nature is repression, not progress, as the palliative.

Machiavelli's genius lies, by contrast, in seeing that men's natural motivations to property may be transformed, by the correct command of circumstances, into the pursuit of glory. This is why virtue, as commentators have rightly pointed out, is so frequently to be encountered in his writings in martial contexts; and why those civilizations possessed, in his view, of the greatest virtue, were martial cultures (Wood, 1967; Hannaford, 1972). It does not mean, as Hannaford rightly points out, that the concept of *virtù* is exhausted by its military content, or that war is in itself glorious. It does mean, however, that virtue stands in a special relation to necessity, and that necessity frequently involves war and conquest. Necessity can mean both the precautions that must be taken to ensure than an otherwise virile culture does not go soft, or it can refer to a course of events forced on a nation from the outside. In the first case necessity arises from the constraints of human nature, in the second from causes that lie outside one's control, constituting the Stoic 'fate', or Hellenistic 'fortune', so beloved of Polybius and Machiavelli to personify remote and unfathomable chains of causation.

15

Machiavelli, the Marcher Lords and War

When Machiavelli reflects in the Preface to book 2 of the *Discourses*, on the ebb and flow of human events, in which everything changes and yet all remains the same, the balance of good and evil hardly affected by changes in its distribution from 'province to province', he finds the significant difference, worthy indeed of his whole treatise, in the fact that 'the world's virtue first found a home in Assyria, then flourished in Media and later in Persia, and at length arrived in Italy and Rome' (1974 edn, 267). Leslie Walker notes the probable source for this passage in Plutarch's more poetic statement in *De fortuna Romanorum* (*Moralia*, 4.4, 317e–f, 1936 edn, 331, noted in Walker, 1975, vol. 2, 92, n.4):

> Fortune, when she had deserted the Persians and the Assyrians, had flitted lightly over Macedonia, and had quickly shaken off Alexander, made her way through Egypt and Syria, conveying kingships here and there; and turning about, she would often exalt the Carthaginians. But when she was approaching the Palatine and crossing the Tiber, it appears that she took off her wings, stepped out of her sandals, and abandoned her untrustworthy and unstable globe. Thus did she enter Rome, as with intent to abide, and in such guise is she present today, as though ready to meet her trial.

Machiavelli's departures from Plutarch, if this is indeed his source, are noteworthy ones. To begin with, it is Virtue and not Fortune, whose transmigrations Machiavelli is tracking. Fortune for him is both a woman and a 'violent river ... wild and dangerous' (*Prince*, 1961 edn, 130), devastating in its path. And here Machiavelli's metaphor outdoes that of Plutarch, for whom 'the pace of Fortune, bold is her spirit and most vaunting her hopes ... outstrips Virtue' (*De fortuna Romanorum*, 317e, 1936 edn, 331). Egypt and Syria are omitted from Machiavelli's account, perhaps because as pacific monarchies they did not demonstrate the martial spirit which characterizes the other candidates. Virtue has also moved on, and although for so long monopolized by the Roman Empire, whose concentration of the 'world's virtue' has never been matched, is now 'distributed among many nations where men lead virtuous lives': the Franks, the Germans, 'the kingdom of the Turks, [i.e.] that of the Sultan; and ... the Saracens, who performed such great exploits and occupied so much of the world, since they broke up the Roman empire in the East' (*Discourses*, 2, Introd., 1974 edn, 267).

These new contestants are important, for Machiavelli's remarks fall in the context of a preface to his discussion of the ways in which the Romans achieved imperial expansion, the subject of book 2, which dismisses glorifications of the past and yearnings for a return to the golden age, as themselves a product of the restlessness of human desire that can never be quenched. Machiavelli mocks the humanists for a romanticization of the past that stands in the way of a sober analysis of the present, and for failure to assess impartially the judgement of the ancient historians, themselves quite frequently partial. In this respect Machiavelli displays an independence with regard to his sources that is quite Polybian, as demonstrated by the latter's attitude to the historians Philinus and Fabius, and his comments on the apparent transparency of events in the past, which 'admit of being tested by naked fact', compared with the difficulty of obtaining insight into the purposes of contemporaries (Polybius 3.31, cited in Walker, 1975, 2.92, n.2).

There is no doubt that the nations in which *virtù*, on Machiavelli's account, was wont to reside, were martial states, from the great marcher lords of the Assyrian Empire, to the bold-faced Saracens. Nor does he reveal orientalist assumptions that the West has a monopoly of virtue, as post-Reformation thinkers were inclined to. Machiavelli's heroes are as often ancient as modern, and as frequently Eastern as Western. Thus the long shadow cast by Alexander, the Persianized prince, is almost matched by the great Hannibal, to whom Machiavelli devotes almost as much attention as Polybius (*Discourses*, 2.9, 2.12, 2.27, 3.32). His attitude to the Turks is surprisingly impartial, given the threat that they posed to the trade of the Italian city-states – although to Venice rather than Florence, primarily. The acquaintance of Italian humanists with the history and culture of the Islamic states, and the impact of Arab incursions on the peninsula, are too easily underestimated. Not only did Arabic sources contribute heavily to Renaissance humanist literature, transmitted through Byzantine scholarship, the teachings of scholars like Pletho, themselves schooled in the Arabic commentaries, as well as medieval Western sources, but Renaissance scholars were attuned to the significance of Islamic culture quite self-consciously.

Marsilio Ficino was acquainted with the important Islamic Platonist commentaries of Avicenna and Averroes, for instance, while Pico della Mirandola made his own translation from the Arabic of that 'jewel of Arabic literature', the *Risalat Hayy ibn Yaqsan* of Ibn Tufayl (Abubacer), the twelfth century 'philosophical novel', known in its Latin version as the *Philosophus autodidactus* later so widely translated and circulated, eventual source of Defoe's *Robinson Crusoe* (Pastor, 1930; Smith, 1939; Anawati, 1974, 386–7; Menocal, 1987). Volumes have been written on the possible sources in Islamic eschatology for Dante's *Divina Commedia*, and the traditions of Arabic literature sponsored at the court of the Spanish ruler Alfonso the Wise that produced a 'golden century' of literary monuments, of which Cervantes *Don Quixote* is later reminiscent (Palacios, 1926; Anawati, 1974, 344–5; Gabrieli, 1974, 93–5). But the legacy of Islamic political thought has gone almost unnoticed (see Lambton, 1954, 1956, 1962, 1974, 1981; E. Rosenthal, 1958, 1965; Daniel, 1960).

Machiavelli evinces an interest in Muslim princes that may be significant, discussing the virtue of Bajazet, Sultan of the Turks, in terms that are highly instructive. Now, Bajazet 'a man who loved peace more than war, was able to enjoy the fruits of his father, Mahomet's labours; for the latter, like David, had defeated his neighbours, and left to him a strong kingdom which he could easily maintain by peaceful methods' (*Discourses*, 1.19, 1974 edn, 166). Machiavelli is referring in fact to Mehmed II (AD 1444–6; 1451–81), known as the Conqueror, who captured Constantinople in 1453, and went on to overrun Asia Minor, Serbia, Bosnia, Albania and the Crimea, Rhodes, and to gain a toehole in Italy by taking the city of Otranto, which he did not, however, hold for long (Walker, 1975, 2.47, n.3; Lapidus, 1988, 310–15). His son, Bajazet II, may have inclined more to peace than to war, but his accomplishments were not negligible either, conquering Styria and Croatia, and giving the Poles a lot of trouble as well.

Selim I, son of Bajazet, of whom Machiavelli speaks as a contemporary, which dates his writing of this section of the *Discourses* to around 1517, certainly outdid his father, defeating the Persians, conquering Kurdistan, entering Cairo as conqueror in 1517 and subsequently becoming Caliph, overrunning not only Egypt but Syria and the Hejaz as well (Walker, 1975, 2.47, n.3). Thus Machiavelli can illustrate the principle that a strong prince may be followed by one weak prince but not by two, stretching the facts a little by claiming that had the 'son, Selim, the present ruler, been like his father, not like his grandfather, this kingdom would have been ruined' (*Discourses*, 1.19, 1974 edn, 166). He was right to predict that Selim would excel his grandfather in glory, which put him in a league with Romulus and the Biblical King David in Machiavelli's book (*Discourses*, I.19, 1974 edn, 166). This does not mean that Bajazet, like Numa Pompilius or Solomon, the other pacific successors to great conquerors, was lacking in virtue either – Machiaveli puts Numa at the top of the list. For when peace is appropriate, virtue is pacific. War may be necessary to prevent men from going soft, but peace has its purposes too.

Indeed, apart from expansionism that permits human aspirations a source of fulfilment, the purposes that war primarily serves are cultural and not political. The intermittent application of force serves to arrest the inevitable decline into *ozio* and *il vivere molle* that peace produces: 'For virtue brings forth peace (*quiete*), peace leisure, (*ozio*), leisure disorder and disorder ruin' (*History of Florence*, 5.1, trans. Waley, 1970, 95). Whatever influence the cycle of expansion and decline of Polybius 6 may have had on Machiavelli's own theory of decadence, the reading he gives of it is psychological and cultural rather than strictly political. The perennial counterpart to his disquisitions on the virtues of war is to be found in his observations on the evils of leisure, so much so that one eighteenth-century anthology of Machiavelli's epigrams includes a section entitled '*Male dell' ozio*' (noted in Waley, 1979, 95). One of the great hazards of the stationary state, should it be so fortunate to escape attack from the outside, is that, having no need to go to war it will atrophy from idleness (*ozio*) and effeminacy, falling prey to factions which will be its ruination (*Discourses*, 1.6, 1974 edn, 123). So pervasive are the threats of *ozio*, that ancient writers were prompted to site their cities on barren land, rather than endure the perpetual menace to all inhabitants of agreeable and fertile places (*paesi amenissimi e fertilissimi*), a solution, Machiavelli observes, which overlooks the importance of wealth and commerce as necessary forms of power and competition for the release of incessant human desires for acquisition and improvement (*Discourses*, 1.1, 1974 edn, 102; Waley, 1970, 95). But even the Romans, whom Machiavelli excuses himself for perhaps seeming to overpraise, and therefore falling 'into the very fault for which I am blaming others' – of praising the past too much and disparaging the present (*Discourses*, 2. Introd., 1974 edn, 268) – were not immune from the vice of *ozio*. Machiavelli repeats Livy's account of the Roman legions garrisoning Capua in 343 BC who 'went rotten through leisure (*marcendo nell 'ozio*)' (*Discourses*, 2.20, 1974 edn, 339; Waley, 1970, 95).

Yet the lesson of war as a palliative for cultural atrophy had not been learned: 'throughout the world the methods and institutions (*modi e ordini*) of war, in comparison with those of the ancients, are exhausted; but in Italy they are totally lost' (Machiavelli, *Arte della Guerra e scritti politici minore*, 1961 edn, 498, trans. Waley, 1970, 94). Machiavelli bemoans the fact 'as clear as the sun', that the virtue prevailing in ancient times has in the present given way to vice (*Discourses*, 2. Introd., 1974 edn, 268). But it is not a fact that lies outside his macro-historical schema. For, with the ancients, Machiavelli believes that institutions, like organisms, have a natural life cycle which can only by the most delicate balance of forces be held in suspension. It follows that the sons of kings become tyrants, of aristocrats, oligarchs, and of democrats, anarchists. In the case of all institutions that wield power, and therefore political institutions above all others, 'it is clearer than daylight that, without renovation, these bodies do not last' (*Discourses*, 3, Introd., 1974 edn, 385; Waley, 1970, 94–5).

War is a cultural purgative, capable of regenerating a culture for a certain period. By espousing its use Machiavelli does not step outside the boundaries of ancient political theory, which bases the virtue of the state on the energies of the hoplite soldier and his corresponding civil rights. Thucydides, too, suggested on many occasions that the honour of the battle field was the source of all civic virtue, and Aristotle appreciated the energy which the enfranchisement of the hoplite soldier released for pacific purposes. Machiavelli constantly inveighed against the use of mercenaries on the same grounds. Not only did mercenaries deprive the state of a citizenry that was fighting fit, but in the Roman case they provided partisans, with no stake in civic order, who were used in the wars of the generals to destabilize the state. By the same processes, citizen soldiers, with no leverage against aggrandizing oligarchs, became dispossessed of their land and flocked to Rome as pauperized plebs. The result was agricultural decline, a decline in the birthrate, manpower shortage in the country, and discontent in the city, that brought about the collapse of the republic (Brunt, 1962, 1965, 1966; Badian, 1972; Anderson, 1974a).

Curiously, Machiavelli did not support the programme of Gracchan reforms, which would have broken up the great *latifundia*; resettled the soldier-citizen on the land; and reduced the ranks of the urban plebs, dependent on state hand-outs, in the form of bread and circuses, for their very subsistence. He thought that, like those of Agis and Cleomenes, they came too late. He was perhaps also mindful of the suspicions of classical writers of demogogues in any form, no matter how good their programmes – for instance, Aristotle's disparagement of Solon and Cleisthenes, which was, however, more moderate than that of Plato or most of his contemporaries (Aristotle, *The Athenian Constitution*, 1984 edn, chs 5–12, 21). More importantly, Machiavelli's Roman sources were overwhelmingly either republicans who themselves numbered among the great oligarchs, like

Cicero and Caesar, or imperial apologists, like Horace, Virgil and Sallust. Their failure to arrive at an analysis of the systemic causes of republican decline was due not only to an individual stake in the status quo, but also to the extreme personalism of Roman political culture.

The aristocratic ethos and its career constituted the source of the moral and political tradition of Rome. The political power of the nobility as a class, based as it was on 'the complex nexus of personal and extra-constitutional relationships' by means of which, through the institution of *clientela*, it tied into the notables of the provincial communities, enabled it to control 'not only the people of Rome, but the whole of Italy' (Earl, 1967, 15). The inward-looking and personalistic preoccupations of this class, consumed with the incessant struggle for status and position within the institutions they controlled as of right, was not challenged from the outside. Roman aristocratic rule enjoyed the virtual absence of sustained popular movements, the emasculated plebs requiring no more of their patrons and masters than protection and stability. And when the nobility ceased to supply them, the Empire fell (Earl, 1967, 15–16). Even new men, Cato, Sallust and Cicero, usually rose to prominence in Rome as representatives of the provincial notability. And Stoicism, as the philosophy of new men, although challenging the traditional aristocratic ethic which defined virtue and nobility in caste terms as preservation of *mos maiorum*, the conservation of custom and precedent, nevertheless did not transcend the personalism which characterized the values of the traditional ruling class.

From Cicero to Sallust and from Tacitus to Augustine, this incapacity of the official historians and rhetoricians to arrive at a systematic analysis of the pressing problems of the age incurred by the acquisition of world empire, the influx of immigrants from the East, massive inflation as a consequence of the wealth and spoils from the Eastern wars, the Hannibalic devastations of the south, continuing depopulation of the countryside and increase in the floating underclass of unemployed in Rome, reflected an inability to break out of this personalistic and moralistic frame of reference (Earl, 1967, 17). (Appian was perhaps the exception, and Appian was an Egyptian.) Political and cultural decline was consistently read as a failure of virtue, and *virtus* entailed *gloria* and *nobilitas*. The invocation of Fortuna, to account for all the vicissitudes for which a simple failure of *virtus* could not account, doubtless raised the stakes of that hapless lady. So even Livy, more independent and less easily bought than the Empire's servants of the Augustan age, Virgil and Horace, could find no overarching principles beyond Virtue and Fortune, by which to hold Rome's failure to account. Only Polybius the Greek, writing for Greeks with a long and superior tradition of historical analysis, was in a position to do so, and even he had limited success.

It is due to the influence of Polybius, rather than that of Livy, that Machiavelli is able to argue for a definition of virtue that includes the ability to bring institutions back to their foundations by pacific means; and a definition of the virtue of institutions that refers to their structural characteristics. In *Discourses* 3.1 (1974 edn, 385), noting that he takes it for granted that 'the life of all mundane things is of finite duration', Machiavelli turns to the more interesting question, how it is that 'composite bodies, such as ... states and religious institutions' can be so constructed as to 'complete the whole of the course appointed them by heaven', as bodies that 'do not disintegrate, but maintain themselves in an orderly fashion so that if there is no change; or, if there be change, it tends rather to their conservation rather than to their destruction'. Polybius, although not rated very highly as an analyst of Roman practice and accused of failing to distinguish between legal competencies and actual powers (Fritz, 1954, 307 ff), nevertheless proved himself capable of posing these structural questions that Roman historians were unable to do. It is to Polybius, then, that Machiavelli owes an account of virtue that is non-moralistic – Polybius, the scathing critic of earlier moralists, in his pragmatism and scepticism a classically Hellenistic figure.

What more then was *virtù* on Machiavelli's account than martial prowess and the pursuit of military honour? To begin with, as the antithesis of Fortune, Virtue was the ability to seize the moment and make opportunities where some would be content to let events take their course. Machiavelli sets out to give 'the loftiest examples' of this sort of 'exceptional prowess', selecting as heroes to be emulated, Moses, Cyrus, Romulus and Theseus (Machiavelli, *Prince*, 6, 1961 edn, 49, 51). Toughened in a hard school, Moses by the Egyptians, Cyrus by the Medes, for instance, each had learned like the archer, to overshoot his mark in order to achieve it. And although these exceptional leaders are chosen to illustrate the superiority of the prophet armed, as opposed to the prophet unarmed, the lessons to be learned from their example are not just military. These men 'who become rulers by prowess', set themselves up to pass the ultimate test of virtue – which involves not only conquering a kingdom but holding it – by the prudence with which they initially proceed: 'The opportunities given them enabled these men to succeed, and their own exceptional prowess enabled them to seize their opportunities; in consequence their countries were renowned and enjoyed great prosperity' (*Prince* 6, 1961 edn, 51). Benefit to the community figures importantly in the assessment of virtue.

Not only does prudence require men to distinguish between military solutions and political solutions, as the situation requires, but it is just in the propensity to equate political virtue with military *virtù* that the tendency toward tyranny lies. In the *Discourses*, 1.10, Machiavelli ranks great leaders into three categories, in order of superiority. They are: founders of religions, founders of republics or kingdoms, and great military commanders, respectively; to which correspond on the scale of infamy: destroyers of religion, subverters of kingdoms and republics, and those who 'make war on virtue, on letters, and on any art that brings advantage and honour to the human race', respectively (*Discourses*, 1.10, 1974 edn, 134–5). 'And yet', he laments:

> notwithstanding this, almost all men, deceived by the false semblance of good and the false semblance of renown ... when they might have founded a republic or a kingdom to their immortal honour, turn their thoughts to tyranny, and fail to see what fame, what glory, security, tranquillity, conjoined with peace of mind, they are missing by adopting this course, and what infamy, scorn, abhorrence, danger and disquiet they are incurring. (*Discourses*, 1.10, 1974 edn, 135)

It is worth noting that his examples of despotism do not feature the 'oriental despots' beloved of the early modern political theorists from Harrington, on. The tyrants, Caesar, Nabis, Phalaris and Dionysius, matched against the good 'princes', Scipio, Agesilaus, Timoleon and Dion, are all Westerners (*Discourses*, 1.10, 1974 edn, 135). Most noteworthy of all is the underlying rationale for this distinction. The good prince has the percipience to see that the only defence against the entropy of all living things is the finely balanced constitution, the securing of a system 'replete with peace and justice', where 'the senate's authority [is] respected, the magistrates honoured, rich citizens [enjoy] their wealth, nobility and virtue [are] held in high esteem, and everything [works] smoothly' (*Discourses*, 1.10, 1974 edn, 137). Tyrants, who cannot make this distinction between the methods of conquest and those of pacification, between virtue on the battlefield, and the benefits of constitutional rule, bring immediately into play those wasting forces which, in an orderly regime of the simple type, do not exert their strength until the institutions mature, and which in a complex regime may be artificially held at bay for a prolonged period. Machiavelli draws his examples from the bad Emperors of Rome: 'distraught with wars, torn by seditions, brutal alike in peace and in war, princes frequently killed by assassins, civil wars constantly occurring, Italy in travail and ever a prey to fresh misfortunes, its cities demolished and pillaged' (*Discourses*, 1.10, 1974 edn, 137).

Only once does Machiavelli refer in the *Discourses* to barbarous devastators of countries and destroyers of civilization, as 'oriental princes' (2.2, 1974 edn, 280). Although unreferenced, this comment on oriental tyranny is made by contrasting militaristic regimes with the benefits of free and pacific states. Again, the benefits of peace and freedom lie in the scope they allow citizens to pursue the satisfaction of their daily needs, the growth of new needs, once subsistence demands are met, and the all-round progress and contentment that result. In autonomous states there is population growth, 'every man is ready to have children, since he believes that he can rear them and feels sure that his patrimony will not be taken away'; there is economic growth, 'riches multiply and abound there, alike those that come from agriculture and those that are produced by the trades' because people take the effort to acquire only what they can freely enjoy; and the public interest is promoted together with the private, because 'in competition one with the other, men look both to their own advantage and to that of the public; so that in both respects wonderful progress is made' (*Discourses*, 2.2, 1974 edn, 280).

Machiavelli's primitivism is, in the end, much more complex than that of the Stoics or Rousseau. Even they had hinted that the rude virtue of rough men, who were never tempted by luxury and so never developed the virtue to overcome it, could not compare to the virtue of the civilized man who would subjugate his needs in order to achieve that tranquillity of soul induced by moral strength (Springborg, 1981, chs 1, 3). Machiavelli, so far from disparaging the benefits of civilization, argues that those who dare to seize the moment, acquire territory and hold it, enriching the state and securing the well-being of every man, are the most esteemed; while those who at the same time know how to exert the levers of pain and hardship to induce fighting spirit and civic fitness are condoned for their prudence. The tyrant is not simply identified by the marks of absolute rule, for absolute rule is sometimes necessary. The tyrant suffers from a failure of nerve, and disability of judgement: he mistakes force for power, and coercion for authority. In this respect he is not fit to rule, and Fortune, always alert to the frailties of the unwary, will bring him down.

The superiority of complex bodies over simple ones in staving off entropy, combined with the advantages which self-government brings in terms of progress and economic growth, do in fact reflect negatively on the oriental system of rule as exercised by the Turks, Machiavelli maintains. And in *The Prince*, 4 (1961 edn, 45) he paints the classic picture of Turkey as the patrimonial regime which, compared with the feudal regime exemplified by the French kingdom, 'is ruled by one man, all the others [being] his servants'. 'This one ruler divides the empire into *sandjaks* in charge of which he places various administrators, whom he changes and varies as it suits him. But the king of France is surrounded by a long-established order of nobles, who are acknowledged in France by their own subjects and loved by them' (*Prince*, 4, 1961 edn, 45). Machiavelli's tone would suggest where his preferences lie, but he certainly does not adjudge Turkey a tyranny by these criteria. Far from it, when assessing the relative merits of these two types of regime, he observes merely that while the Turkish empire, though difficult to win, once conquered can be held with ease, 'the French state can be more easily seized, but it can be held only with great difficulty'. In other words, the dependency induced in the populace by the Turkish form of rule – and it should be pointed out that this lay more in myth than in reality – had its own costs in terms of economic growth and cultural vitality. But it did not demonstrate the failure of judgement, the pointless cruelty, the inability to establish law and order or a stable regime that characterize tyranny. Nor did it produce the malignancy, indolence, corruption and excess that characterized the late Roman Empire in decline, and the tyrannical emperors Machiavelli describes in *Discourses*, 1.10. In this respect Machiavelli, like Montesquieu in his *Considerations on the Causes of the Greatness of the Romans and their Decline* (1734, ch. 9), reserves tyranny as a term for the excesses of Western potentates who have betrayed perfectly constitutional and well-ordered complex political systems.

Those who argue that Machiavelli displayed in *The Prince*, as compared with the *Discourses*, a 'deliberate indifference to the distinction between king and tyrant' (Strauss, 1948, 2; Mansfield, 1979) are vindicated in certain respects. But only if one understands 'tyranny' in the sense in which it was used in fifth-century Greece, and only by focusing on the crucial difference between constitutionality and unconstitutionality. Not only was 'tyrant' an epithet applied to praise kings by fifth-century writers as respectable as Aeschylus and Sophocles, but Isocrates, in his *Address to Nicocles* – that ancient mirror of princes of which Machiavelli's *Prince* is so reminiscent – could without irony or malice advise his master that tyranny was the greatest good to befall any ruler (Andrewes, 1956, 22, 25). Tyranny as a term may first have been applied to Gyges, the Lydian made famous by Plato in the *Republic*, who acquired his throne by force and kept it by deceit; the word itself is possibly Lydian (Andrewes, 1956, 22); but that it conveyed no essential stigma is demonstrated by the fact that in certain religious cults it was an epithet for the gods. What the term conveyed to those who would praise or blame individual tyrants alike, however, was lack of constitutionality:

> Tyranny was not a constitution, and the tyrant held no official position and bore no formal title. If his courtiers called him king or tyrant, it was a recognition of his power and enhanced his prestige, but it made no great difference which word they used. They were able to use these terms because the tyrant did not try to conceal

the fact of his power, but rather advertised it, knowing that the ordinary man would at least half admire him for it. (Andrewes, 1956, 25)

It is in this classical sense that Machiavelli's *Prince* is more a manual for tyrants than a manual for kings. Conventions of beneficence, mercy and goodness, associated with sacral kingship (Springborg, 1990d) are openly flouted, and the prince is advised to practice niggardliness, coercion and deceit – on a scale sufficient for *The Prince* itself to be read as a work of massive deception intended to trick the tyrant into his own demise (Dietz, 1986). But to assume in Machiavelli a post-classical abhorrence of tyranny is to apply to him modern sanitized moral standards for rulers, based on the equation of tyranny and totalitarianism, that he could not possibly have made. Adjudged by all classical criteria, Alexander was a tyrant just as much as Hiero, a marcher lord who just went on conquering because he did not know when to stop or what else to do to hold an empire based on relentless expansion and very little else (Mann, 1986, ch. 8). But a marcher lord was, in Machiavelli's opinion, just what Italy at that juncture needed – as we know from chapter 26, even if a late addition – to regain for Italians the hegemony of Italy. This notwithstanding that Alexander, like most tyrants, succumbed to excess, the occupational hazard of tyrants whose universally agreed upon hallmark was a remarkable capacity, matched by favourable opportunities, for sensual indulgence (Andrewes, 1956, 25–6).

Another of the marks of the lack of constitutionality of the ancient tyrant was his propensity to rule by party as a demagogue. So much so, in fact, that those who follow Aristotle's stipulative definition of tyranny, assume that this is what it meant. F.W. Walbank (1984, 62) notes that for Aristotle (*Politics*, 8.10.3, 1310b9ff) 'kingship is the resource of the better classes against the people, whereas a tyrant is chosen from the people to be their protector against the notables' (see also Fritz, 1954; Andrewes, 1956, 18). It is not surprising that tyranny, when applied to the Pisistratids and their successors who, ruling with a party of the poor and the many, sought to free peasants from oppressive landlords, should in the minds of fourth-century aristocrats have changed from a term of approbation to one of opprobrium. Their genuine fears of tyranny as partisan rule led Plato and Aristotle to believe that the cycle of party infighting was what made a tyrant more oppressive than a king. Kings, by contrast, normally hereditary – which obviated the necessity of party – enjoyed an unmediated attachment to the community, to whom they stood as benefactor and provider (Fritz, 1954, 187–91).

Machiavelli's *Discourses* demonstrate his characteristic emulation of military war lords, his fascination with Alexander, Scipio and Hannibal, although not with Caesar. But different considerations have come to bear, which make constitutionality a central issue in a way that it is not in *The Prince*. Republicanism and despotism did not lie so far apart in the spectrum of Florentine politics. But in the *Discourses* the gap is crucial. Machiavelli's attitude to tyranny was a classical one. When Pericles, in his last speech reported by Thucydides, compared the Athenian empire to a tyranny, showing 'his awareness of the danger and unpopularity of Athens' position, but [concluding] that it was worth while to hold an empire, provided it was a really great empire' (Andrewes,

1956, 26, citing Thucydides 2.63.2, 64.5), Machiavelli would have agreed. It was for reasons of empire, indeed, that he rejected the unconstitutionality of tyranny. In *The Prince*, he makes a distinction between the fundamental alternatives of republicanism or monarchy that implies no distinction between *monarchos* and *tyrannos*, *monarchos* being a descriptive rather than honorific term meaning 'sole ruler' in Greek, which even as used by ancient writers, and especially by Polybius, could encompass monarchies good and bad (Andrewes, 1956, 27).

In the *Discourses*, however, there is an implied distinction between the two which underlies all of Machiavelli's crucial distinctions: between *virtù* and *fortuna*; freedom and stability, the virtues of republicanism; between military leadership as opposed to adventurism; prudent, as opposed to reckless, expansionism. The models of the *Discourses* are Roman and Hellenistic, and not Athenian, which is why the distinctions between monarchy and tyranny, monarchy and republicanism are made in an un-Greek way. For monarchy and republicanism were antithetical to the Greeks, whereas monarchy and tyranny belonged to the same family. Even Aristotle's mixed regime did not include monarchy as a component, but was rather a mix of aristocratic, oligarchic and democratic elements. For the Romans, however, republicanism was not incompatible with constitutional monarchy, and indeed presupposed it. And Florentine republicanism belonged to the Italian tradition on balance. Ironically, the crucial difference between *The Prince* and the *Discourses* may be attributed less to the Roman Livy, and more to the Greek Polybius, and perhaps primarily to Polybius 6. But then, as commentators point out, Livy as much as any Latin historian, relied on Greek sources, among them possibly Hecataeus of Miletus (*c*.500 BC), Hellanicus of Mytilene (*c*.450 BC) and Timaeus of Sicily (*c*.356–260 BC), who made reference to Rome in their histories, and certainly Herodotus and Polybius himself. Not only were many of the incidents Livy incorporated fabrications, but they took the form of 'Greek stories reclothed in Roman dress':

The twins, Romulus and Remus, sons of a god, exposed by the river, suckled by a wolf and discovered by a shepherd, are an adaptation of an old Near Eastern myth, found in Greece in the legend of Neleus and Pelias, sons of the god Poseidon exposed on the river Enipeus and suckled by a bitch and a mare (I.4.3*ff.*). The fatal quarrel between the twins culminating in Remus derisively vaulting Romulus's walls recalls similar Greek legends of Oeneus and Toxeus or Poimander and Leucippus (I.7.2). The treachery and fate of Tarpeia was a familiar Hellenistic motif (I.11.6*ff.*) Sometimes the debt is even more obvious. Two of the most notorious events of Tarquinius Superbus's reign are openly imitated from the Greek historian Herodotus – the lopping of the poppy-heads (I.54.6) was Thrasyboulus's message to Periander (Hdt. 5.92.6) and the infiltration of Gabii by Sextus Tarquinius (I.53.5) was suggested by Zopyrus's ruse against Babylon (Hdt. III.154). (Ogilvie, 1971, 12–13)

16
Machiavelli and Polybius on
the Predatory and Personalistic State

There is no reason to believe, as some scholars do, that *The Prince* shows no Polybian influence. Classicists who emphasize the degree to which Polybius is preoccupied with a binary antithesis, monarchy and republicanism, republicanism and despotism (Cole, 1964, 1967), would provide vindication in Polybian sources for Machiavelli's opening axiom that all forms of dominion are either republics or principalities. Hexter (1956, 76, n.4) has argued, not altogether successfully, that *Prince* 8 contains a piece of information on Hiero for which Polybius 1.9 is the only possible source – the Penguin editor of *The Prince* (1961 edn, 146) giving the source as the historian Justin, who may also have been Machiavelli's source on Philip transferring his subjects from province to province like sheep (Justin 8.5.7, cited in Mansfield, 1979, 100, n.8), and is otherwise known as being among his sources. But Hexter has better reasons than this for believing *The Prince* to be permeated with Polybian preoccupations; and other commentators have remarked on the degree to which the projects of both *The Prince* and the *Discourses* are set by the programme of Polybius; and of the difficulty of reconciling this fact with what we know about Machiavelli's access to Polybian texts (Gilbert, 1953, 1965). Latin translations of the first five books of Polybius were available to Machiavelli, some published as early as 1473 but not the crucial book 6. This has caused some commentators difficulty with Machiavelli's claim in *Prince* 2, already to have written on republics in another place, for it is assumed that, the correspondences between *Discourses* 1.2, and Polybius 6 being too close for coincidence, Machiavelli did get access to Polybius 6, in an unpublished form, and that this provided the catalyst for his work on Livy and a move towards republicanism that post-dates *The Prince*.

Hexter poses an ingenious solution to the problem of the missing translation of Polybius 6 in the person of Janus Lascaris, a Byzantine Greek, whose authorship of a translation of the chapters of Polybius on military matters, which included Polybius 6 and was published in 1529 without his permission, is established (Hexter, 1956, 87). Lascaris had contacts with Cosimo Rucellai and members of the Rucellai Garden circle, to which Machiavelli belonged, and to members of which, Zanobi Buondelmonte and Cosimo Rucellai himself, he dedicated the *Discourses*. Hexter speculates that Lascaris could have met Machiavelli and passed on to him an unpublished translation of Polybius 6 some time during the period that he spent in Florence, but not before 1515, the earliest date at which Machiavelli would have joined the group. This seems to pose problems, though, for Machiavelli's reference in *The Prince*, known to have been written in 1515, to a work on republics, presumed to be the *Discourses*, and assumed to have been written after 1515 (Hexter, 1956). Felix Gilbert has proposed a solution to this problem in turn, which postulates a meeting between Machiavelli and Lascaris in Florence some time before 1494, under the auspices of the friendship between Machiavelli's father and the humanist Bartolomeo Scala; or alternatively, Machiavelli could have made contact with Lascaris through Claude de Seyssel, who had knowledge of Polybius 6 from Lascaris, and whom Machiavelli met in France in 1504 (Gilbert, 1965, 320–1). This would mean that Machiavelli could indeed have commenced writing the first chapter of the *Discourses* before 1515, and perhaps as early 1513.

On the same information a different solution is possible, and one that would explain other aspects of the puzzle of Machiavelli's sources. It is known from the testament of a contemporary that Machiavelli's project on Livy was more or less commissioned by the Rucellai Garden group, and that Machiavelli entered that group no earlier than 1515. We have other sources on the attitudes of this group to the writing of history that are of significance for Machiavelli's project (cited in Gilbert, 1965, 203, n.1). Cosimo Rucellai's predilection for Livy, for which we have evidence in print, may have motivated Machiavelli to reshape a project on republics inspired by Polybius, that was already under way. And perhaps the prevailing view that Greek historians had been superseded by Roman ones, as well as a certain amount of patriotism, caused Machiavelli, otherwise a self-confessed adept at deception – see his witty confession '[For] some time I have never said what I believed and never believed what I said, and if I do sometimes happen to say what I think, I always hide it among so many lies that it is hard to recover' (cited in Dietz, 1986, 777) – to conceal the Polybian source.

The curious structure of the *Discourses* and the relative absence of Livy from the early chapters has been noted. Felix Gilbert, who has undertaken the only detailed structural analysis of the *Discourses* and their relation to the classical sources, assisted by Fr. Walker's notes, observes that no systematic commentary on Livy is undertaken in the first 18 chapters of book 1, or the first 29 chapters of book 3 (Gilbert, 1953, 145–6). Machiavelli's commentary on the first Decad of Livy, which may have constituted a continuous piece of work in its earliest form, appears to have been broken up and redistributed in the final version of the *Discourses*, so that commentary on Livy's first Pentad is to be found in *Discourses*, book 1, 19–56; commentary on Livy 5 and 8 on war are to be found dispersed throughout *Discourses* book 2, devoted also to war and foreign relations; while commentary on Livy 6, 7, 9 and 10 are undertaken almost sequentially in *Discourses*, 3.30–49 (Gilbert, 1953, 142–7). We have internal evidence in *Discourses* 2.10 and 3.27 that date the time of writing to the year 1517. And if 1515 is the *terminus a quo*, references to Cosimo Rucellai and the Emperor Maximilian as still living, suggest 1519, the year in which they both died, as the *terminus ad quem* (Gilbert, 1953, 138). Clearly Machiavelli reworked earlier sections, so that no segment stands out as having been written at the time of *The Prince*, the introduction and the last chapter of which he wrote some time between September 1515 and September 1516, the main body having been written several years earlier, and probably in 1513 (Gilbert, 1965, 326).

What is most striking, as commentators have frequently observed, is the similarity between *The Prince* and the first 18 chapters of the *Discourses*, which are self-contained without containing much of Livy. Felix Gilbert (1953, 148), noting that several chapters contain no reference to Livy at all, observed that in these early chapters 'Machiavelli's "Romanism" is somewhat subdued and that, apart from Rome, Sparta and Venice serve as patterns of republican life.' Moreover, Machiavelli feels compelled to apologize himself that he seems to be rather slow in arriving at a discussion of Livy's subject matter, the founding of Rome and the history of its religious and military institutions (Machiavelli, *Discourses*, 1.9, 1974 edn, 131, cited in Gilbert, 1953, 149). The continuity between this work and Machiavelli's earlier work extends to specific passages, Gilbert (1953, 149) noting that the ideas of *Prince* 19 on the Emperors of Rome and *Discourses* 1.10 'seem like two parts of a rather comprehensive reflection on the same subject' (Gilbert, 1953, 149); that 'the great state founders, Moses, Lycurgus, Solon, who have been characterized as the real heroes of the *Prince*, make their appearance in these chapters'; and that 'most of all, the statements about different kinds of principalities given in *the Prince*, and about different kinds of republics given in the *Discorsi*, complement each other, so that taken together they provide a classification of all forms of government' (Gilbert, 1953, 149).

But none of these similarities strictly requires an acquaintance with book 6, which even in Polybius' work constitutes a set of macro-historical reflections, more or less self-contained, providing a break in his chronological and comparative account of Mediterranean history in the Hellenistic period. It is possible to maintain with Gilbert that Machiavelli was working on a treatise on republics at the time at which he wrote, or refurbished, *The Prince* and that he was influenced by Polybius, without presupposing access to book 6 at this point, although internal evidence in *Discourses* 1.16 would suggest that it is improbable he was unaware of it when writing this chapter. The availability of Latin translations, cross-references in the material and a similarity of purpose, suggest that Machiavelli may well have been familiar with some, or all that survives, of Polybius at the time of writing of *The Prince*, which leaves us with the question what influences or which sources introduced those considerations that undoubtedly do set the *Discourses* apart from *The Prince*?

Grander speculations on the life cycles of regimes, the relation between Fortune (Stoic 'Fate') and the causality of human action, the antiquity of the world and attempts to reconstruct the history of civilization, as well as specific references to the Polybian *anacyclosis* and the mixed constitution as a device to arrest it, are all confined to the *Discourses*, admittedly to those chapters, 1.1–18 and 3.1–29, where the influence of Polybius, and the absence of Livy, are most noticeable. Much of this macro-historical material could have come from Diodorus Siculus, an alternative source on *Kulturgeschichte*, whom Machiavelli names in his chapter on the antiquity of the world, destruction of civilization by flood and fire and the regeneration of culture from primitive vestiges (*Discourses*, 2.5, 1974 edn, 289), a fact that is generally overlooked by Machiavelli commentators. Leslie Walker observes that Diodorus was the probable source for Machiavelli's comments on the kings of Egypt as superior lawgivers (Diodorus

1.1.9 and 1.58.3); his remarks on Semiramis, foundress of the Assyrian Empire at Nineveh (*Discourses*, 3.58; Walker, 1975, vol. 2, 177) and the Egyptian fable of Antaeus (*Discourses*, 2.12; Walker, 1975, vol. 2, 279). He even credits Diodorus as a possible source for Machiavelli's 'new departure' in comparative method, comparing Diodorus 1.1.3–4, on the subject of 'universal historians', with Machiavelli's Preface to book 1 of the *Discourses* (1974 edn, 98–9), which makes the same case for an analogue between the order of the cosmos and the uniformity of the historical world (Walker, 1975, vol. 1, 90–1), but without suggesting Diodorus as a source for the *anacyclosis*, a version of which his *Library of History* also contains.

Diodorus ranks among Hellenistic writers who appear more often than Polybius as sources for Machiavelli's historical *exempla* for this period. Walker also suggests Diodorus as the possible source of Machiavelli's reference to the wonderful story of Alexander and Cleitus Melas, the satrap of Bactria, who had once saved the young Alexander's life, but who, inebriated from feasting, disparaged King Philip, and was run through with a sword by his honour-bound son (Diodorus 17.21.57, cited in Walker, 1975, vol. 2, 88). A deed which he lived to regret, Machiavelli claims, thus proving against Livy that, even in the case of the great Alexander, the masses are not necessarily more fickle than princes (*Discourses*, 1.58, 1974 edn, 253–4). Plutarch's *Life of Alexander*, 16 and 50–2, is another possible source for this particular example (Walker, 1975, vol. 2, 88), as it is for the account, narrated at some length by Machiavelli (*Discourses*, 2.27, 1974 edn, 364–5), of the siege of Tyre by Alexander, undertaken uncertainly but concluded decisively and with enormous loss of life. For this illustration of the behaviour of prudent princes and republics in regard to peace overtures, Machiavelli could also have relied on Diodorus 17.4, although Walker (1975, vol. 2, 138) thinks it unlikely, a more extensive account of the seige being provided by Quintus Curtius Rufus, to whose *de Rebus Gestis Alexandri Magni* Machiavelli refers in *Discourses* 2.10, negatively, for his maxim that 'Money is the sinews of war' (Walker, 1975, vol. 2, 106–7).

If Machiavelli commentary has rather neglected Hellenistic sources such as Plutarch, Diodorus, Quintus Curtius Rufus, Herodian, Procopius, who along with the Roman writers Sallust, Tacitus, Juvenal and Cicero, are actually cited by Machiavelli, in favour of the great Polybius, who was not, there is nevertheless a reason for it. The project of Polybius' 'universal history' shapes the *Discourses* of Machiavelli in a way that the other works do not. For, as Walbank in his Sather Lectures on Polybius summarized it, if the first 30 books of Polybius can be seen as an answer to the question 'How and thanks to what kind of constitution Rome became the ruler of the world', the last ten ask, 'Was Roman rule acceptable?' (Walbank, 1972, 182). This states Machiavelli's project in a way that no questions posed by Livy do. Polybius raised, even if he did not successfully answer, the question of the legitimacy of empire, and in the course of writing he had to adjust his *Histories* to the realities of Roman hegemony that were uncomfortable to him (Walbank, 1972, 179–82). It is Polybius on whom we rely for an account of the reasoning for and against the destruction of Carthage, that heinous act that he sees fit to defend for reasons of *Realpolitik*, but which raises in his mind the spectre of Rome as a tyrant state (Walbank, 1972, 174–9).

Historians have puzzled over the irrationality of an act, endorsed by the great Cato, who had shown mercy to the Rhodians and had even quoted with approval Scipio Africanus' plea to save Hannibal's city, and whose only pretext is found in the anecdote which recalls Cato producing fresh figs and declaring them to have been grown in Carthage (Adcock, 1946, 117). Could Carthaginian trade have posed a threat sufficient to warrant vengeance so great that *Delenda est Carthago* rings down the ages with the dolorous clamour of the earlier *Troianus delenda est?*

Although Walbank (1972, 182–3) is right to say that Polybius gives no answer to the question whether empire was justified that took satisfactory account of the advantages or disadvantages of the ruled, which, as a Greek, was his vantage point; do we have to conclude with him that Polybius added two decades to his *Histories* to include those dramatic events in which he personally participated, under the pretext of answering it? One thing we know, that Polybius would not have answered the question as it was subsequently answered by Cicero in *De re publica* (3.33–41), or by Augustine in *De civitate dei* (19.21), 'that imperial rule is justifiable, as is the rule of god over man, the mind over the body, reason over passion; [following] a universal law equally beneficial to rulers and ruled' (Walbank, 1972, 182); a doctrine attributed to the Stoic Panaetius, on whom Cicero so heavily drew, owing something to the doctrines of the Stoic Posidonius, and perhaps even the oriental sources that fed into Christianity, where it later became dogma.

We have, in fact, a clue to Polybius' probable answer to the question in two fragments of Diodorus, which are believed to draw on him (Adcock, 1946, 127–8). And the answer is Machiavellian, not Peripatetic or Stoic. In the 'Polybian' fragments of Diodorus, the theory is proposed that 'states win power by valour and shrewdness, augment it by reasonableness and generosity, and make it secure by terror and frightfulness (*phobo kai kataplexei*)'. Diodorus adduces examples, significantly, in the careers of Alexander and the Romans who, 'when they were practically onmipotent in the civilized world made their rule secure by terror and by destroying the most eminent cities' (Diodorus Siculus, 32.2 and 4, cited in Adcock, 1946, 117–18). The judgement of Diodorus, and presumably Polybius, on the rationale of the Romans, is Machiavellian in a typically Hellenistic sense. It constitutes a non-moralistic judgement on human motivations and their relation to action that claims to uncover lines of historical causation. But it represents a realism easily confused with cynicism, thought to be characteristic, for instance, of Alexandrian men of letters such as Menander and Menippus of Gadara, the latter of whose work survives only in its imitators, Varro, Seneca and Lucian (Barber, 1970, 58, 70–1).

An acquaintance with Polybius' grand project did not depend, therefore, on access to book 6 – it could be gleaned from the earlier promise of which book 6 is the fulfilment, as well as from Cicero's *Republic* – although it is in book 6 that the theoretical underpinning is laid out. Machiavelli's attention in the *Discourses* to 'complex bodies' and their peculiar properties in holding entropy at bay; and specifically his interest in the structure and development of the Roman constitution, as diversified in space and time, accounting for extraordinary, and in some respects unjustified, hegemony; undoubtedly owe a great deal to the impetus to piece the puzzle together which the discovery of Polybius 6 must have provided. For the Machiavellian 'balance' which is much talked about, is that moment, so hard to define, between healthy expansionism within constitutional bounds, and imperial excess which tips into decline. Polybius, alone among historians, had attempted to isolate the variables involved in imperial atrophy. And if Plato and Aristotle had to some extent laid the groundwork in their theories of the cyclical life of the *polis*, much distance still lay between the fragility of the *polis*, whose problems lay in external security rather than internal government, and the sprawling empires of the Hellenistic period, each a collection of large, heterogeneous cities, like Alexandria and Babylon – an aggregate of *politeumata* or confessional communities, rather than *poleis* – as well as of small closely knit Greek cities of the *polis* type (Tarn, 1952, 148–9).

In each of these Hellenistic kingdoms usurpers had established themselves as preservers of ancient civilization, the Seleucids, who modelled themselves on the Achaemenids as the Achaemenids had modelled themselves on the Assyrians, reviving Babylon, 'whose ancient culture was to the Seleucids what that of Egypt was to the Ptolemies' (Tarn, 1952, 128). Ancient literatures of national liberation, Sumerian hymns and the Babylonian Creation Epic were revived, cuneiform was restored, temples rebuilt, scientific and astronomic work revivified, chronicles written and myths made official, in a task which was a great undertaking of national reunification headquartered in Babylon by the Seleucids (Tarn, 1952, 128–9); and paralleled only by the endeavours of the Ptolemies in Alexandria. If the Seleucids 'regarded their empire as embracing the four categories of subject kings, dynasts, peoples and cities' (Tarn, 1952, 129), the Ptolemaic kingdom was also considerably diversified, between the ancient cities of Abydos, Memphis and Thebes, the relatively modern Alexandria and satrapies in Asia Minor.

The logistical problems of empire faced by Rome were therefore ancient ones, and she faced them in ancient ways. She slipped into the Hellenistic world unobtrusively, establishing dominion here by treaty, there by alliance, taking over the elaborate array of individually negotiated relations, some *symmachic*, others *hegemonic*, that already characterized the Hellenistic monarchies and the collection of cities they controlled (Badian, 1968; Gruen, 1984). For the barbarian West, however, less civilized by the normal criteria of economic and social development, and without yet the Eastern tradition of free cities, she developed the simpler and harsher strategy of conquest and occupation (Badian, 1968, 1984). The Roman *latifundia* proved to be a unique mechanism for bringing into production the virgin soils of Northern Europe, by the application of large infusions of capital and slave labour. Plantation agriculture seized Europe for Rome as it was used by Europe to seize Africa, the Carribean, India, the Americas and Indo-China when, over a millennium later, the Europeans took their turn at Empire. And it did so, in the case of Rome, who pioneered it – but also in the case of the later European imitators – by creating an enormously rich and powerful oligarchic rentier class, with the capacity to corrupt the heartland; whose agrarian aggrandisement dispossessed the citizen soldier, on whom the republic as a widely based regime, at least in principle, was founded. By moving the axis of power to the easily controlled West, Rome allowed the Eastern empire to atrophy and the Italian provinces to suffer irremediable neglect (Weber, 1950; Badian, 1972; Anderson, 1974a).

This process of Roman empire building is Machiavelli's subject. And if he reserves the term tyranny for Tarquinius Superbus, in the first instance (*Discourses*, 3.5), and for the later Roman Emperors (*Discourses*, 1.10), in the last, it is because, whatever the case may be in the oriental and Greek worlds, his preoccupations and sources are Latin. It is taking Westernism and Latinity altogether too far, however, to maintain that Machiavelli, because neither the phenomenon nor the concept existed in Western medieval Christendom, had no notion of the state as a large-scale territorial entity or, as more generous scholars have suggested, that it was a concept towards which he was incipiently groping (Hexter, 1973, 150–78; Skinner, 1979, vol. 1; Mansfield, 1983). '*Lo stato*' may very well still have meant 'condition' of the realm, or the prince's 'estate', something which suffers expansion, diminution, requires maintenance, or is, in other words, relatively fluid, and without connotations of a monolithic entity with fixed boundaries like the modern bureaucratic state (Hexter, 1973, 156). But this did not mean that Machiavelli or his predecessors, even as Latin speakers, were unacquainted with the concepts of *imperium* or *hegemonia*, clearly present in Roman sources. How otherwise could Machiavelli have posed the Polybian question: what was it about the constitution of the Roman state that permitted it to acquire the whole world?; or its corollary: and why did it lose it? Is not the 'predatory' nature of Machiavelli's vision due to the very fact that he conceives the state as an aggressive vehicle for patriotic aspirations and expansionism, so that the state as a territorial entity is compatible with, if not exhausted by, *lo stato* as the notion of 'patrimony' or 'estate'? And while it is true, as Hexter demonstrates from his careful content analysis of *The Prince*, that *lo stato* is a passive object of the predatory prince which suffers things done to it, rather than doing them – it is acquired, held, maintained, taken away, lost – this bespeaks Machiavelli's position, for whom the state, whether *lo stato* or *imperium*, probably did mean 'command over men', rather than 'the body politic' (Hexter, 1973, 156–64).

It is significant that Machiavelli should have used the comparisons good/better/bad to refer to the welfare of the people six times, while he applies this scale to the prince 41 times. And it is equally significant that when, in books 1 to 11, he considers new, old and mixed tenancies of command over men, he should assess them from the point of view of the good of the prince, rather than what is good for the polity (Hexter, 1973, 166). This comes as a surprise only if we consider Machiavelli a benign republican. But of course he is not – he is a ruthless analyst of the realities of state power, and it is only on the basis of the narrowest ethnocentrism that we can argue that the concept of the state was not available to him because the phenomenon did not exist. Or, as Hexter concludes, that 'the emergence of the actual historical phenomenon of the modern state therefore roughly coincides with the emergence of the term universally applied to it' (1973, 152).

Indeed, there is something anachronistic about the search for the original of the word 'state'. Hexter (1973, 166–7) points out in passing that Machiavelli distinguishes between *stato*, *citta* and *patria*, showing him to be much more classically attuned than his commentators. Moreover, and this is highly significant, the latter two entities do not necessarily *belong* to someone. This means that

Machiavelli names republics by their age old name – they were 'cities' to Aristotle, Augustine and Aquinas – while more extensive realms were *patriae*. Republics are those composite bodies, 'bodies politic' in the classical sense, as Hexter admits – locus of '*il vivere libero, il vivere civile, il vivere politico, il bene commune*, and so on' (*Discourses*, 1.2,3,5,6,7, 9, cited in Hexter 1973, 170). But the prince who treats the realm as his estate or patrimony is hardly modern, either, and Hexter cites Machiavelli's example of Ferdinand of Aragon who, ' "in the beginning of his reign attacked Granada, and that enterprise was the foundation *dello stato suo*" ' (*Prince*, 21.43b cited in Hexter, 1973, 164). He adds the example of Egypt, 'where the Mameluke Sultan rules not by inheritance but by election, [and where] "although the prince is new, *gli ordini di quello stato* are old and are arranged to accept him as if he were their hereditary lord" ' (*Prince*, 19.40b, cited in Hexter, 1973, 164). If, as Hexter rightly points out, Machiavelli, in his repost to the Cardinal d'Amboise's claim 'that the Italians did not understand war ... retorted that the French did not understand statecraft', he meant nothing more than that the French, having acquired patrimony, did not know how to keep it (*Prince*, 3, 1961 edn, 44; Hexter, 1973, 164).

But if patrimonial rule was new to the newly emergent European states, its antiquity as a phenomenon was the very reason that Machiavelli, in the steps of Diodorus (1.1.3–4) and Polybius, recommended the study of ancient history as a coping strategy (Machiavelli, *Discourses*, I, Introd.). It is the very type of regime that has for so long been thought, often inaccurately, to characterize oriental states. Turkey is discussed by Machiavelli as a patrimonial state, but so are the kingdoms conquered by Alexander, whom he so greatly admires (*Prince*, 4, 1961 edn, 44–6). Technically, there is a fine line between patrimonial regimes and classical 'tyrannies', since the *stato* of the prince is not ruled constitutionally, or acquired by heredity. But all oriental regimes are not patrimonial, the kingdoms of Egypt and Persia being known for the excellence of their ancient laws (*Discourses*, 1.1, and 1.58). And all patrimonial regimes are not tyrannical.

What is new in *The Prince* is not the concept of the state, but the reassessment of the merits of patrimonial rule. It is for this reason that Machiavelli is believed, with some justice, to display in this work 'a deliberate indifference to the distinction between king and tyrant' (Strauss, 1948, 2). Put differently, Machiavelli does see an important difference between medieval monarchy in the European mould, and the patrimonial regimes established by the marcher lords, the great Alexander, further back the Assyrian kings, and more recently the Muslim conquerors. National liberation, for which in book 26 of *The Prince* he yearns, can only be achieved by great conquerors in the ancient tradition, and not by traditional European kings, shackled by Pope and Emperor. And if the state is their patrimony, it is a small price to pay for independence which can later be institutionalized constitutionally. If his treatment of republics is classical, so is his treatment of tyranny.

Some of the confusion that surrounds Machiavelli's concept of the state turns on evolutionary assumptions of progress on the part of his commentators, as well as a certain romanticization of Renaissance thinkers, so long extolled as the paragon of European high culture. It is believed, on the one hand, that the newly emergent European nation states of the fifteenth and sixteenth centuries ushered in a phenomenon unknown to the ancient world; and, on the other, that the 'impersonal' bureaucratic state of the modern world no longer resembles its small and intimate beginnings. So, for instance, Harvey Mansfield (1983, 849) endorses the distinction made by Quentin Skinner between 'the traditional ideal of the prince maintaining his existing position and range of powers', which Machiavelli is said to defend (Skinner, 1979, vol. 2, 354); and 'the distinctively modern idea of the State as a form of public power separate from both the ruler and the ruled, and constituting the supreme political authority within a certain defined territory'; defended already by Bodin in the late sixteenth century (Skinner, 1979, vol. 2, 353, citing Weber's definition of the modern state; cited in turn by Mansfield, 1983, 849). Mansfield elaborates the distinction further, creating a distinction between the 'personalism' of the ancient polity and the 'impersonal modern state', which compares unfavourably to it.

There is justice in the epithet 'personalism' being ascribed to the *polis*. But a catalogue of 'personalistic' features would include items many classical writers and most writers in the classical republican tradition, including modern ones, would not approve, were they to recognize them. Among them, 'justice', defined as 'benefiting one's friends and harming one's enemies'; the rule of family, affinity and fraternity, through the phratries, hetaries, syssities, gymnasia, ecclesia, symposia, and other all-male clubs; hegemonic aristocratic families and the subjugation of women, that constantly gave the lie in practice to the great aspirations to democracy in theory (Springborg, 1986, 1987a); something which Mansfield (1983, 850) almost concedes by noting that in Aristotle there is no distinction between state and regime: the state is the groups who control it and they are partisan! The aspect of personalism that Mansfield chooses to emphasize concerns the identity of rulers and ruled, the self-referring nature of *politeia* and *politeuma* – this notion of the constitution of the *polis* being nothing but the sum of its rules of everyday life. Put differently, it is due to the absence of a distinction between official and unofficial norms, between public and private life, because of a definition of citizenship, even in Aristotle, that stipulated active participation as a qualification. The personalism of the *polis* can be attributed to the fact that the ancient republics were, at least in principle, representative regimes, and not because of lack of institutionalization.

There is a considerable gap between the intimacy that comes from personal involvement in the day-to-day running of the state, and that of Machiavelli's principalities, which are held in the personal property of the prince. This latter is the very personalism that defined tyrannies, classically, and that still defines patrimonial regimes, characterized by their unincorporated nature, today (Moore, 1974). The whole argument concerning the ancient 'personal' *polis* and the 'impersonal' modern state (Skinner, 1978; Mansfield, 1983) is more efficaciously treated if recast in traditional terms of republican, patrimonial and imperial regimes, which obviate the ambiguities of 'personalism'. But, looked at this way, the referents line up a little differently. The personalism of patrimonialism had its merits, the very ones that Machiavelli hoped to emphasize. Strong and fearless leaders, marcher lords making lightning strikes on enemy country, could rally national support, and effect territorial consolidation, greatly desired in conditions where imperial retrenchment, or a power vacuum, left a people prey to pretenders and usurpers.

These were the conditions in which Machiavelli's Florence found herself, between the jaws of the Emperor, the Papacy and hegemonic princes from the north – the Venetians and the Visconti – simultaneously. Great leaders of the past who carried their people with them, Moses, Solon, Lycurgus, Cyrus, Philip and Alexander, were instructive examples, some of them even making the desired transition to constitutional rule. Patrimonialism also had its darker side, though, at which Mansfield (1983, 854) hints, by pointing out that most of what passed for politics in such regimes took place behind the scenes: what was visible in Machiavelli's *stato* was power, but not its changing modes. What Mansfield (1983, 854) concludes from this fact, rather strangely, is that Machiavelli was 'on the way toward defining the state by its territory and people', rather than by regime. But here Machiavelli is no different from his models, Cicero and Augustine, who knew that empires are defined by territory and *ethnai*; republics, or *poleis*, by regime. Monarchies, like Persia, Egypt and Rome, are defined territorially; republics, as Plato and Aristotle so long ago pointed out, are defined politically. This should not distract us from the fact that the personalism of patrimonial regimes is an intimacy that would not necessarily be wished; while the impersonality of the large-scale nation state, due to bureaucratic apparatuses and political intermediaries, is due to that degree of institutionalization that is believed by some to constitute the conditions of freedom (Huntington, 1968).

The phenomenon of totalitarianism has blurred the lines between institutionalism and constitutionalism, between legitimacy and legality. If praetorian regimes now masquerade as republics, this should not prompt the exaggerated response of assimilating Renaissance despotisms to the modern fascist state (see Jones, 1965, 90). The fact is, there is a significant difference of scale between Renaissance principalities and modern totalitarian governments. The same difference of scale that exists between ancient republics (*poleis*) and modern republics. And because of the different modes of social control, on the one hand, and representation, on the other, that these differences of scale entail, qualitative distinctions divide these ancient social forms from what are believed to be their modern counterparts. If democracy and totalitarianism until recently were seen to be converging, and have now mutually capitulated, it is due perhaps to their similarity of scale, rather than to any other single factor.

That ancient city-republican forms have been transported, with unintended consequences, into the setting of the large territorial nation state, is perhaps due to the factor of scale being overlooked. It is hard to imagine how a people can both rule and be ruled in aggregates that include hundreds of cities larger by many times than a *polis*, states larger than empires of classical times, and populations greater than the then-known world of Aristotle and Pericles. Loss of intimacy is only one of the costs incurred by translating 'democracy' into 'representative republicanism', a development that dates to the second century BC, as we have seen. The concept of the city as a public space; the spatial properties of the *polis* as allowing all its citizens to be gathered together in one place (Plato, *Laws* 738e, 1970 edn, 206); the facilities which the city as a spatial entity affords for communication, interaction and commerce in its widest cultural and economic senses; are all lost when the state ceases to be the city and government is removed to some isolated federal capitol on a hill, with hegemony over lands and seas on which many of its citizens have never even personally cast an eye.

These considerations are worth mentioning for the reason that, as at least one scholar has pointed out (Jones, 1965, 90), the Renaissance state, either 'despotic' or 'republican', is too easily assimilated to the modern state, whether 'democratic' or 'totalitarian'. Republicanism and despotism did not lie as far apart in Renaissance political experience as we like to think democracy and totalitarianism do today; something which the reflections of Mansfield and Skinner on the 'personalism' of older state forms perhaps attempt to capture. The fluidity of Renaissance politics bespeaks the absence of modern economies to scale; the degree of institutionalization now necessary to control large territorial aggregates; the absence of modern efficiencies of communication, and so on. So much so that even to term the Renaissance polity a state is a misnomer in the opinion of some (Sinner, 1978; Mansfield, 1983; but also Jones, 1965). If democracy and totalitarianism are the zenith and the nemesis of the modern state, respectively, the idea of 'the "Renaissance" state, unitary, absolute, and secular, built on new foundations and a new class structure, and serving as a model to the rest of western Europe', does not yet admit of such stark contrasts (Jones, 1965, 90, citing Chabod, 1958, 64ff, 70–2). 'Despotic government was not totalitarian; communal government, although sometimes called *democratia*, knew nothing of manhood suffrage' (Jones, 1965, 74). *Democratia* had, after all, been denaturalized as a term by the Romans from at least the second century BC, carrying only vague intimations of freedom and autonomy any more (Larsen, 1945). But freedom for whom, and autonomy for what?

> By the statutes of most Italian towns, qualification for citizenship, and even more for office, was restricted almost exclusively to property-owning burgesses of local origin and prolonged residence. Rustics, the largest class, though combined in rural communes, were defined by law as inferiors and were almost nowhere granted political rights; nor were the humbler townsmen, the wageworkers and 'plebei' (Giannotti); nor finally were the citizens of independent towns, incorporated by conquest in expanding territorial states ... Representative parliaments, in Italy as elsewhere, were the creation not of urban but of feudal regimes. Under the rule of the richer republics, Venice and still more Florence, subordinate communities were degraded to a position of colonial dependence and ruthlessly exploited in the economic interest of the dominating town. 'Florentina libertas' was for Florentines alone. (Jones, 1965, 74–5).

The political continuities between republican Rome and Renaissance Italy are not confined to Machiavellian theory – they are apparent in practice. And once again it was an extremely conservative and oligarchic republicanism. Despotism, like Roman imperialism, lay close by, and produced some surprises for the starry-eyed republican. Whatever 'constitutional checks and balances' republicanism may have enshrined, 'power in the Italian communes clung obstinately to wealth and migrated with movements of wealth; through all revolutions of political and economic regime, oligarchy, in fact or law, was the predominant form of government' (Jones, 1965, 75), great sections of the community being better off under despots. The *popolo*, for instance, never comprised 'the whole people of a republic, or even the whole commune': it was 'a "party", the *pars populi*, for which the property qualification might be higher than that for the commune' (Jones, 1965, 76).

More recently, Louis Green (1989, 2) has suggested the traditional account of the rise of Renaissance despots out of the decline of the communes to have been contaminated by 'late nineteenth-century historiography of the *Risorgimento* with its tendency to present constitutional government as natural to the original state of Italian society and its decay in the later Middle Ages as an aberration'. As Green (1986, 129–34; 1989, 2) goes on to argue, the rise of the *signoria* had its root in geopolitical and technological developments, the mutually reinforcing increase in professional armies and consolidation of regional states, such that only the richest of the old republican governments, like that of Florence, survived, realizing their own imperial ambitions by hegemonic rule over subject cities. Green's careful analysis of the fourteenth-century chroniclers of seigneurial regimes discloses that, after an initial period in which the *signoria* were viewed either 'as heroic figures fighting against overwhelming odds, or as creatures of insatiable ambition whose greed and vanity made them overreach themselves' (Green, 1989, 2), a period ensued in which 'the princely characteristics of the new "signori" or lords came to be stressed.' And this coincided with the consolidation of the 'autocratic state ruled by a hereditary dynasty' out of the flux of earlier transitional despotic governments which represented 'mere family predominance with factional support'. One might argue, in fact, that what we have here is a development akin to the rise of the oligarchic classes in the Italian provinces, which permitted Rome to transform itself from Republic to Empire. In the fourteenth-century chroniclers of the old communes, Albertino Mussato and Ferreto de' Ferreti (cited in Green, 1989, 3–6), we have the familiar language of nostalgia for the golden age of communal rule, citizens 'being confronted by the choice between dying for freedom or living as slaves', the preservation of liberty being '"indeed a delightful thing"' (Ferreti, *Opere*, 1908–20 edn, vol. 1, 249, cited in Green, 1989, 6). Ferreti's views, it turns out, are instructive: 'the context in which these speeches are placed ... suggests that there was in fact very little hope, in the prevailing circumstances, of having these aspirations to liberty permanently realized' (Ferreti, *Opere*, 1908–20 edn, vol. 1, 276–7, cited in Green, 1989, 6):

> Wealthy republics, such as Venice and Florence, had preserved their freedom, as had Bologna under papal protection, but elsewhere, as in Pisa and Lucca, where there were popular governments Ferreti did not approve of them, considering them to be under the tyrannical sway of mob-rule. However much he might secretly have yearned for the ideal of a pristine civic liberty, he was for all practical purposes reconciled to what must have seemed to him an irresistible trend towards despotism and subjugation of smaller cities such as his own [Vicenza]. He was essentially a provincial intellectual who recognized his need to seek patronage from the rulers of what had become his metropolitan power, and this clearly influenced his judgment of the tyrants with whom he deals in his history.

Republicanism, which had flourished briefly in the interstices between feudalism and despotism – in Florence from 1494 to 1512 and from 1527 to 1530 – had created a mythology, based on classical sources, of freedom and autonomy, celebrated in the rhetoric, and counterposed to the much-vaunted monarchical virtues of order, peace and security (Jones, 1965, 71–3). The gap between republicanism and despotism was, in fact, almost exactly identical to the gap between the Guelphs and the Ghibellines, which was not great – Louis Green, in fact, locates the precise moment, in the work of Matteo Villani (Green, 1972, 81; 1989, 12, citing Villani, *Cronica*, 1846 edn, vol. 2, 3–4), at which this distinction passed from merely designating opposing factions in Italian politics to being 'a qualitative and ideological' one, identifying 'preservation of free institutions with the Guelph cause and tyranny with the Ghibelline one'. Moreover, to stress to the degree to which the distinction was ideologically tilted, if wealthy merchants, guilds of bankers and industrialists were better off under republicanism, the poor and the excluded, as well as those from the old noble families, were usually better off under despotism. For despots were great levellers of potential contenders for their power, at the same time relying on a traditional aristocratic class for support. Thus 'the aristocratic Guicciardini' could argue that 'government belonged properly to the wealthy and wise', and that 'Democracy was a dangerous delusion', while Filippo Maria Visconti, quite characteristically, declared: 'It seems to me that it's better to obey a prince or king, whatever his disposition, than submit to being governed by a rabble of artisans or by rulers of whom we cannot even tell who their fathers were' (cited in Jones, 1965, 78).

If republicanism represented mainly new money, new wealth eventually becomes old, which may have prompted Machiavelli briefly to consider throwing in his lot with the prince, and which probably accounted for the eventual decline of republicanism. Meanwhile the regime which new money represented saw as great a concentration of power as at any time in the history of the Italian city-state, even if the mix was different. For instance, in republican Florence of the 1330s some '70% of all major offices were held by members of the three wealthiest guilds'. The 'popular' revolution of 1343 had given access to members of another 21 guilds, the net effect being 'to render eligible for high office some 3,500 men, from a total urban population of 75,000–80,000 souls'. But 'at no stage was more than one-tenth of the eligible class effectively qualified for office, about 750 persons at most, and of these an excessive proportion were still drawn from the upper guilds or from client lower guildsmen' (Jones, 1965, 76). Thus was Florentine republican government; hardly different from what we understand by democracy today in respect of the right to rule – as distinct from the right to be ruled; but a far remove from the Athenian city-state it is widely believed to have incarnated. And yet, 'described by contemporaries as *democratia* and represented by Florentines as an egalitarian, broadly-based polity ... the Florentine constitution of the mid-Trecento, un-Athenian though it was' – and as long as it lasted – 'was probably as democratic as any regime, in the larger medieval communes' (Jones, 1965, 76–7).

It was the very concentration of economic power under republics that encouraged the faction-fighting, out of which despotism was to re-emerge. For, 'however popular in form, in Italy, unlike the ancient world, the origins of despotism lay in oligarchy rather than democracy' (Jones, 1965, 79). The flight to old families and old forms that brought to power new princes was due to a fear of new money and the ruthlessness that it spelled. Republican Florence showed no embarrassment at treating with, and even flattering, tyrants in diplomacy, and her treatment of subject towns, stripped from the enemy, might well be summed up as 'Tuscany for the Tuscans', or rephrased as 'Tuscany for Florence' (Rubinstein, 1952, 23–7, 45). Something which Machiavelli himself recognized, pointing out that to be the subject people of a republic is the worst slavery of all (*Discourses*, 2.2, 1974 edn, 280; Mansfield, 1983, 855): 'First because it is more lasting, and there is no hope of escape'; but 'secondly', and more importantly, 'because the aim of a republic is to deprive all other corporations of their vitality and to weaken them, to the end that its own body corporate may increase'.

Only to modern ears does such pragmatism sound shocking. In the context of the fourteenth-century chroniclers, reflecting 'a tendency to view politics neutrally, giving credit, on the one hand, to a great despot, but, on the other, also writing with enthusiasm of the peaceful and magnificent state of the republic of Padua in 1310 and the rejoicing of its citizens at their liberation from the oppression of Ezzelino of Romano in 1260' (Green, 1989, 7, referring to Cortusio's chronicle), such a view did not necessarily seem at all strange. 'Despotic states, like republican ones, were caught up in the play of forces ultimately too powerful for them to control but, while they endured, they could be judged by the same kinds of standards of probity, integrity, justice and virtue which applied to other regimes' (Green, 1989, 8). Green (1989, 9) points to cases, in Villani's *Chronicle*, for instance, in which 'the theme of the despot who ultimately fell victim to his own lust for power was combined with another, that of the weakness and indecisiveness of republican government, against which the *virtù* of the heroic, if doomed despot could be contrasted.' He suggests, indeed, that the very vociferousness of the chroniclers' defence of republican liberty and attacks on tyranny bespoke a realization of the futility and anarchronism of their aspirations:

> Earlier in the fourteenth century, despotic power in Italy had been extremely precarious: of the lordships over cities which Ferreti had listed on the eve of the emperor Henry VII's entry into Italy, only one, that of the Scaligeri, had lasted more than two decades. The families in power by about 1340, however, with the exception of the Carrara and Della Scala which were deposed by Gran-Galezzo Visconti at the end of the Trecento, generally continued to govern their states into the fifteenth century. Communes such as Florence, therefore, found themselves confronted from the 1340's onwards by despotisms such as Milan which were both more durable and more formidable than those which had been in existence thirty years before. The greater stability and strength of the great *signorie* therefore made it necessary to find grounds for the justification of traditional liberties in terms other than the superiority of the institutions they guaranteed to short-lived dictatorships based on mere force. (Green, 1989, 12)

At the very moment at which the rule of the *signorie* became normalized, their chroniclers made their own 'contribution to the political culture of future generations in creating what became almost archetypal images of tyrants animated by a single-minded and amoral passion for power that ultimately destroyed them', ensuring 'that, even when the circumstances they described had changed, this figure should survive and take its place in the gallery of stock political types' (Green, 1989, 15). It was precisely a function of the chroniclers' 'capacity to dramatise history' that, just 'at a time when [the *signorie*] were becoming ever more common and firmly established they were seen by all but the committed defenders of autocratic rule as essentially abnormal' (Green 1989, 14). In fact, of course, there was an equally strong tradition capable of assimilating their rule to the just king along Platonist lines. The enduring legacy of the chroniclers was an imaginative recreation of classical categories, already normatively skewed, in terms of which seigneurial rule was appraised:

> Regarded first as expressions of vice, then as illustrations of the instability of politics, [rule of the *signorie*] eventually came either to be condemned or justified on the basis of two alternative myths. The first of these, republican in inspiration, assumed a fundamental incompatibility between the natural inclinations of a people uncorrupted by servitude (or subjection to an absolute authority) and any kind of arbitrary rule which was represented as a perversion of the original and proper condition of the civil community. The second, promoted by the publicists of despots, was that what had initially been created as a tyranny was no longer tyrannical but a just state. Both of these myths evaded the realities of the prevailing *realpolitik* and moral compromises of Italian politics by idealising one or other of the two main institutional forms that had survived the changes and dislocations of the early Trecento – the greater republics and the new regional *signorie*. Thereby, a double standard was created to preserve, in an age of political pragmatism and shifting alliances, something of the moral certitude which had been inspired by the ideological loyalties of the previous century and the sharp distinctions between what had then been seen as absolutes of right and wrong or good and bad. The causes of the Church and of the Empire which had been the pretext for the factionalism out of which tyranny had grown, were – now that it was established – transformed into those of the defence of republican liberty or the creation of a paternalistic order. (Green, 1989, 14)

Machiavelli, who both participated in the recreation of the republicanism/ despotism dichotomy and understood its function and limits, defines the 'common good' of republics in terms as predatory as the private good of princes, making no moral distinction between the acquisitiveness of one *vis à vis* the other (*Discourses*, 2, 2). It is just that the predatory instincts of the many provide the tree of empire a stronger base than the predatory instincts of one, no matter how inflated the appetites of that one may be. In fact, the vulnerability of the prince may prompt him, if he is intelligent, to 'behave constitutionally' and maintain humane institutions: 'he will more often than not be equally fond of all the cities that are subject to him, and will leave them in possession of all their trades and all their ancient institutions so that, if they are unable to increase, as free cities do, they will not be ruined like those that are enslaved' (*Discourses*, 2.2, 1974 edn, 280–1). The sturdy majority – even if belonging to a rather narrowly based citizenry – with none of these inhibitions, can exert the tyranny of numbers, as de Tocqueville, more Machiavellian than we realize, was later to observe.

Mansfield is quite right to emphasize (1983, 855) that Machiavelli's 'republicanism shows no more of the impersonality of the modern state than does his advice to princes. A republic is the *stato* of a certain group as a principality is the *stato* of the prince, in both cases an effectual acquisition'; the great advantage of the republic being that it is an acquisition more widely enjoyed, and therefore more easily maintained. And the clue, although he does not catch it, lies in the fact of Machiavellian, like ancient, republicanism being representative of groups; whereas the impersonality of the modern state rests, as Max Weber long ago observed, on representation of individuals (Weber, 1968, 3. 16, 'The City'). The already constituted groups, family, clan, friendship, fraternal, cultic and occupational, of the ancient and Renaissance republican worlds, set definite limits to the competence of the state, as well as colonizing it for their own purposes. The Athenian citizen entered the public arena not as an individual but as a family member, admitted by free birth and the petition of his father to the phratry which kept the citizen rolls; as a demesman, and therefore tied to a specific locality which afforded him certain rights and duties; as the member of a hetairy, syssity or some other political club, which would give him effective access to power, or not (Ferguson, 1910; Calhoun, 1913; Connor, 1971; Roussel, 1976).

If the *polis* itself was more like a voluntary association, competing in an array of voluntary associations which bound their members by contract and oath, offering material and tangible rewards for loyalty, the Renaissance republics of Italy were little different. 'Though never, like the early *polis*, a coalition of clans, the Italian commune, in all its history, knew no more powerful influence than that defined by Leon Battista Alberti as ' "the strongest of all bonds, the bond of blood" ' (Jones, 1965, 83). The vitality of the Renaissance family, like its classical predecessors, lay in the real power that it exerted over its members, spatially confined within its economic, juridical and political control (F. Kent, 1977a; D. Kent, 1978; D. Kent and F. Kent, 1988). Individual families increased their power by unions in clans, as often artificial as based on consanguinity in any literal sense (Ferguson, 1938; Jones, 1965, 84; Roussel, 1976). Clan codes, defended by militias and the institution of the vendetta, were as ubiquitous in the Italian city-state as in its ancient models. The success of the family, as a viable social entity that could outlive regimes, survive generations and expand territorial and economic control in an impressive manner, encouraged other subordinate groups to model themselves on its practices, as indeed the commune itself was so modelled:

> Beyond the family were other associations – the trade-guild, the social class, and most of all, the party; and it is characteristic that, like the *consorterie*, the guilds, the parties, and even the social classes, all came to assume a corporate organization, modelled on that of the commune. They exacted oaths of fealty, they had laws and jurisdiction, assemblies and officials, and in certain cases they established military or para-military formations. Nominally these groups were all subject to the commune; practically they were rival corporations, which strove to absorb the commune and identify the state with a class or party. By the later-thirteenth century they had generally achieved their aim. In many towns the organization of the *popolo* had in effect replaced the commune, in most the commune had become officially Guelf or Ghibelline, and, however democratic the form of government, membership of a particular class, party or guild, had almost everywhere become a qualification for citizenship or office. (Jones, 1964, 85)

While Mansfield is right to insist that if, indeed, the decisive shift to the modern state comes with Machiavelli, it is not the shift 'from the personal state to the impersonal state' that was decisive, he is on shakier ground when he asserts that 'the decisive shift' rather, was 'from the personal state in the Aristotelian sense to the acquisitive personal state of Machiavelli' (Mansfield, 1983, 855). This simply projects romantic illusions about the origins of the modern state back a phase. Everything that modern classicists have to tell us about the classical *polis* suggests that it was both as personalistic and as predatory as Republican Florence or Venice in the Renaissance period (Bourriot, 1976; Roussel, 1976; Connor, 1981; Davies, 1981; Springborg, 1986). Its fragility, and ultimate demise, were due to its inability to match the personalism or the predations of the subordinate groups of which it was comprised. If Machiavelli's focus was this fragility, and attempts by constitutional engineering to overcome it, betraying an insensitivity to the excesses of state power, this is perhaps not so surprising. What is new about his venture is neither the predatory state nor the praetorian prince, but a willingness to discuss these realities in an open and non-moralistic manner, which to the Roman, if not the Hellenistic or oriental, tradition was entirely foreign.

17

Polybius and Machiavelli on Patronage and Corruption

And here Machiavelli outdoes Polybius, in part because his *floruit* post-dates the Roman Empire, which Polybius intuited without actually witnessing its reality. Machiavelli even outdoes his time and class. For like Polybius he represents the old republicans, which new money and the new prince (*princeps*) threaten to oust. But, unlike Polybius, he does not seek refuge in the conservative definition of freedom which serves his caste; or notions of corruption that would put a brake on wider participation in the benefits of economic expansion. Machiavelli's case against the Gracchan reforms was the same as Cicero's: by stripping the rich proprietors of their possessions it would deprive the republic of its champions (Cicero, *For Sestius*, 48.103, cited in Veyne, 1976, 464). Polybius had been no democrat either.

Like Polybius, Machiavelli makes no distinction between republics with or without kings, reserving the term *monarchia*, a descriptive term meaning literally 'one-man rule', more typically for tyrants. So, if *Discourses* 1.9 is entitled 'That it is necessary to be the Sole Authority if one would constitute a Republic afresh or would reform it thoroughly regardless of its Ancient Institutions'; *Discourses* 1.10 makes the contrast to 'Those who [would] set up a Tyranny [as being] no less Blameworthy than are the Founders of a Republic or a Kingdom Praiseworthy' (Machiavelli, *Discourses*, 1974 edn, 77–8; Crick, 1974, 20). But Machiavelli makes a break with Polybius' moralistic conservatism, that would dissociate Philip and Alexander from their traditional reputations for excess, whereas to Polybius – as to humanists up to Gibbon – corruption took a literally physiological form as depravity of the body. Luxury makes people soft, frugality and fear keep them tough: 'If there is one rule applicable in all cases whether it is a question of the army, of a city, or of our body, it is that one should never permit them to live for long in ease or leisure, above all not in periods of prosperity and material abundance', for indolence and permissiveness engender indiscipline and revolt (Polybius 11.25, cited in Veyne, 1976, 473).

Although Machiavelli carries over some of Polybius' organicist assumptions concerning natural principles of growth and decay; the necessity for frugality, even poverty as discipline-inducing conditions for the masses; he is less prone to conflate moral and physiological principles, or to a fundamental primitivism. He is thus willing to concede that Philip, like Alexander, created a great empire from small beginnings (*Discourses*, 1.26, 1974 edn, 177), providing that military leadership, which is so much more important even than followership (*Discourses*, 3.13, 1974 edn, 445), and yet could harbour a depraved monster, and as such got his final desserts. In *Discourses* 2.28, Machiavelli illustrates his maxim 'How Dangerous is it for a Republic or a Prince not to avenge an Injury done either to the Public or to a Private Person' with the example of Philip, whose companion Attalus was enamoured of a certain 'handsome and noble young man Pausanias ... and had on several occasions sought to get him to assent, but found that he had no liking for such things; so seeing that he could not get what he wanted otherwise, he decided to set a trap for him and to use force.' Attalus threw a party which Pausanias and other barons, as well as the royal 'companions' attended, and, 'when they had had their fill of food and wine, he had him seized and bound; then he not only used force in order to gratify his lust, but, to his greater shame, got others to treat him in the same disgusting way'. Philip was indicted not only by the disgraceful behaviour of the royal companions, but because Pausanias, having 'complained several times to Philip, who, having kept him for a time in expectation of vengeance, not only did not avenge him, but made Attalus governor of a Grecian province'. Philip paid, slain by Pausanias on 'the day of the solemn wedding of [his] daughter' to Alexander of Epirus, as he stood 'between the two Alexanders, his son and his son-in-law' (*Discourses*, 2.28, 1974 edn, 368–9). The chapter which follows is entitled 'Fortune blinds Men's Minds when she does not wish them to obstruct her Designs'! But on the 'companions' Machiavelli is silent.

At least some of the differences between Machiavelli and Polybius on the question of *monarchos*, marcher lord or tyrant, are due to the fact that although Machiavelli too represents an oligarchic republicanism, it is an oligarchy of old money rather than old blood. In his perambulations through the various scenarios that the new prince offers, Machiavelli comes eventually to the conclusion that he too readily represents the threat of a return to rule by the old noble caste, which is why, undoubtedly by a fine attempt at sleight of hand, he advises his prince to abandon the nobles and base his regime on the 'people' (*Prince*, 9, 1961 edn, 67–9; Dietz, 1986, 783–4). At all costs, the prince must be institutionalized, so that the privileges of the new 'republicans', the privileged *popolo*, are maintained, and of the old *ottimati* neutralized. The short shrift that he gives the gentry, or *gentiluomini*, is evidence enough of the distance that lies between him and the Roman republican, a Cicero, Tacitus, Sallust, Livy or even Polybius. The old *rentier* class of Rome and its Renaissance relics, with their power base in the countryside are 'wreckers' of republics, so that 'where the gentry are numerous, no one who proposes to set up a republic can succeed unless he first gets rid of the lot' (*Discourses*, 1.55, 1974 edn, 247; Crick, 1974, 40, 529, n.5).

Machiavelli takes more care with his definition of this social category than most, noting that 'the term "gentry" is used of those who live in idleness on the abundant revenue derived from their estates, without having anything to do either with cultivation or with other forms of labour essential to life. Such men are a pest in any republic', and only 'more pernicious are those who, in addition to the aforesaid revenues, have castles under their command and subjects who are under their obedience' (*Discourses*, 1.55, 1974 edn, 245–6; Crick, 1974, 39). We have a clue, perhaps, to the thread of continuity between *The Prince* and the *Discourses*, in Machiavelli's conclusion that the the new prince may perform, and only he, the useful task of neutralizing the old barons, and that this is the justification for his absolute power. Drawing a distinction that is, in this instance, more Greek than Roman, between republicanism as 'civic' or urban government (*d'ogni civilita*), and the incipient feudalism or decentralization of noble rule, he points to the barons of Naples, the Papal States, the Romagna and Lombardy (Crick, 1974, 40):

> It is owing to [them] that in these provinces there has never arisen any republic or any political life, for men born in such conditions are entirely inimical to any form of civic government. In provinces thus organized no attempt to set up a republic could possibly succeed. To reconstitute them, should anyone want to do so, the only way would be to set up a monarchy there. The reason for this is that, where the material is so corrupt, laws do not suffice to keep it in hand; it is necessary to have, besides laws, a superior force, such as appertains to a monarch, who has such absolute and overwhelming power that he can restrain excesses due to ambition and the corrupt practices of the powerful. (*Discourses*, 1.55, 1974 edn, 246)

To Machiavelli, and this is said to reflect Renaissance Italian experience accurately (Jones, 1965, 79), despotism is an oligarchic phenomenon, democracy following despotism, rather than giving rise to it in the cycle of regimes. Not only is corruption defined by Machiavelli as class stratification that permits the emergence of a parasitic noble class accustomed to *ozio*, but even in a 'free state', which the former can never be, such tendencies are ever present in factions pernicious to the autonomy of the state: 'To such hostile factions will belong all those who held preferment under the tyrannical government and grew fat on the riches of its prince, since, now that they are deprived of these emoluments, they cannot live contented, but are compelled, each of them, to try to restore the tyranny in order to regain their authority' (*Discourses*, 1.16, 1974 edn, 154).

In the conflict between patricians and plebians that threatened to tear apart most newly independent Italian city-republics, Machiavelli, breaking with the Roman republican tradition quite openly, took the part of the plebians – although not when it came to the Roman Republic itself. The withdrawal, everywhere, of the 'large neutral majority, the "homines communes" (Bartolus) who, with a civic spirit far older than humanism, [had] kept the administration going', in favour of a concentration of authority in the hands of specialists, 'for the sake of speed and efficiency, in small executive councils, magistracies, and plenipotentiary committees', presented a tendency difficult to resist (Jones, 1965, 77–8): 'In every way, therefore, institutionally and politically, the irresistible trend, as even republicans recognized, was to restrict supreme office, the unpaid *honores*, to a group of dominant families, the *ottimati*, *principali*, *beneficiati*, and so on', the old class of *euergetai*, or notables, the traditional bastion of classical republican cities, who traded their services for the right to rule, even funding public works from their private resources, and thus earning their titles as benefactors and *honorati*. But this is a tendency that Machiavelli, in a very unclassical manner, hoped to resist. In his ideal 'republican' state the government will not harbour *euergetai*, who rapidly become a ruling caste: 'because a self-governing state assigns honours and rewards only for honest and determinate reasons, and, apart from this, rewards and honours no one; and when one acquires honours or advantages which appear to have been deserved, one does not acknowledge any obligation towards those responsible for the remuneration' (*Discourses*, 1.16, 1974 edn, 154).

Machiavelli seems to have broken out of the constraints of oligarchy and patronage (*euergetism*), as we find them in Rome and in the accounts of her greatest commentators, Polybius and Cicero. Or has he? We know that in *Prince* 9, and *Discourses* 16–18, and 18–32, both seemingly heavily indebted to Polybius 6, the concept of 'beneficence' is crucial to his account of the successful dealings of princes with their subjects, and to his notion of the miscarriage of justice. Here 'beneficence' is also predicated on the assumption of fundamental and radical economic inequality, the refusal to admit possibilities of economic and social development of which there might be a positive outcome in the redistribution of the wealth. But Machiavelli's preoccupation is with the power of oligarchies and patronage to corrupt *republics*. For Polybius corruption, in its most crucial aspect, means the depravity of the ruling oligarchy on whom 'mixed government' is balanced – the corruption of monarchy being redeemable by good councillors, and the people being deemed by him so corruptible that they hardly count. Machiavelli would seem to follow him in construing corruption in a literally physical sense, as bestialization through excess. So he speaks, in terms strikingly Polybian, in *Discourses* 1.16 (1974 edn, 153), of 'a people accustomed to live under a prince' as virtually incapable of preserving its liberty, should it chance to acquire it, due to appetites for economic security and gain that are insatiable:

> for such a people differs in no wise from a wild animal which, though by nature fierce and accustomed to the woods, has been brought up in captivity and servitude and is then loosed to rove the countryside at will, where, being unaccustomed to seeking its own food, and discovering no place in which it can find refuge, it becomes the prey of the first comer who seeks to chain it up again. (Machiavelli, *Discourses*, 1.16, 1974 edn, 153)

But Machiavelli's inference is, nevertheless, a different one. Such a people, like those accustomed to foreign domination, if 'wholly corrupt' are so due to servitude, rather than to greed. The threat they pose to the prince is easily dissipated; by avenging their enemies – typically the nobles, on the one hand; and by diagnosing the root of their desire for economic freedom – since he cannot in fact grant it – on the other. He will find that 'a small section of the populace desire to be free in order to obtain authority over others, but that the vast bulk of those who demand freedom, desire it but to live in security' (*Discourses*, 1.16, 1974 edn, 156). In other words, for 'the possibility of enjoying what one has, freely and without incurring suspicion for instance, the assurance that one's wife and children will be respected, the absence of fear for oneself' (*Discourses*, 1.16, 1974 edn, 154).

Machiavelli admits, in this digression on princes, for which he apologizes as 'distort[ing] the plan of this discourse' on republics (*Discourses*, 1.16, 1974 edn, 155), that when it comes to political equality, even under republics, 'the real rulers do not amount to more than forty or fifty citizens and, since this is a small number, it is an easy thing to make yourself secure in their regard either by doing away with them or by granting them such a share of honours according to their standing, as will for the most part satisfy them' (*Discourses*, 1.16, 1974 edn, 156).

Machiavelli's sensitivity to tyranny is not so great that he hesitates to advise the newly formed republican government, i.e. government by the *popolo*, to 'kill the sons of Brutus', as a handy maxim for dealing with the nobles, traditional class enemies (*Discourses*, 1.16, 1974 edn, 155); or the newly formed principality to emasculate the people, if that is necessary to secure it. Because, as he observed in his discussion of the Polybian question of notorious ingratitude, 'quite rightly do writers on civic government say that peoples bite more savagely when they have just recovered their liberty than when they have had it for some time' (Machiavelli, *Discourses*, 1.28, 1974 edn, 180, a reference to Cicero *De officiis* 2.7.24; cited in Mansfield, 1979, 103).

This concept of ingratitude as 'biting the hand that feeds' causes Machiavelli to note that the Romans were less ungrateful to their citizens than the Athenians, because they had less to fear from them (*Discourses*, 1.28, 1974 edn, 179). He might have added, because they were less free. Here we note that Machiavelli appears to be viewing the problem from the perspective of the ruler, rather than that of the ruled. Ingratitude in republics flows only one way – from subjects to rulers, because the ruled, as fundamentallly inferior, have no beneficence to dispense from which gratitude can accrue. But even in the case of the Florentine Republic citizenship implies ruling and being ruled. So when Machiavelli speaks of the 'people', *popolo*, he is referring neither to the ruling elite, the *ottimati*, nor to the *popolo grasso*, the populace at large, but to that class briefly enfranchised by the *Consiglio Grande*, to which he himself belonged. When Machiavelli raises the rather rhetorical question 'Which is the more ungrateful, a People or a Prince?' (*Discourses*, 1.29, 1974 edn, 180), the only cases in which ingratitude on the part of a prince appears to be endemic, concern his indebtedness to his generals. But in a republic, that is to say 'a city in which freedom prevails', its two characteristic goals, 'one ... to enlarge its dominion; the other ... to keep itself free' (*Discourses*, 1.29, 1974 edn, 182) may both occasion ingratitude toward its prominent citizens, or members of the ruling elite.

The solution to the problem of 'ingratitude', so crucial in Polybius, to which Machiavelli must provide an answer, is simple enough. In the case of princes, they can avoid facing the question of gratitude and indebtedness to generals by conducting their own campaigns, 'as in the beginning the Roman emperors did, as in our own day the Turk does, and as courageous princes [Cyrus, Philip and Alexander] both have done and still do' (*Discourses*, 1.30, 1974 edn, 184). Machiavelli has in mind not only the prestige that accrues from victory, but the spoils of war, of which the generals must at all costs be deprived, for fear of the economic and political power they confer. In the case of republics, they should follow the example of Rome, whose only case of signal ingratitude was to Scipio, whom the people feared in proportion to the greatness of his victory; as Cato made the case, 'a city could not be called free in which there was a citizen of whom the magistrates were afraid' (*Discourses*, 1.29, 1974 edn, 183). Otherwise Rome heeded the advice that all governments must heed, 'whether it be a prince or a republic, but especially if it be a prince', which is that 'a government which thinks that it is only when danger has arisen that it should win men over by the conferring of benefits, is mistaken; for not only will it fail to win them over, but it will hasten its own ruin' (*Discourses*, 1.32, 1974 edn, 189).

Machiavelli, although not entirely standing Polybian beneficence on its head, has produced an account which makes it incumbent on rulers to beware the vengeance of the ruled, when the question of benefits arises. He has thus both morally neutralized and democratized the concept. No longer is beneficence the paradigmatic economic interchange, from whose experience concepts of benefit and injury are inferred as the basis of justice. Rather, gratitude is a matter of strategic concern. He quotes Tacitus ' "One is more inclined to repay injuries than benefits; for it is burdensome to grant favours, but revenge is profitable" ' (Tacitus, *Histories* 4.3, *Discourses*, 1.29, 1974 edn, 181; Mansfield, 1979, 104). And if rights and benefits are still assessed from the point of view of the ruler, with the primary goal of conservation of power in mind, nevertheless this goal requires a certain prudence in ensuring that the people, if dependent, as in the case of absolute princely rule, *potestà assolutà* (*Discourses*, 1.25, 1974 edn, 176), and like a ravaging beast, accustomed to the gratification of its needs from above; or if independent, like that of a republic, and jealous of its powers, is not to be roused to violence and revolution – something which Polybius was not privileged to witness, but which Machiavelli feared in the form of 'Caesarism' (*Discourses*, 1.52, 1974 edn, 237; Mansfield, 1979, 154–5).

Machiavelli notes that the Roman Senate had originally followed a prudent path, according to the maxim that 'A Republic or a Prince should ostensibly do out of Generosity what Necessity Constrains them to do.' So the decision 'to use public money to pay men on military service' seemed to the plebs a gift, so acceptable 'that Rome went mad with delight; for it seemed to them that they had received a great benefaction which they had never expected' (*Discourses*, 1.51, 1974 edn, 234–5). Had the Senate continued on this path the conditions for the ruin of the 'aristocratic party' (*della parte degli Ottimati*) would never have obtained, or the demagogic Caesar, 'the first tyrant', risen to power (*Discourses*, 1.37, 1.52, 1974 edn, 203, 237). For, if it was encumbent on the prince who aspired to absolute power (*una potestà assolutà*) to placate the people while making everything new (*Discourses*, 1.26), how much more so was it incumbent on a republic 'corrupted' by the democratization of wealth (*Discourses*, 1.25). Had the party of nobles, the Roman *optimati*, observed this principle, the people would not have flocked to the warring generals, as to demagogues who, through the distribution of land and booty, could gratify their demands for a steady supply of economic benefits. There would have been no Caesar and no Caesarism, which Machiavelli deplores in the company of the best of Roman oligarchs. A view which modern democrats, rehabilitating Caesar, have reversed (Syme, 1939).

It is important to note that there is no essential difference between *The Prince* and the *Discourses* on the critical questions of the function of beneficence. Felix Gilbert would seem to be correct in his assessment, reiterating a point made by Freidrich Meinecke over half a century ago, that if the first 11 chapters of *The Prince* follow the standard mirror of princes format, with the routine catalogue of princely virtues, the following 15 would seem to provide a critique (Gilbert, 1939, 478–83). Gilbert notes, once again concurring with Meinecke, that chapters 15 to 18 appear to be an integrated addition, constituting ' "a small special treatise on the relations of politics to the ethical values and feelings of the prince's subjects"' (Gilbert, 1939, 482, citing Meinecke, 1923). What he fails to note, however, is that these chapters present a systematic refutation of the values of the *polis*, as elaborated by Aristotle in the *Nicomachean Ethics*, foremost among which are the virtues of magnificence, liberality and beneficence. As symptomatic virtues of the ruling class, that caste of *euergetai*, or notables, who underwrite public works in exchange for the right to rule, magnificence, or beneficence, produces *megalopsuchos*, the Great-Souled one, who walks with a slow gait, talks with a deep voice, to show that nothing moves him, no one can touch him, that he is impervious to either good fortune or fate. Only the highest honours, does he accept, and only on lavish and expensive projects does he expend his energy, his exquisite taste expressing what he is. This was a character whom Machiavelli knew well: 'his name was Lorenzo il Magnifico, and there was room for two ways of looking at him' (Pocock, 1990).

Magnificence, liberality and great-souledness engage Aristotle's attention for a whole book of the *Nicomachean Ethics* (4, 1119b20–1128b35) and significantly that which leads into the famous treatment of justice in book 5. It comes as something of a surprise, then, to find Machiavelli, who has briefly mentioned the role of the prince as benefactor in chapter 9, as among the ploys at his command to win over the people (*Prince*, 1961 edn, 69), in chapter 16 enveighing against its costliness. Once again, it is significant that in chapter 15 Machiavelli should list the ruling virtues and their excesses according to Aristotle's typology – with some characteristic variations:

> So leaving aside imaginary things [Plato's *Republic*], and referring only to those which truly exist, I say that whenever men are discussed (and especially princes, who are more exposed to view), they are noted for various qualities which earn them either praise or condemnation. Some, for example, are held to be generous, and others miserly ... Some are held to be benefactors, others are called grasping; some cruel, some compassionate; one man faithless, another faithful; one man effeminate and cowardly, another fierce and courageous; one man courteous, another proud; one man lascivious, another pure; one grave, another frivolous; one religious, another sceptical; and so forth. (*Prince*, 15, 1961 edn, 91)

We know Machiavelli well enough to be little surprised that for the most part he recommends the unvirtuous alternative, on the rather specious grounds that 'it would be most laudable if a prince possessed all the qualities deemed to be good among those I have enumerated. But, human nature being what it is, princes cannot possess those qualities, or rather they cannot always exhibit them' (*Prince*, 15, 1961 edn, 91–2). The trick, as he points out, is to avoid the *reputation*, for vice, without necessarily avoiding the reality, 'because, taking everything into account, he will find that some of the things that appear to be virtues will, if he practises them, ruin him, and some of the things that appear to be wicked will bring him security and prosperity.' So, if he can *appear* to be virtuous, without being so, and avoid 'the evil reputation attached to those vices which could lose him his state', so much the better. At any rate, 'he must not flinch from being blamed for vices which are necessary for safeguarding the state' (*Prince*, 15, 1961 edn, 92). Liberality is the first candidate for this treatment:

So, starting with the first of the qualities I enumerated above, I say it would be splendid if one had a reputation for generosity; nonetheless if your actions are influenced by the desire for such a reputation you will come to grief. This is because if your generosity is good and sincere it may pass unnoticed and it will not save you from being reproached for its opposite. If you want to acquire a reputation for generosity, therefore, you have to be ostentatiously lavish; and a prince acting in that fashion will soon squander all his resources, only to be forced in the end, if he wants to maintain his reputation, to lay excessive burdens on the people, to impose extortionate taxes, and to do everything else he can to raise money. This will start to make his subjects hate him. (*Prince*, 16, 1961 edn, 92)

If Machiavelli counsels against beneficence on the part of the prince, on the part of the nobles it is downright dangerous, as a ploy to wean the people's loyalty to themselves. Beneficence equals corruption in Machiavelli's book. And if corruption on the part of the prince is bad, on the part of nobles it is intolerable. If it comes to that, get rid of them, he says! So, in *Prince* 9 (1961 edn, 68), Machiavelli advises the conqueror of a new territory that 'a prince must always live with the same people, but that he can well do without the nobles, since he can make and unmake them every day, increasing and lowering their standing at will'. It is difficult to be sure when Machiavelli is using 'people' in the technical sense, *popolo* as a party, and when he means simply inhabitants of a territory. But one may assume that the technical sense is foremost, since non-citizens were of very little account except for the rare occasions on which they were mobilized for revolution, or drafted into the army *in extremis*. The urban bias of the Italian city-states was notorious, Renaissance republicanism, like Aristotelian, being predicated on the assumption that country-dwellers would not often be coming to town to claim their rights; participatory 'democracy' worked only as long as it was confined to a few. Rome, by contrast 'had a number of institutions which assured that they would come quite often' (Pocock, 1990).

The message to the prince is unambiguous: economic dependence is the answer to power. The same principle applied to nobles and people. Of the nobles, 'those who become dependent, and are not rapacious, must be honoured and loved'; those who are independent must be cut down (*Prince* 9, 1961 edn, 68). As for the people, the prince must take them into his economic 'protection'. For 'when men receive favours from someone they expected to do them ill, they are under a greater obligation to their benefactor; just so the people can in an instant become more amicably disposed towards the prince than if he had seized power by their favour' (*Prince*, 9, 1961 edn, 69).

In *Discourses* 1.10 and 1.16, Machiavelli extends the logic of this argument that the new prince, who comes upon a polity corrupted by the servitude of nobles to tyrannical rule, will find 'a people [that] differs in no wise from a wild animal which, though by nature fierce and accustomed to the woods, has been brought up in captivity and servitude and is then loosed to rove the countryside at will, where, being unaccustomed to seeking its own food and discovering no place in which it can find refuge, it becomes the prey of the first comer who seeks to chain it up again' (*Discourses*, 1.16, 1974 edn, 153). Mansfield, noting Walker's reference to Polybius 6.9.9, at this point (Walker, 1975, vol. 2, 40), observes, as we would agree, that 'the reference is made significant only by the difference between Polybius and NM that it confirms. For Polybius the people become bestial and find a despot when corrupted by gifts and violence; for NM the people are naturally ferocious beasts corrupted when kept in captivity, and succumb to a despot out of bewilderment' (Mansfield, 1979, 79–80, n.2). But Mansfield goes on rather strangely to conclude that 'in this section corruption is considered not from the standpoint of the people suffering it, as first seems to be the case, but from that of the prince trying to overcome it'; a standpoint, he goes on to observe, that 'might be thought to cast doubt on the hypothesis that the first eighteen chapters of the *Discourses*, constitute the lengthy reasoning on republics to which NM refers in the second chapter of *The Prince*' [Gilbert, 1953] ... Or does it suggest rather that NM was getting ready to leave writing the *Discourses* and begin *The Prince* [Chabod, 1960, 38n]? Or was the allusion in *The Prince* inserted later than 1513 (but why in 1516 necessarily?) so that it could refer to the entire Discourses [Baron, 1956]? ... Or did NM plan to write the *Discourses* when he wrote *The Prince* because he saw the need to say everything he knew in two different ways?' (Mansfield, 1979, 79, n.1)

But Machiavelli almost always sees the problem of corruption from the point of view of the prince, or at least that of the ruling class, even if that be the 'people' in the technical sense. Thus in *Discourses* 1.10 (1974 edn, 138) he could conclude that 'should a good prince seek worldly renown, he should most certainly covet possession of a city that has become corrupt, not, with Caesar, to complete its spoliation, but, with Romulus, to reform it'. The fine line between the founder prince and the tyrant, which is the subject of this chapter, is that although both require a corrupt people to show their wares, the one slips from the grandeur of the former to the easy stupidity of the latter. The observer of tyranny will 'happily learn how much Rome, Italy, and the world owed to Caesar', Machiavelli sarcastically remarks:

> He will see Rome burnt, its Capitol demolished by its own citizens, ancient temples lying desolate, religious rites grown corrupt, adultery rampant throughout the city. He will find the sea covered with exiles and the rocks stained with blood. In Rome he will see countless atrocities perpetrated; rank, riches, the honours men have won, and, above all, virtue, looked upon as a capital crime. He will find calumniators rewarded, servants suborned to turn against their masters, freed men to turn against their patrons, and those who lack enemies attacked by their friends. (*Discourses*, 1.10, 1974 edn, 137–8)

But this, the condition of Rome under the emperors, is the condition of spoliation that follows a tyrant, rather than the corruption that brings the new prince to power; something on which the latter can capitalize, in fact. Commentators – and this includes Walker (1975, vol. 2, 63–5, see Crick, 1974, 176, 533, n.20) and Mansfield (1979) – have obscured Machiavelli's distinction between tyranny and the legitimate prince, by translating the *potestà assolutà* of the latter as 'despotism'. Corruption as a condition of economic and political servitude, in which the people are deprived of their rights by the excessive power of the nobility, lies leagues away from the world-turned-upside-down, the chaos and reversal of the social orders that describe revolution and social collapse following prolonged tyranny. Polybius knew of the former but not of the latter.

And the similarity between *The Prince* and the *Discourses* on the subject of corruption would seem to confirm the date of writing of the first 18 chapters of the latter as contemporaneous with the former, rather than casting this in doubt; it would seem to suggest, as well, that Machiavelli had access to Polybius 6 at this point, to which reference is clearly made in *Discourses* 1.16 (1974 edn, 153).

Machiavelli's viewpoint on beneficence, the prince, the nobility and corruption is one of the most consistent continuities between *The Prince* and the *Discourses*, in fact. So is his recommendation to the founder prince to foresake the path of the tyrant and choose rather the path of the republican legislator, the great Romulus, Solon or Lycurgus. The reasons he offers appeal to the enlightened self-interest of the prince, rather than the interests of the ruled, although serving both. Once again the stability of a composite body guarantees against the incipient instability of the rule of one man (*monarchia*). Such a sacrifice of ultimate power does not require the prince to resign his principate, for republicanism for Machiavelli, unlike Aristotle, includes monarchy, rather than standing over against it. In their choice of reform, like Romulus, or tyranny, like Caesar, princes face their fate:

> Nor, in very truth can the heavens afford men a better opportunity of acquiring renown; nor can men desire anything better than this. And if in order to reform a city one were obliged to give up the principate, someone who did not reform it in order not to fall from that rank would have some excuse. There is, however, no excuse if one can both keep the principate and reform the city. (*Discourses*, 1.10, 1974 edn, 138)

Machiavelli is very far from Polybius, the conservative oligarch, in his assessment of corruption and its effects. Whatever virile, even bestial, instincts drive the masses to acquisition after acquisition present less of a threat to the state, and may even be effectively harnessed, than the world-turned-upside-down of chaos that may result from abject subjugation under a tyrant. The gap between republicanism and 'despotism', *potestà assolutà* was not this, which is why it involved no radical break for Machiavelli to write at one time from the perspective of the one, at another from that of the other. The very fluidity of the 'state' so-called in Renaissance Italy accounts in part for Machiavelli's apparent ambivalence between republicanism and absolute monarchy (Jones, 1965, 95). Alternation between one strategy and the other in Italian experience accounts for the rest: 'Between republics and despotisms the resemblances seem at least as great as the differences. In political organization both prolonged the past without radical alteration ... and not till the eighteenth century, when despotism became ' 'enlightened'', was any attempt made to impose an egalitarian state' (Jones, 1965, 94–5).

The differences in practice amounted to an urban bias under republicanism, which restricted citizenship to propertied town-dwellers, treating rural communes, as well as artisans, as inferior (Jones, 1965, 74–5). The restoration of *civitas* in Italy from the eleventh to the thirteenth centuries, constituted by the city and its *territorium*, brought certain administrative and fiscal advances, a uniformity in tax laws, economic and commercial regulation between the city-states, but not necessarily internal unity (Jones, 1965, 80–1). As before, the city was constituted by an aggregate of corporate groups, each seeking to maximize its interests, so that the 'state' as such represented little more than a shifting coalition of the personalistic networks for the transmission of economic goods, political power and military protection (Jones, 1965, 83–5). This urbanism, so reminiscent of the Greek *polis*, produced the same intensification of antagonism between the city and countryside, between the poor and the rich, commented on by Machiavelli, who claimed that in the case of Genoa it produced two states (*History of Florence*, 8, cited in Jones, 1965, 82, n.5). Republicanism meant narrow, self-enriching oligarchy, and when oligarchy gave way to despotism, this revolution so-called did not even require a change of constitution, the Visconti, for instance, ruling as salaried magistrates (Jones, 1965, 86). Tax laws and fiscal measures remained unchanged, and despots used mercenaries like republics, the citizen-soldier having been made obsolete by the *condottieri* for technological reasons, rather than due to a failure of *virtù* (Jones, 1965, 87). The differences lay in the despots' personal control of republican institutions, and their discretionary powers with regard to taxation and the law. Other areas escaped their net, however, and it was the despots who, while levelling rival political factions, allowed the 'obstinate survival of diversity and privilege'. 'In much of their policy, indeed, republican Venice and Florence would seem to have been less tolerant than despots of autonomous authority, clerical, feudal, or urban' (Jones, 1965, 91) and much harsher in their treatment of the countryside.

From the point of view of the masses, a point of view that, as we have observed, was rarely represented in Machiavelli, 'power and office were effectively restricted to the same privileged order, and from the mass of people, under republics and despots alike, the same complaints monotonously arise: against unjust taxation, against corrupt and costly justice, against local and personal privilege' (Jones, 1965, 95). Even a 'democrat' in this era spoke not for the masses but for those qualified to rule – as long as it was a qualification based on more than birth alone (Pocock, 1990). Representative government – or government that was representative of more than the oligarchic elite – had to await the development of parliaments, which were a feudal, and not an urban, phenomenon (Jones, 1965, 75):

> In the language of Tudor England [Thomas More, in fact] government [for the masses] was 'nothing but a certein conspiracy of riche men procuringe their own commodities under the name and title of the Common Wealth'. Nor did political writers take a different view: to Bartolus, to Machiavelli, to Francesco Vettori, all Italian governments were 'tyrannies' – of party, of class, of despots. In a more sombre spirit, they shared the opinion later expressed by Dr. Samuel Johnson, when invited to comment on the theme of political liberty: 'Sir, that is all visionary. I would not give half a guinea to live under one form of government rather than another'. (Jones, 1965, 95–6)

Machiavelli's reputation for *étatism*, is not undeserved, but a supporter of tyranny he is not. If there seems to be little precedent in ancient or classical literature for the mirror of princes of the Machiavellian type – a fact which commentators have noted (Gilbert, 1939, 458) – it has its forerunners in the Hellenistic period, the works of Plutarch, the lost histories of Alexander, and the Stoic treatises on law and kingship on which Cicero and Seneca draw. This

Hellenistic legacy was not lost in the hiatus between the Roman Stoics and Epicureans and the Renaissance revival of Platonism, but lived on in the East, the world from which Western Christendom was schismatically divided, and to which it has continued to shut its eyes. Not only was the Renaissance 'state', not a *quattrocento* Italian invention; much more unified and powerful Islamic states challenged it from West and East, from Spain to Syria, as well as knocking on its door in the Kingdom of the Two Sicilies. But the Islamic states drew on the sedentary culture of the great Hellenistic cities, Pergamum, Alexandria and Antioch, which had nurtured Greek philosophical traditions long absent from the 'West' – not because they had died out, but because they had never crossed the language barrier from Greek to Latin. This rich philosophical, theological, legal, scientific and literary heritage, which Eastern cities had largely created under the Hellenistic kings, and which they promoted and developed under the Islamic conquerors, produced a mirror of princes genre in important respects similar to the Machiavellian *Prince*. Although there is no internal evidence to suggest direct acquaintance with this literature, the link through Byzantine Platonism may be sufficient to explain similarities too striking to be coincidental.

18

The Islamic Mirror of Princes

Out of the prolific Islamic mirror of princes literature and its Persian counterpart, certain themes predominate which are found in the Italian Renaissance version of the genre as well. The stance of the Islamic counsellor to the Caliph is *étatist* as dictated both by his posture and purpose: the state being taken for granted, the question was how to ensure its stability through effective government; his function lay in supplying this expertise. Among those who undertook the perennially hazardous occupation of advising princes, there were some whose counsel never left the safer zone of expediency, and others who lost their heads for counselling true justice. In either case the questions were framed within a rather consistently Platonist framework, taking either the Thrasymachan position that the successful ruler is he who wins the struggle for power, and that justice is the art of presenting the interests of the ruling class as universally duty-worthy. (Such strategies tended to enlist princely beneficence, to substitute for the people's loss of freedom and autonomy, enhanced enjoyment of material goods.) Or, more frequently, the Muslim commentator enveighed against short-sighted policies, recommending rather true justice, built upon a stable class structure and division of labour, the virtues of the prince and the integrity of his 'guardians'.

The dominance of Platonism in the Islamic, as well as the Renaissance, mirror of princes literature is due not just to accidents of historical transmission and the long tradition of Neoplatonist metaphysics in the East, or the corresponding excitement these aroused when introduced to the Italian West. Structural similarities between the societies of Plato's *Republic* and the Islamic state, and the efficacy of technocratic rule in the consolidation of new states, were much more compelling reasons. For, if classical Islam was centred on the Imam, the medieval Islamic state was focused on the Caliph (Lambton, 1962, 99). Sholomo Goitein, that doyen of Islamic culture, makes the following observation:

It has often occurred to me that the fabric of the original Muslim state, as it was formed approximately in 'Umar's time, bore a strange resemblance to the various strata of the ideal state conceived by Plato in his *Politeia*. The 'Companions' (*Ashab*), or rather the small circle of noble Meccans, who, or whose parents, had been closely connected with the Prophet, correspond to the 'Rulers' (*archontes*) or the 'Perfect Guardians' (*phylakes panteleis*). The mass of tribesmen, who, by leaving Arabia, became recognized as the Warriors of Allah (*muharjirin fi sabil Allah*) and were registered in fixed diwans, resemble Plato's 'Guardians' (*phylakes*),

262   Renaissance Republicanism and Marcher Lord

while the rest of the population, the non-Muslims, who contributed the means of subsistence to the former two classes, may be compared with Plato's 'Employers' and 'Maintainers' (*misthodotai, tropheis*), of which names the designation of the non-Muslims as maddat al-muslimin 'Helpers of the Muslims' ... is strangely reminiscent. Two further instances of resemblance are the facts that the Muslims used to live together in special camp-cities, separated from the rest of the population, and that a serious attempt was made at preventing them from holding or cultivating land. As is well known, Plato's 'Guardians' were supposed to live in closed communities and not to possess private property. It is needless to say that the Muslim state came into being without any connection with Plato's theories. (Goitein, 1949, 131, n.1)

Or did it? The early Islamic state is separated from Plato's *Republic* by the period of Hellenistic kingship. But, as we have seen, both the Macedonian monarchy, with its caste of royal guardian-like 'companions' and the institutions of the Seleucid kingdoms, bore many similarities to the structure of the state that Plato envisaged. This Goitein more or less concedes, adding: 'The nearest historical parallel was the Sassanid empire, where the nobility, the gentry, the priests, the scribes and other "Servants of the King" were exempted from the poll-tax, which was graded according to the capacity of the taxpayer like the jizya paid by non-Muslims to the Caliph's treasurer' (Goitein, 1949, 131, n.1). Could the similarity have been due to Plato's *Politeia* being in fact modelled on that of Pharaonic Egypt, with its aspirant Divine King, its strict social hierarchy and division of labour, scribal, artisan and agricultural classes? Neoplatonist political writings of the Hellenistic period discuss kingship and its attributes in terms reminiscent both of the pharaoh, 'saviour' and 'benefactor', and the philosopher king, source of light, life and justice (Goodenough, 1928; Nock, 1930, 1947, 1951; Delatte, 1942; Pelletier, 1962; Springborg, 1990d). Direct lines of historical transmission thus connect not only the phenomenon of the empire centred on the 'just king' and patrimonial lord, 'hedged about by a luminous solar deity', and protected by his royal henchmen, but also the tradition of theorizing about it in the Greek, and subsequently Arabic speaking, East.

The fascination of Machiavelli and Renaissance practitioners of the mirror of princes genre with Alexander, proto-type of Hellenistic kingship, was sufficient, in conjunction with certain structural similarities between fluid Renaissance states in the making, and the kingdoms of the Hellenistic marcher lords, to call these connections into play. No direct link is either necessary or probable, although the political content of Gemistus Pletho's Platonism, and that of other Byzantine transmitters, was clearly heavily influenced by Islamic sources, as indeed was medieval European theory of the state. It is not surprising then that we should find in the Arabic literature disquisitions on the virtues of the prince, 'shepherd of his sheep', his justice and beneficence, to which those of the Italian mirror of princes as exemplified by Egidio and others bear great similarity (A. Gilbert, 1938; F. Gilbert, 1939, 1965). Nizam al-Mulk (d. 1092), Persian vizir of the middle period of Islamic medieval theories of the state, in his administrative handbook *Siyasat- nama*, combined images of the king as source of 'divine light' and 'knowledge'; whose 'people may pass their days under [the shadow of] his justice'; whose 'magnificence' and 'beneficence' close 'the doors of corruption, disturbance, and sedition' and fill 'the hearts [of the people] with awe of him'; who 'would answer the tyrannical with the sword, protect the ewe and the lamb from the wolf, shorten the hands of tyrants, root out from the earth the corrupt, and make the world prosperous by equity, justice, and security'; with more practical considerations like 'the improvement of irrigation and communications and the building of new cities' (Lambton, 1962, 101–2). Royal competence depends as much upon maintaining the class structure and bureaucratic hierarchy, 'maintain[ing] his subordinates each according to his rank and giv[ing] to each one, according to his deserts, a rank and status'; punishing each 'according to the measure of his offence', as it depends upon exhibiting the classical catalogue of princely virtues:

> It has been said that if a king wants to have glory and excellence above every other king, let him refine and adorn his morals by keeping far from him bad qualities and adopting good qualities. The former are rancour, envy, pride, anger, lust, greed, desire, obstinacy, lying, miserliness, bad temper, tyranny, wilfulness, haste, in-gratitude, and levity; the latter are modesty, good temper, compassion, forgiveness, humility, generosity, sincerity, forbearance, gratitude, mercy, knowledge, reason and justice. (Lambton, 1962, 101–3, citing the Persian text of *Siyasat-nama*, ed. Schefer, 55–6, 163–4)

The great al-Ghazali (AD 1059–1111), Persian Islamic theologian and former professor and rector at the Nizamiya University of Baghdad, who resigned his position to adopt the Sufi garb and rove the Islamic world as a pilgrim like the Cynic Diogenes before him (Corbin, 1967, 326–8), also compared the just ruler to the good shepherd, who would guard his flock from the wolf, protect the meek from the strong (Ghazali, *Nasihat al-Muluk*, Persian 1923 edn, 248, cited in Lambton, 1962, 94). So strong is al-Ghazali's insistence on justice as the mark of kingship that, like Nizam al-Mulk, he repeats the aphorism: 'kingship remains with the unbeliever but not with injustice', 'kingship remains with unbelief but not with tyranny' (Nizam al-Mulk, 8, al-Ghazali, 1923 edn, 40–1, cited in Lambton, 1962, 104–5). Justice, even more than right religion, is the basis of kingship, and al-Ghazali, like Nizam al-Mulk, attributes to Allah the saying: 'The justice of one day of a just sultan is more excellent than the worship of sixty years', maintaining that 'the person most beloved of God is a just sultan and the person most despised a tyrannical sultan' (al-Ghazali, 1923, edn, 8–9, cited in Lambton, 1962, 105).

Al-Ghazali was not so otherworldly as to be incapable of diagnosing the expedience of justice. 'The efforts of [the Persian kings] to make the world prosperous', he noted 'were because they knew that the greater the mate-rial prosperity the more extensive their dominions and the more numerous their subjects' (al-Ghazali, 1923 edn, 48, cited in Lambton, 1962, 106). Like Machiavelli, he was no primitivist and was willing to trade gratification of the economic demands of the masses as a substitute for the dispersal of power, up to a certain point. He repeats the famous Sasanian aphorism on kingship, first recorded by Ibn Balkhi, chronicler of the pre-Islamic Persian kings, repeated by Nizam al-Mulk, al-Ghazali, Kay Ka'us, and others, which, known as the 'circle of power', 'became one of the stock themes of writers of mirrors' (Lambton,

1962, 100; Morony, 1984, 28–9): 'There is no kingdom without an army, no army without wealth, no wealth without material prosperity, and no material prosperity without justice' (Ibn Balkhi, *Fars-nama*, *c.*1110, ed. G. Le Strange, 4–5, cited in Lambton, 1962, 100).

Al-Ghazali attributes to kingship the creation of economic prosperity as a systemic effect, due to the necessity of beneficence to ensure royal rule. For the same reason wise kings eschewed despotism:

> because they feared that the people would not achieve stability with tyranny and injustice, cities and areas would become ruined, the people flee and go to another kingdom, and material prosperity be turned into ruin, kingship decay, revenue decline, the treasury become empty, and the livelihood of the people be dried up. The people do not love a tyrannical king and always curse him. (al-Ghazali, 1923 edn, 48, cited in Lambton, 106).

If the saintly al-Ghazali did not rule out considerations of expediency, some mirrors, like that of the *Qabus-nama* of Kay Ka'us (*c.*1082) counselled nothing else. Proclaiming the question of 'effective rule' to be his subject, Kay Ka'us declared that to this end the ruler must look to the needs of the masses just as he must look to those of the military, 'because the king is like the sun which cannot shine on one and not the other'. Justice is a necessity, not a virtue: 'for the house of just kings endures and becomes old but the house of the unjust quickly disappears, because justice means prosperity and injustice ruin ... The sages have said "the source of material prosperity and happiness in the world is a just king and the source of ruin and sadness a tyrannical king"' (*Qabus-nama*, ed. R. Levy, 1953 edn, 134, cited in Lambton, 1962, 107–8).

Pragmatism required, on the one hand, that the king exert effective authority over his subjects; but, on the other, that he do so as far as possible by civil and not military means, for military rule was a great disincentive to prosperity: 'if one made the subjects obedient by means of the army, one supported the army by means of the subjects. The kingdom is made prosperous by the subjects, because revenue is acquired through them; and they remain where they are and become prosperous through justice' (Kay, Ka'us, *Qabus-nama*, 1953 ed., 133–4, cited in Lambton, 1962, 107).

A very Machiavellian subject and a very Machiavellian solution. More typical in its synthesis of idealism and pragmatism, is the counsel of al-Muqaffa', author of both a mirror and an administrative handbook, the latter of which cost him his life for his frankness, and whose career curiously parallels that of Machiavelli, as Goitein (1949, 121), observes. The parallel goes further than that, for in his mirror, *Adab al-Kabir*, like the author of *The Prince*, al-Muqaffa' counsels absolute rule and the implicit obedience of subjects. But in his administrative handbook, *Adab as-Saghir*, like the author of the *Discourses*, with different considerations in mind, his counsel is somewhat different: 'the ruling of men was a great calamity (for him that exercised that onle)', or ruled alone (al-Muqaffa', *Al-Adab as-Saghir*, Beirut, 1960 edn, 22, cited in Lambton, 1962, 98). Once again the discrepancy between the two works arises as much from the medium as the message. Mirrors standardly dealt with the virtues and vices of rulers (Goitein, 1949, 121) but in his Memorandum on Government, *Kitab as-Sahaba*, an uncommissioned work, proferred to the Caliph al-Mansur of the newly established Abbasid dynasty, whose open-mindedness combined with austerity, suggested to al-Muqaffa' a man open to advice that had not been put to him before on the principles of good administration (Goitein, 1949, 133, n.12), al-Muqaffa', like the author of the *Discourses*, took liberties that he had not taken in his mirror, and that in his case cost him his neck.

Ethnically non-Arab, a Mawla, al-Muqaffa' was also for most of his life a non-Muslim, probably a Manichean (Lambton, 1962, 98); but, schooled in Arabic by the savants of Basra, his exquisite Arabic prose has been a model ever since. Although 'adopt[ing] the social ideals of Arab high society most diligently and surpass[ing] it by lavishing stupendous sums on poets and singers, helping friends in distress and by rescuing complete strangers who applied to him for assistance' (Goitein, 1949, 121), al-Muqaffa' did not hesitate to teach a lesson whenever he could, demonstrating to the Arabs the most refined manners of the Persian aristocrat and his elaborate table ceremonial, even correcting the Arabic of the Arab aristocrats, including the Emir, who in 759 put him to death for his literary audacity (Goitein, 1949, 121, 133, n.12).

Only very strong political convictions could have prompted this citizen of a subject race to speak out. Like Machiavelli, he observed the state at a cross-roads, and hoped that the Abbasids, succeeding to the Caliphate in AD 750, and shifting its seat from Damascus, the Umayyad capital, to Baghdad, would learn from the mistakes of their predecessors. As marcher lords in the old Assyrian and Persian traditions, the Arabs were faced with the eternal problem of converting military into civilian power, maintaining religious integrity and inducing stability and prosperity, without compromising territory or fighting readiness. These are problems that Polybius raised as being classically Hellenistic, and Machiavelli as being classically Renaissance. The answers in each case are much the same: classical and republican, in both the Platonic and Roman senses. Al-Muqaffa' is concerned, first of all, with the upkeep of the army and the purity of its shock troops, whose loss of *virtù* under the Ummayads had cost them the disintegration of their empire. He is concerned with religion, as the bond between army and caliph. He is concerned with legal codification, that would institutionalize justice and take it out of the personal power of the ruler. And he is concerned with the recruitment to the administrative elite, its organization and function, methods of tax collection and jurisdiction that would ensure stable and consistent rule.

To all these questions, al-Muqaffa' gives answers that are both Platonist and curiously Machiavellian. The Abbasids had replaced the Syrian imperial guard of the Umayyads with Khorasanians, 'warriors ... from the north-eastern march of Iran, who brought with them a great military tradition owing to the incessant border warfare with the peoples of Central Asia' (Goitein, 1949, 123). Lacking the racial ties that bound the Syrians to the Umayyads, the Khorasanians were bound to the Abbasids by ties of religious conviction, and these were the only ties that bound them. Al-Muqaffa' makes much of the function of a 'systematic religious education' as a method by which the Caliph might discipline the imperial guard; and in his recommendations for the provisioning of the troops he insists that they should not be permitted to collect land tax (Goitein, 1949, 123–5), mindful perhaps that Platonic auxiliaries might too easily, like the Roman *equites*, end their days, not as fighting-fit guardians of the state, but as flaccid tax-farmers, parasitic upon it. Al-Muqaffa''s advice was not heeded, perhaps because few commentators were percipient enought to see the beginnings of a 'feudal' system which, combining military and fiscal power, was 'destined to shape the social structure of the Near East down to the end of the nineteenth century' (Goitein, 1949, 125). Abu Yusuf, in the *Kitab al-Kharaj*, written when the Khorasanians had already been replaced by Turkish slaves, although dealing with tax-farming, does not so much as mention involvement by the imperial guard.

And if the shock troops of Islam, the equivalent of Plato's auxiliaries, should not be permitted to break the rule against property, how much more important is it that the imperial 'companions', *as-sahaba*, the main subject of Ibn al-Muqaffa''s book, should be unpolluted. He bemoans the democratization of the elite, in violation of a strict functional division of labour, and the admission to its ranks of those 'who were neither educated, nor of noble birth, persons of poor intelligence, well known for their crimes, without merits in either peace or war and – most shocking of all – persons who passed most of their lives as labourers having done manual work with their hands' (al-Muqaffa', *Kitab as-Sahaba*, 125, cited in Goitein, 1949, 126) – an elitism which we associate with Hellas, and prescriptions against manual labour as equivalent to slavery and unthinkable for all but non-citizens, which Herodotus (2.166, 1972 edn, 195–6) nevertheless attributes to Egyptian origins and the strict division of labour into seven classes.

Al-Muqaffa' laid down rules for administrative recruitment to the companion-ship of the Caliph in this syncretic tradition, stipulating three admissable categories of candidates: distinguished military officers ' "who should be pro-moted from the military service to the Companionship" '; *faqihs*, whose religious training and ability to serve as judges qualified them; and indigenous aristocrats (Goitein, 1949, 127). Al-Muqaffa', showing a rare objectivity, favoured the indigenous Iraqi aristocracy as a potential administrative recruitment pool. More generally, however, he belongs to the rank of thinkers who favoured syncretism – a long-standing tradition of the Assyrian and Sasanian empires – rather than racial purity; a tradition to which Ibn Khaldun, who in the *Maqaddimah* 2.9 remarks somewhat maliciously that only very primitive tribes are racially pure; and al-Jahiz who, in his treatise 'Against the Christians', 'incidentally describes the Jews of his time as rude and incapable of philosophical thinking "because an Israelite never marries any but a Jewish woman, which inbreeding leads to stupidity" ' (cited in Goitein, 1949, 134, n.26), also belonged. Al-Muqaffa' hoped for a racial synthesis in Baghdad similar to the Khorasanian blend of Arab and Iranian, that proved to be 'the backbone of the empire' (Goitein, 1949, 126). Ironically, when this syncretism ran its course, the racial integration of Khorasanian and Iraqi elements made them unreliable as an imperial guard, forcing the Caliph to employ mercenaries with solely pecuniary attachment to him, against all the rules of the good republic (Goitein, 1949, 126).

Al-Muqaffa''s whole discussion of the imperial 'companions' lies within the boundaries of the canon set in Hellenic and Hellenistic thought for the Royal *philos* or 'friend'. As Goitein (1949, 134, n.27) observes, it is a tradition that finds its origins in the ancient Near East, the Egyptian, Mesopotamian or

Hebrew 'Friend of the King', but whose attenuations stretch far into the future, producing the Richelieu, Rasputin, Kissinger and Brzezhinski; Mandarins of East and West, the Vanguard of the Party, the Politbureau and Kitchen Cabinet. Astute Aristotle treated *philia* as the paradigmatic form of political relations, most extensively and, in the *Nicomachean Ethics*, books 8 and 9, at greater length even than his treatment of justice, thus giving the lie to modern assumptions, dating at least from Weber, that democracy – politics properly speaking – requires men to set aside affinal, ascriptive and traditional bonds of family, clan, tribe and friendship, in favour of more rational criteria of merit, achievement and the good of the whole as more than a sum of its parts (Springborg, 1986). The *philos*, as a type, received its archetypal expression in a later period, with the Macedonian 'friends' or royal 'companions', among whom were dispersed the lands of great Alexander, in a distribution remarkable for its strategic tough-mindedness, arrived at collegially, when the great king was dead.

Marcher lords in their turn, the new kings were royal by election and achievement, rather than by blood. They 'relied on their armies and mostly ruled in lands where monarchy was traditional', for, in the words of the *Suda*:

> 'it is neither descent nor legitimacy which gives monarchies to men but the ability to command an army and govern a state wisely, as was the case with Philip and Alexander's Successors. For Alexander's natural son got no help from his kinship with him owing to his weak character, whereas those who were in no way related became kings over virtually the whole inhabited world' (Walbank, 1984, 63, citing the *Suda*, s.v. *Basileia*, Austin, 37).

These 'companions'-cum-marcher-lords, most of whom died on campaign, or as victims of violence at home, set the pattern for the Islamic warrior and his institutionalized successor, the Vizier. The mystery that surrounds the surprising emergence of the Islamic conquerors and their lightning strikes across the Maghreb and into the heart of Europe (Hall, 1986, 86; Mann, 1986, 345, 364, 502) is not so surprising at all if one looks for precedents in the right place. For Islamic culture drew on more than the barbarian tribes of Arabia, the highly articulated culture of the sedentary populations providing a fund of ancient and Hellenistic experience on which to draw.

Nor were Islamic political theorists blind to the vulnerability of the warrior state. The rich proliferation of mirrors, legal and administrative treatises, unmatched in Western literature until the seventeenth century, and even then never approximating the sheer volume of material, or the degree of theoretical specialization, owes its origins to just these exigencies: the reflections of savants on the state-building processes taking place around them, in which they had the opportunity to participate. Once again the prevailing *ethos* of *Realpolitik* is due less to calculated power-mongering than to the posture of the political analyst who has technical expertise to dispense in what seem to be technical matters. That politics involves ethics and values is not thereby ruled out, any more than it is in the case of Machiavelli, although deep background moral problems are converted into long-range political problems, and take a back seat to immediate questions of organization and administration, on which the advisor to princes is called to supply an answer. What is surprising by modern standards, where the democratization of advisors has produced more vicious competition for the government ear, is not the opportunism of these commentators, but the degree of their objectivity, under very testing conditions where heads literally rolled.

Al Muqaffa', for instance, in his handbook on the 'Companions', hoped to persuade the Caliph to employ rational criteria, substituting for the Sasanian ruling aristocratic caste, a technocratic elite recruited and maintained according to Platonist principles. In the same tradition, he hoped to see the institutionalization, by legal codification, of power wrested from the personal control of the ruler, a practice of the Persian empire that had not been adopted by the Sasanians. Peculiarly attentive to the special problems of subject peoples, al-Muqaffa' advised the Caliph to combine '(a) precedents and usage (*siyar*), (b) tradition and analogy, (c) his own decisions', as the basis of a comprehensive legal code – for which Roman law supplied directives in local practice, although not precedent as a code (Goitein, 1949, 128). And true to the aristocratic bias of Plato and Aristotle, where aristocracy meant rule by the *aristoi*, or the 'best', al-Muqaffa' deplored the inroads of the merchant in administrative life, due both to 'economic and social developments in general and ... the role played by the neo-Muslim merchants and industrialists who did propaganda for the Abbasids prior to their rise to power' (Goitein, 1949, 130). Like Machiavelli, although out of a somewhat different mind-set, al-Muqaffa' hoped to see the integrity of the ruler and his administrators founded on the sure bases of right (civic) religion, law and the nobility of a virtuous elite, underpinned always by the purity and courage of the imperial shock-troops.

The bias towards urbanism, and the mutually entailed sedentariness that accompanied institutionalization – the subject of undoubtedly the greatest author of mirrors, the *Maqaddimah* of Ibn Khaldun, whose version of the genre transcended its very limits, and which bears striking similarities to Machiavelli's *Discourses* – is less evident in the work of al-Muqaffa'. A Fars from the provincial notability, his special interest is rather the welfare, protection from rapacious tax-gatherers, and legal rights of subject peoples on the periphery of the Islamic kingdoms, as well as the syncretic blending of cultures. It is far more evident in the work of the *Falasifa*, who, with two exceptions only, those of the Westerners Ibn Bajja and Ibn Tufayl, universally saw the good of man to presuppose the city (Rosenthal, 1948, 6). These, the great Islamic transmitters of Plato and Aristotle to medieval Europe by way of their commentaries, perpetuated the classical 'republican' tradition, not for academic reasons, but as a model for the Islamic state. Less concerned than the authors of the Persian mirrors with the *techne* of the ruler, and the Machiavellian problem of inducing fear and respect (Rosenthal, 1948, 5), they addressed themselves rather to the classical 'political' problem of the good life and its social and economic frameworks. Similarities that may not have been accidental between the ideal of the *Shar'ia*, the Islamic legal code and the Platonic *Republic*, suggested the equation of the Islamic Imam with the Platonist philosopher-king-cum-legislator which we find in Alfarabi, the Jewish Maimonides, who bases his identification of philosopher and prophet on Alfarabi, and Averroes (Rosenthal, 1948, 6–8). And if the shift from the Umayyad to the Abbasid Caliphate is generally read as a step in the process of secularization, so is the work of the *Falasifa*, to whom the political ideal is less theocracy than the rule of law (Rosenthal, 1948, 9; Goitein, 1949, 120).

Alfarabi (*c*.873–950), known as 'the second master' after Aristotle, and trained by Ibn Yunus, the most prominent of the Christian Aristotelians at the Abbasid court in Baghdad, wrote commentaries on the *Republic* and the *Laws*, Aristotle's *Politics* being unavailable to him. He also wrote his own treatises, the *Madina Fadila*, or 'Ideal City', and the *Kitab al-Siyasat*, also known as the *Kitab al-Mabadi*, which combine Aristotelian psychology and metaphysics, in a Platonized form, with Platonic politics (Rosenthal, 1948, 7; Watt, 1967, 179–80). Averroes, or Ibn Rushd (*c*.1126–1198), author of commentaries on Plato's *Politeia* and Aristotle's *Ethica Nicomachea*, in his reading of the Aristotelian epithet *zoon politikon*, went far beyond the general assumption of the *Falasifa* that human needs for basic subsistence necessitate a communal existence. Reasoning, like Plato, from differentiated human capacities, to the division and specialization of labour and the development of latent characteristically human powers, he concluded that, 'if the state were nothing but the provider of the material needs of man and the protector of life and property against the superior force of the stronger, then man would never reach his goal' (Rosenthal, 1948, 7; Rahman, 1967, 220–1). It being the case that virtue is the end of politics, the ruler is empowered to make the citizens ' "good, excellent and submissively bent under the laws" ' to the point of absolute rule. But this great power is justified only while the ruler remains the ' "guardian of equity; [for] when he guards equity he guards justice; [and] political equity is identical with legal equity" ' (Rosenthal, 1948, 9). Islam had a long tradition of the right of resistance to tyrants, in theory if not always in practice.

True to Platonist precepts Averroes shared the view that the guardian class should be deprived of property rights, hoping to forestall incipient feudalism, by his time now apparent in the tax-farming janissary class. At the same time, he upheld Plato's principle of 'one man, one job' and the strict division of labour that it entailed. No rigid Platonist, however, he upbraided Galen for his ahistorical critique of Plato's stipulation of a certain limited size for the *polis*, and the necessity to confine the guardian class to one thousand members – were Plato to have lived under the *oikoumeme* he too would have thought differently. Averroes endorsed Plato's principle that women should be educated as men for a specialist occupation, deploring squandering of talent by confining them to the tasks of procreation and housekeeping – as a slave-owning society, Muslim women were not, of course, much required to perform manual household tasks (Rosenthal, 1948, 10–11).

19

Ibn Khaldun and the Cycle of Regimes

The application of Platonic and Aristotelian principles to an indigenous body of thought on the nature of the state and the good prince, in the hands of the *Falasifa* had produced a Renaissance of Islam that had its Western counterpart in quattrocento Italy some centuries later. It was, of course, no coincidence, for not only did the Islamic transmitters of Plato and Aristotle have a profound influence on medieval European political thought in its Latin form, but some of the most influential *Falasifa* were themselves Western Muslims, for instance, the great Ibn Tufayl (d.1185), who moved between Spain and Morocco; his teacher Ibn Bajja (d.1138), known to the West as Avempace; and the Jewish Ibn-Gabirol, who trod the same path. Muslim Andalusia and the court at Granada had exercised a profound influence on the culture of Renaissance Italy and France, the former of which experienced Islamic rule at first hand, the latter having suffered Muslim incursions as far north as Poitiers.

The links established by contiguity and direct, if intermittent, contact, did not require specific lines of transmission, which is perhaps why Islamic influence is so infrequently acknowledged. The citation of authorities had its own conventions, as it still does, and was carefully calculated to impress. The revivification of Western European thought that the Renaissance reception of Plato, in particular, produced, led authors to cite him, who had barely even read him, while the more standard Aristotle of the Schoolmen, who was more thoroughly known, was less fashionable to cite. And yet the *Falasifa* found more favour as authorities than they do now, despite the tension between Islamic culture and the Latin culture that prevailed. They were widely cited by commentators of Aristotle when the *Politics* was first readmitted to the tradition (Dunbabin, 1982, 724–5), and, with the enthusiastic re-entry of Plato, by Renaissance Platonists such as Marsilio Ficino, of whom it is noted that his references to Avicenna and Averroes outnumber those to medieval Latin sources (Kristeller, 1944a, 39, 46–7, 50, 54; 1944–5, 579–80; 1946, 271).

Islamic authors of mirrors and treatises on law include the voluminous works of the Hanafi school, Abu Hanifa (d.767), Abu Yusuf (d.798), and Shaybani (d.803); the 30-volume legal compendium of Sarakhsi (d.1090), the works of as-Samarqandi (d.1144), Kasani (d.1191), Malik b. Anas (d.795), founder of the Maliki school of law, his student al-Qasim (d.806), and Sahnun (d.854), his student in turn; as well as of Shafi'i, founder of the Shafi'i school (d.820) and his disciples (see Udovitch, 1970, 10, 15–16). But of all the legal and administrative handbooks and mirrors, that work which stands above all others in its analytical and theoretical excellence, is the *Maqaddimah* of Ibn Khaldun (1332–1406).

Born in Tunis of a family that migrated from Saudi Arabia to Andalusia in the eighth century, and that had established a reputation for scholarship and statesmanship, Ibn Khaldun personally suffered all the vicissitudes of the counsellor to princes, in favour at one moment and in jail the next, studying, teaching and serving in the Caliphal administration variously in Tunis, Algeria, Morocco, southern Spain and Egypt (Saab, 1967, 107–9). Of all the Muslim political commentators, his analysis structurally most closely resembles that of both Polybius and Machiavelli, to a surprising and barely remarked upon degree.

Like Polybius, Ibn Khaldun, who had completed a classical education in the texts and commentaries of Plato and Aristotle, reversed Aristotle's famous judgement of the *Poetics* that while history dealt with the particular, only poetry could deal with the universal – a judgement that probably requires one to read for 'poetry', Homer, and works in the great epic cycle that constituted a literature of national liberation for the Greeks, source of all the myths of nationhood on which Greek culture, like any other, rested (Gordon, 1953, 54–6). At any rate, by the Hellenistic period, when history had too often declined into chronicle, Polybius effected the surprising reversal by which it, and poetry, no longer laid claim to the universal. This example Ibn Khaldun, claiming no precedents, followed, undertaking the study of 'universal history' in order to establish the rules that govern the rise and decline of states. But Ibn Khaldun is too frequently taken at his word on the question of antecedents: it is clear that an acquaintance with the works of Plato and Aristotle as close as his would have attuned him to their speculations, especially those of Plato, on cyclical history, the principles of state formation and disintegration. In fact, his work contains internal evidence to suggest that this was so. This leaves him in possession of some of the material out of which Polybian methodology is constructed, although how much more was accessible to him in the works of Democritus, Epicurus, Diodorus Siculus and Polybius himself, we do not know (but see al-Azmeh, 1981).

And perhaps this is where the genius of Ibn Khaldun lies, for out of incomparably fewer remnants of the long Greek tradition of *historia*, and the rather selective heritage of Greek philosophical works available to him, he creates an incomparably richer macro-historical account than Polybius or any of the Greeks, apart from Plato and Aristotle themselves. Speaking of his chosen subject, which is nothing less than the history and dynamics of forms of human association in general, he remarks, with some justice:

> It should be known that the discussion of this topic is something new, extraordinary, and highly useful. Penetrating research has shown the way to it. It does not belong to rhetoric, one of the logical disciplines (represented in Aristotle's *Organon*), which are concerned with convincing words whereby the mass is moved to accept or reject a particular opinion. It is also not politics, because politics is concerned with the administration of home or city in accordance with ethical and philosophical requirements, for the purpose of directing the mass toward a behaviour that will result in the preservation and permanence of the species. The subject here is different from those two disciplines which, however, are often

similar to it. In a way, it is an entirely original science. In fact, I have not come across a discussion along these lines by anyone. I do not know if this is because people have been unaware of it, but there is no reason to suspect them of having been unaware of it. Perhaps they have written exhaustively on the topic and their work did not reach us. (*al-Maqaddimah*, 1967 edn, 39)

Ibn Khaldun's humility in refusing to take credit for having discovered a science which could have been discovered by earlier civilizations, the Persians, Chaldeans, Syrians, Babylonians, even the Copts, to name those he names (1967 edn, 39), is a refreshing change from the cultural arrogance of most Greek writers. But, like Polybius, the stranger, and Machiavelli, whose same fluctuating fortunes as a diplomat and advisor made this a matter of personal interest, he was preoccupied with the question: what constitutes the formula for cultural hegemony, and what causes it eventually to ebb away?

There are primitivist elements in Ibn Khaldun's writings, that, like those in Machiavelli, cause him to be read simplistically. For the Tunisian, well acquainted with the Berber, and indeed author of their authoritative history for this period in the sixth and seventh books of the *Kitab al-'Ibar*, or Universal History, to which the *Maqaddimah* was the Prolegomena, understood the energy which a tribal society exhibits in its thrust for power, and which accounted for the extraordinary success of warrior shock troops in the Islamic conquests. The unworldliness of tribal society, locale of the most rigorous religious observances and desert mysticism; its nomadic way of life and relative lack of hindrances in the way of property; the simple life far from the luxury of the cities; impressed him as the source of this cultural energy, or *asabiyah*. For that phenomenon on which he, like Polybius and Machiavelli, focused, and for which he uses the term *asabiyah*, solidarity, or group feeling – the will to power, in a word – is the same phenomenon represented by Alexander and the Macedonian monarchy, the marcher lords of Assyria, more remotely, and the Visconti, Medici and new princes of Italy, in their smaller way. And if the tribe, with its ability to mobilize kinship and territorial ties, might seem to have some organizational advantages over the *princeps* and his 'companions', in fact, as Ibn Khaldun fully realized, power even by the tribe, could not be consolidated without institutionalization in formal political – that means sedentary – structures. But it is not sedentariness itself that is the critical factor: 'desert civilization is inferior to urban civilization because not all the necessities of civilization are to be found among the people of the desert' (Ibn Khaldun, 1967 edn, 122); they are dependent on the city for their needs. And Ibn Khaldun gives an extensive treatment of the economic underpinnings of civilization, in human insufficiency and the necessity for communal life for the satisfaction of needs, requiring in turn the division and specialization of labour, the production of use-values and exchange-values. His text draws very clearly on Plato and Aristotle's accounts of needs and the city and, in its centrality, looks forward to the Aristotelian economics of Marx (Ibn Khaldun, 1967 edn, ch. 5).

The dependence of desert dwellers on the city is, it turns out, a reciprocal one. For not only is the city economically dependent on the countryside for 'conveniences and luxuries', but Islamic culture is dependent on the desert for the dynamism to which its conquests are owed, 'because aggressive and defensive strength is obtained only through group feeling which means affection and willingness to fight and die for each other' (Ibn Khaldun, 1967 edn, 122–3). *Asabiyah* in turn requires leadership, the consolidation of leadership leads to dynasty, and thence to royalty. Monarchy, shored up by religion can, at a certain point, dispense with the fraternal solidarity of the tribe, but religion itself cannot initially emerge without *asabiyah*. Moreover, the sedentary state always faces the possibility that that delicate balance between the satisfaction of needs and luxury, the solvent of *virtù* or *asabiyah*, its equivalent, will cause the fabric to disintegrate, and decline set in. The higher economic, cultural, intellectual and spiritual needs of the city, by virtue of the institutions generated to service them, create on-going structures with built-in interests that can erode the solidarity of the state, by supplying alternative centres of power. The dynamism of a subsistence economy geared to simple need-furnishing, essential for survival, is thus lost in the complexity of institutions competing for power.

In a way that is both curiously Hellenic, as well as representing the realities of early Islam, Ibn Khaldun upbraids Ibn Rushd (Averroes) and those who for whom civilization means urbanism in the *polis* tradition:

'prestige', [Averroes] states, 'belongs to people who are ancient settlers in a town'. He did not consider the things we have just mentioned. I should like to know how long residence in a town can help (anyone to gain prestige), if he does not belong to a group that makes him feared and causes others to obey him. (Ibn Khaldun, 1967 edn, 103)

Averroes has made the fatal mistake of confusing nobility with birth, power with prestige: 'Averroes considers prestige as depending exclusively on the number of forefathers. Yet rhetoric means to sway the opinions of those whose opinions count, that is, the men in command. It takes no notice of those who have no power. They cannot sway anyone's opinions, and their own opinions are not sought. The sedentary inhabitants of cities fall into that catetgory', because at a certain point they are deluded by the lure of prestige, acquired by the sheer passage of time, into thinking they have power, mistaking a functional nobility for its metaphorical form (Ibn Khaldun, 1967 edn, 103).

If luxury can bring down states, it takes more than a few capitalists to bring down a civilization: 'a sedentary person who has a great deal of capital and has acquired a great number of estates and farms and become one of the wealthiest inhabitants of a particular city, who is looked upon as such and lives in luxury and is accustomed to luxury, competes in this respect with amirs and rulers.' The threat to his possessions which the amir, in turn, poses to his property, induces the rich man to seek private protection and rank to secure his position (Ibn Khaldun, 1967 edn, 281–2). Thus begins the endless struggle, a centrifugal force which disperses power to the periphery. Ibn Khaldun, who is as interested as Polybius or Machiavelli in the phenomenon of expansionism, reaches similar conclusions about its obstacles, in an analytical and non-moralistic way.

A culture in the broader sense, however, has the capacity to outlive the states that are its bearers, and Ibn Khaldun, who experienced the high culture of a civilization that stretched almost to the limits of the then-known world, at a time at which the individual states which were its bearers were in decline, appreciated the force of the term 'The House of Islam', *dar al-Islam*. Human aptitude or habit, *malakah*, permits individuals to maintain the benefits of a culture, long after its political forms have decayed, and to imitate previous dynasties. The power of imitation and the dynamism of group solidarity are moral forces, equivalent to Machiavelli's *virtù*, that account for the micro-processes of civilization on which macro-forms are built. Ibn Khaldun believes in an equilibrium of virtue, similar to that which Machiavelli postulated – past civilizations were neither better nor worse than those of today, but virtue was differently distributed.

As a mirror of princes, of which the *Maqaddamah* is a superior analytical form, it contains all the advice we would expect to hear about caliphs and viziers, dynasties and their natural life spans, the succession of judges and religious officials, the police, court procedures, regulation of the market, the money supply, tax collection, the important offices of scribe and door-keeper, the role of symbols in politics, the throne, the royal seal, large tents to impress, trumpets and banners to overwhelm. Whatever the Hellenic content, at the end of the day, when the analysis of macro-processes has been concluded, Ibn Khaldun confesses to subscribe to the old Sasanian 'circle of power'. In a *Book on Politics*, strangely attributed to Aristotle, he finds the old Persian aphorisms arranged 'in a remarkable circle':

> It runs as follows: 'The world is a garden the fence of which is the dynasty. The dynasty is an authority through which life is given to proper behaviour. Proper behaviour is a policy directed by the ruler. The ruler is an institution supported by the soldiers. The soldiers are helpers who are maintained by money. Money is sustenance brought together by the subjects. The subjects are servants who are protected by justice. Justice is something [harmonious], and through it the world persists. The world is a garden ...' – and then it begins again from the beginning. These are eight sentences of political wisdom. They are connected with each other, the end of each one leading into the beginning of the next. They are held together in a circle with no definite beginning or end. The author of this *Book on Politics* said to be Aristotle was proud of what he had hit upon and made much of the significance of the sentences. (Ibn Khaldun, 1967 edn, 41)

Ibn Khaldun admits quite frankly that 'when our discussion in the section on royal authority and dynasties has been studied and due critical attention given to it, it will be found to constitute an exhaustive, very clear, fully substantiated interpretation and detailed exposition of these sentences.' He adds proudly: 'We became aware of these things with God's help and without the instruction of Aristotle or the [Persians]' (Ibn Khaldun, 1967, 41).

And if in the Islamic mirrors there is one thing conspicuously lacking that we find in Polybius or Machiavelli – that being references to republicanism or 'democracy' – we should not be misled by appearances. Islamic writers, as the 'circle of power' enjoins, were as capable as any other of understanding the mutual dependence between rulers and ruled, which could accommodate the interests of both if the bond between them were one of justice. Islam provided its own representative institutions: the communal assembly, planted in the locale of the old Greek *agora*, which later became the mosque (Grabar, 1969, 27–8; Hourani, 1970, 22); instruments for the registering of public complaints

(Morony, 1984, 74, 83–5, 432); the redress of grievances and the institutionalization of the ruler's function as seat of equity, that are to be found in the courts of Islamic princes today. And if the administrative forms of Islam represented a synthesis of those of the Sasanian kingdom and Roman administration of the Eastern provinces, this too was deemed representative, even 'democratic', by the standards of the day (Springborg, 1987a). Continuities between the social forms instituted by the great Alexander, Seleucid successor states, and the Islamic kingdoms are greater than the discontinuities. And in understanding the hiatus between classical republics of antiquity and the Renaissance city-state, the Hellenistic kingdoms and their successors are significant interventions.

20

La Serenissima and the Sublime Porte

Modern theories of oriental despotism have served to obscure the nature of early modern European commentary on the Orient and specifically on the Ottoman Empire. For the years 1501–1550 over one thousand European publications on the Ottoman Empire have been counted, and for the second half of the sixteenth century, some 2,500 (Golner, 1961–8; Heywood, 1972; cited in Valensi, 1987, 73, 136, n.118). One of the richest archives of European commentary on Constantinople, the reports of Venetian ambassadors to the *Sublime Porte* have recently been the subject of an important study by the *Annales* historian, Lucette Valensi (1987). From 1453, the republic of Venice maintained a permanent embassy in Constantinople, interrupted only in time of war, re-established after the Battle of Lepanto, and lasting well into the seventeenth century (Valensi, 1987, 11).

The ambassadorship, carrying the title of *bailo*, represented the highest post to which patricians, who had entered on the Venetian *cursus honorum* with membership of the Great Council at the age of 25, could aspire (Valensi, 1987, 24). Many of them, members of the great merchant families, were graduates of the University of Padua, imbued with humanist values. Venice, Valensi (1987, 16) reminds us, was the home of the first Italian translation of Aristotle's *Politics*, undertaken by the Florentine, Antonio Brucioli, who was in exile there; a work made compulsory reading in the schools of Padua by a senate decree, a few years later. As we will have cause to note, the impact of Aristotle among the Venetians should not be minimized, and certainly not his analysis of the East, perhaps his most significant contribution in the *quattrocento* – not to neglect indigenous influences on the thought of the Venetian patrician class, either. Some ambassadors made collections of the political writings of humanists from other Italian states, for instance – one of which included Machiavelli (Valensi, 1987, 19).

Marcantonio Barbaro, appointed ambassador to the *Sublime Porte* in 1573, is a fine example of the type of *bailo*. Son of a patrician merchant family, with a doctorate from the University of Padua, he had a similarly distinguished brother, who published a critical edition of Vitruvius in 1556 and was connected to the architect Palladio (Valensi, 1987, 16). Another, Giambattista Dona, named ambassador in 1680, became fluent in Turkish, made a collection of sources on the flora and fauna, archaeology and literature of Constantinople, and on the completion of his tour of duty published a comprehensive work on the language and educational system, cultural climate and literature of the Ottoman Empire under the title, *Literature of the Turks* (Valensi, 1987, 17–18).

Our most important source, apart from the writings and reminiscences of the ambassadors, is the formal speech that each delivered to the senate at the completion of his tour of duty, required under the system of scrutiny and accountability of magistrates in this self-styled Platonic republic (whose institutions more closely resembled those of Plato's *Laws*). The occasion of spectacle and ritual in the public life of Venice, speeches of returning ambassadors, sometimes up to four hours long (Valensi, 1987, 19–20), undertook an analysis of the foreign power in question that was often circulated well beyond the confines of the Most Serene Republic. Copies of the texts of some of the most famous *bailo*'s speeches, including those of Marcantonio Barbaro and the speech on Suleyman the Magnificent of 1535 by Gasparo Contarini, author of the influential *De magistratibus et republica Venetorum* of 1520, which proclaimed Venice a Platonic Republic, serene by virtue of its peace and concord assured by rule of law, could be bought in Rome; and in 1616 the library of Oxford held several, including that of Barbaro (Valensi, 1987, 20–1). An indication of the demand for these works can be seen in the career of a particular collection of speeches and instructions of Venetian ambassadors with the title *Tresoro politico*, published successively in Bologna in 1595 and 1598, republished in Milan in 1600, in Bologna again in 1603, translated into Latin in Frankfurt in 1618, and published in several French editions, notably those of 1602 and 1611 (Valensi, 1987, 22). Valued not just as exemplary analyses of the political realities of their day (Valensi, 1987, 23), the Venetian ambassadorial instructions on the Sublime Porte opened a window onto the greatest empire of the age. And this is precisely the perspective of the long line of orations on the Ottomans, 39 between 1503 and the end of the seventeenth century, as opposed to '27 describing the pontifical court, 23 the court of France, and 18 the courts of the [Holy Roman] Empire and Spain' (Valensi, 1987, 24).

The tone of the ambassadors to *La Serenissima*, up to the break point of 1575 which we will discuss, is almost uniformly, and befittingly, superlative. The Ottoman Empire is characterized by greatness in the following aspects: by the greatness of its Lord and Master, '*Questo Gran-Signor e potentissimo*'; by the vastness of its lands, '*vastissimo impero dei Turchi*', encompassing 'all Asia Minor', 'all Greece', 'all the coast of Asia', 'all the shores of Africa up to the straits of Gibraltar', 'three quarters of the entire world', in fact, being dominated by 'the Grand Lord of Asia, Africa and Europe' (Valensi, 1987, 34). Beneath the superlatives one finds persistent themes of analysis, notable for their acuity and for the fact that they are re-echoed in the political writings of thinkers from Machiavelli to Bodin.

According to the ambassadors, the empire of the Turks is founded on three pillars: the magnitude of its receipts, the vastness of its manpower and the obedience of its citizens enjoined by religion (Valensi, 1987, 35). With the exception of one speech among the 39 between 1503 and 1600 – that of 1562 – all the others reported Ottoman receipts exceeding expenses, 'by 30% according to Pietro Zen in 1530, by more than 20% according to Erizzo in 1557, by 47% in the estimate of Babarigo in the following year, by 20% still in the reports of the

1570s' (Valensi, 1987, 36). The system of tax-farming, known as the *timar*, which in a later period attracts condemnation, in this period receives praise. The *timar* was a concession granted to a cavalier (*timariot*) to raise taxes in a given territory, on condition that a fixed return was made to the central government (Valensi, 1987, 132, n.39). Providing the cavalry with the means both to raise and provision troops, the *timar* eventually gave rise to a system of tax-farming similar to the Roman, also monopolized by the cavalry class, or *equites*, known in their tax-farming capacity as the notorious *publicani*. But these comparisons await the future. The considerable attention paid in the ambassadorial orations to the Turkish military at this point serves to emphasize the funds at its disposal through the tax-farming system and the vast manpower capable of being mobilized (Valensi, 1987, 36–7).

It is worth remembering that the Serene Republic, as a self-consciously Platonizing state, would have seen the Ottoman Empire through the same lens. Not without justice, we might add. In the early days of Islam, the *Falasifa*, who were also the transmitters of Plato and Aristotle to the West, conceived of the Islamic state on Platonist lines, one of the reasons for the initial refusal to allow janissaries to farm taxes, as we have pointed out, being Plato's remonstrations against guardians or auxilliaries owning property or undertaking commercial ventures. It was only in a later age that the tendency towards feudalization incipient in the *timar* system became apparent to foreign eyes.

Meanwhile the Platonic *unanimitas* induced by the architectonic Ottoman state, buttressed by the admirable discipline of its troops and a finely graduated military hierarchy, were sources of admiration to the Venetians, for whom order and harmony were governing values (Valensi, 1987, 38). Edifice metaphor, an idiom of great antiquity expressed in notions of *fondement* and *fundamentum*, and transferred in late sixteenth-century France to the structure of law (Condren 1989), is dominant in the characterization of the Ottoman state, suggesting that it was seen as 'law-governed', at least in the Platonic sense. Insistent that it was ' "not founded on force alone, whether that be power of numbers or the power of the court" ', the ambassadors saw the Ottoman Empire as 'an imposing structure whose architecture appeared to correspond to the canons of beauty as Palladio defined them' (Valensi, 1987, 41):

> Whether they were describing the seances of the Divan, the regular ceremonial of the court, the extraordinary ceremonies for the reception of an ambassador, or the institution of the harem, they saw the same logic at work, which achieved a perfect orchestration and a complete mobilization of energies in the service of the supreme power of the sultan. (Valensi, 1987, 41–2)

Needless to say these ambassadors were aware that at palaces (*seraglios*) in Adrinople, Constantinople, Pera and the personal residences of the Sultan – just to mention those which Navagero actually entered and described – the children of 'forty nations, from Russia to Spain, furnished children to the Great Turk', cause of Christian outcry everywhere (Valensi, 1987, 42). But when Navagero notes that the provision of Christian children to the Sultan's court has been the fruit of wars by land and sea, in what clearly furnished a white slave trade, he passes in silence over the scandal to Christians, focusing instead on the advantages of constant war, describing in detail the care and education lavished on the slave children, their daily routines and their preparation for public life. Navagero is representative, for as Valensi (1987, 71–2) well demonstrates:

> Up to the 1570s, the political and military institutions of the Ottoman Empire, and the men who served the sultan, generally inspired in the Venetians words expressing the ideas of order, beauty and perfection. The imperial edifice presented a rigorous and imposing structure. The abstract categories to which the Venetian ambassadors had recourse to designate the Turkish regime, are those of *governo, dominio, regno, imperio*, all neutral appellations, normally applicable to other European regimes with which la Serenissima maintained relations. At the same time, the titulary and the honorific qualifiers which accompanied mention of the sultan and his viziers – magnificent, most serene, etc. – belonged to the same family as those which are applied to the princes and grandees within the horizons of Christianity.

The appellations the Venetian ambassadors invoke in their accounts of the *governo, dominio, regno, imperio*, indicate a preoccupation with sovereignty and power, which is perhaps the only constant in the premodern political literature on the Orient. From Machiavelli to Bodin, one may say, the exploration of the range and limits of sovereignty, describes a field that can accommodate both monarchy and republicanism – or both, barely differentiated, as in the case of these two writers. Admiration for empire is admiration for sovereignty on the most extensive scale. When factionalism among citizens of a republic, or corruption in a monarchy, threaten sovereignty, then and only then is the legitimacy of the state in question. But at this point the Ottoman Empire is still a great empire, one of the four great empires of the world, according to some, and there is no question of its legitimacy. As Valensi has remarked, from Machiavelli to Bodin a certain anachronism in the portrayal of the Turks ruling in the lands of the ancient empires of the East – those of the Assyrians, the Medes and the Persians – is highly suggestive. Language which assimilates the rule of the sultans to that of Alexander the Great, the popularity of the Alexander romance, and other signs suggest the lens through which the Great Turk, not only in the Renaissance period, but up to Bodin, was viewed. By both Machiavelli and Bodin the Ottoman Empire was seen to be the legitimate successor to the Roman. Bodin, in *The Six Books of the Republic*, in a chapter entitled 'Refutation of the Theory of the Four Monarchies', actually scoffs at German pretensions, in the form of the Holy Roman Empire, to the claim, 'using in favour of the Turks, and in the same order, exactly the arguments used in the ambassadorial addresses: territorial power, abundance of resources, manpower and, lastly, the annexation of the great empires of the past' (Valensi, 1987, 82–3, citing Bodin, 1986 edn):

> In just what way would the German sovereign dare to compare himself with the sultan of the Turks? And who could have more rights under the title of monarchy than the latter? But why discuss evidence which is so conclusive in the judgement of everyone? If there ever existed anywhere an authority worthy of the name of empire or of authentic monarchy, it is certainly the sultan who holds it in his hands. He occupies all the richest countries in Asia, in Africa and in Europe, he extends his dominion around the entire Mediterranean, with the exception only of a few islands. His military might is sufficient to balance that of all the other princes: he

has pushed the troops of the Persians and Muscovites back far from his borders, he has conquered the Christian kingdoms and the Byzantine empire and is about to ravage the German provinces ... How much juster it would be to consider as heir to the Roman empire the sultan of the Turks, who after having taken Byzantium, capital of the Empire, from the Christians, went on to conquer from the Persians, the region of Babylon, of which Daniel rightly spoke, adding to the ancient provinces of Rome all the lands of the outer Danube up to the banks of the Boristhene, which constitutes today the greatest part of his territory.

The language of imperialism is everywhere to be seen in discussions of the Great Turk, not only by political theorists demonstrably devoted to the question of sovereignty, but also in comments of the Venetian ambassadors, who may well have been their source. 'Rome may be the epitome of the world', claimed one, 'but Constantinople is the world of all worlds' (cited in Valensi, 1987, 89–90). One, Agostino Nani, declared, 'it is more a world than a state'; another more ominously observed, 'the Turk has arrived at the gates of our Italy, garden of the world and centre of Christianity, and he aspires to universal monarchy' (cited in Valensi, 1987, 90). The Turkish empire had risen to power quickly on the three pillars of 'religion, parsimony and obedience', and its 'religious unity, virile frugality and warrior ardour' were specifically compared by the ambassadors to the foundations of Roman *virtus* (Valensi, 1987, 90–1).

Fascination with the power of the Ottoman Empire among her observers turned once again on the mystery of sovereignty and what type of regime, monarchy or republicanism, best achieves it. As Valensi (1987, 74–5) points out, it is very far from being the case that one can trace a straight line from Machiavelli and Bodin to Montesquieu and Marx in the evolution of a theory of oriental despotism. As she shows (Valensi, 1987, 79), neither Machiavelli nor Bodin lists the Ottoman Empire among tyrannical forms of regime. It is true that both consider the Turkish regime essentially different from European monarchy, and that in the analysis of each a concept of patrimonialism is latent; a concept developed, perhaps with the authority of Aristotle, in the theories of the Venetians also, after the turning point of 1575. Machiavelli's point in *The Prince* (cited in Valensi, 1987, 75) was to distinguish between rule of the Turk and rule of feudal European princes as constituting two types 'to which all the principalities known to history' conform: 'either by a prince to whom everyone is subservient and whose ministers, with his favour and permission, help govern, or by a prince and by nobles whose rank is established not by favour of the prince but by their ancient lineage' (*Prince*, 1961 edn, 44). Machiavelli points out that 'such nobles have states and subjects of their own, and these acknowledge them as lords and bear a natural affection towards them', whereas 'in states governed by a prince and his servants, the prince has greater authority' (*Prince*, 1961 edn, 44–5): 'Contemporary examples of these two different kinds of government are the Turk and the king of France.'

Now it is not at all clear that this comparison is prejudicial to the Ottomans. We know very well Machiavelli's antipathy to hereditary aristocracies. Moreoever the context of the analysis is highly significant: it is with regard to the question which forms the chapter title, 'Why the kingdom of Darius conquered by Alexander did not rebel against his successor after his death?' The answer is that 'if you will consider the kind of government which Darius administered, you will find that it resembled that of the Turk; so first of all Alexander had to crush him utterly and seize his country. Then, afer he had won that victory and Darius was dead, the state rested securely in Alexander's hands' (*Prince*, 1961 edn, 46). By contrast, feudal regimes, easy to conquer because of the opportunities for foment that feudal barons promise, are, for the same reason, never secure. Monarchies of the type of Alexander, which survived his death as kingdoms ruled by his companions – a point which Machiavelli expressly made – exercise a sovereignty that feudal monarchies because of their very decentralization cannot. It is only later that the rule of the prince's servants or companions – of the same type, we should note, as the Platonic and Islamic 'guardians' – become the hallmark of patrimonial regimes. At this point the rule of the prince and his servants conforms positively to the Platonic or Eastern type which attracts the admiration of Venetians, and even of less Platonizing Florentines.

What is the cause of the break, we may ask? In the Venetian case, as Valensi demonstrates, it is marked. From around 1575, four years after the Battle of Lepanto of 1571, in which the Venetians vanquished the Turks, all the former signs of Ottoman greatness are seen to be reversed. Religious unity, economic parsimony and fighting readiness are said to be in decline. Far from being a regime animated by a unanimity which binds the hierarchies together, the Grand Turk has become a ruler over slaves. Perhaps most revealing of all is the way in which the typology to which Machiavelli and Bodin both subsequently subscribe, of the rule of the prince and guardians versus the rule of king and feudal lords, is turned against the Turk. What in the eyes of the Venetian ambassadors characterizes the superiority of European Christian rule? It is precisely freedom, preserve of 'stable institutions founded on rule of law' and *a hereditary nobility* (Valensi, 1987, 94). What are the marks of inferiority of the Turk but precisely 'the extirpation of the nobility in all the conquered lands, the reduction of all the subjects to servitude, and consequently a levelling which abases the citizen body to the lowest degree' (Valensi, 1987, 94). Never mind that in the revisionist histories of the Ottoman Empire now being written, far from the absence of a hereditary nobility being the cause of the abasement of the people, it is now regarded as being the very ground for their freedom. Much lies in the failure of European observers to understand the land tenure system of the Ottoman Empire, which like the Byzantine (Ostrogorsky, 1969, 90, 134–7), and for that matter the Sasanian, Assyrian and Babylonian, rested upon a contract between the tenant farmer and the crown, construed in the willingness of the farmer to pay taxes. This *quid pro quo*, which gave the hundreds of thousands of Ottoman tenant farmers the usufruct of, if not the title to, Crown land, guaranteeing their loyalty, at the same time guaranteed revenues to the sultan, and ensured that no power base for an independent nobility could be created on the basis of vassalage (Keyder, 1987, ch. 1).

There is much to suggest the ideological nature of the 'break', of which Valensi gives her own phenomenology. Along with a good deal of carping by the ambassadors about the barbarity of the Turks, their lack of table manners, deficiencies of their architecture, their inaptitude in the sciences and the arts, their incapacity for speculative thought, the fact that they are 'vile, abject, ignoble, rustic, uncultured, barbarous, liars, proud, insolent, inhumane, faithless, untrue to their word', and the fact that their sorbets do not taste as good the Italians' (Valensi, 1987, 92–3) – and other reversals of opinion on the very attractions the Turks once offered – we have a developing line of analysis on the patrimonial regime and its shortcomings. Many of these may well be based in fact, but it is worth remembering that the Battle of Lepanto did not spell the end of Ottoman supremacy in the Mediterranean, and that Venice herself, exhausted by war, was in decline. Lepanto, 7 October, 1571, saw the Ottoman fleet decimated, three thousand of the enemy killed, another three thousand taken prisoner, and a victory celebrated which 'mobilized the Church and the people, poets and painters, composers and choirs', as Valensi (1987, 110–11) points out; but the balance of forces between the Christians and the Turks was not fundamentally changed. Once the treaty was concluded, Venice re-established normal relations with the Ottomans that lasted until the reign of Murad IV. And while the Christian fleet retreated from the Eastern Mediterranean allowing the Turks to re-establish control, the Ottoman fleet went on to attack Sicily and southern Italy in 1574, and in the same year to take Tunis (Lapidus, 1988, 315). Having consolidated power in North Africa, the Ottomans turned their attention to Persia and the Hapsburg Empire. Venice, on the other hand, entered a decline and finally, after 25 years of warring, between 1645 and 1669, with the Turks whose superior manpower and resources the ambassadors had never ceased extolling, lost Crete which it had held since the thirteenth century (Valensi, 1987, 111). The truce of 1580, signed by the Hapsburgs and Ottomans, established a frontier between Christian and Muslim civilizations that has endured, in fact, to the present (Lapidus, 1988, 315).

The Sublime Porte had suffered, too, from the high cost of incessant warfare. From its campaigns against the Persians it had gained territory in the Caucasus, Kurdistan and Azerbaidjan between 1578 and 1590, only to lose it in 1603–4 (Valensi, 1987, 102). Its long campaign against the Hapsburgs from 1593 to 1606 had won for the sultan the suzereignty of principalities on the Danube, but at the cost of much loss of life and 'corruption of the administration from top to bottom' (Valensi, 1987, 102). Once again comparisons with the decline of the Roman Empire were apt. Much of the idiom in which Ottoman decline was expressed was sexual, invoking the feminine principle by which the Near East had been characterized from antiquity (Springborg, 1990d), and would continue to be in even greater volume in the early modern period, reaching a crescendo with Gibbon, Flaubert and Renan (Said, 1978; Grosrichard, 1979). Among the ambassadors much emphasis was laid on 'the sultanate of women' or the power of women behind the throne (Valensi, 1987, 102); on the withdrawal of the sultans into the harem; and their cruelty directed at male members of the household who would challenge their power in the palaces. But, from Aristotle on, characterizations of tyranny have always included a component of outrageous sexual appetite, depravity and corruption, whose truth or falsity has rarely been documented empirically.

The declining power of the Ottomans was based in fact on the hard realities of feudalization – precisely the causes of the decline of the Roman Empire. The sultanate was no longer able to control the insolent janissaries, who converted the *timar* from the basis of state revenues which they had the concession to farm into personal fiefdoms which they exploited for their own gains (Valensi, 1987, 1030) – precisely the strategy of the *equites*, or *publicani* of Rome, and with similar results. Worldwide inflation with the Spanish price rise of the sixteenth century, and the depopulation of the countryside caused by aggrandizing feudal barons, caused a rapid swelling of the urban proletariat ready for revolt. But the exigencies of inflation and a central administration dependent for revenues on fixed rents, often not delivered, deprived the state of economic stimulus which might have allowed it to fight its way out of the impasse. Its solution, like that of the janissaries, was increasing extortion, cruelty and a regime based on violence. The much-extolled and frequently honoured ancient precepts concerning the 'circle of power': 'no sovereignty without an army, no army without wealth, no wealth without subjects, no loyal subjects without a just society, no justice without social harmony, no harmony without the state, no state without law and no maintaining law without sovereign authority' (Valensi, 1987, 105) was allowed to lapse. It is interesting not only that Machiavelli and Bodin did not refer to the Ottoman Empire as a tyranny, but that when Francis Bacon, who is singular for having done so, defined the term, what made it so was the absence of a landed nobility. In *The Essayes or Counsels, Civill and Morall*, written between 1597 and 1625, he declared: 'A Monarchy, where there is no Nobility at all, is ever a pure and absolute Tyranny; As that of the Turkes' (Bacon, 1985 edn, 41, cited in Valensi, 1987, 142). Technically, we should note, this is a version of the ancient definition of tyranny: the prince who comes to rule by party rather than heredity, since parties refer to rule by the *popolo*, as opposed to the old social order. But, as we have shown, this protest, also made by the Venetian ambassadors, was barely true of the Ottoman system by the time of Bacon's writing. The feudalization of the *timar* created the real possibility of the development of an hereditary nobility. Valensi raises the question whether these developments are not proof that the system was not after all hermetically sealed in its hierarchies and functions, and might not after all admit the janissaries to participation in the economic life of towns (Valensi, 1987, 104) as the European nobility did. But the military solution to political problems – for instance, the violence with which the Ottomans put down the simmering revolt in Anatolia, which threatened Istanbul itself, before being finally crushed in 1608 – arrested these possibilities (Valensi, 1987, 104–5).

Islamic mirrors and treatises on the 'virtuous city' had always emphasized rule of law, both the *sharia* and secular legislation introduced by the sultanate, *kanun*. Contemporary writers made dire predictions about the consequences of departure from rule of law as the only stable basis of political institutions; among them the historian Mustafa 'Ali (1541–1600) and Kinalizade 'Ali Celebi (d.1572). The latter attributed to Suleyman the Magnificent the creation of the *medina i fazili*, the Platonist's law-based 'city of virtue'; while the former articulated a version of the cycle of regimes, marked by expansion, decline and fall, with serious implications for Islamic history (Valensi, 1987, 106). Tyranny was on the minds of Turkish commentators too. A poet in 1608 dreamt up a conversation between Alexander the Great and Ahmed I, the latter whom he adjudged to be a 'worse tyrant than even the pharaoh' – an interesting reflection on Egypt, a traditional enemy – because 'God's word is no longer respected, the cadis are corrupt, the *timars* are given to royal favourites, women and minors rule behind the scenes, the janissaries are in revolt, all the functaries of the state are perverted and tyrannical' (Valensi, 1987, 107). Suddenly, the categories of Aristotle seem to have been mobilized by both the Venetian ambassadors and by contemporary political theorists to give an account of the Ottomans as patrimonial rulers; an account at first technical and non-perjorative, but increasingly prejudicial as the career of the term *despotic* would suggest. Valensi (1987, 142, n.183) points out that Koebner (1951), in his excellent essay on the vicissitudes of this term, credits Thomas Hobbes with being the first among the Europeans to apply the Greek word with Aristotle's meaning; a claim that ignores the fact that in Italy the term was widely used much earlier, and among the Venetian ambassadors themselves. Put into circulation by William of Moerbeke's translation of Aristotle's *Politics*, the terms *despoticus, despotica, despoticum*, were used by Thomas Aquinas, Marsilius of Padua and William of Occam in the thirteenth century, and in the fourteenth introduced into the Italian vernacular by the Dominican Giordano, who wrote of '*il quale dispoticamente governava*' (Valensi, 1987, 117). Nicolas Oresme, in his French critical edition of Aristotle, included the term in his glossary: '*Despotie est princey ou seigneruie sur serfz*' (Koebner, 1951, 281–2; Valensi, 1987, 117–18, 142, n.180). Interestingly, Oresme qualified his definition with the proviso that 'if they were justly serfs the prince was just, but if they were placed in servitude by violence or fraud, then is the prince despotic, oligarchic, tyrannical or the like' (cited in Valensi, 1987, 118).

More typically, however, 'despotic government', where it was used at all, was given a value-neutral definition. This would accord with general Latin practice, where the term was replaced by *dominus* – and here I disagree with Valensi (1987, 118) that it was due to a repugnance for the Greek word; rather it had to do with considerations of sovereignty. The Italian humanists had delayed the entry of 'despotism' into the political lexicon, preferring to translate Aristotle's terms with *dominus, dominatio*, abjuring *despoticum, despotica*, while the French preferred to speak of '*monarchie seigneuriale*', '*empire seigneuriale*' (Valensi, 1987, 118). So Loys Le Roy, in his new translation of Aristotle's *Politics*, commented on the latter's notion of despotic rule as being 'like that of the barbarian kingdoms, which even when they are legitimate and hereditary, nevertheless rule a seigneurial empire, like that of the Turks … [and] Muscovites' (cited in Valensi, 1987, 118). Le Roy's translation of Aristotle retranslated into English yielded '*maisterlike sway*' in the rendering of 'empire seigneurial'; Knolles translated Bodin's '*monarchie seigneuriale*' as 'lordly monarchy'. Indeed it was not until Hobbes's *Elements of Law* and *Leviathan*, written between 1640 and 1651, that government 'despotic' and 'despoticall' was said to have made its début, referring to the power of a master over a servant, which characterizes government based on conquest as opposed to one based on indigenous institutions (Valensi, 1989, 118–19). It is ironic that Hobbes, for whom Aristotle is publicly much despised, should be held responsible for this innovation. But, as Valensi shows, the claim ignores the Italian writings of the time. Giovanni Botero, in his *Raison d'État* of 1583 – which shows him to be author of the concept later credited to Machiavelli – his *Relationi universali* of 1591, and his life's work, the *Discorso della legua contro il Turco* of 1614, while defending monarchy as the form of government closest to the celestial model, and therefore the most perfect, claim that at the hands of the Turk it is 'in fact despotic' (Valensi, 1987, 120–1). When Botero's work is translated into French, however, the term 'despotic' is once again avoided, and the 'absolute' government of the Great Turk, as that of a master over his slaves, is neither *'governo despotico'* nor *'dominio cosi assoluto'*, but *'cette seigneurie absolue'*, proof, as Valensi (1987, 121) suggests, that the term despotism was not yet assimilated in France at the end of the seventeenth century.

Why? My suggestion is that this reflects a positive rather than a negative disposition toward absolute power, consistent with the exploration of sovereignty that we find in fact in the works of Hobbes, Bodin and their contemporaries. Humanists who avoided the term up to their time may have done so less out of ignorance of its usage by Aquinas and Marsilius, than out of the wish to explore the wider parameters of power that *dominus* connoted. They might also have wished to avoid the negative connotations of the term in Aristotle. Hobbes and Bodin were simply bold enough in their approbation of absolute power not to care. Was the situation in Italy very different? The answer is yes, I think, after 1575; not because of the victory of Lepanto, but because of losses in the Eastern Mediterranean and other Ottoman gains. Why not before 1575? Because it did not fit. Aristotle had used the term despotic government with specific reference to the Asiatic powers. As long as Venetians perceived the Ottoman Empire to be a Platonist law-governed entity, whose military guardians and auxiliaries scrupulously served their functions, there was no Asiatic power on the horizon which fit the description. But once violence became manifest as a foundation of rule and corruption widespread, the 'virtuous city' became a 'despotism' consistent with Aristotle's description.

When it comes to the condemnation of tyranny as such, the Venetian ambassadors were not averse to accusing the Florentines as readily as the Turk, and more than rhetoric underlay the denunciation. Florentines were charged outright by the Venetian ambassadors with 'incarnating tyranny' (Valensi, 1987, 114), and what they meant was that Florentine rule was the rule of men rather than the rule of law, 'government by the will of one man, secret government, where each spied on his neighbours and citizens were debased, deprived of their freedom' (Valensi, 1987, 114). The oration of ambassador Vicenso Fedeli of 1561 accused the Florentine prince of enslaving his subjects, while that of Priuli in 1566 charged him with being a tyrant over three republics, and one to whom the name liberty was anathema (Valensi, 1987, 114). The Medici dynasty was referred to by Contarini in 1588, in the same language as that by which the Turks had been accused: they accorded favours to their partisans but ruled the rest by terror; they had sided with the people to destroy the nobility; the free city of Florence had been subjugated (Valensi, 1987, 114–15).

Nor were the Florentines, the old enemy of Venice, the only European tyranny. The privilege was shared by the English, who suffered after James I, the ambassador Nicolo Molin declared, from 'the tyrannical origins of government ... the king being an absolute master in all things, even though he was assisted by a council' (cited in Valensi, 1987, 115). The ambassador Giovanni Sagredo, in turn described the rule of Cromwell in terms usually reserved for the Turk: 'he took power by force and holds the people in servitude. He is feared more than he is loved and lives surrounded by suspicion' (Valensi, 1987, 115); language repeated several times by ambassadors who commented on the fall of Charles I and the rule of Cromwell, his successor.

There was, moreover, a hidden agenda in the identification of absolute monarchy, under whose umbrella the Turkish despotism fell. As Valensi points out, the consistent depiction of the Great Turk ruling in the lands of the ancient empires was not merely antiquarian rhetoric. Millennarians interpreting the book of Daniel according to the theory of the Four Monarchies had a purpose in projecting the Ottoman Empire as true successor to the Roman. The rise of universal monarchy, and its ultimate demise, was to herald the Second Coming and the Last Judgement. Thus in 1573, the ambassador Marcantonio Barbaro wrote (cited in Valensi, 1987, 67):

> Serene Prince and excellent lords, since, by the grace of God, the Ottoman emperor in the course of continued victories, has taken over so many provinces and subdued so many realms, and by this fact is rendered formidable to the entire world, it is not unreasonable to ask ourselves if he has not finally achieved universal monarchy.

The Battle of Lepanto was a sign marking the beginning of the end for the Ottoman Empire, a great and legitimate empire soon to dissolve into tyranny and decline. Such a view fitted well with chiliastic predictions. The question of universal monarchy was one that was asked over and over in the next decades, and almost always in connection with the Great Turk.

Conclusion

The story of Western republicanism and the myth of the oriental prince, which tells the deep origins of orientalism and anti-Semitism, has turned on five basic categories: race, property, oligarchy, aetiology and economy. An early distinction between Greeks and barbarians coincided with justification of slavery as fitting for Asiatics (Semites), freedom for the Greeks. Slaves, as living tools, property of their masters, forfeited their rights to life and liberty precisely because they lacked property in themselves; an argument, first recorded in Aristotle, but famously repeated by Locke. The particular condition of slavery was deemed to stem from a general lack of entitlement in property systems where oriental subjects were already seen as slaves of the Great King, members of his household, rather than citizens of a state, because they owned no property in land. In other words, the Greeks, and later the Romans, in enslaving barbarians merely treated them as they were accustomed to being treated – or so they said. It has been my purpose to show that this argument, to the degree that it made any serious truth claims, rested on a confusion between ownership and usufruct as bases of entitlement.

It is the greatest of ironies that property, among the liberties on which the 'freedom of the Greeks' was said to depend, should have been the jealously guarded right of ruling oligarchies within Graeco-Roman systems. Freedom for the many was defined politically, for the ruling few it was defined politically and economically. Thus freedom of speech, freedom to debate in the assembly, negative freedoms, early became definitive, while economic freedoms were narrowly circumscribed. The turn from participatory to representative democracy did not await the nineteenth century; it had already been made in the second century BC; and this precisely was what 'the freedom of the Greeks' was deemed by the Romans to constitute: a system of rule by a hegemonic oligarchy, with representative councils at the municipal level. To see how neatly the political freedom of subjects matched their economic unfreedom in the ancient world, we have only to examine the system of patronage, beneficence or *euergetism*, whereby the right to rule accrued to those willing and able to foot the cost of public works from private means. In the writings of Aristotle, Polybius, the Roman Stoics, some less famous precursors and successors, scarcely veiled oligarchy is the ruling principle, as it was in the world in which they lived.

Michel Foucault, in *The History of Sexuality* (1982, 1986), has pointed out that, were the problem of hunger to have received the same degree of attention that the control of sexuality has received from the Greeks through to the Christian era, our moral universe would look very different. But one could answer that indeed the problem of hunger was treated similarly. If manuals on approved sexual practices seem to have a more trivial counterpart in the books of etiquette concerning the proper way to eat – a claim with which Norbert Elias (1978) perhaps would not agree – the complex legal structures and moral strictures by means of which sexual access was confined to allow patriarchal families to constitute the building blocks of the state have a striking parallel in the practices and institutions, public and private – *euergetism* among them – through which the ruling class was filtered. Basic human strivings to satisfy the needs for food, shelter, a female and sleep, as Rousseau was so nicely to put it in the *Second Discourse* (1913 edn, 163), are, among other things, levers of power. They have always faced the labyrinth of cultural, structural, political and moral constraints which more or less guarantee that their satisfaction takes a *human* form.

My attempts to expose the specifics of some of these constraints is not, however, a protestation, which Foucault's sometimes seem to be, that a simpler and less culturally and politically mediated private life in its alimentary, sexual and psychic aspects is possible, any more than one could hope to claim that a more unmediated public life, in its social, economic, political, religious and cultic aspects were possible – something absurd on the face of it. Nor would I wish to claim that the historically rooted, formal and informal, institutions and practices by means of which cultural and political discrimination is made possible are thereby immune from moral scrutiny. It is a sign, if not of moral progress, then at least of moral sensibility, that human beings are able to engage in behaviour modification on the basis of moral reflection. In this respect, in at least one area of our conduct we have shown increasing sensitivity, if not perhaps the actual results that one would wish, and that is attentiveness to racial discrimination. The great volume of recent literature on the origins of the American slave trade, if still tending to treat slaves as objects of European enslavement and European emancipation, neglecting their role as active subjects, especially in the latter (Blackburn, 1988), is some testimony to this. It is my purpose to show, in fact, that racial stereotypes, especially in that form of racial discrimination among the least understood and most horrendous of our century, anti-Semitism, go back as far as recorded history. Moreover, as others (Astour, 1976a; Bernal, 1987a) have pointed out, they have involved a tissue of distortions as elaborately crafted, as embroidered with myth and romance, and as overlaid with legal sanctions, as the fabric from which the control of sexuality is cut.

Racial superiority, as basis for political mastery, faced some rather unpalatable facts in Greek myths of origin, for instance. Frequent allusions in Homer and a literal reading of Hesiod, would suggest, in fact, that Greece had been colonized from the Semitic–Hamitic East, by Cadmus the Phoenician and Danaus the Egyptian, subjects of much earlier epic and dramatic works. How to account for these culturally unaccountable facts? A vigorous historical tradition saw case and countercase mounted by the mythographers and logographers debating the question of aetiology, among whom Herodotus is merely the most famous. Relics of the story of Graeco-oriental synoecism are to be found as late as Plato, whose *Timaeus* and *Critias* tell the tale the Egyptian priest told to Solon about the origins of Greek civilization, battles between the barbarians and the Giants – stories of gods and heroes, floods and fires, that are still being told as late as Diodorus and Polybius himself, although in approved didactic form.

It is a further irony that when emergent modern Western European states faced the problem of legitimation in turn, they should have adopted the Graeco-Roman mode. Not only did Renaissance city-states and their successors claim legitimacy as rightful heirs to the Athenian and Roman *poleis*, but they did so in the context of their own versions of the battle of the Giants, predicated once again on the East/West divide. This time it was the conquest of the Northern Europeans over the barbarian Muslim hordes. Once again, 'freedom of the Greeks', to which the Northern Europeans now fell heir, was the differentiating axiom. But two things have been noted. First, how late, in fact, the threat of the East was preceived in Renaissance Italian eyes – postdating the Battle of Lepanto of 1571, in fact. And, secondly, how differently 'freedom of the Greeks' was now construed. A real shift can be seen between Machiavelli, for instance, and Polybius, in many respects his model, on the subject of economic freedom. For Machiavelli the prospect of wider popular participation in economic freedoms gave to the expansionist state the dynamism and prospect of progress that the ancient stationary state, based on oligarchy, lacked. The secret to empire was republican rule based on moderation and the middle classes: the politics of balance. Moreover, Machiavelli, as to a certain extent Polybius, was capable of an impartial assessment of the Eastern systems, which in fact intrigued him. Between East and West the lines were once again more fluid, yet to be sedimented when realities of Ottoman power and the impact of Protestant Reformation thought coincided in the positive identification of Turk and Antichrist; part of my story as yet untold.

Bibliography

Aalders, G.J.D. 1950. The Political Faith of Democritus. *Mnemosyne*, ser. 4, vol. 3: 302–13.

El-Abbadi, M.A.H. 1962. The Alexandrian Citizenship. *Journal of Egyptian Archaeology*, 48: 106–23.

Abdel-Malek, Anouar. 1981a. *Civilisation and Social Theory*. London: Macmillan.

Abdel-Malek, Anouar. 1981b. *Social Dialectics*. London: Macmillan.

Abu-Lughod, Lila. 1986. *Veiled Sentiments: Honour and Poetry in Bedouin Society*. Berkeley, CA: University of California Press.

Ackroyd, Peter R. 1983. Goddesses, Women and Jezebel. In Averil Cameron and Amélie Kuhrt, eds. *Images of Women in Antiquity*. London: Croom Helm, 245–59.

Adams, R. MacC. 1981. *Heartland of Cities*. Chicago: University of Chicago Press.

Adams, R. MacC., ed. 1960. *City Invincible: a Symposium*. Chicago: University of Chicago Press.

Adcock, Frank E. 1946. Delenda est Carthago. *Cambridge Historical Journal*, 8: 117–28.

Adcock, Frank E. 1953. Greek and Macedonian Kingship. *British Academy Proceedings*, 39, 1: 163–80.

Adcock, Frank E. 1964. *Roman Political Ideas and Practice*. Ann Arbor, Michigan: Michigan University Press.

Adkins, Arthur W.H. 1960. *Merit and Responsibility*. Oxford: Clarendon Press.

Adkins, Arthur W.H. 1963. 'Friendship' and 'Self-sufficiency' in Homer and Aristotle. *Classical Quarterly*, n.s. 13, 1: 30–45.

Allen Jr, Walter. 1944. Cicero's House and *Libertas*. *American Philological Association Proceedings*, 75: 1–9.

Allison, J. 1979. Thucydides and *Polypragmosyne*. *American Journal of Ancient History*, 4: 10–22.

Anawati, Georges C. 1974. Philosophy, Theology and Mysticism. In Joseph Schacht and C.E. Bosworth, eds. *The Legacy of Islam*. 2nd edn. Oxford: Clarendon Press.

Anderson, Andrew R. 1932. *Alexander's Gate, Gog and Magog and the Enclosed Nations*. Cambridge, Mass.: Mediaeval Academy of America.

Anderson, Perry. 1974a. *Passages from Antiquity to Feudalism*. London: NLB.

Anderson, Perry. 1974b. *Lineages of the Absolutist State*. London: NLB.

Andrewes, Anthony. 1956. *The Greek Tyrants*. London: Hutchinson.

Andrewes, Anthony. 1961a. Philochoros on Phratries. *Journal of Hellenic Studies*, 81: 1–15.

Andrewes, Anthony. 1961b. Phratries in Homer. *Hermes*, 89: 129–40.

Anglo, Sydney. 1969. *Machiavelli: a Dissection*. London: Paladin.

Anthes, Rudolf. 1954. Note Concerning the Great Corporation of Heliopolis. *Journal of Near Eastern Studies*, 13: 191–2.

Anthes, Rudolf. 1961. Mythology in Ancient Egypt. In Samuel N. Kramer, ed. *Mythologies of the Ancient World*. New York: Doubleday: 15–92.

Apollodorus (of Athens). 1975 edn. *The Library of Greek Mythology*. Keith Aldrich, trans. and ed. Lawrence, Kansas: Coronado Press.

Apuleius of Madauros. 1975 edn. *Metamorphoses, Book 11, The Isis Book*. J. Gwyn Griffiths, trans., notes and commentary. Leiden: Brill.

Arbeitman, Y. and Rendsburg, G. 1981. Adana Revisited: 30 Years Later. *Archiv Orientalni*, 49: 145–57.

Archer, Leonie J. 1983. The Role of Jewish Women in the Religion, Ritual and Cult of Graeco-Roman Palestine. In Averil Cameron and Amélie Kuhrt, eds. *Images of Women in Antiquity*. London: Croom Helm, 273–87.

Aristotle. 1932 edn. *The Politics*. H. Rackham, trans. Loeb edn. London: Heinemann.

Aristotle. 1941 edn. *The Poetics*. Ingram Bywater, trans. In *The Basic Works of Aristotle*. Richard McKeon, ed. New York: Random House: 1455–87.

Aristotle. 1956 edn. *The Nicomachean Ethics*. H. Rackham, trans. Loeb edn. London: Heinemann.

Aristotle 1955 edn. *De Mundo and On Sophistical Refutations*. E.S. Forster trans. D.J. Furley, ed. Cambridge, Mass.: Harvard University Press.

Aristotle. 1976 edn. *The Ethics of Aristotle: the Nicomachean Ethics*. J.A.K. Thomson, trans. Revised with Notes and Appendices by Hugh Tredennick and Jonathan Barnes. Harmondsworth: Penguin.

Aristotle. 1981 edn. *The Politics*. T.A. Sinclair and Trevor J. Saunders, trans. Harmondsworth: Penguin.

Aristotle. 1984 edn. *The Athenian Constitution*. P.J. Rhodes, trans. Harmondsworth: Penguin.

Arnold, E. Vernon. 1911. *Roman Stoicism*. Cambridge: Cambridge University Press.

Arthur, Marylin B. 1973. Early Greece: the Origins of the Western Attitude toward Women. *Arethusa*, 6, 1: 7–58.

Arthur, Marylin B. 1977. Politics and Pomegranates: an Interpretation of the Homeric Hymn to Demeter. *Arethusa*, 10: 7–47.

Arthur, Marylin B. 1982. Cultural Strategies in Hesiod's *Theogony*: Law, Family, Society. *Arethusa*, 15: 63–82.

Arthur, Marylin B. 1983. The Dream of a World without Women: Poetics and Circles of Order in the *Theogony* Prooemium. *Arethusa*, 16, 1–2: 97–116.

Astin, A.E. 1956. Scipio Aemilianus and Cato Censorius. *Latomus*, 15: 159–80.

Astour, Michael. 1964. Semitic Names in the Greek World and Greek Names in the Semitic World. *Journal of Near Eastern Studies*, 23: 193–201.

Astour, Michael. 1967a. *Hellenosemitica: an Ethnic and Cultural Study on West Semitic Impact on Mycenaean Greece*. Leiden: Brill.

Astour, Michael. 1967b. The Problem of Semitic in Ancient Crete. *Journal of the American Oriental Society*, 87: 290–5.

Attar, Samar. 1989. Female Sexuality and the 'Civilizing Mission': the Boxwoman and Shaharazad. Unpublished paper, Australian Middle East Studies Association Conference, 23 September 1989.

Augustine, Saint, 1957 edn. *The City of God Against the Pagans*. 7 vols. George E. McCracken, trans. Loeb edn. London: Heinemann.

Austin, Michel M. and Vidal–Naquet, Pierre. 1977. *Economic and Social History of Ancient Greece*. Berkeley, CA: University of California Press.

Al-Azmeh, Aziz. 1981. *Ibn Khaldun in Modern Scholarship: a Study in Orientalism*. London: Third World Centre for Research and Publishing.

Bacon, Francis. 1985 edn. *The Essayes or Counsels, Civill and Morall* (1597–1625). M. Kiernan, ed. Oxford: Oxford University Press.

Bacon, Helen. 1961. *Barbarians in Greek Tragedy*. New Haven, Conn.: Yale University Press.

Badian, Ernst. 1968. *Roman Imperialism in the Late Republic*. Oxford: Blackwell.

Badian, Ernst. 1972. Tiberius Gracchus and the Beginnings of the Roman Revolution. In Hildegard Temporini, ed. *Aufsteig und Niedergang der Römischen Welt*. Berlin: De Gruyter: 268–731.

Badian, Ernst. 1981. The Deification of Alexander the Great. In *Ancient Macedonian Studies in Honor of Charles F. Edson*. Thessaloniki: Institute for Balkan Studies: 27–71.

Badian, Ernst. 1982. Eurydice. In W. Lindsay Adams and Eugene N. Borza, eds. *Phillip II, Alexander the Great, and the Macedonian Heritage*. Washington, DC: University of America: 99–110.

Badian, Ernst. 1984. *Foreign Clientelae*. 2nd edn. Oxford: Oxford University Press.

Baer, Gabriel. 1960. *Studies in the Social History of Modern Egypt*. Chicago: University of Chicago Press.

Baer, Gabriel. 1964. *Population and Society in the Arab East*. New York: Praeger.

Baille, M.G.L. and Munro, M.A.R. 1988. Irish Tree Rings, Santorini and Volcanic Dust Veils. *Nature*, 332: 334–6.

Baillet, Jules. 1912, 1913. *Le Régime Pharaonique dans ses Rapports avec l'Évolution de la Morale en Égypte*. 2 vols. Paris: Blois.

Baldry, H.C. 1965. *The Unity of Mankind in Greek Thought*. Cambridge: Cambridge University Press.

Balsdon, J.P.V. 1950. The 'Divinity' of Alexander. *Historia*, 1: 363–88.

Barb, Alphonse A. 1952. Bois du Sang, Tantale. *Syria*, 29: 271–84.

Barb, Alphonse A. 1953. Diva Matrix. *Journal of the Warburg and Courtauld Institutes*, 16: 193–238.

Barber, E.A. 1923. Alexandrian Literature. In J.B. Bury et al., eds. *The Hellenistic Age: Aspects of Hellenistic Civilization*. New York: Norton (1970 reprint): 31–78.

Barker, Ernest. 1947. *The Political Thought of Plato and Aristotle*. Oxford: Clarendon Press.

Barker, Ernest. 1957. *Social and Political Thought in Byzantium*. Oxford: Oxford University Press.

Barker, Ernest. 1966. *The Development of Public Services in Western Europe*. Hamden, Conn.: Archon Books.

Baron, Hans. 1938a. Cicero and the Roman Civic Spirit in the Middle Ages and Early Renaissance. *Bulletin of the John Rylands Library*, 22: 72–97.

Baron, Hans. 1938b. Franciscan Poverty and Civic Wealth as Factors in the Rise of Humanism. *Speculum*, 13: 1–37.

Baron, Hans. 1955. *Humanistic and Political Literature in Florence and Venice at the Beginning of the Quattrocento*. Cambridge, Mass.: Harvard University Press.

Baron, Hans. 1960. The Social Background of Political Liberty in the Early Italian Renaissance. *Comparative Studies in Society and History*, 2: 440–51.

Baron, Hans. 1961. Machiavelli: the Republican Citizen and Author of 'The Prince'. *English Historical Review*, 76: 217–53.

Baron, Hans. 1966. *The Crisis of the Early Italian Renaissance*. 2nd edn. Princeton, NJ: Princeton University Press.

Barthold, V.V. 1963. Khalif i Sultan. N.S. Doniach, trans. In *Islamic Quarterly*, 7: 117–35.

Bassett, S., ed. 1989. *The Origins of Anglo-Saxon Kingdoms*. Leicester: Leicester University Press.

Batatu, Hannah. 1978. *The Old Social Classes and the Revolutionary Movements of Iraq*. Princeton, NJ: Princeton University Press.

Bayley, C.C. 1942. Petrarch, Charles IV and the *Renovatio Imperii*. *Speculum*, 17: 323–41.

Bayley, C.C. 1961. *War and Society in Renaissance Florence: the 'De Militia' of Leonardo Bruni*. Toronto: University of Toronto Press: 178–240.

Becker, Marvin B. 1960a. The Republican City State in Florence: an Inquiry into its Origin and Survival (1280–1434). *Speculum*, 35: 39–50.

Becker, Marvin B. 1960b. Some Aspects of Oligarchical, Dictatorial and Popular Signorie in Florence, 1282–1382. *Comparative Studies in Society and History*, 2: 421–39.

Becker, Marvin B. 1962a. Florentine *Libertas*: Political Independents and *Novi Cives*, 1372–1378. *Traditio*, 18: 393–407.

Becker, Marvin B. 1962b. Florentine Popular Government (1343–1382). *Proceedings of the American Philosophical Society*, 106: 360–82.

Becker, Marvin B. 1966. Economic Change and the Emerging Florentine Territorial State. *Studies in the Renaissance*, 13: 7–39.

Becker, Marvin B. 1967, 1968. *Florence in Transition*. 2 vols. *Studies in the Rise of the Territorial State*. Baltimore, MD: Johns Hopkins Press.

Bell, H. Idris. 1953. *Cults and Creeds in Graeco-Roman Egypt*. Liverpool: University of Liverpool Press.

Bell, Lanny. 1985a. Luxor Temple and the Cult of the Royal *Ka*. *Journal of Near Eastern Studies*, 44, 4: 251–94.

Bell, Lanny. 1985b Aspects of the Cult of the Deified Tutankhamen. In *Me'langes Gamal Eddin Mokhtar*. Cairo: Institut Français d'Archéologie Orientale: 31–61.

Bendix, Reinhard. 1968. *Nation-Building and Citizenship*. Berkeley, CA: University of California Press.

Bendix, Reinhard. 1978. *Kings or People*. Berkeley, CA: University of California Press.

Bérard, Jean. 1952. Les Hyksos et la Légende d'Io. *Syria*, 29: 1–43.

Bérard, Jean. 1957. De la Légende Grecque à la Bible: Phaéton et les Sept Vaches Maigres. *Revue de l'Histoire des Religions*, 151: 221–28.

Bérard, Victor. 1927. *Les Phénices et l'Odyssée*. 2nd edn. 2 vols. Paris: Bibliothèque des Écoles Françaises d'Athènes et de Rome.

Bergren, Ann L.T. 1982. Sacred Apostrophe: Re-Presentation and Imitation in the Homeric Hymns. *Arethusa*, 15: 83–108.

Bergren, Ann L.T. 1983. Language and the Female in Early Greek Thought. *Arethusa*, 16: 97–116.

Berman, Lawrence V. 1961. The Political Interpretation of the Maxim: the Purpose of Philosophy is the Imitation of God. *Studia Islamica*, 15: 53–61.

Bermant, Chaim and Weitzman, Michael. 1979. *Ebla*. London: Weidenfeld and Nicolson.

Bernal, Martin. 1985a. Black Athena: the African and Levantine Roots of Greece. In *African Presence in Early Europe. Journal of African Civilizations*, 7, 5: 66–82.

Bernal, Martin. 1985b. Sign, Symbol, Script: an Exhibition of the Origins of Writing and the Alphabet. *Journal of the American Oriental Society*, 105, 4: 736–7.

Bernal, Martin. 1986. Black Athena Denied: the Tyranny of Germany over Greece. *Comparative Criticism*, 8: 3–69.

Bernal, Martin. 1987a. *Black Athena: the Afro-Asiatic Roots of Classical Civilization*. London: Free Association Books.

Bernal, Martin. 1987b. First Land then Sea: Thoughts about the Social Formation of the Mediterranean and Greece. In E. Genovese and L. Hochberg, eds. *Geography in Historical Perspective*. Oxford: Blackwell.

Bernard, J. 1987. *The Female World from a Global Perspective*. Bloomington, Ind.: Indiana University Press.

Bernardi, Aurelio. 1970. The Economic Problems of the Roman Empire at the Time of its Decline. In Carlo Cipolla, ed. *The Economic Decline of Empires*. London: Methuen: 16–83.

Besold, Christopher. 1626. *De magistate in genere*. Frankfurt.

Betancourt, P.P. 1985. *The History of Minoan Pottery.* Princeton, NJ: Princeton University Press.
Betancourt, P.P. 1987. Dating the Aegean Late Bronze Age with Radiocarbon. *Archaeometry*, 29: 45–9.
Betancourt, P.P. and Michael, H.B. 1987. Dating the Aegean Late Bronze Age with Radiocarbon: Addendum. *Archaeometry*, 29: 212–13.
Betancourt, P.P. and Weinstein, G.A. 1976. Carbon-14 and the Beginning of the Late Bronze Age in the Aegean. *American Journal of Archaeology*, 80: 329–48.
Bevan, Edwyn. 1923. Hellenistic Popular Culture. In J.B. Bury et al., eds. *The Hellenistic Age, Aspects of Hellenistic Civilization.* New York: Norton (1970 reprint): 79–107.
Bietak, Manfred. 1979a. Avaris and Piramese: Archaeological Exploration in the Eastern Nile Delta. *British Academy Proceedings*, 65: 225–90.
Bietak, Manfred. 1979b. Urban Archaeology and the 'Town' Problem. In Kent R. Weeks, ed. *Egyptology and the Social Sciences.* Cairo: American University in Cairo Press.
Bietak, Manfred. 1984. Problems of Middle Bronze Age Chronology: New Evidence from Egypt. *American Journal of Archaeology*, 88: 471–85.
Bill, James and Springborg, Robert. 1990. *Politics of the Middle East.* 3rd edn. New York: Little Brown/Scott Foresman.
Binder, Leonard. 1955. Al-Ghazali's Theory of Islamic Government. *The Muslim World*, 45: 229–41.
Black, Anthony. 1984. *Guilds and Civil Society in European Political Thought from the Twelfth Century to the Present.* Ithaca, NY: Cornell University Press.
Blackburn, Robin. 1988. *The Overthrow of Colonial Slavery 1776–1848.* London: Verso.
Blackman, Aylward M. 1918a. Sacramental Ideas and Usages. *Proceedings of the Society of Biblical Archaeology*, 40, 3: 57–91.
Blackman, Aylward M. 1918b. Some Notes on the Ancient Egyptian Practice of Washing the Dead. *Journal of Egyptian Archaeology*, 5: 117–24.
Blackman, Aylward M. 1918c. The House of the Morning. *Journal of Egyptian Archaeology*, 5: 148–65.
Blackman, Aylward M. 1921. On the Position of Women in the Ancient Egyptian Hierarchy. *Journal of Egyptian Archaeology*, 7: 8–30.
Bleeker, C.J. 1973. *Hathor and Thoth. Two Key Figures of the Ancient Egyptian Religion.* Leiden: Brill.
Bloch, Marc. 1961. *Feudal Society.* 2 vols. Chicago: University of Chicago Press.
Blochet, E. 1935, 1936. De l'Autonomie de l'Évolution de la Philosophie Grecque. *Muséon*, 1935: 323–64; 1936: 115–38.
Bloom, Allan. 1987. *The Closing of the American Mind.* New York: Simon and Schuster.
Bloomfield, Morton. 1957. Joachim of Flora. A Critical Study of his Canon, Teachings, Sources, Biography and Influence. *Traditio*, 13: 249–311.
Boas, George. 1950. *The Hieroglyphics of Horapollo.* New York: Bollingen Series 23.
Bodin, Jean. 1941 edn. *La Méthode de l'Histoire.* Pierre Mesnard, ed. Paris: Presses Universitaires de France.
Bodin, Jean. 1955 edn. *Six Books of the Commonwealth.* M.J. Tooley, ed. Oxford: Blackwell.
Bodin, Jean. 1975 edn. *Colloquium of the Seven about the Secrets of the Sublime.* M.L.D. Kuntz, ed. Princeton, NJ: Princeton University Press.
Bodin, Jean. 1986 edn. *Les Six Livres de la République.* 6 vols. Paris: Fayard.
Boesche, Roger. 1987. The Politics of Pretence: Tacitus and the Political Theory of Despotism. *History of Political Thought*, 8, 2: 189–210.
Bond, A. and Sparks, R.S.J. 1976. The Minoan Eruption of Santorini, Greece. *Journal of the Geological Society of London.* 132: 1–16.

Born, Lester Kruger. 1965. *Erasmus: Education of a Christian Prince*. New York: Octogon Books.
Bourriot, Felix. 1976. *Recherches sur la Nature du Génos: Étude d'Histoire Sociale Athénienne – Périodes Archaïque et Classique*. Lille: Université Lille III, Librarie Honoré Champion.
Bouwsma, William. 1968. *Venice and the Defence of Republican Liberty*. Berkeley, CA: University of California Press.
Bouzek, J. 1985. *The Aegean, Anatolia and Europe: Cultural Interrelations in the Second Millennium B.C.* Studies in Mediterranean Archaeology 29. Göteburg: Paul Aström Förlag.
Bowman, Alan K. 1971. *The Town Councils of Roman Egypt*. Toronto: A.M. Hakkert.
Bowski, W. 1900. *The Finances of the Commune of Siena 1284–1355*. Oxford: Oxford University Press.
Bradbrook, M.C. 1936. *The School of Night. A Study of the Literary Relationships of Sir Walter Raleigh*. Cambridge: Cambridge University Press.
Brady, T.A. 1970. Busiris. *Oxford Classical Dictionary*. 2nd edn. Oxford: Oxford Universiy Press: 185.
Braudel, Fernand. 1972. *The Mediterranean and the Mediterranean World in the Age of Philip II*. 2 vols. New York: Harper and Row.
Braudel, Fernand. 1973. *Capitalism and Material Life, 1400–1800*. London: Weidenfeld and Nicolson.
Braudel, Fernand. 1977. *Afterthoughts on Material Civilization and Capitalism*. Patricia Ranum, trans. Baltimore, MD: Johns Hopkins University Press.
Braudel, Fernand. 1980. *On History*. Chicago: University of Chicago Press.
Braudel, Fernand. 1981. *The Structures of Everyday Life: the Limits of the Possible*. London: Collins.
Braudel, Fernand. 1983. *The Wheels of Commerce: Civilization and Capitalism*. New York: Harper and Row.
Braudel, Fernand. 1984. *Perspective of the World*. London: Collins.
Braund, David C. 1984. *Rome and the Friendly King: the Character of Client Kingship*. London: Croom Helm.
Breasted, James H. 1906. *Ancient Records of Egypt, Historical Documents*. 4 vols. Chicago: University of Chicago Press.
Breasted, James H. 1912. *Development of Religion and Thought in Ancient Egypt*. New York: Scribner.
Bremmer, Jan, ed. 1987. *Interpretations of Greek Mythology*. London: Croom Helm.
Brink, C.O. and Walbank, F.W. 1954. The Construction of the Sixth Book of Polybius. *Classical Quarterly*, n.s. 4: 97–122.
Brown, Alison. 1979. *Bartolomeo Scala, 1430–1497, Chancellor of Florence. The Humanist as Bureaucrat*. Princeton, NJ: Princeton University Press.
Brown, Alison. 1986. Platonism in Fifteenth Century Florence and its Contribution to Early Modern Political Thought. *Journal of Modern History*, 58: 383–413.
Brown, Blanche R. 1981. Novelty, Ingenuity, Self-aggrandizement, Ostentation, Extravagance, Gigantism and Kitsch in the Art of Alexander the Great and his Successors. In M. Barasch et al., eds. *Art, the Ape of Nature: Studies in Honor of H.W. Janson*. Englewood Cliffs, NJ: Prentice Hall.
Brown, Peter. 1967. *Augustine of Hippo*. London: Faber and Faber.
Brown, Peter. 1971. *The World of Late Antiquity: from Marcus Aurelius to Muhammad*. London: Thames and Hudson.
Brown, Peter. 1978. *The Making of Late Antiquity*. Cambridge, Mass.: Harvard University Press.

Brown, Peter. 1981. *The Cult of the Saints.* Chicago: University of Chicago Press.
Brown, Peter. 1982. *Society and the Holy in Late Antiquity.* Berkeley, CA: University of California Press.
Brown, Truesdell S. 1962. The Greek Sense of Time in History as Suggested by their Accounts of Egypt. *Historia,* 11, 3: 257–70.
Browning, Robert. 1964. Byzantine Scholarship. *Past and Present,* 28: 3–22.
Browning, Robert. 1975. Enlightenment and Repression in Byzantium in the Eleventh and Twelfth Centuries. *Past and Present,* 69: 3–23.
Brucker, Gene. 1977. *The Civic World of Early Renaissance Florence.* Princeton, NJ: Princeton University Press.
Brundage, Burr C. 1958. Herakles the Levantine: a Comprehensive View. *Journal of Near Eastern Studies,* 17, 4: 225–36.
Bruni, Leonardo. 1968. *Laudatio Florentinae Urbis.* In H. Baron. ed. *From Petrarch to Leonardo Bruni.* Chicago: University of Chicago Press: 217–63.
Brunner, Helmut. 1964. *Die Geburt des Gottkönigs.* Wiesbaden: Ägyptologische Abhandlungen 10.
Brunner, Helmut. 1977. *Die Südliche Räume des Tempels von Luxor.* AV 18. Mainz am Rhein: Philip von Zabern.
Brunt, Peter A. 1962. The Army and the Land in the Roman Revolution. *Journal of Roman Studies,* 52: 69–86.
Brunt, Peter A. 1965. 'Amicitia' in the Late Republic. *Cambridge Philological Society Proceedings,* n.s. 11: 1–20.
Brunt, Peter A. 1966. The Roman Mob. *Past and Present,* 35: 3–27.
Brunt, Peter A. 1971. *Social Conflicts in the Roman Republic.* New York: W.W. Norton.
Brunt, Peter A. 1973. Aspects of the Thought of Dio Chrysostom and of the Stoics. *Cambridge Philological Society Proceedings,* n.s. 19: 9–34.
Burkert, Walter, 1985. *Greek Religion.* Cambridge, Mass.: Harvard University Press.
Burkert, Walter. 1987. *Ancient Mystery Cults.* Cambridge, Mass.: Harvard University Press.
Burn, Andrew R. 1930. *Philistines and Greeks.* London: Kegan Paul, Tench, Trubne and Co.
Burn, Andrew R. 1973. *Alexander the Great and the Middle East.* 2nd edn. Harmondsworth: Penguin.
Burrow, John Wyon. 1966. *Evolution and Society. A Study in Victorian Social Theory.* Cambridge: Cambridge University Press.
Burrow, John Wyon. 1985. *Gibbon.* Oxford: Oxford University Press.
Bury, J.B. 1923. The Hellenistic Age and the History of Civilization. In J.B. Bury et al., eds. *The Hellenistic Age, Aspects of Hellenistic Civilization.* New York: Norton (1970 reprint): 1–30.
Butzer, Karl W. 1976. *Early Hydraulic Egypt: a Study in Cultural Ecology.* Chicago: University of Chicago Press.
Cadogan, G. 1987. Unsteady Date of a Big Bang. *Nature:* 328: 473.
Cahen, Claude. 1958–9. Mouvements Populaires et Autonomisme Urbain dans l'Asie Musulmane du Môyen Age. *Arabica,* 5, 3: 225–50; 6, 1: 25–56; 6, 3: 223–65.
Cahen, Claude. 1970. Y a-t-ileu des Corporations Professionelles dans le Monde Musulman Classique? In A. Hourani and S.M. Stern, eds. *The Islamic City.* Oxford: Oxford University Press.
Calhoun, George M. 1913. *Athenian Clubs in Politics and Litigation.* New York: Burt Franklin.
Callisthenes (Pseudo). 1969 edn. *The Romance of Alexander the Great.* Albert Mugrdich Wolohojian, trans. New York: Columbia University Press.

Campbell, Blair. 1986. Constitutionalism, Rights and Religion: the Athenian Example. *History of Political Thought*, 7: 239–73.

Campbell, Lewis. 1867. *The Sophists and Politicus of Plato*. Oxford: Oxford University Press. (New York: Arno Reprint, 1973.)

Cantarella, E. 1987. *Pandora's Daughters*. Baltimore, MD: Johns Hopkins University Press.

Carney, T.F. 1973. Prosopography: Payoffs and Pitfalls. *Phoenix*, 27: 156–79.

Carpenter, Rhys. 1965. *Discontinuity in Greek History*. Cambridge: Cambridge University Press.

Cary, George. 1956. *The Medieval Alexander*. Cambridge: Cambridge University Press.

Ceffi, F. 1942 edn. *Dicerie*. G. Giannardi, ed. In *Studi di Filologia Italiana*, 6: 27–63.

Cerfaux, L. and Tondriau, J.L. 1957. *Un Concurrent de Christianisme: Le Culte des Souverains dans la Civilisation Gre'co-Romaine*. Paris [Tournai]: Desclée Series: Bibliotheque de Théologie, ser. 3, vol. 5.

Cerny, Jeroslav. 1954. Consanguineous Marriages in Pharaonic Egypt. *Journal of Egyptian Archaeology*, 40: 23–9.

Chabod, Federico. 1958. Y a-t-il un État de la Renaissance? *Actes du Colloque sur la Renaissance*: 64–72.

Chabod, Federico. 1960. *Machiavelli and the Renaissance*. David Moore, trans. Cambridge, Mass.: Harvard University Press.

Chadwick, Henry. 1947. Origen, Celsus and the Stoa. *Journal of Theological Studies*, 48: 34–49.

Charlesworth, M.P. 1937. The Virtues of the Roman Emperor: Propaganda and the Creation of Belief. *British Academy Proceedings*, 23: 105–33.

Chastel, André, et al., eds. 1982. *The Renaissance: Essays in Interpretation*. London: Methuen.

Chew, Samuel C. 1937. *The Crescent and the Rose: Islam and England during the Renaissance*. Oxford: Oxford University Press.

Chrimes, S.B. 1936. *English Constitutional Ideas in the Fifteenth Century*. Cambridge: Cambridge University Press.

Cicero. 1913 edn. *De officiis*. Walter Miller, trans. Loeb edn. London: Heinemann.

Cicero. 1923 edn. *De amicitia*. W.A. Falconer, trans. Loeb edn. London: Heinemann.

Cicero. 1928 edn. *De re publica*. C.W. Keyes, trans. Loeb edn. London: Heinemann.

Cicero. 1931 edn. *De finibus bonorum et malorum*. H. Rackham, trans. Loeb edn. London: Heinemann.

Clarke, M.L. 1968. *The Roman Mind. Studies in the History of Thought from Cicero to Marcus Aurelius*. New York: W.W. Norton.

Cohn, Norman R.C. 1970. *The Pursuit of the Millennium*. Oxford: Oxford University Press.

Coldstream, J.N. and Huxley, G.L. 1984. The Minoans of Kythera. In R. Hägg and N. Marinatos, eds. *The Minoan Thalassocracy*: Myth and Reality. Stockholm: Paul Aström Förlag: 107–10.

Cole, Thomas. 1964. The Sources and Camposition of Polybius VI. *Historia*, 13: 440–86.

Cole, Thomas. 1967. *Democritus and the Sources of Greek Anthropology*. (American Philological Association Monograph 25). Western Reserve University Press.

Coleman, Janet. 1983. Medieval Discussions of Property: *Ratio* and *Dominium* according to John of Paris and Marsiglio of Padua. *History of Political Thought*, 4: 209–28.

Coleman, Janet. 1985. *Dominium* in Thirteenth and Fourteenth Century Political Thought and its Seventeenth Century Heirs: John of Paris and Locke. *Political Studies*, 33: 73–100.

Coles, J.M. and Harding, A.F. 1979. *The Bronze Age in Europe: an Introduction to the Prehistory of Europe c.2000–700 BC.* London: Methuen.

Comfort, William Wistar. 1940. The Literary Role of the Saracens in the French Epic. *Proceedings of the Modern Language Association,* 55: 628–59.

Condren, Conal. 1984. Rhetoric, Historiography and Political Theory: Some Aspects of the Poverty Controversy Reconsidered. *Journal of Religious History,* 13, 1: 15–34.

Condren, Conal. 1985. *The Status and Appraisal of Classical Texts.* Princeton, NJ: Princeton University Press.

Condren, Conal. 1989. Metaphor and Reification: Episodes in the Conceptualization of Power. Unpublished paper delivered to the History of Ideas Seminar, Department of Philosophy, University of Sydney.

Connor, Walter Robert. 1970. Theseus in Classical Athens. In A.G. Ward, W.R. Connor et al., eds. *The Quest for Theseus.* New York: Praeger: 243–74.

Connor, Walter Robert. 1971. *The New Politicians of Fifth-century Athens.* Princeton, NJ: Princeton University Press.

Cook, Alfred S. 1980. *Myth and Language.* Bloomington, Ind.: Indiana University Press.

Cook, M.A. 1974. Economic Developments. In Joseph Schacht, ed. *The Legacy of Islam.* 2nd edn. Oxford: Clarendon Press.

Cook, M.A., ed. 1976. *A History of the Ottoman Empire to 1730.* Cambridge: Cambridge University Press.

Corbin, Henry. 1967. Ghazali, Abu Hamid Muhammad. *Encyclopedia of Philosophy.* London: Collier Macmillan: 3.326–8.

Cornford, Francis. 1950. A Ritual Basis for Hesiod's *Theogony.* In F. Cornford, *The Unwritten Philosophy and Other Essays.* Cambridge: Cambridge University Press: 45–116.

Cornford, Francis. 1975. *Plato's Cosmogony.* Indianapolis: Bobbs Merrill.

Costello, D.P. 1938. Notes on the Athenian *Gene. Journal of Hellenic Studies,* 57: 171–9.

Crick, Bernard. 1974. *Machiavelli's Discourses* (with Introduction and Notes). Harmondsworth: Penguin.

Cumont, Franz. 1956. *The Oriental Religions in Roman Paganism.* New York: Dover.

Curtius Rufus, Quintus. 1971 edn. *The Actes of the Greate Alexander.* Amsterdam: Theatrum Orbis Terrarum (English facsimile edn. of 1553 trans. of *Historia Alexandri Magni*).

Dack, E. van't, et al., eds. 1983 *Egypt and the Hellenistic World. Studia Hellenistica.* Leuven: Lovanii.

Dagger, Richard. 1981. Metropolis, Memory and Citizenship. *American Journal of Political Science,* 25, 4: 715–37.

Damascius (the Syrian). 1959 edn. *Lectures on the Philebus Text.* Trans. and notes by L.G. Westerink. Amsterdam: North-Holland Publishing Co.

Daniel, Norman. 1960. *Islam and the West. The Making of an Image.* Edinburgh: University of Edinburgh Press.

Danker, Frederick, W. 1977. *Benefactor: Epigraphic Study of a Graeco-Roman and New Testament Field.* St Louis, Mo.: Clayton Publishing.

Daube, David. 1943–4. Review of P.W. Duff: *Personality in Roman Law* (Cambridge: Cambridge University Press, 1938). *Journal of Roman Studies,* 33: 86–93; 34: 125–35.

Davies, John K. 1977–8. Athenian Citizenship: the Descent Group and its Alternatives. *Classical Journal,* 73, 2: 105–21.

Davies, John K. 1981. *Wealth and the Power of Wealth in Classical Athens.* New York: Arno.

Davis, Charles T. 1967. Brunetto Latini and Dante. *Studi Medievali,* 8: 421–50.

Davis, Natalie Zemon. 1975. *Society and Culture in Early Modern France.* Stanford, CA: Stanford University Press.

Delatte, Armand. 1915. *Études sur la Littérature Pythagoricienne*. Paris: É. Champion.
Delatte, Armand. 1922. *Essai sur la Politique Pythagoricienne*. Paris: É. Champion. (Liège: Bibliothèque de la Faculté de Philosophie et Lettres de l'Université de Liège. Fascicule 29.)
Delatte, Louis. 1942. *Les Traités de la Royauté d'Ecphante, Diotogène et Sthénidas*. Paris: E. Droz (Liège: Bibliothèque de la Faculté de Philosophie et Letters de l'Universite de Liège.)
Demett, J.D. 1965. Gemisthus Plethon, the Essenes and More's Utopia. *Bibliotèque d'Humanisme et Renaissance*, 27: 579–606.
Derchain, P. 1962. L'Authenticité de l'Inspiration Égyptienne dans le 'Corpus Hermeticum'. *Revue de l'Histoire des Religions*, 161: 175–98.
Detienne, Marcel. 1977. *The Gardens of Adonis. Spices in Greek Mythology*. Janet Lloyd, trans. Highlands, NJ: Humanities Press.
Diakonoff, Igor M. 1956. Main Features of the Economy in the Monarchies of Ancient Western Asia. Third International Conference of Economic History, Munich. Paris: Mouton.
Diakonoff. Igor M. 1974. *Structure of Society and State in Early Dynastic Sumer*. Los Angeles: Undena.
Dietz, Mary G. 1986. Trapping the Prince: Machiavelli and the Politics of Deception. *American Political Science Review*, 80, 3: 777–99.
Dietz, Mary G. 1987. Context is All: Feminism and Theories of Citizenship. *Daedalus*, 116, 4: 1–24.
Diodorus Siculus. 1933 edn. *Library of History*. 10 vols. C.H. Oldfather, trans. Loeb edn. London: Heinemann.
Diop, Chiek Anta. 1977. *Parente Genetique de l'Égyptien Pharaonique et des Langues Negro-Africaines: Processus de Semitisation*. Ifan-Dakar: Les Nouvelles Éditions Africaines.
Djait, Hichem. 1985. *Europe and Islam*. Peter Heinegg, trans. Berkeley, CA: University of California Press.
Dod, Bernard C. 1982. Aristoteles Latinus. In Norman Kretzmann et al., eds. *The Cambridge History of Later Medieval Philosophy*. Cambridge: Cambridge University Press: 45–79.
Dodd, Charles Harold. 1935. *The Bible and the Greeks*. London: Hodder and Stoughton.
Dodds, E.R. 1951. *The Greeks and the Irrational*. Berkeley, CA: University of California Press.
Dodds, E.R. 1965. *Pagan and Christian in an Age of Anxiety*. New York: W.W. Norton.
Donelan, James. 1989. The Argument from Noise: Review of *Black Athena: The Afroasiatic Roots of Classical Civilization*. Vol. 1: *The Fabrication of Ancient Greece, 1785–1985*. *Critical Texts*, 6, 3: 98–108.
Doresse, Marianne. 1971, 1973, 1979. Le Dieu Violé dans sa Châsse et la Fête du Début de la Décade. *Revue d'Égyptologie*, 23: 113–36; 25: 92–135; 31: 36–65.
Dossa, Shiraz, 1987. Political Philosophy and Orientalism: the Classical Origins of a Discourse. *Alternatives*, 15: 343–57.
Douglas, A.E. 1968. *Cicero*. Oxford: Clarendon Press.
Doumas, C. 1974. The Minoan Eruption of the Santorini Volcano. *Antiquity*, 48: 110–15.
Doumas, C., ed. 1978. *Thera and the Aegean World I*. London: Thera and the Aegean World.
Doumas, C., ed. 1980. *Thera and the Aegean World II*. London: Thera and the Aegean World.
Doumas, C. 1983. *Thera: Pompeii of the Aegean*. London: Thames and Hudson.
Dover, Kenley J. 1974. *Greek Popular Morality*. Berkeley, CA: University of California Press.

Driver, Godfrey Rolles and Miles, John C., eds. 1935. *The Assyrian Laws*. Oxford: Clarendon Press.
Driver, Godfrey Rolles and Miles, John C., eds. 1952–5. *The Babylonian Laws*. 2 vols. Oxford: Clarendon Press.
Drucker, Peter F. 1979. The First Technological Revolution and its Lessons. In John G. Burke and Marshall C. Eakin, eds. *Technology and Change*. San Francisco, CA: Boyd and Fraser: 39–46.
Dubler, C.E. 1957. Suivances de l'Ancien Orient dans l'Islam. *Studia Islamica*, 7: 47–75.
Duff, P.W. 1938. *Personality in Roman Law*. Cambridge: Cambridge University Press.
Dugas, L. 1894. *L'Amité Antique d'après les Moeurs Populaires: les Théories des Philosophes*. Paris: Félix Alcan.
Dunbabin, Jean. 1982. The Reception and Interpretation of Aristotle's *Politics*. In Norman Kretzmann et al., eds. *The Cambridge History of Later Medieval Philosophy*. Cambridge: Cambridge University Press: 723–37.
Dunleavy, P. and O'Leary, B. 1987. *Theories of the State. The Politics of Liberal Democracy*. London: Macmillan.
Dussaud, René. 1946–8. L'Origine de l'Alphabet et son Évolution Première d'après les Découvertes de Byblos. *Syria*, 25: 36–52.
Earl, Donald. 1967. *The Moral and Political Tradition of Rome*. Ithaca, NY: Cornell University Press.
Edelstein, Ludwig. 1936. The Philosophical System of Posidonius. *American Journal of Philology*, 57: 286–325.
Edelstein, Ludwig and Kidd, I. 1972. *Posidonius I: the Fragments*. Cambridge: Cambridge University Press.
Edmunds, Lowell. 1985. *Oedipus: the Ancient Legend and its Later Analogues*. Baltimore, MD: Johns Hopkins University Press.
Edwards, Ruth B. 1979. *Kadmos the Phoenician: a Study in Greek Legends and the Mycenaean Age*. Amsterdam: A.M. Hakkert.
Ehrenberg, Victor, 1938. *Alexander and the Greeks*. Oxford: Blackwell.
Ehrenberg, Victor, 1947. *Polypramosyne*: a Study in Greek Politics. *Journal of Hellenic Studies*, 67: 46–67.
Ehrenberg, Victor. 1950. The Origins of Democracy. *Historia*, 1, 4: 515–48.
Ehrenberg, Victor. 1954. *Sophocles and Pericles*. Oxford: Oxford University Press.
Ehrenberg, Victor, 1960. *The Greek State*. New York: W.W. Norton.
Elderkin, George Wicker. 1924. *Kantharos: Studies in Dionysiac and Kindred Cults*. Princeton, NJ: Princeton University Press.
Eliade, Mircea. 1975. *Myth and Reality*. Willard R. Trask, trans. New York: Harper and Row.
Elias, Norbert. 1978, 1982. *The Civilizing Process*. 2 vols. *The History of Manners*, vol. 1. *Power and Civility*, vol. 2. New York: Pantheon.
Emerton, Ephraim. 1964 edn. *Humanism and Tyranny. Studies in the Italian Trecento*. Gloucester, Mass.: Peter Smith (reprint of the 1925 Harvard University Press edn.).
Eneyat, Hamid. 1982. *Modern Islamic Political Thought*. Austin, Texas: University of Texas Press.
Engels, Donald W. 1978. *Alexander the Great and the Logistics of the Macedonian Army*. Berkeley, CA: University of California Press.
Engnell, Ivan. 1967. *Studies in Divine Kingship in the Ancient Near East*. Oxford: Blackwell.
Enuma Elish. The Babylonian Epic of Creation, Restored from the Recently Recovered Tablets of Assur. 1923 edn. S. Langdon, trans. Oxford: Clarendon Press.
Epicorum Graecorum Fragmenta. 1988 edn. Malcolm Davies, ed. Göttingen: Vandenhoeck and Ruprecht.

Ermatinger, C.J. 1954. Averroism in Early Fourteenth Century Bologna. *Medieval Studies*, 16: 36–56.

Faba, G. 1889 edn. *Parlamenti ed Epistole*. In A. Gaudenzi, ed. *I suoni, le forme e le parole dell' odierno dialetto della citta di Bolonga*. Turin: E. Loescher.

Faba, G. 1971a. *Dictamina Rhetorica*. A. Gaudenzi, ed. In *Il propugnatore*, 1892–3. Reprinted in G. Vecchi, ed. Bologna: Medium Aevum Monographs, n.s.

Faba, G. 1971b. *Epistole*. A. Gaudenzi, ed. In *Il propugnatore*, 1892–3. Reprinted in G. Vecchi, ed. Bologna: Medium Aevum Monographs, n.s.

Farrar, Cynthia. 1988. *The Origins of Democratic Thinking*. Cambridge: Cambridge University Press.

Ferreti, Ferreto de'. 1908–20 edn. *Opere*. C. Cipolla, ed. Rome.

Ferguson, William Scott. 1910. The Athenian Phratries. *Classical Philology*, 5, 3: 257–84.

Ferguson, William Scott. 1912. Legalized Absolutism en Route from Greece to Rome. *American Historical Review*, 18: 29–47.

Ferguson, William Scott. 1932. *Athenian Tribal Cycles in the Hellenistic Age*. Cambridge, Mass.: Harvard University Press.

Ferguson, William Scott. 1936. The Athenian Law Code and the Old Attic Trittys. In *Classical Studies Presented to E. Capps*. Princeton, NJ: Princeton University Press.

Ferguson, William Scott. 1938. The Salaminioi of Heptaphylai and Sounion. *Hesperia*, 1: 1–74.

Ferguson, William Scott. 1944. The Attic Orgeones. *Harvard Theological Review*, 37, 2: 61–140.

Festugière, A.-J. 1946–50. *Corpus Hermeticum*. 4 vols. Paris: Les Belles Lettres.

Ficino, Marsilio. 1944 edn. *Questiones de Luce et Asie Multe Marsilii*. In Paul Oskar Kristeller, 'The Scholastic Background of Marsilio Ficino'. *Traditio*, 2: 257–318. Reprinted in P.O. Kristeller, *Studies in Renaissance Thought and Letters*. Rome: Edizione di Storia e Letteratura, 1969: 67–97.

Figgis, F.N. 1934. *The Divine Right of Kings*. 2nd edn. Cambridge: Cambridge University Press.

Fink, Zera Silver. 1945. *The Classical Republicans: an Essay in the Recovery of a Seventeenth Century Pattern of Ideas*. Evanston, Ill.: Northwestern University Press.

Finley, Moses I. 1952. *Studies in Land and Credit in Ancient Athens*. New Brunswick, NJ: Rutgers University Press.

Finley, Moses I. 1954. *The World of Odysseus*. Harmondsworth: Penguin.

Finley, Moses I. 1955. Marriage, Sale and Gift in the Homeric World. *Revue Internationale des Droits de l'Antiquité*. 3rd series, 2: 167–94.

Finley, Moses I., ed. 1960. *Slavery in Classical Antiquity*. Cambridge: Cambridge University Press.

Finley, Moses I. 1970a. Aristotle and Economic Analysis. *Past and Present*, 47: 3–25.

Finley, Moses I. 1970b. Manpower and the Fall of Rome. In Carlo Cippola, ed. *The Economic Decline of Empires*. London: Methuen: 84–91.

Finley, Moses I. 1973a. *The Ancient Economy*. Berkeley, CA: University of California Press.

Finley, Moses I. 1973b. *Democracy Ancient and Modern*. New Brunswick, NJ: Rutgers University Press.

Finley, Moses I. 1974. Myth, Memory and History. The Ancestral Constitution. In M. Finley, *The Use and Abuse of History*. New York: Viking Press.

Finley, Moses I. 1980. *Ancient Slavery and Modern Ideology*. London: Chatto and Windus.

Finley, Moses I. 1981. *Economy and Society in Ancient Greece*. London: Chatto and Windus.

Finley, Moses I. 1983. *Politics in the Ancient World.* Cambridge: Cambridge University Press.

Fisher, N.R.E. 1979. Review of Felix Bourriot, *Recherches sur la nature du genos. Journal of Hellenic Studies,* 99: 193–5.

Fisher, N.R.E. 1981. Review of *Tribu et Cité* by Denis Roussel. *Journal of Hellenic Studies,* 101: 189–90.

Flanagan, Thomas. 1972. The Concept of *Fortuna* in Machiavelli. In A. Parel, ed. *The Political Calculus.* Toronto: Toronto University Press: 127–56.

Fleischer, Cornell. 1984. Royal Authority, Dynastic Cyclism and 'Ibn Khaldunism' in Sixteenth Century Ottoman Letters. *Journal of Asian and African Studies,* 18: 218–37.

Fleisher, Martin, ed. 1972. *Machiavelli and the Nature of Political Thought.* New York: Atheneum.

Foley, Helene P. 1981. The Concept of Women in Athenian Drama. In Helene P. Foley, ed. *Reflections of Women in Antiquity.* London: Gordon and Breach: 127–68.

Fontenrose, Joseph E. 1959. *Python: a Study of Delphic Myth and its Origins.* Berkeley, CA: University of California Press.

Fontenrose, Joseph E. 1970. Cecrops. *Oxford Classical Dictionary.* 2nd edn. Oxford: Oxford University Press: 218.

Fontenrose, Joseph E. 1971. *The Ritual Theory of Myth.* Berkeley, CA: University of California Press.

Forrest, William G. 1960. The Tribal Organisation of Chios. *The Annual of the British School at Athens,* 55: 172–89.

Forsyth, Phyllis Young. 1980. *Atlantis: the Making of Myth.* London: Croom Helm.

Fortenbaugh, W.W. 1977. Aristotle on Slaves and Women. In Jonathan Barnes et al., eds. *Articles on Aristotle.* London: Duckworth: 135–9.

Foucault, Michel. 1980, 1986. *The History of Sexuality.* Volume 1, *An Introduction.* Volume 2, *The Pursuit of Pleasure.* New York: Vintage.

Fowden, Garth. 1977. The Platonist Philosopher and his Circle in Late Antiquity. *Philosophia,* 7: 359–83.

Fowden, Garth. 1981. Late Antique Paganism Reasoned and Revealed. *Journal of Roman Studies,* 71: 178–82.

Fowden, Garth. 1982. The Pagan Holy Man in Late Antique Society. *Journal of Hellenic Studies,* 102: 33–59.

Fowden, Garth. 1986. *The Egyptian Hermes.* Cambridge: Cambridge University Press.

Fragmenta Graecorum et Romanorum.

Fragmenta Historicorum Graecorum. 1841–70. C. Muller, ed.

Fragmente der Griechischen Historiker. 1923–58. F. Jacoby, ed. Berlin.

Franceschi, D. 1966 edn. Oculus pastoralis. *Memorie del'accademia delle scienze di Torino,* 11: 3–70.

Frankfort, Henri. 1933. *The Cenotaph of Seti I at Abydos.* London: Egypt Exploration Society.

Frankfort, Henri. 1934. Gods and Myths on Sargonid Seals. *Iraq,* 1: 2–29.

Frankfort, Henri. 1944. A Note on the Lady of Birth. *Journal of Near Eastern Studies,* 3: 198–200.

Frankfort, Henri. 1948. *Kingship and the Gods.* Chicago: University of Chicago Press.

Franklin, Julian H. 1963. *Jean Bodin and the Sixteenth-Century Revolution in the Methodology of Law and History.* New York: Columbia University Press.

Frati, C. 1913. 'Flore de parlare' o 'Somma d'arengare' attribuita a Ser Giovanni Fiorentino da Vignano'. *Giornale storico della letteratura italiana,* 61: 1–31; 228–65.

Friedrich, Paul. 1978. *The Meaning of Aphrodite.* Chicago: University of Chicago Press.

Fritz, Kurt von. 1954. *The Theory of the Mixed Constitution in Antiquity: a Critical Analysis of Polybius' Political Ideas.* New York: Columbia University Press.

Froidefond, C. 1971. *Le Mirage Égyptien dans la Littérature Grecque d'Homère à Aristote.* Aix-en Provence: Université de Lettres et Sciences.

Frost, K.T. 1913. The *Critias* and Minoan Crete. *Journal of Hellenic Studies*, 33: 189–206.

Fustel de Coulanges, N.D. 1873 edn. *The Ancient City, a Study on the Religion, Laws and Institutions of Greece and Rome.* Willard Small, trans. New York: Dover (reprint).

Gabrieli, Francesco. 1974. Islam in the Mediterranean World. In Joseph Schacht and C.E. Bosworth, eds. *The Legacy of Islam.* 2nd edn. Oxford: Clarendon Press: 63–103.

Gardiner, Sir Alan H. 1947. *Ancient Egyptian Onomastica.* 3 vols. Oxford: Oxford University Press.

Gardner, Jane F. 1986. *Women in Roman Law and Society.* Bloomington: Indiana University Press.

Garin, Eugenio. 1965. *Italian Humanism: Philosophy and Civic Life in the Renaissance.* Peter Munz, trans. Oxford: Oxford University Press.

Garvie, A.F. 1969. *Aeschylus' Supplices, Play and Trilogy.* Cambridge: Cambridge University Press.

Gaster, Theodor. 1969. *Myth, Legend and Custom in the Old Testament.* New York: Harper and Row.

Gauthier, David. 1977. The Social Contract as Ideology. *Philosophy and Public Affairs*, 6, 2: 130–64.

Gauthier, Phillipe. 1978. Review of *Tribu et Cité* by Denis Roussel. *Revue Historique*, 237: 509–15.

Gauthier, R.A. 1951. *Magnanimité.* Paris: Bibliothèque Thomiste.

Geanakoplos, Deno J. 1966. *Byzantine East and Latin West.* Oxford: Oxford University Press.

Geanakoplos, Deno J. 1967. Pletho, Georgius Gemistus (*c.*1355–1452). *Encyclopedia of Philosophy.* London: Collier Macmillan: 6.350–1.

Geanakoplos, Deno J. 1974a. The Discourse of Demetrius Chalcondyles on the Inauguration of Greek Studies at the University of Padua in 1463. *Studies in the Renaissance*, 21: 18–44.

Geanakoplos, Deno J. 1974b. The Italian Renaissance and Byzantium: the Career of the Greek Humanist-Professor John Argyropoulos in Florence and Rome (1415–87). In *Conspectus of History* (Muncie, Indiana) 1: 12–28.

Geanakoplos, Deno J. 1976. *Interaction of the 'Sibling' Byzantine and Western Cultures in the Middles Ages and Italian Renaissance (1330–1600).* New Haven, Conn.: Yale University Press.

Geanakoplos, Deno J. 1978. *Byzantium and the Renaissance.* New Haven, Conn.: Yale University Press.

Geanakoplos, Deno J. 1984. Theodore Gaza, a Byzantine Scholar from the Palaeologan 'Renaissance' in the Italian Renaissance. *Medievalia et humanistica*, n.s. 12: 61–81.

Geanakoplos, Deno J. 1988. Italian Humanism and Byzantine Emigré Scholars. In Albert Rabil, Jr, ed. *Renaissance Humanism: Foundations, Forms, and Legacy.* 3 vols. Philadelphia, PA: University of Pennsylvania Press, vol. 3: 350–81.

Gellner, Ernst. 1969. A Pendulum Swing Theory of Islam. In Roland Robertson, ed. *Sociology of Religion.* Harmondsworth: Penguin.

Gelzer, Matthias. 1975. *The Roman Nobility.* Robin Seager, trans. Oxford: Blackwell.

Genovese, Eugene D. 1979. *From Rebellion to Revolution: Afro-American Slave Revolts in the Making of the Modern World.* Baton Rouge, LA: University of Louisiana Press.

Gentillet, Innocent. 1968 edn. *Anti-Machiavel (1576). Commentaire et Notes.* C. Edward Pathé, ed. Geneva: Droz.

Al-Ghazali. 1964 edn. *Nasihat al-Muluk.* F.F.C. Bagley, trans. *Ghazali's Book of Counsel for Kings.* Oxford: Oxford University Press.

Ghirshman, R. 1954. *Iran.* Harmondsworth: Penguin.

Giannardi, S. 1942 edn. Le 'Dicerie' di Filippo Ceffi. *Studi di filologie italiana*, 6: 5–63.

Gibb, Sir H.A.R. 1937. Al-Mawardi's Theory of the Caliphate. *Islamic Culture*, 11, 3: 291–302.

Gibb, Sir H.A.R. 1955. The Evolution of Government in Early Islam. *Studia Islamica*, 4: 1–17.

Gibbon, Edward. 1896–1903. *Decline and Fall of the Roman Empire*. J.B. Bury, ed. London: Methuen.

Gierke, Otto von. 1990. *Political Theories of the Middle Ages*. F.W. Maitland, ed. Cambridge: Cambrige University Press.

Gierke, Otto von. 1934. *Natural Law and the Theory of Society 1500–1800*. E. Barker, ed. Cambridge: Cambridge University Press.

Gilbert, Alan. 1938. *Machiavelli's Prince and its Forerunners*. Durham, North Carolina: University of Carolina Press.

Gilbert, Felix. 1939. The Humanist Concept of the Prince and *The Prince* of Machiavelli. *Journal of Modern History*, 11, 4: 449–83.

Gilbert, Felix. 1949. Bernardo Rucellai and the Orti Oricellari ... *Journal of the Warburg and Courtauld Institutes*, 12: 101–31.

Gilbert, Felix. 1953. The Composition and Structure of Machiavelli's *Discorsi*. *Journal of the History of Ideas*, 14: 136–56.

Gilbert, Felix. 1957. Florentine Political Assumptions in the Period of Savonarola and Soderini. *Journal of the Warburg and Courtauld Institutes*, 20: 187–214.

Gilbert, Felix. 1965. *Machiavelli and Guicciardini: Politics and History in Sixteenth Century Florence*. Princeton, NJ: Princeton University Press.

Gilbert, Felix. 1968. The Venetian Constitution in Florentine Republican Thought. In Nicolai Rubinstein, ed. *Florentine Studies: Politics and Society in Renaissance Florence*. Evanston, Ill.: Northwestern University Press: 463–500.

Gill, Christopher. 1976. The Origin of the Atlantis Myth. *Trivium*, 11: 1–11.

Gill, Christopher. 1977. The Genre of the Atlantis-story. *Classical Philology*, 72: 287–304.

Gill, Joseph. 1959. *The Council of Florence*. Cambridge: Cambridge University Press.

Gilmore, Myron P. 1963. The Renaissance Conception of the Lessons of History. In M.P. Gilmore, *Humanists and Jurists: Six Studies in the Renaissance*. Cambridge, Mass.: Harvard University Press.

Gimbutas, Marija. 1982. *The Goddesses and Gods of Old Europe 6500–3500 BC., Myths and Cult Images*. Berkeley, CA: University of California Press.

Gimbutas, Marija. 1989. *The Language of the Goddess*. San Francisco, CA: Harper and Row.

Glanville, S.R.L. and Skeat, T.C. 1954. Eponymous Priesthoods of Alexandria from 211 B.C. *Journal of Egyptian Archaeology*, 40: 45–58.

Glotz, Gustave. 1904. *La Solidarité de la Famille dans le Droit Criminel en Grèce*. Paris: Librarie des Écoles Françaises d'Athènes.

Godel, R. 1956. Platon à Heliopolis d'Égypte. *Bulletin de l'Association Guillaume Budé*: 69–118.

Goitein, Sholomo D. 1949. A Turning Point in the History of the Muslim State. *Islamic Culture*, 23: 120–35.

Goitein, Sholomo D. 1957. The Rise of the Near-Eastern Bourgeoisie in Early Islamic Times. *Journal of World History*, 3: 583–604.

Goitein, Sholomo D. 1964. Commercial and Family Partnerships in the Countries of Medieval Islam. *Islamic Studies*, 3: 315–37.

Goitein, Sholomo D. 1967–83. *A Mediterranean Society: the Jewish Communities of the Arab World as Portrayed in the Documents of the Cairo Geniza*. 4 vols. Berkeley, CA: University of California Press.

Goitein, Scholomo D. 1969. Cairo: an Islamic City in the Light of the Geniza Documents. In Ira M. Lapidus, ed. *Middle Eastern Cities*. Berkeley, CA: University of California Press.

Goldthwaite, Richard. 1968. *Private Wealth in Renaissance Florence*. Princeton, NJ: Princeton University Press.

Gombrich, E.H. 1945. Botticelli's Mythologies: a Study in the Neoplatonic Symbolism of his Circle. *Journal of the Warburg and Courtauld Institutes*, 8: 16.

Gombrich, E.H. 1948. *Icones Symbolicae*: the Visual Image in Neo-Platonic Thought. *Journal of the Warburg and Courtauld Institutes*, 11: 163–92.

Gombrich, E.H. 1972. *Symbolic Images: Studies in the Art of the Renaissance*. London: Phaedon.

Gomme, A.W. 1913. The Legend of Cadmus and the Logograph. I and II. *Journal of Hellenic Studies*, 33: 53–72; 223–45.

Goodenough, Erwin R. 1928. The Political Philosophy of Hellenistic Kingship. *Yale Classical Studies*, 1: 55–102.

Goodenough, Erwin R. 1935. *By Light, Light*. New Haven, Conn.: Yale University Press.

Goodenough, Erwin R. 1938. *The Politics of Philo Judaeus*. New Haven, Conn.: Yale University Press.

Goody, Jack. 1962. *Death, Property and the Ancestors*. Stanford, CA: Stanford University Press.

Goody, Jack. 1969. Inheritance, Property and Marriage in Africa and Eurasia. *Sociology*, 3: 55–76.

Goody, Jack. 1973. *The Character of Kinship*. Cambridge: Cambridge University Press.

Goody, Jack. 1983. *The Development of the Family and Marriage in Europe*. Cambridge: Cambridge University Press.

Goody, Jack. 1990. *Oriental, the Ancient and the Primitive Systems of Marriage and the Family in the Pre-industrial Societies of Eurasia*. Cambridge: Cambridge University Press.

Goody, Jack and Tambiah, S.J. 1973. *Bridewealth and Dowry*. Cambridge: Cambridge University Press.

Gordon, Cyrus H. 1953. Homer and the Bible. *Hebrew Union College Annual*, 26: 43–108.

Gordon, Cyrus H. 1958. Minoan Linear A. *Journal of Near Eastern Studies*, 17: 245–55.

Gordon, Cyrus H. 1981. The Semitic Language of Minoan Crete. In Y. Arbeitman and A.R. Bombard, eds. *Buono Homini Donum: Essays in Historical Linguistics in Memory of J. Alexander Kerns*. 2 vols. Amsterdam: John Benjamin: 761–82.

Gordon, William. 1978. *Change and Decline, Roman Literature in the Early Empire*. Berkeley, CA: University of California Press.

Gould, J.P. 1980. Law, Custom and Myth: Aspects of the Social Position of Women in Classical Athens. *Journal of Hellenic Studies*, 100: 38–59.

Grabar, Oleg. 1963. Umayyad 'Palace' and the 'Abbasid 'Revolution'. *Studia Islamica*, 18: 5–18.

Grabar, Oleg. 1969. The Achitecture of the Middle Eastern City. In Ira Lapidus, ed. *Middle Eastern Cities*. Berkeley, CA: University of California Press.

Gramsci, Antonio. 1971 edn. *Selections from the Prison Notebooks*. Q. Hoare and G. Nowell-Smith, trans. New York: International Publisher.

Green, Louis. 1972. *Chronicle into History*. Cambridge: Cambridge University Press.

Green, Louis. 1986. *Castruccio Castracani*. Oxford: Clarendon Press.

Green, Louis. 1989. The Image of Tyranny in Early Fourteenth Century Italian Historical Writing. Paper presented to the Conference on Political Discourse in Early Modern Europe, Humanities Research Centre, Australian National University, Canberra, 14–16 April.

Greene, Thomas M. 1976. Petrarch and the Humanist Hermeneutic. In Giose Rimanelli and Kenneth J. Atchity, eds. *Italian Literature: Roots and Branches*. New Haven, Conn.: Yale University Press: 210–24.

Gresseth, G.K. 1975. The Gilgamesh Epic and Homer. *Classical Journal*, 71: 1–18.

Griffith, Guy T. 1966. *Alexander the Great: the Main Problems*, Cambridge: Heffer.

Griffiths, John Gwyn. 1953. The Egyptian Derivation of the Name Moses. *Journal of Near Eastern Studies*, 12: 225–31.

Griffiths, John Gwyn, 1960. *The Conflict of Horus and Seth: from Egyptian and Classical Sources*. Liverpool: Liverpool University Press.

Griffiths, John Gwyn. 1961. The Death of Cleopatra VII. *Journal of Egyptian Archaeology*, 47: 113–18.

Griffiths, John Gwyn. 1966. Hecataeus and Herodotus on 'A Gift of the River', *Journal of Near Eastern Studies*, 25: 57–61.

Griffiths, John Gwyn, 1970. *Plutarch's 'De Iside et Osiride'*. Cambridge: Cambridge University Press.

Griffiths, John Gwyn, 1975. *Apuleius of Madauros, the Isis Book*. Leiden: Brill.

Griffiths, John Gwyn. 1980. *The Origins of Osiris and his Cult*. Leiden: Brill.

Grosrichard, Alain. 1979. *Structure du Sérail. La Fiction du Despotisme Asiatique dans l'Occident Classique*. Paris: Éditions du Seuil.

Gruen, Erich S. 1984. *The Hellenistic World and the Coming of Rome*. 2 vols. Berkeley, CA: University of California Press.

Gruen, Erich S. 1985. Review of David C. Braund, *Rome and the Friendly King: The Character of Client Kingship* (London: Croom Helm, 1984). *Ancient Society: Resources for Teachers* (Macquarie Ancient History Association), 15, 2: 102–6.

Grunebaum, G.E. von. 1946. *Medieval Islam*. Chicago: University of Chicago Press.

Güterbock, Hans Gustav. 1948. The Hittite Version of the Hurrian Kumarbi Myths: Oriental Forerunners of Hesiod. *American Journal of Archaeology*, 52: 123–34.

Guiccardini, Francesco. 1932 edn. A Dialogue on Florentine Government. In Roberto Palmarocchi, ed. *Dialogo e Discorsi del Reggimento di Firenze*. Bari: 1–172.

Guiccardini, Francesco. 1965 edn. Considerations on the '*Discourses*' of Machiavelli. In C. and M. Grayson, eds. *Francesco Guicciardini: Selected Writings*. Oxford: Oxford University Press: 107–19.

Gutas, Dimitri. 1975. *Greek Wisdom Literature in Arabic Translation: A Study of the Graeco-Arabic Gnomologia*. New Haven, Conn.: American Oriental Society.

Guthrie, W.K.C. 1962. *A History of Greek Philosophy. Vol. 1: The Earlier Presocratics and the Pythagoreans*. Cambridge: Cambridge University Press.

Hale, John Rigby. 1961. *Machiavelli and Renaissance Italy*. Harmondsworth: Penguin.

Hale, John Rigby. 1971. *Renaissance Europe, 1480–1520*. London: Collins.

Hall, H.R. 1901–2. Keftiu and the Peoples of the Sea. *Annual of the British School at Athens*, 8: 157–89.

Hall, H.R. 1905. The Two Labyrinths. *Journal of Hellenic Studies*, 25: 320–37.

Hall, John A. 1986. *Powers and Liberties: the Causes and Consequences of the Rise of the West*. Harmondsworth: Penguin.

Hamilton, J.R. 1969. *Plutarch, Alexander: a Commentary*. Oxford: Clarendon Press.

Hammer, C.U., Clausen, H.B. and Dansgaard, W. 1980. Greenland Ice Sheet Evidence of Post Glacial Volcanism and its Climatic Impact. *Nature*, 288: 230–35.

Hammer, C.U., Clausen, H.B., Friedrich, W.L. and Tauber, H. 1987. The Minoan Eruption of Santorini in Greece Dated to 1645 BC? *Nature*, 328: 517–19.

Hammer, William. 1944. The New or Second Rome in the Middle Ages. *Speculum*, 19: 50–62.

Hammond, N.G.L. 1961. Land Tenure in Athens and Solon's *Seisachtheia*. *Journal of Hellenic Studies*, 81: 76–98.

Hannaford, I. 1972. Machiavelli's Concept of Virtù in *The Prince* and *The Discourses* Reconsidered. *Political Studies*, 20, 2: 185–9.

Hankey, V. 1987. The Chronology of the Aegean Late Bronze Age. In P. Aström, ed. *High, Middle or Low?* Studies in Mediterranean Archaeology, Pocketbook 56, part II: 39–59. Gothenburg, Paul Aström Förlag.

Hankey, V. and Warren, P. 1974. The Absolute Chronology of the Aegean Late Bronze Age. *Bulletin of the Institute of Classical Studies*, 21: 142–52.

Hardie, W.F.R. 1978. Magnanimity in Aristotle's Ethics. *Phronesis*, 23: 69–70.

Harding, A.F. 1984. *The Mycenaeans and Europe*. London: Academic Press.

Harris, William V. 1979. *War and Imperialism in Republican Rome 327–70 BC*. Oxford: Oxford University Press.

Harrison, A.R.W. 1968. *The Law of Athens: the Family and Property*. Oxford: Clarendon Press.

Harrison, Jane Ellen. 1903. Mystica Vannus Iacchi. *Journal of Hellenic Studies*, 23: 292–324.

Harrison, Jane Ellen. 1957. *Prolegomena to the Study of Greek Religion*. New York: Harper and Row (reprint of 1921 3rd edn).

Harrison, Jane Ellen. 1962. *Themis. A Study of the Social Origins of Greek Religion*. New York: Harper and Row (reprint of 1927 2nd edn).

Hartog, François. 1988. *The Mirror of Herodotus. The Representation of the Other in the Writing of History*. Janet Lloyd, trans. Berkeley, CA: University of California Press.

Hartsock, Nancy. 1983. The Erotic Dimension and the Heroic Ideal. In N. Hartsock, *Money, Sex and Power*. London: Longman.

Harvey, F.D. 1965. Two Kinds of Equality. *Classica et Mediaevala*, 26: 101–40.

Hay, Denys. 1982. Historians and the Renaissance in the Last Twenty-five Years. In André Chastel et al., eds. *The Renaissance: Essays in Interpretation*. London: Methuen: 1–32.

Heers, Jacques. 1974. *Le Clan Familial au Moyen Age. Étude sur les Structures Politiques et Sociales des Milieux Urbains*. Paris: Presses Universitaires de France.

Heers, Jacques. 1977. *Parties and Political Life in the Medieval West*. David Nicholas, trans. Amsterdam: North Holland Publishing Co.

Heidel, William Arthur. 1935. Hecataeus and the Egyptian Priests in Herodotus Book II. *American Academy of Arts and Sciences*. Memoirs, 18, 2: 50–134.

Helck, W. 1987. Was kann die Ägyptologie wirklick zum Problem der absoluten Chronologie in der Bronzezeit beitragen? Chronologische Annäherungswerte in der 18 Dynastie. In P. Aström, ed. *High, Middle or Low?* Studies in Mediterranean Archaeology, Pocketbook 56, Part I: 18–26. Gothenburg: Paul Aström Förlag.

Henrichs, Albert. 1978. Greek Maenedism from Olympus to Messalina. *Harvard Studies in Classical Philology*, 82: 121–60.

Henrichs, Albert. 1979. Greek and Roman Glimpses of Dionysus. In C. Houser, ed. *Dionysus and his Circle: Ancient through Modern*. Cambridge, Mass.: Harvard University Press: 1–11.

Herlihy, David. 1962. Land, Family and Women in Continental Europe. *Traditio*, 18: 89–120.

Herlihy, David and Klapisch-Zuber, Christiane. 1985. *Tuscans and their Families: a Study of the Florentine Catasto of 1427*. New Haven, Conn.: Yale University Press.

Herodotus. 1972 edn. *The Histories*. Aubrey de Sélincourt, trans. Rev. with notes by A.R. Burn. Harmondsworth: Penguin.

Herzog, Don. 1986. Some Questions for Republicans. *Political Theory*, 14, 3: 473–93.

Heurgnon, Jacques. 1950. *The Rise of Rome*. Berkeley, CA: University of California Press.

Hesiod. 1959 edn. *The Works and Days, Theogony, the Shield of Herakles*. Richard Lattimore, trans. Ann Arbor: Michigan University Press.

Hexter, John H. 1956. Seyssel, Machiavelli and Polybius VI: the Mystery of the Missing Translation. *Studies in the Renaissance*, 3: 75–96.

Hexter, John H. 1973. The Predatory Vision: Niccolo Machiavelli, *Il Principe* and *lo Stato*. In J.H. Hexter, *The Vision of Politics on the Eve of the Reformation*. New York: Basic Books: 150–78.

Hexter, John H. 1977. Review of J.G.A. Pocock, *The Machiavellian Moment*. *History and Theory*, 16: 306–18.

Heywood, C.J. 1972. Sir Paul Rycaud, a Seventeenth Century Observer of the Ottoman State: Notes for a Study. In E.K. Shaw and C.J. Heywood, eds. *English and Continental Views of the Ottoman Empire, 1500–1800*. Los Angeles, CA: University of California, Clark Memorial Library: 31–59.

Hill, Enid. 1987. *Al-Sanhuri and Islamic Law*. Cairo: American University in Cairo. Cairo Papers in Social Science, vol. 10, no. 1.

Hill, Enid. 1989a. The Cultural Dimensions of Science. Unpublished paper presented to the American Social Science Research Council Committee on Islam, Aix-en-Provence, May 1989.

Hill, Enid. 1989b. *The Islamic Philosophers*. Unpublished manuscript. Cairo: Department of Political Science, American University in Cairo.

Hirsch, Steven W. 1985. *The Friendship of the Barbarians: Xenophon and the Persian Empire*. Hanover, NH.: University Press of New England.

Hodgson, Marshall G.S. 1960. The Unity of Later Islamic History. *Journal of World History*, 5: 879–914.

Hodgson, Marshall G.S. 1964. Islam and Image. *History of Religions*, 3: 220–60.

Hoffman, Michael M. 1979. *Egypt before the Pharaohs. The Prehistoric Foundations of Egyptian Civilization*. New York: Knopf.

Holmes, George. 1973. The Emergence of an Urban Ideology at Florence *c*.1250–1450. *Transactions of the Royal Historical Society*, 23: 111–34.

Holmes, S.T. 1979. Aristippus in and out of Athens. *American Political Science Review*, 73: 113–28.

Homer. 1980 edn. *The Odyssey*. Walter Shewring, trans. Oxford: Oxford University Press.

Hont, Istvan and Ignatieff, Michael, eds. 1983. *Wealth and Virtue*. Cambridge: Cambridge University Press.

Hood, Sinclair. 1971. *The Minoans*. London: Thames and Hudson.

Hooker, Richard. 1965 edn. *The Laws of Ecclesiastical Polity* (1600). London: Dent.

Höpfl, Harro and Thompson, Martyn P. 1979. The History of Contract as a Motif in Political Thought. *American Historical Review*, 84: 919–44.

Hornblower, G.D. 1929. Predynastic Figures of Women and their Successors. *Journal of Egyptian Archaeology*, 15: 29–47.

Hornung, Erik. 1983. *Conceptions of God in Ancient Egypt: the One and the Many*. John Baines, trans. London: Routledge.

Hornung, Erik. 1987. Lang order Kurz? – das Mittlere und Neue Reich Ägyptens als Prüfstein. In P. Aström, ed. *High, Middle or Low?* Studies in Mediterranean Archaelogy, Pocketbook 56, Part I: 27–36. Gothenburg: Paul Aström Förlag.

Hourani, Albert. 1968. Ottoman Reform and the Politics of Notables. In William Polk and Richard L. Chambers, eds. *Beginnings of Modernization in the Middle East*. Chicago: University of Chicago Press.

Hourani, Albert. 1970. The Islamic City in the Light of Recent Research. In Albert Hourani and S.M. Stern, eds. *The Islamic City*. Oxford: Oxford University Press.

Hughes, M.Y. 1944. England's Eliza and Spenser's Medina. *Journal of English and Germanic Philology*, 46: 1–15.

Hughs, D. Owen. 1972. Kinsmen and Neighbors in Medieval Genoa. In H.A. Miskimin et al., eds. *The Medieval City*. New Haven, Conn.: Yale University Press: 95–111.

Hughs, D. Owen. 1974. Toward Historical Ethnography: Notarial Records and Family History in the Middle Ages. *Historical Methods Newsletter*, 7, 2: 61–8.
Hughs, D. Owen. 1975. Urban Growth and Family Structure in Medieval Genoa. *Past and Present*, 66: 3–78.
Hulliung, Mark. 1983. *Citizen Machiavelli*. Princeton, NJ: Princeton University Press.
Humphrey, John. 1689. *A Plain, Honest Easy and Brief Determination of the Late Controversy*. London.
Humphreys, S.C. 1977. Public and Private Interests in Classical Athens. *The Classical Journal*, 73: 97–104.
Huntington, Samuel P. 1968. *Political Order in Changing Societies*. New Haven, Conn.: Yale University Press.
Hyde, J.K. 1965. Medieval Descriptions of Cities. *Bulletin of the John Rylands Library*, 48: 308–40.
Hyde, J.K. 1978. *Society and Politics in Medieval Italy*. London: Macmillan.
IG *Inscriptiones Graecae*. 1873–.
Ibn Khaldun. 1967 edn. *The Maqaddimah. An Introduction to History*. Franz Rosenthal, trans. N.J. Dawood, ed. Princeton, NJ: Princeton University Press.
Ignatieff, Michael. 1985. *The Needs of Strangers*. London: Chatto and Windus.
Inalcik, Halil. 1955. Land Problems in Turkish History. *The Muslim World*, 45: 221–4.
Inalcik, Halil. 1973. *The Ottoman Empire. The Classical Age, 1300–1600*. London: Weidenfeld and Nicolson.
Inalcik, Halil. 1980. State, Sovereignty and Law during the Reign of Suleyman. In H. Inalcik and H. Lowry, eds. *Suleyman and his Age*. Institute of Turkish Studies.
Irwin, T.H. 1985. Permanent Happiness: Aristotle and Solon. In J. Annas, ed. *Oxford Studies in Ancient Philosophy, III*. Oxford: Clarendon Press: 89–124.
Iskandarnamah: a Persian Medieval Alexander Romance. 1978 edn. Mindo S. Southgate, trans. New York: Columbia University Press.
Isocrates. 1945 edn. *Busiris*. L. van Hook, trans. Loeb edn. London: Heinemann.
Issawi, Charles. 1969. Economic Change and Urbanization in the Middle East. In Ira M. Lapidus, ed., *Middle Eastern Cities*. Berkeley, CA: University of California Press: 102–19.
Iversen, Erik. 1961. *The Myth of Egypt and its Hieroglyphics in European Tradition*. Copenhagen: Gad.
Iversen, Erik. 1968. Diodorus' Account of the Egyptian Canon. Journal of Egyptian Archaeology, 54: 215–18.
Iversen, Erik. 1971. The Hieroglyphic Tradition. In J.R. Harris, ed. *The Legacy of Egypt*. 2nd edn. Oxford: Clarendon Press.
Iversen, Erik. 1984. *Egyptian and Hermetic Doctrine*. Copenhagen: Gad.
Jacob, Margaret C. 1976. *The Newtonians and the English Revolution 1689–1720*. Ithaca, NY: Cornell University Press.
Jacobsen, Thorkild. 1970. Toward the Image of Tammuz. In W.L. Moran, ed. *Toward the Image of Tammuz and Other Essays on Mesopotamian History and Culture*. Cambridge, Mass.: Harvard University Press.
Jacobsen, Thorkild. 1976. *The Treasures of Darkness: a History of Mesopotamian Religion*. New Haven, Conn.: Yale University Press.
Jaeger, Werner. 1961. *Aristotle. Fundamentals of the History of his Development*. 2nd edn. Oxford: Oxford University Press.
James, George G.M. 1974. *The Stolen Legacy: the Greeks were not the Authors of Greek Philosophy, but the Peoples of North Africa, Commonly Called the Egyptians*. New York: Philosophical Library.
Janssen, J.J. 1982. Gift-giving in Ancient Egypt as an Economic Feature. *Journal of Egyptian Archaeology*, 68: 253–8.

Janssen, J.J. 1978. The Early State in Ancient Egypt. In H. Claessen and P. Skalnik, eds. *The Early State*. The Hague: Mouton.

Jonas, Hans. 1959. *The Gnostic Religion*. Boston: Beacon Press.

Jones, A.H.M. 1937. *The Cities of the Eastern Roman Provinces*. Oxford: Clarendon Press.

Jones, A.H.M. 1940. *The Greek City from Alexander to Justinian*. Oxford: Clarendon Press.

Jones, A.H.M. 1942. Egypt and Rome. In S.R.K. Glanville, ed. *The Legacy of Egypt*. Oxford: Oxford University Press.

Jones, A.H.M. 1970. *Augustus*. New York: W.W. Norton.

Jones, P.J. 1965. Communes and Despots: the City State in Late-Medieval Italy. *Royal Historical Society Transactions*, 15: 71–96.

Kantorowicz, Ernst. 1931. *Frederick II*. E.O. Lorimer, trans. London. New York: Ungar, reprint, 1967.

Kantorowicz, Ernst. 1946. *Laudes Regiae*. Berkeley, CA: University of California Press.

Kantorowicz, Ernst. 1957. *The King's Two Bodies. A Study in Medieval Political Theology*. Princeton, NJ: Princeton University Press.

Kantorowicz, Ernst. 1965. The Quinity of Winchester. In *Selected Essays*, New York: J.J. Augustin.

Kaplony, Peter. 1975–. Ka. In Wolfgang Helck et al., eds. *Lexikon der Ägyptologie*. Wiesbaden: Otto Harrassowitz, vol. 3: 275–82.

Karageorghis, V. ed. 1973. *The Mycenaeans in the East Mediterranean*. Acts of the International Archaeological Symposium, Nicosia, Crete: Department of Antiquities.

Karageorghis, V., ed. 1979. *The Relations between Cyprus and Crete, c.2000–500 B.C.* Acts of the International Archaeological Symposium, Nicosia, Crete: Department of Antiquities.

Kay, Ka'us. 1951 edn. *Qabus Nama*. Reuben Levy, trans. *A Mirror for Princes*. London: Cresset.

Keen, M.H. 1965. The Political Thought of the Fourteenth Century Civilians. In Beryl Smalley, ed. *Trends in Medieval Political Thought*. Oxford: Oxford University Press: 105–26.

Kelley, Donald R. 1964. *De Origine Feudorum*: the Beginnings of an Historical Problem. *Speculum*, 39, 2: 207–28.

Kemp, Barry J. 1977. A Building of Amenophis III at Kom El-Abd. *The Journal of Egyptian Archaeology*, 63: 71–82.

Kemp, Barry J. 1983. Old Kingdom, Middle Kingdom and Second Intermediate Period c.2686–1552 BC. In Brian Trigger et al., eds. *Ancient Egypt: a Social History*. Cambridge: Cambridge University Press: 71–182.

Kemp, Barry J. and Merrillees, R.S. 1980. *Minoan Pottery in Second Millennium Egypt*. Mainz: Phillip von Zabern.

Kent, Dale V. 1975. The Florentine *Reggimento* in the Fifteenth Century. *Renaissance Quarterly*, 28: 575–638.

Kent, Dale V. 1978. *The Rise of the Medici: Faction in Florence 1426–34*. Oxford: Oxford University Press.

Kent, Dale V. 1979. The Importance of Being Eccentric: Giovanni Cavalcanti's View of Cosimo de' Medici's Florence. *The Journal of Medieval and Renaissance Studies*, 9: 101–32.

Kent, Dale V. and Kent, Francis W. 1988. *Neighbours and Neighbourhood in Renaissance Florence*. New York: J.J. Augustin.

Kent, Francis W. 1972. The Rucellai Family and its Loggia. *Journal of the Warburg and Courtauld Institutes*, 35: 397–401.

Kent, Francis W. 1977a. *Household and Lineage in Renaissance Florence. The Family Life of the Capponi, Ginori and Rucellai*. Princeton, NJ: Princeton University Press.

Kent, Francis W. 1977b. A la Recherche du Clan Perdue: Jacques Heers and 'Family Clans' in the Middle Ages. *Journal of Family History*, 2: 77–86.

Kent, Francis W. 1981. The Making of a Renaissance Patron of the Arts. In F.W. Kent et al., eds. *A Florentine Patrician and his Palace*. London: Warburg Institute.

Kerford, G.B. 1967. Peripatetics. *Encyclopedia of Philosophy*. London: Collier Macmillan: 5.92–3.

Kerschensteiner, Jula. 1945. *Platon und der Orient*. Stuttgart: Kohlhammer Verlag.

Keuls, Eva C. 1985. *The Reign of the Phallus. Sexual Politics in Ancient Athens*. New York: Harper and Row.

Keyder, Caglar. 1987. *State and Class in Turkey: a Study in Capitalist Development*. London: Verso.

Khaduri, Majid. 1984. *The Islamic Conception of Justice*. Baltimore, MD: Johns Hopkins University Press.

Khuri, Fuad I. 1975. *From Village to Suburb, Order and Change in Greater Beirut*. Chicago: University of Chicago Press.

Khuri, Fuad I. 1976. A Profile of Family Associations in Two Suburbs of Beirut. In Jean G. Péristiany, ed. *Mediterranean Family Structures*. Cambridge: Cambridge University Press.

Khuri, Fuad I. 1980. *Tribe and State in Bahrain*. Chicago: University of Chicago Press.

King, David A. 1978. Islamic Mathematics and Astronomy. *Journal for the History of, Astronomy*, 9: 212–18.

King, David A. 1980. The Exact Sciences in Medieval Islam: Some Remarks on the Present State of Research. *Middle East Studies Association of North America, Bulletin*, 14, 1: 10–26.

King, L.W. 1916. *Legends of Babylon and Egypt in Relation to Hebrew Tradition*. London: British Academy (Schweich Lectures).

Kirk, Geoffrey. 1975. *Myth: its Meaning and Function in Ancient and Other Cultures*. Cambridge: Cambridge University Press.

Kirshner, Julius and Molho, Anthony. 1978. The Dowry Fund and the Marriage Market in Early *Quattrocento* Florence. *Journal of Modern History*, 50: 403–38.

Kitchen, K.A. 1987. The Basics of Egyptian Chronology in Relation to the Bronze Age. In P. Aström, ed. *High, Middle or Low?*. Studies in Mediterranean Archaeology, Pocketbook 56, Part I: 37–55. Gothenburg: Paul Aström Förlag.

Klapisch, Christina. 1976. 'Parenti, Amici e Vicini': il territorio urbano d'una famiglia mercantile nel xv secolo. *Quaderni Storici*, 33: 953–82.

Knapp, A. Bernard. 1982. The Onomastica of Alashiya. *New Journal of Cyprian Studies*, 1: 1–30.

Knapp, A. Bernard. 1985a. Alashiya, Caphtor/Keftiu, and East Mediterranean Trade: Recent Studies in Cypriote Archaeology and History. *Journal of Field Archaeology*, 12: 231–50.

Knapp, A. Bernard. 1985b. Production and Exchange in the Aegean and East Mediterranean: an Overview. In A. Bernard Knapp and Tamara Stech, eds. *Prehistoric Production and Exchange: the Aegean and the East Mediterranean*. Los Angeles, CA: UCLA Institute of Archeology, Monograph 25: 1–11.

Knapp, A. Bernard. 1988a. *The History and Culture of Ancient Western Asia and Egypt*. Chicago: Dorsey Press.

Knapp, A. Bernard. 1988b. Reader's Comments on Patricia Springborg, *Western Republicanism and the Oriental Prince*.

Knight, G. Wilson. 1961. *The Imperial Theme. Further Interpretations of Shakespeare's Tragedies*. London: Methuen.

Koebner, R. 1951. Despot and Despotism: Vicissitudes of a Political Term. *Journal of the Warburg and Courtauld Institutes*, 14: 275–302.

Koenig, John 1982. War and Taxes in Northern Italy, 1350–1400. In C. Condren and R. Pesman Cooper, eds. *Altro Polo: a Volume of Italian Renaissance Studies.* Sydney: University of Sydney Press: 51–78.

Kornemann, E. 1931. Zum Staatsrecht des Polybios. *Philologus,* 86: 169–84.

Krader, Lawrence. 1974. Introduction to *The Ethnological Notebooks of Karl Marx.* Assen: Van Gorcum.

Kramer, Samuel Noah. 1963. *The Sumerians.* Chicago: University of Chicago Press.

Kramnick, Isaac. 1982. Republican Revisionism Revisited. *American Historical Review,* 87: 629–64.

Kristeller, Paul Oskar. 1943a. *The Philosophy of Marsilio Ficino.* New York: Columbia University Press.

Kristeller, Paul Oskar. 1943b. The Place of Classical Humanism in Renaissance Thought. *Journal of the History of Ideas,* 4: 59–63. Reprinted in P.O. Kristeller, *Studies in Renaissance Thought and Letters.* Rome: Edizioni di Storia e Letteratura, 1969: 11–15.

Kristeller, Paul Oskar. 1944a. Augustine and the Early Renaissance. *Review of Religion* 8: 339–58. Reprinted in P.O. Kristeller, *Studies in Renaissance Thought and Letters.* Rome: Edizioni di Storia e Letteratura, 1969: 355–72.

Kristeller, Paul Oskar, 1944b. The Scholastic Background of Marsilio Ficino. *Traditio,* 2: 257–318. Reprinted in P.O. Kristeller, *Studies in Renaissance Thought and Letters.* Rome: Edizioni di Storia e Letteratura, 1969: 35–97.

Kristeller, Paul Oskar. 1944–5. Humanism and Scholasticism in the Italian Renaissance. *Byzantion,* 17: 346–74. Reprinted in P.O. Kristeller, *Studies in Renaissance Thought and Letters.* Rome: Edizioni di Storia e Letteratura, 1969: 553–83.

Kristeller, Paul Oskar. 1946. Francesca de Diacceto and Florentine Platonism in the Sixteenth Century. In *Miscellenea Giovanni Mercati,* 4.260–304. (Vatican City). Reprinted in P.O. Kristeller, *Studies in Renaissance Thought and Letters.* Rome: Edizioni di Storia e Letteratura, 1969: 287–336.

Kristeller, Paul Oskar. 1951. Matteo de' Libri, Bolognese Notary of the Thirteenth Century, and his *Artes Dictaminis.* In *Miscellanea Giovanni Galbiati,* ii (Fontes Ambrosiani 26), Milan: 283–320.

Kristeller, Paul Oskar. 1967. Marsilio Ficino (1433–1499). *Encyclopedia of Philosophy.* London: Collier Macmillan: vol. 3: 196–201.

Kristeller, Paul Oskar. 1969. Lay Religious Traditions and Florentine Platonism. In P.O. Kristeller, *Studies in Renaissance Thought and Letters.* Rome: Edizioni di Storia e Letteratura: 99–122.

Kristeller, Paul Oskar. 1969. Philosophical Movements of the Renaissance. In P.O. Kristeller, *Studies in Renaissance Thought and Letters.* Rome: Edizioni di Storia e Letteratura: 17–31.

Kristeller, Paul Oskar. 1972. The Renaissance and Byzantine Learning. In P.O. Kristeller, *Renaissance Concepts of Man.* New York: Harper and Row.

Kristeller, Paul Oskar. 1979. Byzantine and Western Platonism in the 15th Century. In M. Mooney, ed. *Renaissance Thought and its Sources.* New York: Columbia University Press.

Krzyszkowska, O. and Nixton, L. eds. 1983. *Minoan Society: Proceedings of the Cambridge Colloquium, 1981.* Bristol, UK: Bristol Classical Press.

Lacey, W.K. 1966. Homeric *Hedna* and Penelope's *Kyrios. Journal of Hellenic Studies,* 86: 55–68.

Lacey, W.K. 1968. *The Family in Classical Greece.* London: Methuen.

Ladner, Gerhart B. 1940. The Symbolism of the Biblical Cornerstone in the Medieval West. *Medieval Studies,* 2: 43–60.

Lafrance, Guy, ed. 1987. *Pouvoir et Tyrannie.* Ottowa: University of Ottowa Press.

LaMarche, V.C. Jr and Hirschboeck, K.K. 1984. Frost Rings in Trees as Records of Major Volcanic Eruptions. *Nature*, 307: 121–6.

Lambert, M.B. 1961. *Franciscan Poverty*. London: SPCK.

Lambton, Ann K.S. 1953. *Landlord and Peasant in Persia. A Study of Land Tenure and Land Revenue Administration*. Oxford: Oxford University Press.

Lambton, Ann K.S. 1954. The Theory of Kingship in the *Nasihat ul-Muluk* of Ghazali. *Islamic Quarterly*, 1: 47–55.

Lambton, Ann K.S. 1956. 'Quis Custodiet Custodes'. Some Reflections on the Persian Theory of Government. *Studia Islamica*, 5: 125–48; 6: 125–46.

Lambton, Ann K.S. 1962. Justice in the Medieval Persian Theory of Kingship. *Studia Islamica*, 17: 91–119.

Lambton, Ann K.S. 1974. Islamic Political Thought. In Joseph Schacht and C.E. Bosworth, eds. *The Legacy of Islam*. 2nd edn. Oxford: Clarendon Press: 404–24.

Lambton, Ann K.S. 1981. *State and Government in Medieval Islam*. Oxford: Oxford University Press.

Lambton, Ann K.S. 1988. *Continuity and Change in Medieval Persia. Aspects of Administration, Economic and Social History, 11–14th Century*. London: I.B. Taurus and Co.

Landsberger, Benno. 1976. *The Conceptual Autonomy of the Babylonian World*. Thorkild Jacobsen et. al., trans. Malibu, CA: Undena.

Lapidus, Ira M. 1967. *Muslim Cities in the Later Middle Ages*. Cambridge, Mass.: Harvard University Press.

Lapidus, Ira M. 1969. Muslim Cities and Islamic Societies. In Ira M. Lapidus, ed. *Middle Eastern Cities: a Symposium on Ancient Islamic and Contemporary Middle Eastern Urbanism*. Berkeley, CA: University of California Press: 47–74.

Lapidus, Ira M. 1986. Cities and Societies. A Comparative Study of the Emergence of Urban Civilization in Mesopotamia and Greece. *Journal of Urban History*, 12, 3: 257–92.

Lapidus, Ira M. 1988. *History of Islamic Societies*. Cambridge: Cambridge University Press.

Larsen, J.A.O. 1945. Representation and Democracy in Hellenistic Federalism. *Classical Philology*, 40: 65–97.

Larsen, J.A.O. 1954. The Judgement of Antiquity on Democracy. *Classical Philology*, 49: 1–14.

Larsen, J.A.O. 1955. *Representative Government in Greece and Rome*. Berkeley, CA: University of California Press.

Larsen, Mogens Trolle. 1967. *Old Assyrian Caravan Procedures*. Istanbul: Nederlands Historisch-Archeologisch Institut in Het Nabije Oosten.

Larsen, Mogens Trolle. 1976. *The Old Assyrian City-State and its Colonies*. Copenhagen: Akademisk Forlag.

Laslett, Peter. 1964. Introduction and Notes to Locke's *Two Treatises of Government (1690)*. Cambridge: Cambridge University Press.

Lateiner, Donald. 1982. 'The Man who does not Meddle in Politics': a Topos in Lysias. *Classical World*, 76: 1–12.

Latini, B. 1948 edn. *Li Livres dou Trésor*. F. Carmody, ed. Berkeley, CA: University of California Press.

Lawson, George. 1660. *Politica Sacra et Civilis*. London.

Lee, Desmond. 1971. An Appendix on Atlantis. In Desmond Lee, ed. *Plato's Timaeus and Critias*. Harmondsworth: Penguin: 144–67.

Lefkowitz, Mary R. 1986. *Women in Greek Myth*. London: Duckworth.

Lefkowitz, Mary R. and Fant, Maureen B. 1982. *Women's Life in Greece and Rome*. London: Duckworth.

Lerner, Gerda. 1986. *The Creation of Patriarchy*. vol. 1. Oxford: Oxford University Press.
Lerner, Ralph and Mahdi, Muhsin, eds. 1972. *Medieval Political Philosophy, a Sourcebook*. Ithaca, NY: Cornell University Press.
Lesko, Barbara S. 1978. *The Remarkable Women of Ancient Egypt*. Berkeley, CA: B.L. Scribe Publications.
Lesure, Michel. 1986. Les Relations franco-ottomanes à l'épreuve des guerres de Religion (1560–1594). In Hâmit Batu et J.–L. Bacqué-Grammont, eds. *L'Empire ottoman, la République de Turquie et la France*. Istanbul-Paris: Isis (Varia Turcica 3): 37–57.
Levi-Strauss, Claude. 1964–8. *Mythologies*. Paris: Plon.
Levin, Samuel. 1978. The Perfumed Goddess. *Bucknell Review*, 24: 49–58. (Special issue, *Women, Literature, Criticism*, ed. Harry R. Garvin.)
Lewis, Bernard. 1937. The Islamic Guilds. *Economic History Review*, 8: 20–37.
Lewis, Bernard. 1962. Ottoman Observers of Ottoman Decline. *Islamic Studies*, 1: 71–87.
Lewis, Bernard. 1982. *The Muslim Discovery of Europe*. New York: W.W. Norton.
Lewis, Bernard. 1984. *The Jews of Islam*. Princeton, NJ: Princeton University Press.
Lewis, Bernard. 1988. *The Political Language of Islam*. Chicago: University of Chicago Press.
Lewy, H. 1978. *Chaldean Oracles and Theurgy: Mysticism, Magic and Platonism in the Later Roman Empire*. M. Tardieu, ed. Cairo: Institut Français d'Archéologie Orientale.
Libri, Matteo de'. 1974 ed. *Arringhe*. E. Vincenti, ed. Milan: 3–227.
Lichtenstadter, Ilse. 1949. From Particularism to Unity: Race, Nationality and Minorities in the Early Islamic Empire. *Islamic Culture*, 23: 251–80.
Lichtheim, Miriam. 1973, 1976, 1980. *Ancient Egyptian Literature*. 3 vols. Berkeley, CA: University of California Press.
Liebeschutz, Hans. 1943. John of Salisbury and Pseudo Plutarch. *Journal of the Warburg and Courtauld Institutes*, 6: 33–9.
Liebeschutz, J.H.W.G. 1972. *Antioch: City and Imperial Administration in the Later Roman Empire*. Oxford: Oxford University Press.
Littleton, C. Scott. 1980. *The New Comparative Mythology: an Anthropological Assessment of the Theories of Georges Dumézil*. 3rd edn. Berkeley, CA: University of California, Press.
Littman, Robert J. 1974. *The Greek Experience*. London: Thames and Hudson.
Littwak, Edward N. 1976. *The Grand Strategy of the Roman Empire from the 1st Century AD to the 3rd century*. Baltimore, MD: Johns Hopkins University Press.
Livy (Titus Livius). 1971 edn. *The Early History of Rome* (Books 1–5 of *The History of Rome from its Foundation*). Aubrey de Sélincourt, trans. Harmondsworth: Penguin.
Livy (Titus Livius). 1972 edn. *The War with Hannibal* (Books 21–30 of *The History of Rome from its Foundation*). Aubrey de Sélincourt, trans. Harmondsworth: Penguin.
Livy (Titus Livius). 1976 edn. *Rome and the Mediterranean* (Books 31–45 of *The History of Rome from its Foundation*). Henry Bettenson, trans. Harmondsworth: Penguin.
Lloyd, Alan B. 1969. Perseus and Chemmis (Herodotus II, 91). *Journal of Hellenic Studies*, 89: 79–86.
Lloyd, Alan B. 1975, 1976. *Herodotus Book II. Introduction Commentary*. 2 vols. Leiden: E.J. Brill.
Lloyd, Alan B. 1983. The Late Period, 664–323 B.C. In B.G. Trigger et al., eds. *Ancient Egypt: a Social History*. Cambridge: Cambridge University Press: 279–364.
Lloyd, Geoffrey E.R. 1966. *Polarity and Analogy*. Cambridge: Cambridge University Press.
Locke, John. 1964 edn. *Two Treatises of Government (1690)*. P. Laslett, ed. Cambridge: Cambridge University Press.
Lohr, C.H. 1982. The Medieval Interpretation of Aristotle. In Norman Kretzmann et al.,

eds. *The Cambridge History of Later Medieval Philosophy.* Cambridge: Cambridge University Press: 80–98.

Long. A.A. 1967. Carneades and the Stoic Telos. *Phronesis,* 12: 59–90.

Long, A.A. 1970. Morals and Values in Homer. *Journal of Hellenic Studies,* 90: 121–39.

Long, A.A. 1971. *Problems in Stoicism.* London: Athlone Press.

Long, A.A. 1974. *Hellenistic Philosophy, Stoics, Epicureans, Sceptics.* New York: Charles Scribner.

L'Orange, H.P. 1947. *Apotheosis in Ancient Portraiture.* Oslo: Aschehoug.

L'Orange. H.P. 1953. *Studies in the Iconography of Cosmic Kingship.* Osle: Aschehoug.

Loraux, Nicole. 1978. Sur la Race des Femmes et Quelques-Unes de ses Tribus. *Arethusa,* 11: 43–87.

Loraux, Nicole. 1986. *The Invention of Athens. The Funeral Oration in the Classical City.* Alan Sheridan, trans. Cambridge, Mass.: Harvard University Press.

Lord, C. 1978. Politics and Philosophy in Aristotle's *Politics. Hermes,* 40: 336–59.

Lovejoy, Arthur O. and Boas, George. 1935. *Primitivism and Related Ideas in Antiquity.* Baltimore, MD: Johns Hopkins University Press.

Luce, J.V. 1969. *The End of Atlantis.* London: Thames and Hudson.

Luce, J.V. 1976. Thera and the Devastation of Minoan Crete: a New Interpretation of the Evidence. *American Journal of Archaeology,* 80: 1–16.

Lutz, Cora E. 1942. Musonius Rufus, the 'Roman Socrates'. *Yale Classical Studies,* 10: 1–147.

McEwan, C.W. 1934. *The Oriental Origin of Hellenistic Kingship.* (Chicago Studies in Ancient Oriental Civilization, no. 13). Chicago: University of Chicago Press.

McEwan, G.U.P. 1981. *Priest and Temple in Hellenistic Babylonia.* Wiesbaden: Steiner.

MacGillivray, J.A. and Barber, R.N.L., eds. 1984. *The Prehistoric Cyclades.* Edinburgh: Department of Classical Archaeology, University of Edinburgh.

Machiavelli, Niccolo, 1961 edn. *The Prince.* George Bull, ed. Harmondsworth: Penguin.

Machiavelli, Niccolo. 1974 edn. *The Discourses.* Bernard Crick, ed. Harmondsworth: Penguin.

Macmullan, Ramsey. 1980. Women in Public in the Roman Empire. *Historia,* 29: 208–18.

McNally, Sheila. 1978. The Maenad in Early Greek Art. *Arethusa,* 11: 101–30.

Macurdy, Grace. 1932. *Hellenistic Queens. A Study of Woman-Power in Macedonia, Seleucid Syria and Ptolemaic Egypt.* Baltimore, MD: Johns Hopkins University Press. (Reprinted 1975, Westport, Conn.: Greenwood Press.)

Magoun, F.B. 1929. *The Gests of King Alexander of Macedon.* Cambridge: Cambridge University Press.

Mahdi, Muhsin. 1963. Alfarabi. In Leo Strauss and Joseph Cropsey, eds. *History of Political Thought.* Chicago: Rand McNally: 160–80.

Maine, Henry James Sumner. 1861. *Ancient Law.* London: Routledge.

Maitland, Frederic W. 1990. Introduction to Otton von Gierke's *Political theories of the Middle Ages.* Cambridge: Cambridge University Press.

Maitland, Frederic W. 1936. The King as Corporation, and Moral Personality and Legal Personality. In H.D. Hazeltine, G. Lapsley and P.H. Winfield, eds. *Selected Essays.* Cambridge: Cambridge University Press.

Mango, Cyril, 1965. Byzantium and Romantic Hellenism. *Journal of the Warburg and Courtauld Institutes,* 28: 29–43.

Mango, Cyril. 1984. Byzantine Literature as a Distorting Mirror. In Cyril Mango, *Byzantium and its Image.* London: Variorum Reprints: 3–18.

Mango, Cyril. 1984. Discontinuity in the Classical Past in Byzantium. Reprinted in Cyril Mango, *Byzantium and its Image.* London: Variorum Reprints: 48–57.

Mann, Michael. 1986. *The Sources of Social Power. Vol. 1. A History of Power from the Beginning to A.D. 1760.* Cambridge: Cambridge University Press.

Manning, Sturt. 1988. The Bronze Age Eruption of Thera: Absolute Dating, Aegean Chronology and Mediterranean Cultural Interrelations. *Journal of Mediterranean Archaeology*, 1, 1: 17–82.

Mansfield, Harvey C. Jr. 1964. Party Government and the Settlement of 1688. *American Political Science Review*, 58: 933–46.

Mansfield, Harvey C. Jr. 1968. Modern and Medieval Representation. In J.R. Pennock and C. Chapman, eds. *Representation. Nomos*, 11: 55–82.

Mansfield, Harvey C. Jr. 1971. Hobbes and the Science of Indirect Government. *American Political Science Review*, 65: 97–110.

Mansfield, Harvey C. Jr. 1979. *Machiavelli's New Modes and Orders. A Study of 'The Discourses on Livy'*. Ithaca, NY: Cornell University Press.

Mansfield, Harvey C. Jr. 1983. On the Impersonality of the Modern State: a Comment on Machiavelli's use of *Stato. American Political Science Review*, 77: 849–57.

Manuel, Frank E. 1965. *Shapes of Philosophical History*. Stanford, CA: Stanford University Press.

Marcovich, M. 1975. How to Flatter Women: P. Oxy. 2891. *Classical Philology*, 70: 123–4.

Mardin, Serif. 1969. Power, Civil Society and Culture in the Ottoman Empire. *Comparative Studies in Society and History*, 11: 258–81.

Marinatos, Spyridon. 1939. The Volcanic Destruction of Minoan Crete. *Antiquity*, 13: 425–39.

Marinatos, Spyridon. 1968–76. *Excavations at Thera I-VII*. Athens: Archaeological Society of Athens.

Marinatos, Spyridon and Hirmer, Max. 1960. *Crete and Mycenae*. New York: Harry N. Abrams, Inc.

Marinatos, Spyridon and Ninkovich, D., eds. 1971. *Acta of the 1st International Scientific Congress on the Volcano of Thera*. Athens: Archaeological Services of Greece.

Marsh, D. 1980. *The Quattrocento Dialogue. The Classical Tradition and Humanist Innovation*. Cambridge, Mass.: Harvard University Press.

Martin, Paul M. 1982. *L'Idée de Royauté à Rome*. Clermont-Ferrand: Aposa.

Marx, Karl. n.d. *Capital*, vol. 1. Moscow: Progress Publishers.

Marx, Karl. 1973. *Grundrisse*. Martin Nicolaus, trans. Harmondsworth: Penguin.

Marx, Karl. 1974. *The Ethnological Notebooks*. Lawrence Krader, ed. Assen: Van Gorcum.

Marx, Karl and Engels, Frederick. 1953 edn. *The Russian Menace in Europe*. London: George Allen and Unwin.

Marx, Karl and Engels, Frederick. 1975–. *The Collected Works*. London: Lawrence and Wishart.

Masai, F. 1956. *Pléthon et le Platonisme de Mistra*. Paris: 'Al-Mawardi.

Matthiae, Paolo, 1980. *Ebla: An Empire Rediscovered*. London: Hodder and Stoughton.

Maxwell, Bishop John. 1644. *Sacro-Sancta Regnum Majestas*. Oxford.

Meinecke, Friedrich. 1923. Machiavelli, *Der Furst*. (German translation of *The Prince*, with an Introduction). Berlin: Klassiker der Politik, 8.

Menocal, Maria Rosa. 1987. *The Arabic Role in Medieval Literary History. A Forgotten Heritage*. Philadelphia, PA.: University of Pennsylvania Press.

Mercer, Samuel A.B. 1939. *The Tell el Amarna Tablets*. 2 vols. Toronto: Macmillan.

Merkelbach, R. and West, M.L. 1967. *Fragmente Hesiodea*. Oxford: Clarendon Press.

Merlan, Philip. 1967. The Alexandrian School. *Encyclopedia of Philosophy*. Vol. 1. London: Collier Macmillan: 75–6.

Merlan, Philip. 1968. *From Platonism to Neoplatonism*. The Hague: Martinus Nijhoff.

Metlitzski, Dorothee. 1977. *The Matter of Araby in Medieval England*. New Haven Conn.: Yale University Press.

Meyer, Eduard. 1906. *Die Israeliten und Ihre Nachbarstämme. Altestamentliche Untersuchungen*. Halle A.S.: Niemeyer.

Meyer, Reinhold. 1981–2. The Declaration of War Against Cleopatra. *Classical Journal,* 77: 97–103.

Michael, H.N. 1978. Radiocarbon Dates from the Site of Akrotiri, Thera, 1967–1977. In C. Doumas, ed. *Thera and the Aegean World I.* London: Thera and the Aegean World: 791–5.

Mill, James. 1972 edn. *The History of British India.* London and New Delhi Associated Publishing House.

Millar, Fergus, 1971. Paul of Somosata, Zenobia and Aurelian: the Church, Local Culture and Political Allegiance in Third-Century Syria. *Journal of Roman Studies,* 61: 1–17.

Millar, Fergus. 1977. *The Emperor in the Roman World.* London: Duckworth.

Millar, Fergus. 1981. *The Roman Empire and its Neighbours.* 2nd edn. London: Duckworth.

Mitford, T.B. 1960. Ptolemy Son of Pelops. *Journal of Egyptian Archaeology,* 46: 109–11.

Molho Anthony. 1971. *Florentine Public Finances in the Early Renaissance, 1400–1433.* Cambridge, Mass.: Harvard University Press.

Momigliano, A. 1975. *Alien Wisdom: the Limits of Hellenization.* Cambridge: Cambridge University Press.

Mommsen, T.E. 1942. Petrarch's Conception of the Dark Ages. *Speculum,* 17: 226–42.

Money, J.H. 1973. The Destruction of Akrotiri. *Antiquity,* 47: 50–3.

Montesquieu. 1964 edn. *The Persian Letters* (1721). George Healy, trans. New York: Bobbs-Merrill (Library of the Liberal Arts).

Montesquieu. 1968 edn. *Considerations on the Causes of the Greatness of the Romans and their Decline* (1734). Ithaca, NY: Cornell University Press.

Moore, Barrington, 1969. *Social Origins of Dictatorship and Democracy.* Harmondsworth: Penguin.

Moore, Clement Henry. 1974. Authoritarian Politics in Unincorporated Society. *Comparative Politics,* 6, 2: 193–218.

Moore, Clement Henry. 1977. Clientelist Ideology and Political Change: Fictitious Networks in Egypt and Tunisia. In Ernest Gellner and John Waterbury, eds. *Patrons and Clients in Mediterranean Society.* London: Duckworth.

Mooren, L. 1981. Ptolemaic Families. In Robert S. Bagnal, ed. *Proceedings of the XVI International Congress of Papyrology.* Chico, California: 289–301.

Morgan, Lewis Henry. 1877. *Ancient Society, or Researches into the Lines of Human Progress from Savagery through Barbarism to Civilization.* Chicago: Charles H. Kerr and Co.

Morony, Michael G. 1984. *Iraq after the Muslim Conquest.* Princeton, NJ: Princeton University Press.

Morrison, J.S. 1941. The Place of Protagoras in Athenian Public Life. *Classical Quarterly,* 35: 1–15.

Morrow, Glen R. 1941. Plato and the Rule of Law. *Philosophical Review,* 50: 105–26.

Morrow, Glen R. 1960. *Plato's Cretan City. A Historical Interpretation of the 'Laws'.* Princeton, NJ: Princeton University Press.

Movers, F.C. 1841–50. *Die Phönizier.* 2 vols, 4 books. Bonn and Berlin.

Muhly, J.D. 1972. The Land of Alashiya: References to Alashiya in the Texts of the Second Millennium B.C., and the History of Cyprus in the Late Bronze Age. In V. Karageorghis, ed. *Acts of the First International Cyprological Congress.* Nicosia: Department of Antiquities: 201–19.

Muhly, J.D. 1982 The Nature of Trade in the Late Bronze Age Eastern Mediterranean: The Organization of the Metals Trade and the Role of Cyprus. In J.D. Muhly, R. Maddin and V. Karageorghis, eds. *Acts of the International Archaeological Symposium: Early Metallurgy in Cyprus, 4000–500 BC.* Larnaca: Pierides Foundation: 251–69.

Muir, Edward, 1981. *Civic Ritual in Renaissance Venice*. Princeton, NJ: Princeton University Press.

Mulgan, Richard G. 1970. Aristotle's Sovereign. *Political Studies*, 18: 518–22.

Mulgan, Richard G. 1974a. Aristotle's Doctrine that Man is a Political Animal. *Hermes*, 102: 438–45.

Mulgan, Richard G. 1974b. Aristotle and Absolute Rule. *Autichthon*, 8: 21–8.

Mulgan, Richard G. 1977. *Aristotle's Political Theory*. Oxford: Oxford University Press.

Mulgan, Richard G. 1979. Lycophron and Greek Theories of Social Contract. *Journal of the History of Ideas*, 40: 121–8.

Mulgan, Richard G. 1981. Machiavelli, Aristotle and Pocock – a Question of Evidence. *The New Zealand Journal of History*, 15, 1: 61–7.

Mulgan, Richard G. 1984. Liberty in Ancient Greece. In Z. Pelcyznski and J. Gray, eds. *Conceptions of Liberty in Political Philosophy*. London: Athlone Press.

Mulgan, Richard G. 1989. Aristotle in the Antipodes. Armidale: University of New England, unpublished paper.

Mulgan, Richard G. 1990. Aristotle and the Value of Political Participation. *Political Theory*, 18, 2: 195–215.

Murnane, William J. 1975–. Opetfest. In Wolfgang Helck and E. Otto, eds. *Lexikon der Ägyptologie*. Wiesbaden: Otto Harrassowitz, vol. 4: 574.

Murnane, William J. 1981. The Sed Festival: a Problem in Historical Method. *Mitteilungen des Deutschen Archeologischen Instituts Abteilung, Kairo*, 37: 369–76.

Mussato, A. 1727. edn. *De Gestis Italicorum Post Mortem Henrici VII Caesaris Historia*. L. Muratori, ed. In *Rerum Italicarum Scriptores*, vol. 10, cols, 569–768.

Na'aman, N. 1984. Statements of Time-spans by Babylonian and Assyrian Kings and Mesopotamian Chronology. *Iraq*, 46: 115–23.

Nachtergael, G. 1980. Berenice II, Arsinoë III, et l'Offrance de la Boucle. *Chronique d'Égypte*, 55: 240–53.

Naff, Thomas and Roger Owen, eds. 1977. *Studies in Eighteenth Century Islamic History*. Carbondale, Ill.: Southern Illinois University Press.

Nagler, Michael. 1967. Towards a Generative View of the Oral Formula. *Transactions of the American Philological Society*, 98: 269–311.

Nagler, Michael. 1974. *Spontaneity and Tradition. A Study of the Oral Art of Homer*. Berkeley, CA: University of California Press.

Najemy, J. 1982. *Corporatism and Consensus in Florentine Electoral Politics 1280–1400*. Chapel Hill, North Carolina: University of North Carolina Press.

Nederman, Cary J. 1987. Aristotle as Authority: Alternative Aristotelian Sources of Late Medieval Political Theory. *History of European Ideas*, 8, 1: 31–44.

Nederman, Cary J. 1988. Nature, Sin and the Origins of Society: the Ciceronian Tradition in Medieval Political Thought. *Journal of the History of Ideas*, 49: 3–26.

Nelson, Harold H. 1942. The Identity of Amon-Re of United-with-Eternity. *Journal of Near Eastern Studies*, 1, 2: 127–55.

Nelson, Harold H. 1949. Certain Reliefs at Karnak and Medinet Habu and the Ritual of Amenophis I. *Journal of Near Eastern Studies*, 8: 201–21, 343–5.

Neumann, Erich. 1956. *The Great Mother: an Analysis of an Archetype*. New York: Pantheon.

Nicolet, Claude. 1980. *The World of the Citizen in Republican Rome*. London: Batisford Academic and Educational Books.

Nieuwenhuijze, C.A.O. 1977. *Commoners, Climbers and Notables: A Sampler of Studies on Social Ranking in the Middle East*. Leiden: Brill.

Nilsson, Nils M.P. 1950. *The Minoan–Mycenaean Religion*. 2nd edn. Lund: D.W.K. Gleerup.

Nilsson, Nils M.P. 1970. Apaturia. *Oxford Classical Dictionary*. 2nd edn. Oxford: Oxford University Press: 79.
Nilsson, Nils M.P. 1972. *Cults, Myths, Oracles and Politics in Ancient Greece*. New York: Cooper Square Books.
Nims, Charles. 1965. *Thebes of the Pharaohs: Pattern for Every City*. London: Elek Books.
Nims, Charles F. 1966. The Date of the Dishnouring of Hatshepsut. *Zeitschrift für Ägytologische Sprache und Altertumskunde*, 93: 97–100.
Nock, Arthur Darby, 1928. Notes on Ruler Cult I-IV. *Journal of Hellenic Studies*, 48: 21–43.
Nock, Arthur Darby. 1930. *Sunnaos Theos*. Harvard Studies in Classical Philology, 41: 1–62.
Nock, Arthur Darby. 1942. Ruler Worship and Syncretism. *American Journal of Philology*, 63: 217–24.
Nock, Arthur Darby. 1947. The Emperor's Divine *Comes*. *Journal of Roman Studies*, 37: 102–16.
Nock, Arthur Darby. 1951. *Soter* and *Euergetes*. In S.L. Johnson, ed. *The Joy of Study ... to Honor F.C. Grant*. New York: Macmillan: 127–48.
Nock, Arthur Darby. 1952. Hellenistic Mysteries and Christian Sacraments. *Menosyne*, 5: 177–213.
Nock, Arthur Darby. 1953. Neotera, Queen or Goddess? *Aegyptus*, 33: 283–96.
Nock, Arthur Darby. 1957. Deification and Julian. *Journal of Roman Studies*, 47: 115–23.
Nock, Arthur Darby. 1962. The Exegesis of *Timaeus* 28C. *Virginia Chronicle*, 16: 79–86.
Nock, Arthur Darby. 1972. *Essays on Religion and the Ancient World*. 2 vols. Oxford: Clarendon Press.
Nowicka, Maria. 1969. La Maison Privée dans l'Égypte Ptolemaique. Warsaw: Institute de la Culture Materielle, Bibliographa Antiqua, 9.
OED. 1971 edn. *The Compact Edition of the Oxford English Dictionary* (Complete Text Reproduced Micrographically). Oxford: Oxford University Press.
OGIS Orientis Graeci Inscriptiones Selectae. Wilhelm Dittenberger, ed. 1903–5.
Obermann, J. 1935. Political Theology in Early Islam: Hasan al-Basri's Treatise on *Qadar*. *Journal of the American Oriental Society*, 55: 138–62.
Ocshorn, Judith. 1981. *The Female Experience and the Nature of the Divine*. Bloomington, Ind.: Indiana University Press.
O'Flaherty, Wendy Doniger. 1980. *Women, Androgynes and Other Mythical Beasts*. Chicago: University of Chicago Press.
Ogilvie, R.M. 1969. *The Romans and their Gods in the Age of Augustus*. New York: W.W. Norton.
Ogilvie, R.M. 1971. Introduction to Livy, *The Early History of Rome*, Books 1–5 of *The History of Rome from its Foundation*. Harmondsworth: Penguin: 7–29.
Okin, Susan Moller. 1977. Philosopher Queens and Private Wives: Plato on Women and the Family. *Philosophy and Public Affairs*, 6: 345–69.
Okin, Susan Moller. 1979. *Women in Western Political Thought*. Princeton, NJ: Princeton University Press.
Okin, Susan Moller, 1982. Women and the Making of the Sentimental Family. *Philosophy and Public Affairs*, 11, 1: 65–88.
Olson, Mancur. 1971. *The Logic of Collective Action: Public Goods and the Theory of Groups*. Cambridge, Mass.: Harvard University Press.
Oppenheim, Adolf L. 1969. Mesopotamia – Land of Many Cities. In Ira M. Lapidus, ed. *Middle Eastern Cities: a Symposium on Ancient Islamic and Contemporary Middle Eastern Urbanism*. Berkeley, CA: University of California Press.
Oppenheim, Adolf L. 1977. *Ancient Mesopotamia*. Chicago: University of Chicago Press.

Orr, Robert, 1972. The Time Motif in Machiavelli. In *Machiavelli and the Nature of Political Thought*. M. Fleisher, ed. New York: Atheneum: 185–208.

Osborne, Robin. 1985. *Demos: the Discovery of Classical Attica*. Cambridge: Cambridge University Press.

Ostrogorsky, George. 1969. *History of the Byzantine State*. New Brunswick, NJ: Rutgers University Press.

Ostwald, Martin, 1969. *Nomos and the Beginnings of Athenian Democracy*. Oxford: Clarendon Press.

Otto, Eberhard. 1968. *Egyptian Art and the Cults of Osiris and Amon*. Kate Bosse Griffiths, trans. London: Thames and Hudson.

Otto, Eberhard. 1975–. Dualismus. In Wolfgang Helck et al., eds. *Lexikon der Agyptologie*. Wiesbaden: Otto Harrassowitz, vol. 1: 1148–50.

Palacios, Asin, 1926. *Islam and the Divine Comedy*. Harold Sunderland, trans. London.

Palmer, L.R. 1963. *The Interpretation of Mycenaean Greek Texts*. Oxford: Oxford University Press.

Palmer, L.R. 1981. The Khyan Lid Deposit at Knossos. *Kadmos*, 20: 108–28.

Palmer, L.R. 1984. The Linear B Palace at Knossos. In P. Aström, L.R. Palmer and L. Pomerance, eds. *Studies in Aegean Chronology*. Studies in Mediterranean Archaeology, Pocketbook 25. Gothenburg: Paul Aström Förlag: 26–119.

Panofsky, E. 1962. *Studies in Iconology: Humanistic Themes in the Art of the Renaissance*. New York: Harper.

Parke, Herbert William. 1970. Dodona. *Oxford Classical Dictionary*. 2nd edn. Oxford: Oxford University Press: 358.

Parronchi, A. 1964. The Language of Humanism and the Language of Sculpture. *Journal of the Warburg and Courtauld Institutes*, 27: 108–36.

Parry, V.J. 1962. Renaissance Historical Literature in Relation to the Near and Middle East (with special reference to Paolo Giovio). In Bernard Lewis and P.M. Holt, eds. *Historians of the Middle East*. Oxford: Oxford University Press.

Pastor, Antonio R. 1930. *The Idea of Robinson Crusoe*. Watford: The Gongora Press.

Pateman, Carole. 1980. Women and Consent. *Political Theory*, 8: 149–68.

Pateman, Carole, 1988. *The Sexual Contract*. Cambridge: Polity Press.

Pateman, Carole and Brennan, Teresa. 1979. 'Mere Auxiliaries to the Commonwealth': Women and the Origins of Liberalism. *Political Studies*, 27: 183–200.

Pearson, Lionel. 1960. *The Lost Histories of Alexander the Great*. American Philological Association Monographs, 20.

Pellat, C. 1961. L'Imamat dans la Doctrine de Gahiz. *Studia Islamica*, 15: 23–52.

Pelletier, André, ed. 1962. *Letter d'Aristé à Philocrate. Introduction, Texte Critique, Traduction*. Paris: Éditions du Cerf, 29.

Peradotto, John and Sullivan, John P., eds. 1984. *Women in the Ancient World: the Arethusa Papers*. Albany, NY: SUNY Press.

Péristiany, Jean G., ed. 1965. *Honour and Shame: the Values of Mediterranean Society*. London: Weidenfeld and Nicolson.

Péristiany, Jean G., ed. 1968. *Contributions to Mediterranean Sociology*. Paris: Mouton.

Péristiany, Jean G., ed. 1976. *Mediterranean Family Structure*. Cambridge: Cambridge University Press.

Pestman, Pieter W. 1961. *Marriage and Matrimonial Property in Ancient Egypt*. Leiden: Papyrological Lugbundbatava, no. 9.

Pestman, Pieter W. 1968. *A History of Classical Scholarship from the Beginnings to the End of the Hellenistic Age*. Oxford: Oxford University Press.

Pestman, Pieter W. 1983. Some Aspects of Egyptian Law in Graeco-Roman Egypt. Title-deeds and *Hupallagma*. In E. van't Dack et al., eds. *Egypt and the Hellenistic World*. Leuven: Lovanii: 281–302.

Peters, Emrys Lloyd. 1976. Aspects of Affinity in a Lebanese Maronite Village. In J.G. Péristiany, ed. *Mediterranean Family Structure*. Cambridge: Cambridge University Press.

Peters, Francis E. 1968. *Aristotle and the Arabs: the Aristotelian Tradition in Islam*. New York: New York University Press.

Phillipson, Nicholas. 1983. Adam Smith as Civic Moralist. In Istvan Holt and Michael Ignatieff, eds. *Wealth and Virtue*. Cambridge: Cambridge University Press.

Pickard-Cambridge, A.W. and Winnington-Ingram, R.P. 1970. Aeschylus. *Oxford Classical Dictionary*. 2nd edn. Oxford: Oxford University Press: 17–19.

Pickles, Dorothy. 1970. *Democracy*. London: Methuen.

Pigman, G.W., III. 1979. Imitation and the Renaissance Sense of the Past: the Reception of Erasmus' *Ciceronianus*. *The Journal of Medieval and Renaissance Studies*, 9, 2: 155–77.

Pitkin, Hanna. 1981. Justice: on Relating Public and Private. *Political Theory*, 9, 3: 327–52.

Pitkin, Hanna. 1984. *Fortune is a Woman*. Berkeley, CA: University of California Press.

Pitkin, Hanna. 1988. Are Freedom and Liberty Twins? *Political Theory*, 16, 4: 523–52.

Pitt-Rivers, Julian. 1977. *The Fate of Sechem or the Politics of Sex: Essays in the Anthropology of the Mediterranean*. Cambridge: Cambridge University Press.

Plato. 1926 edn. *The Laws*. 2 vols. R.G. Bury, trans. Loeb edn. London: Heinemann.

Plato. 1930, 1935. *The Republic*. 2 vols. Paul Shorey, trans. Loeb edn. London: Heinemann.

Plato. 1956 edn. *The Protagoras and Meno*. W.K.C. Guthrie, trans. Harmondsworth: Penguin.

Plato. 1961 edn. *Collected Dialogues*. Edith Hamilton and Huntington Cairns, eds. Princeton, NJ: Bollingen.

Plato. 1970 edn. *The Laws*. Trevor J. Saunders, trans. Harmondsworth: Penguin.

Plato. 1971 edn. *The Timaeus and Critias*. Desmond Lee, trans. Harmondsworth: Penguin.

Plato. 1975 edn. *Timaeus*. Francis McDonald Cornford, trans. and commentary. Indianapolis: Bobbs-Merrill.

Plato. 1978 edn. *The Republic*. H.D.P. Lee, trans. Harmondsworth: Penguin.

Plutarch. 1936 edn. Discourse to an Unlearned Prince. *Moralia X* (799c–783a). F.C. Babbitt, trans. Loeb edn. London: Heinemann.

Plutarch. 1936 edn. Isis and Osiris. *Moralia V* (351c–384c). F.C. Babbitt, trans. Loeb edn. London: Heinemann: 6–191.

Plutarch. 1936 edn. On the Fortune of the Romans. *Moralia IV* (305a–316b). F.C. Babbitt, trans. Loeb edn. London: Heinemann: 320–77.

Plutarch. 1936 edn. On the Fortune or the Virtue of Alexander. *Moralia IV* (316b–326d). F.C. Babbitt, trans, Loeb edn. London: Heinemann: 379–487.

Plutarch. 1936 edn. On the Genius of Socrates. *Moralia VII* (575a–599a). F.C. Babbitt, trans. Loeb edn. London: Heinemann.

Plutarch, 1970 edn. *De Iside et Osiride. Moralia V*. J. Gwyn Griffiths, trans., notes and commentary. Swansea: University of Wales Press.

Pocock, John G.A. 1968. Time, History and Eschatology in the Thought of Thomas Hobbes. *Politics, Language and Time*. London: Methuen.

Pocock, John G.A. 1975. *The Machiavellian Moment*. Princeton, NJ: Princeton University Press.

Pocock, John G.A. 1977. *The Political Writings of James Harrington*. Cambridge: Cambridge University Press.

Pocock, John G.A. 1978. Contexts for the Study of James Harrington. *Il Pensiero Politico*, 11, 1: 20–35.

Pocock, John G.A. 1981. The *Machiavellian Moment* Revisited. *Journal of Modern History*, 53: 49–72.

Pocock, John G.A. 1984. *Virtue, Commerce and History*. Cambridge: Cambridge University Press.
Pocock, John G.A. 1990. Reader's Comments on P. Springborg, *Western Republicanism and the Oriental Prince*.
Poggio Bracciolini. 1966 edn. Historiae Florentini Populi. In R. Fubini, ed. *Opera Omnia*. 4 vols. Turin. vol. 2: 81–493.
Polanyi, Karl. 1944. *The Great Transformation*. Boston: Beacon Press.
Polanyi, Karl. 1957. Aristotle Discovers the Economy. In K. Polanyi, C.M. Arensberg and H.W. Pearson, eds. *Trade and Market in the Early Empires*. Glencoe: Free Press.
Polybius. 1979 edn. *The Rise of the Roman Empire*. Ian Scott-Kilvert, trans. Introduction by Frank W. Walbank. Harmondsworth: Penguin.
Pomerance, L. 1973. The Possible Role of Tomb Robbers and Viziers of the 18th Dynasty in Confusing Minoan Chronology. In G.P. Carratelli and G. Rizza, eds. *Antichità Cretesi*. Catania: Institute of Archaeology, University of Catania: 21–30.
Pomerance, L. 1984a. A Note on the Carved Stone Ewers from the Khyan Lid Deposit. In P. Aström, L.R. Palmer and L. Pomerance, eds. *Studies in Aegean Chronology*. Studies in Mediterranean Archaeology, Pocketbook 25. Gothenburg: Paul Aström Förlag: 15–26.
Pomerance, L. 1984b. The Mythogenesis of Minoan Chronology. In P. Aström, L.R. Palmer and L. Pomerance, eds. *Studies in Aegean Chronology*. Studies in Mediterranean Archaeology, Pocketbook 25. Gothenburg: Paul Aström Förlag: 8–14.
Pomeroy, Sarah B 1984. *Women in Hellenistic Egypt. From Alexander to Cleopatra*. New York: Schocken Books.
Ponet, John. 1942 edn. *A Shorte Treatise of Politick Power*. In W.S. Hudson, ed. *John Ponet (1516?–1556), Advocate of Limited Monarchy*. Chicago: University of Chicago Press.
Popham, M.R. 1970a. Late Minoan Chronology. *American Journal of Archaeology*, 74: 266–28.
Popham, M.R. 1970b. *The Destruction of the Palace at Knossos. Pottery of the LMIIIA Period*. Studies in Mediterranean Archaeology, 12. Gothenburg: Paul Aström Förlag.
Posener, Georges. 1960. *De la Divinité du Pharaon*. Cahiers de la Société Asiatique, 11.
Post, Gaines. 1964. *Studies in Medieval Legal Thought: Public Law and the State, 1100–1322*. Princeton, NJ: Princeton University Press.
Poulantzas, Nicos. 1974. *Fascism and Dictatorship*. London: NLB.
Préaux, Claire. 1939. *L'Économie Royale des Lagides*. Brussels: Édition de la Fondation Égyptologique Reine Elizabeth.
Préaux, Claire. 1959. Le Statut de la Femme a l'Époque Hellénistique, Principalement en Égypte. *Receuils de la Société J. Bodin*, 11: 127–75.
Préaux, Claire. 1978. *Le Monde Hellénistique. La Grèce et l'Orient (323–146 av. J.-C.)*. 2 vols. Paris: Presses Universitaires de France.
Preston, Joseph H. 1977. Was There an Historical Revolution? *Journal of the History of Ideas*, 38: 353–64.
Price, Russell. 1973. The Senses of Virtù in Machiavelli. *European Studies Review*, 3: 315–45.
Price, Russell. 1977. The Theme of *Gloria* in Machiavelli. *Renaissance Quarterly*, 30: 588–631.
Price, Simon R.F. 1986. *Rituals and Power: the Roman Imperial Cult in Asia Minor*. Cambridge: Cambridge University Press.
Price, Simon and Cannadine, David, eds. 1987. *Rituals of Royalty: Power and Ceremonial in Traditional Society*. Cambridge: Cambridge University Press.
Pritchard, James Bennett. 1950. *Ancient Near Eastern Texts Relating to the Old Testament*. Princeton, NJ: Princeton University Press.

Puhvel, Jaan. 1988. *Comparative Mythology*. Baltimore, MD: Johns Hopkins Press.
Pullan, Brian. 1971. *Rich and Poor in Renaissance Venice*. Oxford: Oxford University Press.
Pusey, Nathan M. 1940. Alcibiades and *To Philopoli*. *Harvard Studies in Classical Philology*, 51: 215–31.
The Pyramid Texts. 1968 edn. *The Pyramid of Unas*. Texts translated with commentary by Alexandre Piankoff. Princeton, NJ: Bollingen.
Quaegebeur, Jan. 1970. Ptolémée II en Adoration Devant Arsinoé II Divinisée. *Bulletin de l'Institute Français d'Archéologie Orientale, le Caire*, 69: 191–217.
Quaegebeur, Jan. 1971. Documents Concerning a Cult of Arsinoë Philadelphos at Memphis. *Journal of Near Eastern Studies*, 30: 239–70.
Quaegebeur, Jan 1972. Contribution à la Prosopographie des Prêtres Memphites à l'Époque Ptolémaique. *Ancient Society*, 3: 77–109.
Quaegebeur, Jan. 1978. Reines Ptolémaiques et Traditions Égyptiennes. In H. Maehler and V.M. Strocka, eds. *Das Ptolemaïsche Ägypten*. Mainz am Rhein: Von Zabern: 245–62.
Queller, Donald E. 1986. *The Venetian Patriciate. Reality versus Myth*. Urbana and Chicago, Ill.: University of Illinois Press.
Raab, Felix. 1964. *The English Face of Machiavelli*. London: Routledge and Kegan Paul.
Rabil, Albert, ed. 1988. *Renaissance Humanism: Foundations, Forms and Legacy*. 3 vols. Philadelphia, PA: University of Pennsylvania Press.
Rahe, Paul A. 1984. The Primacy of Politics in Classical Greece. *American Historical Review*, 89: 265–93.
Rahman, Fazlur. 1967. Islamic Philosophy. *Encyclopedia of Philosophy*. London: Collier Macmillan, vol. 4: 219–24.
Raubitschek, Antony. 1976. Plato and Minos. *Quaderni di Storica*, 3: 233–8.
Ray, J.D. 1976. *The Archive of Hor*. London: Egypt Exploration Society.
Raymond, André. 1957. Une Liste des Corporations de Métiers au Caire en 1801. *Arabica*, 4: 150–63.
Raymond, André. 1984. *The Great Arab Cities in the 16th–18th Centuries: an Introduction*. New York: New York University Press.
Redford, Donald B. 1984. *Akhenaten, the Heretic King*. Princeton, NJ: Princeton University Press.
Rees, D.A. 1967. Platonism and the Platonic Tradition. *Encyclopedia of Philosophy*. London: Collier Macmillan, vol. 6: 333–41.
Reesor, Margaret E. 1951. *The Political Theory of the Old and Middle Stoa*. New York: J.J. Augustin.
Reeves, Marjorie. 1969. *The Influence of Prophecy in the Late Middle Ages. A Study in Joachism*. Oxford: Oxford University Press.
Reeves, Marjorie. 1976. *Joachim of Fiore and the Prophetic Future*. London: SPCK.
Renfrew, Colin. 1972. *The Emergence of Civilization: The Cyclades and the Aegean in the Third Millennium B.C.* London: Methuen.
Renfrew, Colin. 1979. The Eruption of Thera and Minoan Crete. In P.D. Sheets and D.K. Grayson, eds. *Volcanic Activity and Human Ecology*. New York: Academic Press: 565–85.
Richter, Melvin. 1975. Despotism. *Dictionary of the History of Ideas*. Philip Wiener, ed. New York: Charles Scribner, vol. 2: 1–18.
Rist, J.M. 1969. *Stoic Philosophy*. Cambridge: Cambridge University Press.
Robb, N.A. 1968. *Neoplatonism of the Italian Renaissance*. New York: Octagon Books.
Robertson Smith, William. 1894. *The Religion of the Semites. The Fundamental Institutions*. 2nd edn (reprinted 1959). New York: Schocken.

Robbins, Kittye Delle. 1983. Tiamat and her Children: an Enquiry into the Persistence of Mythic Archetypes of Woman as Monster/Villainess/Victim. In Meg McGarvan Murray, ed. *Face to Face: Fathers, Mothers, Masters, Monsters*. Westport, Conn.: Greenwood Press.

Robins, Gay. 1983. The God's Wife of Amun in the 18th Dynasty in Egypt. In Averil Cameron and Amélie Kuhrt, eds. *Images of Women in Antiquity*. London: Croom Helm.

Robinson, James M. ed. 1977. *The Nag Hammadi Library*. Leiden: Brill.

Rodinson, Maxime. 1988. *The Mystique of Islam in Europe*. Seattle: University of Washington Press.

Rorty, A.O. 1980. *Essays on Aristotle's Ethics*. Berkeley, CA: University of California Press.

Rose, Herbert Jennings. 1964. *Handbook of Greek Literature*. London: Methuen.

Rose, Herbert Jennings. 1970a. Danaus. *Oxford Classical Dictionary*. 2nd edn. Oxford: Oxford University Press: 311–12.

Rose, Herbert Jennings. 1970b. Erichthonius. *Oxford Classical Dictionary*. 2nd edn. Oxford: Oxford University Press: 406.

Rose, Herbert Jennings. 1970c. Europa. *Oxford Classical Dictionary*. 2nd edn. Oxford: Oxford University Press: 421–2.

Rose, Herbert Jennings. 1970d. Io. *Oxford Classical Dictionary*. 2nd edn. Oxford: Oxford University Press: 549.

Rose, Herbert Jennings and Robertson, C.M. 1970a. Aethra. *Oxford Classical Dictionary*. 2nd edn. Oxford: Oxford University Press: 20.

Rose, Herbert Jennings and Robertson, C.M. 1970b. Heracles. *Oxford Classical Dictionary*. 2nd edn. Oxford: Oxford University Press: 498–9.

Rosenmeyer, Thomas G. 1949. The Family of Critias. *American Journal of Philology*, 70: 404–10.

Rosenthal, Erwin Isak J. 1948. Some Aspects of Islamic Political Thought. *Islamic Culture*, 22: 1–17.

Rosenthal, Erwin Isak J. 1958. *Political Thought in Medieval Islam*. Cambridge: Cambridge University Press.

Rosenthal, Erwin Isak J. 1965. *Islam in the Modern National State*. Cambridge: Cambridge University Press.

Rosenthal, Franz. 1974. Literature. In Joseph Schacht and C.E. Bosworth, eds. *The Legacy of Islam*. Oxford: Clarendon Press: 318–49.

Ross, David. 1949. *Aristotle*. 5th revised edn. London: Methuen.

Ross, David John Athole. 1963. *Alexander Historians: a Guide to Medieval Illustrated Literature*. London: Warburg Institute.

Ross, G.M. 1974. Seneca's Philosophical Influence. In C.D.N. Costa, ed. *Seneca*. London: Routledge: 116–65.

Ross, J.M. 1977. Is There Any Truth in Atlantis? *The Durham University Journal*, 69, (n.s. 38), 2: 189–99.

Rostovtzeff, Mikhail. 1932. *Caravan Cities*. Oxford: Clarendon Press.

Rostovtzeff, Mikhail. 1941. *The Social and Economic History of the Hellenistic World*. 3 vols. Oxford: Clarendon Press.

Rostovtzeff, Mikhail, 1954. *The Social and Economic History of the Roman Empire*. 3 vols. Oxford: Clarendon Press.

Roth, Gunther. 1968. Personal Rulership, Patrimonialism and Empire-Building in the New States. *World Politics*, 20, 2: 194–206.

Rouillard, C.D. 1941. *The Turk in French History, Thought and Literature*. Paris: Presses Universitaires de France.

Rousseau, J.-J. 1913 edn. *The Social Contract and Discourses*. G.D.H. Cole, trans. London: J.M. Dent and Sons.

Roussel, Denis. 1976. *Tribu et Cité. Études sur les Groupes Sociaux dans les Cités Grecques aux Époques Archaïque et Classique*. Paris: Les Belles Lettres.

Rubinstein, Nicolai. 1942. The Beginnings of Political Thought in Florence. A Study in Medieval Historiography. *Journal of the Warburg and Courtauld Institutes*, 5: 198–222.

Rubinstein, Nicolai. 1952. FLorence and Despots: some Aspects of Florentine Despotism in the Fourteenth Century. *Royal Historical Society Transactions*, 2 (5th series): 21–45.

Rubinstein, Nicolai. 1957. Municipal Progress and Decline in the Italy of the Communes. In D.J. Gordon, ed. *Fritz Saxl, 1890–1948: a Volume of Memorial Essays*. London: Thomas Nelson: 165–83.

Rubinstein, Nicolai. 1966. *The Government of Florence under the Medici (1434–1494)*. Oxford: Oxford University Press.

Rubinstein, Nicolai, ed. 1968. *Florentine Studies: Politics and Society in Renaissance Florence*. London: Faber.

Rubinstein, Nicolai. 1982. Political Theories in the Renaissance. In André Chastel et al., eds. *The Renaissance: Essays in Interpretation*. London: Methuen: 153–200.

Rucellai, Bernardo. 1727 edn. *Sylloges Epistolarum a Viris Illustribus Scriptarum*. Petrus Bermannus, ed. Leyden.

Runciman, W.G. 1982. Origins of States: the Case of Archaic Greece. *Comparative Studies in Society and History*, 24: 351–77.

Runciman, W.G. 1983. Capitalism without Classes: the Case of Classical Rome. *British Journal of Sociology*, 34: 157–81.

Rustow, Alexander. 1980. *Freedom and Domination. A Historical Critique of Civilization*. Salvator Attanasio, trans. Dankwart A. Rustow, introd. Princeton, NJ: Princeton University Press.

Rutherford, Samuel. 1644. *Lex, Rex*. London.

Ryffel, H. 1949. *Metabole Politeion. Der Wandel der Staatsverfassungen*. Bern: Noltes Romanische Forschungen Über die Kultur der Antike, 2.

SIG Sylloge Inscriptionum Graecarum. W. Dittenberg, ed. 1915–24.

Saab, Hassan. 1967. Ibn Khaldun. *Encyclopedia of Philosophy*. London: Collier Macmillan: 107–9.

Sabloff, J. and Lamberg-Karlovsky, C.C., eds. 1976. *Ancient Civilization and Trade*. Albuquerque: University of New Mexico Press.

Sadowski, Yahya. 1987. Is this Society Civil? Rethinking the Logic of State Formation in Egypt. Unpublished paper, The Brookings Institution, Washington, DC.

Said, Edward. 1978. *Orientalism*. London: Routledge and Kegan Paul.

Sainte Croix, G.E.M. de. 1954. Suffragium: from Vote to Patronage. *British Journal of Sociology*, 5: 33–48.

Sainte Croix, G.E.M. de. 1970. Some Observations on the Property Rights of Athenian Women. *Classical Review*, 20: 273–8.

Sainte Croix, G.E.M. de. 1983. *The Class Struggle in the Ancient Greek World*. London: Duckworth.

Sallust. 1921a edn. *Bellum Catilinae*. J.C. Rolfe, trans. Loeb edn. London: Heinemann.

Sallust. 1921b edn. *Bellum Jugurthinum*. J.C. Rolfe, trans. Loeb edn. London: Heinemann.

Salmon, E.T. 1974. *The Nemesis of Empire*. Oxford: Oxford University Press.

Salvemini, G. 1903 edn. Il 'Liber de reminine civitatum' di Giovanni da Viterbo. *Giornale storico della letteratura italiana*, 41: 284–303.

Samson, Julia. 1985. *Nefertiti and Cleopatra: Queen Monarchs of Ancient Egypt*. London: Rubicon Press.

Samuel, Deborah H. 1980. Women as Property Owners in Roman Egypt. American Philological Association Conference, New Orleans, December 1980.

Sanchez, Sonia. 1984. Nefertiti: Queen to a Sacred Mission. *Journal of African Civilizations (Black Women in Antiquity)*, 6, 1: 49–55.

Sancisi-Weerdenburg, Heleen. 1983. Exit Atossa; Images of Women in Greek Historiography on Persia. In Averil Cameron and Amélie Kuhrt, eds. *Images of Women in Antiquity*. London: Croom Helm.

Saunders, John J. 1963. The Problem of Islamic Decadence. *Journal of World History*, 7: 701–20.

Sauneron, Serge. 1960. *The Priests of Ancient Egypt*. Ann Morrissett, trans. New York: Grove Press.

Saxonhouse, Arlene W. 1980. Men, Women, War and Politics: Family and Politics in Aristophanes and Euripides. *Political Theory*, 8, 1: 65–81.

Saxonhouse, Arlene W. 1985. *Women in the History of Political Thought: Ancient Greece to Machiavelli*. New York: Praeger.

Schachermeyr, Fritz. 1949. Welche Historische Ereignisse führten zu der Entstehung der Mykenischen Kultur? *Archiv Orientalni* 17, 2: 331–50.

Schachermeyr, Fritz. 1964. *Das Minoische Kultur des Alten Kreta*. Stuttgart: Kohlhammer.

Schaeffer, Claude F.-A. 1938. Les Fouilles de Ras Shamra-Ugarit, Neuvième Campagne (Printemps, 1937). Rapport Sommaire. *Syria*, 19: 193–255.

Schaps, David M. 1977. The Women Least Mentioned: Etiquette and Women's Names. *Classical Quarterly*, n.s. 27: 323–30.

Schaps, David M. 1979. *Economic Rights of Women in Ancient Greece*. Edinburgh: University of Edingurgh Press.

Scherer, Jacques. 1987. *Dramaturgies d'Oedipe*. Paris: Puf.

Schlaifer, Robert. 1960. Greek Theories of Slavery from Homer to Aristotle. In M.I. Finley, ed. *Slavery in Classical Antiquity*. Cambridge: Cambridge University Press.

Schmitt, Charles B. 1972. *Cicero Scepticus: a Study of the Influence of the Academica in the Rennaissance*. The Hague: Martinus Nijhoff.

Schmitt, Charles B. 1983. *Aristotle and the Renaissance*. Cambridge, Mass.: Harvard University Press.

Schochet, Gordon J. 1975. *Patriarchalism in Political Thought: The Authoritarian Family and Political Speculation and Attitudes Especially in Seventeenth Century England*. Oxford: Basil Blackwell.

Schwartz, Nancy L. 1979. Distinction between Public and Private Life. Marx on the *Zoon Politikon*. *Political Theory*, 7, 2: 245–66.

Schweitzer, Ursula. 1956. *Das Wesen des Ka in Diesseits und Jenseits der Alten Agypter*. Gluckstadt: J.J. Augustin.

Schwoebel, R. 1967. *The Shadow of the Crescent. The Renaissance Image of the Turk (1453–1517)*. Nieuwkoop: De Graaf.

Scullard, Hugh H. 1982. *From the Gracchi to Nero: a History of Rome from 133 B.C. to A.D. 68*. 5th edn. London: Methuen.

Seager, J. and Olson, A. 1986 *Women in the World: an International Atlas*. New York: Simon and Schuster.

Sealey, Ralph. 1987. *The Athenian Republic: Democracy or Rule of Law*. University Park, PA: Pennsylvania State University Press.

Segal, Charles. 1974. The Homeric Hymn to Aphrodite: a Structuralist Approach. *Classical World*, 67: 205–12.

Segal, Charles. 1978. The Menace of Dionysus: Sex Roles and Reversals in Euripides' *Bacchae*. *Arethusa*, 11: 185–202.

Segall, B. 1956. Some Syrian and Syro-Hittite Elements in the Art of the West. *American Journal of Archeology*, 60: 165–70.

Seigel, J.E. 1966. 'Civic Humanism' or Ciceronian Rhetoric? The Culture of Petrarch and Bruni. *Past and Present*, 34: 3–48.

Seltman, Charles T. 1956. *Women in Antiquity*. New York: Thames and Hudson.
Seneca. 1925 edn. *Epistolae Morales*, vol. 3. R. Gummere, trans. Loeb edn. London: Heinemann.
Shaffer, E.S. 1975. *Kubla Khan and the Fall of Jerusalem: the Mythological School of Biblical Criticism and Secular Literature 1770–1880*. Cambridge: Cambridge University Press.
Shahid, Irfan. 1984a. *Rome and the Arabs*. Washington, DC: Dumbarton Oaks.
Shahid, Irfan. 1984b. *Byzantium and the Arabs in the Fourth Century*. Washington, DC: Dumbarton Oaks.
Shaw, Stanford. 1976. *History of the Ottoman Empire and Modern Turkey*. Vol. 1. *Empire of the Gazis*. Cambridge: Cambridge University Press.
Shboul, Ahmad M.H. 1979. *Al Mas'udi and his World: a Muslim Humanist and his Interest in Non-Muslims*. London: Ithaca Press.
Sherk, Robert K. 1984. *Rome and the Greek East to the Death of Augustus*. Cambridge: Cambridge University Press.
Siegel, J.H. 1968. *Rhetoric and Philosophy in Renaissance Humanism*. Princeton, NJ: Princeton University Press.
Silverberg, R. 1964. *Akhnaten, the Rebel Pharaoh*. Philadelphia: Hamilton.
Simon, Virginia Spottswood. 1984. Tiye: Nubian Queen of Egypt. *Journal of African Civilizations (Black Women in Antiquity)*: 6, 1: 56–63.
Sinclair, R.K. 1988. *Democracy and Participation in Athens*. Cambridge: Cambridge University Press.
Sinclair, T.A. 1962. Introduction and Notes to Aristotle's *Politics*. Harmondsworth: Penguin.
Singerman, Diane. 1986. A Study of the Disposable Income of Lower to Lower-Middle Class Families in Modern Cairo. Unpublished lecture, American Research Center in Egypt, Cairo.
Sivard, R. 1985. *Women: a World Survey*. Washington: World Priorities.
Skinner, Quentin. 1979. *The Foundations of Modern Political Thought*. 2 vols. *The Renaissance*, vol. 1. *The Age of Reformation*, vol. 2. Cambridge: Cambridge University Press.
Skinner, Quentin. 1981. *Machiavelli*. (Past Master Series). New York: Hill and Wang.
Skinner, Quentin. 1983: Machiavelli on the Maintenance of Liberty. *Politics*, 18, 2: 3–15.
Skinner, Quentin. 1986. Ambrogio Lorenzetti: the Artist as Political Philosopher. *Proceedings of the British Academy*, 72: 1–56.
Skinner, Quentin. 1989. Greece and Rome in Renaissance Political Thought. Paper presented to the Conference on Political Discourse in Early Modern Europe, Humanities Research Centre, Australian National University, Canberra, 14–16 April.
Skinner, Quentin, 1990. Reader's Report on P. Springborg, *Western Republicanism and the Oriental Prince*.
Slater, Philip. 1968. *The Glory of Hera. Greek Mythology and the Greek Family*. Boston: Beacon Press.
Smith, Bruce James. 1985. *Politics and Remembrance: Republican Themes in Machiavelli, Burke and de Tocqueville*. Princeton, NJ: Princeton University Press.
Smith, Byron Porter. 1939. *Islam in English Literature*. Beirut: American University Press (2nd edn. New York: Caravan Books, 1977).
Smith, Charles Forster. 1906–7. What Constitutes a State? *Classical Journal*, 2: 299–302.
Smith, W.S. 1965. *Interconnections in the Ancient Near East*. New Haven, Conn.: Yale University Press.
Sniderek, A. 1953–4. La Société Indigène en Égypte au IIIe Siècle avant notre Ère après les Archives de Zénon. *Journal of Juristic Papyrology*, 7–8: 231–84.
Snodgrass, A.M. 1985. The New Archaeology and the Classical Archaeologist. *American Journal of Archaeology*, 89: 31–7.

Snyder, Jane McIntosh. 1981. The Web of Song: Weaving Imagery in Homer and the Lyric Poets. *Classical Journal*, 76: 193–6.

Soudek, Joseph. 1952. Aristotle's Theory of Exchange. *American Philosophical Society Proceedings*, 96, 1: 45–75.

Southern, R.W. 1962. *Western Views of Islam in the Middle Ages*. Cambridge, Mass.: Harvard University Press.

Sparks, R.S.J. 1985. Archaeomagnetism, Santorini Volcanic Eruptions and Fired Destruction Levels on Crete. *Nature*, 313: 74–5.

Springborg, Patricia. 1976. *Leviathan*, Christian Commonwealth Incorporated. *Political Studies*, 24, 2: 171–83.

Springborg, Patricia. 1981. *The Problem of Human Needs and the Critique of Civilization*. London: George Allen and Unwin.

Springborg, Patricia. 1984a. Aristotle and the Problem of Needs. *History of Political Thought*, 5, 3: 393–424.

Springborg, Patricia. 1984b. Democracy, Method or Praxis? *Thesis Eleven*, 9: 108–25.

Springborg, Patricia. 1984c. Karl Marx on Democracy, Participation, Voting and Equality. *Political Theory*, 12, 4: 537–56.

Springborg, Patricia. 1984d. Marx, Democracy and the Ancient Polis. *Critical Philosophy*, 1, 1: 47–66.

Springborg, Patricia. 1986. Politics, Primordialism and Orientalism: Marx, Aristotle and the Myth of the *Gemeinschaft*. *American Political Science Review*, 80, 1: 185–211.

Springborg, Patricia. 1987a. The Contractual State: Reflections on Orientalism and Despotism. *History of Political Thought*, 8, 3: 395–433.

Springborg, Patricia, 1987b. Early History of the State: West and East. *Politics*, 22, 2: 105–13.

Springborg, Patricia. 1988. Pandora and Hatshepsut: Ancient Archetypes in the Iconography of Kingship. Submitted Paper Participant, International Political Science Association Convention, Washington, DC.

Springborg, Patricia. 1989a. Arendt, Republicanism and Patriarchalism. *History of Political Thought*, 10, 3: 499–523.

Springborg, Patricia. 1989b. Hannah Arendt and the Classical Republican Tradition. In Gisela T. Kaplan and Clive S. Kessler, eds. *Hannah Arendt: Thinking, Judging, Freedom*. Sydney, Australia: Allen and Unwin: 9–17.

Springborg, Patricia. 1990a. The Feminine Principle in 'The Birth of the State'. *Political Theory Newsletter*, 2, 1: 45–63.

Springborg, Patricia. 1990b. His Majesty is a Baby? *Political Theory*, 18, 4: 673–89.

Springborg, Patricia. 1990c. The Primacy of the Political: Rahe and the Myth of the *Polis*. *Political Studies*: 38, 1: 83–104.

Springborg, Patricia. 1990d. *Royal Persons: Patriarchal Monarchy and the Feminine Principle*. London: Unwin Hyman.

Springborg, Robert. 1975. Patterns of Association in the Egyptian Political Elite. In George Lenczowski, ed. *Political Elites in the Middle East*. Washington: American Enterprise Institute.

Springborg, Robert. 1982. *Family, Power, and Politics in Egypt: Sayed Bey Marei – his Clan, Clients and Cohorts*. Philadelphia, PA: University of Pennsylvania Press.

Stalley, R.F. 1983. *An Introduction to Plato's Laws*. Indianapolis, Ind.: Hackett.

Stanley, D.J. and Sheng, H. 1986. Volcanic Shards from Santorini (Upper Minoan Ash) in the Nile Delta, Egypt. *Nature*, 320: 733–5.

Starn, R. 1971. Francesco Guicciardini and his Brothers. In A. Mohlo and J.A. Tedeschi, eds. *Renaissance Studies in Honor of Hans Baron*. Florence: G.C. Sansoni.

Stewart, Desmond. 1981. *The Foreigner: a Search for the First Century Jesus*. London: Hamish Hamilton.

Stock, Hanns. 1948. Das Ostdelta Ägyptens in Seiner Entscheidenden Rolle für die Politische und Religiöse Entwicklung des Alten Reiches. *Die Welt des Orients*, 1, 3: 135–45.

St. V. Fr. Stoicorum Veterum Fragmenta. 1964 edn. H. von Arnim, ed. Leipzig, 1903–24, reprinted, Stuttgart, 1964. 4 vols.

Stone, Lawrence. 1971. Prosopography. *Daedalus*, 100, 1: 46–79.

Strabo. 1989 edn. *The Geography of Strabo*. H.L. Jones and J.R.S. Sterrett, trans. Cambridge, Mass.: Harvard University Press.

Strange, J. 1980. *Caphtor/Keftiu, A New Investigation*. (Acta Theologica Danica 14). Leiden: E.J. Brill.

Strasburger, Hermann. 1965. Poseidonios on Problems of the Roman Empire. *Journal of Roman Studies*, 55: 40–53.

Strauss, Leo. 1948. *On Tyranny. An Interpretation of Xenophon's 'Hiero'*. Glencoe, Ill.: Free Press.

Strayer, Joseph R. 1969. France: the Holy Land, the Chosen People, and the Most Christian King. In Theodore K. Rabb and Jerrold E. Siegel, eds. *Action and Conviction in Early Modern Europe: Essays in Honor of E.H. Harrison*. Princeton, NJ: Princeton University Press: 3–16.

Strayer, Joseph R. 1970. *On the Medieval Origins of the Modern State*. Princeton, NJ: Princeton University Press.

Ström, I. 1984. Aspects of Minoan Foreign Relations, LMI–LMII. In R. Hägg and N. Marinatos, eds. *The Minoan Thalassocracy: Myth and Reality*. Stockholm: Paul Aström Förlag: 191–5.

Stubbings, Frank H. 1962. The Aegean Bronze Age. *Cambridge Ancient History*. 2nd edn. fasc. 4. Cambridge: Cambridge University Press.

Stubbings, Frank H. 1963. The Rise of Mycenaean Civilization. *Cambridge Ancient History*. 2nd edn. fasc. 18. Cambridge: Cambridge University Press.

Sussman, Linda S. 1978. Workers and Drones; Labor, Idleness and Gender in Hesiod's Beehive. *Arethusa*, 11: 27–41.

Svoboda, K. 1913. Die Abfassungszeit des Geschichtswerkes des Polybios. *Philologus*, 72: 465–83.

Syme, Sir Ronald. 1939. *The Roman Revolution*. Oxford: Clarendon Press.

Syme, Sir Ronald. 1950. *A Roman Post-Mortem, Inquest on the Fall of the Roman Republic*. (Todd Memorial Lecture no. 3). Sydney: Australasian Medical Publishing Co.

Tacitus, Publius (Gaius) Cornelius. 1972 edn. *The Annals of Tacitus. Books 1–6*. Edited with a commentary by F.R.D. Goodyear. Volume 1: *Annals 1.1–54*. Cambridge: Cambridge University Press.

Tacitus, Publius (Gaius) Cornelius. 1977 edn. *The Annals of Imperial Rome*. Michael Grant, trans. Harmondsworth: Penguin.

Taeger, Fritz. 1957. *Charisma: Studien zur Geschichte des Antiken Herrscherkultes*. Stuttgart: Kohlhammer.

Tanner, R. Godfrey. 1990a. Ancient Lists of Aristotle's Works. Paper Presented to the Greek Philosophy Conference, University of Sydney, Sydney, Australia, 10 July 1990.

Tanner, R. Godfrey. 1990b. Aristotle's Non-Scientific Writings. Paper Presented to the Greek Philosophy Conference, University of Sydney, Sydney, Australia, 10 July 1990.

Tarn, W.W. 1927. The Hellenistic Ruler Cult. *Journal of Hellenic Studies*, 47: 53–62.

Tarn, W.W. 1933. Alexander the Great and the Unity of Mankind. *British Academy Proceedings*, 19: 123–66.

Tarn W.W. 1948. *Alexander the Great*. Cambridge: Cambridge University Press.

Tarn, W.W. 1952. *Hellenistic Civilization*. 3rd edn. London: Arnold.

Tarrant, H.A.S. 1985. Review of Phyllis Young Forsyth, *Atlantis: the Making of Myth*

(London: Croom Helm, 1980). *Ancient Society: Resources for Teachers* (Macquarie Ancient History Association) 15, 2: 94–7.

Tate, J. 1929. Plato and Allegorical Interpretation. *Classical Quarterly*, 23: 142–54.

Taubenschlag, R. 1937. The Ancient Greek City-Laws in Ptolemaic Egypt. *Actes du Vme Congres International de Papyrologie, Oxford*: 471–89.

Taubenschlag, R. 1938. La Competence du Kyrios dans le Droit Greco-Égyptien. *Archives d'Histoire du Droit Oriental*, 2: 293–314. (Reprinted in R. Taubenschlag, *Opera Minora*, 2 (Warsaw, 1959): 353–77).

Taylor, A.E. 1928. *A Commentary on Plato's 'Timaeus'*. Oxford: Clarendon Press.

Taylor, Lily Ross. 1949. *Party Politics in the Age of Caesar*. Berkeley, CA: University of California Press.

Taylor, Lily Ross. 1975. *The Divinity of the Roman Emperor*. Philadelphia, PA: Porcupine Press (reprint of 1931 edn).

Tcherikover, V. 1937. Palestine under the Ptolemies. *Mizraim*, 4–5: 9–69.

Tcherikover, V. 1959. *Hellenistic Civilization and the Jews*. S. Applebaum, trans. Philadelphia, PA: Jewish Publishing Society of America.

Telfer, E. 1970–1. Friendship. *Aristotelian Society Proceedings*, 71: 223–41.

Terray, Emmanuel. 1979. *Marxism and Primitive Societies*. Mary Klopper, trans. New York: Monthly Review Press.

Thesleff, Holger. 1961. *An Introduction to the Pythagorean Writings of the Hellenistic Period*. Oslo: Abo.

Thesleff, Holger. 1965. *The Pythagorean Texts of the Hellenistic Period*. Oslo: Abo.

Thompson, Martyn P. 1977. Hume's Critique of Locke and the 'Original Contract'. *Il Pensiero Politico*, 10, 2: 189–201.

Thompson, Reginald C. 1928. *The Epic of Gilgamesh*. London: Luzac.

Thompson, Wesley. 1982. Weaving, A Man's Work. *Classical World*, 75: 217–22.

Thomson, George. 1961. *Studies in Ancient Greek Society, I, The Prehistoric Aegean*. London: Lawrence and Wishart.

Tierny, Brian. 1982. *Religion, Law and the Growth of Constitutional Thought*. Cambridge: Cambridge University Press.

Tilly, Charles, ed. 1975. *The Formation of Nation States in Western Europe*. Princeton, NJ: Princeton University Press.

Tilly, Charles. 1984. *Big Structures, Large Processes, Huge Comparisons*. New York: Russell Sage Foundation.

Tilly, Charles. 1985. War Making and State Making as Organized Crime. In Peter B. Evans, Dietrich Rueschemeyer and Theda Skocpol, eds. *Bringing the State Back In*. Cambridge: Cambridge University Press.

Tönnies, Ferdinand. 1955 edn. *Community and Association*. C. Loomis, trans. London: Routledge and Kegan Paul.

Tönnies, Ferdinand. 1971. Hobbes and the *Zoon Politikon*. In F. Tonnies, *On Sociology: Pure, Applied and Empirical*. Chicago: Chicago University Press.

Tondrian, L. 1948. Princesses Ptolémaïques Comparées ou Identifiées à des Déesses. *Bulletin, Société Archéologique d'Alexandrie*, 37: 12–33.

Treggiari, S.M. 1976. Jobs for Women. *American Journal of Ancient History*, 1: 76–104.

Trexler, R.C. 1978. Honor among Thieves. The Trust Function of the Urban Clergy in the Florentine Republic. In S. Bertelli and G. Ramakus, eds. *Essays Presented to Myron P. Gilmore*. 2 vols. Florence: La Nuova Italia, vol. 1: 317–34.

Trigger, Brian J. 1983. The Rise of Egyptian Civilization. In B.J. Trigger and B. Kemp, eds. *Ancient Egypt: a Social History*. Cambridge: Cambridge University Press: 1–70.

Trigger, Brian J. and Kemp, Barry, eds. 1983. *Ancient Egypt: a Social History*. Cambridge: Cambridge University Press.

Trinkaus, Charles. 1965. *Adversity's Noblemen, the Italian Humanists on Happiness.* New York: New York University Press.

Trinkaus, Charles. 1970. *In our Image and Likeness: Humanity and Divinity in Italian Humanist Thought.* Chicago: University of Chicago Press.

Trinkaus, Charles. 1976. Protagoras in the Renaissance, an Exploration. In E.P. Mahoney, ed. *Philosophy and Humanism.* Leiden: Brill.

Trinkaus, Charles. 1979. *The Poet as Philosopher, Petrarch and the Formation of Renaissance Consciousness.* New Haven, Conn.: Yale Univeristy Press.

Trinkaus, Charles. 1982. Themes for a Renaissance Anthropology. In André Chastel et al., ed. *The Renaissance: Essays in Interpretation.* London: Methuen: 83–125.

Trinkaus, Charles. 1983. The Question of Truth in Renaissance Rhetoric and Anthropology. In James J. Murphy, ed. *Renaissance Eloquence: Studies in the Theory and Practice of Renaissance Rhetoric.* Berkeley, CA: University of California Press.

Trompf, Garry W. 1979. *The Idea of Historical Recurrence in Western Thought. From Antiquity to the Reformation.* Berkeley, CA: University of California Press.

Tuchman, Gaye. 1975. Women and the Creation of Culture. In Marcia Millmann and Rosebeth Moss Kantner, eds. *Another Voice: Feminist Perspectives on Social Life and Social Science.* New York: Doubleday: 171–201.

Turner, Bryan S. 1974a. Islam, Capitalism and Weber's Theses. *British Journal of Sociology,* 25: 230–43.

Turner, Bryan S. 1974b. *Weber and Islam: a Critical Study.* London: George Alen and Unwin.

Turner, Bryan S. 1978. *Marx and the End of Orientalism.* London: George Allen and Unwin.

Turner, Bryan S. 1984. Orientalism and the Problem of Civil Society in Islam. In Asaf Hussain et al., eds, *Orientalism, Islam and Islamists.* Brattleboro, Vermont: Amana Press: 23–42.

Udovitch, Abraham L. 1970. *Partnership and Profit in Medieval Islam.* Princeton, NJ: Princeton University Press.

Udovitch, Abraham L., ed. 1981. *The Islamic Middle East, 700–1900: Studies in Economic and Social History.* Princeton, NJ: The Darwin Press.

Ugaritic Manual. 1953 edn. Newly Revised Grammar, Texts in Transliteration, etc. Cyrus H. Gordon, ed. Rome: Pontificium Institutum Biblicum.

Ullmann, Walter. 1949. The Development of the Medieval Idea of Sovereignty. *English Historical Review,* 64: 1–33.

Valensi, Lucette. 1987. *Venise et la Sublime Porte. La Naissance du Despote.* Paris: Hachette.

Vander Waerdt, Paul A. 1985. Kingship and Philosophy in Aristotle's Best Regime. *Phronesis,* 30: 249–73.

Vander Waerdt, Paul A. 1990. The Plan and Intention of Aristotle's Ethical and Political Writings. Unpublished paper delivered to the University of Sydney Philosophy Seminar, 3 September 1990.

Vernant, J.–P. 1982. From Oedipus to Periander: Lameness, Tyranny, Incest in Legend and History. *Arethusa,* 15: 19–38.

Vernant, J.–P. 1983. *Myth and Thought among the Greeks.* London: Routledge and Kegan Paul.

Vercoutter, J. 1956. *L'Égypte et le monde égéen préhellénique.* Bibliothéque d'Étude 22. Cairo: Institut Français d'Archéologie Orientale.

Veyne, Paul. 1976. *Le Pain et le Cirque: Sociologie Historique d'un Pluralisme Politique.* Paris: Éditions du Seuil.

Veyne, Paul. 1983a. *L'Elegie Erotique Romaine: L'Amour, La Poesie et l'Occident.* Paris: Éditions du Seuil.

Veyne, Paul. 1983b. *Les Grecs ont-ils Cru a leurs Mythes? Essai sur l'Imagination Constitutante*. Paris: Éditions du Seuil.

Veyne, Paul, ed. 1987. *A History of Private Life*. Vol. 1. Cambridge, Mass.: Harvard University Press.

Veyne, Paul. 1988. *Did the Greeks Believe in their Myths? An Essay on the Constitutive Imagination*. Paula Wissing, trans. Chicago: University of Chicago Press.

Vidal-Naquet, Pierre. 1964. Athènes et l'Atlantide. *Revue des Études Grecques*, 77: 420–44.

Vidal-Naquet, Pierre. 1965. Economie et société dans la Grèce ancienne: L'Oeuvre de Moses I. Finley. *Archives européennes de sociologie*, 6: 111–48.

Vignano, Giovanni da. 1974 edn. *Flore de parlare*. E. Vincenti, ed. In Matteo de' Libri, *Arringhe*. Milan: 229–325.

Villani, Giovanni. 1844–5 edn. *Cronica*. F.G. Dragomanni, ed. Florence.

Vincent, A. 1987. *Theories of the State*. Oxford: Basil Blackwell.

Viterbo, Giovanni da. 1901 edn. *Liber de regimine civitatum*. C. Salvemini, ed. In *Bibliotheca juridica medii aevi*. 3 vols. Bologna, vol. 3: 215–80.

Vivanti, Corrado. 1967. Henry IV, the Gallic Hercules. *Journal of the Warburg and Courtauld Institutes*, 30: 176–97.

Vlastos, Gregory. 1953. Isonomia. *American Journal of Philology*, 74, 4: 337–66.

Vogt, Joseph. 1974. The Structure of Ancient Slave Wars. In J. Vogt, *Ancient Slavery and the Ideal of Man*. Oxford: Oxford University Press: 39–92.

Wachsmann, S. 1987. *Aegeans in the Theban Tombs*. Louvain: Katholieke Universiteit.

Wade-Gery, Henry T. 1931. Studies in the Structure of Attic Society: I. Demotionidai. *Classical Quarterly*, 25: 129–43.

Wade-Gery, Henry T. 1933. Studies in the Structure of Attic Society: II. The Laws of Kleisthenes. *Classical Quarterly*, 27: 17–29.

Walbank, Frank W. 1940. *Philip V of Macedon*. Cambridge: Cambridge University Press.

Walbank, Frank W. 1943. Polybius on the Roman Constitution. *Classical Quarterly*, 37: 73–82.

Walbank, Frank W. 1957–67. *A Historical Commentary on Polybius*. 3 vols. Oxford: Oxford University Press.

Walbank, Frank W. 1960. History and Tragedy. *Historia*, 9: 216–34.

Walbank, Frank W. 1964. Polybius and the Roman State. *Greek, Roman and Byzantine Studies*, 5: 239–60.

Walbank, Frank W. 1967. The Scipionic Legend. *Cambridge Philological Society, Proceedings*, 13: 54–69.

Walbank, Frank W. 1972. *Polybius*. Berkeley, CA: University of California Press.

Walbank, Frank W. 1984. Monarchies and Monarchic Ideas. In *Cambridge Ancient History VII*. 2nd edn. Cambridge: Cambridge University Press.

Walcot, Peter. 1966. *Hesiod and the Near East*. Cardiff: University of Wales Press.

Waley, Daniel. 1970. The Primitivist Element in Machiavelli's Thought. *Journal of the History of Ideas*, 31: 91–9.

Waley, Daniel. 1988. *The Italian City-Republics*. 3rd edn. London: Longman.

Walker, A.D.M. 1979. Aristotle's Account of Friendship in the Nicomachean Ethics. *Phronesis*, 24: 180–96.

Walker, B. 1952. *The Annals of Tacitus: a Study in the Writing of History*. Manchester: Manchester University Press.

Walker, Barbara G. 1983. *The Woman's Encyclopedia of Myths and Secrets*. San Francisco: Harper and Row.

Walker, D.P. 1953. Orpheus the Theologian and Renaissance Platonists. *Journal of the Warburg and Courtauld Institutes*, 16: 100–20.

Walker, D.P. 1954. The *Prisca Theologica* in France. *Journal of the Warburg and Courtauld Institutes*, 17: 1–21.

Walker, D.P. 1958. *Spiritual and Demonic Magic from Ficino to Campenella*. London: Warburg Institute, University of London.

Walker, Leslie J. 1972. *The Ancient Theology: Studies in Christian Neoplatonism from the 15th to the 18th Century*. Ithaca, NY: Cornell University Press.

Walker, Leslie J. 1975. *The Discourses of Niccolo Machiavelli*. 2 vols. London: Routledge and Kegan Paul.

Wallace-Hadrill, A. 1982. Civilis-Princeps: Between Citizen and King. *Journal of Roman Studies*, 72: 32–48.

Wallerstein, Immanuel. 1974. *The Modern World System I: Capitalist Agriculture and the World-Economy in the Sixteenth Century*. Orlando, Florida: Academic Press.

Walter, Pierre. 1957. Jean Louis Guez de Balzac's le Prince. *Journal of the Warburg and Courtauld Institutes*, 20: 215–47.

Walzer, Michael. 1965. *Revolution of the Saints*. Cambridge, Mass.: Harvard University Press.

Walzer, Michael, ed. 1974. *Regicide and Revolution: Speeches at the Trial of Louis XVI*. Cambridge: Cambridge University Press.

Walzer, Richard. 1962a. On the Legacy of the Classics in the Islamic World. In R. Walzer, *Greek into Arabic: Essays on Islamic Philosophy*. Oxford: Bruno Cassirer.

Walzer, Richard. 1962b. Platonism in Islamic Philosophy. In R. Walzer, *Greek into Arabic: Essays on Islamic Philosophy*. Oxford: Bruno Cassirer.

Warren, P.M. 1984. Absolute Dating of the Bronze Age Eruption of Thera (Santorini). *Nature*, 308: 492–3.

Warren, P.M. 1985. Minoan Pottery from Egyptian Sites. *Classical Review*, 35: 147–51.

Waters, K.H. 1985. *Herodotus the Historian*. London: Croom Helm.

Watkins, N.D., Sparks, R.S.J., Sigurdsson, H., Huang, T.C., Federman, A., Carey, S. and Ninkovich, D. 1978. Volume and Extent of the Minoan Tephra from Santorini Volcano; New Evidence from Deep Sea Sediment Cores. *Nature*, 271: 122–26.

Watt, W. Montgomery. 1967. Al-Farabi. *Encyclopedia of Philosophy*. London: Collier Macmillan: 3.179–80.

Weber, Max. 1950. Social Causes of the Decline of Ancient Civilization. *Journal of General Education* 5, 1: 75–88.

Weber, Max. 1958. *The Protestant Ethic and the Spirit of Capitalism*. New York: Scribner.

Weber, Max. 1968. *Economy and Society: an Outline of Interpretive Sociology*. 3 vols. G. Roth and Claus Wittich, eds. New York: Bedminster Press.

Wehrli, C. 1964. Phila, Fille d'Antipater et Épouse de Demetrius, Roi des Macédoniens. *Historia*, 13: 140–7.

Weill, Raymond. 1918. *La Fin du Moyen Empire Égyptien. Étude sur les Monuments et l'Histoire de la Periode Comprise entre la XIIe et la XVIIIe Dynastie*. 2 vols. Paris.

Weinstein, Donald. 1958. Savonarola, Florence and the Millennarian Tradition. *Church History*, 27: 3–17.

Weinstein, Donald. 1962. Millennarianism in a Civic Setting. The Savonarola Movement in Florence. In Sylvia Thrupp, ed. *Millennial Dreams in Action. Comparative Studies in Society and History, Supplement 2* (The Hague): 187–203.

Weinstein, Donald. 1968. The Myth of Florence. In Nicolai Rubinstein, ed. *Florentine Studies: Politics and Society in Renaissance Florence*. Evanston, Ill.: Northwestern University Press: 15–48.

Weinstein, Donald. 1970. *Savonarola and Florence. Prophecy and Patriotism in the Renaissance*. Princeton, NJ: Princeton University Press.

Weinstein, Donald. 1972. Savonarola and Machiavelli. In Myron P. Gilmore, ed. *Studies on Machiavelli*. Florence: G.D. Sansoni.

Weinstein, J.M. 1981. The Egyptian Empire in Palestine: a Reassessment. *Bulletin of the American Schools of Oriental Research*, 241: 1–28.

Weiss, Roberto. 1969. *The Renaissance Discovery of Classical Antiquity*. Oxford: Oxford University Press.

Weissman, Ronald. 1982. *Ritual Brotherhood in Renaissance Florence*. New York: Academic Press.

Welliver, W. 1977. *Character, Plot and Thought in Plato's 'Timaeus–Critias'*. Leiden: Brill.

Wells, Evelyn. 1969. *Hatshepsut*. New York: Anchor Doubleday.

Wente, Edward F. 1967. *Late Ramesside Letters*. (Studies in Ancient Oriental Civilization, no.33.) Chicago: University of Chicago Press.

West, Martin L. 1966. *Hesiod, Theogony*. Edited with a Prologemena and Commentary. Oxford: Clarendon Press.

West, Martin L. 1968. Near Eastern Material in Hellenistic and Roman Literature. *Harvard Studies in Classical Philology*, 73: 113–34.

West, Martin L. 1985. *The Hesiodic Catalogue of Women: its Nature, Structure and Origins*. Oxford: Clarendon Press.

Wheaton, R. 1975. Family and Kinship in Western Europe: the Problem of the Joint Family Household. *Journal of Interdisciplinary History*, 5: 601–28.

Whitfield, J.H. 1947. *Machiavelli*. Oxford: Oxford University Press.

Whitfield, J.H. 1969, Savonarola and the Purpose of *The Prince*. In J.H. Whitfield, *Discourses on Machiavelli*. Cambridge: W. Heffer and Sons.

Wickert, Elizabeth. 1990. For those who Sail to Heaven: the Mouled of Abu'l Hajjaj. Unpublished Lecture and Documentary Film. Canadian Institute in Cairo. 12 February, 1990.

Wieland, George. 1982. The Reception and Interpretation of Aristotle's *Ethics*. In Norman Kretzmann et al., eds. *Cambridge History of Later Medieval Philosophy*. Cambridge: Cambridge University Press: 657–72.

Williams, Gordon Willis. 1970. Marriage Ceremonies, Roman. *Oxford Classical Dictionary*. 2nd edn. Oxford: Oxford University Press: 651–2.

Williams, Oliver, P. 1984. Urbanism. Unpublished manuscript, Department of Political Science, University of Pennsylvania, Philadelphia, PA.

Wilson, John A. 1951. *The Burden of Egypt*. Chicago: University of Chicago Press.

Wilson, John A. 1973. Akh-en-aton and Nefert-iti. *Journal of Near Eastern Studies*, 32, 1–2: 235.

Wimby, Diedre. 1984. The Female Horuses and Great Wives of Kemet. *Journal of African Civilizations* (*Black Women in Antiquity*), 6, 1: 36–48.

Winks, Robin W. 1972. *Slavery: a Comparative Perspective*. New York: New York University.

Winnington-Ingram, Reginald Pedus. 1948. *Euripides and Dionysus, an Interpretation of the Bacchae*. Cambridge: Cambridge University Press.

Wirszubski, Chaim. 1954. Cicero's *Cum Dignitate Otium*: a Reconsideration. *Journal of Roman Studies*, 44: 1–13.

Wirszubski, Chaim. 1969. *Libertas as a Political Idea at Rome During the Late Republic and Early Principate*. Cambridge: Cambridge University Press.

Witt, R. 1971. The Rebirth of the Concept of Republican Liberty in Italy. In A. Molho and J. Tedeschi, eds. *Renaissance Studies in Honor of Hans Baron*. Florence: G.C. Sansoni: 173–99.

Witt, R. 1982. Medieval 'Ars dictaminis' and the Beginnings of Humanism: a New Construction of the Problem. *Renaissance Quarterly*, 35: 1–35.

Witt, R.E. 1971. *Isis in the Graeco-Roman World*. Ithaca, NY: Cornell University Press.

Wittfogel, Karl A. 1957. *Oriental Despotism*. New Haven, Conn.: Yale University Press.

Wolff, H.J. 1944. Marriage Law and Family Organization in Ancient Athens. *Traditio*, 2: 43–95.

Wolin, Sheldon. 1985. Postmodern Society and the Absence of Myth. *Social Research*, 52: 217–39.

Wood, Ellen, M. 1988. *Peasant–Citizen and Slave: the Foundations of Athenian Democracy*. London: Verso.

Wood, Neal. 1967. Machiavelli's Concept of *Virtù* Reconsidered. *Political Studies*, 15: 159–72.

Wood, Neal and Ellen, M. 1978. *Class, Ideology and Political Theory: Socrates, Plato and Aristotle in Social Context*. Oxford: Oxford University Press.

Woodward, A.M. and Forrest, W.G. 1970. Sparta. *Oxford Classical Dictionary*. 2nd edn. Oxford: Oxford University Press: 1006–7.

Xenophon. 1921 edn. *Cyropaedia*. Walter Miller, trans. 2 vols. Loeb edn. London: Heinemann.

Xenophon. 1922 edn. *Anabasis*. C.L. Brownson, trans. Loeb edn. London: Heinemann.

Yates, Frances Amelia. 1964. *Giordano Bruno and the Hermetic Tradition*. London: Routledge and Kegan Paul.

Yates, Frances Amelia. 1966. *The Art of Memory*. London: Routledge and Kegan Paul.

Yates, Frances Amelia. 1975. *Astraea: the Imperial Theme in the Sixteenth Century*. London: Routledge and Kegan Paul.

Yates, Frances Amelia. 1979. *The Occult Philosophy in the Elizabethan Age*. London: Routledge.

Yavetz, Z. 1969. *Plebs and Princeps*. Oxford: Oxford University Press.

Yoffee, Norman. 1977. *The Economic Role of the Crown in the Old Babylonian Period*. Malibu, CA: Udena Publications.

Yoffee, Norman. 1981. *Explaining Trade in Ancient Western Asia*. Malibu, CA: Udena Publications.

Yoffee, Norman and Cogill, George. 1988. *The Collapse of Ancient States and Civilizations*. Tucson, Ariz.: University of Arizona Press.

Youtie, H.C. 1971. Atrammatos: an Aspect of Greek Society. *Harvard Studies in Classical Philology*, 75: 161–76.

Zabkar, Louis V. 1963. Herodotus and the Egyptian Idea of Immortality. *Journal of Near Eastern Studies*, 22: 57–63.

Zanker, G. 1977. Callimachus' Hecale: a New Kind of Epic Hero? *Antichthon*, 11: 68–77.

Zeitlin, Froma I. 1978. The Dynamics of Misogyny: Myth and Mythmaking in the *Oresteia*. *Arethusa*, 11: 149–84.

Zeitlin, Froma I. 1982. Cultic Models of the Female: Rites of Dionysus and Demeter. *Arethusa*, 15: 129–57.

Index